HACKERS
Updated
TOEFL LISTENING

학습을 위한
추가 혜택

교재 MP3   단어암기 MP3   쉐도잉 프로그램   iBT 리스닝 실전모의고사

이용방법 해커스인강(HackersIngang.com) 접속 ▶
상단 메뉴 [토플 → MP3/자료 → 무료 MP3/자료] 클릭 ▶ 본 교재 선택하여 이용하기

MP3/자료 바로 가기 ▶

토플 보카 외우기

이용방법 고우해커스(goHackers.com) 접속 ▶
상단 메뉴 [TOEFL → 토플보카외우기] 클릭하여 이용하기

토플 스피킹/라이팅 첨삭 게시판

이용방법 고우해커스(goHackers.com) 접속 ▶
상단 메뉴 [TOEFL → 스피킹게시판/라이팅게시판] 클릭하여 이용하기

토플 공부전략 강의

이용방법 고우해커스(goHackers.com) 접속 ▶
상단 메뉴 [TOEFL → 토플공부전략] 클릭하여 이용하기

토플 자료 및 유학 정보

이용방법 고우해커스(goHackers.com)에 접속하여 다양한 토플 자료 및 유학 정보 이용하기

고우해커스 바로 가기 ▶

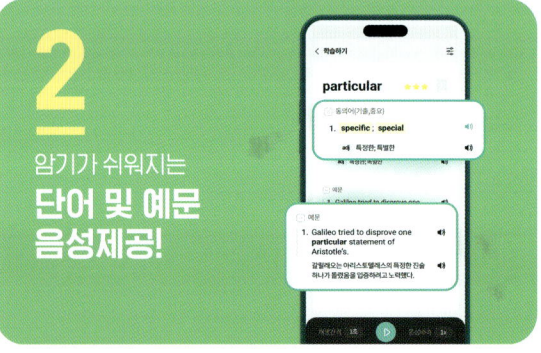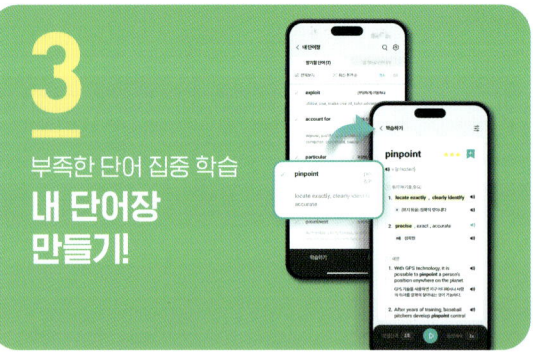

2026년 1월 21일 시행
Updated TOEFL

심층 분석,
이렇게 바뀐다

시대의 변화에 따라 영어 사용 환경이 달라진 것을 반영하여, 2026년 1월 21일 TOEFL 시험이 대대적으로 바뀐다.

『Hackers Updated TOEFL』은 수험자들이 **Updated TOEFL** 시험에도 철저히 대비할 수 있도록, 시험 변경사항과 새로운 문제 유형을 철저히 분석하여 가장 효과적인 핵심 전략과 출제 경향을 완벽 반영한 실전문제를 수록하고 있다.

Updated TOEFL, 얼마나 알고 계신가요?

	YES	NO
Q1. 시험 소요시간이 줄어들었다.	☐	☐
Q2. 리딩/리스닝 영역에서는 전반부 채점 결과에 따라 후반부 구성과 난이도가 달라진다.	☐	☐
Q3. 스피킹 영역이 시험의 마지막 순서다.	☐	☐

*정답은 모두 YES! 자세한 시험 변경사항은 이어지는 페이지에서 확인할 수 있습니다.

Updated TOEFL, 이렇게 바뀐다!

영역	문제 유형	문항 수 Module1	문항 수 Module2 Lower	문항 수 Module2 Upper	예상 시간	점수
Reading 총 35문항 *더미 문제가 출제될 경우, 최대 48문항	TASK1 Complete the Words 단어의 철자 완성하기	10문항	10문항	10문항	18~27분	1~6점
	TASK2 Read in Daily Life 일상 지문 읽고 문제 풀기	5문항	5문항	0문항		
	TASK3 Read an Academic Passage 학술 지문 읽고 문제 풀기	5문항	0문항	5문항		
Listening 총 35문항 *더미 문제가 출제될 경우, 최대 45문항	TASK1 Listen and Choose a Response 문장 듣고 이어질 응답 고르기	8문항	7문항	3문항	18~27분	1~6점
	TASK2 Listen to a Conversation 대화 듣고 문제 풀기	4문항	4문항	4문항		
	TASK3 Listen to an Announcement 공지 듣고 문제 풀기	4문항	4문항	0문항		
	TASK4 Listen to an Academic Talk 강의 듣고 문제 풀기	4문항	0문항	8문항		
Writing 총 12문항	TASK1 Build a Sentence 단어 배열하여 문장 완성하기	10문항			23분	1~6점
	TASK2 Write an Email 이메일 쓰기	1문항				
	TASK3 Write for an Academic Discussion 학술 토론 의견 쓰기	1문항				
Speaking 총 11문항	TASK1 Listen and Repeat 문장 듣고 따라 말하기	7문항			8분	1~6점
	TASK2 Take an Interview 인터뷰 질문에 답변하기	4문항				
	Total				1시간 30분 내외	1~6점

시험 응시 72시간 이내 성적 발표

일상 지문이 추가되고, 단계별 적응형 구조가 도입된다.
- 단어 완성하기 유형과 일상 지문 읽기 유형이 추가되고, 학술 지문의 길이 감소
- Module 1의 결과에 따라 Module 2의 난이도와 구성이 달라지는 단계별 적응형 구조(multistage adaptive testing) 도입
- Module 1에 채점되지 않는 더미 문제 출제 가능 (Reading/Listening 영역 중 한 영역에서 출제)

일상 대화와 교내 공지가 추가되고, 단계별 적응형 구조가 도입된다.
- 짧은 일상 대화와 교내 공지 유형이 추가되고, 강의 지문의 길이 감소
- Module 1의 결과에 따라 Module 2의 난이도와 구성이 달라지는 단계별 적응형 구조(multistage adaptive testing) 도입
- Module 1에 채점되지 않는 더미 문제 출제 가능 (Reading/Listening 영역 중 한 영역에서 출제)

문장 완성 유형과 이메일 쓰기 유형이 추가된다.
- 문장 완성 유형과 이메일 쓰기 유형 추가
- 기존의 토론 글쓰기 유형은 그대로 유지
- 시험의 마지막 영역에서 세 번째 영역으로 순서 변경

문제 유형이 모두 바뀌고, 준비 시간이 없어진다.
- 따라 말하기 유형과 인터뷰 유형 추가
- 모든 유형에서 별도의 답변 준비 시간 없이 바로 답변 시작
- 시험의 세 번째 영역에서 마지막 영역으로 순서 변경

시험 소요 시간과 성적 발표 기간이 줄고, 점수 체계가 바뀐다.
- 시험 전체 소요 시간과 성적 발표 기간 감소
- 성적 체계가 0~120점 체계에서 1~6점 체계로 변경되고, 전체 점수 계산 방식이 영역별 합계에서 평균으로 변경

Updated TOEFL, 이렇게 대비하라!

■ READING

TASK 1	**Complete the Words** 단어의 철자 완성하기 (1지문 10문항)	
	• 학술 지문에서 앞부분 절반의 철자만 제시되는 단어 10개의 뒷부분을 채워 완성하는 유형이다.	
	• 다양한 학술 분야 주제의 지문이 70~100단어 분량으로 출제된다.	
TASK 2	**Read in Daily Life** 일상 지문 읽고 문제 풀기 (1지문 2~3문항)	
	• 이메일, 문자메시지, 광고, 공지, 기사, SNS 포스팅, 양식 등 다양한 형태의 지문이 출제된다.	
	• 지문 길이는 15~100단어 분량으로 짧은 편이며, 일상적인 주제와 소재를 다룬다.	
TASK 3	**Read an Academic Passage** 학술 지문 읽고 문제 풀기 (1지문 5문항)	
	• 기존의 리딩 유형과 가장 유사하지만, 지문의 길이가 175~200단어로 감소했다.	
	• 전공 심화 수준의 까다로운 내용은 출제되지 않으며, 문화적 편향 없는 보편적인 주제와 소재가 출제된다.	

영역 심층 분석

1. 학술 지문의 비중이 줄고, 기본적인 어휘력과 일상생활에서 접하는 다양한 글을 읽고 이해하는 능력이 중요해진다.
2. 단계별 적응형 구조(multistage adaptive testing)가 도입된다.
   - 두 단계(Module)로 구성되며, Module 1의 결과에 따라 Module 2의 난이도와 구성이 조정된다.
   - Module 2에서 낮은 난이도의 구성이 나오면 리딩 영역 만점(6점)을 받는 것은 불가능하다.
3. 문항 당 풀이 시간은 줄어든다.
   - 전체 문항 수는 20문항에서 35~48문항으로 증가하고, 소요 시간은 약 35분에서 18~27분으로 감소했다.

핵심 대비 전략

TASK 1 풀이 시간을 단축하기 위해 어휘력을 키우고, 단어의 앞부분 철자만 보고 뒤에 이어질 철자를 채우는 연습을 한다.
- 평소에 영어로 된 글을 자주 읽으면서 다양한 단어에 익숙해진다. 특히, 단어의 정확한 철자까지 알아 둔다.
- 앞부분의 철자만 주어지고 뒷부분은 빈칸으로 주어지는 TASK 1 문제 형태에 익숙해지도록 많은 문제를 풀어 본다.

TASK 2 정답의 근거를 빠르게 찾을 수 있도록, 다양한 일상 지문의 형태와 흐름을 익힌다.
- 이메일, 메시지 대화문, 공지, 각종 양식 등, 다양한 일상 지문의 형태와 일반적인 흐름을 익힌다.

TASK 3 다양한 배경지식을 쌓고, 빠르고 정확한 독해를 통해 정답의 근거를 찾는 연습을 한다.
- 지문의 길이가 줄어도, TASK 3의 학술 지문은 여전히 난이도가 높기 때문에 빠르고 정확한 독해가 관건이다.
- 다양한 배경지식을 쌓으면 친숙하지 않은 주제의 지문을 보더라도 쉽고 빠르게 지문의 내용을 이해할 수 있다.

LISTENING

TASK 1 | **Listen and Choose a Response** 문장 듣고 이어질 응답 고르기
- 7~8단어로 이루어진 한 문장을 듣고 이어질 응답을 고르는 유형이다.
- 일상적인 대화 상황이 출제되며, 종종 구어체도 나온다.
- 문항 당 풀이 시간은 최대 20초이다.

TASK 2 | **Listen to a Conversation** 대화 듣고 문제 풀기 (1지문 2문항)
- 식사, 쇼핑, 약속 등 일상적인 주제에 관한 두 사람 사이의 대화가 출제된다.
- 대화 길이는 약 23초, 문항 당 풀이 시간은 최대 20초이다.

TASK 3 | **Listen to an Announcement** 공지 듣고 문제 풀기 (1지문 2문항)
- 대학 캠퍼스 내에서 행사, 강의, 시설 등에 대해 안내하는 공지가 출제된다.
- 공지 길이는 약 21초, 문항 당 풀이 시간은 최대 20초이다.

TASK 4 | **Listen to an Academic Talk** 강의 듣고 문제 풀기 (1지문 4문항)
- 기존의 리스닝 강의 유형과 유사하지만, 지문의 길이가 약 1분 20초로 감소했다.
- 전공 심화 수준의 까다로운 내용은 출제되지 않으며, 문화적 편향 없는 보편적인 주제와 소재가 출제된다.
- 문항 당 풀이 시간은 최대 30초이다.

영역 심층 분석

1. 학술적인 내용뿐 아니라, 일상적인 주제에 대한 짧은 대화나 공지를 듣고 화자의 의도를 이해하는 능력도 평가한다.
2. 북미, 영국, 호주, 뉴질랜드 발음이 골고루 출제된다.
3. 단계별 적응형 구조(multistage adaptive testing)가 도입된다.
   - 두 단계(Module)로 구성되며, Module 1의 결과에 따라 Module 2의 난이도와 구성이 조정된다.
   - Module 2에서 낮은 난이도의 구성이 나오면 리스닝 영역 만점(6점)을 받는 것은 불가능하다.

핵심 대비 전략

TASK 1 질문을 확실하게 듣는 연습을 하고, 자주 출제되는 오답 패턴에 대비한다.
- 짧고 빠르게 지나가는 질문 문장을 놓치지 않고 들을 수 있도록 집중력을 강화한다.
- 자주 출제되는 오답 패턴을 확실히 익히고, 자주 틀리는 문제에 대해 자신이 오답을 선택한 이유를 꼼꼼하게 분석한다.

TASK 2&3 정확한 근거를 갖고 정답을 고를 수 있도록, 지문의 흐름과 내용을 정확히 파악하여 듣는 연습을 한다.
- 대화와 공지의 앞부분을 놓치지 않고 듣는 연습을 통해 주제를 확실히 파악할 수 있도록 한다.
- 일상 대화에서 자주 출제되는 구어체 표현에 익숙해진다.
- 공지의 빈출 주제와 일반적인 흐름, 자주 나오는 표현을 익힌다.

TASK 4 다양한 배경지식을 쌓고, 강의의 핵심 내용을 정리하며 듣는 연습을 한다.
- 지문의 길이가 줄어도, TASK 4의 강의는 여전히 난이도가 높기 때문에 핵심 내용을 놓치지 않고 정확히 듣는 것이 중요하다.
- 다양한 배경지식을 쌓으면 친숙하지 않은 주제의 강의를 듣더라도 내용을 정확히 파악할 수 있다.
- 평소에 문제를 풀 때 집중해서 들으며 주요 내용을 노트테이킹하는 연습을 한다.

Updated TOEFL, 이렇게 대비하라!

WRITING

TASK 1
Build a Sentence 단어 배열하여 문장 완성하기
- 완전한 형태로 주어지는 한 문장을 보고, 보기 단어를 배열하여 이어질 응답 문장을 완성하는 유형이다.
- 문법적으로 정확하면서도 문맥에 맞는 자연스러운 응답이 될 수 있는 문장을 완성해야 한다.
- 10문항이 출제되고, TASK 전체 제한 시간은 약 5분 50초이다.

TASK 2
Write an Email 이메일 쓰기
- 학교나 일상에서 일어날 법한 상황과 이메일을 쓰는 목적이 주어지고, 그에 맞춰 이메일을 작성하는 유형이다.
- 일반적인 이메일의 구조에 맞게 작성해야 하며, 초대, 추천, 문제점 전달, 해결책 제안 등의 다양한 의사소통 목적에 맞는 형식과 표현을 적절히 활용해야 한다.
- 7분 동안 최대한 길게 작성하도록 요구되는데, 110~130 단어 분량이 적절하다.

TASK 3
Write for an Academic Discussion 학술 토론 의견 쓰기
- 기존 토플에서 그대로 유지되는 유일한 유형이다.
- 교수가 토론 주제를 간단히 설명하며 던진 질문과, 다른 학생 두 명의 의견을 읽고, 자신의 의견을 작성하는 유형이다.
- 10분 동안 최소 100단어 이상 작성해야 한다.

영역 심층 분석

1. **기본적인 문법 규칙에 따라 문장을 쓰는 능력을 평가한다.**
   - 전달하고자 하는 의미를 제대로 전달하기 위해 지켜야 할 문법 규칙들을 잘 알고 있는지를 평가한다.

2. **온라인 의사소통 형식에 적절한 글을 쓰는 역량이 중요하다.**
   - 글을 쓰는 목적, 상대방과의 관계 등에 따라 적절한 문장 구조와 표현을 구사할 수 있어야 한다.

핵심 대비 전략

TASK 1 기본적인 영어 어순과 문법 규칙을 지키며 문장을 쓰는 연습을 한다.
- 수 일치, 시제 일치, 대명사와 접속사의 쓰임 등 기본적인 문법 규칙을 익혀 둔다.

TASK 2 이메일의 기본 구조를 익히고, 일상적인 의사소통 목적에 따라 자주 쓰는 표현을 익힌다.
- 인사말, 목적, 세부사항, 맺음말로 이어지는 이메일의 기본 구조를 지켜 답안을 작성하는 연습을 한다.
- 문의, 부탁, 항의, 감사 등 다양한 의사소통 목적 별로 자주 쓰이는 표현을 익혀 둔다.
- 평소에 많은 문제를 풀어 보며, 1~2분 동안 아웃라인을 잡고, 4~5분 동안 실제 답안을 쓰는 연습을 한다.

TASK 3 평소에 다양한 주제에 대해 브레인스토밍해 보고, 논리적인 답안을 쓰는 연습을 한다.
- 자신의 주장에 대해 논리적으로 타당한 이유와 근거를 생각해내는 연습을 한다.
- 다양한 주제에 대해 나올 수 있는 질문들과 답안에 활용할 수 있는 아이디어를 정리해 둔다.
- 평소에 2~3분 동안 답변 내용을 구상하고, 7분 동안 답안을 작성하는 연습을 한다.

SPEAKING

TASK 1	**Listen and Repeat** 문장 듣고 따라 말하기 • 음성으로만 들려주는 문장 7개를 한 개씩 듣고 그대로 따라 말하는 유형이다. • 일상 및 학교에서 접할 수 있는 시설, 행사, 절차 등에 대해 사람들에게 안내하는 상황이 제시되고, 배경이 되는 장소를 묘사한 그림이 제시된다. • 각 문장은 한 번씩만 들려주고, 3초의 간격 후에 8~12초의 답변 시간이 주어진다.
TASK 2	**Take an Interview** 인터뷰 질문에 답변하기 • 특정 주제에 대한 인터뷰 질문 4개에 답변하는 유형이다. • 교육, 사회, 과학기술, 여가 등 다양한 주제로 인터뷰가 진행된다. • 인터뷰 질문은 음성으로만 들려주고, 준비 시간 없이 바로 답변해야 한다. • 한 질문에 대한 답변 시간은 45초가 주어진다.

영역 심층 분석

1. 실생활에서의 의사소통 방식을 반영하여, 즉각적으로 적절한 말을 하는 능력을 평가한다.
   - 상대방의 말을 정확히 듣고 기억하여 그대로 전달할 수 있어야 한다.
   - 상대방의 질문에 대해 즉각적으로 자신의 의견을 타당한 이유나 근거와 함께 말할 수 있어야 한다.
2. 북미, 영국, 호주, 뉴질랜드 발음이 골고루 출제된다.

핵심 대비 전략

TASK 1 문장을 들으면서 정확히 기억하고 그대로 따라 말하는 연습을 한다.
- 쉐도잉 연습을 통해 들리는 문장을 그대로 따라 말할 수 있도록 한다.
- 다양한 안내 상황 별로 자주 출제되는 표현을 익힌다.

TASK 2 질문을 듣는 동시에 답변 내용을 생각하고 바로 말할 수 있도록 충분히 연습한다.
- 기본적인 답변 구조를 익히고 그에 맞춰 말하는 연습을 충분히 해 둔다.
- 다양한 인터뷰 주제에 대해 나올 수 있는 질문들과 답변에 활용할 수 있는 아이디어를 정리해 둔다.

해커스 토플이 제공하는 토플 정복을 위한 특별한 혜택!

01 토플 적중 예상특강
(HackersIngang.com)

해커스어학원 선생님들의 이번 달 토플 적중 예상특강 제공

02 온라인 실전모의고사
(HackersIngang.com)

출제 경향을 완벽 반영한 온라인 모의고사로 실전 완벽 대비

03 단어암기 MP3
(HackersIngang.com)

단어암기 MP3로 언제, 어디서든 효과적인 단어 학습 가능

04 토플 스피킹/라이팅 첨삭 게시판
(goHackers.com)

무제한 1:1 첨삭을 통한 확실한 실력 향상

05 토플 쉐도잉 & 말하기 연습 프로그램
(goHackers.com)

쉐도잉 & 말하기 반복 훈련으로 빠른 실력 향상

06 토플 자료 및 유학 정보
(goHackers.com)

성공적인 토플 학습방법부터 유학 정보와 다양한 무료 학습자료까지 풍부한 정보 제공

HACKERS

Updated
TOEFL
LISTENING

해커스 어학연구소

무료 토플자료·유학정보 공유
goHackers.com

PREFACE

『Hackers Updated TOEFL LISTENING』을 내면서

해커스 토플은 단순한 시험 대비를 넘어, 여러분의 실질적인 영어 실력 향상에 도움이 되고자 하는 작은 진심으로 출발했습니다. 해커스 토플 전 시리즈가 오랜 세월 **베스트셀러를 넘어 스테디셀러로 자리**할 수 있었던 이유는, 늘 **처음과 같은 마음**으로 더 좋은 책을 만들기 위해 고민하고, 최신 경향을 반영하기 위해 끊임없이 노력하기 때문입니다.

이번 『Hackers Updated TOEFL』 시리즈 또한 해커스의 전문성과 축적된 노하우를 바탕으로, 변화된 시험의 모든 유형을 면밀히 분석하고 정교한 문제 해결 전략을 담아 **실전 대비의 완결판**으로 완성하였습니다.

Updated TOEFL 경향을 반영한 방대한 양의 실전 문제를 수록하였으며, 실전과 동일한 난이도와 구성의 실전모의고사를 온라인으로 제공하여 보다 철저히 실전에 대비할 수 있도록 하였습니다. 이 교재의 학습 과정을 충실히 따라간다면 누구나 실전에 철저히 대비할 수 있으며, 궁극적으로 **고득점 달성**으로 이어질 것이라 확신합니다.

『Hackers Updated TOEFL LISTENING』이 여러분의 토플 목표 점수 달성에 확실한 해결책이 될 뿐 아니라, 실질적인 영어 실력의 향상과 함께 더 큰 꿈을 향해 나아가는 길에서 **든든한 동반자**가 되기를 소망합니다.

David Cho
& 해커스어학연구소

Hackers Updated TOEFL LISTENING

CONTENTS

『해커스 토플 리스닝』이 특별한 이유!	6
TOEFL iBT 소개	10
TOEFL iBT LISTENING 소개	12
TOEFL iBT LISTENING 화면 구성	14
성향별 맞춤 공부 방법	16
해커스 학습플랜	18
DIAGNOSTIC TEST	21

TASK 1 Listen and Choose a Response

Introduction — 30

Section I. Wh- Questions
1. What & Which Questions — 34
2. Who & Where/When Questions — 40
3. Why & How Questions — 46

Section II. Non Wh- Questions
1. Be/Auxiliary Verb Questions — 54
2. Tag Questions — 58
3. Alternative Questions — 62
4. Suggestion/Offer/Request Questions — 66

Section III. Statements
1. Informative Statements — 72
2. Advisory Statements — 76

TASK 2 Listen to a Conversation

Introduction — 82

Section I. Question Types
1. Main Topic/Purpose Questions — 86
2. Suggestion/Offer Questions — 94
3. Problem Questions — 102
4. Do Next Questions — 110
5. Detail Questions — 118
6. Intention/Attitude Questions — 126
7. Inference Questions — 134

Section II. Conversation Topics
1. Daily Life — 144
2. Campus Life — 152
3. Work & Service — 160

TASK 3 Listen to an Announcement

Introduction 170

Section I. Question Types
1. Main Topic/Purpose Questions 174
2. To Do Questions 182
3. Detail Questions 190
4. Intention Questions 198
5. Inference Questions 206

Section II. Announcement Topics
1. Campus Events 216
2. Student Activities 224
3. Lectures & Facilities 232

TASK 4 Listen to an Academic Talk

Introduction 242

Section I. Question Types
1. Main Topic/Purpose Questions 246
2. Discuss Next Questions 254
3. Detail Questions 262
4. Intention Questions 270
5. Organization Questions 278
6. Inference Questions 288

Section II. Academic Topics
1. Humanities 298
2. Arts 308
3. Social Science 320
4. Physical Science 332
5. Life Science 344

ACTUAL TEST 1 356
ACTUAL TEST 2 368
TASK별 실전 필수 어휘 [부록] 383
미국식 영어와 영국식 영어의 차이 [부록] 405

정답·스크립트·해석·정답단서 [책 속의 책] 413

실전모의고사(온라인) 2회분
해커스인강(HackersIngang.com) 접속 → [MP3/자료] 클릭 → [무료 MP3/자료] 클릭하여 이용

『해커스 토플 리스닝』이 특별한 이유!

01 Updated TOEFL 출제 경향 완벽 반영!

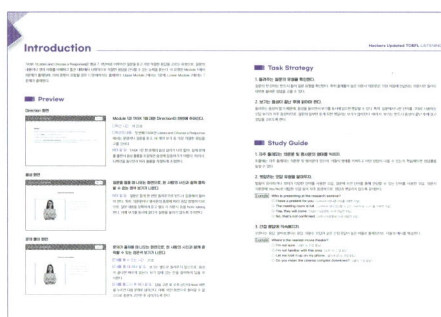

Task Introduction
Updated TOEFL Listening의 각 Task 별 특징, 시험 진행 방식을 확인하고, 실전에서 고득점을 달성하기 위한 전략과 학습 방법을 확인할 수 있다.

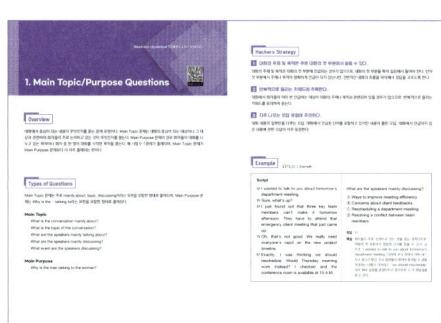

Hackers Strategy
모든 문제 유형에 대해 문제 풀이에 실질적인 도움이 되는 핵심 전략과 자주 나오는 정답 및 오답 패턴을 학습할 수 있다.

Topics & Expressions
대화 상황, 공지 주제, 강의 주제별로 꼭 알아야 할 빈출 표현과 배경지식을 효과적으로 습득할 수 있다.

풍부한 문제 풀이로 실전에 철저하게 대비!

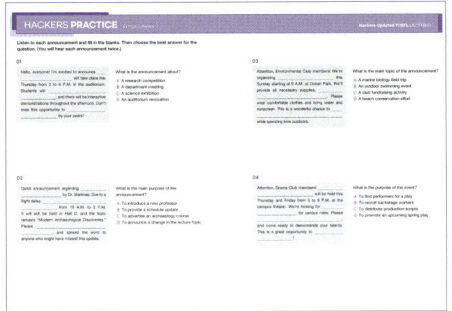

Hackers Practice

딕테이션 연습과 유형별 전략을 문제에 적용하는 연습을 통해 실전 토플에 필요한 탄탄한 실력을 다질 수 있다.

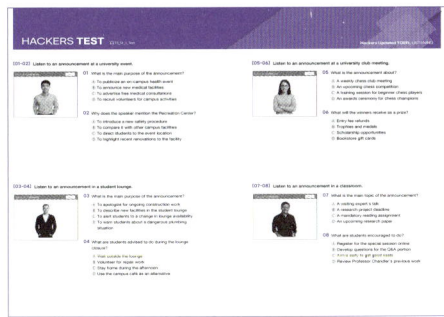

Hackers Test

출제 경향을 완벽 반영한 실전 문제들을 집중적으로 풀어 봄으로써 실전 감각을 키울 수 있다.

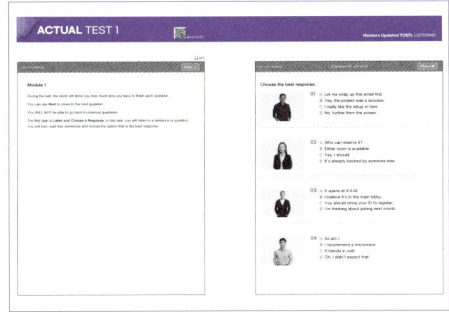

Actual Test

실제 시험의 구성과 난이도를 그대로 반영한 Actual Test 2회분을 풀어보며 자신의 실력을 최종 점검할 수 있다.

『해커스 토플 리스닝』이 특별한 이유!

03 체계적이고 탄탄한 단계별 학습 구성!

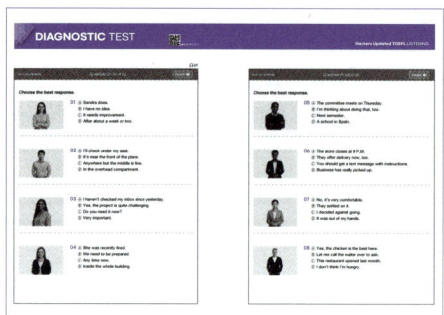

Diagnostic Test
Updated TOEFL Listening 시험의 전반적인 유형 및 난이도 등을 이해하고, 현재 자신의 실력을 진단하여 더욱 효과적인 학습을 계획할 수 있다.

문제 유형별 학습
각 Task의 문제 유형을 하나씩 학습하며 각 유형별로 최적화된 전략을 확실히 자신의 것으로 만들 수 있다.

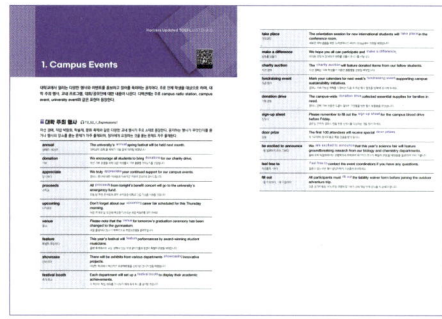

지문 주제별 학습
각 Task의 빈출 지문 주제를 확인하고 꼭 알아야 할 표현을 학습할 수 있다.

Hackers Updated **TOEFL** LISTENING

04 다양한 부가학습자료로 확실한 복습!

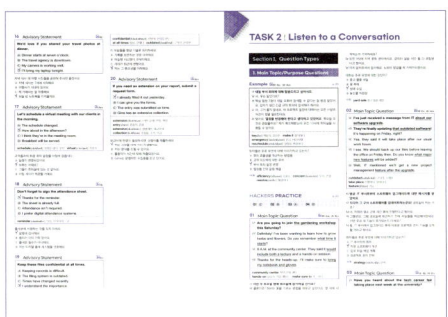

정답·스크립트·해석·정답단서 [책속의 책]

교재에 수록된 모든 지문과 문제의 스크립트, 정확한 해석, 정답의 단서, 발음 정보를 제공한다. 이를 통해 학습자가 지문을 보다 쉽게 이해하고 정답과 오답의 근거를 스스로 파악할 수 있다.

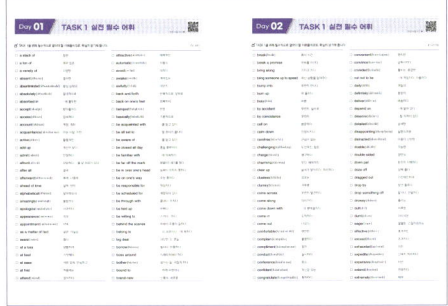

TASK별 실전 필수 어휘 [부록]

각 Task의 핵심 어휘를 정리한 부록과 온라인으로 제공하는 단어암기 MP3로, 이동할 때나 자투리 시간에 효율적으로 단어를 암기할 수 있다.

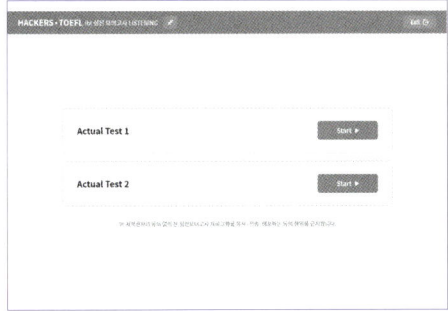

온라인 실전모의고사 [온라인]
& 쉐도잉 연습 프로그램 [온라인]

온라인 실전모의고사 2회분을 풀어보며 실전에서 흔들림 없이 실력을 발휘할 수 있다. 또한, 교재에 수록된 핵심 문장을 복습할 수 있는 쉐도잉 연습 프로그램으로 듣기 실력을 빠르게 향상시킬 수 있다.

TOEFL iBT 소개

■ TOEFL iBT란?

TOEFL(Test of English as a Foreign Language) iBT(Internet-based test)는 미국의 비영리기관인 ETS(Educational Testing Service)에서 주관하는 국제 공인 영어 시험으로, 영어가 모국어가 아닌 수험자의 영어 실력을 읽기·듣기·쓰기·말하기 네 영역으로 나누어 평가한다. 2026년 1월 21일부터 바뀌는 Updated TOEFL 시험은 Reading, Listening, Writing, Speaking 영역의 순서로 진행된다. Reading과 Listening 영역은 각 응시자의 Module 1 채점 결과에 따라 Module 2의 난이도와 구성이 달라지는 단계별 적응형 구조(multistage adaptive testing)로 진행된다.

■ TOEFL iBT 시험 구성

영역	TASK		문항 수	시험 시간	점수
Reading	TASK 1	Complete the Words	35~48문항 · Module 1: 20~33문항 · Module 2: 15문항	약 18~27분	1~6점
	TASK 2	Read in Daily Life (1지문 2~3문항)			
	TASK 3	Read an Academic Passage (1지문 5문항)			
Listening	TASK 1	Listen and Choose a Response	35~45문항 · Module 1: 20~30문항 · Module 2: 15문항	약 18~27분	1~6점
	TASK 2	Listen to a Conversation (1지문 2문항)			
	TASK 3	Listen to an Announcement (1지문 2문항)			
	TASK 4	Listen to an Academic Talk (1지문 4문항)			
Writing	TASK 1	Build a Sentence	12문항	약 23분	1~6점
	TASK 2	Write an Email			
	TASK 3	Write for an Academic Discussion			
Speaking	TASK 1	Listen and Repeat (1세트 7문항)	11문항	약 8분	1~6점
	TASK 2	Take an Interview (1세트 4문항)			
				약 2시간	1~6점

· Reading 또는 Listening 중 한 영역의 Module 1에서 더미 문제가 출제된다.
· Reading과 Listening 영역의 Module 1에서는 모든 TASK가 출제되지만, Module 2에서는 난이도에 따라 일부 TASK만 출제된다.

■ TOEFL iBT 점수 체계

2026년 1월 21일 시행되는 Updated TOEFL은 세계적으로 널리 쓰이는 외국어 능력 공통 기준인 CEFR(Common European Framework of Reference for Languages) 6단계와 직관적으로 연계되는 1~6점 구간 점수제(banded scoring scale)를 도입한다. 각 영역 점수와 총점은 0.5점 단위로 올라가는 1~6점 점수대로 표시되고, 총점은 4개 영역 점수의 평균값을 가장 가까운 0.5 단위로 반올림하여 산출한다. (예: 4개 영역 점수 평균이 5.25이면, 총점은 5.5로 표기)

* Updated TOEFL 시행 2년 동안은 기존의 0~120점 점수대도 함께 표기된다.

TOEFL 점수와 CEFR Level 환산표

TOEFL 점수	1.0	1.5	2.0	2.5	3.0	3.5	4.0	4.5	5.0	5.5	6.0
CEFR Level	A1		A2		B1		B2		C1		C2

■ TOEFL iBT 접수 및 성적 확인

실시일	· ETS Test Center 시험: 일주일에 약 2~3일 실시 · 홈에디션 시험: 일주일에 약 4~5일 실시
시험 장소	· ETS Test Center에서 치르거나, 집에서 홈에디션 시험으로 응시 가능
접수 방법	· ETS 토플 웹사이트 또는 전화상으로 접수
시험 당일 준비물	· 공인된 신분증 원본 반드시 지참 (자세한 신분증 규정은 ETS 토플 웹사이트에서 확인 가능) · 홈에디션 시험에 응시할 경우, 사전에 ETS 토플 웹사이트에서 필요한 프로그램 설치 및 준비물 확인하여 지참
성적 및 리포팅	· 시험 응시 후 바로 Reading/Listening 영역 비공식 점수 확인 가능 · 시험 응시일로부터 72시간 후에 온라인으로 성적 확인 가능 · 시험 접수 시, 자동으로 성적 리포팅 받을 기관 선택 가능 · MyBest Scores 제도 시행 (최근 2년간의 시험 성적 중 영역별 최고 점수 합산하여 유효 성적으로 인정)

TOEFL iBT LISTENING 소개

TOEFL iBT LISTENING 영역은 영어를 사용하는 국가의 대학 또는 일상 생활에서 일어날 수 있는 대화, 공지, 강의를 듣고 이해하는 능력을 평가한다. 대화, 공지, 강의는 실제 상황처럼 매우 자연스러우며, 구어체도 종종 사용된다. 음성은 미국, 영국, 호주, 뉴질랜드 네 가지 발음이 골고루 출제된다. 노트테이킹이 허용되므로 필요한 경우에는 음성을 들으면서 주요 키워드를 메모하는 것이 도움이 된다.

■ TOEFL iBT LISTENING 구성

TOEFL iBT LISTENING 영역은 두 개의 Module로 구성되며, Module 1의 결과에 따라 Module 2의 구성과 난이도가 달라지는 단계별 적응형 구조(multistage adaptive testing)로 진행된다. Module 1에서는 네 가지 TASK가 모두 출제되지만, Module 2에서는 난이도에 따라 출제되는 TASK가 달라진다. 또한, Module 1에서는 더미 문제가 출제될 수 있다.

Module 1		
TASK 1	Listen and Choose a Response	8~12문항
TASK 2	Listen to a Conversation	4~6문항 (2~3지문)
TASK 3	Listen to an Announcement	4~8문항 (2~4지문)
TASK 4	Listen to an Academic Talk	4~8문항 (1~2지문)
		총 20~30문항

Module 1의 결과에 따라 Module 2의 구성과 난이도가 달라진다.

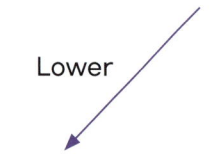 Lower    Upper

Module 2: Lower		
TASK 1	Listen and Choose a Response	7문항
TASK 2	Listen to a Conversation	4문항 (2지문)
TASK 3	Listen to an Announcement	4문항 (2지문)
TASK 4	Listen to an Academic Talk	0문항
		총 15문항

Module 2: Upper		
TASK 1	Listen and Choose a Response	3문항
TASK 2	Listen to a Conversation	4문항 (2지문)
TASK 3	Listen to an Announcement	0문항
TASK 4	Listen to an Academic Talk	8문항 (2지문)
		총 15문항

■ TOEFL iBT LISTENING TASK별 특징

TASK 1 Listen and Choose a Response
의문문 또는 평서문 형태의 한 문장을 듣고 화면에 제시된 네 개의 보기 중 이어질 응답으로 가장 적절한 것을 고르는 유형이다. 들려주는 문장이 평균 7~8단어로 짧은 편이고 한 번만 들려주므로 집중력을 유지하며 내용을 정확하게 파악하는 것이 중요하다. 한 문제 당 제한 시간은 20초이다.

TASK 2 Listen to a Conversation (1지문 2문항)
두 사람의 대화를 듣고 대화 내용과 관련된 문제의 답을 고르는 유형이다. 대화를 듣는 동안은 문제를 볼 수 없고, 대화가 끝나면 문제와 보기 네 개가 화면에 제시된다. 대화의 길이는 약 23초이며, 주로 대학이나 일상생활에서 일어날 법한 상황으로 구성된다. 한 문제 당 제한 시간은 20초이다.

TASK 3 Listen to an Announcement (1지문 2문항)
한 사람이 말하는 공지를 듣고 공지 내용과 관련된 문제의 답을 고르는 유형이다. 공지가 끝나면 문제와 보기 네 개가 화면에 제시된다. 공지 길이는 약 21초이며, 주로 대학 내에서 강의, 행사, 시설 등에 대한 안내를 하는 내용이 출제된다. 한 문제 당 제한 시간은 20초이다.

TASK 4 Listen to an Academic Talk (1지문 4문항)
한 사람이 말하는 강의를 듣고 강의 내용과 관련된 문제의 답을 고르는 유형이다. 강의가 끝나면 문제와 보기 네 개가 화면에 제시된다. 강의 길이는 약 1분 20초 정도이며 한 문제당 제한 시간은 30초이다.

TOEFL iBT LISTENING 화면 구성

1. 음량 조정 화면

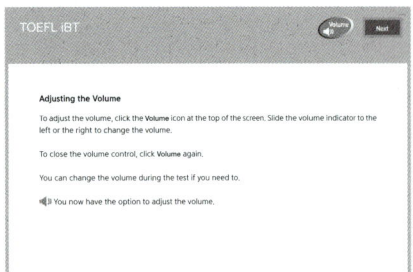

시험을 시작하기 전에 음량을 조절하는 방법을 알려주는 화면이다. Volume 버튼을 클릭하면 소리를 조절할 수 있는 창이 나타난다. 시험을 보는 동안에도 계속해서 음량을 조절할 수 있다.

2. Listening Direction 화면

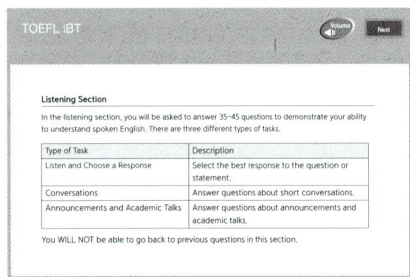

리스닝 시험에 대한 전반적인 설명이 주어지는 화면이다. 총 35~45문항이 출제되는 것, 크게 3가지 TASK로 구성된다는 것, 앞 문제로 돌아갈 수 없다는 설명이 나온다.

3. Module 시작 화면

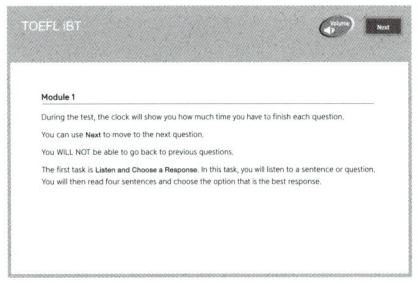

Module 진행 방식에 대한 설명이 주어지는 화면이다. 화면에서 문항 별 제한 시간이 표시된다는 것, Next 버튼을 클릭하여 다음 문제로 이동할 수 있다는 내용과 함께 TASK 1 진행 방식에 대한 설명이 나온다.

4. TASK 1 문제 화면

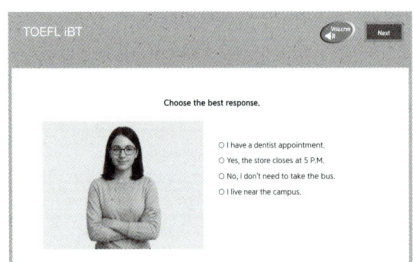

TASK 1은 문제 음성을 들을 때 대화하는 사람들의 사진과 보기 4개가 나온다. 문제 음성이 끝나면, 보기 앞에 있는 칸을 클릭하여 답을 표시한다. 답을 표시한 후 Next 버튼을 클릭하면 답이 확정되고 다음 문제로 넘어간다.

5. TASK 2~4 지문을 들을 때 나오는 화면

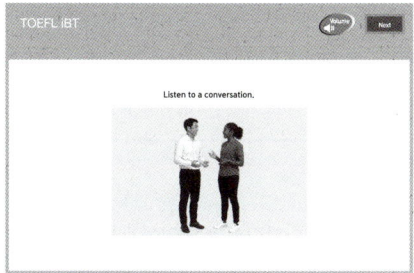

TASK 2의 대화를 들을 때는 두 화자의 사진이 나오고, TASK 3~4의 공지나 강의를 들을 때는 한 명의 화자의 사진이 나온다.

6. TASK 2~4 문제 화면

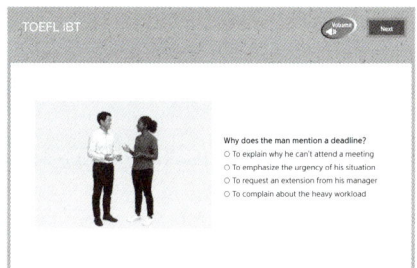

TASK 2~4에서 지문 음성이 끝난 후 나오는 문제 화면이다. 문제와 보기 4개가 화면에 나오면, 보기 앞에 있는 칸을 클릭하여 답을 표시한다. 답을 표시한 후 Next 버튼을 클릭하면 답이 확정되고 다음 문제로 넘어간다.

7. Module 종료 화면

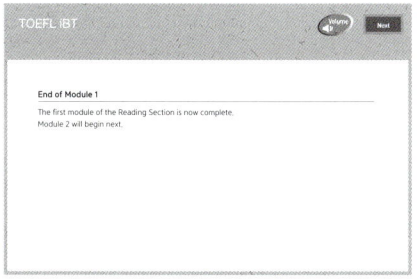

각 Module이 끝나고 나오는 디렉션 화면에서 Next 버튼을 누르면 다음 Module이나 다음 영역으로 넘어간다.

성향별 맞춤 공부 방법

* 해커스 학습플랜은 p.18~19에 수록되어 있습니다.

개별학습 혼자서 공부할 때 가장 집중이 잘 된다!

1. 나만의 학습플랜을 세운다!
p.21의 DIAGNOSTIC TEST를 통하여 자신의 현재 실력을 확인하고, 해커스 학습플랜을 참고하여 본인에게 맞는 학습 계획을 세운다.

2. 매일매일 정해진 학습 분량을 공부한다!
학습플랜에 따라 매일의 정해진 분량을 반드시 마치도록 하고, 만약 그러지 못했을 경우에는 계속 진도를 나가되 일주일이 지나기 전에 해당 주의 학습 분량을 모두 끝낸다.

3. 문제를 미리 보지 않고 풀며 오답 분석을 한다.
문제를 풀 때에는 항상 문제를 미리 보지 않고 푸는 것을 원칙으로 하며, 문제를 다 푼 후에는 스크립트와 본인이 들은 내용을 비교하며 확인하고 정답과 오답을 분석한다.

* 고우해커스(goHackers.com)의 [해커스 Books > 토플 리스닝 Q&A]에서 궁금한 사항을 질문할 수 있습니다.

스터디학습 다른 사람과 함께 공부할 때 더 열심히 한다!

1. 개별 예습으로 스터디를 준비한다!
본문 내용을 예습하고 문제를 미리 풀어 본다.

2. 토론 학습으로 완벽하게 이해한다!
미리 예습해 온 문제를 함께 토론하면서 답을 수렴해 나간다. 서로의 답을 공개하고 왜 그것을 답으로 선택하게 되었는지 토론한 후, 책의 정답과 스크립트를 확인한다.

3. 개별 복습으로 마무리한다!
스터디가 끝난 후, 해커스인강(HackersIngang.com)에서 무료로 다운로드 받을 수 있는 단어암기 MP3를 활용하여 단어를 학습하고, 스터디했던 내용을 개별 복습한다.

▶ 인강학습 원하는 시간, 원하는 장소에서 강의를 듣고 싶다!

1. 나만의 학습플랜을 세운다!
해커스인강(HackersIngang.com)에서『샘플강의보기』를 통해 강의 구성을 미리 파악하고,『스터디플랜』에 따라 자신의 학습 계획을 세운다.

2. 이해될 때까지 반복해서 듣는다!
학습플랜에 따라 오늘 공부해야 할 강의를 집중해서 듣고, 잘 이해가 되지 않는 부분은 완전히 이해될 때까지 반복해서 시청한다.

3.『선생님께 질문하기』를 적극 활용한다!
강의를 듣다가 모르는 부분이 있거나 질문할 것이 생기면『선생님께 질문하기』를 이용하여 확실히 이해하도록 한다.

학원학습 선생님의 강의를 직접 들을 때 가장 효과적이다!

1. 100% 출석을 목표로 한다!
자신의 스케줄에 맞는 수업을 등록하고, 개강일부터 종강일까지 100% 출석을 목표로 빠짐없이 수업에 참여한다.

2. 예습과 복습을 철저히 한다!
수업 전에 미리 그날 배울 내용을 훑어본다. 수업이 끝난 후에는 자신이 취약한 부분을 확인하고 복습한다.

3. 적극적으로 질문한다!
수업 시간에 잘 이해되지 않은 부분은 쉬는 시간이나 해커스어학원(Hackers.ac)의『반별게시판』을 이용해 선생님께 질문함으로써 확실히 짚고 넘어간다.

해커스 학습플랜

p.21의 DIAGNOSTIC TEST를 풀어 본 후, 그 결과에 따라 본인의 실력에 적합한 학습플랜에 맞게 공부한다.
- 맞은 개수 0~5개 : 40일 동안 학습한다. (20일 완성 학습플랜의 1일 분량을 이틀에 나누어 학습)
- 맞은 개수 6~11개 : 30일 완성 학습플랜에 따라 학습한다.
- 맞은 개수 12~17개 : 20일 완성 학습플랜에 따라 학습한다.
- 맞은 개수 18~20개 : 10일 동안 학습한다. (20일 완성 학습플랜의 2일 분량을 하루에 학습)

■ 20일 완성 학습플랜

DAY 1	DAY 2	DAY 3	DAY 4	DAY 5
□ DIAGNOSTIC TEST □ 어휘 Day 01	□ T1 Sec.I-1 □ T1 Sec.I-2 □ T1 Sec.I-3 □ 어휘 Day 02	□ T1 Sec.II-1 □ T1 Sec.II-2 □ T1 Sec.II-3 □ 어휘 Day 03	□ T1 Sec.II-4 □ T1 Sec.III-1 □ T1 Sec.III-2 □ 어휘 Day 04	□ T2 Sec.I-1 □ T2 Sec.I-2 □ T2 Sec.I-3 □ 어휘 Day 05
DAY 6	**DAY 7**	**DAY 8**	**DAY 9**	**DAY 10**
□ T2 Sec.I-4 □ T2 Sec.I-5 □ T2 Sec.I-6 □ 어휘 Day 06	□ T2 Sec.I-7 □ T2 Sec.II-1 □ T2 Sec.II-2 □ 어휘 Day 07	□ T2 Sec.II-3 □ T3 Sec.I-1 □ 어휘 Day 08	□ T3 Sec.I-2 □ T3 Sec.I-3 □ 어휘 Day 09	□ T3 Sec.I-4 □ T3 Sec.I-5 □ 어휘 Day 10
DAY 11	**DAY 12**	**DAY 13**	**DAY 14**	**DAY 15**
□ T3 Sec.II-1 □ T3 Sec.II-2 □ 어휘 Day 11	□ T3 Sec.II-3 □ T4 Sec.I-1 □ 어휘 Day 12	□ T4 Sec.I-2 □ T4 Sec.I-3 □ 어휘 Day 13	□ T4 Sec.I-4 □ T4 Sec.I-5 □ 어휘 Day 14	□ T4 Sec.I-6 □ T4 Sec.II-1 □ 어휘 Day 15
DAY 16	**DAY 17**	**DAY 18**	**DAY 19**	**DAY 20**
□ T4 Sec.II-2 □ T4 Sec.II-3 □ 어휘 Day 16	□ T4 Sec.II-4 □ T4 Sec.II-5 □ 어휘 Day 17	□ Actual Test 1 □ 어휘 Day 18	□ Actual Test 2 □ 어휘 Day 19	□ 온라인 모의고사 1 □ 온라인 모의고사 2 □ 어휘 Day 20

T: TASK   Sec: Section   어휘: TASK별 실전 필수 어휘[부록]
매일 학습이 완료된 부분에 체크(v) 표시한다.

■ 30일 완성 학습플랜

DAY 1	DAY 2	DAY 3	DAY 4	DAY 5
☐ DIAGNOSTIC TEST ☐ 어휘 Day 01	☐ T1 Sec.I-1 ☐ T1 Sec.I-2 ☐ 어휘 Day 02	☐ T1 Sec.I-3 ☐ T1 Sec.II-1 ☐ 어휘 Day 03	☐ T1 Sec.II-2 ☐ T1 Sec.II-3 ☐ 어휘 Day 04	☐ T1 Sec.II-4 ☐ T1 Sec.III-1 ☐ 어휘 Day 05
DAY 6	**DAY 7**	**DAY 8**	**DAY 9**	**DAY 10**
☐ T1 Sec.III-2 ☐ 어휘 Day 06	☐ T2 Sec.I-1 ☐ T2 Sec.I-2 ☐ 어휘 Day 07	☐ T2 Sec.I-3 ☐ T2 Sec.I-4 ☐ 어휘 Day 08	☐ T2 Sec.I-5 ☐ T2 Sec.I-6 ☐ 어휘 Day 09	☐ T2 Sec.I-7 ☐ T2 Sec.II-1 ☐ 어휘 Day 10
DAY 11	**DAY 12**	**DAY 13**	**DAY 14**	**DAY 15**
☐ T2 Sec.II-2 ☐ T2 Sec.II-3 ☐ 어휘 Day 11	☐ T3 Sec.I-1 ☐ T3 Sec.I-2 ☐ 어휘 Day 12	☐ T3 Sec.I-3 ☐ T3 Sec.I-4 ☐ 어휘 Day 13	☐ T3 Sec.I-5 ☐ T3 Sec.II-1 ☐ 어휘 Day 14	☐ T3 Sec.II-2 ☐ T3 Sec.II-3 ☐ 어휘 Day 15
DAY 16	**DAY 17**	**DAY 18**	**DAY 19**	**DAY 20**
☐ T4 Sec.I-1 ☐ 어휘 Day 16	☐ T4 Sec.I-2 ☐ 어휘 Day 17	☐ T4 Sec.I-3 ☐ 어휘 Day 18	☐ T4 Sec.I-4 ☐ 어휘 Day 19	☐ T4 Sec.I-5 ☐ 어휘 Day 20
DAY 21	**DAY 22**	**DAY 23**	**DAY 24**	**DAY 25**
☐ T4 Sec.I-6 ☐ 어휘 Day 01-02 복습	☐ T4 Sec.II-1 ☐ 어휘 Day 03-04 복습	☐ T4 Sec.II-2 ☐ 어휘 Day 05-06 복습	☐ T4 Sec.II-3 ☐ 어휘 Day 07-08 복습	☐ T4 Sec.II-4 ☐ 어휘 Day 09-10 복습
DAY 26	**DAY 27**	**DAY 28**	**DAY 29**	**DAY 30**
☐ T4 Sec.II-5 ☐ 어휘 Day 11-12 복습	☐ Actual Test 1 ☐ 어휘 Day 13-14 복습	☐ Actual Test 2 ☐ 어휘 Day 15-16 복습	☐ 온라인 모의고사 1 ☐ 어휘 Day 17-18 복습	☐ 온라인 모의고사 2 ☐ 어휘 Day 19-20 복습

T: TASK   Sec: Section   어휘: TASK별 실전 필수 어휘[부록]
매일 학습이 완료된 부분에 체크(v) 표시한다.

무료 토플자료·유학정보 공유
goHackers.com

**Hackers
Updated TOEFL
LISTENING**

DIAGNOSTIC TEST

실제 TOEFL 리스닝 시험과 유사한 Diagnostic Test를 통해 본인의 실력을 평가해 봅니다.
그리고 본인에게 맞는 학습플랜(p.18)을 확인한 후, 본 교재를 효율적으로 학습합니다.

DIAGNOSTIC TEST

🎧 DT

TOEFL iBT LISTENING Questions 01~04 of 20 Volume 🔊

Choose the best response.

01 Ⓐ Sandra does.
Ⓑ I have no idea.
Ⓒ It needs improvement.
Ⓓ After about a week or two.

02 Ⓐ I'll check under my seat.
Ⓑ It's near the front of the plane.
Ⓒ Anywhere but the middle is fine.
Ⓓ In the overhead compartment.

03 Ⓐ I haven't checked my inbox since yesterday.
Ⓑ Yes, the project is quite challenging.
Ⓒ Do you need it now?
Ⓓ Very important.

04 Ⓐ She was recently fired.
Ⓑ We need to be prepared.
Ⓒ Any time now.
Ⓓ Inside the whole building.

TOEFL iBT LISTENING Questions 05~08 of 20

Choose the best response.

05 Ⓐ The committee meets on Thursday.
Ⓑ I'm thinking about doing that, too.
Ⓒ Next semester.
Ⓓ A school in Spain.

06 Ⓐ The store closes at 9 P.M.
Ⓑ They offer delivery now, too.
Ⓒ You should get a text message with instructions.
Ⓓ Business has really picked up.

07 Ⓐ No, it's very comfortable.
Ⓑ They settled on it.
Ⓒ I decided against going.
Ⓓ It was out of my hands.

08 Ⓐ Yes, the chicken is the best here.
Ⓑ Let me call the waiter over to ask.
Ⓒ This restaurant opened last month.
Ⓓ I don't think I'm hungry.

[09-10] Listen to a conversation.

09 What event are the speakers discussing?

Ⓐ A barbecue party
Ⓑ A dinner reservation
Ⓒ A cooking class
Ⓓ A restaurant opening

10 What does the woman plan to bring to the event?

Ⓐ Music equipment
Ⓑ Some beverages
Ⓒ Her potato salad
Ⓓ Barbecue ingredients

[11-12] Listen to a conversation.

11 What reason does the man give for his suggestion to use public transportation?

Ⓐ It is more convenient.
Ⓑ It saves time during busy hours.
Ⓒ It helps save money.
Ⓓ It is better for the environment.

12 What does the woman say about driving to campus?

Ⓐ It would make her commute more stressful.
Ⓑ It would reduce her travel time.
Ⓒ It would fit her schedule better.
Ⓓ It would prevent her from being late.

[13-14] Listen to an announcement at a university club meeting.

13 What is the main topic of the announcement?

Ⓐ A guest presentation
Ⓑ A weekly schedule
Ⓒ A photography exhibition
Ⓓ An upcoming workshop

14 What should students do according to the announcement?

Ⓐ Submit entries by the deadline
Ⓑ Attend the next workshop
Ⓒ Vote for photographs online
Ⓓ Sign up to display their photos

[15-16] Listen to an announcement at a school event.

15 What is the main purpose of the announcement?

Ⓐ To introduce career counselors
Ⓑ To promote internship opportunities
Ⓒ To announce a job fair schedule
Ⓓ To explain college application procedures

16 What should students submit to apply by this Friday?

Ⓐ A résumé and internship application form
Ⓑ College transcripts and test scores
Ⓒ Recommendation letters from professors
Ⓓ A portfolio of academic projects

[17-20] Listen to a talk in an economics class.

17 What is the main topic of the talk?

   Ⓐ The challenges faced by technology markets
   Ⓑ The history of communication networks and telephone systems
   Ⓒ An idea to develop the social media market
   Ⓓ A market phenomenon in the technology and communication sectors

18 Why does the speaker mention social media platforms and messaging apps?

   Ⓐ To give examples of digital services that are affected by network effects
   Ⓑ To describe how companies reduce their initial costs
   Ⓒ To identify which new services have been successful in the market
   Ⓓ To illustrate the technical features of communication technologies

19 According to the speaker, what is a problem caused by network effects?

   Ⓐ High network access costs
   Ⓑ Complicated platform interfaces
   Ⓒ Competitive barriers to entry
   Ⓓ Insufficient initial user attraction

20 What will the speaker discuss next?

   Ⓐ The benefits of building network platforms
   Ⓑ The strategic management of network effects by companies
   Ⓒ The technical aspects of communication networks
   Ⓓ The psychological reasons why people join monopolistic networks

Answers p.414

*채점 후 p.18을 보고 본인의 맞은 개수에 해당하는 학습 플랜을 참고하세요.

무료 토플자료·유학정보 공유
goHackers.com

무료 토플자료·유학정보 공유
goHackers.com

Hackers
Updated TOEFL
LISTENING

TASK 1

Listen and Choose a Response

Introduction

Section I. Wh- Questions
  1. What & Which Questions
  2. Who & Where/When Questions
  3. Why & How Questions

Section II. Non Wh- Questions
  1. Be/Auxiliary Verb Questions
  2. Tag Questions
  3. Alternative Questions
  4. Suggestion/Offer/Request Questions

Section III. Statements
  1. Informative Statements
  2. Advisory Statements

Introduction

TASK 1(Listen and Choose a Response)은 평균 7~8단어로 이루어진 질문을 듣고 가장 적절한 응답을 고르는 유형으로, 질문의 내용이나 영어 어휘를 이해하고 짧은 대화에서 사회적으로 적절한 응답을 인식할 수 있는 능력을 묻는다. 이 유형은 Module 1에서 8문제가 출제되며, 더미 문항이 포함될 경우 12문제까지도 출제된다. Upper Module 2에서는 3문제, Lower Module 2에서는 7문제가 출제된다.

■ Preview

Direction 화면

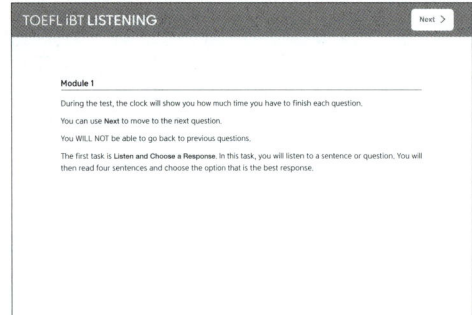

Module 1과 TASK 1에 대한 Direction이 한번에 주어진다.

디렉션 시간 : 약 20초

디렉션의 내용 : 첫 번째 TASK인 Listen and Choose a Response에서는 문장이나 질문을 듣고, 네 개의 보기 중 가장 적절한 응답을 고를 것이다.

해야 할 일 : TASK 1은 한 문제의 음성 길이가 너무 짧아, 실제 문제를 풀면서 음성 볼륨을 조정하면 음성에 집중하기가 어렵다. 따라서, 디렉션을 들으면서 미리 볼륨을 적절하게 조정한다.

음성 화면

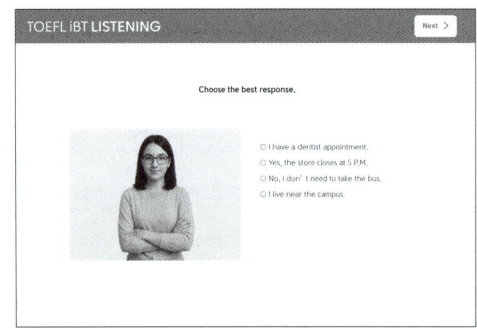

질문을 들을 때 나오는 화면으로, 한 사람의 사진과 함께 클릭할 수 없는 회색 보기가 나온다.

해야 할 일 : 질문은 짧게 한 번만 들려주므로 반드시 집중해서 들어야 한다. 특히, 의문문이나 평서문의 종류에 따라 응답 방법이 다르므로, 질문 내용을 정확하게 듣고 필요 시 의문사 등을 Note-taking 한다. 이때 보기를 동시에 읽다가 질문을 놓치지 않도록 주의한다.

문제 풀이 화면

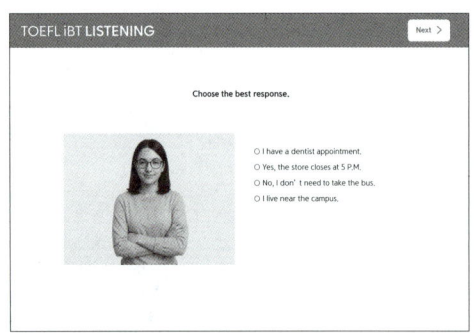

문제가 출제될 때 나오는 화면으로, 한 사람의 사진과 함께 클릭할 수 있는 검은색 보기가 나온다.

문제를 풀 수 있는 시간 : 20초

문제를 풀 때 해야 할 일 : 보기는 별도로 들려주지 않으므로, 음성이 끝나면 빠르게 읽는다. 보기 앞에 있는 칸을 클릭하여 답을 표시한다.

문제를 풀고 난 후 해야 할 일 : 답을 고른 후 우측 상단의 Next 버튼을 누르면 다음 문제로 넘어간다. 이때, 이전 화면으로 돌아갈 수 없으므로 충분히 고민한 후 넘어가도록 한다.

Task Strategy

1. 들려주는 질문의 유형을 확인한다.
질문의 첫 단어는 반드시 들어 질문 유형을 확인한다. 특히 출제율이 높은 의문사 의문문은 가장 처음에 언급되는 의문사만 들어도 대부분 올바른 정답을 고를 수 있다.

2. 보기는 음성이 끝난 후에 읽어야 한다.
들려주는 음성이 짧기 때문에, 음성을 들으면서 보기를 동시에 읽으면 헷갈릴 수 있다. 특히, 질문에서 나온 단어를 그대로 사용하는 오답 보기가 자주 등장하므로, 질문의 일부만 듣게 되면 헷갈리는 보기가 많아진다. 따라서, 보기는 반드시 음성이 끝난 후에 읽고 정답을 고르도록 한다.

Study Guide

1. 자주 출제되는 의문문 및 평서문의 형태를 익히자.
토플에는 자주 출제되는 의문문 및 평서문이 있으며, 이들의 형태를 익혀두고 어떤 정답이 나올 수 있는지 학습해두면 정답률을 높일 수 있다.

2. 헷갈리는 오답 유형을 알아두자.
발음이 유사하거나 의미가 다양한 단어를 사용한 오답, 질문에 쓰인 단어를 통해 연상할 수 있는 단어를 사용한 오답, 의문사 의문문에 Yes/No로 대답한 오답 등이 자주 등장하므로, 정답과 헷갈리지 않도록 유의한다.

Example Who is presenting at the research seminar?
  ○ I have a present for you. ['present'의 다른 의미를 사용한 오답]
  ○ The meeting room is full. ['seminar'에서 연상할 수 있는 'meeting room'을 사용한 오답]
  ○ Yes, they will come. [의문사 의문문에 Yes로 대답한 오답]
  ○ No, that's not confirmed. [의문사 의문문에 No로 대답한 오답]

3. 간접 응답에 익숙해지자.
모른다는 응답, 알아보겠다는 응답, 되묻는 응답과 같은 간접 응답이 높은 비율로 출제되므로, 이들의 예시를 학습한다.

Example Where's the nearest movie theater?
  ○ I'm not sure. [모른다는 간접 응답]
  ○ I'm not familiar with this area. [모른다는 간접 응답]
  ○ Let me look it up on my phone. [알아보겠다는 간접 응답]
  ○ Do you mean the cinema complex downtown? [되묻는 간접 응답]

무료 토플자료·유학정보 공유
goHackers.com

Section I
Wh- Questions

Section I에서는 TASK 1에 출제되는 의문사 의문문을 What, Which, Who, Where, When, Why, How로 나누어 각 의문문의 특징과 질문 형태, 빈출 정답 및 오답을 소개하고 있다. 또한 연습 문제 및 실전 문제를 통해 각 문제 유형을 효과적으로 공략할 수 있도록 하였다.

TASK 1의 Wh- Questions는 아래와 같이 나눌 수 있다.

1. What & Which Questions
2. Who & Where/When Questions
3. Why & How Questions

Hackers Updated TOEFL LISTENING

1. What & Which Questions

① What Questions

Overview

의문사 What을 이용하여 시간, 종류, 비용, 의견 등을 묻는 문제 유형이다. What 뒤에 나오는 내용까지 잘 들어야 올바른 응답을 고를 수 있다. 매 시험 0~1문제가 출제되며, 이 유형에서는 시간을 묻는 문제가 특히 자주 출제된다.

Hackers Strategy

· What 의문문은 뒤에 오는 명사 또는 동사에 따라 시간, 종류, 비용, 의견 등을 묻는다. What 뒤의 명사 또는 동사를 반드시 듣고 무엇에 대한 정보를 묻고 있는지 파악한다.

Example T1_S1_1_Example1

What time does the pharmacy close tonight?
오늘 밤 약국은 몇 시에 닫나요?

· At 10 P.M. 오후 10시에요. [시간]
· We should check their schedule.
  그들의 일정을 확인해야 해요. [간접 응답]

What kind of apps do you use for taking notes?
필기를 위해 어떤 종류의 앱을 쓰시나요?

· I use NoteWave. 저는 NoteWave를 써요. [종류]
· I prefer using pen and paper.
  저는 펜과 종이를 쓰는 것을 선호해요. [간접 응답]

What's the delivery charge?
배달료가 얼마인가요?

· It's five dollars per order. 주문 당 5달러예요. [비용]
· We don't offer that service.
  저희는 그 서비스를 제공하지 않아요. [간접 응답]

What do you think of the new marketing strategy?
새 마케팅 전략을 어떻게 생각하세요?

· It is quite innovative. 꽤 독창적이에요. [의견]
· I haven't checked it yet. 아직 확인을 안 했어요. [간접 응답]

② Which Questions

Overview

의문사 Which를 이용하여 다수 중 하나를 고르게 하는 문제 유형이다. 매 시험 0~1문제가 출제된다.

Hackers Strategy

· Which 또는 Which of 뒤에 나오는 명사가 질문의 핵심이므로 주의해서 듣는다.
· the one, either, both를 포함한 응답이 정답으로 자주 출제되는 점을 알아둔다.

Example

🎧 T1_S1_1_Example2

Which bus goes to the shopping mall?
어느 버스가 쇼핑몰에 가나요?

· **Number 45 stops there.** 45번이 그곳에 서요. [하나 선택]
· **Sorry, I don't know.** 죄송하지만, 저도 몰라요. [간접 응답]

Which of these two desserts do you prefer?
이 두 디저트 중 어떤 것을 선호하시나요?

· **The one with blueberry.**
  블루베리가 있는 것이요. [둘 중 하나 선택]
· **Either is fine.** 둘 중 아무거나 괜찮아요. [둘 중 하나 선택]
· **Both seem delicious.** 둘 다 맛있어 보여요. [둘 다 선택]
· **I need more time to decide.**
  결정할 시간이 더 필요해요. [간접 응답]

⚠ **Wrong Answers**

· **Yes, it's on the table.** 네, 그것은 식탁 위에 있어요.
  [의문사 의문문에 Yes/No로 대답한 오답]
· **Because I like sweets.** 제가 단 것을 좋아해서요.
  [다른 의문문에 대한 내용으로 대답한 오답]

HACKERS PRACTICE 🎧 T1_S1_1_Practice

Listen to each question and fill in the blanks. Then choose the best response. (You will hear each question twice.)

01

_____ are _____ at the gym?

Ⓐ Personal training and group classes.
Ⓑ I go there every morning.
Ⓒ Yes, it stays open all year.
Ⓓ How much is the membership fee?

02

_____ of this _____ ?

Ⓐ That's smart thinking.
Ⓑ The warranty lasts three years.
Ⓒ It costs nine hundred dollars.
Ⓓ It has excellent battery life.

03

_____ is hosting the _____ ?

Ⓐ On the second floor.
Ⓑ The Human Resources team.
Ⓒ Every new employee must attend.
Ⓓ Sure, I'll send you the schedule.

04

_____ is your _____ ?

Ⓐ Yes, with Dr. Williams.
Ⓑ At the downtown clinic.
Ⓒ It's at 2:30 P.M.
Ⓓ I think I need a new medicine.

05

_____ should we _____ ?

Ⓐ Yes, it started last week.
Ⓑ The deadline was extended.
Ⓒ The client presentation.
Ⓓ Let's hire another developer.

06

_____ the new club room?

Ⓐ We opened last month.
Ⓑ Was it renovated?
Ⓒ It's pretty old now.
Ⓓ Which club are you joining?

07

_____ is your _____ _____?

Ⓐ Standard shipping is fine.
Ⓑ The package arrives tomorrow.
Ⓒ I ordered it last Tuesday.
Ⓓ There's a delivery fee.

08

_____ has the most _____?

Ⓐ The interviews started at noon.
Ⓑ I'll have to check their résumés.
Ⓒ We hired three new employees.
Ⓓ Experience is an important factor.

09

_____ the _____ _____ in the engine?

Ⓐ The traffic is usually bad this time.
Ⓑ No, it's really noisy outside.
Ⓒ I'll have to ask the mechanic.
Ⓓ I just got it serviced last month.

10

_____ would you _____?

Ⓐ It has been upgraded.
Ⓑ The warranty expires next week.
Ⓒ Computer prices have increased.
Ⓓ Depends on what you need it for.

Answers p.418

HACKERS TEST 🎧 T1_S1_1_Test

Choose the best response.

01 Ⓐ It's closed on Mondays.
    Ⓑ Tickets are half-price for students.
    Ⓒ The special exhibition ends next month.
    Ⓓ At 8 A.M., two hours earlier than on weekdays.

02 Ⓐ We take credit cards and cash.
    Ⓑ The total comes to 45 dollars.
    Ⓒ Please sign the receipt.
    Ⓓ How much do I need to pay?

03 Ⓐ The one on top of the pile.
    Ⓑ No, it hasn't been signed yet.
    Ⓒ The copy machine is out of ink.
    Ⓓ The management class starts soon.

04 Ⓐ It takes effect next month.
    Ⓑ HR sent an email about it.
    Ⓒ I'd say it's reasonable.
    Ⓓ The meeting ended earlier than I expected.

05 Ⓐ It's non-refundable.
    Ⓑ The deadline is next Friday.
    Ⓒ You need a recommendation letter.
    Ⓓ I'm not familiar with that detail.

06 Ⓐ My class starts at 9 A.M. sharp.
    Ⓑ The campus tour takes two hours.
    Ⓒ Yes, the express train is arriving soon.
    Ⓓ Let me check my GPS app.

07 Ⓐ How many countries have you visited?
    Ⓑ Transportation and guided tours.
    Ⓒ I'm planning to travel in June.
    Ⓓ The flights are quite expensive.

08 Ⓐ At the downtown gallery.
    Ⓑ Over ten thousand dollars.
    Ⓒ It's an original oil painting.
    Ⓓ The auction ended yesterday.

09 Ⓐ It came just after noon.
    Ⓑ The delivery service is reliable.
    Ⓒ It's in the mailroom.
    Ⓓ Yes, I signed for it.

10 Ⓐ The interview ends at 5 P.M.
    Ⓑ Both had excellent qualifications.
    Ⓒ No, we still have three more to see.
    Ⓓ The position closed yesterday.

11 Ⓐ I've already submitted my report.
   Ⓑ The deadline is next Friday.
   Ⓒ The committee prefers PDF files.
   Ⓓ Do you need more time to finish?

12 Ⓐ The home team is playing well.
   Ⓑ Tickets are still available.
   Ⓒ It was canceled due to heavy rain.
   Ⓓ In the downtown stadium.

13 Ⓐ Between 20 and 30 dollars.
   Ⓑ The dress code requires business casual attire.
   Ⓒ It has been in business for decades.
   Ⓓ Reservations are highly recommended.

14 Ⓐ You'll have to ask Jonathan.
   Ⓑ We need to update the figures.
   Ⓒ No, the marketing team will send it.
   Ⓓ This cabinet contains office supplies.

15 Ⓐ Your insurance will expire next month.
   Ⓑ Please fill out the form and wait in the lobby.
   Ⓒ How long have you been with your current provider?
   Ⓓ We have health and auto plans.

16 Ⓐ Applications are due next Friday.
   Ⓑ The scholarship covers full tuition.
   Ⓒ Check the guidelines on the website.
   Ⓓ Yes, they require several documents.

17 Ⓐ Our rates are competitive for leather goods.
   Ⓑ Would you like to schedule a fitting?
   Ⓒ We can have them ready by Friday.
   Ⓓ Hemming starts at fifteen dollars.

18 Ⓐ It's detailed in the employee handbook.
   Ⓑ The Internet connection is quite stable.
   Ⓒ Have you seen the remote control?
   Ⓓ No, the policy was updated last year.

19 Ⓐ Please respond to my email immediately.
   Ⓑ There are two I'm considering.
   Ⓒ I'll be on vacation next week.
   Ⓓ The team is working remotely now.

20 Ⓐ Are you asking about monthly or annual rates?
   Ⓑ You can watch videos on multiple devices.
   Ⓒ Let's streamline the whole process.
   Ⓓ New shows are added weekly.

Answers p.419

Hackers Updated TOEFL LISTENING

2. Who & Where/When Questions

① Who Questions

Overview

의문사 Who를 이용하여 행동의 주체를 묻는 문제 유형이다. 매 시험 1~2문제가 출제되며, 의문사 의문문 중 출제 비율이 높은 편에 속한다.

Hackers Strategy

· Who 의문문의 정답으로 사람 이름뿐만 아니라 직책 이름이나 부서 이름이 자주 등장하므로, 관련 표현들을 알아둔다.

professor 교수	manager 관리자, 부장	assistant 조수, 보조
academic advisor 지도 교수	supervisor 감독자	president 사장
sales department 영업부	IT department 기술부	maintenance department 관리부
accounting office 회계부	customer service 고객 서비스	marketing department 마케팅 부서

· Whose(누구의)로 시작하는 문제가 가끔 출제되기도 하며, 이때 주로 사람 이름이 정답이 되는 점을 알아둔다.

Example T1_S1_2_Example1

Who is leading the product demonstration?
제품 시연을 누가 이끄나요?

· It's Mr. Schmidt. Mr. Schmidt예요. [사람 이름]
· The department manager. 부서장이요. [직책 이름]
· The marketing team is. 마케팅팀이요. [부서 이름]

⚠ **Wrong Answers**

· No, Jake isn't here. 아니요, Jake는 여기 없어요.
 [의문사 의문문에 Yes/No로 대답한 오답]
· At 7 P.M. 오후 7시예요.
 [다른 의문문에 대한 내용으로 대답한 오답]

Whose jacket is this?
이것은 누구의 재킷인가요?

· It's probably Ms. Kim's. Ms. Kim의 것일 거예요. [사람 이름]
· You should ask him. 그에게 물어보세요. [간접 응답]

② Where/When Questions

Overview

의문사 Where를 이용하여 위치 및 장소를 묻거나, When을 이용하여 시간 및 날짜를 묻는 문제 유형이다. 매 시험 2~3문제가 출제되며, 특히 Where는 의문사 의문문 중 출제 비율이 가장 높다.

Hackers Strategy

- Where 의문문의 정답으로 자주 등장하는 위치 및 장소 관련 표현들을 알아둔다.

over there 저쪽에	in the auditorium 강당 안에	on the second floor 2층에
on the counter 카운터 위에	near the station 역 근처에	across the street 길 건너
in the cabinet 캐비닛 안에	at the corner of ~의 코너에	next to the park 공원 옆에

- When 의문문의 정답으로 자주 등장하는 시간 및 날짜 관련 표현들을 알아둔다.

in an hour 한 시간 후에	by the end of the month 월말까지	two months ago 두 달 전에
the day after tomorrow 내일 모레에	in September 9월에	after the meeting 회의 후에
by next Monday 다음 주 월요일까지	last week 지난주에	soon 곧

Example 🎧 T1_S1_2_Example2

Where is the nearest gas station?
가장 가까운 주유소가 어디인가요?

- There's one at the corner of Maple Street.
  Maple가의 모퉁이에 하나가 있어요. [장소]
- I'll help you find it. 찾는 것을 도와드릴게요. [간접 응답]

⚠️ **Wrong Answers**

- Yes, some more gas. 네, 더 많은 기름이요.
  [의문사 의문문에 Yes/No로 대답한 오답]

When is the student council meeting scheduled?
학생회 회의는 언제인가요?

- In about an hour. 약 한 시간 후요. [시간]
- At the end of the month. 월말이요. [날짜]
- It has been canceled. 취소되었어요. [간접 응답]

⚠️ **Wrong Answers**

- On the third floor. 3층에요.
  [다른 의문문에 대한 내용으로 대답한 오답]

HACKERS PRACTICE 🎧 T1_S1_2_Practice

Listen to each question and fill in the blanks. Then choose the best response. (You will hear each question twice.)

01

_____ at the graduation ceremony?

Ⓐ It begins at 2 P.M.
Ⓑ In the auditorium.
Ⓒ Professor Lee, I think.
Ⓓ Yes, my parents are attending.

02

_____ can I _____ ?

Ⓐ The newest model was released last week.
Ⓑ Most items have a one-year warranty.
Ⓒ Take the escalator to the third floor.
Ⓓ No, my smartphone is broken.

03

_____ us at the _____ ?

Ⓐ It will end soon.
Ⓑ The conference room is booked.
Ⓒ We discussed the budget yesterday.
Ⓓ Someone from the marketing department.

04

_____ me _____ _____ classes?

Ⓐ Registration ends this Friday.
Ⓑ I'm unsure, but I can find out.
Ⓒ I'm taking four courses this semester.
Ⓓ No, the classroom is in Building B.

05

_____ am I _____ my research proposal?

Ⓐ The deadline is next Friday.
Ⓑ Through the department's online portal.
Ⓒ Dr. Williams wrote the research proposal.
Ⓓ Research methods are covered in chapter five.

06

_____ the leadership _____ ?

Ⓐ The manager usually does.
Ⓑ Yes, she is the new leader.
Ⓒ About project management techniques.
Ⓓ Registration closes this afternoon.

07

_____ does _____ to Chicago _____ ?

Ⓐ Platform number five.
Ⓑ It takes about three hours.
Ⓒ In 20 minutes.
Ⓓ Tickets are still available.

08

_____ should we _____ this year?

Ⓐ Magnolia Park has nice facilities.
Ⓑ No more than 30 minutes.
Ⓒ It's scheduled for June 15th.
Ⓓ Yes, we need to order catering.

09

_____ was _____ you visited _____ downtown?

Ⓐ The tickets are reasonably priced.
Ⓑ The visitor center is over there.
Ⓒ Actually, I've never been there.
Ⓓ Yes, it's located close to the campus.

10

_____ tonight?

Ⓐ Actually, we're going out to eat.
Ⓑ Yes, Harry will clean the kitchen.
Ⓒ I prefer chicken over fish.
Ⓓ Did you already have dinner?

Answers p.422

HACKERS TEST T1_S1_2_Test

Choose the best response.

01 Ⓐ I believe it's the HR department.
    Ⓑ Next month in Colorado.
    Ⓒ The budget was increased.
    Ⓓ You need to register online.

02 Ⓐ From the new café on Third Street.
    Ⓑ I usually drink tea in the morning.
    Ⓒ It contains special Colombian beans.
    Ⓓ This mug was a birthday gift.

03 Ⓐ You can check them online tomorrow.
    Ⓑ The test was very difficult.
    Ⓒ We had thirty questions to answer.
    Ⓓ I think I did well on it.

04 Ⓐ The logo was unveiled last month.
    Ⓑ We hired an outside firm.
    Ⓒ I prefer the old design.
    Ⓓ It's for our website.

05 Ⓐ The client meeting is at 2 P.M.
    Ⓑ No, from twelve countries.
    Ⓒ Which specific region are you asking about?
    Ⓓ Yes, the presentation was successful.

06 Ⓐ It starts at 9 A.M. sharp.
    Ⓑ In Conference Room C.
    Ⓒ The training lasts for two days.
    Ⓓ Five new hires are starting today.

07 Ⓐ The exhibition closes on Sunday.
    Ⓑ I wasn't at the awards ceremony.
    Ⓒ I submitted three photos in total.
    Ⓓ The prizes will be awarded tomorrow.

08 Ⓐ It's in the fridge.
    Ⓑ At our new store.
    Ⓒ Please wait while I check.
    Ⓓ This model has excellent reviews.

09 Ⓐ Michael volunteered.
    Ⓑ The goal is to raise 10,000 dollars.
    Ⓒ It's scheduled for next Saturday.
    Ⓓ We're supporting the local shelter.

10 Ⓐ The CEO approved it yesterday.
    Ⓑ We need to include the budget analysis.
    Ⓒ Let me check with my manager.
    Ⓓ I'm working with the design team.

11 Ⓐ The printer is working fine now.
    Ⓑ It took some time to repair the laptop.
    Ⓒ I know a great repair shop downtown.
    Ⓓ No, I don't need any help.

12 Ⓐ Yes, it's on the website.
    Ⓑ The lecture has been canceled.
    Ⓒ You should arrive early to get a seat.
    Ⓓ The auditorium is near the science building.

13 Ⓐ The first meeting went very well.
    Ⓑ Do we need another meeting?
    Ⓒ We discussed the project timeline.
    Ⓓ The conference room is booked all day.

14 Ⓐ Yes, I'm free after 6 P.M.
    Ⓑ I don't think so.
    Ⓒ Probably the usual place.
    Ⓓ The meeting agenda looks good.

15 Ⓐ It's always crowded there.
    Ⓑ Finals begin next Monday.
    Ⓒ Group study sessions help most students.
    Ⓓ The fourth floor of the library.

16 Ⓐ The library will be closing soon.
    Ⓑ I'm afraid we're at full capacity.
    Ⓒ We met twice last week.
    Ⓓ I'm interested in economics.

17 Ⓐ It will start at 1 o'clock.
    Ⓑ The exhibits were really innovative.
    Ⓒ It hasn't been announced yet.
    Ⓓ I'm planning to attend the lectures.

18 Ⓐ In the science building.
    Ⓑ Every Tuesday at 2 P.M.
    Ⓒ No, Dr. Hayes is not in his office.
    Ⓓ I don't know, but I can find out.

19 Ⓐ After we finish the kitchen renovation.
    Ⓑ The backyard is quite spacious.
    Ⓒ We're using an online listing service.
    Ⓓ Property values have increased lately.

20 Ⓐ The student lounge gets a lot of foot traffic.
    Ⓑ Our meeting is next Thursday.
    Ⓒ We should order more supplies.
    Ⓓ The club president approved the design.

Answers p.424

Hackers Updated TOEFL LISTENING

3. Why & How Questions

① Why Questions

Overview

의문사 Why를 이용하여 어떤 일의 이유나 원인, 목적을 묻는 문제 유형이다. 매 시험 0~1문제가 출제된다.

Hackers Strategy

· '~ 때문에'라는 의미의 because (of)를 생략하고 바로 이유나 목적을 설명하는 응답이 정답으로 자주 출제되는 점을 알아둔다. because (of)로 시작하지만 그 뒤에 질문의 맥락과 관계없는 내용으로 대답하는 오답이 종종 출제되므로, because (of)만 보고 답으로 고르지 않도록 주의한다.

Example T1_S1_3_Example1

Why did Cameron relocate to London?
Cameron은 왜 런던으로 이주했나요?

· **He received a job offer there.** 그곳에서 일자리 제의를 받았어요. [이유]
· **Let's ask him.** 그에게 물어봅시다. [간접 응답]

⚠ **Wrong Answers**

· **No, to London.** 아니요, 런던으로요.
  [의문사 의문문에 Yes/No로 대답한 오답]

· **Next month.** 다음 달에요.
  [다른 의문문에 대한 내용으로 대답한 오답]

· **Because he lost his wallet.** 지갑을 잃어버렸기 때문이에요.
  [Because 뒤에 질문의 맥락과 관계없는 내용으로 대답한 오답]

② How Questions

Overview

의문사 How를 이용하여 가격, 개수, 기간, 빈도, 방법 등을 묻는 문제 유형이다. How 뒤에 나오는 내용까지 잘 들어야 올바른 응답을 고를 수 있다. 매 시험 1~2문제가 출제된다.

Hackers Strategy

- How 의문문은 뒤에 오는 형용사 또는 부사에 따라 가격, 개수, 기간, 빈도 등을 묻는다. How 뒤의 형용사 또는 부사를 반드시 듣고 무엇에 대한 정보를 묻고 있는지 파악한다.
- How 뒤에 can, do, should와 같은 조동사가 이어지는 경우 방법을 물으며, 이때 명령문이 정답으로 자주 출제되는 점을 알아둔다.

Example 🎧 T1_S1_3_Example2

How much is a monthly bus pass?
월간 버스 정기 승차권은 얼마인가요?

· It costs 55 dollars. 55달러예요. [가격]

How many copies of the proposal should I print?
제안서를 몇 부 뽑아야 할까요?

· One for each team member. 각 팀원 당 한 부요. [개수]

How long does orientation for new students last?
신입생을 위한 오리엔테이션은 얼마나 지속되나요?

· For the entire first week. 첫 주 전체 동안요. [기간]

How often should I water these plants?
이 식물에 얼마나 자주 물을 줘야 하나요?

· About once a week should be fine.
일주일에 한 번이면 될 거예요. [빈도]

How can I get this software to work properly?
이 소프트웨어를 어떻게 제대로 작동시키나요?

· Try reinstalling it. 재설치를 해보세요. [방법]
· I don't know, either. 저도 모르겠어요. [간접 응답]

HACKERS PRACTICE 🎧 T1_S1_3_Practice

Listen to each question and fill in the blanks. Then choose the best response. (You will hear each question twice.)

01

_____ was the project _____ _____?

Ⓐ I had some technical difficulties.
Ⓑ The new deadline is next month.
Ⓒ I'll work overtime to finish it.
Ⓓ Because I finished it early.

02

_____ is the _____ _____ today?

Ⓐ Sure, you can borrow my phone.
Ⓑ We should make fast decisions.
Ⓒ Seems like the router needs repairs.
Ⓓ I need to send some large files.

03

_____ did the _____ _____?

Ⓐ Classes begin next week.
Ⓑ Actually, it was rescheduled.
Ⓒ We offer ten different courses.
Ⓓ How about another time?

04

_____ aren't the _____ _____ yet?

Ⓐ To the finance department.
Ⓑ Yes, I've read through all of them.
Ⓒ The quarterly results were positive.
Ⓓ Some data needs revision.

05

_____ didn't you _____ _____?

Ⓐ It was very informative.
Ⓑ The trainer is an expert in the field.
Ⓒ I had a conflicting appointment.
Ⓓ Yes, it will be offered again.

06

_____ reserve a _____
_____?

Ⓐ Yes, it's a group project.
Ⓑ Through the student portal.
Ⓒ The study was conducted last month.
Ⓓ I finished my project yesterday.

07

_____ will it cost to _____
_____?

Ⓐ The garage closes at 6 P.M.
Ⓑ Between 200 and 250 dollars.
Ⓒ I can give you a ride tomorrow.
Ⓓ Your warranty expired last month.

08

_____ does the _____
_____ on weekends?

Ⓐ Did you take a bus?
Ⓑ It's at the main entrance.
Ⓒ Let's go jogging this weekend.
Ⓓ Every thirty minutes.

09

_____ participants registered
_____?

Ⓐ Registration closes on Friday.
Ⓑ You can register online.
Ⓒ So far, almost 100.
Ⓓ The venue has limited capacity.

10

_____ will the _____
_____ take?

Ⓐ According to the email, last month.
Ⓑ The center is located near the library.
Ⓒ You need your student ID to enter.
Ⓓ I didn't know it was being renovated.

Answers p.427

HACKERS TEST

Choose the best response.

01 Ⓐ Press the red button to start brewing.
  Ⓑ The machine was quite expensive.
  Ⓒ The coffee beans are in the cabinet.
  Ⓓ The old one broke down.

02 Ⓐ Yes, the schedule is fixed.
  Ⓑ Let's join the book club.
  Ⓒ We used to meet every Thursday.
  Ⓓ The original room was unavailable.

03 Ⓐ The kitchen is busy tonight.
  Ⓑ I ordered today's special.
  Ⓒ The menu has many options.
  Ⓓ The restaurant isn't closed yet.

04 Ⓐ The show starts at 8 P.M.
  Ⓑ Four, one for each of us.
  Ⓒ The venue is downtown.
  Ⓓ I prefer classical music.

05 Ⓐ No, their quality declined.
  Ⓑ Our current one increased its prices.
  Ⓒ I'm considering applying for another position.
  Ⓓ Deliveries are made weekly.

06 Ⓐ It depends on the season.
  Ⓑ The produce is always fresh.
  Ⓒ I buy organic vegetables there.
  Ⓓ It's located near the park.

07 Ⓐ Park near the humanities building.
  Ⓑ The parking lot operates 24 hours.
  Ⓒ No, I usually take the shuttle bus.
  Ⓓ You should ask Mr. Jenson about that.

08 Ⓐ I paid it last week.
  Ⓑ The lights are too dim.
  Ⓒ That's a mystery to me, too.
  Ⓓ It's in the kitchen drawer.

09 Ⓐ Yes, we have our own policy.
  Ⓑ Client meetings are scheduled on Tuesday.
  Ⓒ For a maximum of seven years by law.
  Ⓓ The file room was recently reorganized.

10 Ⓐ The construction will finish next month.
  Ⓑ Yes, it's the newest building on campus.
  Ⓒ Have you seen the architectural plans?
  Ⓓ To create additional laboratory space.

11 Ⓐ I thought someone else would handle it.
    Ⓑ The problem started last week.
    Ⓒ The IT department is down the hall.
    Ⓓ Do you know their contact information?

12 Ⓐ Some young consumers.
    Ⓑ It was launched two months ago.
    Ⓒ Let's check the feedback reports.
    Ⓓ The marketing campaign was successful.

13 Ⓐ The print shop is closing soon.
    Ⓑ I need to print my essay.
    Ⓒ You can save files on the cloud.
    Ⓓ It's better to call a professional.

14 Ⓐ No, a week ago.
    Ⓑ The presentation is prepared.
    Ⓒ The meeting room on the third floor.
    Ⓓ Do you mean the budget meeting?

15 Ⓐ The training room is reserved.
    Ⓑ Approximately 8% of our annual budget.
    Ⓒ New employees start next Monday.
    Ⓓ The workshop lasts three days.

16 Ⓐ Professor Johnson is in room 302.
    Ⓑ The minimum is three hours weekly.
    Ⓒ You should email them first.
    Ⓓ No, the requirement isn't that strict.

17 Ⓐ The ceremony was quite emotional.
    Ⓑ It exceeded our expectations.
    Ⓒ The venue is located downtown.
    Ⓓ We sent invitations three months in advance.

18 Ⓐ The library opened an hour ago.
    Ⓑ Because I didn't know about it.
    Ⓒ Some members asked me to.
    Ⓓ I'm sorry that you lost it.

19 Ⓐ The bus station is under renovation.
    Ⓑ The parking garage opens quite early.
    Ⓒ Because I drive to work every day.
    Ⓓ There's a construction project causing traffic delays.

20 Ⓐ Because it's a newly updated one.
    Ⓑ I've been wondering about that myself.
    Ⓒ Registration begins next Monday.
    Ⓓ It is too late to implement a new policy.

Answers p.428

무료 토플자료·유학정보 공유
goHackers.com

Section II
Non Wh- Questions

Section II에서는 의문사 의문문을 제외한 Be동사/조동사 의문문, 부가 의문문, 선택 의문문, 제안/제공/요청 의문문으로 나누어 각 의문문의 특징과 질문 형태, 빈출 정답 및 오답을 소개하고 있다. 또한 연습 문제 및 실전 문제를 통해 각 문제 유형을 효과적으로 공략할 수 있도록 하였다.

TASK 1의 Non Wh- Questions는 아래와 같이 나눌 수 있다.

1. Be/Auxiliary Verb Questions
2. Tag Questions
3. Alternative Questions
4. Suggestion/Offer/Request Questions

**Hackers
Updated TOEFL
LISTENING**

1. Be/Auxiliary Verb Questions

Overview

be동사와 조동사를 이용하여 의문사 없이 묻는 문제 유형이다. 매 시험 2~3문제가 출제된다.

Hackers Strategy

· Yes/No로 대답하거나 Yes/No를 생략하고 적절한 부연 설명으로 대답한 응답이 정답이 될 수 있다.
· 질문이 부정형이더라도, 확인하고자 하는 사실이 맞는 말이거나 의견에 동의하면 Yes, 사실을 부인하거나 의견에 반대하면 No로 시작하고 그에 맞는 적절한 부연 설명이 나온 내용을 정답으로 고른다.

Example   T1_S2_1_Example

| Are you attending Dr. Palmer's guest lecture?
Palmer 박사님의 초청 강연에 참석하시나요? | · Yes, I'm planning to arrive early to get a seat.
네, 자리를 맡기 위해 일찍 도착할 계획이에요. [Yes 사용]
· I am busy that day. 저는 그날 바빠요. [No 생략] |

So the mall is open until 10 P.M.?
쇼핑몰은 오후 10시까지 열려 있는 거죠?

· No, they changed their hours.
아니요, 그들의 운영시간을 바꿨어요. [No 사용]
· You should check their website.
그들의 웹사이트를 확인해보세요. [간접 응답]

Didn't the maintenance team fix the elevator?
유지보수팀이 엘리베이터를 고치지 않았나요?

· Yes, they did. 네, 고쳤어요. [Yes 사용]
· Actually, they're scheduled to come next week.
사실, 그들은 다음 주에 올 예정이에요. [간접 응답]

⚠ **Wrong Answers**

· Yes, the stairway is over there. 네, 계단은 저기에 있어요.
[Yes/No 뒤에 질문의 맥락과 관계없는 내용이 나오는 오답]

HACKERS PRACTICE 🎧 T1_S2_1_Practice

Listen to each question and fill in the blanks. Then choose the best response. (You will hear each question twice.)

01

_____ you _____ with your
_____?

Ⓐ The project is due tomorrow.
Ⓑ Yes, I could use some assistance.
Ⓒ Yes, I think I can handle it on my own.
Ⓓ The research lab isn't open now.

02

_____ the _____
_____ this week?

Ⓐ I'm looking for some used textbooks.
Ⓑ Yes, they were really expensive.
Ⓒ We should check their website.
Ⓓ It is near the city library.

03

_____ the _____
_____?

Ⓐ Yes, it did.
Ⓑ I'm not so sure.
Ⓒ Include at least five sources.
Ⓓ No, you should turn it in tomorrow.

04

_____ the _____
on Friday?

Ⓐ It begins on Thursday.
Ⓑ The registration fee is 150 dollars.
Ⓒ Yes, it has been canceled.
Ⓓ Are you available on the weekend?

05

_____ you able to _____ the
online _____?

Ⓐ No, I downloaded every material.
Ⓑ Our professor required three textbooks.
Ⓒ No, the website was under maintenance.
Ⓓ The library was inaccessible after 10 P.M.

Answers p.431

HACKERS TEST

Choose the best response.

01
Ⓐ Yes, I'm going on vacation.
Ⓑ Did you check the attendance?
Ⓒ It takes place in the auditorium.
Ⓓ I've already registered online.

02
Ⓐ I'd recommend it.
Ⓑ The staff lounge is closed.
Ⓒ Are you applying for the position?
Ⓓ Some additional office supplies.

03
Ⓐ The semester ends in June.
Ⓑ The registration desk is downstairs.
Ⓒ I should clear my schedule.
Ⓓ The psychology course was full.

04
Ⓐ The financial report is ready.
Ⓑ Yes, but I had to leave early.
Ⓒ Yes, it's scheduled for tomorrow.
Ⓓ Actually, due to a lack of funding.

05
Ⓐ Yes, I've been looking forward to visiting it.
Ⓑ Yes, the renovation will be finished next month.
Ⓒ No, the visitor center is on the ground level.
Ⓓ No, I think the paintings are in the east wing.

06
Ⓐ The cafeteria opens at 7 A.M.
Ⓑ I need to return this tray.
Ⓒ Let's ask for the menu.
Ⓓ The new diner downtown.

07
Ⓐ The exam will cover many chapters.
Ⓑ You need to bring your student ID.
Ⓒ I haven't heard anything yet.
Ⓓ Are you going to drop the course?

08
Ⓐ Ten copies, please.
Ⓑ What do you need it for?
Ⓒ I'm writing a research paper.
Ⓓ Books must be returned by Friday.

09
Ⓐ Customer feedback is always valuable.
Ⓑ Yes, some people can't attend tomorrow.
Ⓒ I prepared all the presentation slides.
Ⓓ No, the meeting room is on the fifth floor.

10
Ⓐ No, it has been moved to Thursday.
Ⓑ No, I didn't study biology in high school.
Ⓒ The science building is across from the library.
Ⓓ Dr. Miller is a renowned biologist.

11. Ⓐ Yes, I went to see a play there.
    Ⓑ No, the movie starts at 8:30 tonight.
    Ⓒ No, it wasn't as great as I expected.
    Ⓓ Yes, I prefer watching films at home.

12. Ⓐ The plane is landing soon.
    Ⓑ Yes, it was so frustrating.
    Ⓒ Luggage weight limit is 23 kilograms.
    Ⓓ I'm taking the train instead.

13. Ⓐ I was assigned a different task.
    Ⓑ Prepare for the acceptance speech.
    Ⓒ Only if you have a valid medical excuse.
    Ⓓ The office is closing early today.

14. Ⓐ The meeting was last week.
    Ⓑ I've worked with the client for years.
    Ⓒ Actually, some revisions were requested.
    Ⓓ The proposal included three price options.

15. Ⓐ Someone from the financial department.
    Ⓑ When is the department meeting scheduled?
    Ⓒ We requested new equipment.
    Ⓓ I think they're still reviewing it.

16. Ⓐ No, the park has many facilities.
    Ⓑ Yes, the fare is the same for all routes.
    Ⓒ No, you are on the wrong one.
    Ⓓ Yes, I usually take the subway.

17. Ⓐ Yes, I'd be happy to help you.
    Ⓑ The meeting was informative.
    Ⓒ Let's check the reservation system.
    Ⓓ I've prepared all the documents.

18. Ⓐ No, it was sent to all employees.
    Ⓑ No, the change begins tomorrow.
    Ⓒ I don't think I received one.
    Ⓓ I prefer phone calls to emails.

19. Ⓐ My professor is out this week.
    Ⓑ Yes, the classroom is locked.
    Ⓒ I already finished my assignment.
    Ⓓ The morning courses are always crowded.

20. Ⓐ I'm about halfway through it.
    Ⓑ The discussion will be held in Room 302.
    Ⓒ Peter suggested three scholarly sources.
    Ⓓ Reading is my favorite hobby.

Answers p.432

2. Tag Questions

Overview

평서문 뒤에 didn't you, is it, right 등의 꼬리말을 덧붙여 사실을 확인하거나 의견에 동의를 구하는 문제 유형이다. 매 시험 0~1문제가 출제된다.

Hackers Strategy

· Yes/No로 대답하거나 Yes/No를 생략하고 적절한 부연 설명으로 대답한 응답이 정답이 될 수 있다.
· 꼬리말의 형태와 관계없이, 그 앞의 내용이 맞는 말이거나 그 내용에 동의하면 Yes, 틀린 말이거나 그 내용에 반대하면 No라고 한 후 그에 맞는 적절한 부연 설명이 나온 내용을 정답으로 고른다.

Example T1_S2_2_Example

Jonathan is graduating this semester, isn't he?
Jonathan은 이번 학기에 졸업해요, 그렇지 않나요?

· Yes, I believe so. 네, 그런 것 같아요. [Yes 사용]
· He still has a few more classes to take.
  그는 들어야 하는 몇몇 수업이 여전히 있어요. [No 생략]
· Let's ask him. 그에게 물어봅시다. [간접 응답]

⚠ **Wrong Answers**

· Yes, it was a difficult semester. 네, 어려운 학기였어요.
  [Yes/No 뒤에 질문의 맥락과 관계없는 내용이 나오는 오답]

HACKERS PRACTICE 🎧 T1_S2_2_Practice

Listen to each question and fill in the blanks. Then choose the best response. (You will hear each question twice.)

01

The _____ is _____ today, _____?

Ⓐ Yes, perfect for a walk outside.
Ⓑ What is your favorite season?
Ⓒ Yes, this heat is unbearable.
Ⓓ I'm not sure whether I will attend.

02

Ms. Lawson _____ yesterday, _____?

Ⓐ Her assistant quit last week.
Ⓑ She called in sick.
Ⓒ She works late on Tuesdays.
Ⓓ Her office is on the second floor.

03

This _____ pastries, _____?

Ⓐ Would you like some iced coffee?
Ⓑ It's open from 9 A.M. to 10 P.M.
Ⓒ I haven't had the chance to try them.
Ⓓ How much did you pay for that?

04

_____ every 15 minutes, _____?

Ⓐ The blue line goes downtown.
Ⓑ It is in front of the student center.
Ⓒ No, I missed the last one yesterday.
Ⓓ Yes, but only on the weekdays.

05

_____ last week, _____?

Ⓐ I am free next weekend.
Ⓑ I needed some more time.
Ⓒ This form is complicated.
Ⓓ Where is the admissions office?

Answers p.435

HACKERS TEST 🎧 T1_S2_2_Test

Choose the best response.

01 Ⓐ I went there last month.
　　Ⓑ It's next to City Hall.
　　Ⓒ No, they close at 5 P.M.
　　Ⓓ Some art exhibitions.

02 Ⓐ The final exam was difficult.
　　Ⓑ No, they'll be up tomorrow.
　　Ⓒ No, I couldn't study that much.
　　Ⓓ The classroom is on the third floor.

03 Ⓐ The meeting will begin at noon.
　　Ⓑ It lasted about three hours.
　　Ⓒ I had a doctor's appointment.
　　Ⓓ The meeting room is empty.

04 Ⓐ No, it didn't take that long.
　　Ⓑ Yes, I submitted it yesterday.
　　Ⓒ The library has research materials.
　　Ⓓ Is the deadline going to be extended?

05 Ⓐ Are the tickets sold out?
　　Ⓑ I watched it last weekend.
　　Ⓒ The cinema is downtown.
　　Ⓓ I like watching horror movies.

06 Ⓐ The building opens at 8 A.M.
　　Ⓑ I think it's in Room 305 today.
　　Ⓒ Professor Kim teaches history.
　　Ⓓ The class started last week.

07 Ⓐ The food is quite expensive there.
　　Ⓑ No, I'm going to order the special.
　　Ⓒ Actually, they started accepting them.
　　Ⓓ Yes, it's on Main Street.

08 Ⓐ Did you see Nina's posting?
　　Ⓑ I need to mail this package.
　　Ⓒ I bought a stamp booklet.
　　Ⓓ Yes, we should go tomorrow.

09 Ⓐ You need your student ID card.
　　Ⓑ I borrowed three books.
　　Ⓒ Actually, it's open until midnight.
　　Ⓓ The café is on the first floor.

10 Ⓐ Do you mean your expense report?
　　Ⓑ The Internet is working fine.
　　Ⓒ Did you have any feedback?
　　Ⓓ I'll send you a copy now.

11 Ⓐ I did it online last night.
    Ⓑ The semester ends in May.
    Ⓒ Registration fees will increase soon.
    Ⓓ My advisor is out of town next week.

12 Ⓐ I'll meet you at the station.
    Ⓑ No, it departs at 7 P.M.
    Ⓒ The ticket costs five dollars.
    Ⓓ I prefer taking the train.

13 Ⓐ Not everyone was present.
    Ⓑ The professor speaks clearly.
    Ⓒ We do have more time.
    Ⓓ Your slides look great.

14 Ⓐ Where is your car key?
    Ⓑ My office is far from here.
    Ⓒ Yes, it's in the back seat.
    Ⓓ I'm heading that way anyway.

15 Ⓐ IT scheduled it for tomorrow.
    Ⓑ The computers are quite new.
    Ⓒ I prefer the older version.
    Ⓓ Our team needs training.

16 Ⓐ The deadline is next week.
    Ⓑ All three months need to be covered.
    Ⓒ Did you already email it to me?
    Ⓓ The numbers looked promising.

17 Ⓐ Yes, it's my first time.
    Ⓑ The contract expires next month.
    Ⓒ Yes, they're very reliable.
    Ⓓ Let me contact them tomorrow.

18 Ⓐ Her office is in Taylor Hall.
    Ⓑ No, she's available from 2 to 4.
    Ⓒ I need to ask her about the exam.
    Ⓓ Why did you cancel it?

19 Ⓐ The client was quite upset.
    Ⓑ When is the deadline?
    Ⓒ Nobody expects it.
    Ⓓ We finished ahead of schedule.

20 Ⓐ His lectures are really engaging.
    Ⓑ The classroom is in the engineering building.
    Ⓒ Registration opens next Monday.
    Ⓓ I need to check my schedule.

Answers p.436

3. Alternative Questions

Overview

두 가지 선택 사항을 or로 연결한 'A or B(A 또는 B)' 형태를 사용하여 둘 중 하나를 선택하도록 요구하는 문제 유형이다. 매 시험 0~1문제가 출제된다.

Hackers Strategy

· 두 가지 선택 사항 중 하나를 선택하는 응답, 둘 다 선택하거나 둘 다 선택하지 않는 응답, 제3의 선택을 하는 응답이 정답으로 자주 출제되는 점을 알아둔다.

Example 🎧 T1_S2_3_Example

Should we schedule the meeting for Monday or Tuesday? 회의를 월요일로 잡을까요, 화요일로 잡을까요?

- I prefer the latter. 후자를 더 선호해요. [둘 중 하나를 선택]
- Either is fine. 둘 중 아무 때나 괜찮아요. [둘 다 선택]
- How about Thursday? 목요일은 어때요? [제3의 선택]
- I'm unavailable all week.
  저는 주 전체가 안돼요. [간접 응답]

⚠ **Wrong Answers**

- Yes, the meeting room is on the third floor.
  네, 회의실은 3층이에요. [선택 의문문에 Yes/No로 대답한 오답]

HACKERS PRACTICE 🎧 T1_S2_3_Practice

Listen to each question and fill in the blanks. Then choose the best response. (You will hear each question twice.)

01

Would you like to _____
or _____ ?

Ⓐ At the department store.
Ⓑ I'll meet you after dinner.
Ⓒ They serve Italian food.
Ⓓ What time is the movie?

02

Do you prefer _____
or _____ ?

Ⓐ The campus is nearby.
Ⓑ Classes start next week.
Ⓒ I find online more convenient.
Ⓓ The professor is very strict.

03

Would you rather _____
or _____ ?

Ⓐ I'll bring the presentation files.
Ⓑ That's my driver's license.
Ⓒ The conference starts at 9 A.M.
Ⓓ I prefer public transportation.

04

Do you _____ or _____ ?

Ⓐ Yes, thank you.
Ⓑ I don't mind.
Ⓒ I think I do.
Ⓓ The café closes at 5 P.M.

05

Is the _____
or _____ ?

Ⓐ I'll prepare the agenda.
Ⓑ The room is booked for an hour.
Ⓒ It's been rescheduled to next week.
Ⓓ Let's review what was discussed.

Answers p.439

HACKERS TEST

T1_S2_3_Test

Choose the best response.

01 Ⓐ I usually go on weekends.
    Ⓑ The library closes at 9 P.M.
    Ⓒ I feel more comfortable at home.
    Ⓓ My textbooks are expensive.

02 Ⓐ The deadline is next Friday.
    Ⓑ Teamwork is more efficient.
    Ⓒ The report needs revision.
    Ⓓ Our manager approved it.

03 Ⓐ Let's use the conference room instead.
    Ⓑ The meeting starts at noon.
    Ⓒ I'll bring the presentation slides.
    Ⓓ Your report was excellent.

04 Ⓐ The campus is beautiful.
    Ⓑ I'd rather walk when it's nice out.
    Ⓒ The bus arrives every ten minutes.
    Ⓓ My class has been canceled.

05 Ⓐ The museum opens at 10 A.M.
    Ⓑ The exhibit ends next month.
    Ⓒ The artwork was interesting.
    Ⓓ The subway will be faster.

06 Ⓐ The flight is three hours long.
    Ⓑ The plane has already departed.
    Ⓒ My luggage is overweight.
    Ⓓ I always choose the window.

07 Ⓐ We meet on a monthly basis.
    Ⓑ Yes, it's written in French.
    Ⓒ Neither seems suitable for me.
    Ⓓ He's the captain of the debate team.

08 Ⓐ Is there another option?
    Ⓑ Yes, I'm allergic to nuts.
    Ⓒ Outside the cafeteria.
    Ⓓ I didn't eat any lunch.

09 Ⓐ The projector isn't working.
    Ⓑ I need more time to prepare.
    Ⓒ Professor Kim graded our papers.
    Ⓓ The deadline was yesterday.

10 Ⓐ The total is 40 dollars including tax.
    Ⓑ Can I use these coupons?
    Ⓒ The store closes at 8 P.M.
    Ⓓ I need a receipt, please.

11 Ⓐ The exam schedule was posted.
    Ⓑ I get nervous speaking in public.
    Ⓒ No, the exam was very difficult.
    Ⓓ The presentation is next week.

12 Ⓐ The deadline is next Friday.
    Ⓑ I've already completed it.
    Ⓒ Digital would be more convenient.
    Ⓓ The professor grades fairly.

13 Ⓐ The meeting starts at noon.
    Ⓑ Either option works for me.
    Ⓒ I already ate lunch.
    Ⓓ The cafeteria is downstairs.

14 Ⓐ I enjoy reading about real events.
    Ⓑ The library closes at 9 P.M.
    Ⓒ I haven't read that book yet.
    Ⓓ My professor assigned three chapters.

15 Ⓐ Everything on the menu looks good.
    Ⓑ It was difficult to park outside.
    Ⓒ Sharon will arrive by five o'clock.
    Ⓓ Looks like it's going to rain.

16 Ⓐ Let's wait until we're done.
    Ⓑ The discussion lasted an hour.
    Ⓒ The meeting room is reserved.
    Ⓓ I prepared my presentation.

17 Ⓐ We need to fix this computer.
    Ⓑ Yes, I would really appreciate it.
    Ⓒ Whichever is more convenient for you.
    Ⓓ I found the manual quite helpful.

18 Ⓐ The class lasts two hours.
    Ⓑ The professor speaks clearly.
    Ⓒ I'm not good with devices.
    Ⓓ My laptop is quite new.

19 Ⓐ Their office closes at 5 P.M.
    Ⓑ Their email address changed.
    Ⓒ I sent the document yesterday.
    Ⓓ A call would be more personal.

20 Ⓐ I want some outdoor activities.
    Ⓑ The museum closes at 6 P.M.
    Ⓒ That is a high mountain.
    Ⓓ Weekend tickets are expensive.

Answers p.440

4. Suggestion/Offer/Request Questions

Overview

무언가를 하라고 제안하거나, 무엇을 해주겠다고 제공하거나, 무엇을 해달라고 요청하는 문제 유형이다. 매 시험 1~2 문제가 출제된다.

Hackers Strategy

- 제안 의문문은 Why don't we, How about의 형태, 제공 의문문은 Would you like (me to), Do you need me to의 형태, 요청 의문문은 Could you, Would you mind의 형태를 주로 가진다는 점을 알아둔다.
- 각 의문문의 내용에 대해 이를 수락하거나 거절하는 응답이 정답으로 자주 출제되는 점을 알아둔다.

Example

🎧 T1_S2_4_Example

How about trying that new restaurant downtown? 시내의 새 식당을 시도해보는 게 어때요?	• Sure, I'd like that. 좋아요. [수락] • I have other plans tonight. 오늘 밤 다른 계획이 있어요. [거절]
Would you like me to give you a receipt for your purchase? 구매에 대한 영수증을 드릴까요?	• Yes, I'll need it for expense reimbursement. 네, 비용 변제를 위해 그것이 필요해요. [수락] • That won't be necessary. 필요하지 않아요. [거절]
Can you help me with my science project? 제 과학 프로젝트를 도와주시겠어요?	• I'd be happy to look at it. 기꺼이 살펴 볼게요. [수락] • What aspect do you need help with? 어떤 측면에서 도움이 필요한가요? [간접 응답]

HACKERS PRACTICE T1_S2_4_Practice

Listen to each question and fill in the blanks. Then choose the best response. (You will hear each question twice.)

01

_____ our study group?

Ⓐ Sure, when do you meet?
Ⓑ The library closes at 9 P.M.
Ⓒ I studied for three hours.
Ⓓ Yes, these study materials.

02

_____ some extra _____?

Ⓐ The slides look colorful.
Ⓑ That's a great idea.
Ⓒ In the conference room.
Ⓓ Three cups of coffee.

03

_____ a good café _____?

Ⓐ The mall opens at 9 A.M.
Ⓑ I prefer tea to coffee.
Ⓒ The cups are in the cabinet.
Ⓓ There is one close to the park.

04

_____ these documents at the _____?

Ⓐ Not at all, I'm heading that way.
Ⓑ The desk needs to be cleaned.
Ⓒ They were delivered this morning.
Ⓓ Did you drop these on the floor?

05

_____ your report for _____?

Ⓐ Yesterday at midnight.
Ⓑ It was reported in the news.
Ⓒ The printer is acting up.
Ⓓ I already submitted it.

Answers p.443

HACKERS TEST

T1_S2_4_Test

Choose the best response.

01 Ⓐ I already ordered lunch.
   Ⓑ That sounds great to me.
   Ⓒ The meeting room is too small.
   Ⓓ Do you have the results?

02 Ⓐ Is the repair shop open now?
   Ⓑ Sure, it's getting warm in here.
   Ⓒ The technician took a look at it.
   Ⓓ The new model is quite reliable.

03 Ⓐ You are very diligent.
   Ⓑ Yes, I'll give him your message.
   Ⓒ I'm afraid I can't.
   Ⓓ The schedule was posted yesterday.

04 Ⓐ It's on your right.
   Ⓑ I joined a morning class.
   Ⓒ Some sugar, please.
   Ⓓ Not right now.

05 Ⓐ Yes, this is comfortable.
   Ⓑ I'll take you there.
   Ⓒ We need more sofas.
   Ⓓ I'll call the event organizer.

06 Ⓐ I received questions about the course.
   Ⓑ The science building is closed.
   Ⓒ Is she in her office now?
   Ⓓ Do you want me to help you?

07 Ⓐ Some safety goggles.
   Ⓑ No, I'm very curious.
   Ⓒ Yes, I'd love to see it.
   Ⓓ The equipment needs updating.

08 Ⓐ I prefer classical music.
   Ⓑ Sorry, I didn't realize it was so loud.
   Ⓒ He turned down the job offer.
   Ⓓ I downloaded a new album.

09 Ⓐ The dormitory is closed for renovation.
   Ⓑ I'll be free on Saturday morning.
   Ⓒ The elevator is out of service.
   Ⓓ You'll need a key card to enter.

10 Ⓐ No, I'm not prepared.
   Ⓑ That seems necessary.
   Ⓒ Put all the materials on the desk.
   Ⓓ The department has five teams.

11 Ⓐ I'm free on Tuesday.
    Ⓑ The schedule is on the wall.
    Ⓒ Yes, I went there last week.
    Ⓓ They're working late today.

12 Ⓐ Downtown is very crowded.
    Ⓑ I don't really like their menu.
    Ⓒ Can I try on this pair?
    Ⓓ Two cups of tea, please.

13 Ⓐ The chef is excellent.
    Ⓑ I'm all set with what I have.
    Ⓒ Medium-rare, please.
    Ⓓ The table needs cleaning.

14 Ⓐ What exactly do you need help with?
    Ⓑ The presentation was excellent.
    Ⓒ It starts in five minutes.
    Ⓓ That would be helpful.

15 Ⓐ I prefer the previous version.
    Ⓑ The software needs updating.
    Ⓒ The manual is available online.
    Ⓓ It's quite an expensive program.

16 Ⓐ Yes, the vase is broken.
    Ⓑ I need to finish this chapter first.
    Ⓒ The library is closed now.
    Ⓓ My study group meets weekly.

17 Ⓐ The clients arrived early.
    Ⓑ The meeting room is booked.
    Ⓒ New projects can be challenging.
    Ⓓ I'd be happy to handle that.

18 Ⓐ The professor extended the deadline.
    Ⓑ No, I didn't get any information.
    Ⓒ Yes, I don't understand it.
    Ⓓ It needs to be submitted soon.

19 Ⓐ The lecture hall is quite large.
    Ⓑ Actually, I didn't receive one.
    Ⓒ You should go straight and turn right.
    Ⓓ Do you have the schedule?

20 Ⓐ Don't you have a doctor's appointment?
    Ⓑ No, he is on a business trip this week.
    Ⓒ The airport has been renovated.
    Ⓓ Yes, it's my driver's license.

Answers p.444

무료 토플자료·유학정보 공유
goHackers.com

Section III
Statements

Hackers Updated TOEFL LISTENING

Section III에서는 의문문이 아닌 평서문의 특징과 형태, 빈출 정답 및 오답을 소개하고 있다. 또한 연습 문제 및 실전 문제를 통해 각 문제 유형을 효과적으로 공략할 수 있도록 하였다.

TASK 1의 Statements는 아래와 같이 나눌 수 있다.

1. Informative Statements
2. Advisory Statements

1. Informative Statements

Overview

정보를 제공하거나 의견을 전달하는 평서문에 대한 적절한 반응을 묻는 문제 유형이다. 매 시험 2~3문제가 출제된다.

Hackers Strategy

· 평서문의 의도에 따라 정답으로 자주 출제되는 응답이 다른데, 정보를 제공하는 경우 해당 정보를 확인했다는 내용이나 추가 정보를 문의하는 응답이 정답으로 자주 출제되는 점을 알아둔다. 의견을 전달하는 경우에는 해당 의견에 동의 또는 반대하거나, 필요 시 해결책을 제시하는 응답이 정답으로 자주 출제되는 점을 알아둔다.

Example   T1_S3_1_Example

I'm afraid I'm not available tomorrow.
유감이지만 저는 내일 시간이 안 될 것 같아요.

· I understand. 이해해요. [정보 확인]
· How about next week then?
  그럼 다음 주는 어때요? [추가 정보 문의]

Janet's speech was too technical for beginners.
Janet의 연설은 초심자에게는 너무 전문적이었어요.

· The content was far too advanced.
  내용이 수준이 너무 높았어요. [동의]
· Actually, her examples made it accessible.
  사실, 그녀의 예시들은 그것을 이해하기 쉽게 만들었어요. [반대]

I'm not sure about the current investment strategy. 저는 현재 투자 전략에 대해 확실하지 않아요.

· That's unfortunate. 유감이네요. [공감]
· Perhaps we should reconsider our options.
  저희 선택지들을 다시 고려해 볼까 봐요. [해결책 제시]

⚠ **Wrong Answers**

· I think you have it. 당신이 그것을 가지고 있다고 생각해요.
  [평서문 내용과 다른 주제의 내용으로 대답하는 오답]

HACKERS PRACTICE 🎧 T1_S3_1_Practice

Listen to each statement and fill in the blanks. Then choose the best response. (You will hear each statement twice.)

01

_____ on the highway _____.

Ⓐ That must have been stressful.
Ⓑ I usually take the subway.
Ⓒ Yes, traffic was terrible.
Ⓓ 80 kilometers per hour.

02

_____ twenty minutes.

Ⓐ I'll grab my coat and we can go.
Ⓑ The theater is being renovated.
Ⓒ Films are expensive these days.
Ⓓ She started working there last week.

03

_____ right now.

Ⓐ In the fridge.
Ⓑ Every Sunday.
Ⓒ Can I come with you?
Ⓓ The clothing store is not open.

04

_____ in town.

Ⓐ No, it's a seafood place.
Ⓑ The town hall is nearby.
Ⓒ He is out of town now.
Ⓓ I didn't really like it.

05

I'm _____.

Ⓐ It is exactly right.
Ⓑ I already finished them.
Ⓒ What's a better time for you?
Ⓓ How much is this item?

Answers p.447

HACKERS TEST T1_S3_1_Test

Choose the best response.

01 Ⓐ Let's try to get there early.
    Ⓑ I don't feel comfortable about that.
    Ⓒ Use the temporary pass system.
    Ⓓ They identified the problem.

02 Ⓐ I should return my books now.
    Ⓑ The librarian is very helpful.
    Ⓒ The new books arrived yesterday.
    Ⓓ On the other side of campus.

03 Ⓐ It closes at 5 P.M.
    Ⓑ How about joining them?
    Ⓒ The exhibit starts in May.
    Ⓓ Admission is ten dollars.

04 Ⓐ Ask Jonathan.
    Ⓑ The map is available online.
    Ⓒ Those buildings are inaccessible.
    Ⓓ I usually take the bus to campus.

05 Ⓐ It's getting warmer.
    Ⓑ It was last week.
    Ⓒ I haven't met her yet.
    Ⓓ Did she reschedule it?

06 Ⓐ Your present is on the table.
    Ⓑ Thanks, I worked hard on it.
    Ⓒ Today is Tuesday, right?
    Ⓓ I'm impressed by this sculpture.

07 Ⓐ What's your weekend schedule like?
    Ⓑ The mail carrier is really friendly.
    Ⓒ That's only a few days from now.
    Ⓓ I called in sick last Friday.

08 Ⓐ I think so, too.
    Ⓑ Yes, it was quiet last night.
    Ⓒ No, this is a dining room.
    Ⓓ Let's rent this car.

09 Ⓐ I'm allergic to seafood.
    Ⓑ It's on the second floor.
    Ⓒ The server is not on the clock.
    Ⓓ I'll have to try them sometime.

10 Ⓐ The deadline was last Friday.
    Ⓑ Did you fill out the forms?
    Ⓒ Well, I didn't know about that.
    Ⓓ I'm interested in environmental science.

11 Ⓐ The research paper is due soon.
    Ⓑ Textbooks are too heavy to carry.
    Ⓒ I borrowed some from the library.
    Ⓓ Let's take advantage of it.

16 Ⓐ It's next Friday at noon.
    Ⓑ There are many forms to fill out.
    Ⓒ The science building is across the street.
    Ⓓ I've already selected my courses.

12 Ⓐ The weight limit is 50 pounds.
    Ⓑ I apologize for that.
    Ⓒ How long will you stay?
    Ⓓ Those people are waiting in line.

17 Ⓐ That's excellent news.
    Ⓑ I report to the CEO directly.
    Ⓒ The quarter ends next week.
    Ⓓ They're improving the facilities.

13 Ⓐ About 20 clients.
    Ⓑ Don't move anything on my desk.
    Ⓒ That works better for me.
    Ⓓ This meeting room is empty.

18 Ⓐ The market conditions are challenging.
    Ⓑ Let me check my calendar.
    Ⓒ Let's review it this afternoon.
    Ⓓ Teams should work together.

14 Ⓐ I can go and pick him up.
    Ⓑ The airline serves good food.
    Ⓒ When does the train arrive?
    Ⓓ I'm sorry to hear that.

19 Ⓐ Did you submit your assignment?
    Ⓑ Please move your car to another spot.
    Ⓒ Will you look for a new one?
    Ⓓ I had a really busy semester.

15 Ⓐ I lost a lot of weight.
    Ⓑ Some new equipment.
    Ⓒ I've never seen you there.
    Ⓓ At the center of the campus.

20 Ⓐ November is a cold month.
    Ⓑ We should start looking for partners.
    Ⓒ Projects are quite time-consuming.
    Ⓓ Did you already finish your project?

Answers p.447

2. Advisory Statements

Overview

권고하거나 요청하는 평서문에 대한 적절한 반응을 묻는 문제 유형이다. 매 시험 1~2문제가 출제된다.

Hackers Strategy

· 주로 Let's로 시작하거나 명령문의 형태를 가지며, 명령문 앞에 조건절(If ~)이 붙는 형태도 자주 나오므로 유의한다.
· 권고 및 요청에 수락 또는 거절하거나 추가 정보를 문의하는 응답이 정답으로 자주 출제되는 점을 알아둔다.

Example 🎧 T1_S3_2_Example

Let's grab lunch after the lecture.
강의가 끝나고 점심을 먹어요.

· That sounds good to me. 좋아요. [수락]
· I need to meet with my advisor.
  제 지도교수님을 만나야 해요. [거절]
· Do you know any good places nearby?
  근처에 좋은 곳을 알고 있나요? [추가 정보 문의]

If you want to register, go to the front desk.
등록하고 싶다면, 안내 데스크로 가세요.

· I'll do that. 그럴게요. [수락]
· Can you tell me where it is?
  어디에 있는지 말씀해주시겠어요? [추가 정보 문의]

Tell me if you have any questions.
질문이 있다면 말해주세요.

· OK, I have one. 네, 저는 하나 있어요. [수락]
· I'm fine for now. 지금은 괜찮아요. [거절]

⚠ **Wrong Answers**

· I'll print out the handouts. 제가 유인물을 인쇄할게요.
  [질문에서 암시하는 적절한 후속 행동과 일치하지 않는 오답]

HACKERS PRACTICE 🎧 T1_S3_2_Practice

Listen to each statement and fill in the blanks. Then choose the best response. (You will hear each statement twice.)

01

You should _____ _____ after use.

Ⓐ Equipment is expensive.
Ⓑ The lab opens at 8 A.M.
Ⓒ I'll make sure to do that.
Ⓓ Using microscopes is fun.

02

Please _____ when _____ _____.

Ⓐ Do you need any help?
Ⓑ You have a lot of questions.
Ⓒ No, my phone is working fine.
Ⓓ I don't have your number.

03

If you _____, contact _____ directly.

Ⓐ I'll call them this afternoon.
Ⓑ The office is on the second floor.
Ⓒ Yes, I received the confirmation email.
Ⓓ Can I call my friends over?

04

_____ at the new _____ tonight.

Ⓐ Did you make a reservation?
Ⓑ Why not tonight instead?
Ⓒ They're on the counter.
Ⓓ Maybe it is.

05

I'd love _____ the holiday party _____.

Ⓐ The holidays are in December.
Ⓑ I'll bring a dessert to share.
Ⓒ Your house has a nice garden.
Ⓓ They loved the gift you sent.

Answers p.450

HACKERS TEST 🎧 T1_S3_2_Test

Choose the best response.

01 Ⓐ I'm pretty sure about it.
　　Ⓑ My inbox is always empty.
　　Ⓒ I'll look right away.
　　Ⓓ Are you going to cancel it?

02 Ⓐ The event starts at 8 A.M.
　　Ⓑ I won't be able to go there.
　　Ⓒ Friday works for everyone.
　　Ⓓ Registration desk is on the first floor.

03 Ⓐ I can volunteer next weekend.
　　Ⓑ The charity raised lots of money.
　　Ⓒ Events are scheduled monthly.
　　Ⓓ Organizing requires leadership skills.

04 Ⓐ He started working here in 2021.
　　Ⓑ Where should we do it?
　　Ⓒ I like this chocolate cake better.
　　Ⓓ I haven't prepared the report yet.

05 Ⓐ Research requires extensive funding.
　　Ⓑ The conference is in Chicago.
　　Ⓒ I'm honored by the invitation.
　　Ⓓ The presentation room is booked.

06 Ⓐ Let's meet in person.
　　Ⓑ What is his number?
　　Ⓒ Do you want me to help you?
　　Ⓓ I already completed my courses.

07 Ⓐ We don't need to document them.
　　Ⓑ I prefer the second floor.
　　Ⓒ Where exactly on that floor?
　　Ⓓ The elevator is out of order.

08 Ⓐ How are the reviews of that diner?
　　Ⓑ The printer is out of paper.
　　Ⓒ I'm really into journalism.
　　Ⓓ I don't have enough time today.

09 Ⓐ I'll call you immediately.
　　Ⓑ Shipping costs are too high.
　　Ⓒ The package was damaged.
　　Ⓓ We need more inventory.

10 Ⓐ That would be really helpful.
　　Ⓑ The professor canceled the class.
　　Ⓒ What time is the study group meeting?
　　Ⓓ I prefer to study in the library.

11 Ⓐ When is the deadline?
    Ⓑ I'll take it off the calendar.
    Ⓒ The university has many programs.
    Ⓓ How much is your tuition fee?

12 Ⓐ I haven't received any feedback.
    Ⓑ Which part is confusing you?
    Ⓒ Assignments are due next Friday.
    Ⓓ I finished my work early.

13 Ⓐ Do you need more information?
    Ⓑ Where can I find the manual?
    Ⓒ The questions are too difficult.
    Ⓓ Let me answer that for you.

14 Ⓐ You can use my notes.
    Ⓑ That's what I'll do.
    Ⓒ Here is the agenda.
    Ⓓ Tomorrow morning.

15 Ⓐ I'm revising my paper.
    Ⓑ The deadline is next Friday.
    Ⓒ I'll email you my feedback.
    Ⓓ There are five sections in total.

16 Ⓐ Dinner starts at seven o'clock.
    Ⓑ The travel agency is downtown.
    Ⓒ My camera is working well.
    Ⓓ I'll bring my laptop tonight.

17 Ⓐ The schedule changed.
    Ⓑ How about in the afternoon?
    Ⓒ I think they're in the meeting room.
    Ⓓ Breakfast will be served.

18 Ⓐ Thanks for the reminder.
    Ⓑ The sheet is already full.
    Ⓒ Attendance isn't required.
    Ⓓ I prefer digital attendance systems.

19 Ⓐ Keeping records is difficult.
    Ⓑ The filing system is outdated.
    Ⓒ Times have changed recently.
    Ⓓ I understand the importance.

20 Ⓐ I already filled it out yesterday.
    Ⓑ I can give you the forms.
    Ⓒ The entry was submitted on time.
    Ⓓ Gina has an extensive collection.

Answers p.451

무료 토플자료·유학정보 공유
goHackers.com

TASK 2

Listen to a Conversation

Hackers Updated TOEFL LISTENING

Introduction

Section I. Question Types
1. Main Topic/Purpose Questions
2. Suggestion/Offer Questions
3. Problem Questions
4. Do Next Questions
5. Detail Questions
6. Intention/Attitude Questions
7. Inference Questions

Section II. Conversation Topics
1. Daily Life
2. Campus Life
3. Work & Service

Introduction

TASK 2(Listen to a Conversation)는 평균 70~71단어로 이루어진 대화를 듣고 주어지는 문제의 답을 고르는 유형으로, 대화의 주제 및 중요한 세부 내용을 파악하고 화자의 태도, 의도, 목적을 이해하는 능력을 묻는다. 각 대화에는 2개의 문제가 출제되는데, Module 1에서 대화 2개가 출제되며, 더미 문항이 포함될 경우 대화가 3개까지도 출제된다. Module 2에서는 난이도와 상관없이 대화가 2개씩 출제된다.

■ Preview

Direction 화면

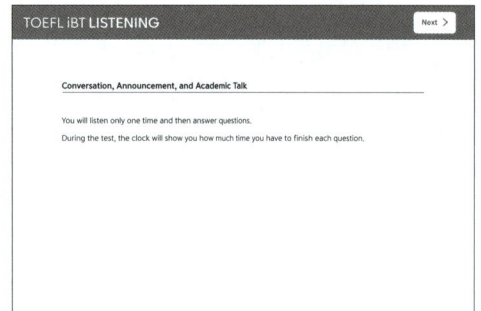

TASK 2, 3, 4 시험에 대한 Direction이 한 번에 주어진다.

디렉션 시간 : 약 11초

디렉션의 내용 : 대화, 공지, 학술 강의를 한 번만 듣고 문제를 풀 것이며, 시계가 문제를 풀 수 있는 시간을 표시할 것이다.

해야 할 일 : Note-taking을 할 펜과 종이를 앞에 가져다 두고, 대화를 들을 준비를 마친다. 필요한 경우 음성 볼륨을 조정한다.

음성 화면

대화를 들을 때 나오는 화면으로, 두 화자의 사진이 나온다.

해야 할 일 : 대화의 첫 부분에서 대화의 전반적인 주제를 파악할 수 있으므로, 첫 부분을 놓치지 않도록 주의 깊게 듣는다. 문제 풀이를 할 때 대화의 주요한 정보를 기억할 수 있도록, 음성을 들으며 Note-taking을 해둔다.

문제 풀이 화면

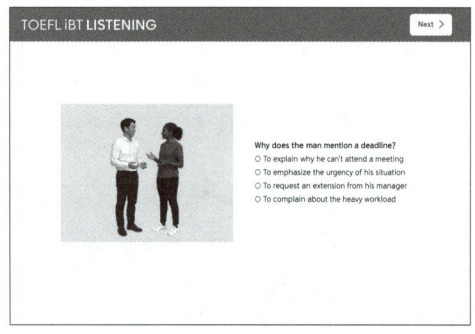

문제가 출제될 때 나오는 화면으로, 문제와 보기가 나온다.

문제를 풀 수 있는 시간 : 20초

문제를 풀 때 해야 할 일 : 문제와 보기는 별도로 들려주지 않으므로, 화면이 전환되면 빠르게 읽는다. 보기 앞에 있는 칸을 클릭하여 답을 표시한다.

문제를 풀고 난 후 해야 할 일 : 답을 고른 후 우측 상단의 Next 버튼을 누르면 다음 문제 또는 다음 대화로 넘어간다. 이때, 이전 화면으로 돌아갈 수 없으므로 충분히 고민한 후 넘어가도록 한다.

Task Strategy

1. 대화가 어떤 상황인지 파악하며 듣는다.
대화의 전반적인 상황을 파악하면 중간중간 세부 내용을 놓치더라도 풀 수 있는 문제가 생기므로, 대화를 들으면서 화자들이 중점적으로 얘기하고 있는 소재나 화자들의 관계를 파악한다.

2. 중요한 세부 정보를 Note-taking한다.
대화를 듣는 동안에는 어떤 문제가 나올지 모르지만, TASK 2에서는 대화의 내용에서 알 수 있는 세부적인 사실을 묻는 문제가 자주 출제된다. 특히, 화자가 제안하거나 제공하는 것, 화자가 가진 문제점, 화자가 다음에 할 일, 화자가 예로 들거나 나열한 세부 정보는 문제로 연결될 가능성이 크므로 이러한 정보들은 반드시 Note-taking해둔다.

3. paraphrasing된 정답을 고른다.
대부분 문제의 정답은 대화의 내용을 paraphrasing해서 나오므로, 제대로 paraphrasing된 정답을 고른다. 대화에서 들은 단어 및 일부 표현을 그대로 쓴 선택지는 오히려 오답일 가능성이 많다는 것도 염두에 둔다.

Study Guide

1. 문제 유형별로 알맞은 듣기 전략을 익히자.
정답을 잘 고르기 위해 집중해서 들어야 하는 정답의 단서가 문제 유형에 따라 다르므로, 각 유형별로 알맞은 듣기 전략을 익혀두면 정답을 더 정확하게 고를 수 있다.

2. 대화 주제별로 등장하는 표현에 익숙해지자.
일상 생활, 캠퍼스 생활, 업무 상황 등으로 출제되는 다양한 대화의 주제별로 자주 등장하는 표현을 알아두면 실제 시험에서 대화 내용을 더욱 빠르게 파악할 수 있다.

3. 화자의 의도를 파악하는 연습을 하자.
대화에 직접적으로 언급되지 않는 화자의 의도를 파악하는 전략을 익히고 이를 연습해두면, 화자의 의도를 파악하는 질문을 더 쉽게 풀이할 수 있다.

무료 토플자료·유학정보 공유
goHackers.com

Hackers
Updated TOEFL
LISTENING

Section I
Question Types

Section I에서는 TASK 2에 출제되는 문제 유형을 7가지로 구분하여 각 유형의 특징과 질문 형태, 실제 문제 풀이에 적용 가능한 전략들을 소개하고 있다. 또한 연습 문제 및 실전 문제를 통해 각 문제 유형을 효과적으로 공략할 수 있도록 하였다.

TASK 2의 Question Types에는 다음의 7가지가 있다.

1. Main Topic/Purpose Questions
2. Suggestion/Offer Questions
3. Problem Questions
4. Do Next Questions
5. Detail Questions
6. Intention/Attitude Questions
7. Inference Questions

1. Main Topic/Purpose Questions

Overview

대화에서 중심이 되는 내용이 무엇인지를 묻는 문제 유형이다. Main Topic 문제는 대화의 중심이 되는 대상이나 그 대상과 관련하여 화자들이 주로 논의하고 있는 것이 무엇인지를 묻는다. Main Purpose 문제의 경우 화자들이 대화를 나누고 있는 목적이나 화자 중 한 명이 대화를 시작한 목적을 묻는다. 매 시험 0~1문제가 출제되며, Main Topic 문제가 Main Purpose 문제보다 더 자주 출제되는 편이다.

Types of Questions

Main Topic 문제는 주로 mainly about, topic, discussing이라는 표현을 포함한 형태로 출제되며, Main Purpose 문제는 Why is the ~ talking to라는 표현을 포함한 형태로 출제된다.

Main Topic
    What is the conversation mainly about?
    What is the topic of the conversation?
    What are the speakers mainly talking about?
    What are the speakers mainly discussing?
    What event are the speakers discussing?

Main Purpose
    Why is the man talking to the woman?

Hackers Strategy

1 대화의 주제 및 목적은 주로 대화의 첫 부분에서 들을 수 있다.

대화의 주제 및 목적은 대화의 첫 부분에 언급되는 경우가 많으므로, 대화의 첫 부분을 특히 집중해서 들어야 한다. 만약 첫 부분에서 주제나 목적이 명확하게 언급이 되지 않는다면, 전반적인 대화의 흐름을 파악해서 정답을 고르도록 한다.

2 반복적으로 들리는 키워드에 주목한다.

대화에서 화자들이 여러 번 언급하는 대상이 대화의 주제나 목적과 관련되어 있을 경우가 많으므로, 반복적으로 들리는 키워드를 유의하여 듣는다.

3 자주 나오는 오답 유형에 주의한다.

대화 내용의 일부만을 다루는 오답, 대화에서 언급된 단어를 포함하고 있지만 내용이 틀린 오답, 대화에서 언급되지 않은 내용에 관한 오답이 자주 등장한다.

Example

🎧 T2_S1_1_Example

Script

M I wanted to talk to you about tomorrow's department meeting.
W Sure, what's up?
M I just found out that three key team members can't make it tomorrow afternoon. They have to attend that emergency client meeting that just came up.
W Oh, that's not good. We really need everyone's input on the new project timeline.
M Exactly. I was thinking we should reschedule. Would Thursday morning work instead? I checked and the conference room is available at 10 A.M.

What are the speakers mainly discussing?

Ⓐ Ways to improve meeting efficiency
Ⓑ Concerns about client feedbacks
Ⓒ Rescheduling a department meeting
Ⓓ Resolving a conflict between team members

정답 Ⓒ

해설 화자들이 주로 논의하고 있는 것을 묻는 문제이므로, 대화의 첫 부분에서 정답의 단서를 찾을 수 있다. 남자가 "I wanted to talk to you about tomorrow's department meeting."이라며 부서 회의에 대해 얘기하고 싶다고 했다. 주요 팀원들이 회의에 참석할 수 없을 것이라는 내용이 이어지고, "we should reschedule"에서 회의 일정을 변경하자고 했으므로 Ⓒ가 정답임을 알 수 있다.

HACKERS PRACTICE 🎧 T2_S1_1_Practice

Listen to each conversation and fill in the blanks. Then choose the best answer for the question. (You will hear each conversation twice.)

01

M Are you going to join _____ _____ this Saturday?
W Definitely! I've been wanting to learn how to grow herbs and flowers. Do you remember _____?
M 9 A.M. at the community center. They said it _____ and a hands-on session.
W Thanks for the heads-up. I'll make sure to _____.

What is the conversation mainly about?
Ⓐ A yard sale
Ⓑ A flower festival
Ⓒ A gardening class
Ⓓ A farmers' market

02

M I've just received a message from IT _____.
W They're finally updating _____ _____! It's happening on Friday, right?
M Yes, they said it will take place after our usual work hours.
W I see. We should back up our files before leaving the office on Friday then. Do you know _____ will be added?
M Well, IT mentioned we'll get a new project management feature _____.

What are the speakers mainly discussing?
Ⓐ A meeting with the IT department
Ⓑ A workplace software improvement
Ⓒ A backup plan for work files
Ⓓ A project management strategy

03

W Have you heard about the _____ _____ taking place next week at the university?
M Yes! I'm definitely planning to attend. _____ _____ my résumé this weekend.
W Great idea. I heard there will be more than 30 companies looking _____ _____.
M That's exciting! Why don't we meet up and go together?

What event are the speakers discussing?

Ⓐ A career fair
Ⓑ A résumé workshop
Ⓒ A job interview
Ⓓ A networking dinner

04

M You're taking Professor Austin's advanced statistics course, right? _____ _____?
W Challenging but fascinating. The workload is _____ _____ though.
M I'm considering signing up for the course next semester. _____ _____ for someone who just barely passed basic statistics?
W Honestly, you might want to _____ _____ first. Professor Austin assumes you're already comfortable with regression analysis.

Why is the man talking to the woman?

Ⓐ To borrow the woman's notes from a class
Ⓑ To discuss a professor's teaching style
Ⓒ To find a study partner
Ⓓ To get advice about course selection

Answers p.455

HACKERS TEST 🎧 T2_S1_1_Test

[01-02] Listen to a conversation.

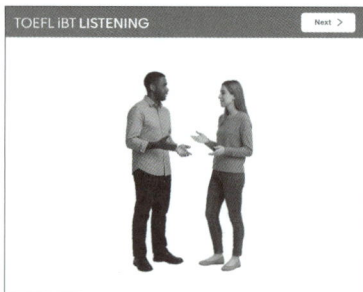

01 What is the conversation mainly about?

Ⓐ A family picnic
Ⓑ A beach party
Ⓒ A farewell dinner
Ⓓ A departmental seminar

02 What is the woman planning to do on Saturday morning?

Ⓐ Attend a department gathering
Ⓑ Talk with her colleagues
Ⓒ Make desserts for the party
Ⓓ Take her sister to the airport

[03-04] Listen to a conversation.

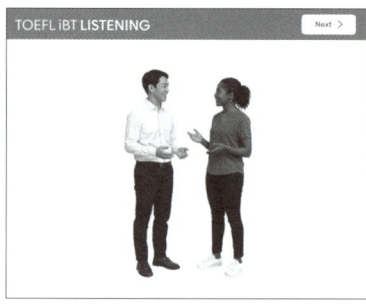

03 What event are the speakers discussing?

Ⓐ A book fair
Ⓑ A downtown festival
Ⓒ A weekend market
Ⓓ A book club meeting

04 What does the woman plan to bring to the event?

Ⓐ Author biographies
Ⓑ Lunch containers
Ⓒ Reading glasses
Ⓓ Personal books

[05-06] Listen to a conversation.

05 What is the topic of the conversation?

Ⓐ A work-related gathering
Ⓑ A weekend career fair
Ⓒ A summer music celebration
Ⓓ A concert of a famous band

06 What will the man most likely do next?

Ⓐ Obtain tickets for the festival
Ⓑ Reschedule his work deadlines
Ⓒ Text the woman his arrival time
Ⓓ Research the performing bands

[07-08] Listen to a conversation.

07 What are the speakers mainly discussing?

Ⓐ A budget proposal for marketing
Ⓑ Social media platform selection
Ⓒ TV commercial production schedules
Ⓓ Competitor analysis results

08 What does the woman suggest they do?

Ⓐ Increase the overall budget
Ⓑ Shift focus to digital influencers
Ⓒ Postpone the campaign launch
Ⓓ Focus on traditional advertising

HACKERS TEST

[09-10] Listen to a conversation.

09 What are the speakers mainly talking about?

Ⓐ A technology workshop
Ⓑ Problems with a website
Ⓒ An online marketing strategy
Ⓓ Some changes to a presentation

10 What department does the man most likely work in?

Ⓐ Human Resources
Ⓑ Accounting
Ⓒ Marketing
Ⓓ Information Technology

[11-12] Listen to a conversation.

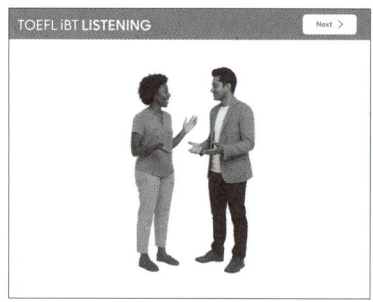

11 Why is the woman talking to the man?

Ⓐ To invite him to a party
Ⓑ To discuss campus activities
Ⓒ To find a celebration venue
Ⓓ To plan her own birthday party

12 What does the man mention about the restaurant?

Ⓐ They provide complimentary appetizers.
Ⓑ They offer special celebration treats.
Ⓒ They have live band performance.
Ⓓ They allow outside decorations.

[13-14] Listen to a conversation.

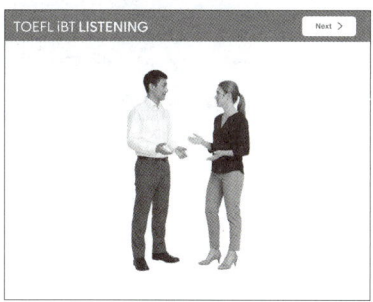

13 What event are the speakers discussing?

Ⓐ A food fair
Ⓑ A charity fundraiser
Ⓒ A wine tasting event
Ⓓ A local farmers' market

14 Why does the woman want to attend the event on Saturday?

Ⓐ Restaurants offer special foods on weekends.
Ⓑ Her family will come to the Saturday session.
Ⓒ She has to work late on Friday
Ⓓ She already has other plans for Friday.

[15-16] Listen to a conversation.

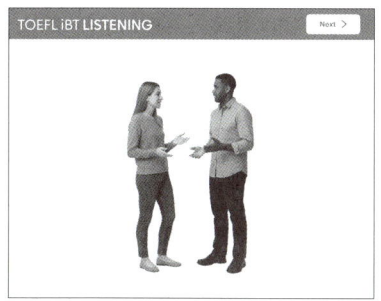

15 What are the speakers mainly discussing?

Ⓐ A professor's teaching style
Ⓑ Library study rooms
Ⓒ A study group for an exam
Ⓓ Economics course requirements

16 What does the woman suggest about the exam?

Ⓐ It requires collaborative preparation.
Ⓑ It focuses on recent lectures only.
Ⓒ It's easier than that of previous years.
Ⓓ It includes practical applications.

Answers p.456

2. Suggestion/Offer Questions

Overview

한 화자가 다른 화자에게 제안하거나 제공하는 내용을 묻는 문제 유형이다. Suggestion 문제는 화자가 제안하는 내용, Offer 문제는 화자가 제공하는 내용을 묻는다. 보기는 대부분 명령문의 형태를 가지며, 동명사구가 나오기도 한다. 매 시험 0~1문제가 출제된다.

Types of Questions

Suggestion 문제는 주로 suggest, encourage, advise, advice라는 표현을 포함한 형태로 출제되며, Offer 문제는 주로 offer라는 표현을 포함한 형태로 출제된다.

Suggestion
  What does the woman suggest the man do?
  What does the man encourage the woman to do?
  What does the woman advise the man to do?
  What advice does the man give the woman?
  What is the woman's advice about exercising?

Offer
  What does the man offer to help with?
  What does the woman offer to do?

Hackers Strategy

1 제안이나 제공을 나타내는 표현에 귀를 기울인다.

Suggestion 문제는 주로 What/How about, Why don't you, You can/should, You might want to와 같은 표현 뒤에, Offer 문제는 주로 Do you need, Do you want me to와 같은 표현 뒤에 정답의 단서가 나온다. 이러한 표현들이 대화에서 들리면 Suggestion이나 Offer 문제가 출제될 것임을 예상할 수 있다.

2 남자가 한 말과 여자가 한 말을 명확하게 구분한다.

대화에서 남자와 여자 중 한 화자가 제안하거나 제공한 것을 묻기 때문에, 남자와 여자가 각각 한 말을 명확하게 구분해야 Suggestion/Offer 문제를 정확하게 풀 수 있다.

3 자주 나오는 오답 유형에 주의한다.

대화에서 언급된 단어를 포함하고 있지만 내용이 틀린 오답이나 대화에서 언급된 사실과 전혀 관련이 없는 오답이 자주 등장한다. 특히, 다른 성별의 화자가 대화에서 언급한 내용이 오답으로 자주 출제되므로 주의한다.

Example   🎧 T2_S1_2_Example

Script

W Have you registered for next semester's classes yet?

M Not yet. I was planning to do it this weekend when I have time to think about my schedule.

W You might want to do it sooner. I just talked to Professor Martinez, and he mentioned that the environmental science seminar is almost full already.

M Really? But registration just opened two days ago!

W The department gave early registration access to environmental studies majors, but now it's open to everyone. There were only about eight spots left when I checked the system an hour ago.

What does the woman suggest the man do?

Ⓐ Change his major to environmental studies
Ⓑ Speak with the professor about reserving a spot
Ⓒ Think thoroughly about the course schedule
Ⓓ Sign up for classes before the weekend

정답 Ⓓ

해설 여자가 남자에게 제안하는 것을 묻는 문제이므로, 여자가 제안을 하는 표현에서 정답의 단서를 찾을 수 있다. 남자가 "I was planning to do it this weekend"라며 그것, 즉 수강 신청을 이번 주말에 할 것이라고 했고, 여자가 "You might want to do it sooner."라며 더 빨리 하는 것이 좋겠다고 했으므로 Ⓓ가 정답임을 알 수 있다.

HACKERS PRACTICE 🎧 T2_S1_2_Practice

Listen to each conversation and fill in the blanks. Then choose the best answer for the question. (You will hear each conversation twice.)

01

M I've been so _____
   _____ lately.
W You really need to take care of yourself. How
   about _____?
M I don't know… There's still so much to do,
   and the _____
   _____.
W Trust me, even a short break can boost your
   productivity.
M You're probably right. Maybe I'll _____
   _____.

What does the woman suggest the man do?

Ⓐ Work from home
Ⓑ Take some time off
Ⓒ Complete the project quickly
Ⓓ Extend his deadline

02

W I've been trying to update the new employees'
   information on the company intranet, but
   _____
   the new HR system.
M I took a training session on that system last
   week. Do you want me _____
   _____ the new hires' profiles?
W That _____.
   I've been struggling with it all morning.
M No problem. Let's set up a time this afternoon
   to _____.

What does the man offer to help with?

Ⓐ Setting up a meeting schedule
Ⓑ Scheduling additional training sessions
Ⓒ Adding content to a new system
Ⓓ Recruiting additional staff members

03

W Have you decided if you're _____ _____ on Saturday? We're going to Oakwood Trail.
M I want to, but I'm a bit worried. I've only hiked once before.
W Why don't you _____?
Oakwood isn't as challenging as people say.
M I'm still a bit nervous about _____ _____.
W Don't worry about that. We always _____ _____ as a group.

What does the woman encourage the man to do?

Ⓐ Join a hiking trip
Ⓑ Buy hiking equipment
Ⓒ Train before a hike
Ⓓ Choose an easier trail

04

W I've been reading this textbook for hours, but _____. I have a final exam on Monday and I'm starting to panic.
M Don't try to memorize _____ _____. Break the material into smaller sections and focus on understanding one concept before _____ _____.
W That makes sense. I've been trying to learn everything all at once.
M That rarely works. Remember, _____ _____—it's much more effective.

What is the man's advice about studying?

Ⓐ Study with a group of classmates.
Ⓑ Memorize as much as possible.
Ⓒ Regular breaks are important.
Ⓓ Learn gradually rather than all at once.

Answers p.460

HACKERS TEST 🎧 T2_S1_2_Test

[01-02] Listen to a conversation.

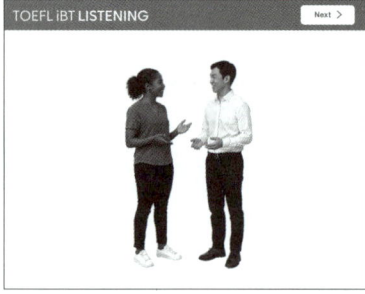

01 What does the woman say about PowerFit?

Ⓐ It offers discounted memberships.
Ⓑ It has updated fitness equipment.
Ⓒ It provides weekend training sessions.
Ⓓ It is close to where she lives.

02 What does the man encourage the woman to do?

Ⓐ Prioritize location over equipment quality
Ⓑ Focus exclusively on strength training
Ⓒ Create a specific workout schedule
Ⓓ Try both gyms before deciding

[03-04] Listen to a conversation.

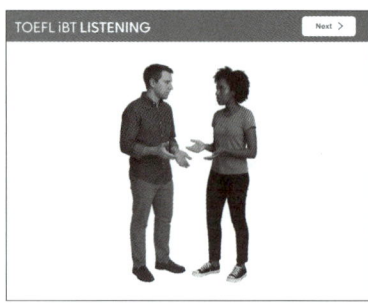

03 What will the woman do tomorrow?

Ⓐ See a doctor
Ⓑ Finish her project
Ⓒ Attend a virtual meeting
Ⓓ Forward the emails to the man

04 What does the man offer to do?

Ⓐ Schedule a doctor's appointment
Ⓑ Take care of urgent emails
Ⓒ Attend meetings alone
Ⓓ Contact the HR department

[05-06] Listen to a conversation.

05 Why does the man mention community service hours?

Ⓐ To suggest extending the cleanup duration
Ⓑ To explain why he missed previous sessions
Ⓒ To share his motivation for joining the event
Ⓓ To ask if there's a minimum number of hours required

06 What does the woman suggest the man do?

Ⓐ Purchase new cleaning supplies
Ⓑ Sign up for another event
Ⓒ Bring his own beverage
Ⓓ Arrive early to set up the equipment

[07-08] Listen to a conversation.

07 Why does the woman mention blue light?

Ⓐ To explain why screens interfere with sleep
Ⓑ To recommend a specific type of lighting
Ⓒ To suggest buying blue light glasses
Ⓓ To criticize modern technology

08 What is the woman's advice about falling asleep?

Ⓐ Take sleeping medication nightly.
Ⓑ Avoid using screens before bedtime.
Ⓒ Exercise right before sleeping.
Ⓓ Don't drink coffee in the evening.

HACKERS TEST

[09-10] Listen to a conversation.

09 What does the man suggest the woman do?

Ⓐ Join forces on the assignment
Ⓑ Ask the professor for an extension
Ⓒ Focus more on data analysis
Ⓓ Change her research topic

10 What will the woman most likely focus on?

Ⓐ Data collection methods
Ⓑ Statistical analysis
Ⓒ Past events and context
Ⓓ Research conclusions

[11-12] Listen to a conversation.

11 What is the woman's problem?

Ⓐ She doesn't own good cooking utensils.
Ⓑ Her meals lack flavor.
Ⓒ She burns food frequently.
Ⓓ She can't follow recipes exactly.

12 What advice does the man give the woman?

Ⓐ Take an advanced cooking class
Ⓑ Stick to recipes more carefully
Ⓒ Buy better kitchen equipment
Ⓓ Taste food while preparing it

[13-14] Listen to a conversation.

13 Why has the man been focusing on one area?

Ⓐ It is a safe neighborhood.
Ⓑ It is close to where he works.
Ⓒ It has the lowest rent prices.
Ⓓ It is near public transportation.

14 What does the woman advise the man to do?

Ⓐ Lower his expectations
Ⓑ Negotiate the rent
Ⓒ Find a roommate
Ⓓ Expand his search area

[15-16] Listen to a conversation.

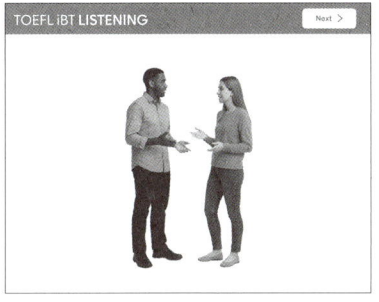

15 What does the man offer to help with?

Ⓐ Designing a new department logo
Ⓑ Sending the slides to the directors
Ⓒ Fixing the inconsistent chart formatting
Ⓓ Arranging refreshments for the meeting

16 What will the woman do before they meet?

Ⓐ Make copies of her slides
Ⓑ Schedule a meeting
Ⓒ Share her presentation file
Ⓓ Reserve the conference room

Answers p.461

3. Problem Questions

Overview

화자가 겪고 있는 문제점을 묻는 문제 유형이다. 매 시험 0~1문제가 출제되며, 특히 기기의 고장과 관련된 대화에서 자주 출제된다.

Types of Questions

주로 problem이라는 표현을 포함한 형태로 출제된다.

Problem

What is the man's problem?

What is the woman's problem with her computer?

What problem are the speakers discussing?

What problem is the man experiencing with online classes?

Hackers Strategy

1 부정적인 표현에 귀를 기울인다.

대화에서 but, trouble, issue, frustrating, concerned, worried와 같은 부정적인 표현이 언급되면 Problem 문제가 출제될 확률이 높다. 특히, act up, freeze, shut down과 같이 기기에 발생할 수 있는 문제점이 들리면, 어떤 기기가 문제인지 Note-taking해둔다.

2 남자가 한 말과 여자가 한 말을 명확하게 구분한다.

대화에서 남자와 여자 중 한 화자가 겪고 있는 문제점을 묻기 때문에, 남자와 여자가 각각 한 말을 명확하게 구분해야 Problem 문제를 정확하게 풀 수 있다.

3 자주 나오는 오답 유형에 주의한다.

대화에서 언급된 단어를 포함하고 있지만 내용이 틀린 오답이나 대화에서 언급된 사실과 전혀 관련이 없는 오답이 자주 등장한다. 특히, 대화에서 언급된 문제가 있는 대상이 주어로 등장하지만, 뒤에 문제가 되는 부분이 대화의 내용과 일치하지 않아 틀린 오답에 주의한다.

Example

🎧 T2_S1_3_Example

Script

W Are you still planning to drive to the conference tomorrow?
M I was, but my car started making a strange noise when I drove it this morning. I'm concerned about taking it on a long trip.
W Oh. Have you called a mechanic yet?
M Yes, I called one an hour ago. He said he could look at it tomorrow afternoon, but that's too late.
W We could carpool if you want. I'm leaving early in the morning.
M That would be great. I really appreciate the offer.

What is the man's problem?

Ⓐ His vehicle has run out of fuel.
Ⓑ His car is making an unusual sound.
Ⓒ His coworker can't attend the conference.
Ⓓ The conference venue has changed.

정답 Ⓑ

해설 남자의 문제점을 묻는 문제이므로, 남자가 언급하는 부정적인 표현에서 정답의 단서를 찾을 수 있다. 남자가 "but my car started making a strange noise"라며 그의 차가 이상한 소리를 내기 시작했다고 했으므로 Ⓑ가 정답임을 알 수 있다.

HACKERS PRACTICE 🎧 T2_S1_3_Practice

Listen to each conversation and fill in the blanks. Then choose the best answer for the question. (You will hear each conversation twice.)

01

M I'm _____ the company email system. It keeps _____ when I try to attach files. Are you having the same issue?
W Yes, it's so frustrating! We _____ about it.
M I already called them. They said they were working on it, but they didn't give a timeline for the fix.
W That's not good. I have _____ to clients before noon.

What problem are the speakers discussing?

Ⓐ A tight deadline for sending reports
Ⓑ A malfunctioning email system
Ⓒ A canceled meeting with clients
Ⓓ A missing important document

02

W You look stressed today. Is everything okay?
M Not really. I just found out I have three exams _____ next week.
W Wow, that's _____. Have you talked to any of your professors about it?
M Not yet. I'm not sure if they'd _____ the schedule this late in the semester.
W Why don't you _____ anyway? It doesn't hurt to ask.
M You're right. Thanks for the advice.

What is the man's problem?

Ⓐ He failed an important exam.
Ⓑ He received poor grades on the test.
Ⓒ He has multiple tests on one day.
Ⓓ He skipped many classes this semester.

03

W Hey, _____ just opened downtown, and I signed up.
M Really? I'm still going to the one near my apartment, but it's always so _____.
W That's why I switched gyms. I could _____ I wanted.
M Oh, is the new one any better?
W Much better! It's even offering a temporary discount. The only downside is the parking situation. It's really _____ sometimes.

What problem is the woman experiencing with her new gym?

Ⓐ It has fewer fitness machines.
Ⓑ It is too crowded after work.
Ⓒ It charges high membership fees.
Ⓓ It lacks sufficient parking spaces.

04

M I'm not sure what to do about my smartphone. The _____ in just a few hours.
W Have you checked which apps are _____?
M I did, and I've closed everything unnecessary.
W Hmm... Could your phone be running _____?
M I don't think so. I still have more than 50GB left.
W That's strange. How old is it?
M About three years now. I'm wondering if I should _____.

What is the man's problem with his smartphone?

Ⓐ It runs out of battery very quickly.
Ⓑ It doesn't have enough storage space left.
Ⓒ It has too many unnecessary apps running.
Ⓓ It overheats when using multiple applications.

Answers p.465

HACKERS TEST

[01-02] Listen to a conversation.

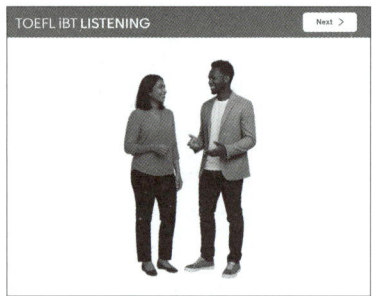

01 What is the man's problem?

Ⓐ He doesn't have enough time to practice yoga.
Ⓑ He doesn't know where the community center is.
Ⓒ He has scheduling conflicts between work and yoga class.
Ⓓ He didn't bring the equipment he needs for the yoga class.

02 What can be inferred about the woman?

Ⓐ She always arrives early to yoga class.
Ⓑ She teaches yoga at the community center.
Ⓒ She hasn't purchased a yoga mat for herself.
Ⓓ She is more experienced at yoga than the man.

[03-04] Listen to a conversation.

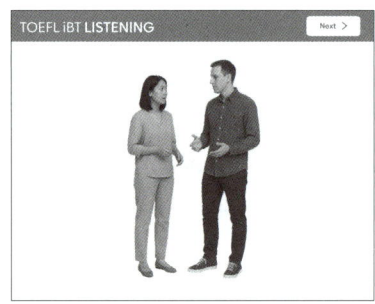

03 What is the woman's problem with her laptop?

Ⓐ Its keyboard is broken.
Ⓑ Its screen doesn't turn on.
Ⓒ Its battery needs replacement.
Ⓓ It won't connect to other devices.

04 Why does the man mention same-day repairs?

Ⓐ To explain why the tech center is expensive
Ⓑ To inform the woman of an available solution
Ⓒ To complain about the tech center's limited hours
Ⓓ To encourage the woman to visit the tech center immediately

[05-06] Listen to a conversation.

05 What problem are the speakers discussing?

Ⓐ Some camping equipment needs fixing.
Ⓑ The budget for the weekend trip is too tight.
Ⓒ The campground booking system isn't working.
Ⓓ Their weekend plan might be ruined by rain.

06 What will the man most likely do next?

Ⓐ Buy some tickets
Ⓑ Repair some supplies
Ⓒ Contact a camping site
Ⓓ Look for an indoor venue

[07-08] Listen to a conversation.

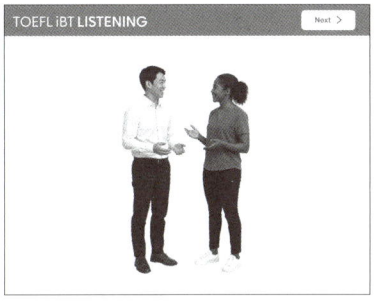

07 What problem is the man experiencing with the air conditioner?

Ⓐ It is making loud noises.
Ⓑ It is not producing cold air.
Ⓒ It is using too much electricity.
Ⓓ It is not turning on.

08 What does the woman offer to do?

Ⓐ Contact building maintenance.
Ⓑ Check his air conditioner.
Ⓒ Lend a cooling device.
Ⓓ Help him move to another room.

HACKERS TEST

[09-10] Listen to a conversation.

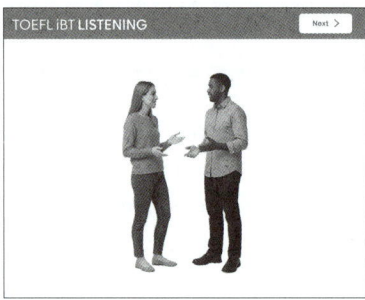

09 What is the woman's problem?

Ⓐ She cannot reduce her screen time.
Ⓑ She suffers from intense headaches.
Ⓒ She misunderstood the presentation date.
Ⓓ She feels stressed about medication side effects.

10 When does the woman expect to resume working on the presentation?

Ⓐ Monday
Ⓑ Tuesday
Ⓒ Thursday
Ⓓ Friday

[11-12] Listen to a conversation.

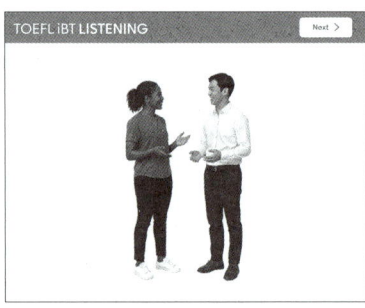

11 What problem are the speakers discussing?

Ⓐ Dormitory safety concerns
Ⓑ Poor lighting in the rooms
Ⓒ Lack of time for council meetings
Ⓓ Excessive noise after dark

12 What reason does the man give for his suggestion?

Ⓐ It will save time during the meeting.
Ⓑ It will help them write a formal report.
Ⓒ It will make their complaint more convincing.
Ⓓ It will allow them to propose a specific solution.

[13-14] Listen to a conversation.

13 What is the man's problem with his bicycle?

    Ⓐ Its tires need to be replaced.
    Ⓑ Its brakes are making a noise.
    Ⓒ Its chain keeps falling off.
    Ⓓ Its seat is uncomfortable.

14 What does the woman offer to do?

    Ⓐ Recommend a cheaper repair shop
    Ⓑ Help transport the bicycle to a repair shop
    Ⓒ Contact a family member for help
    Ⓓ Lend the man her brother's repair tool

[15-16] Listen to a conversation.

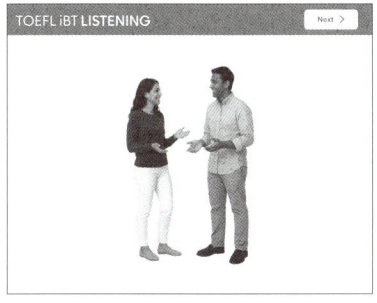

15 What problem are the speakers experiencing with the printer?

    Ⓐ It prints pages too slowly.
    Ⓑ It experiences constant jamming.
    Ⓒ It makes loud noises when operating.
    Ⓓ It shuts down unexpectedly.

16 What will the woman probably do next?

    Ⓐ Purchase a new printer
    Ⓑ Arrange for professional repair services
    Ⓒ Train colleagues on basic troubleshooting
    Ⓓ Transfer printing tasks to another department

Answers p.466

4. Do Next Questions

Overview

대화가 끝난 후 화자가 다음에 할 일을 묻는 문제 유형이다. 매 시험 0~1문제가 출제된다.

Types of Questions

주로 do next나 do after라는 표현을 포함한 형태로 출제된다.

Do Next

What will the woman do next?
What will the man most likely do next?
What will the woman probably do next?
What will the man do after the meeting?

Hackers Strategy

1 다음에 할 일은 주로 대화의 마지막 부분에서 들을 수 있다.

Do Next 문제는 대화가 끝난 후에 화자가 할 일을 묻기 때문에, 정답의 단서는 대부분 대화의 마지막 부분에 언급된다. 따라서, 마지막까지 대화를 집중해서 잘 들어야 한다.

2 미래를 나타내는 표현에 귀를 기울인다.

will, be going to 등의 미래 시제나 later, next, after 등의 미래와 관련된 표현이 포함된 문장을 들으면 Do Next 문제가 출제될 것을 예상할 수 있으며, 주로 해당 표현들 뒤에서 정답의 단서를 들을 수 있다.

3 자주 나오는 오답 유형에 주의한다.

대화에서 언급된 단어를 포함하고 있지만 내용이 틀린 오답이나 대화에서 언급된 사실과 전혀 관련이 없는 오답이 자주 등장한다.

Example T2_S1_4_Example

Script

M Hey, what are you thinking about bringing to the neighborhood potluck?
W I completely forgot about that! When exactly is it again?
M It's tomorrow at noon.
W I have no idea what to bring. What are you planning to contribute?
M I'm bringing a chocolate cake. You could make a pasta salad. It won't take too much to prepare.
W That's a good idea. I will head out to the supermarket and buy the ingredients.

What will the woman most likely do next?

Ⓐ Go to the supermarket
Ⓑ Make a chocolate cake
Ⓒ Ask someone else for help
Ⓓ Start preparing a meal

정답 Ⓐ

해설 여자가 다음에 할 일을 묻는 문제이므로, 대화 마지막 부분의 미래를 나타내는 표현에서 정답의 단서를 찾을 수 있다. 여자가 "I will head out to the supermarket and buy the ingredients."라며 지금 슈퍼마켓에 가서 재료를 사겠다고 했으므로 Ⓐ가 정답임을 알 수 있다.

HACKERS PRACTICE 🎧 T2_S1_4_Practice

Listen to each conversation and fill in the blanks. Then choose the best answer for the question. (You will hear each conversation twice.)

01

M Have you had a chance to look at _____?
W Not really, why?
M The ancient pottery collection _____ this Friday, and I really wanted to check it out.
W Oh, that's only two days away! I'm also interested in pottery, so _____ tomorrow after lunch?
M Great! I _____ on the museum website right away.

What will the man do next?

Ⓐ Make an online reservation
Ⓑ Cancel his afternoon class
Ⓒ Meet the woman at the museum
Ⓓ Eat lunch with his friend

02

M How's _____ for tomorrow's client meeting?
W I've got most of it done, but I'm _____ in the conference room. It keeps shutting down randomly.
M That's frustrating. Have you tried _____?
W All the other rooms are booked tomorrow. I _____ to get this fixed.
M Good idea. They're usually pretty quick with these kinds of issues.

What will the woman most likely do next?

Ⓐ Finalize the presentation materials
Ⓑ Find another conference room
Ⓒ Reschedule the client meeting
Ⓓ Contact technical support

03

W I missed Professor Hart's lecture yesterday because I had a doctor's appointment. Did he _____?

M He went over the key concepts for next week's exam. It _____.

W Oh no, that sounds crucial. Would you mind _____?

M Of course, but I can't get to them right now since class is about to start. I'll scan them and _____.

W No worries, thank you!

What will the man do after the class?

Ⓐ Meet with the professor
Ⓑ Study for an exam
Ⓒ Send the woman his notes
Ⓓ Take the woman to see a doctor

04

W I just received an email about _____ I applied for.

M Really? What did it say?

W I got approved! So, I need to sign the lease and _____ by tomorrow.

M Congratulations! Do you _____?

W Not yet. I need to _____ first.

What will the woman probably do next?

Ⓐ Look for another dormitory
Ⓑ Ask the man for a loan
Ⓒ Access her bank account
Ⓓ Call the dormitory administration

HACKERS TEST 🎧 T2_S1_4_Test

[01-02] Listen to a conversation.

01 What is the woman's problem?

Ⓐ She borrowed too many books.
Ⓑ She can't access the library website.
Ⓒ She didn't expect her books to be due.
Ⓓ She forgot to pay the overdue fine.

02 What will the woman do next?

Ⓐ Extend her borrowing period
Ⓑ Return her books immediately
Ⓒ Look for a book at home
Ⓓ Check the new policy online

[03-04] Listen to a conversation.

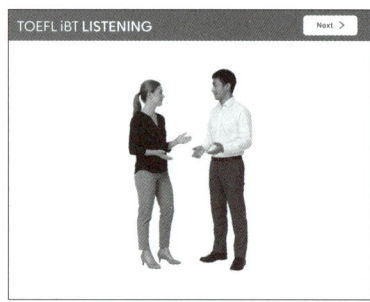

03 What does the woman imply when she says, "Our customers aren't engineers"?

Ⓐ The company should target more engineers.
Ⓑ The description needs to be simpler.
Ⓒ They must hire more technical writers.
Ⓓ Their products are overpriced.

04 What will the man most likely do next?

Ⓐ Schedule a follow-up meeting
Ⓑ Research customer preferences
Ⓒ Develop easier infographics
Ⓓ Edit the text descriptions

[05-06] Listen to a conversation.

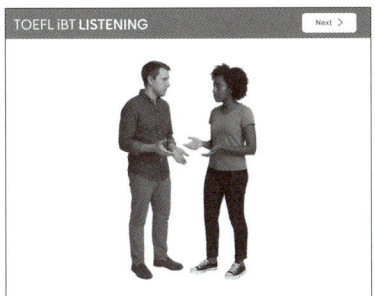

05 Why does the woman suggest meeting at 2 P.M.?

Ⓐ The restaurant does not open until 2 P.M.
Ⓑ She plans to meet someone else before lunch.
Ⓒ She cannot meet earlier due to her schedule.
Ⓓ The restaurant offers discounts after 2 P.M.

06 What will the man probably do next?

Ⓐ Change the meeting time
Ⓑ Book a table for two people
Ⓒ Look for another restaurant
Ⓓ Make an inquiry about the menu

[07-08] Listen to a conversation.

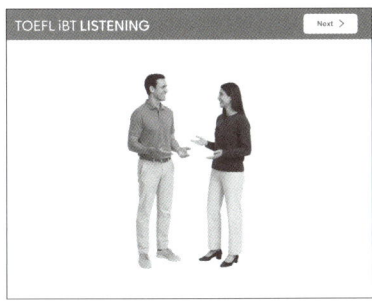

07 Why does the woman mention computers?

Ⓐ To advise the man to take computer classes
Ⓑ To describe necessary skills for a position
Ⓒ To suggest submitting an application online
Ⓓ To identify a problem with the library system

08 What will the man most likely do next?

Ⓐ Fill out a form
Ⓑ Call the woman
Ⓒ Clean up some books
Ⓓ Change his schedule

HACKERS TEST

[09-10] Listen to a conversation.

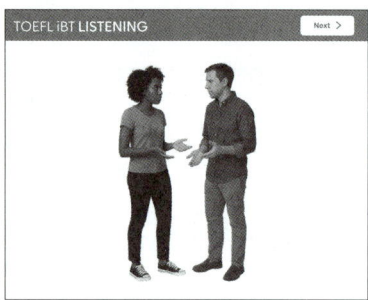

09 What problem is the woman experiencing?

Ⓐ She missed the deadline for the report.
Ⓑ Her computer has been freezing repeatedly.
Ⓒ Her report contains too many errors.
Ⓓ She doesn't have the man's contact information.

10 What will the man do next?

Ⓐ Drive her to the downtown repair shop
Ⓑ Show her how to prevent computer freezing
Ⓒ Call the shop to make an appointment for her
Ⓓ Share the repair shop's contact details

[11-12] Listen to a conversation.

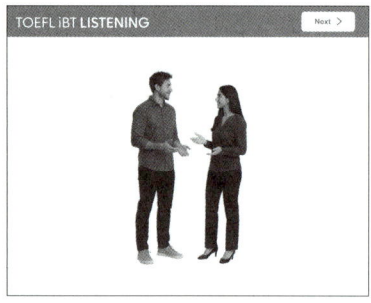

11 What does the woman imply about renewable energy?

Ⓐ It offers many topic options to select from.
Ⓑ It requires expensive equipment to study.
Ⓒ It is not covered well in their textbook.
Ⓓ It is becoming more popular among students.

12 What will the speakers most likely do next?

Ⓐ Attend the lecture together
Ⓑ Consult with their professor
Ⓒ Schedule a meeting time
Ⓓ Change their presentation topics

[13-14] Listen to a conversation.

13 What can be inferred about the regular bus line?

    Ⓐ It makes at least four stops on the way to the beach.
    Ⓑ It provides a more scenic route to the beach.
    Ⓒ It is twice as cheap as the express bus.
    Ⓓ It requires reservations in advance.

14 What will the woman most likely do next?

    Ⓐ Look for alternative transportation options
    Ⓑ Check the bus schedule for departure times
    Ⓒ Purchase tickets for a weekend beach trip
    Ⓓ Inform her parents about the new bus service

[15-16] Listen to a conversation.

15 What does the woman say about catering services?

    Ⓐ They are too expensive.
    Ⓑ They require a minimum purchase.
    Ⓒ They are unavailable for large groups.
    Ⓓ They don't provide vegetarian options.

16 What will the woman do after the meeting?

    Ⓐ Set up conference equipment
    Ⓑ Contact a food service provider
    Ⓒ Send out workshop invitations
    Ⓓ Sign a contract with a client

Answers p.472

5. Detail Questions

Overview

대화를 통해 알 수 있는 다양한 세부 사실을 묻는 문제 유형이다. 질문에서 묻는 내용과 질문 형태가 매우 다양하다. 매 시험 4~5문제가 출제되어, 출제 비율이 가장 높은 문제 유형이다.

Types of Questions

Detail 문제는 세부적으로 묻고자 하는 내용에 따라 다양한 형태로 출제된다. say about이나 mention about이라는 표현을 포함한 형태로 출제되어 특정 대상에 대해 화자가 언급한 사항을 묻거나, why나 reason이라는 표현을 포함한 형태로 출제되어 이유를 묻는다. 그 외에도 대화 안의 세부 사항에 대해 묻는 다양한 문제가 출제된다.

Mention
  What does the man say about his roommate?
  What does the woman mention about the assignment?

Reason
  Why did the woman call a technician?
  Why is the man asking about the library hours?
  Why do the speakers want to leave early?
  What reason does the man give for his suggestion?

Etc.
  What is the man trying to decide between?
  What do the speakers dislike about the hotel room?
  When will the book fair begin?
  Where will the seminar be held?

Hackers Strategy

1 화자가 주요한 화제와 관련하여 언급하는 사실들을 Note-taking한다.

대화의 주요한 화제에 대해 화자가 몇 가지 사실을 설명하는 경우에는 이에 대한 문제가 출제될 확률이 높으므로, 주요한 내용을 Note-taking해두는 것이 중요하다.

2 화자가 한 말을 paraphrasing한 것을 정답으로 고른다.

대화에서 출제되는 Detail 문제의 정답에서는 화자가 했던 말을 그대로 인용하기보다 다른 표현으로 바꾸어 쓰는 경우가 많다.

3 자주 나오는 오답 유형에 주의한다.

대화에서 언급된 단어를 포함하고 있지만 내용이 틀린 오답이나 대화에서 언급된 사실과 전혀 관련이 없는 오답이 자주 등장한다.

Example 🎧 T2_S1_5_Example

Script

W I just finished that new science fiction novel, *Beyond the Stars*.
M Oh, what did you think of it? I read it last month.
W It was really fascinating! The character development was incredible.
M I agree. What impressed me most was the author's detailed world-building. The alien cultures she created were so unique and well-thought-out.
W I hadn't focused as much on the world-building, but you're right! I'm definitely going to read her other books now.
M You should. Her first trilogy received several literary awards for innovative storytelling.

What does the man say about the novel?

Ⓐ It received poor reviews from critics.
Ⓑ It contains too many characters.
Ⓒ It is better than the author's previous works.
Ⓓ It features distinct alien cultures.

정답 Ⓓ

해설 남자가 소설에 대해 언급한 것을 묻는 문제이므로, 소설과 관련하여 남자가 대화에서 언급한 사실에서 정답의 단서를 찾을 수 있다. 남자가 "The alien cultures she created were so unique"라며 작가가 창조한 외계인 문화는 매우 독창적이라고 했으므로 Ⓓ가 정답임을 알 수 있다.

HACKERS PRACTICE 🎧 T2_S1_5_Practice

Listen to each conversation and fill in the blanks. Then choose the best answer for the question. (You will hear each conversation twice.)

01

W Did you see the flyer _____ _____? I'm interested in the outdoor movie screening and the campus e-sports tournament finals _____ _____.

M Wow, they both sound fun! But I can't make it to either of them. I _____ _____ with my family.

W That's okay, I can go with Jane instead. How about _____ on Saturday night? This looks pretty interesting.

M Sounds great! I'm _____.

What event are the speakers planning to attend together?

Ⓐ A campus art showcase
Ⓑ A live music performance
Ⓒ An outdoor movie screening
Ⓓ A game tournament

02

M I've been looking for _____ _____. Do you know any good stores?

W There's a _____ that has a great selection. It just opened last month, and they have _____ _____.

M That sounds perfect! How much are the discounts?

W It's 15% off _____. I bought my phone case there and saved quite a bit.

M Great! I'll _____ this weekend.

What does the woman say about the tech shop?

Ⓐ It has been open since last year.
Ⓑ It is located in a shopping center.
Ⓒ It provides student discounts on digital devices.
Ⓓ It offers free accessories with a student ID.

03

M I'm _____ my sister's surprise birthday party.
W What's the problem?
M The restaurant I reserved just _____ _____, so now I need to find another place.
W Was there a system error at the restaurant?
M No. Apparently, they had _____ _____.
W No way, that's unfortunate. In that case, how about the café downtown that John runs? I _____.

Why does the man need a new venue?

Ⓐ He failed to confirm the reservation in advance.
Ⓑ His original booking wasn't properly processed.
Ⓒ The restaurant was damaged by a recent fire.
Ⓓ John refused the man's request to use his café.

04

W Have you checked the company intranet? There are several _____ _____.
M Which parts?
W The staff directory _____ _____ who left months ago, and our pricing guidelines are from last year.
M I see. I'll _____ _____ today. Could you send me a detailed list of all the changes?
W Yes, I'll _____ and email it to you by the end of the day.

Why does the man plan to contact a web developer?

Ⓐ To create a new pricing strategy for their products
Ⓑ To learn how to update the website himself
Ⓒ To discuss creating a staff directory from scratch
Ⓓ To request updates to outdated information

HACKERS TEST T2_S1_5_Test

[01-02] Listen to a conversation.

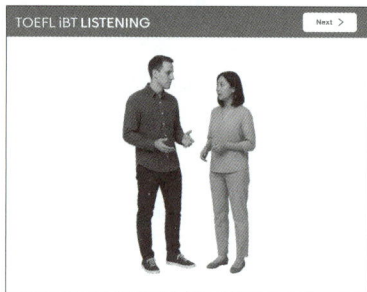

01 What do the speakers say about the reservation?

Ⓐ It was made through the website.
Ⓑ It was confirmed twice by email.
Ⓒ It was canceled by the woman.
Ⓓ It was made three months ago.

02 Why does the woman choose to accept the smaller room?

Ⓐ She prefers smaller hotel rooms.
Ⓑ She wishes to save money on accommodation.
Ⓒ She thinks finding another place will be difficult.
Ⓓ She wants to avoid dealing with the hotel staff.

[03-04] Listen to a conversation.

03 Why did the man want to talk to the woman?

Ⓐ To provide feedback on her previous reports
Ⓑ To assign her new research responsibilities
Ⓒ To check her availability for a conference
Ⓓ To discuss her academic performance

04 What does the man say about the woman's responsibilities?

Ⓐ She will work in the laboratory every day.
Ⓑ She will focus on literature reviews.
Ⓒ She will gather data and make reports.
Ⓓ She will present her findings at conferences.

[05-06] Listen to a conversation.

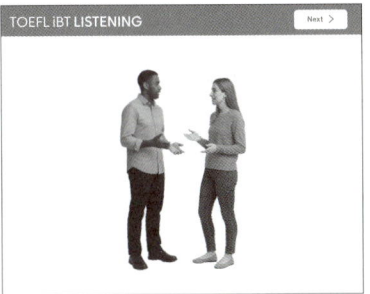

05 Where will the photography club meeting be held?

    Ⓐ In an auditorium
    Ⓑ In an art gallery
    Ⓒ In a student center
    Ⓓ In a photography studio

06 Why does the woman mention her study group?

    Ⓐ To give a reason why she might be late
    Ⓑ To invite the man to join the study group
    Ⓒ To ask if the meeting time can be changed
    Ⓓ To explain why she can't attend the meeting

[07-08] Listen to a conversation.

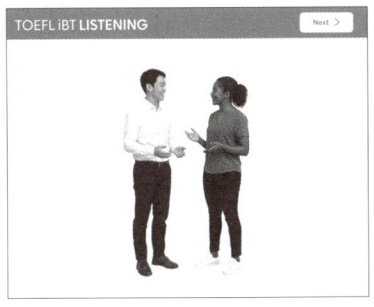

07 What day are the speakers likely to depart to Chicago?

    Ⓐ Monday
    Ⓑ Friday
    Ⓒ Saturday
    Ⓓ Sunday

08 What will the woman most likely do next?

    Ⓐ Look for restaurants near their hotel
    Ⓑ Check the weather forecast for Chicago
    Ⓒ Research train departure times and costs
    Ⓓ Find a suitable hotel in downtown Chicago

HACKERS TEST

[09-10] Listen to a conversation.

09 What do the speakers say about the office printer?

Ⓐ It is still covered by warranty.
Ⓑ It needs new cartridges installed.
Ⓒ It was very expensive when purchased.
Ⓓ It was purchased more than two years ago.

10 What does the man encourage the woman to do?

Ⓐ Purchase a replacement printer
Ⓑ Look for alternative repair shops
Ⓒ Arrive at the service center early
Ⓓ Check if the warranty is still valid

[11-12] Listen to a conversation.

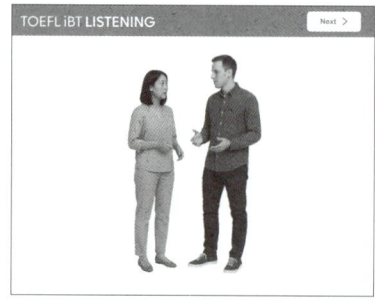

11 What are the speakers mainly discussing?

Ⓐ Schedule conflicts
Ⓑ Recent HR policy changes
Ⓒ Negative customer feedback
Ⓓ A mandatory training program

12 When will the man attend the training session?

Ⓐ 8 A.M.
Ⓑ 9 A.M.
Ⓒ 1 P.M.
Ⓓ 2 P.M.

[13-14] Listen to a conversation.

13 What does the woman say about the BookPro bag?

Ⓐ It is the most popular model.
Ⓑ It has additional storage pockets.
Ⓒ It costs more than the man's budget.
Ⓓ It was designed for his laptop model.

14 What will the man most likely do next?

Ⓐ Ask an employee about pricing
Ⓑ Compare different bag features
Ⓒ Look for other laptop bags
Ⓓ Purchase the first option

[15-16] Listen to a conversation.

15 What is the man's problem?

Ⓐ His computer screen needs adjustment.
Ⓑ He is allergic to some painkillers.
Ⓒ He cannot focus on his work tasks.
Ⓓ He has been experiencing health issues.

16 Why does the woman recommend that the man see Dr. Parker?

Ⓐ She offers affordable treatment options.
Ⓑ She has flexible appointment scheduling.
Ⓒ She has expertise in his type of condition.
Ⓓ She works close to his office location.

Answers p.477

6. Intention/Attitude Questions

Overview

대화에서 화자가 한 말의 기저에 놓인 화자의 의도 및 태도를 묻는 문제 유형이다. Intention 문제는 화자가 한 말의 일부를 인용해서 해당 말을 한 의도를 묻거나, 대화 안에서 언급된 대상을 문제에 제시해서 해당 대상을 언급한 의도를 묻는다. Attitude 문제는 대화 안에서 언급된 대상에 대해 화자가 어떤 태도 및 의견을 가지고 있는지를 묻는다. 매 시험 0~1문제가 출제되며, 특히 Attitude 문제는 출제 빈도가 Intention 문제에 비해 낮은 편이다.

Types of Questions

화자가 한 말의 일부를 인용하거나 대화에서 언급한 대상을 질문에 제시한다. Intention 문제는 Why does ~ say/mention 또는 What does ~ imply when이라는 표현을 포함한 형태로 출제되며, Attitude 문제는 attitude라는 표현을 포함한 형태로 출제된다.

Intention

Why does the man say "I already contacted them twice"?

Why does the man mention a study group?

What does the woman imply when she says, "That sounds familiar"?

Attitude

What is the woman's attitude toward remote work?

How does the man seem to feel about living downtown?

Hackers Strategy

1 화자가 언급하는 주장, 예시, 문제점 등에 주목한다.

화자는 주로 대화에서 특정 대상을 언급하면서 본인의 주장을 뒷받침하거나, 예시를 들어주거나, 문제점을 제시하는데, 이때 언급된 대상이 질문에 제시되는 경우가 많다. 따라서, 화자의 주장이나 화자가 들어주는 예시, 화자가 제시하는 문제점을 집중해서 들으면, 언급된 대상의 목적을 유추할 수 있다.

2 대화의 맥락 속에서 화자의 말을 이해한다.

화자의 의도 및 태도는 대화의 전체적인 맥락 안에서 파악하는 것이 가장 중요하며, 이를 위해서는 대화에서 오가는 말을 통해 그 사이에 함축된 화자의 의도 및 태도를 파악해야 한다.

3 자주 나오는 오답 유형에 주의한다.

대화에서 알 수 있는 화자의 의도가 아닌 표면적 의미만을 제시한 오답이나 전후 문맥을 잘못 파악한 오답이 자주 등장한다.

Example

🎧 T2_S1_6_Example

Script

W Have you finished your part of our group presentation for Professor Kim's class?
M Almost. I just need to add a few more slides, but I'm having trouble finding reliable sources for the last section.
W I might be able to help with that. I did a similar research project last semester and saved all my references.
M Thank you! Could you send me those sources and look over what I've done so far this evening?
W Tomorrow would be better. I have a study group for my calculus exam at 6 P.M., and I don't know how long we'll be working on practice problems.

Why does the woman mention a study group?

Ⓐ To show off her academic commitments
Ⓑ To explain her scheduling conflict
Ⓒ To highlight the importance of teamwork
Ⓓ To suggest the man join her calculus class

정답 Ⓑ

해설 여자가 스터디 그룹을 언급한 의도를 묻는 문제이므로, 해당 대상을 언급하면서 함께 한 말에서 정답의 단서를 찾을 수 있다. 여자가 "Tomorrow would be better. I have a study group for my calculus exam at 6 P.M."라며 스터디 그룹이 오후 6시에 있어서 내일이 더 낫겠다고 했다. 따라서, 일정에 충돌이 있다는 것을 설명하기 위해 스터디 그룹을 언급한 것이므로 Ⓑ가 정답임을 알 수 있다.

HACKERS PRACTICE 🎧 T2_S1_6_Practice

Listen to each conversation and fill in the blanks. Then choose the best answer for the question. (You will hear each conversation twice.)

01

M Did you _____ in the campus library for our group project meeting tomorrow?
W I tried earlier, but all the rooms were already reserved. Is there any chance we could _____?
M Well, I don't think that's a good idea. My _____ with my little brothers always around.
W Oh, I see. I should call the library and see if we can be _____ for any canceled rooms.

What is the man's attitude toward studying at his place?

Ⓐ He feels it lacks adequate space.
Ⓑ He thinks it will be too distracting.
Ⓒ He expresses concerns about privacy issues.
Ⓓ He worries about disturbing his neighbors.

02

W Excuse me, I'm trying to track down this sociology journal article _____, but I can't seem to find it anywhere.
M Let me check for you. Hmm, it looks like that particular journal is not part of _____.
W Oh no, my paper is _____, and I really need that article.
M Don't worry. We can request it through interlibrary loan.
W But doesn't that usually _____?
M You're right. But for academic articles, we can get them within 24 hours. Just _____ before you leave.

What does the woman imply when she says, "But doesn't that usually take several days?"

Ⓐ She is concerned the article won't arrive before her deadline.
Ⓑ She has tried interlibrary loan before.
Ⓒ She believes the man is exaggerating the service speed.
Ⓓ She thinks the interlibrary loan process is inefficient.

03

M Have you heard about _____ _____ that just opened downtown?
W Yeah, I actually went there yesterday. The pasta was amazing, but the _____ _____.
M Oh, really? My roommate had _____ _____. He said the food was just okay, but the staff was really attentive.
W Well, I guess it's tough to _____ _____ when a place just opens.

Why does the man mention his roommate?

Ⓐ To encourage another restaurant visit
Ⓑ To illustrate why new restaurants often fail
Ⓒ To present a contrasting opinion
Ⓓ To plan a group dinner at the restaurant

04

M What do you think of _____ _____? The marketing department wants our feedback by tomorrow morning.
W I like the overall layout, but the color scheme doesn't really _____ _____.
M You can _____. Our company's logo is blue and silver, but they've used orange accents throughout the site.
W Exactly. Let's _____ now before we forget.

Why does the man mention the company's logo?

Ⓐ To recommend creating a new logo
Ⓑ To criticize the placement of it on the website
Ⓒ To praise the marketing department's creativity
Ⓓ To suggest changing website colors

Answers p.481

HACKERS TEST 🎧 T2_S1_6_Test

[01-02] Listen to a conversation.

01 Why does the man mention a chemistry lab?

  Ⓐ To provide context for his possible delay
  Ⓑ To explain why he cannot attend the meeting
  Ⓒ To demonstrate his commitment to his studies
  Ⓓ To emphasize his time management challenges

02 What does the woman say about the baseball club meeting tonight?

  Ⓐ It is going to be held indoors.
  Ⓑ It will feature a video of a historical game.
  Ⓒ It requires bringing baseball equipment.
  Ⓓ It will involve recording game scores.

[03-04] Listen to a conversation.

03 What is the woman's attitude toward the seminar?

  Ⓐ She thinks the instructor is qualified.
  Ⓑ She has concerns about the presenter.
  Ⓒ She prefers online seminars instead.
  Ⓓ She believes it starts too late.

04 What will the woman probably do next?

  Ⓐ Research the speaker's background
  Ⓑ Sign up for the seminar
  Ⓒ Ask friends for their opinions
  Ⓓ Look for alternative events

[05-06] Listen to a conversation.

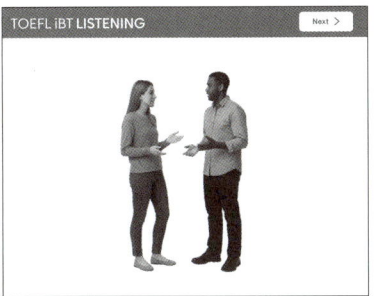

05 Why does the man mention the midterm period?

Ⓐ To explain why students are physically stressed
Ⓑ To show understanding of the woman's situation
Ⓒ To remind the woman about upcoming tests
Ⓓ To compliment the workshop's scheduling

06 What does the man encourage the woman to do?

Ⓐ Organize a pre-workshop meetup
Ⓑ Share workshop information online
Ⓒ Register for the workshop without delay
Ⓓ Research stress management techniques

[07-08] Listen to a conversation.

07 What does the man imply when he says, "My mind is all over the place these days"?

Ⓐ He couldn't remember the museum's location.
Ⓑ He is planning to visit multiple museums.
Ⓒ He has seen too many art exhibitions lately.
Ⓓ He confused the exhibition's opening date.

08 What does the woman imply about the new interactive art exhibition?

Ⓐ It will close soon due to high demand.
Ⓑ It offers discounts for early reservations.
Ⓒ It is the largest one in the museum.
Ⓓ It encourages advance booking.

HACKERS TEST

[09-10] Listen to a conversation.

09 What is the man's attitude toward the apartment?

    Ⓐ He thinks it's going to be noisy.
    Ⓑ He dislikes the downtown location.
    Ⓒ He is worried about whether he can afford it.
    Ⓓ He prefers a larger kitchen.

10 Why does the woman mention transportation costs?

    Ⓐ To explain why the rent is cheap
    Ⓑ To describe her own living situation
    Ⓒ To suggest buying a new car
    Ⓓ To justify the higher housing cost

[11-12] Listen to a conversation.

11 Why does the man mention his client?

    Ⓐ To delay tomorrow's department meeting
    Ⓑ To explain why he can't fulfill his responsibility
    Ⓒ To share information about an important visitor
    Ⓓ To highlight the significance of the presentation

12 What will the woman do next?

    Ⓐ Call a client
    Ⓑ Create additional slides
    Ⓒ Make copies of handouts
    Ⓓ Repair a broken projector

[13-14] Listen to a conversation.

13 How does the woman seem to feel about the cooking class?

Ⓐ She is confident she will excel.
Ⓑ She is anxious but motivated to learn.
Ⓒ She regrets signing up for it.
Ⓓ She thinks it will be too easy for her.

14 What does the man say about the instructor?

Ⓐ She works well with new cooks.
Ⓑ She is very demanding with students.
Ⓒ She specializes in advanced techniques.
Ⓓ She only teaches baking classes.

[15-16] Listen to a conversation.

15 Why does the woman mention her roommate?

Ⓐ To explain why she is quitting her job
Ⓑ To suggest an alternative transportation option
Ⓒ To recommend someone else for the position
Ⓓ To offer additional information about the job

16 When is the application deadline?

Ⓐ Next month
Ⓑ Next week
Ⓒ This Friday
Ⓓ This Saturday

Answers p.482

7. Inference Questions

Overview

대화에서 직접적으로 언급되지 않았으나 대화 내용을 통해 논리적으로 추론할 수 있는 사실을 묻는 문제이다. 대화에서 주어진 정보들을 종합적으로 이해하는 것뿐만 아니라 전체적인 맥락도 이해하는 능력이 요구된다. 매 시험 0~1문제가 출제되어 출제율은 낮은 편이지만, 고득점을 위해서는 반드시 맞춰야 하는 문제 유형이다.

Types of Questions

kind of job, work in이라는 표현을 포함한 형태로 출제되어 화자의 신분을 묻거나, inferred, concluded라는 표현을 포함한 형태로 출제되어 화자 또는 대화에 언급된 대상에 대해 추론할 수 있는 바를 묻는다. imply, indicate라는 표현을 포함한 형태로 출제되어 대화에 언급된 대상에 대해 화자가 암시하는 바를 묻기도 한다.

Speaker

What kind of job does the man most likely have?
What department of the company does the woman most likely work in?

Inference

What can be inferred about the woman?
What can be concluded about a restaurant?

Implication

What does the man imply that he was planning to do?
What do the speakers imply about a professor?
What does the man imply when he mentions a new book?
What does the woman indicate about the gym?

Hackers Strategy

1 화자의 어조는 추론의 근거가 된다.
Inference 문제는 화자에 대해 묻거나 화자가 특정 대상에 대해 암시하는 바를 묻는데, 화자의 어조는 말로 하지 않은 화자의 생각을 드러내주는 좋은 단서가 된다. 따라서, 화자가 사용한 특정한 어조를 통해 화자의 생각을 파악한다.

2 화자가 암시하는 바를 paraphrasing한 것을 정답으로 고른다.
화자가 직접적으로 말하지는 않았으나, 화자가 한 말을 통해 간접적으로 알 수 있는 사실이 있다. 이렇듯 화자의 말에 함축된 의미를 바르게 paraphrasing한 것이 정답이 된다. 특히, 대화에서 화자가 반복해서 한 말을 통해서 화자의 말이나 행동에 대한 근거를 찾는다.

3 자주 나오는 오답 유형에 주의한다.
대화에서 언급된 단어를 포함하고 있지만 내용이 틀린 오답, 대화에서 언급되지 않은 오답, 충분한 근거 없이 확대해서 해석한 오답이 자주 등장한다. 특히, Inference 문제는 높은 수준의 추리력이나 논리력을 요구하지 않으므로, 반드시 화자의 말 안에서 근거를 찾도록 한다.

Example
🎧 T2_S1_7_Example

Script

W How's the preparation going for the industry conference next month?
M We still need to confirm the keynote speaker.
W Didn't Dr. Holt already agree to speak? I thought that was settled weeks ago.
M She did initially, but her assistant called yesterday mentioning some scheduling conflicts with her research project.
W That's concerning. The promotional materials have already gone out with her name featured prominently.
M I know. I'm meeting with Dr. Chen this afternoon to discuss his availability.

What does the man imply about Dr. Holt?

Ⓐ She is not able to speak at the conference.
Ⓑ She is a recognized expert in her field.
Ⓒ She plans to bring her assistant to the conference.
Ⓓ She requested a different time slot for her presentation.

정답 Ⓐ

해설 남자가 Holt 박사님에 대해 암시하는 바를 묻는 문제이므로, 해당 대상에 대해 언급한 말에서 정답의 단서를 찾을 수 있다. 남자가 "We still need to confirm the keynote speaker"라며 기조 연설자를 확정해야 한다고 했고, "her assistant called ~ mentioning some scheduling conflicts"라며 그녀, 즉 Holt 박사님의 조수가 Holt 박사님이 일정 충돌이 있다고 했다. 따라서, Holt 박사님이 회의에서 연설을 하지 못할 것임을 추론할 수 있으므로 Ⓐ가 정답임을 알 수 있다.

HACKERS PRACTICE 🎧 T2_S1_7_Practice

Listen to each conversation and fill in the blanks. Then choose the best answer for the question. (You will hear each conversation twice.)

01

W I'm _____ _____ later. Do you need anything?
M Actually, could you pick up some vegetables for me? I'm _____ this month.
W Sure, any specific ones you prefer? They have a great _____ _____.
M Maybe some spinach and bell peppers? I found some recipes online _____ _____.

What can be inferred about the man?

Ⓐ He dislikes grocery shopping.
Ⓑ He grows his own vegetables.
Ⓒ He has allergies to certain foods.
Ⓓ He plans to change his eating habits.

02

M Excuse me, I _____ _____ last week. Can I renew them?
W Yes, _____ for another two weeks, as long as no one else has requested them. Do you want to _____ _____?
M I especially need to keep the biology reference book for my new project.
W Okay, let me check… Sorry, you can't renew that one. Three other students _____ _____.

What kind of job does the woman most likely have?

Ⓐ Bookstore clerk
Ⓑ Biology professor
Ⓒ Librarian
Ⓓ Editor

03

M The student council said _____
_____ is on Thursday.
Are you coming too?
W Yes, I really need to get funding for _____
_____ for my drama club.
M I heard several clubs are competing for limited funds this semester. Sounds like it won't be an easy decision.
W True. That's why we've prepared _____
_____ how that equipment would benefit multiple student productions throughout the year.
M That sounds like a solid plan. I hope you ____
_____.

What does the woman imply about her club's proposal?

Ⓐ It focuses on one performance only.
Ⓑ It was prepared thoroughly.
Ⓒ It exceeds the budget limit.
Ⓓ It was submitted late.

04

M Are you _____
the farmers' market this weekend?
W I'm thinking about it. The _____
_____ than at the supermarket.
M Definitely. Parking is _____
_____, though. Last time, I had to circle the lot for half an hour to get a spot.
W That's why I usually take my bike. Bicycle parking is way easier. Plus, it forces me to be _____
_____, since I can only put a limited amount in my basket.

What do the speakers indicate about the farmers' market?

Ⓐ It has limited parking availability.
Ⓑ It offers better prices than supermarkets.
Ⓒ It is only open on weekends.
Ⓓ It provides free parking.

Answers p.486

HACKERS TEST 🎧 T2_S1_7_Test

[01-02] Listen to a conversation.

01 Why does the man mention a family commitment?

Ⓐ To justify arriving late to the museum
Ⓑ To inform the woman about his unavailability
Ⓒ To suggest rescheduling to a weekday instead
Ⓓ To explain why he needs to leave early

02 What do the speakers imply about the history museum?

Ⓐ It offers online ticket purchasing options.
Ⓑ It recently added an additional building.
Ⓒ It limits visitor numbers in the afternoon.
Ⓓ It displays modern art exhibitions year-round.

[03-04] Listen to a conversation.

03 What is the man trying to decide between?

Ⓐ A laptop and a tablet
Ⓑ A speaker and a microphone
Ⓒ Wired and wireless headphones
Ⓓ Headphones and a portable speaker

04 What can be inferred about the man?

Ⓐ He does not usually listen to music in his room.
Ⓑ He often invites friends to his dorm room.
Ⓒ He prefers studying with other people.
Ⓓ He already owns another headphone.

[05-06] Listen to a conversation.

05 What kind of job does the woman most likely have?

Ⓐ Library employee
Ⓑ College professor
Ⓒ Bookstore manager
Ⓓ Career center director

06 Why does the man mention his high school?

Ⓐ To explain why he left his previous job
Ⓑ To mention his educational background
Ⓒ To prove he has necessary skills for the job
Ⓓ To compare high school and college classes

[07-08] Listen to a conversation.

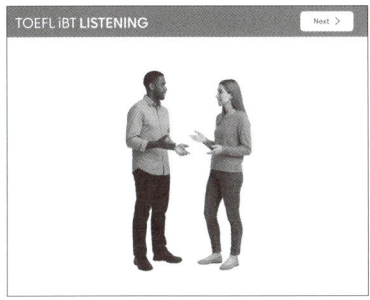

07 What does the woman imply about the weather forecast?

Ⓐ It might change by the weekend.
Ⓑ It will prevent their outdoor plans.
Ⓒ It affects rock-climbing activities.
Ⓓ It is usually inaccurate.

08 What can be inferred about the speakers?

Ⓐ They live near Mount Cedar.
Ⓑ They have visited the climbing center before.
Ⓒ They do not have much climbing experience.
Ⓓ They prefer indoor activities to outdoor ones.

HACKERS TEST

[09-10] Listen to a conversation.

09 What is the woman's problem?

Ⓐ She lacks the necessary technical skills.
Ⓑ She has too much work to finish on time.
Ⓒ She disagrees with the marketing team's vision.
Ⓓ She cannot contact the design team.

10 What can be inferred about the woman?

Ⓐ She frequently misses project deadlines.
Ⓑ She works independently on most projects.
Ⓒ She needs to collaborate with multiple teams.
Ⓓ She is faster at working on photos than text.

[11-12] Listen to a conversation.

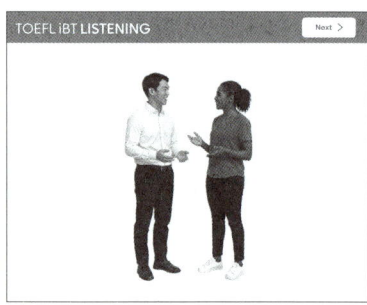

11 What can be concluded about the woman?

Ⓐ She is experienced with technical equipment.
Ⓑ She will not attend tonight's performance.
Ⓒ She needs help setting up the projector.
Ⓓ She is worried about the event's success.

12 Why does the man mention last semester's event?

Ⓐ To suggest hiring a technician
Ⓑ To show his concern about equipment
Ⓒ To praise the woman's preparation skills
Ⓓ To recommend attracting a larger audience

[13-14] Listen to a conversation.

13. What department of the company does the woman most likely work in?

   Ⓐ Accounting
   Ⓑ Advertising
   Ⓒ Human Resources
   Ⓓ Research and Development

14. What does the woman want to discuss with the managers?

   Ⓐ Evaluation procedures
   Ⓑ Employee scheduling conflicts
   Ⓒ Professional growth opportunities
   Ⓓ Division restructuring plans

[15-16] Listen to a conversation.

15. What does the woman imply that she was about to do?

   Ⓐ Attend Lisa's birthday party
   Ⓑ Meet a friend at a mall
   Ⓒ Drive to an art gallery
   Ⓓ Go shopping for a present

16. Why does the man recommend the art book?

   Ⓐ It matches Lisa's interests.
   Ⓑ It comes with free art supplies.
   Ⓒ It costs less than the jewelry box.
   Ⓓ It has really good reviews.

Answers p.487

Hackers Updated TOEFL LISTENING

Section II
Conversation Topics

Section II에서는 TASK 2에 자주 등장하는 주제들을 중심으로 세부 단원을 구성하였다. TOEFL에는 일상 생활, 캠퍼스 생활, 업무 및 서비스와 관련된 대화가 중점적으로 출제된다.

TASK 2의 Conversation Topics에는 다음의 3가지가 있다.

1. Daily Life
2. Campus Life
3. Work & Service

1. Daily Life

일상에서 필수적으로 접하게 되는 상황 및 장소에서 이루어지는 대화이다. 식사, 쇼핑, 취미, 가정/건강, 이동/숙박과 같은 소재가 등장하며, 일상 생활에서 접할 수 있는 다양한 표현을 알아두면 도움이 된다. 대화 주제 중 가장 출제 비율이 높다.

식사 🎧 T2_S2_1_Expressions1

식사 약속을 잡거나, 새로운 식당에 가보자고 제안하거나, 근처 식당을 추천받거나, 식사 메뉴를 고민하는 내용이 나온다. 특정 대상을 언급한 의도를 묻는 문제가 종종 출제되는데, 주로 식사 약속을 거절하는 이유를 제시하거나 식당을 추천받는 이유를 제시하기 위한 내용이 정답이 되는 경우가 많다.

buzz 이야기, 소문, 웅성거림	There's a lot of **buzz** about the new restaurant downtown. 시내의 새 식당에 대해 많은 이야기가 있어요.
vegetarian options 채식 메뉴	Does the restaurant have **vegetarian options** on their menu? 그 식당의 메뉴에 채식 메뉴가 있나요?
make a reservation 예약하다	I can **make a reservation** for this Saturday. 제가 이번 주 토요일로 예약할 수 있어요.
by any chance 혹시	Have you heard about the new Chinese place **by any chance**? 혹시 새로운 중국 음식점에 대해 들어봤나요?
catering company 출장연회 업체	Which **catering company** are you using for the wedding reception? 결혼 피로연을 위해 어느 출장연회 업체를 이용하시나요?
daily special 일일 특선 요리	They have a **daily special**, which is usually seafood. 그들은 일일 특선 요리가 있는데, 보통 해산물이에요.
a wide variety of options 다양한 선택지	We can choose from **a wide variety of options**, everything from snacks to full meals. 저희는 간식부터 정식까지 다양한 선택지 중에서 선택할 수 있어요.

쇼핑 🎧 T2_S2_1_Expressions2

제품을 구매하기 전 장단점을 비교해보며 고민하거나, 교환이나 환불 등을 요청하는 내용이 나온다. 구매를 고민하고 있는 대상이나 화자가 요청하는 것을 묻는 문제가 자주 출제된다.

vendor 판매업체, 판매상	The market has a new vendor selling specialty items. 그 시장에는 특별한 물품을 파는 새로운 판매업체가 있어요.
portable 휴대가 쉬운	If you want something portable, a smartphone is better than a tablet. 만약 당신이 휴대가 쉬운 무언가를 원한다면, 스마트폰이 태블릿보다 나아요.
go shopping 쇼핑을 가다	Are you planning to go shopping this weekend? 이번 주말에 쇼핑하러 갈 계획인가요?
stock up on ~을 많이 사다	I'm going to stock up on coffee while it's on sale. 세일 중에 커피를 많이 사둘 거예요.
plenty of 많은	There are plenty of options in this price range. 이 가격대에 많은 선택지들이 있어요.
on the go 이동 중에	I make my shopping list on my phone so I can check it on the go. 저는 이동 중에 확인할 수 있도록 제 휴대폰에 쇼핑 목록을 작성해요.
product description 제품 설명	Could you please clarify this part of the product description? 제품 설명의 이 부분을 명확히 설명해 주시겠어요?
torn between ~ 사이에서 고민하는	I'm torn between the cheaper model and the one with better features. 저는 더 저렴한 모델과 더 좋은 기능을 가진 모델 사이에서 고민하고 있어요.
explore all the stalls 모든 가판대를 둘러보다	Maybe we can go together and explore all the stalls. 저희는 함께 가서 모든 가판대를 둘러볼 수도 있어요.
check out 계산하다	We should check out these items before the store closes. 저희는 가게가 문을 닫기 전에 이 물품들을 계산해야 해요.
pick up 사다, 구매하다	I still need to pick up some snacks and drinks. 저는 아직 간식과 음료를 사야 해요.
a few extra 여분의	I will get a few extra pairs of socks just in case. 혹시 모르니 여분의 양말을 살 거예요.
out of stock 품절이 된	The yoga mats are out of stock, but we're expecting a new shipment soon. 요가 매트가 품절됐지만, 곧 새 상품이 입고될 예정입니다.
go with 고르다, 선택하다	Let's go with the organic cereal since it's on sale this week. 이번 주에 할인하니까 유기농 시리얼로 고릅시다.

취미

취미 생활의 일정을 변경하거나 추후 계획에 대해 논의하고, 취미에 대해 고민하거나 문화 생활을 같이 하자는 내용이 나온다. 어떤 행사에 대해 화자들이 대화하고 있는지, 화자들의 계획이 무엇인지를 묻는 문제가 자주 출제된다.

suit ~에게 편리하다	The evening yoga class would **suit** me better since I work during the day. 낮에 일하기 때문에 저녁 요가 수업이 저에게 더 편리할 것 같아요.
instructor 강사	The pottery **instructor** will demonstrate different glazing techniques today. 도예 강사가 오늘 다양한 유약 기법을 시연할 예정이에요.
slog (꾸준히 하는) 지루하고 힘든 일	Learning to play piano can be a **slog**, but it's worth it in the end. 피아노 배우기는 지루하고 힘든 일이 될 수 있지만, 결국에는 그만한 가치가 있어요.
sidetrack 딴 길로 빠지다, (일을) 회피하다	I got **sidetracked** by social media and forgot to call you. 소셜 미디어 때문에 딴 길로 빠져서 당신에게 전화하는 것을 까먹었어요.
diverse 다양한	The art workshop teaches **diverse** painting styles from watercolor to oil. 미술 워크숍에서는 수채화부터 유화까지 다양한 그림 스타일을 가르쳐요.
discover 발견하다	I **discovered** a new hiking trail that leads to a beautiful waterfall. 아름다운 폭포로 이어지는 새로운 하이킹 코스를 발견했어요.
unique 독특한	This photography club focuses on capturing **unique** perspectives of city life. 이 사진 동아리는 도시 생활의 독특한 관점을 포착하는 데 중점을 둬요.
sporting goods store 운동용품점	I need to stop by the **sporting goods store** to buy new tennis balls. 저는 새 테니스 공을 사러 운동용품점에 들려야 해요.
demonstration 시연	The chef will give a cooking **demonstration** at the food festival tomorrow. 요리사가 내일 요리 축제에서 요리 시연을 할 예정이에요.
fascinating 흥미로운, 매력적인	The documentary about underwater photography was absolutely **fascinating**. 수중 사진에 관한 다큐멘터리는 정말 흥미로웠어요.
craft fair 공예품 박람회	Are you going to the **craft fair** this weekend? 이번 주말에 공예품 박람회에 갈 건가요?
well known 잘 알려진	The chef is **well known** throughout the culinary world. 그 요리사는 요리계 전체에서 잘 알려져 있어요.
on-site registration 현장 등록	I forgot to register online, but they offer **on-site registration**. 저는 온라인 등록을 깜빡했지만, 그곳은 현장 등록을 받아요.
get back into ~을 다시 시작하다	I'm trying to **get back into** basketball after taking a break for two years. 저는 2년 동안 쉰 후에 농구를 다시 시작하려고 해요.

■ 가정/건강 🎧 T2_S2_1_Expressions4

집으로의 초대, 이사 계획에 대한 논의, 집 유지보수, 건강 관련 조언과 같은 내용이 나온다. 화자들이 주로 논의하고 있는 대상이나 문제점을 묻거나, 화자가 제안하는 것을 묻는 문제가 자주 출제된다.

move in 이사를 들어오다	I discovered several issues after I **moved in**. 저는 이사를 들어온 후에 여러 문제점을 발견했어요.
call a plumber 배관공을 부르다	My landlord said he'd **call a plumber** to fix the leaking bathroom pipe. 집주인이 새는 화장실 파이프를 고치기 위해 배관공을 부르겠다고 했어요.
housing office 주거 관리 사무실	Please fill out the request form at the **housing office**. 주거 관리 사무실에서 신청서를 작성해주세요.
diagnose 진단하다	The doctor needs to run more tests before she can **diagnose** my knee pain. 의사가 제 무릎 통증을 진단하기 전에 더 많은 검사를 해야 해요.
feeling under the weather 몸이 좋지 않은	I've been **feeling under the weather** lately, so I should rest. 최근에 몸이 좋지 않아서, 쉬어야겠어요.

■ 이동/숙박 🎧 T2_S2_1_Expressions5

대중교통이나 셔틀 버스 탑승 관련 문의, 숙박 시설 예약 및 변경에 대해 이야기하는 내용이 나온다. 화자의 문제점이나 화자가 다음에 할 일을 묻는 문제가 자주 출제된다.

access 접근하다; 입장, 접근	The subway station is closed for maintenance, so we can't **access** the downtown area easily. 지하철역이 보수공사로 닫혀있어서, 저희는 시내 지역에 쉽게 접근할 수 없어요.
transfer 환승하다	You need to **transfer** at Central Station to get to the airport. 공항에 가려면 중앙역에서 환승해야 해요.
split the fare 요금을 나눠내다	If we **split the fare** among the four of us, it won't be that expensive. 만약 저희 넷이서 요금을 나눠내면, 그렇게 비싸지 않을 거예요.
rideshare 승차 공유	Let's try to recruit Michael and Sarah to come with us and take a **rideshare**. Michael과 Sarah를 같이 오게 해서 승차 공유를 이용해봐요.
commute time 통근 시간, 통학 시간	My **commute time** doubled since they started construction on the main highway. 주요 고속도로에서 공사를 시작한 이후로 통근 시간이 두 배가 됐어요.
head down to ~로 내려가다	I'll **head down to** the parking garage and bring the car around. 주차장으로 내려가서 차를 가져올게요.
stop by 가는 길에 들르다	There's a grocery store just a few blocks away, so I'll **stop by** on my way. 몇 블록 떨어진 곳에 식료품점이 있으니까, 제가 가는 길에 들를게요.
make it to ~에 이르다, 도착하다	If we leave by 6, we should **make it to** our seats before kickoff. 6시까지 출발하면, 킥오프 전에 저희 자리에 도착할 수 있을 거예요.

HACKERS TEST 🎧 T2_S2_1_Test

[01-02] Listen to a conversation.

01 Why does the man mention his last visit?

Ⓐ To explain why he prefers a different restaurant
Ⓑ To suggest they should leave earlier
Ⓒ To indicate why he can't make it tonight
Ⓓ To recommend the woman see the same dentist

02 What does the woman say about the restaurant?

Ⓐ It serves high-quality seafood dishes.
Ⓑ It is too expensive for most people.
Ⓒ It requires reservations in advance.
Ⓓ It is located far from their area.

[03-04] Listen to a conversation.

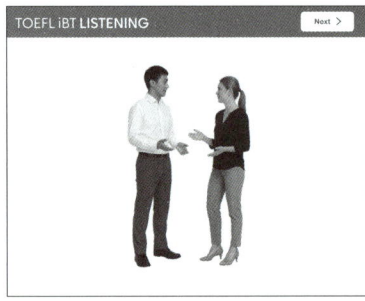

03 What event are the speakers discussing?

Ⓐ A photography workshop
Ⓑ A stargazing event
Ⓒ A science lecture
Ⓓ A camping trip

04 What will the man most likely bring to the event?

Ⓐ Photography equipment
Ⓑ Professional telescopes
Ⓒ Food and beverages
Ⓓ Portable flashlights

[05-06] Listen to a conversation.

05 What is the woman trying to decide between?

Ⓐ Two job opportunities
Ⓑ Two interview times
Ⓒ Two professional outfits
Ⓓ Two different hairstyles

06 Why does the man recommend the blazer?

Ⓐ It costs less than the suit.
Ⓑ It makes a better first impression.
Ⓒ It is easier to clean and maintain.
Ⓓ It offers more styling flexibility.

[07-08] Listen to a conversation.

07 What is the woman's problem?

Ⓐ She missed her regular bus to school.
Ⓑ Her usual bus route has been modified.
Ⓒ She lost her monthly transit pass.
Ⓓ She cannot find the correct bus stop.

08 What does the man say about the express subway?

Ⓐ It requires advance booking.
Ⓑ It runs less frequently than buses.
Ⓒ It costs more than taking the bus.
Ⓓ It stops at fewer stations than before.

HACKERS TEST

[09-10] Listen to a conversation.

09 What are the speakers mainly discussing?

   Ⓐ A home repair issue
   Ⓑ A bathroom renovation
   Ⓒ A guest room decoration
   Ⓓ A safety inspection

10 What does the man suggest the woman do?

   Ⓐ Get multiple repair estimates first
   Ⓑ Indicate that the repair is time-sensitive
   Ⓒ Ask neighbors for a company recommendation
   Ⓓ Wait until the weekend for better rates

[11-12] Listen to a conversation.

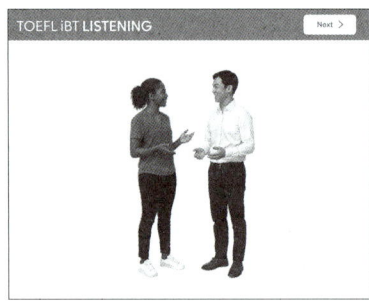

11 Why is the woman asking for restaurant recommendations?

   Ⓐ She forgot to pack lunch for work.
   Ⓑ She wants to try a new type of cuisine.
   Ⓒ She is throwing a party for her friend.
   Ⓓ She is planning a family celebration.

12 What will the woman most likely do next?

   Ⓐ Visit the restaurant's website
   Ⓑ Ask about the restaurant's prices
   Ⓒ Contact the restaurant to book a table
   Ⓓ Look for other restaurant options

[13-14] Listen to a conversation.

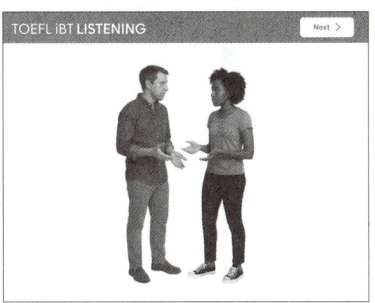

13 Why does the man want to start reading?

   Ⓐ To complete a school assignment
   Ⓑ To develop a new hobby
   Ⓒ To prepare for a book club meeting
   Ⓓ To research a specific topic

14 What does the woman say about fantasy novels?

   Ⓐ They are typically very expensive.
   Ⓑ They are shorter than other genres.
   Ⓒ They have complex storylines.
   Ⓓ They help reduce everyday tension.

[15-16] Listen to a conversation.

15 What is the man's problem?

   Ⓐ He lost his receipt for a purchase.
   Ⓑ A piece of equipment is not working.
   Ⓒ He cannot afford the headphones he wants.
   Ⓓ The store doesn't carry his preferred brand.

16 What does the woman offer to do?

   Ⓐ Contact the manufacturer
   Ⓑ Provide a store credit
   Ⓒ Reserve an item
   Ⓓ Recommend a different brand

Answers p.491

2. Campus Life

대학 생활 중 일어날 법한 상황에서 이루어지는 대화이다. 학업/과제, 캠퍼스 업무, 캠퍼스 시설, 동아리 모임과 같은 소재가 등장하며, 학생들이 캠퍼스에서 겪을 수 있는 다양한 상황에 대한 표현을 알아두면 도움이 된다.

■ 학업/과제 🎧 T2_S2_2_Expressions1

수업 자료를 요청하거나 과제 협업을 제안하는 내용이 나온다. 과제물과 관련된 문의를 하거나 제출 기한이 변경되어 다음 계획을 세우는 내용도 나온다. 다양한 문제가 출제될 수 있으며, 주로 화자가 맡을 특정 업무나 화자들이 모일 장소를 묻는 문제가 출제된다.

resources 자료	I need more resources to finish our project. 저는 저희의 프로젝트를 끝내기 위해 더 많은 자료가 필요해요.
collaborate 협업하다	I'd love to collaborate with you on this assignment. 저는 이 과제에 당신과 협업하고 싶어요.
deadline extension 기한 연장	I need to request a deadline extension for my research paper. 저는 연구 논문에 대한 기한 연장을 요청해야 해요.
in the middle of ~을 하는 중인	I'm in the middle of a project I need to finish tonight. 저는 오늘 밤에 끝내야 하는 프로젝트를 하는 중이에요.
catch up 따라잡다	I missed two weeks of lectures due to illness, so I need to catch up on the material before the exam. 저는 병으로 2주간 강의를 빠져서, 시험 전에 수업 내용을 따라잡아야 해요.
data collection 데이터 수집	The professor extended the deadline for our research project because we need more time for data collection. 데이터 수집에 더 많은 시간이 필요해서 교수님께서 연구 프로젝트 마감일을 연장해 주셨어요.
office hours 면담 시간	Professor Singh's office hours are from 2 to 4 P.M. on Wednesdays. Singh 교수님의 면담 시간은 수요일 오후 2시부터 4시까지예요.

■ 캠퍼스 업무 🎧 T2_S2_2_Expressions2

학생 아르바이트 지원, 연구 조교 업무 논의, 캠퍼스 내 봉사활동 신청과 같이 캠퍼스에서 일어날 법한 다양한 업무에 대한 내용이 나온다. 화자들이 주로 논의하고 있는 내용이나 화자가 맡게 될 업무를 묻는 문제가 자주 출제된다.

manageable 감당할 수 있는	The professor said the research project would be more manageable if we divide it into smaller sections. 교수님께서 연구 프로젝트를 더 작은 섹션으로 나누면 더 감당할 수 있을 거라고 하셨어요.
teaching assistant 조교	She works as a teaching assistant for the introductory psychology course. 그녀는 심리학 입문 과목의 조교로 일하고 있어요.
research assistant 연구 조교	The professor is looking for a research assistant for the project. 교수님께서 프로젝트를 위한 연구 조교를 찾고 있어요.
student employment 학생 고용	Are there any student employment opportunities available this semester? 이번 학기에 학생 고용 기회가 있나요?
application deadline 지원 마감일	What's the application deadline for the internship program? 인턴십 프로그램의 지원 마감일이 언제인가요?
part-time position 아르바이트 자리	I'm looking for a part-time position that fits my class schedule. 저는 제 수업 일정에 맞는 아르바이트 자리를 찾고 있어요.
volunteer opportunity 봉사활동 기회	There's a great volunteer opportunity at the campus cafeteria. 캠퍼스 구내식당에 좋은 봉사 활동 기회가 있어요.
make sure to 반드시 ~하다	The teaching assistant told us to make sure to submit our lab reports before the deadline next week. 조교가 다음 주 마감일 전에 실험 보고서를 반드시 제출하라고 했어요.
heavy workload 과도한 업무량	I am struggling with the heavy workload from both coursework and research responsibilities. 저는 수업과 연구 책임 모두에서 오는 과도한 업무량으로 어려움을 겪고 있어요.

캠퍼스 시설 🎧 T2_S2_2_Expressions3

도서관 정책 변경, 구내 식당 메뉴 변경, 실험실 사용 계획, 시설 이용 방법에 대한 문의와 같이 캠퍼스 안의 시설과 관련된 내용이 나온다. 화자가 겪고 있는 문제점이나 화자가 다음에 할 일을 묻는 문제가 자주 출제된다.

policy 정책	The library changed the **policy**, and now we can keep the books for four weeks. 도서관은 정책을 변경해서, 저희는 이제 책을 4주 동안 가지고 있을 수 있어요.
expand 확장하다	The university plans to **expand** the study space to accommodate more students. 대학교는 더 많은 학생들을 수용하기 위해 학습 공간을 확장할 계획이에요.
hours of operation 운영 시간	Excuse me, what are the **hours of operation** for the cafeteria? 실례지만, 교내 식당의 운영 시간이 어떻게 되나요?
facility hours 운영 시간	I need to check the **facility hours** for the recreation center before planning my workout schedule. 제 운동 스케줄을 계획하기 전에 레크리에이션 센터의 운영 시간을 확인해야 해요.
library resources 도서관 자료	Jim recommended using the **library resources** instead of online sources. Jim이 온라인 자료 대신 도서관 자료를 사용하라고 추천했어요.
reserve a study room 스터디룸을 예약하다	I tried to **reserve a study room** for tonight, but they're all booked. 오늘 밤에 스터디룸을 예약하려고 했는데, 모두 예약이 찼어요.
computer lab 컴퓨터실	The **computer lab** in the engineering building has the latest software for our programming assignments. 공과대학 건물의 컴퓨터실에는 저희 프로그래밍 과제를 위한 최신 소프트웨어가 있어요.
maintenance request 수리 요청	I submitted a **maintenance request** for the broken printer in the student lounge. 저는 학생 라운지의 고장 난 프린터에 대한 수리 요청을 제출했어요.
access card 출입카드	You need an **access card** to enter the building after hours. 운영 시간 이후에 건물에 들어가려면 출입카드가 필요해요.
parking permit 주차 허가증	Please display your **parking permit** on the dashboard when parking on campus. 캠퍼스에 주차할 때 대시보드에 주차 허가증을 보이게 놓아주세요.
printing service 인쇄 서비스	The library's **printing service** is available 24 hours during finals week. 도서관의 인쇄 서비스는 기말시험 주간 동안 24시간 이용 가능해요.
lost and found 분실물 보관소	I checked the **lost and found**, but my backpack wasn't there. 분실물 보관소를 확인했는데, 제 배낭은 거기에 없었어요.
security office 보안실	Report any suspicious activity to the **security office** immediately. 의심스러운 활동은 즉시 보안실에 신고하세요.
emergency procedures 비상 절차	Make sure you're familiar with the **emergency procedures**. 비상 절차를 잘 알고 있는지 확인하세요.

동아리 모임 🎧 T2_S2_2_Expressions4

동아리 정기 모임 참석 여부를 확인하거나 활동 계획을 논의하는 내용이 나온다. 모임에서 다룰 주제에 대한 의견을 나누거나 행사 준비를 위한 역할 분담과 관련된 대화도 나온다. 화자가 회의에 참석하지 못하는 이유를 묻거나 동아리 활동 또는 행사의 세부 사항에 대해 묻는 문제가 자주 출제된다.

attend 참석하다	Are you planning to **attend** the book club meeting tonight? 오늘 밤 독서 동아리 모임에 참석할 예정인가요?
sign up 가입하다	Where can I **sign up** for the photography club? 사진 동아리에 어디서 가입할 수 있나요?
club activities 동아리 활동	What kind of **club activities** do you organize throughout the year? 일 년 동안 어떤 종류의 동아리 활동을 조직하나요?
recruit new members 새 부원을 모집하다	Our debate club needs to **recruit new members** before October. 10월 전에 저희 토론 동아리는 새 부원을 모집해야 해요.
make arrangements 준비하다, 주선하다	The club president asked me to **make arrangements** for the venue for our end-of-semester party. 동아리 회장이 저에게 학기말 파티를 위한 장소를 준비하라고 했어요.
check availability 사용 가능 여부를 확인하다	You should **check availability** for the conference room before scheduling our monthly club meeting. 당신은 월례 동아리 모임을 계획하기 전에 회의실 사용 가능 여부를 확인해야 해요.
mandatory attendance 의무 출석	There is **mandatory attendance** for the first three club sessions for new members. 신입 회원들은 처음 세 번의 동아리 세션에 의무적으로 출석해야 해요.
regular attendance 정기 모임 출석	**Regular attendance** at meetings is required for active membership. 정기 모임 출석은 회원 자격을 위해 필요해요.
community service 지역사회 봉사활동	Our club participates in **community service** projects every semester. 저희 동아리는 매 학기 지역사회 봉사활동 프로젝트에 참여해요.
leadership position 임원직	I'm interested in running for a **leadership position** in the club. 저는 동아리에서 임원직에 출마하는 데 관심이 있어요.
social events 친목 행사	Our club organizes various **social events** to bring members together. 저희 동아리는 부원들 간의 친목을 도모하기 위해 다양한 친목 행사를 조직해요.
club constitution 동아리 회칙	All new members must read and agree to the **club constitution** before they can participate in activities. 모든 새 부원들은 활동에 참여하기 전에 동아리 회칙을 읽고 동의해야 해요.
club newsletter 동아리 소식지	Have you checked the latest **club newsletter**? 최신 동아리 소식지를 확인해봤나요?

HACKERS TEST 🎧 T2_S2_2_Test

[01-02] Listen to a conversation.

01 Why is the man talking to the woman?

Ⓐ To borrow the woman's notes from a class
Ⓑ To discuss their midterm study plan
Ⓒ To ask about Professor Becker's office hours
Ⓓ To invite her to a study group

02 What does the woman say about the slides?

Ⓐ They are outdated.
Ⓑ They are not accessible online.
Ⓒ They are too difficult to understand.
Ⓓ They need to be purchased separately.

[03-04] Listen to a conversation.

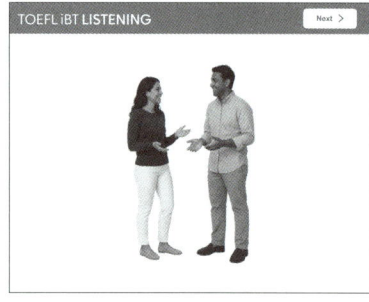

03 What does the man say about the current food selection?

Ⓐ It offers small portions.
Ⓑ It is too expensive for students.
Ⓒ It becomes monotonous over time.
Ⓓ It doesn't offer healthy choices.

04 Why does the woman mention student requests?

Ⓐ To explain why certain changes are being made
Ⓑ To encourage the man to complain more
Ⓒ To criticize the dining hall management
Ⓓ To gather more student feedback

[05-06] Listen to a conversation.

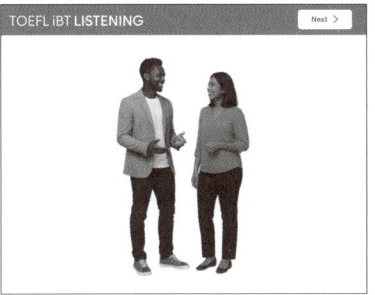

05 What will the man primarily be responsible for?

Ⓐ Grading undergraduate students
Ⓑ Managing the laboratory budget
Ⓒ Writing research grant proposals
Ⓓ Handling experimental data

06 What does the woman imply about the workload?

Ⓐ It remains the same throughout the semester.
Ⓑ It can increase during certain periods.
Ⓒ It requires weekend availability.
Ⓓ It conflicts with regular coursework.

[07-08] Listen to a conversation.

07 Why does the man mention a report?

Ⓐ To explain why he cannot attend the meeting
Ⓑ To ask for help with his assignment
Ⓒ To suggest postponing the tournament
Ⓓ To invite the woman to study together

08 What does the woman say about the chess club?

Ⓐ It only accepts experienced players.
Ⓑ It is looking for additional members.
Ⓒ It meets three times a week.
Ⓓ It requires membership fees.

HACKERS TEST

[09-10] Listen to a conversation.

09 What is the man's problem?

  Ⓐ He is not good at using the online booking system.
  Ⓑ He has not completed the required safety training.
  Ⓒ He is unable to reserve a laboratory space.
  Ⓓ He does not have the necessary equipment.

10 What does the woman suggest the man do?

  Ⓐ Try a different time slot
  Ⓑ Contact the lab coordinator
  Ⓒ Complete the safety training first
  Ⓓ Use another lab in a different building

[11-12] Listen to a conversation.

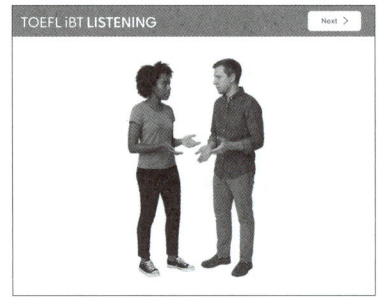

11 What are the speakers mainly discussing?

  Ⓐ A campus volunteer opportunity
  Ⓑ A painting exhibition
  Ⓒ A weekend art class
  Ⓓ A building renovation

12 What will the man probably do next?

  Ⓐ Contact the project coordinator
  Ⓑ Register for the program
  Ⓒ Visit the student center
  Ⓓ Check for more information

[13-14] Listen to a conversation.

13 What does the man suggest they do?

Ⓐ Request a deadline extension
Ⓑ Divide the work more effectively
Ⓒ Find additional team members
Ⓓ Change their research topic

14 When will the speakers complete their individual tasks?

Ⓐ By the end of the month
Ⓑ In three weeks
Ⓒ Next Thursday
Ⓓ Next Friday

[15-16] Listen to a conversation.

15 Where will the field trip most likely take place?

Ⓐ At the State Forest
Ⓑ At the Natural History Museum
Ⓒ At the Riverside Nature Center
Ⓓ At the Botanical Gardens

16 What does the woman offer to do?

Ⓐ Organize transportation
Ⓑ Plan group activities
Ⓒ Bring some equipment
Ⓓ Contact the center

Answers p.495

3. Work & Service

Hackers Updated TOEFL LISTENING

회사나 다양한 서비스가 필요한 곳에서 이루어지는 대화이다. 회사 업무, 인사/사내 행사, 수리와 같은 소재가 등장하며, 직장이나 서비스 업종에서 사용되는 실무적인 표현을 알아두면 도움이 된다.

■ 회사 업무 🎧 T2_S2_3_Expressions1

회의 준비, 회사 웹사이트 수정, 보고서 작성과 같이 다양한 회사 업무에 대한 내용이 나온다. 주로 화자들이 논의하고 있는 대상이나 다음에 할 일을 묻는 문제가 출제된다. 또, 화자가 업무를 언제 진행할지, 누가 그 업무를 진행할지 세부적인 내용을 묻는 문제도 종종 출제된다.

strategy 전략, 계획	Have you reviewed the marketing strategy for the mobile app launch? 모바일 앱 출시에 대한 마케팅 전략을 검토해봤나요?
illustrate 보여주다	I will use charts and graphs to illustrate our quarterly sales performance. 저는 분기별 매출 성과를 보여주기 위해 차트와 그래프를 사용할 거예요.
emphasize 강조하다	During the meeting, the manager emphasized the importance of meeting our project deadlines. 회의 중에, 관리자가 프로젝트 마감일 준수의 중요성을 강조했어요.
handout 인쇄물	Please prepare a handout with the quarterly budget information for tomorrow's board meeting. 내일 이사회 회의를 위해 분기별 예산 정보가 담긴 인쇄물을 준비해 주세요.
finalize 마무리 짓다	I need to finalize my presentation slides before tomorrow's meeting. 저는 내일 회의 전에 발표 슬라이드를 마무리 지어야 해요.
adjustment 조정	The project timeline requires some adjustments due to the unexpected issues. 예상치 못한 문제로 인해 프로젝트 일정에 조정이 필요해요.
implement 도입하다, 시행하다	The company plans to implement the new software system across all departments next month. 회사가 다음 달 모든 부서에 새로운 소프트웨어 시스템을 도입할 계획이에요.
be similar to ~과 비슷하다	The new strategy is similar to what we discussed in last quarter's meeting. 새로운 전략은 지난 분기 회의에서 논의한 것과 비슷해요.
be supposed to ~하기로 되어있다	I'm supposed to bring some drinks to my team's lunch meeting tomorrow. 제가 내일 팀 점심 회의에 음료를 가져가기로 되어있어요.

set up ~을 준비하다	Did you finish **setting up** the online store for our new product next month? 다음 달 저희 신제품을 위한 온라인 상점을 준비하는 것을 끝냈나요?	
sales figures 판매 수치	Fortunately, the quarterly **sales figures** look promising. 다행히도, 분기별 판매 수치가 유망해 보여요.	
double-check 재확인하다	Could you **double-check** the quarterly report before we submit it to the marketing team? 마케팅팀에 제출하기 전에 분기 보고서를 재확인해 주시겠어요?	
back-to-back 연이은	I have **back-to-back** client meetings this afternoon, so I won't be available until after 5 P.M. 저는 오늘 오후에 연이은 고객 미팅이 있어서, 오후 5시 이후까지는 시간이 없어요.	
product launch event 제품 출시 행사	The **product launch event** has been moved to the Grand Hotel downtown. 제품 출시 행사가 시내 Grand 호텔로 옮겨졌어요.	
customer feedback 고객 의견	The **customer feedback** from our social media campaign has been overwhelmingly positive so far. 저희 소셜 미디어 캠페인에 대한 고객 의견이 지금까지 압도적으로 긍정적이에요.	
be unable to ~을 할 수 없다	I'm **unable to** attend the conference call with our overseas partners. 저는 해외 파트너들과의 전화 회의에 참석할 수 없어요.	
manage to ~을 해내다	Did you **manage to** gather all the contact information of the new clients? 새 고객들의 연락처를 모두 모으는 것을 해냈나요?	
quarterly report 분기 보고서	I'm working on the **quarterly report** for the management team. 경영진을 위한 분기 보고서를 작성하고 있어요.	
budget proposal 예산 제안서	Have you reviewed the **budget proposal** for next year? 내년도 예산 제안서를 검토해봤나요?	
conference call 전화 회의	The **conference call** with the overseas team is at 9 A.M. tomorrow. 해외 팀과의 전화 회의가 내일 오전 9시에 있어요.	
workflow process 업무 프로세스	We need to streamline the **workflow process** to improve efficiency. 효율성을 높이기 위해 업무 프로세스를 간소화해야 해요.	
business trip 출장	I have a **business trip** next week to meet with the guest speaker from the product strategy team. 저는 제품 전략팀의 초청 강연자를 만나기 위해 다음 주에 출장을 가요.	

인사/사내 행사 🎧 T2_S2_3_Expressions2

채용 고민, 인사 이동 안내, 직원 교육 참석, 사내 행사 계획과 같은 내용이 나온다. 화자가 고민하는 구체적인 내용을 묻는 문제, 화자의 태도를 묻는 문제, 화자가 다음에 할 일을 묻는 문제가 자주 출제된다.

obligation 의무, 책무	All employees have an **obligation** to attend the training session next Friday. 모든 직원은 다음 주 금요일 교육 세션에 참석할 의무가 있어요.
promotion 승진	Liam's **promotion** will be announced during tomorrow's team meeting. 내일 팀 회의 동안 Liam의 승진이 발표될 거예요.
hands-on 실습의, 직접 해보는	The new employee training workshop will include **hands-on** practice with our customer service software. 신입사원 교육 워크숍은 고객 서비스 소프트웨어 실습을 포함할 예정이에요.
recruit 채용하다	We need to **recruit** at least five new engineers before the fourth quarter. 저희는 4분기 전에 최소 5명의 새로운 엔지니어를 채용해야 해요.
hiring process 채용 과정	The **hiring process** for the marketing position will take approximately six weeks to complete. 마케팅 직책의 채용 과정은 완료하는 데 약 6주가 걸릴 예정이에요.
safety training 안전교육	All new hires must complete the **safety training** program before they can access the laboratory facilities. 모든 신입사원은 실험실 시설에 접근하기 전에 안전 교육 프로그램을 완료해야 해요.
narrow it down to ~으로 좁히다	We've **narrowed it down to** three candidates for the product manager position. 저희는 제품 매니저 직책 후보자를 3명으로 좁혔어요.
need attention 주목할 필요가 있다	The employee feedback survey results **need attention**. 직원 피드백 설문조사 결과에 주목할 필요가 있어요.
award recipient 수상자	The CEO personally congratulated all **award recipients** during the company celebration. 최고 경영자는 회사 축하 행사에서 모든 수상자들을 개인적으로 축하했어요.
employee recognition 직원 인정	The new **employee recognition** program will include performance bonuses. 새로운 직원 인정 프로그램은 성과 보너스를 포함할 거예요.
performance evaluation 성과 평가	Each department manager must submit **performance evaluation** reports. 각 부서 매니저는 성과 평가 보고서를 제출해야 해요.
training workshop 교육 워크숍	The leadership **training workshop** will cover project management skills. 리더십 교육 워크숍은 프로젝트 관리 기술을 다룰 예정이에요.
company retreat 회사 야유회	The annual **company retreat** will include team-building activities and presentations from each department head. 연례 회사 야유회는 팀 빌딩 활동과 각 부서장의 발표를 포함할 예정이에요.

수리

기기가 고장 나서 수리 방안을 논의하거나 수리점에 방문할 계획을 세우는 이야기가 나온다. 화자가 겪고 있는 문제점이나 화자가 제안하는 것이 무엇인지를 묻는 문제가 자주 출제된다.

troubleshoot 문제를 해결하다	I spent two hours troubleshooting the printer issue before finding the solution. 저는 해결책을 찾기 전에 프린터 문제를 해결하기 위해 2시간을 썼어요.
technician 기술자	I called a technician this morning to fix the air-conditioning system. 저는 오늘 아침 에어컨 시스템을 수리하기 위해 기술자를 불렀어요.
replacement part 교체 부품	We'll need to order replacement parts for the copy machine. 복사기의 교체 부품을 주문해야 할 거예요.
properly 제대로	The laptop won't function properly until you update the software. 소프트웨어를 업데이트할 때까지 노트북은 제대로 작동하지 않을 거예요.
fiddle (세부사항을) 조작하다	Henry tried fiddling with the printer settings, but it still doesn't work. Henry가 프린터 설정을 조작해봤지만 여전히 제대로 작동하지 않아요.
repair estimate 수리 견적	Mr. Clarkson will give us a repair estimate for the damaged equipment. Mr. Clarkson이 저희에게 손상된 장비에 대한 수리 견적을 줄 거예요.
act up 제 기능을 못하다	My computer has been acting up all week, freezing during important presentations and meetings. 제 컴퓨터는 중요한 발표와 회의 중에 멈추면서, 일주일 내내 제 기능을 못하고 있어요.
shut down 멈추다	The server will shut down automatically tonight for scheduled maintenance. 서버는 예정된 유지보수를 위해 오늘 밤 자동으로 멈출 예정이에요.
repair shop 수리점	I know a great repair shop downtown that fixed my laptop really quickly. 제 노트북을 정말 빠르게 고쳐준 시내의 훌륭한 수리점을 알고 있어요.
have trouble with ~에 어려움을 겪다	Several employees have trouble with the new software system since the recent update. 최근 업데이트 이후 여러 직원들이 새로운 소프트웨어 시스템에 어려움을 겪고 있어요.
flat tire 바람 빠진 타이어	I'll be late because I discovered a flat tire this morning. 저는 오늘 아침에 바람 빠진 타이어를 발견해서 늦을 것 같아요.
out of order 고장 난	The elevator is out of order, so we'll need to use the stairs. 엘리베이터가 고장 나서, 저희는 계단을 이용해야 해요.
technical support 기술 지원팀	Please contact technical support immediately if the video conference system stops working during the presentation. 발표 중에 화상 회의 시스템이 작동을 멈추면 즉시 기술 지원팀에 연락하세요.
warranty coverage 보증 기간	The warranty coverage for this equipment expires next month, so we should address any issues now. 이 장비의 보증 기간이 다음 달에 만료되므로, 저희는 지금 문제들을 해결해야 해요.

HACKERS TEST 🎧 T2_S2_3_Test

[01-02] Listen to a conversation.

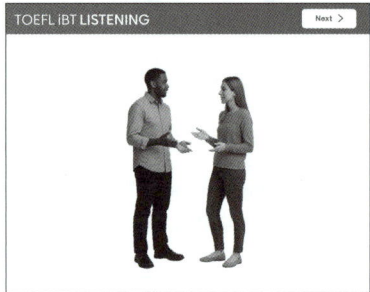

01 What has the woman completed?

Ⓐ Updating sales data
Ⓑ Printing presentation materials
Ⓒ Checking the final participant list
Ⓓ Reviewing the proposal section

02 When will the speakers meet to review their work?

Ⓐ Tuesday
Ⓑ Wednesday
Ⓒ Thursday
Ⓓ Friday

[03-04] Listen to a conversation.

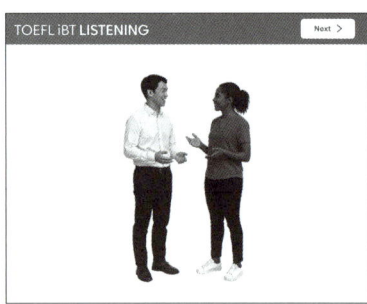

03 Why did the man call a technician?

Ⓐ His computer keeps acting up.
Ⓑ He needs new software installed.
Ⓒ His Internet connection is unstable.
Ⓓ He cannot access his work files.

04 What does the woman suggest the man do?

Ⓐ Visit the repair shop
Ⓑ Work from home today
Ⓒ Use an alternative device
Ⓓ Contact the IT department again

[05-06] Listen to a conversation.

05 What can be inferred about last year's training?

Ⓐ It included hands-on practice sessions.
Ⓑ Employees watched instructional materials.
Ⓒ It was conducted by external experts.
Ⓓ It focused primarily on evacuation routes.

06 What will the man do next?

Ⓐ Upgrade safety equipment
Ⓑ Review compliance reports
Ⓒ Contact the safety coordinator
Ⓓ Schedule emergency drills

[07-08] Listen to a conversation.

07 What are the speakers mainly discussing?

Ⓐ A networking session
Ⓑ A product reveal event
Ⓒ A monthly staff meeting
Ⓓ A client appreciation dinner

08 Why does the man mention upgrading the refreshments?

Ⓐ To accommodate the larger group size
Ⓑ To impress potential customers
Ⓒ To meet dietary restrictions
Ⓓ To satisfy catering requirements

HACKERS TEST

[09-10] Listen to a conversation.

09 What is the woman's problem?

Ⓐ She lost her research paper files.
Ⓑ She needs to charge her laptop.
Ⓒ She cannot access the Internet.
Ⓓ She missed the deadline for her assignment.

10 What does the man say about the library?

Ⓐ It has extended hours during exam week.
Ⓑ It requires advance booking for computer use.
Ⓒ It has computers on a different network.
Ⓓ It charges fees for printing services.

[11-12] Listen to a conversation.

11 Why does the man mention his client?

Ⓐ To suggest hiring more customer service staff
Ⓑ To provide evidence of the form's complexity
Ⓒ To explain why sales have decreased recently
Ⓓ To propose a new marketing strategy

12 What does the woman suggest they do?

Ⓐ Reduce the number of required fields
Ⓑ Hire more customer service representatives
Ⓒ Remove the feedback section completely
Ⓓ Disable unnecessary pop-up messages

[13-14] Listen to a conversation.

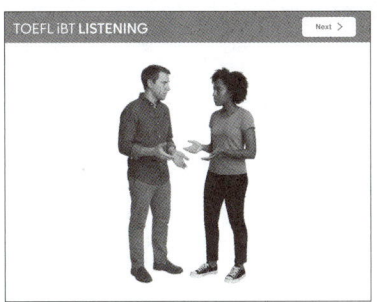

13 What is the woman's attitude toward the job candidates?

   Ⓐ She considers them perfect for the role.
   Ⓑ She is worried about their qualifications.
   Ⓒ She prefers to hire experienced professionals.
   Ⓓ She is disappointed with the application pool.

14 What will the speakers most likely do next?

   Ⓐ Post additional job postings
   Ⓑ Contact the university career center
   Ⓒ Review the company's training programs
   Ⓓ Arrange the interview schedule with applicants

[15-16] Listen to a conversation.

15 Why does the woman mention the executives?

   Ⓐ To emphasize the importance of the meeting
   Ⓑ To explain why the elevator repair is urgent
   Ⓒ To propose changing the meeting agenda
   Ⓓ To recommend hiring additional staff

16 What does the woman suggest they do?

   Ⓐ Cancel the board meeting entirely
   Ⓑ Reschedule the executives' visit
   Ⓒ Use a different meeting location
   Ⓓ Contact the elevator manufacturer directly

Answers p.499

무료 토플자료·유학정보 공유
goHackers.com

TASK 3
Listen to an Announcement

Hackers Updated TOEFL LISTENING

Introduction

Section I. Question Types
1. Main Topic/Purpose Questions
2. To Do Questions
3. Detail Questions
4. Intention Questions
5. Inference Questions

Section II. Announcement Topics
1. Campus Events
2. Student Activities
3. Lectures & Facilities

Introduction

TASK 3(Listen to an Announcement)는 평균 47~48단어로 이루어진 공지를 듣고 주어지는 문제의 답을 고르는 유형으로, 한 명의 화자가 전달하는 공지의 주요 목적 및 중요한 세부 내용을 파악하는 능력을 묻는다. 각 공지에는 2개의 문제가 출제되는데, Module 1에서 공지 2개가 출제되며, 더미 문항이 포함될 경우 공지가 4개까지도 출제된다. Upper Module 2에서는 이 유형이 출제되지 않으며, Lower Module 2에서만 공지 2개가 출제된다.

Preview

음성 화면

공지를 들을 때 나오는 화면으로, 화자의 사진이 나온다.

주의 사항 : TASK 3의 Direction 화면은 별도로 나오지 않으므로 TASK 2가 끝난 후 바로 공지를 들을 준비를 해야 한다.

해야 할 일 : 공지가 이루어지는 장소를 통해 대략적인 공지 내용을 예측할 수 있으므로 각 공지의 Direction부터 집중해서 듣는다. 공지의 첫 부분에서 공지의 목적을 파악할 수 있으므로, 첫 부분을 놓치지 않도록 주의 깊게 듣는다. 문제 풀이를 할 때 공지의 주요한 정보를 기억할 수 있도록, 음성을 들으며 Note-taking을 해둔다.

문제 풀이 화면

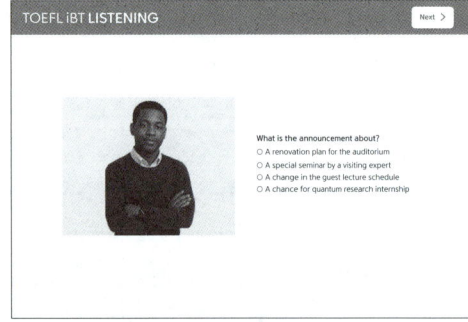

문제가 출제될 때 나오는 화면으로, 문제와 보기가 나온다.

문제를 풀 수 있는 시간 : 20초

문제를 풀 때 해야 할 일 : 문제와 보기는 별도로 들려주지 않으므로, 화면이 전환되면 빠르게 읽는다. 보기 앞에 있는 칸을 클릭하여 답을 표시한다.

문제를 풀고 난 후 해야 할 일 : 답을 고른 후 우측 상단의 Next 버튼을 누르면 다음 문제 또는 다음 공지로 넘어간다. 이때, 이전 화면으로 돌아갈 수 없으므로 충분히 고민한 후 넘어가도록 한다.

Task Strategy

1. 공지가 이루어지는 장소를 통해 공지 내용을 유추한다.
Direction에서 공지가 이루어지는 장소를 먼저 확인할 수 있으며, 장소에 따라 공지 내용이 달라지므로 이를 파악해두면 앞으로 이어질 공지 내용을 더 쉽게 들을 수 있다. 예를 들어, university event에서는 주로 교내에서 일어날 법한 행사를 소개하며 참여를 독려하고, classroom에서는 주로 초청 강연이나 강의실 변경에 대한 안내를 한다.

2. 공지의 첫 부분과 마지막 부분은 반드시 듣는다.
공지에는 주제 및 목적이나 청자에게 요청하는 내용을 묻는 문제가 자주 출제된다. 따라서, 공지의 첫 부분에서 공지에서 중점적으로 다룰 내용이나 목적을 듣고, 공지의 마지막 부분에서 청자에게 요구되는 행동 지침을 반드시 듣는 연습을 한다.

3. 중요한 세부 정보를 Note-taking한다.
TASK 3에서는 특히 화자가 청자들에게 요청하는 행동 지침, 화자가 예로 들거나 나열한 세부 정보가 문제로 연결될 가능성이 크므로 공지를 들으면서 이러한 세부 정보들은 반드시 Note-taking해둔다.

4. paraphrasing된 정답을 고른다.
대부분 문제의 정답은 공지의 내용을 paraphrasing해서 나오므로, 제대로 paraphrasing된 정답을 고른다. 공지에서 들은 단어 및 일부 표현을 그대로 쓴 선택지는 오히려 오답일 가능성이 많다는 것도 염두에 둔다.

Study Guide

1. 문제 유형별로 알맞은 듣기 전략을 익히자.
정답을 잘 고르기 위해 집중해서 들어야 하는 정답의 단서가 문제 유형에 따라 다르므로, 각 유형별로 알맞은 듣기 전략을 익혀두면 정답을 더 정확하게 고를 수 있다.

2. 공지 유형별로 등장하는 표현에 익숙해지자.
교내 행사, 학생 활동, 강의 및 시설 등으로 출제되는 다양한 공지의 주제별로 자주 등장하는 표현을 알아두면 실제 시험에서 공지 내용을 더욱 빠르게 파악할 수 있다.

3. 중요한 세부 정보를 듣고 파악하는 능력을 기르자.
공지에서는 구체적인 시간, 장소, 변경사항 등의 핵심 정보를 빠르게 파악하는 능력이 중요하므로, 이를 제대로 듣는 연습을 집중적으로 한다.

Section I
Question Types

Section I에서는 TASK 3에 출제되는 문제 유형을 5가지로 구분하여 각 유형의 특징과 질문 형태, 실제 문제 풀이에 적용 가능한 전략들을 소개하고 있다. 또한 연습 문제 및 실전 문제를 통해 각 문제 유형을 효과적으로 공략할 수 있도록 하였다.

TASK 3의 Question Types에는 다음의 5가지가 있다.

1. Main Topic/Purpose Questions
2. To Do Questions
3. Detail Questions
4. Intention Questions
5. Inference Questions

1. Main Topic/Purpose Questions

Overview

공지에서 중심이 되는 내용이 무엇인지를 묻는 문제 유형이다. Main Topic 문제는 공지에서 안내하고자 하는 중점적인 내용이 무엇인지를 묻는다. Main Purpose 문제의 경우 화자가 공지를 하는 주요 목적을 묻는다. 매 시험 3~4문제가 출제되며, Main Topic 문제가 Main Purpose 문제보다 더 자주 출제되는 편이다.

Types of Questions

Main Topic 문제는 주로 mainly about, topic이라는 표현을 포함한 형태로 출제되며, Main Purpose 문제는 main purpose라는 표현을 포함한 형태로 출제된다.

Main Topic

What is the announcement about?
What is the announcement mainly about?
What is the main topic of the announcement?

Main Purpose

What is the main purpose of the announcement?

Hackers Strategy

1 공지의 주제 및 목적은 주로 공지의 첫 부분에서 들을 수 있다.

공지의 주제 및 목적은 공지의 첫 부분에 언급되는 경우가 많으므로, 공지의 첫 부분을 특히 집중해서 들어야 한다. 만약 첫 부분에서 주제나 목적이 명확하게 언급이 되지 않는다면, 전반적인 공지의 흐름을 파악해서 정답을 고르도록 한다.

2 반복적으로 들리는 키워드에 주목한다.

공지에서 화자가 여러 번 언급하는 대상이 공지의 주제나 목적과 관련되어 있을 경우가 많으므로, 반복적으로 들리는 키워드를 유의하여 듣는다. 특히, 공지에서 날짜, 시간, 장소 정보가 강조되는 경우 일정 변경이나 행사 관련 공지일 경우가 많다.

3 자주 나오는 오답 유형에 주의한다.

공지 내용의 일부만을 다루는 오답, 공지에서 언급된 단어를 포함하고 있지만 내용이 틀린 오답, 공지에서 언급되지 않은 내용에 관한 오답이 자주 등장한다.

Example

🎧 T3_S1_1_Example

Script

Good afternoon, everyone. This is a reminder that the annual university career fair will take place next Thursday in the Student Union Ballroom. Over 50 companies from various industries will be present, including tech giants, financial institutions, and healthcare organizations. This is an excellent opportunity to explore internship and job opportunities, so bring multiple copies of your résumé and dress professionally.

What is the announcement mainly about?

Ⓐ A job opening at the university
Ⓑ An upcoming career fair
Ⓒ A résumé-writing workshop
Ⓓ A change in financial services

정답 Ⓑ

해설 공지가 주로 무엇에 관한 것인지를 묻는 문제이므로, 공지의 첫 부분에서 정답의 단서를 찾을 수 있다. 화자가 "the annual university career fair will take place next Thursday"라며 다음 주 목요일에 대학 취업 박람회가 열릴 것이라고 했으므로 Ⓑ가 정답임을 알 수 있다.

HACKERS PRACTICE 🎧 T3_S1_1_Practice

Listen to each announcement and fill in the blanks. Then choose the best answer for the question. (You will hear each announcement twice.)

01

Hello, everyone! I'm excited to announce _____ _____ will take place this Thursday from 2 to 6 P.M. in the auditorium. Students will _____ _____, and there will be interactive demonstrations throughout the afternoon. Don't miss this opportunity to _____ _____ by your peers!

What is the announcement about?

Ⓐ A research competition
Ⓑ A department meeting
Ⓒ A science exhibition
Ⓓ An auditorium renovation

02

Quick announcement regarding _____ _____ by Dr. Martinez. Due to a flight delay, _____ _____ from 10 A.M. to 2 P.M. It will still be held in Hall C, and the topic remains "Modern Archaeological Discoveries." Please _____ _____, and spread the word to anyone who might have missed this update.

What is the main purpose of the announcement?

Ⓐ To introduce a new professor
Ⓑ To provide a schedule update
Ⓒ To advertise an archaeology course
Ⓓ To announce a change in the lecture topic

03

Attention, Environmental Club members! We're organizing _____ this Sunday starting at 9 A.M. at Ocean Park. We'll provide all necessary supplies, _____ _____. Please wear comfortable clothes and bring water and sunscreen. This is a wonderful chance to _____ _____ while spending time outdoors.

What is the main topic of the announcement?

Ⓐ A marine biology field trip
Ⓑ An outdoor swimming event
Ⓒ A club fundraising activity
Ⓓ A beach conservation effort

04

Attention, Drama Club members! _____ _____ will be held this Thursday and Friday from 3 to 6 P.M. at the campus theater. We're looking for _____ _____ for various roles. Please _____, and come ready to demonstrate your talents. This is a great opportunity to _____ _____!

What is the purpose of the event?

Ⓐ To find performers for a play
Ⓑ To recruit backstage workers
Ⓒ To distribute production scripts
Ⓓ To promote an upcoming spring play

HACKERS TEST 🎧 T3_S1_1_Test

[01-02] Listen to an announcement at a university event.

01 What is the main purpose of the announcement?

　Ⓐ To publicize an on-campus health event
　Ⓑ To announce new medical facilities
　Ⓒ To advertise free medical consultations
　Ⓓ To recruit volunteers for campus activities

02 Why does the speaker mention the Recreation Center?

　Ⓐ To introduce a new safety procedure
　Ⓑ To compare it with other campus facilities
　Ⓒ To direct students to the event location
　Ⓓ To highlight recent renovations to the facility

[03-04] Listen to an announcement in a student lounge.

03 What is the main purpose of the announcement?

　Ⓐ To apologize for ongoing construction work
　Ⓑ To describe new facilities in the student lounge
　Ⓒ To alert students to a change in lounge availability
　Ⓓ To warn students about a dangerous plumbing situation

04 What are students advised to do during the lounge closure?

　Ⓐ Wait outside the lounge
　Ⓑ Volunteer for repair work
　Ⓒ Stay home during the afternoon
　Ⓓ Use the campus café as an alternative

[05-06] Listen to an announcement at a university club meeting.

05 What is the announcement about?

Ⓐ A weekly chess club meeting
Ⓑ An upcoming chess competition
Ⓒ A training session for beginner chess players
Ⓓ An awards ceremony for chess champions

06 What will the winners receive as a prize?

Ⓐ Entry fee refunds
Ⓑ Trophies and medals
Ⓒ Scholarship opportunities
Ⓓ Bookstore gift cards

[07-08] Listen to an announcement in a classroom.

07 What is the main topic of the announcement?

Ⓐ A visiting expert's talk
Ⓑ A research project deadline
Ⓒ A mandatory reading assignment
Ⓓ An upcoming research paper

08 What are students encouraged to do?

Ⓐ Register for the special session online
Ⓑ Develop questions for the Q&A portion
Ⓒ Arrive early to get good seats
Ⓓ Review Professor Chandler's previous work

HACKERS TEST

[09-10] Listen to an announcement in a classroom.

09 What is the main purpose of the announcement?

Ⓐ To announce a change in teaching assistants
Ⓑ To request student feedback about the class
Ⓒ To collect midterm answer sheets from students
Ⓓ To remind students about attendance requirements

10 What will the speaker most likely do next?

Ⓐ Dismiss the class early
Ⓑ Explain a new concept
Ⓒ Distribute questionnaires
Ⓓ Show an adjusted course schedule

[11-12] Listen to an announcement in a student lounge.

11 What is the main topic of the announcement?

Ⓐ New cafeteria options
Ⓑ A healthy eating campaign
Ⓒ The availability of refreshments
Ⓓ A lounge renovation schedule

12 Why does the speaker mention the survey?

Ⓐ To encourage additional participation
Ⓑ To announce another upcoming survey
Ⓒ To apologize for the delayed implementation
Ⓓ To explain the basis for product additions

[13-14] Listen to an announcement at a university club meeting.

13 What is the main purpose of the announcement?

   Ⓐ To explain how to submit photos for the contest
   Ⓑ To recruit new members for a photography club
   Ⓒ To promote an upcoming gallery exhibition
   Ⓓ To seek participants for a photography workshop

14 Who will determine the winning entries?

   Ⓐ Event attendees
   Ⓑ The club president
   Ⓒ The faculty advisor
   Ⓓ Professional photographers

[15-16] Listen to an announcement on the school radio.

15 What is the announcement mainly about?

   Ⓐ A university facility's operating hours
   Ⓑ Information about the shuttle bus route
   Ⓒ New on-campus transportation options
   Ⓓ Adjustments to the shuttle bus schedule

16 When will the last bus depart under the new schedule?

   Ⓐ 10 P.M.
   Ⓑ 10:30 P.M.
   Ⓒ 11 P.M.
   Ⓓ 11:30 P.M.

Answers p.505

2. To Do Questions

Overview

화자가 청자들에게 요청하거나 권고하는 내용을 묻는 문제 유형이다. 매 시험 4~5문제가 출제되어 출제 비율이 높은 편이다. 이 유형은 주로 공지에서만 볼 수 있다.

Types of Questions

주로 hope, urge, suggest라는 표현을 포함한 형태로 출제되어 화자가 청자에게 바라는 행동을 묻거나, encourage/advised to do, should ~ do라는 표현을 포함한 형태로 출제되어 청자가 해야 할 일을 묻는다.

To Do

What does the speaker hope the listeners will do?
What does the speaker urge the listeners to do?
What does the speaker suggest students do?
What are students encouraged to do?
What are students advised to do in response to the announcement?
What should students do according to the announcement?

Hackers Strategy

1 정답의 단서는 주로 공지의 마지막 부분에서 들을 수 있다.

To Do 문제는 TASK 3에서 출제 비율이 높은 편이고 정답의 단서는 대부분 공지의 마지막 부분에 언급되므로, 공지의 마지막을 잘 들으면 정답률을 높일 수 있다.

2 요청 및 권고를 나타내는 표현에 귀를 기울인다.

please, hope, recommend, make sure to, be sure to, feel free to와 같은 표현이 포함된 문장을 들으면 To Do 문제가 출제될 것을 예상할 수 있으며, 주로 해당 표현들 뒤에서 정답의 단서를 들을 수 있다.

3 자주 나오는 오답 유형에 주의한다.

공지에서 언급된 단어를 포함하고 있지만 내용이 틀린 오답이나 대화에서 언급된 사실과 전혀 관련이 없는 오답이 자주 등장한다.

Example

🎧 T3_S1_2_Example

Script

Attention, class. As you've probably noticed, we've had several issues with the classroom projector during the last few presentations. To avoid these problems in your presentations next week, I strongly recommend that you come to class at least 10 minutes early on your presentation day to test the projector.

What does the speaker suggest students do?

Ⓐ Reschedule their presentations
Ⓑ Submit their slides before class
Ⓒ Arrive early to test the equipment
Ⓓ Bring personal laptops for their presentations

정답 Ⓒ

해설 화자가 학생들이 했으면 하는 것을 묻는 문제이므로, 공지 마지막 부분의 요청 및 권고를 나타내는 표현에서 정답의 단서를 찾을 수 있다. 화자가 "I strongly recommend that you come to class at least 10 minutes early on your presentation day to test the projector"라며 발표 날에는 수업에 10분 일찍 와서 프로젝터를 점검할 것을 권장한다고 했으므로 Ⓒ가 정답임을 알 수 있다.

HACKERS PRACTICE T3_S1_2_Practice

Listen to each announcement and fill in the blanks. Then choose the best answer for the question. (You will hear each announcement twice.)

01

Movie lovers, get ready for our _____ _____! This Friday, _____ _____ under the stars at the main plaza starting at 7 P.M. _____ _____ for a cozy evening. In case of rain, we'll move to the Student Union Theater. Make sure to arrive early if you want to _____!

What does the speaker hope the listeners will do?

Ⓐ Bring blankets and refreshments
Ⓑ Give blankets to other attendees
Ⓒ Spread the word about the movie night
Ⓓ Arrive early to purchase tickets

02

Good morning, everyone. Our campus library is implementing _____ _____ for the group study rooms starting next Monday. Instead of offering walk-in availability, the library will require that rooms _____ at least two hours in advance. The _____ _____ will be three hours per day per student. Instructions for the new system are posted near the circulation desk. Please _____ to avoid any inconvenience when booking a study room.

What are students encouraged to do?

Ⓐ Visit the circulation desk
Ⓑ Submit feedback about the system
Ⓒ Read the posted instructions
Ⓓ Arrive two hours before using a room

03

Good afternoon, everyone! Our _____ _____ is scheduled for Thursday at 7 P.M. in Conference Room B. This year's topic is "School uniforms: Necessary or outdated?" Teams _____ to argue for either side. Make sure to _____ _____ _____ and be ready for intense discussions. Registration closes ____ _____.

What does the speaker suggest students do?

Ⓐ Conduct research on the history of school uniforms
Ⓑ Bring research materials
Ⓒ Submit research materials in advance
Ⓓ Request a specific debate topic

04

Attention, students. Next Wednesday, we're hosting our _____ in the gymnasium from 10 A.M. to 4 P.M. Over 50 companies will be present, including major tech firms and local businesses. To make the most of this opportunity, please _____ _____ and dress professionally. Don't miss this chance to _____ _____!

What should students do according to the announcement?

Ⓐ Register online and pay the entrance fee
Ⓑ Sign up for time slots with employers
Ⓒ Practice interview questions beforehand
Ⓓ Get their résumés ready and dress professionally

Answers p.508

HACKERS TEST 🎧 T3_S1_2_Test

[01-02] Listen to an announcement at a university event.

01 What is the main topic of the announcement?

Ⓐ A cooking competition
Ⓑ A fundraising activity
Ⓒ An upcoming festival
Ⓓ A food safety notice

02 What does the speaker hope the listeners will do?

Ⓐ Join a cooking class
Ⓑ Volunteer for the event
Ⓒ Purchase international dishes
Ⓓ Experience different cuisines

[03-04] Listen to an announcement in a classroom.

03 What is the reason for the change described in the announcement?

Ⓐ Scheduling conflicts
Ⓑ A classroom renovation
Ⓒ A weather-related emergency
Ⓓ Facility maintenance

04 What are students advised to do in response to the announcement?

Ⓐ Submit their assignments early
Ⓑ Modify their study schedule
Ⓒ Download new study materials
Ⓓ Complete extra practice problems

[05-06] Listen to an announcement at a university club meeting.

05 Why does the speaker mention the university's homecoming event?

Ⓐ To highlight university traditions
Ⓑ To provide the reason for the postponement
Ⓒ To cancel the cultural dinner completely
Ⓓ To encourage students to attend both events

06 What does the speaker hope the listeners will do?

Ⓐ Confirm their attendance
Ⓑ Bring international dishes
Ⓒ Prepare cultural presentations
Ⓓ Pass along the schedule change

[07-08] Listen to an announcement at a student meeting.

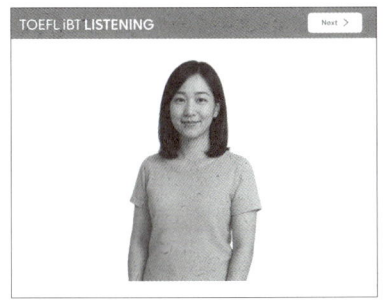

07 What is the main topic of the announcement?

Ⓐ A leadership workshop
Ⓑ A campus facility
Ⓒ A university policy
Ⓓ A student election

08 What should interested students do according to the announcement?

Ⓐ Recruit supporters for their campaigns
Ⓑ Turn in candidacy forms before the deadline
Ⓒ Present their ideas to current council members
Ⓓ Declare their interest during Wednesday's meeting

HACKERS TEST

[09-10] Listen to an announcement at a university event.

09 What is the reason for the change described in the announcement?

Ⓐ Budget constraints
Ⓑ Unfavorable weather
Ⓒ Unscheduled maintenance
Ⓓ Increased attendance

10 What does the speaker hope the listeners will do?

Ⓐ Return unused tickets
Ⓑ Arrive early for the ceremony
Ⓒ Register for the indoor ceremony
Ⓓ Notify guests of the location change

[11-12] Listen to an announcement in a classroom.

11 What is the main purpose of the announcement?

Ⓐ To remind students about a change in office hours
Ⓑ To scold students for inadequate research
Ⓒ To offer a chance to improve grades
Ⓓ To explain the grading criteria for research papers

12 What are students who received a grade below C encouraged to do?

Ⓐ Write a summary of project feedback
Ⓑ Compare their grades with other students
Ⓒ Submit initial drafts and request extensions
Ⓓ Meet with the instructor and submit revised papers

[13-14] Listen to an announcement at a university event.

13 What is the announcement about?

Ⓐ A venue change
Ⓑ An event cancellation
Ⓒ A facility upgrade
Ⓓ A fee increase

14 What does the speaker suggest students do?

Ⓐ Print their tickets by Saturday
Ⓑ Prepare questions in advance
Ⓒ Confirm their attendance online
Ⓓ Arrive early at the convention center

[15-16] Listen to an announcement at a university club meeting.

15 What is the main purpose of the announcement?

Ⓐ To advertise a science exhibition
Ⓑ To share news of an approved initiative
Ⓒ To describe plant species on campus
Ⓓ To discuss budget allocation procedures

16 What does the speaker hope the listeners will do?

Ⓐ Visit the science building
Ⓑ Propose additional projects
Ⓒ Participate in the garden project
Ⓓ Photograph the planting process

Answers p.509

3. Detail Questions

Overview

공지를 통해 알 수 있는 다양한 세부 사실을 묻는 문제 유형이다. 질문에서 묻는 내용과 질문 형태가 매우 다양하다. 매 시험 1~2문제가 출제된다.

Types of Questions

Detail 문제는 세부적으로 묻고자 하는 내용에 따라 다양한 형태로 출제된다. say about이나 true about이라는 표현을 포함한 형태로 출제되어 특정 대상에 대해 화자가 언급하여 사실인 사항을 묻거나, why나 reason이라는 표현을 포함한 형태로 출제되어 이유를 묻는다. 그 외에도 공지 안의 세부 사항에 대해 묻는 다양한 문제가 출제된다.

Mention

What does the speaker say about the music festival?
Which of the following is true about the tutoring program?

Reason

Why is the student lounge being renovated?
What is the reason for the change described in the announcement?

Etc.

What will the authors do at the book fair?
What should students submit when signing up?
When will the art exhibition start?
Where will the charity event take place?

Hackers Strategy

1 화자가 주요한 화제와 관련하여 언급하는 사실들을 Note-taking한다.
공지의 주요한 화제에 대해 화자가 몇 가지 사실을 설명하는 경우에는 이에 대한 문제가 출제될 확률이 높으므로, 주요한 내용을 Note-taking해두는 것이 중요하다.

2 화자가 한 말을 paraphrasing한 것을 정답으로 고른다.
공지에서 출제되는 Detail 문제의 정답에서는 화자가 했던 말을 그대로 인용하기 보다 다른 표현으로 바꾸어 쓰는 경우가 많다.

3 자주 나오는 오답 유형에 주의한다.
공지에서 언급된 단어를 포함하고 있지만 내용이 틀린 오답이나 공지에서 언급된 사실과 전혀 관련이 없는 오답이 자주 등장한다.

Example 🎧 T3_S1_3_Example

Script

Good morning, class. I want to provide some details about the reference requirements for your final research project that's due at the end of the semester. For this assignment, you'll need to include a minimum of five academic sources, with at least three of them being peer-reviewed journal articles. The other two sources can be books or reliable websites, but please avoid using general encyclopedia sites and non-academic web resources as sources.

What does the speaker say about acceptable sources for the project?

Ⓐ Only peer-reviewed articles are allowed.
Ⓑ All websites can be used as sources.
Ⓒ All sources must be books or journal articles.
Ⓓ Some sources must be peer-reviewed articles.

정답 Ⓓ

해설 화자가 과제를 위해 허용 가능한 출처에 대해 언급한 것을 묻는 문제이므로, 출처와 관련하여 화자가 공지에서 언급한 사실에서 정답의 단서를 찾을 수 있다. 화자가 "at least three of them being peer-reviewed journal articles"라며 최소 셋은 동료 심사를 받은 학술지 논문이어야 한다고 했으므로 Ⓓ가 정답임을 알 수 있다.

HACKERS PRACTICE 🎧 T3_S1_3_Practice

Listen to each announcement and fill in the blanks. Then choose the best answer for the question. (You will hear each announcement twice.)

01

May I have your attention? The main computer lab will be unavailable Thursday through Sunday for _____. Please note that alternative _____ _____ in the east wing of the IT Building. If you need further assistance, please contact the IT Help Center.

What is the reason for the lab closure?

Ⓐ Building renovation
Ⓑ Virus scanning
Ⓒ System upgrades
Ⓓ Network security issues

02

Good morning, freshmen! The Student Mentoring Program is now accepting applications for next semester. Experienced upper-year students ___ _____ _____ and campus life. Mentors will meet their mentees _____ for one-on-one sessions. A _____ _____ will also be held for program participants. Don't miss this opportunity to adapt successfully to college life!

Who will serve as mentors in the program?

Ⓐ Senior students
Ⓑ Professional counselors
Ⓒ Selected professors
Ⓓ First-year students

03

Attention, Robotics Club members. _____ _____ the National Robotics Competition is due by this Wednesday. We need to _____ _____ and submit the technical specifications. Practice sessions will be held daily in the engineering lab next week from 6 to 9 P.M. to _____ _____ qualifying round.

What should students submit when registering a team?

Ⓐ Consent forms
Ⓑ Technical details
Ⓒ Safety checklists
Ⓓ Practice schedules

04

Photography Club members, we're hosting a _____ _____ this Saturday at Riverside Nature Park. Professional photographer Marian Lee will _____ _____. We will depart at 8:00 A.M. from the campus's main gate on a chartered bus. Lunch and _____ _____ for the workshop will be provided.

Which of the following is true about the workshop?

Ⓐ Participants need to bring their own cameras.
Ⓑ It is held on campus.
Ⓒ It focuses on portrait photography techniques.
Ⓓ Transportation and a meal are included.

HACKERS TEST 🎧 T3_S1_3_Test

[01-02] Listen to an announcement in a student lounge.

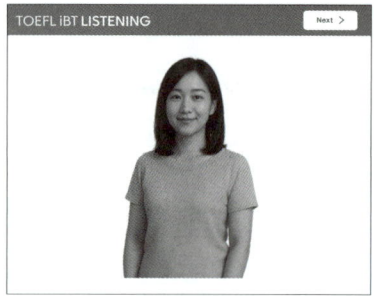

01 What is the reason for the closure of the student lounge?

   Ⓐ A remodeling project
   Ⓑ A safety inspection
   Ⓒ A carpet installation
   Ⓓ A cleaning operation

02 Why does the speaker mention the Student Union Building?

   Ⓐ To explain the purpose of recent renovations
   Ⓑ To inform students about ongoing construction
   Ⓒ To recommend an alternative space to students
   Ⓓ To encourage students to explore different areas

[03-04] Listen to an announcement at a university club meeting.

03 What is the main topic of the announcement?

   Ⓐ A university writing contest
   Ⓑ A call for event volunteers
   Ⓒ A regional debate competition
   Ⓓ A change in a club meeting's location

04 What should students submit when signing up?

   Ⓐ A one-page application
   Ⓑ An academic transcript
   Ⓒ A list of preferred topics
   Ⓓ A debate strategy outline

[05-06] Listen to an announcement at a university event.

05 What is the reason for the change described in the announcement?

   Ⓐ Budget constraints
   Ⓑ High demand for the event
   Ⓒ An unexpected renovation
   Ⓓ An increase in participating companies

06 Why does the speaker mention the university website?

   Ⓐ To provide professional networking tips
   Ⓑ To explain details about the venue change
   Ⓒ To direct students to the registration platform
   Ⓓ To post profiles of participating companies

[07-08] Listen to an announcement at a university event.

07 What is the main purpose of the announcement?

   Ⓐ To advertise an upcoming film festival
   Ⓑ To remind students about a rescheduled event
   Ⓒ To celebrate award-winning student filmmakers
   Ⓓ To encourage participation in a global film contest

08 What will directors do at the festival?

   Ⓐ Recruit students for internships
   Ⓑ Judge a student film competition
   Ⓒ Answer questions from attendees
   Ⓓ Present lectures on global cinema trends

HACKERS TEST

[09-10] Listen to an announcement in a classroom.

09 What is the main topic of the announcement?

Ⓐ An orientation for a recently hired instructor
Ⓑ A visiting professor's talk
Ⓒ A change in course requirements
Ⓓ A collaborative research project

10 What does the speaker say about the lecture?

Ⓐ It will last for two hours.
Ⓑ It will be held at Northwestern University.
Ⓒ It is required for all students to attend.
Ⓓ It will cover a topic related to the curriculum.

[11-12] Listen to an announcement in a student lounge.

11 What is the reason for the lounge closure described in the announcement?

Ⓐ Locker removal
Ⓑ Floor cleaning
Ⓒ Structural repairs
Ⓓ Furniture installation

12 What does the speaker hope the listeners will do?

Ⓐ Sign up for lounge access
Ⓑ Retrieve their own belongings
Ⓒ Avoid the second floor entirely
Ⓓ Submit their furniture preferences

[13-14] Listen to an announcement in a classroom.

13 What is the main purpose of the announcement?

Ⓐ To inform students of a schedule change
Ⓑ To announce a change in the classroom
Ⓒ To remind students about midterm exams
Ⓓ To describe the presentation format

14 Which of the following is true about Room 619?

Ⓐ It is available only during the midterm exam period.
Ⓑ It has been recently renovated for humanities students.
Ⓒ It has equipment that will be useful for presentations.
Ⓓ It has a limited capacity compared to current classroom.

[15-16] Listen to an announcement at a university event.

15 What day will the event take place?

Ⓐ Tuesday
Ⓑ Thursday
Ⓒ Friday
Ⓓ Sunday

16 Where can the listeners purchase tickets?

Ⓐ James Hall
Ⓑ The Student Union Building
Ⓒ The children's hospital
Ⓓ The charity's headquarters

Answers p.514

4. Intention Questions

Overview

공지에서 화자가 특정 대상을 언급한 의도를 묻는 문제 유형이다. 매 시험 0~1문제가 출제되어, 공지에서는 출제 비중이 낮은 편이다.

Types of Questions

Why does ~ mention이라는 표현을 포함한 형태로 출제되며, 화자가 공지에서 언급한 대상을 질문에 제시한다.

Intention

Why does the speaker mention the west wing?

Why does the professor mention the guest speaker?

Hackers Strategy

1 화자가 언급하는 주장, 예시, 문제점 등에 주목한다.

화자는 주로 공지에서 특정 대상을 언급하면서 본인의 주장을 뒷받침하거나, 예시를 들어주거나, 문제점을 제시하는데, 이때 언급된 대상이 질문에 제시되는 경우가 많다. 따라서, 화자의 주장이나 화자가 들어주는 예시, 화자가 제시하는 문제점을 집중해서 들으면, 언급된 대상의 목적을 유추할 수 있다.

2 공지의 맥락 속에서 화자의 말을 이해한다.

화자의 의도를 전체적인 맥락 안에서 파악하는 것이 가장 중요하며, 이를 위해서는 공지에서 언급된 말을 통해 그 사이에 함축된 화자의 의도를 파악해야 한다.

3 자주 나오는 오답 유형에 주의한다.

공지에서 알 수 있는 화자의 의도가 아닌 표면적 의미만을 제시한 오답이나 전후 문맥을 잘못 파악한 오답이 자주 등장한다.

Example

🎧 T3_S1_4_Example

Script

Starting next week, the campus shuttle service will be adding new stops at the Science Building. The route expansion was implemented because many students with evening labs in the Science Building had to walk back to their dorms in the dark. The updated route information is available on the university website.

Why does the speaker mention students with evening labs?

Ⓐ To explain the reason for adding a new stop
Ⓑ To announce a new evening course
Ⓒ To justify additional funding for the shuttle service
Ⓓ To introduce a campus safety initiative

정답 Ⓐ

해설 화자가 저녁 실험이 있는 학생을 언급한 의도를 묻는 문제이므로, 해당 대상을 언급하면서 함께 한 말에서 정답의 단서를 찾을 수 있다. 화자가 "The route expansion was implemented because many students with evening labs ~ had to walk back to their dorms in the dark."라며 저녁 실험이 있는 학생들이 어둠 속에서 기숙사까지 걸어가야 했기 때문에 노선 확장이 시행되었다고 했다. 따라서, 새 정류장을 추가한 이유를 설명하기 위해 저녁 실험이 있는 학생을 언급한 것이므로 Ⓐ가 정답임을 알 수 있다.

HACKERS PRACTICE 🎧 T3_S1_4_Practice

Listen to each announcement and fill in the blanks. Then choose the best answer for the question. (You will hear each announcement twice.)

01

The library's Wi-Fi system will _____ _____ this weekend. The network will be unavailable _____ until Monday morning. We recommend _____ _____ on the second floor if you need an Internet connection during this time. We're sorry for any inconvenience this may cause.

Why does the speaker mention the computer lab?

Ⓐ To announce new software installations
Ⓑ To highlight recent renovations to the building
Ⓒ To indicate where the Internet can be accessed
Ⓓ To advertise extended weekend hours

02

The Regional Sculpture Exhibit opens tomorrow in our campus gallery, featuring works by _____ _____. The exhibit will run for three weeks, with _____ _____ every Friday at noon. Visitors can _____ during the exhibit, and a portion of the proceeds will go to our university's art scholarship fund.

Why does the speaker mention five nearby cities?

Ⓐ To specify where the artists come from
Ⓑ To explain transportation arrangements for visitors
Ⓒ To announce expansion plans for next year
Ⓓ To promote tourism partnerships with nearby areas

03

During finals week, the library will _____
_____
to better serve students. We'll be open 24 hours per day on weekdays, while _____
_____. Additional study spaces have been set up on the third floor to _____
_____. Good luck with your exams!

Why does the speaker mention the third floor?

Ⓐ To recommend weekend study options
Ⓑ To indicate the location of extra study areas
Ⓒ To specify where refreshments will be provided
Ⓓ To highlight recent building renovations

04

Important update for all chemistry students. _____ will be implemented in all laboratories starting next week. Safety goggles and lab coats are _____
_____ during experiments. Room 201 has _____
_____ in all sizes, so please pick up your gear before Monday's session.

Why does the speaker mention Room 201?

Ⓐ To show which room has been renovated
Ⓑ To designate the return location
Ⓒ To indicate where to submit the lab report
Ⓓ To direct students to safety equipment

HACKERS TEST ⌂ T3_S1_4_Test

[01-02] Listen to an announcement in a student lounge.

01 What is the reason for the lounge closure described in the announcement?

Ⓐ Budget constraints
Ⓑ Seasonal renovation
Ⓒ Electrical system maintenance
Ⓓ Regular cleaning

02 Why does the speaker mention the South Building?

Ⓐ To explain the source of the electrical problem
Ⓑ To offer students an alternative location
Ⓒ To describe the maintenance schedule
Ⓓ To highlight a new campus facility

[03-04] Listen to an announcement at a university event.

03 What is the announcement about?

Ⓐ An exhibition of musical instruments
Ⓑ A fundraising event for the music department
Ⓒ An upcoming a cappella championship
Ⓓ An interview with famous a cappella singers

04 Why does the speaker mention the rapid pace of ticket sales?

Ⓐ To encourage the immediate purchase of tickets
Ⓑ To promote additional performance dates
Ⓒ To apologize for the high price of tickets
Ⓓ To explain the limited seating capacity

[05-06] Listen to an announcement at a university club meeting.

05 What does the speaker hope the listeners will do?

Ⓐ Discuss event management strategies
Ⓑ Promote the event to other clubs
Ⓒ Provide their names for attendance records
Ⓓ Register as volunteers for the event

06 Why does the speaker mention the $10 voucher?

Ⓐ To motivate club members to commit their time
Ⓑ To announce a new partnership with the campus store
Ⓒ To explain the budget allocation to club members
Ⓓ To introduce new products available at the campus store

[07-08] Listen to an announcement on the school radio.

07 Why does the speaker mention feedback surveys?

Ⓐ To announce a survey deadline extension
Ⓑ To show how student input influenced decisions
Ⓒ To request additional feedback from students
Ⓓ To explain why the menu changes were delayed

08 What does the speaker hope the listeners will do?

Ⓐ Visit the dining hall more often
Ⓑ Try the new menu options
Ⓒ Share opinions about the changes
Ⓓ Volunteer at the dining hall

HACKERS TEST

[09-10] Listen to an announcement at a university event.

09 What is the main topic of the announcement?

Ⓐ A virtual reality lecture
Ⓑ A research competition
Ⓒ A technology showcase
Ⓓ A networking opportunity

10 Why does the speaker mention Dr. Robertson?

Ⓐ To specify who will evaluate student projects
Ⓑ To highlight the featured presenter at the event
Ⓒ To congratulate the founder of the Innovation Center
Ⓓ To thank the organizer of the event

[11-12] Listen to an announcement at a university club meeting.

11 What is the main purpose of the announcement?

Ⓐ To encourage participation in drama auditions
Ⓑ To explain the plot of Shakespeare's play
Ⓒ To assign specific roles to club members
Ⓓ To announce changes to the theater space

12 Why does the speaker mention scripts?

Ⓐ To explain why preparation is not necessary
Ⓑ To let students know the audition requirements
Ⓒ To highlight script changes from the original play
Ⓓ To suggest studying Shakespeare before auditions

[13-14] Listen to an announcement at a university club meeting.

13 Why does the speaker mention the Science Building?

　Ⓐ To announce building renovations
　Ⓑ To suggest an alternative meeting place
　Ⓒ To identify where the trees will be planted
　Ⓓ To indicate where equipment will be stored

14 What does the speaker suggest members bring?

　Ⓐ Snacks and reusable water containers
　Ⓑ Digging tools and refreshments
　Ⓒ Working gloves and sturdy shoes
　Ⓓ Student ID cards and signed permission forms

[15-16] Listen to an announcement at a university event.

15 What does the speaker hope the listeners will do?

　Ⓐ Help with the renovation work
　Ⓑ Attend the additional practice sessions
　Ⓒ Form a team for the debate tournament
　Ⓓ Submit their topic selections on time

16 Why does the speaker mention Room 304?

　Ⓐ To announce the competition location
　Ⓑ To explain why renovations are necessary
　Ⓒ To indicate where debate practices will be held
　Ⓓ To describe the advantages of the new space

Answers p.518

5. Inference Questions

Overview

공지에서 직접적으로 언급되지 않았으나 공지 내용을 통해 논리적으로 추론할 수 있는 사실을 묻는 문제이다. 매 시험 0~1문제가 출제되어 출제율은 낮은 편이지만, 고득점을 위해서는 반드시 맞춰야 하는 문제 유형이다.

Types of Questions

inferred라는 표현을 포함한 형태로 출제되어 공지에 언급된 대상에 대해 추론할 수 있는 바를 묻거나, suggest, imply, indicate라는 표현을 포함한 형태로 출제되어 언급된 대상에 대해 화자가 암시하는 바를 묻기도 한다.

Inference

What can be inferred about the computer lab?
What can be concluded about Dr. Brown?

Implication

What does the speaker suggest about the competition?
What does the speaker imply about the new location?
What does the speaker indicate about the final exam?

Hackers Strategy

1 화자가 언급하는 내용의 결론을 생각한다.
공지에서 화자가 언급하는 말을 그대로만 받아들이지 말고, 결론적으로 화자가 말하고자 하는 바가 무엇인지를 염두에 두어야 한다.

2 화자가 암시하는 바를 paraphrasing한 것을 정답으로 고른다.
화자가 직접적으로 말하지는 않았으나, 화자가 한 말을 통해 간접적으로 알 수 있는 사실이 있다. 이렇듯 화자의 말에 함축된 의미를 바르게 paraphrasing한 것이 정답이 된다. 특히, 대화에서 화자가 반복해서 한 말을 통해서 화자의 말이나 행동에 대한 근거를 찾는다.

3 자주 나오는 오답 유형에 주의한다.
대화에서 언급된 단어를 포함하고 있지만 내용이 틀린 오답, 대화에서 언급되지 않은 오답, 충분한 근거 없이 확대해서 해석한 오답이 자주 등장한다. 특히, Inference 문제는 높은 수준의 추리력이나 논리력을 요구하지 않으므로, 반드시 화자의 말 안에서 근거를 찾도록 한다.

Example
🎧 T3_S1_5_Example

Script

Welcome, everyone. Just a quick announcement about our film club's movie night this Friday. We'll be seeing *The Pursuit of Knowledge*, which won several awards at independent film festivals last year. The screening will start at 7 P.M. in our usual meeting spot. Since the film runs for almost three and a half hours, we won't have time for our usual discussion afterward. Instead, we'll discuss it at next week's meeting.

What can be inferred about the film club's regular meetings?

Ⓐ They are held in different locations each week.
Ⓑ They typically include both a film screening and discussion.
Ⓒ They only feature award-winning films.
Ⓓ They attract many attendees.

정답 Ⓑ

해설 영화 동아리의 정기 모임에 대해 암시되는 것을 묻는 문제이므로, 해당 대상에 대해 언급된 말에서 정답의 단서를 찾을 수 있다. 화자가 "Since the film runs for almost three and a half hours, we won't have time for our usual discussion afterward."라며 영화가 거의 3시간 반 동안 상영되므로 그 후에 평소처럼 토론할 시간이 없을 것이라고 했다. 따라서, 모임은 보통 영화 상영과 토론을 둘 다 포함한다는 것을 추론할 수 있으므로 Ⓑ가 정답임을 알 수 있다.

HACKERS PRACTICE 🎧 T3_S1_5_Practice

Listen to each announcement and fill in the blanks. Then choose the best answer for the question. (You will hear each announcement twice.)

01

Hello students! We are hosting our university's first-ever gaming tournament next weekend. We've _____ _____ to offer exciting prizes, including gaming equipment and software. Registration closes next Monday, but spots are _____.
This tournament is open to people of _____ _____, so don't hesitate to participate!

What can be inferred about the gaming tournament?

Ⓐ It has generated significant student interest.
Ⓑ It demands professional gaming experience.
Ⓒ It will be held in multiple locations on campus.
Ⓓ It requires participants to bring their own equipment.

02

Good afternoon, everyone! The university is _____ this year's Student Film Festival. We welcome all kind of films _____.
The creators of the winning entries will receive not only cash prizes but also the opportunity to screen _____ _____. The submission deadline is March 15, and all entries must be _____ _____.

What does the speaker imply about the film festival?

Ⓐ It is being held for the first time this year.
Ⓑ It provides screening opportunities beyond the campus.
Ⓒ It requires films be at least 20 minutes in duration.
Ⓓ It awards individual and team participants separately.

03

An important update regarding _____
_____. Due to technical issues in the computer lab, you will be able to _____
_____ to take the test. It will _____ on Tuesday at 2 P.M., but you can take it in your dorm or any location with reliable Internet access. _____
_____ for detailed instructions.

What does the speaker indicate about the exam?

Ⓐ Its format will be announced by email.
Ⓑ It will take place in the computer lab.
Ⓒ It will start at the originally scheduled time.
Ⓓ Its questions will be revised shortly.

04

Good morning, students! Next weekend, the university is hosting its _____
_____ to support local homeless shelters. The 5K run begins at 8 A.M. from the _____, with registration starting at 7 A.M. The entry fee is only ten dollars, and all proceeds _____
_____. Even if you're not running, come cheer on your fellow students and _____
_____!

What does the speaker suggest about the breakfast?

Ⓐ It will be served in the fitness center.
Ⓑ It will be made by student volunteers.
Ⓒ It will be offered for a price of ten dollars.
Ⓓ It will be available to all event attendees.

HACKERS TEST 🎧 T3_S1_5_Test

[01-02] Listen to an announcement in a classroom.

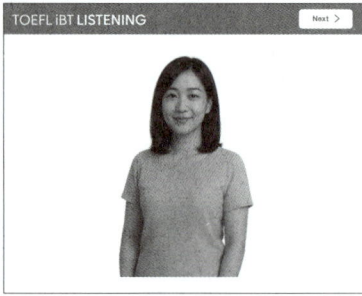

01 What is the main topic of the announcement?

Ⓐ A new equipment policy
Ⓑ A change to booking procedures
Ⓒ An update on facility improvements
Ⓓ An expansion of the music department

02 What can be inferred about the available practice rooms?

Ⓐ They require a fee to reserve.
Ⓑ They will likely be more crowded than usual.
Ⓒ They are located in a different building.
Ⓓ They will be temporarily closed for cleaning.

[03-04] Listen to an announcement in a classroom.

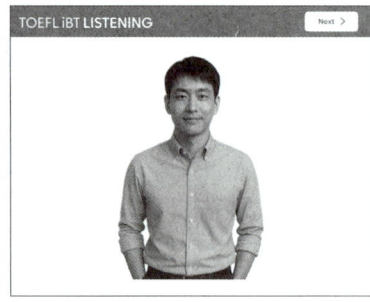

03 What is the reason for the change described in the announcement?

Ⓐ Lack of exam supervisors
Ⓑ Changes to the curriculum requirements
Ⓒ Maintenance issues in the testing facility
Ⓓ Insufficient time for students to prepare

04 What does the speaker suggest about the postponement?

Ⓐ It follows university emergency protocols.
Ⓑ It can affect the difficulty of the exam questions.
Ⓒ It provides an academic advantage for students.
Ⓓ It may lead to further scheduling complications.

[05-06] Listen to an announcement at a university event.

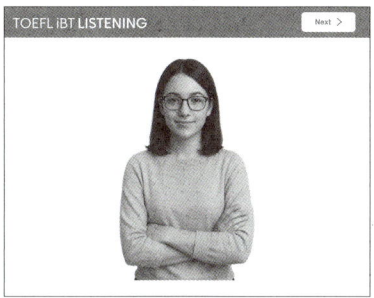

05 What is the main purpose of the announcement?

Ⓐ To advertise a campus job fair
Ⓑ To explain new research guidelines
Ⓒ To announce the opening of a research facility
Ⓓ To promote an academic showcase

06 What can be inferred about the event?

Ⓐ It features foreign guest speakers.
Ⓑ Attendance is mandatory for graduation.
Ⓒ Registration requires the advisor's approval.
Ⓓ People from outside the university will be present.

[07-08] Listen to an announcement in a student lounge.

07 What does the speaker suggest about the work?

Ⓐ It will improve the building's appearance.
Ⓑ It supports environmental goals.
Ⓒ It will require a budget increase.
Ⓓ It will enhance natural lighting.

08 What are students advised to do during the lounge closure?

Ⓐ Suggest improvements to the lounge
Ⓑ Request temporary access to a facility
Ⓒ Take their belongings in advance
Ⓓ Find alternative study spaces on campus

HACKERS TEST

[09-10] Listen to an announcement at a university club meeting.

09 What time should the members be ready for departure?

Ⓐ 9:30 A.M.
Ⓑ 10:00 A.M.
Ⓒ 1:30 P.M.
Ⓓ 2:00 P.M.

10 What can be inferred about the volunteer opportunity?

Ⓐ It involves delivering food to individual homes.
Ⓑ It requires special training before students participate.
Ⓒ It benefits both the community and the students.
Ⓓ It operates as a program with weekly commitment.

[11-12] Listen to an announcement in a classroom.

11 Why does the speaker mention the department's website?

Ⓐ To encourage frequent visits
Ⓑ To share new course schedules
Ⓒ To direct students to the booking page
Ⓓ To announce extended office hours

12 What does the speaker imply about the new system?

Ⓐ It will enable professors to serve students better.
Ⓑ It will replace existing email communications entirely.
Ⓒ It will create longer wait times for appointments.
Ⓓ It will reduce the available time for meetings.

[13-14] Listen to an announcement in a classroom.

13 What is the main purpose of the announcement?

Ⓐ To change the venue for Thursday's lecture
Ⓑ To promote the special psychology program
Ⓒ To publicize an expert's academic seminar
Ⓓ To explain cognitive behavioral therapy techniques

14 What can be inferred about the event?

Ⓐ It will be mandatory for psychology majors.
Ⓑ It will include multiple guest speakers.
Ⓒ It will be recorded for future reference.
Ⓓ It will involve interactions with a speaker.

[15-16] Listen to an announcement at a university club meeting.

15 What is the main topic of the announcement?

Ⓐ A telescope maintenance workshop
Ⓑ An orientation for new members
Ⓒ A space mission celebration
Ⓓ A talk on Mars exploration by an expert

16 What does the speaker indicate about the telescope observations?

Ⓐ They require advance registration.
Ⓑ They will be optional for participants.
Ⓒ They depend on weather conditions.
Ⓓ They will be managed by graduate students.

Answers p.522

무료 토플자료·유학정보 공유
goHackers.com

Hackers
Updated TOEFL
LISTENING

Section II
Announcement Topics

Section II에서는 TASK 3에 자주 등장하는 주제들을 중심으로 세부 단원을 구성하였다. TOEFL에는 교내 행사, 학생 활동, 강의 및 시설 공지와 관련된 내용이 중점적으로 출제된다.

TASK 3의 Announcement Topics에는 다음의 3가지가 있다.

1. Campus Events
2. Student Activities
3. Lectures & Facilities

1. Campus Events

Hackers Updated TOEFL LISTENING

대학교에서 열리는 다양한 행사와 이벤트를 홍보하고 참여를 독려하는 공지이다. 주로 전체 학생을 대상으로 하며, 대학 주최 행사, 교내 프로그램, 대회/공모전에 대한 내용이 나온다. 디렉션에는 주로 campus radio station, campus event, university event와 같은 표현이 등장한다.

■ 대학 주최 행사 🎧 T3_S2_1_Expressions1

자선 경매, 직업 박람회, 학술제, 문화 축제와 같은 다양한 교내 행사가 주요 소재로 등장한다. 공지하는 행사가 무엇인지를 묻거나 행사의 장소를 묻는 문제가 자주 출제되며, 청자에게 요청하는 것을 묻는 문제도 자주 출제된다.

annual 연례의, 매년의	The university's **annual** spring festival will be held next month. 대학교의 연례 봄 축제가 다음 달에 개최될 예정입니다.
donation 기부 (물품)	We encourage all students to bring **donations** for our charity drive. 자선 기부 운동을 위해 모든 학생들이 기부 물품을 가져오기를 권장합니다.
appreciate 감사하다	We truly **appreciate** your continued support for our campus events. 캠퍼스 행사에 대한 여러분의 지속적인 지원에 진심으로 감사드립니다.
proceeds 수익금	All **proceeds** from tonight's benefit concert will go to the university's emergency fund. 오늘 밤 자선 콘서트의 모든 수익금은 대학교 긴급 기금을 지원할 것입니다.
upcoming 다가오는	Don't forget about our **upcoming** career fair scheduled for this Thursday morning. 이번 주 목요일 오전에 예정된 다가오는 취업 박람회를 잊지 마세요.
venue 장소	Please note that the **venue** for tomorrow's graduation ceremony has been changed to the gymnasium. 내일 졸업식의 장소가 체육관으로 변경되었음을 알려드립니다.
feature 특별히 포함하다	This year's festival will **feature** performances by award-winning student musicians. 올해 축제에서는 수상 경력이 있는 학생 음악가들의 공연이 특별히 포함될 예정입니다.
showcase 선보이다	There will be exhibits from various departments **showcasing** innovative projects. 다양한 학과에서 혁신적인 프로젝트들을 선보이는 전시가 있을 예정입니다.
festival booth 축제 부스	Each department will set up a **festival booth** to display their academic achievements. 각 학과는 학업 성취를 전시하기 위해 축제 부스를 설치할 것입니다.

take place 개최되다	The orientation session for new international students will take place in the conference room. 새로운 유학생들을 위한 오리엔테이션 세션이 회의실에서 개최될 예정입니다.
make a difference 변화를 만들다	We hope you all can participate and make a difference. 여러분 모두가 참여하여 변화를 만들어 주시기를 바랍니다.
charity auction 자선 경매	The charity auction will feature donated items from our fellow students. 자선 경매는 저희 학생들이 기증한 물품들을 선보일 예정입니다.
fundraising event 모금 행사	Mark your calendars for next week's fundraising event supporting campus sustainability initiatives. 캠퍼스 지속가능성 계획을 지원하는 다음 주 모금 행사 일정을 달력에 표시해 두세요.
donation drive 기부 운동	The campus-wide donation drive collected essential supplies for families in need. 캠퍼스 전체 기부 운동은 도움이 필요한 가정들을 위한 필수 용품들을 모았습니다.
sign-up sheet 신청서	Please remember to fill out the sign-up sheet for the campus blood drive before Friday. 금요일 전까지 캠퍼스 헌혈 운동 신청서를 작성하는 것을 잊지 마세요.
door prize 경품	The first 100 attendees will receive special door prizes. 첫 100명의 참석자들은 특별 경품을 받게 됩니다.
be excited to announce ~을 발표하게 되어 기쁘다	We are excited to announce that this year's science fair will feature groundbreaking research from our biology and chemistry departments. 올해 과학 박람회에서는 생물학과와 화학과의 획기적인 연구가 특별히 포함될 예정임을 발표하게 되어 기쁩니다.
feel free to 자유롭게 ~하다	Feel free to contact the event coordinators if you have any questions. 질문이 있으시면 행사 담당자에게 자유롭게 문의하세요.
fill out ~을 작성하다, ~에 기입하다	All participants must fill out the liability waiver form before joining the outdoor adventure trip. 모든 참가자들은 야외 모험 여행에 참가하기 전에 책임 면제 양식을 작성해야 합니다.

교내 프로그램 🎧 T3_S2_1_Expressions2

멘토링 프로그램, 과외 프로그램, 리더십 워크숍과 같이 대학교에서 제공하는 다양한 프로그램이 주요 소재로 등장한다. 공지의 목적을 묻는 문제나 청자에게 요청하는 것을 묻는 문제가 자주 출제되며, 프로그램의 세부 사항을 묻는 문제도 종종 출제된다.

support 지원	The academic center will **support** struggling students through personalized sessions. 학업 센터에서는 개인 맞춤형 세션을 통해 어려움을 겪는 학생들을 지원할 것입니다.
encourage 권장하다, 격려하다	We **encourage** all international students to participate in our peer mentoring program this semester. 모든 유학생들이 이번 학기 동료 멘토링 프로그램에 참여하기를 권장합니다.
general audience 일반 청중	The study skills workshop is designed for a **general audience** regardless of academic background. 학습 기술 워크숍은 학문적 배경에 관계없이 일반 청중을 대상으로 설계되었습니다.
take advantage of ~을 이용하다	Students can **take advantage of** our free editing services every Wednesday. 학생들은 매주 수요일에 제공되는 무료 첨삭 서비스를 이용할 수 있습니다.
tutoring 개인 지도	The writing center offers one-on-one **tutoring** sessions to help improve essay writing skills. 작문 센터에서는 에세이 작성 기술 향상을 돕기 위해 일대일 개인 지도 세션을 제공합니다.
gain insight into ~에 대한 통찰력을 얻다	This workshop will help you **gain insight into** effective study strategies. 이 워크숍은 효과적인 학습 전략에 대한 통찰력을 얻는 데 도움이 될 것입니다.
make sure that ~을 확실히 하다	Please **make sure that** you complete the prerequisite courses before enrolling in the advanced seminar. 고급 세미나에 등록하기 전에 선수과목을 이수했는지 확실히 하시기 바랍니다.
highly recommend 적극 권하다	We **highly recommend** joining the graduate student study groups for comprehensive exam preparation. 종합시험 준비를 위해 대학원생 스터디 그룹에 참여할 것을 적극 권합니다.
study abroad program 유학 프로그램	Applications for next year's **study abroad program** are due by the end of this month. 내년 유학 프로그램 신청서는 이번 달 말까지 제출해야 합니다.
behind schedule 예정보다 늦은	The language immersion program is currently **behind schedule** due to the late arrival of the instructor. 어학 몰입 프로그램은 강사 도착 지연으로 인해 현재 예정보다 늦어지고 있습니다.

대회/공모전 🎧 T3_S2_1_Expressions3

대학교에서 진행하는 다양한 대회나 공모전이 주요 소재로 등장한다. 대회나 공모전의 세부 사항을 묻는 문제, 청자들이 대회를 신청하는 방법, 대회의 우승자들이 얻을 수 있는 혜택 등을 묻는 문제가 자주 출제된다.

competition 대회	The university is now accepting submissions from undergraduate students for its annual writing competition. 대학교의 연례 작문 대회에서 현재 학부생들의 출품작을 접수하고 있습니다.
deadline 마감일	Please note that the deadline for photography contest entries is this Friday. 사진 공모전 출품작 마감일이 이번 주 금요일임을 유의하시기 바랍니다.
guideline 지침, 안내	All participants must carefully review the competition guidelines before submitting their projects. 모든 참가자들은 프로젝트를 제출하기 전에 대회 지침을 신중히 검토해야 합니다.
judge 심사위원	Distinguished faculty members and industry professionals serve as contest judges. 저명한 교수진과 업계 전문가들이 공모전 심사위원으로 활동합니다.
entry 출품작	Each entry will be evaluated by a panel of expert judges. 각 출품작은 전문가 심사위원단에 의해 평가될 것입니다.
criteria 기준	Projects will be evaluated based on specific criteria, including innovation and presentation. 프로젝트들은 혁신성과 발표를 포함한 특정 기준에 따라 평가될 것입니다.
scholarship 장학금	Competition winners are eligible for merit-based scholarships. 경진대회 우승자들은 성적 우수 장학금을 받을 자격이 있습니다.
finalist 결선 진출자	The three finalists in the poster competition will present their work next week. 포스터 공모전의 세 명의 결선 진출자들은 다음 주에 작품을 발표할 예정입니다.
eligibility 자격, 적격	All undergraduate students meet the eligibility requirements for this competition. 모든 학부생들이 이 경진대회의 자격 요건을 충족합니다.
observe 준수하다, 관찰하다	All contestants must observe the time limits during their presentations at the speech contest. 모든 참가자들은 연설 대회에서 발표하는 동안 제한 시간을 준수해야 합니다.
be sure to 반드시 ~하다	Be sure to include your student ID number when submitting your entry for the design competition. 디자인 공모전에 출품작을 제출할 때 반드시 학번을 포함하시기 바랍니다.
present an award 상을 수여하다	The dean will present an award to the outstanding student researcher at next week's ceremony. 학장이 다음 주 시상식에서 우수 학생 연구자에게 상을 수여할 예정입니다.

HACKERS TEST 🎧 T3_S2_1_Test

[01-02] Listen to an announcement on the school radio.

01 What is the main topic of the announcement?

Ⓐ A temporary facility closure
Ⓑ A free vaccination program
Ⓒ A wellness center relocation
Ⓓ A mandatory health screening

02 What does the speaker hope the listeners will do?

Ⓐ Show up for the vaccination
Ⓑ Contact the wellness center
Ⓒ Volunteer in the east wing lobby
Ⓓ Make an appointment beforehand

[03-04] Listen to an announcement at a university event.

03 What can winners of the competition gain?

Ⓐ Headphones and a microphone
Ⓑ An opportunity to record with professionals
Ⓒ A gold medal and a ribbon
Ⓓ Prize money and a trophy

04 Why does the speaker mention the university's mobile app?

Ⓐ To indicate the application submission method
Ⓑ To promote its event notification system
Ⓒ To advertise the new digital platform features
Ⓓ To announce the deadline change

[05-06] Listen to an announcement on the school radio.

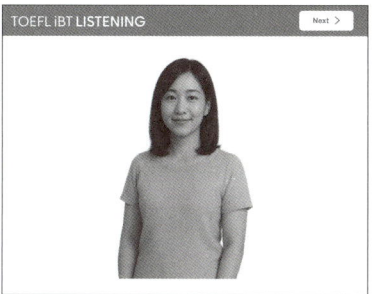

05 What is the main topic of the announcement?

ⓐ Academic advisor meetings
ⓑ First-year student requirements
ⓒ Available tutoring sessions
ⓓ Course registration information

06 What are students encouraged to do?

ⓐ Participate in the program
ⓑ Submit their course schedules
ⓒ Schedule individual meetings
ⓓ Meet with academic advisors

[07-08] Listen to an announcement at a university event.

07 What is the main purpose of the announcement?

ⓐ To advertise a university art exhibition
ⓑ To publicize an upcoming literary event
ⓒ To announce the winners of a literary contest
ⓓ To encourage students to submit their poetry

08 Why does the speaker mention Maya Richardson's fame?

ⓐ To recommend securing seats early
ⓑ To explain why tickets are expensive
ⓒ To convince students to study literature
ⓓ To persuade attendees to purchase her book

HACKERS TEST

[09-10] Listen to an announcement at a university event.

09 Where are the finance companies located?

Ⓐ North section
Ⓑ East section
Ⓒ West section
Ⓓ South section

10 What does the speaker suggest listeners bring?

Ⓐ Student IDs
Ⓑ Recommendation letters
Ⓒ Résumés
Ⓓ Academic transcripts

[11-12] Listen to an announcement at a university event.

11 What is the main purpose of the announcement?

Ⓐ To recruit new players for the football team
Ⓑ To encourage attendance at a campus event
Ⓒ To request volunteers for the upcoming game
Ⓓ To announce a new rivalry with another school

12 Why does the speaker mention free T-shirts?

Ⓐ To introduce a new school mascot
Ⓑ To persuade students to show up early
Ⓒ To reward players for their performance
Ⓓ To create a unified appearance for attendees

[13-14] Listen to an announcement at a university event.

13 What is the main purpose of the announcement?

Ⓐ To request volunteers for campus events
Ⓑ To distribute free water bottles to students
Ⓒ To inform students of eco-awareness activities
Ⓓ To announce location changes for events

14 What does the speaker hope the listeners will do?

Ⓐ Register for the scheduled workshops
Ⓑ Promote the event to other students
Ⓒ Practice sustainable eating habits
Ⓓ Volunteer for the workshops

[15-16] Listen to an announcement at a university event.

15 What is the main topic of the announcement?

Ⓐ A change in concert scheduling
Ⓑ An academic conference
Ⓒ A student band audition
Ⓓ An upcoming musical event

16 Why does the speaker mention ID cards?

Ⓐ To track participation for course credit
Ⓑ To promote the university's ID system
Ⓒ To enable free entrance for students
Ⓓ To ensure security at the event

Answers p.525

2. Student Activities

동아리나 학생회와 같은 학생 활동과 관련된 공지이다. 주로 특정 그룹의 구성원들을 대상으로 하며, 동아리 모임, 사회 활동, 학생회 회의에 대한 내용이 나온다. 디렉션에는 주로 university club meeting, student meeting과 같은 표현이 등장한다.

■ 동아리 모임 🎧 T3_S2_2_Expressions1

동아리에서 안건에 대해 회의를 하거나 동아리에서 주최하는 행사에 대한 안내를 하는 내용이 주로 나오며, 동아리의 신규 회원을 모집하는 내용도 나온다. 공지하고 있는 행사가 무엇인지 묻는 문제가 자주 출제되며, 특히 동아리에서 대회를 개최할 경우 우승자들이 얻을 수 있는 것을 묻는 문제도 종종 출제된다.

finalize 마무리 짓다	We need to finalize the details for our club's upcoming event by tomorrow. 우리 동아리의 다가오는 행사 세부 사항을 내일까지 마무리 지어야 합니다.
get together 모이다	All drama club members will get together this Friday to rehearse for the performance. 모든 연극 동아리 회원들이 공연을 위한 리허설을 하기 위해 이번 금요일에 모일 예정입니다.
don't miss out on ~을 놓치지 마세요	Don't miss out on our annual hiking trip this Saturday! 이번 토요일 우리의 연례 하이킹 여행을 놓치지 마세요!
be in charge of ~을 담당하다	Sarah will be in charge of organizing the charity bake sale for our volunteer club. Sarah가 우리 자원봉사 동아리의 자선 제빵 판매 조직을 담당할 것입니다.
be dedicated to ~에 헌신하다	Our environmental club is dedicated to promoting sustainability initiatives across the campus. 우리 환경 동아리는 캠퍼스 전체에 지속가능성 계획을 홍보하는 데 헌신하고 있습니다.
around the corner 코앞에 와 있는	With the spring festival around the corner, we need to start preparing our club's booth display. 봄 축제가 코앞에 와 있어서, 우리 동아리의 부스 전시를 준비하기 시작해야 합니다.
bring up (문제 등을) 언급하다	During today's meeting, please bring up any concerns about the upcoming camping trip. 오늘 회의에서 다가오는 캠핑 여행에 대한 우려 사항이 있으면 언급해 주세요.
call off ~을 취소하다	We had to call off the outdoor movie night due to the weather forecast. 날씨 예보로 인해 야외 영화 상영의 밤을 취소해야 했습니다.
share details 세부 사항을 공유하다	The president will share details about the new community service project at next week's meeting. 회장이 다음 주 회의에서 새로운 지역사회 봉사 프로젝트에 대한 세부 사항을 공유할 예정입니다.

secure permission 허락을 받다	We still need to secure permission from the administration before hosting the talent show. 장기자랑 행사를 주최하기 전에 아직 행정부로부터 허락을 받아야 합니다.
as soon as possible 가능한 한 빨리	Please submit your participation forms for the cultural night as soon as possible. 문화의 밤 참가 신청서를 가능한 한 빨리 제출해 주세요.
as usual 늘 그렇듯이	As usual, our weekly book club meeting will be held in the library. 늘 그렇듯이, 우리의 주간 독서 클럽 회의는 도서관에서 열릴 예정입니다.
be about to 막 ~하려 하다	Our debate team is about to start the final preparations for the inter-university competition. 우리 토론팀이 막 대학 간 경쟁을 위한 최종 준비를 시작하려 합니다.
be done with ~을 마치다, 끝내다	Once we are done with the membership drive, we'll focus on planning our first major event. 회원 모집을 마치면, 첫 번째 주요 행사 계획에 집중할 것입니다.
be likely to ~할 것 같다	New members are likely to find our photography club's workshops both informative and enjoyable. 새로운 회원들은 우리 사진 동아리의 워크숍이 유익하고 즐거울 것 같다고 여길 것입니다.
be subject to ~의 대상이 되다	All club activities are subject to approval by the student activities office. 모든 동아리 활동은 학생 활동 사무소의 승인 대상이 됩니다.
come up with ~을 제안하다	We need to come up with creative fundraising ideas for our music club's new equipment. 우리 음악 동아리의 새로운 장비를 위한 창의적인 모금 아이디어를 제안해야 합니다.
get a move on 서두르다	We need to get a move on with the decorations if we want everything ready for tomorrow's event. 내일 행사를 위해 모든 것을 준비하려면 장식 작업을 서둘러야 합니다.
get down to ~에 착수하다	Let's get down to discussing the budget for our club's annual conference this year. 올해 우리 동아리의 연례 컨퍼런스 예산 논의에 착수합시다.

■ 사회 활동 🎧 T3_S2_2_Expressions2

학생들이 주체가 되는 다양한 사회 활동이 소재로 등장하며, 주로 행사에 대해 안내하거나 행사를 운영할 인원을 모집하는 내용이 나온다. 어떤 행사가 진행되는지 묻는 문제나 청자들에게 요청하는 내용을 묻는 문제가 자주 출제된다.

impact 영향	Our project has had a huge **impact** on improving literacy rates in local schools. 우리 프로젝트는 지역 학교의 문해율 향상에 큰 영향을 미쳤습니다.
make our way to ~로 함께 가다	After the volunteer orientation, we'll **make our way to** the dog shelter to begin our work. 자원봉사 오리엔테이션 후에, 우리는 활동을 시작하기 위해 유기견 보호소로 함께 갈 것입니다.
raise funds for ~을 위한 기금을 모으다	The student government is organizing a charity concert to **raise funds for** disaster relief efforts. 학생회에서는 재해 구호 활동을 위한 기금을 모으기 위해 자선 콘서트를 조직하고 있습니다.
contribute to ~에 공헌을 하다	Every volunteer hour you complete will **contribute to** building a stronger community partnership. 여러분이 완료하는 모든 자원봉사 시간은 더 강한 지역사회 파트너십 구축에 공헌할 것입니다.
take a moment to ~할 시간을 잠시 내다	Please **take a moment to** sign up for our upcoming blood drive scheduled for next Tuesday. 다음 주 화요일로 예정된 우리의 다가오는 헌혈 행사에 등록할 시간을 잠시 내주세요.
awareness material 교육 자료, 홍보 자료	We'll be distributing **awareness material** about mental health resources during the campus wellness fair. 캠퍼스 건강 박람회 동안 정신 건강 자원에 대한 교육 자료를 배포할 예정입니다.
be concerned with ~에 관여하다	Our environmental action group is primarily **concerned with** promoting sustainable practices on campus. 우리 환경 행동 그룹은 주로 캠퍼스에서 지속 가능한 관행을 홍보하는 데 관여하고 있습니다.
count on ~에 기대다, ~에 의지하다	We can **count on** the support of local businesses for our annual charity fundraising event. 우리의 연례 자선 모금 행사를 위해 지역 기업들의 지원에 기대할 수 있습니다.
give back 환원하다	This program provides students with meaningful ways to **give back** to the community. 이 프로그램은 학생들에게 지역사회에 환원할 수 있는 의미 있는 방법들을 제공합니다.

학생회 회의 🎧 T3_S2_2_Expressions3

학생회 회의에서 나올 수 있는 다양한 안건이 주요 소재로 등장한다. 주로 행사나 프로그램을 개최하면서 필요한 내용이나 교내 이슈와 관련된 내용이 나온다. 회의의 주된 목적이나 주제를 묻는 문제가 자주 출제되며, 회의 세부 내용에 대해 묻는 문제도 종종 출제된다.

facilitate 촉진하다, 용이하게 하다	The student government will **facilitate** discussions between students and faculty. 학생회는 학생과 교수진 간의 논의를 촉진할 것입니다.
funding 자금, 기금	We need to discuss the allocation of **funding** for next semester's student activities and programs. 다음 학기 학생 활동과 프로그램을 위한 자금 배정에 대해 논의해야 합니다.
call a meeting 회의를 소집하다	The student body president will **call a meeting** to address concerns about dining hall services. 학생회장이 식당 서비스에 대한 우려 사항을 다루기 위해 회의를 소집할 것입니다.
remind A of B A에게 B를 다시 알려주다	I'd like to **remind** everyone **of the upcoming deadline** for budget proposal submissions. 예산 제안서 제출 마감일이 다가오고 있음을 모든 분들에게 다시 알려드리고 싶습니다.
initiative 계획	Our new sustainability **initiative** aims to reduce plastic waste across all campus facilities. 우리의 새로운 지속 가능성 계획은 모든 캠퍼스 시설에서 플라스틱 폐기물을 줄이는 것을 목표로 합니다.
administration 행정부	We've scheduled a meeting with the **administration** to discuss improvements to student housing. 학생 주거 시설 개선에 대해 논의하기 위해 행정부와 회의 일정을 잡았습니다.
take steps 조치를 취하다	We must **take steps** to improve communication between different student organizations on campus. 캠퍼스 내 다양한 학생 단체 간의 의사소통을 개선하기 위한 조치를 취해야 합니다.
approve plans 계획을 승인하다	The student senate will vote to **approve plans** for the new mental health support program. 학생 의회는 새로운 정신 건강 지원 프로그램에 대한 계획을 승인하기 위해 투표할 것입니다.
get ~ started ~을 시작하다	Let's **get** the discussion **started** with the first item on today's agenda about campus safety. 캠퍼스 안전에 대한 오늘 안건의 첫 번째 항목으로 논의를 시작합시다.
it's important to ~하는 것이 중요하다	**It's important to** gather student feedback before implementing any major policy changes. 주요 정책 변경을 시행하기 전에 학생 피드백을 수집하는 것이 중요합니다.

HACKERS TEST 🎧 T3_S2_2_Test

[01-02] Listen to an announcement at a student meeting.

01 What is the main topic of the announcement?

    Ⓐ Student portal update
    Ⓑ Office building renovation
    Ⓒ Leadership training event
    Ⓓ Camp Wildwood facilities

02 Why does the speaker mention the Student Affairs office?

    Ⓐ To mention the registration location
    Ⓑ To show where the retreat will take place
    Ⓒ To tell students where to make payments
    Ⓓ To explain where to report registration issues

[03-04] Listen to an announcement at a university event.

03 What is the main purpose of the announcement?

    Ⓐ To celebrate winners of the writing contest
    Ⓑ To announce the delay in the submission deadline
    Ⓒ To suggest a new theme for monthly meetings
    Ⓓ To explain submission guidelines for the competition

04 What are students encouraged to do?

    Ⓐ Bring printed copies
    Ⓑ Submit multiple stories
    Ⓒ Complete their entries
    Ⓓ Attend the workshop

[05-06] Listen to an announcement at a university club meeting.

05 What is the main topic of the announcement?

Ⓐ A tennis equipment sale
Ⓑ A university sports event
Ⓒ A tennis lesson schedule
Ⓓ A court maintenance notice

06 What can winners receive as a prize?

Ⓐ A special tennis racket
Ⓑ A tennis visor
Ⓒ A cash reward
Ⓓ A trophy and medal

[07-08] Listen to an announcement in a classroom.

07 What is the main topic of the announcement?

Ⓐ Language proficiency test registration
Ⓑ International student orientation
Ⓒ Graduation requirement updates
Ⓓ Study abroad application due date

08 Why does the speaker mention Room 302?

Ⓐ To inform students of the location change
Ⓑ To specify where the event will take place
Ⓒ To indicate where to submit applications
Ⓓ To show a room available for study groups

HACKERS TEST

[09-10] Listen to an announcement at a university club meeting.

09 What is the main purpose of the announcement?

Ⓐ To organize a chess competition
Ⓑ To change the tournament date
Ⓒ To demonstrate chess-playing techniques
Ⓓ To announce plans to buy new equipment

10 What does the speaker hope the listeners will do?

Ⓐ Share the delivery cost
Ⓑ Attend the next tournament
Ⓒ Contact equipment suppliers
Ⓓ Recommend equipment brands

[11-12] Listen to an announcement at a university club meeting.

11 What point does the speaker make about complete blueprints?

Ⓐ They will be reviewed by industry professionals.
Ⓑ They will be discussed in detail at the next meeting.
Ⓒ They show examples of previous successful projects.
Ⓓ They are required submissions for the contest.

12 What can the winning team receive as a prize?

Ⓐ Exemption from next semester's tuition fees
Ⓑ Automatic entry into national competitions
Ⓒ Financial support for future projects
Ⓓ Professional mentorship opportunities

[13-14] Listen to an announcement at a university club meeting.

13 What is the main purpose of the announcement?

   Ⓐ To recruit new members for the club
   Ⓑ To launch an environmental awareness campaign
   Ⓒ To explain the benefits of recycling on campus
   Ⓓ To announce the approval of the club's proposal

14 What does the speaker hope the listeners will do?

   Ⓐ Promote the initiative on social media
   Ⓑ Develop new environmental proposals
   Ⓒ Participate in the campus recycling effort
   Ⓓ Monitor the use of new recycling stations

[15-16] Listen to an announcement at a university club meeting.

15 What is the main topic of the announcement?

   Ⓐ A new photography contest
   Ⓑ A purchase of photography equipment
   Ⓒ The annual photography exhibition
   Ⓓ Updated membership requirements

16 Why does the speaker mention the Student Center?

   Ⓐ To indicate where the exhibition is held
   Ⓑ To illustrate the progress the club has made
   Ⓒ To describe where registration will take place
   Ⓓ To advise where to find additional information

Answers p.528

3. Lectures & Facilities

Hackers Updated TOEFL LISTENING

강의 및 과제와 관련된 내용이나 캠퍼스 시설 및 서비스와 관련된 내용을 발표하는 공지이다. 주로 특정 강의를 듣는 학생들이나 시설 및 서비스를 이용하는 학생들을 대상으로 하며, 강의/과제, 초청 강연, 시설/서비스 변경에 대한 내용이 나온다. 디렉션에는 주로 classroom, student lounge와 같은 표현이 등장한다.

■ 강의/과제 🎧 T3_S2_3_Expressions1

강의나 과제와 관련된 공지 사항이 주요 소재로 등장하며, 시험 일정 변경, 시험 범위 안내, 강의실 변경, 과제 평가 기준 안내와 같은 내용이 나온다. 공지의 목적을 묻거나 청자에게 요청하는 것을 묻는 문제가 자주 출제된다.

citation 인용	Please remember to include proper citation format for all sources used in your research paper. 연구 논문에 사용된 모든 자료에 대해 적절한 인용 형식을 포함하는 것을 기억하시기 바랍니다.
submission 제출	The submission deadline for your final project has been extended to next Friday. 기말 프로젝트 제출 마감일이 다음 금요일로 연장되었습니다.
enrollment 등록	Due to increased enrollment in this course, we will be moving to a larger lecture hall. 이 과목의 등록이 증가하여 더 큰 강의실로 이동할 예정입니다.
instead of ~ 대신에	Instead of a written exam, you will be required to complete a group presentation for your midterm. 필기시험 대신, 여러분은 중간고사를 위해 그룹 발표를 완료해야 할 겁니다.
at least 적어도	Students must complete at least three lab assignments before the end of the semester. 학생들은 학기말 전에 적어도 세 개의 실험 과제를 완료해야 합니다.
inform A of B A에게 B를 알리다	I need to inform you of the changes to next week's assignment requirements. 다음 주 과제 요구 사항의 변경 사항을 여러분에게 알려드려야 합니다.
go over 살펴보다	We'll go over the exam format and key topics during our review session tomorrow. 내일 복습 세션 동안 시험 형식과 주요 주제들을 살펴보겠습니다.
give instructions 설명하다	The teaching assistant will give instructions on how to access the online learning platform. 조교가 온라인 학습 플랫폼에 접속하는 방법에 대해 설명할 것입니다.

figure out 알아내다	You'll need to figure out which research methodology works best for your thesis topic. 논문 주제에 가장 적합한 연구 방법론이 무엇인지 알아내야 합니다.	
be cut out for ~에 자질이 있다	Students who struggle with complex mathematical concepts may not be cut out for advanced engineering courses. 복잡한 수학 개념을 어려워하는 학생들은 고급 공학 과정에 자질이 없을 수 있습니다.	
adhere to ~을 준수하다	All students must adhere to the academic integrity policy when completing their assignments. 모든 학생들은 과제를 완료할 때 학업 성실성 정책을 준수해야 합니다.	
be counted toward ~에 포함되다	Your participation in class discussions will be counted toward your final grade. 수업 토론 참여는 최종 성적에 포함될 것입니다.	
in time 제시간에	Please make sure to submit your research proposals in time for the faculty review committee meeting. 교수 심사위원회 회의에 맞춰 연구 제안서를 제시간에 제출하시기 바랍니다.	
in terms of ~의 측면에서 보면	In terms of grading criteria, participation will account for 20% of your final score. 채점 기준의 측면에서 보면 참여도가 최종 점수의 20퍼센트를 차지할 것입니다.	
keep up with ~에 뒤처지지 않다	Students are expected to keep up with the assigned reading schedule throughout the semester. 학생들은 학기 내내 지정된 읽기 일정에 뒤처지지 않을 것이 기대됩니다.	
look over ~을 검토하다	I encourage you to look over your essay drafts carefully before submitting the final version. 최종 버전을 제출하기 전에 에세이 초안을 신중히 검토할 것을 권장합니다.	
make up for ~을 만회하다	Extra credit assignments are available to help make up for any missed quiz grades. 놓친 퀴즈 점수를 만회하는 데 도움이 되도록 추가 학점 과제가 제공됩니다.	

■ 초청 강연 🎧 T3_S2_3_Expressions2

초청 강연에 대해 안내하는 내용이 나오며, 주로 강연자의 정보, 강연 위치, 강연에서 얻을 수 있는 것들이 세부적인 내용으로 나온다. 이와 관련된 세부 사항을 묻는 문제가 자주 출제된다.

expert 전문가	Please welcome Dr. Johnson, a leading **expert** in artificial intelligence research. 인공지능 연구 분야의 선도적인 전문가인 Johnson 박사를 환영해 주십시오.
renowned 유명한, 명성 있는	This afternoon we'll be hosting a lecture by Professor Lee, a **renowned** scholar in contemporary literature. 오늘 오후 현대 문학 분야의 명성 있는 학자인 Lee 교수의 강연을 개최할 것입니다.
guest speaker 초청 연사	The psychology department has arranged a **guest speaker** for next Friday's research workshop. 심리학과에서 다음 주 금요일 연구 워크숍을 위해 초청 연사를 섭외했습니다.
limited seating 좌석 제한	Please note that there will be **limited seating** available for the presentation. 발표에는 좌석 제한이 있음을 알려드립니다.
secure a spot 자리를 맡다	I encourage you to arrive early to **secure a spot** for the highly anticipated economics lecture. 매우 기대되는 경제학 강연에서 자리를 맡기 위해 일찍 도착할 것을 권장합니다.
join in ~에 참여하다	We invite all students to **join in** the discussion following Professor Martinez's keynote address. Martinez 교수의 기조 연설 후 토론에 모든 학생들을 참여시키고자 합니다.
be recognized for ~으로 인정받다	She **is recognized for** her groundbreaking research in marine biology. 그녀는 해양 생물학 분야의 획기적인 연구로 인정받고 있습니다.
award-winning 상을 받은	Tomorrow's seminar will be presented by an **award-winning** journalist. 내일의 세미나는 상을 받은 기자가 진행할 것입니다.
in the area of ~의 분야에서	Our distinguished speaker has made significant contributions **in the area of** renewable energy. 우리의 저명한 연사는 재생 에너지 분야에서 중요한 기여를 했습니다.
Q&A session 질의응답 시간	There will be a thirty-minute **Q&A session** following the main presentation on climate policy. 기후 정책에 관한 주요 발표 후 30분간의 질의응답 시간이 있을 것입니다.
auditorium 강당	The guest speaker's presentation will begin at 3 P.M. in the main **auditorium**. 초청 연사의 발표는 오후 3시에 대강당에서 시작합니다.

■ 시설/서비스 변경 🎧 T3_S2_3_Expressions3

교내 시설이나 서비스와 관련하여, 시설 보수 안내, 서비스 변경 또는 중단 안내와 같은 내용이 나온다. 왜 변경이 생기는지를 묻는 문제가 자주 출제되며, 그로 인해 청자들이 앞으로 해야 할 일을 묻는 문제도 종종 출제된다.

alternative 대안, 대체	We recommend using the library as an **alternative** study space while the student lounge is under renovation. 학생 라운지가 보수 공사 중인 동안 도서관을 대체 학습 공간으로 사용할 것을 권장합니다.
reminder 조언, 주의, 상기시키는 것	This is a **reminder** that the campus bookstore will have extended hours during finals week. 이것은 기말고사 주간 동안 캠퍼스 서점이 연장 운영할 것이라는 조언입니다.
closure 폐쇄	The temporary **closure** of the main cafeteria will last until the new kitchen equipment is installed. 주요 구내식당의 임시 폐쇄는 새로운 주방 장비가 설치될 때까지 지속될 것입니다.
accordingly 그에 맞춰	The reading room schedule has been modified, so please plan your study time **accordingly**. 열람실 일정이 변경되었으므로, 그에 맞춰 학습 시간을 계획하시기 바랍니다.
be due to ~할 예정이다	The gymnasium renovation project **is due to** begin next Monday morning. 체육관 보수 공사 프로젝트는 다음 주 월요일 아침에 시작할 예정입니다.
apologize for ~에 대해 사과하다	We **apologize for** any inconvenience caused by the parking lot closure. 주차장 폐쇄로 인한 불편에 대해 사과드립니다.
go into effect 시행되다	The new campus security measures will **go into effect** starting this weekend. 새로운 캠퍼스 보안 조치는 이번 주말부터 시행될 것입니다.
be equipped with ~을 갖추다	The renovated lecture hall will **be equipped with** state-of-the-art audio-visual technology. 보수된 강의실은 최첨단 시청각 기술을 갖출 것입니다.
be closed for repairs 보수 공사로 폐쇄되다	The east wing elevator will **be closed for repairs** from Tuesday through Thursday. 동관 엘리베이터는 화요일부터 목요일까지 보수 공사로 폐쇄될 것입니다.
accommodate the needs 요구를 수용하다	The new study spaces are designed to **accommodate the needs** of both individual and group study. 새로운 학습 공간은 개인 학습과 그룹 학습 모두의 요구를 수용하도록 설계되었습니다.

HACKERS TEST 🎧 T3_S2_3_Test

[01-02] Listen to an announcement in a student lounge.

01 What is the reason for the lounge closure described in the announcement?

Ⓐ Emergency safety repairs
Ⓑ Electrical system upgrades
Ⓒ Wi-Fi system maintenance
Ⓓ Regular weekend maintenance

02 What are students advised to do in response to the announcement?

Ⓐ Study outdoors instead
Ⓑ Volunteer with maintenance
Ⓒ Use alternative study spaces
Ⓓ Reschedule their weekend plans

[03-04] Listen to an announcement in a classroom.

03 What is the main purpose of the announcement?

Ⓐ To introduce the new supervising professor
Ⓑ To notify students about attendance requirements
Ⓒ To promote a campus environmental initiative
Ⓓ To publicize an upcoming academic event

04 Why does the speaker mention a Q&A session?

Ⓐ To explain why the lecture will be longer than usual
Ⓑ To advise students to formulate their inquiries beforehand
Ⓒ To demonstrate how participation grades will be calculated
Ⓓ To encourage students to participate in the event

[05-06] Listen to an announcement in a classroom.

05 What is the reason for the change described in the announcement?

Ⓐ Weather-related concerns
Ⓑ Campus construction work
Ⓒ Equipment maintenance issues
Ⓓ Experiential learning opportunity

06 What does the speaker suggest members bring?

Ⓐ USB storage drives
Ⓑ Digital media projects
Ⓒ Completed assignments
Ⓓ Personal identification cards

[07-08] Listen to an announcement in a student lounge.

07 What is the main topic of the announcement?

Ⓐ A lounge closure
Ⓑ A cleaning schedule
Ⓒ A change in lounge hours
Ⓓ Coffee shop menu changes

08 What are students encouraged to do?

Ⓐ Keep noise levels down
Ⓑ Dispose of trash properly
Ⓒ Report any issues to the staff
Ⓓ Turn off the lights when leaving

HACKERS TEST

[09-10] Listen to an announcement in a classroom.

09 What is the main purpose of the announcement?

Ⓐ To introduce a new assignment for the class
Ⓑ To inform students about extended office hours
Ⓒ To announce a change in the submission format
Ⓓ To remind students about the midterm paper deadline

10 Why does the speaker mention the syllabus?

Ⓐ To suggest that students review attendance policies
Ⓑ To explain how to access course materials online
Ⓒ To guide students on paper formatting standards
Ⓓ To highlight recently made changes to the course

[11-12] Listen to an announcement in a student lounge.

11 What is the announcement about?

Ⓐ A delay in the cafeteria renovation
Ⓑ A survey about student satisfaction
Ⓒ A construction project in the student facility
Ⓓ A new coffee shop opening in the city

12 What are students advised to do during the lounge closure?

Ⓐ Apply for jobs at the new coffee shop
Ⓑ Participate in the online voting system
Ⓒ Contribute ideas for the lounge re-design
Ⓓ Use alternate campus facilities temporarily

[13-14] Listen to an announcement in a classroom.

13 What is the main topic of the announcement?

Ⓐ A book signing event
Ⓑ A registration deadline
Ⓒ A leadership conference
Ⓓ A psychology course enrollment

14 Why does the speaker mention the website?

Ⓐ To describe speaker qualifications
Ⓑ To provide registration information
Ⓒ To share details about conference location
Ⓓ To distribute digital conference materials

[15-16] Listen to an announcement in a classroom.

15 What is the reason for the change described in the announcement?

Ⓐ A guest lecture
Ⓑ Schedule conflicts
Ⓒ Facility maintenance
Ⓓ Software access needs

16 What does the speaker emphasize students should bring?

Ⓐ Project data
Ⓑ Course syllabus
Ⓒ Reference books
Ⓓ Student ID cards

Answers p.531

무료 토플자료·유학정보 공유
goHackers.com

**Hackers
Updated TOEFL
LISTENING**

TASK 4

Listen to an Academic Talk

Introduction

Section I. Question Types
1. Main Topic/Purpose Questions
2. Discuss Next Questions
3. Detail Questions
4. Intention Questions
5. Organization Questions
6. Inference Questions

Section II. Academic Topics
1. Humanities
2. Arts
3. Social Science
4. Physical Science
5. Life Science

Introduction

TASK 4(Listen to an Academic Talk)는 평균 199~200단어로 이루어진 강의를 듣고 주어지는 문제의 답을 고르는 유형으로, 대학 수준의 강의 내용 및 학술 용어를 파악하고 강의의 구조와 정보가 전달되는 방식을 이해하는 능력을 묻는다. 각 강의에는 4개의 문제가 출제되는데, Module 1에서 강의 1개가 출제되며, 더미 문항이 포함될 경우 강의가 2개까지도 출제된다. Lower Module 2에서는 이 유형이 출제되지 않으며, Upper Module 2에서만 강의 2개가 출제된다.

Preview

음성 화면

강의를 들을 때 나오는 화면으로, 화자의 사진이 나온다.

주의 사항 : TASK 4의 Direction 화면은 별도로 나오지 않으므로 TASK 3가 끝난 후 바로 강의를 들을 준비를 해야 한다.

해야 할 일 : 강의의 첫 부분에서 강의의 전반적인 주제를 소개하므로, 첫 부분을 놓치지 않도록 주의 깊게 듣는다. 문제 풀이를 할 때 강의의 주요한 정보를 기억할 수 있도록, 음성을 들으며 Note-taking을 해둔다.

문제 풀이 화면

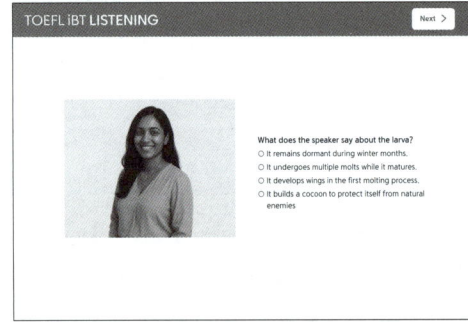

문제가 출제될 때 나오는 화면으로, 문제와 보기가 나온다.

문제를 풀 수 있는 시간 : 30초

문제를 풀 때 해야 할 일 : 문제와 보기는 별도로 들려주지 않으므로, 화면이 전환되면 빠르게 읽는다. 보기 앞에 있는 칸을 클릭하여 답을 표시한다.

문제를 풀고 난 후 해야 할 일 : 답을 고른 후 우측 상단의 Next 버튼을 누르면 다음 문제 또는 다음 강의로 넘어간다. 이때, 이전 화면으로 돌아갈 수 없으므로 충분히 고민한 후 넘어가도록 한다.

Task Strategy

1. 강의의 첫 부분과 마지막 부분은 반드시 듣는다.
TASK 4에서는 강의의 주제를 묻거나 다음에 설명할 내용을 묻는 문제가 상당히 높은 비율로 출제된다. 따라서, 강의의 첫 부분에서 강의에서 중점적으로 다룰 핵심 소재를 듣고, 강의의 마지막 부분에서 화자가 앞으로 설명할 내용을 반드시 듣는 연습을 한다.

2. 중요한 세부 정보를 Note-taking하면서 강의의 큰 구조를 파악한다.
TASK 4에서는 화자가 다음에 다룰 내용, 화자가 예로 들거나 나열한 세부 정보가 문제로 연결될 가능성도 크지만, 화자가 특정 개념을 소개하는 방식이나 강의의 전체 구조를 묻는 문제도 자주 출제된다. 따라서, 세부 정보들을 Note-taking하면서 강의가 어떤 구조로 전개되는지도 함께 파악해야 한다.

3. 핵심적인 용어의 개념 정의에 집중한다.
강의에서는 특정 개념이나 용어에 대한 정의와 설명이 이루어지며, 이 개념에 대한 질문이 자주 출제된다. 따라서, 화자가 특히 강조하거나 "이것은 중요합니다", "핵심은", "정의하자면" 등의 표현을 사용할 때 집중해서 들어야 한다.

4. paraphrasing된 정답을 고른다.
대부분 문제의 정답은 강의의 내용을 paraphrasing해서 나오므로, 제대로 paraphrasing된 정답을 고른다. 강의에서 들은 단어 및 일부 표현을 그대로 쓴 선택지는 오히려 오답일 가능성이 많다는 것도 염두에 둔다.

Study Guide

1. 강의의 일반적인 구조에 익숙해지자.
강의는 주제 소개→개념 설명→예시 제공→다음에 다룰 내용 등의 일반적인 구조를 가지므로, 이러한 구조를 익히면 주요 정보를 효율적으로 파악할 수 있다.

2. 학술 용어와 기초 배경 지식을 알아두자.
강의를 들으며 많은 정보를 소화해야 하는데, TOEFL에 자주 출제되는 학문 분야의 용어와 기본적인 배경 지식을 알아두면 강의의 내용을 이해하기 더욱 수월해진다.

3. 개념과 예시를 연결 짓는 연습을 하자.
대부분의 강의는 개념을 설명한 후 그에 대한 구체적인 예시나 사례를 제시하며, 개념과 예시 간의 관계를 묻는 문제가 자주 출제된다. 따라서, 예시가 언급될 때는 그것이 어떤 개념이나 원리를 설명하기 위한 것인지 연결 짓는 것을 연습하면 문제를 더 정확하게 풀 수 있다.

무료 토플자료·유학정보 공유
goHackers.com

Section I
Question Types

Section I에서는 TASK 4에 출제되는 문제 유형을 6가지로 구분하여 각 유형의 특징과 질문 형태, 실제 문제 풀이에 적용 가능한 전략들을 소개하고 있다. 또한 연습 문제 및 실전 문제를 통해 각 문제 유형을 효과적으로 공략할 수 있도록 하였다.

TASK 4의 Question Types에는 다음의 6가지가 있다.

1. Main Topic/Purpose Questions
2. Discuss Next Questions
3. Detail Questions
4. Intention Questions
5. Organization Questions
6. Inference Questions

Hackers Updated TOEFL LISTENING

1. Main Topic/Purpose Questions

Overview

강의에서 중심이 되는 내용이 무엇인지를 묻는 문제 유형이다. Main Topic 문제는 강의에서 가르치고자 하는 중점적인 내용이 무엇인지를 묻는다. Main Purpose 문제의 경우 강의를 진행하는 주요 목적을 묻는다. 매 시험 3~4문제가 출제되며, 강의의 첫 번째 문제로 자주 출제된다. Main Purpose 문제는 출제 빈도가 비교적 낮다.

Types of Questions

Main Topic 문제는 주로 mainly about, topic, mainly discuss라는 표현을 포함한 형태로 출제되며, Main Purpose 문제는 main purpose라는 표현을 포함한 형태로 출제된다.

Main Topic

What is the talk mainly about?

What aspect of jazz is the talk mainly about?

What is the topic of the talk?

What is the main topic of the talk?

What does the speaker mainly discuss?

Main Purpose

What is the purpose of the talk?

What is the main purpose of the lecture?

Hackers Strategy

1 강의의 주제 및 목적은 주로 강의의 첫 부분에서 들을 수 있다.

강의의 주제 및 목적은 강의의 첫 부분에 언급되는 경우가 많으므로, 강의의 첫 부분을 집중해서 들어야 한다. 특히 첫 부분에서 앞으로의 강의에서 핵심적으로 다루는 용어에 대한 정의를 설명하는 경우가 많으므로, 이를 잘 들으면 주제를 쉽게 파악할 수 있다.

2 주제를 언급할 때 자주 쓰는 표현을 기억한다.

강의에서는 주로 We're going to discuss ~, I want to talk about ~, Let's explore ~, The focus of the lecture is ~, The key point is ~ 뒤에 주제가 언급되므로, 이러한 표현들을 알아두고 귀를 기울여 듣는다.

3 자주 나오는 오답 유형에 주의한다.

강의 내용의 일부만을 다루는 오답, 강의에서 언급된 단어를 포함하고 있지만 내용이 틀린 오답, 강의에서 언급되지 않은 내용에 관한 오답이 자주 등장한다. 특히, 강의의 핵심 개념을 설명하기 위한 세부 사항을 이용한 오답은 헷갈릴 수 있으므로 주의한다.

Example

🎧 T4_S1_1_Example

Script

Today, we are going to discuss bird development post-hatching. Specifically, we will talk about the two categories of hatching birds, precocial and altricial hatchlings. As we've already discussed, most birds begin life in an egg and enter the world through a process called hatching. Well, that seems obvious enough to any of us who eat eggs, but what happens to the chicks once they're hatched? It depends on what kind of bird they are.

What is the talk mainly about?

Ⓐ Formation of bird embryos before hatching
Ⓑ Evolution of egg-laying animals
Ⓒ Two types of hatchling development
Ⓓ Survival advantages of each hatching strategy

정답 Ⓒ

해설 강의가 주로 무엇에 관한 것인지를 묻는 문제이므로, 강의의 첫 부분에서 정답의 단서를 찾을 수 있다. 화자가 "we are going to discuss bird development post-hatching."라며 부화 후 새의 발달에 대해 논의한다고 했고, "we will talk about the two categories of hatching birds"라며 부화한 새의 두 범주에 대해 이야기 할 것이라고 했으므로 Ⓒ가 정답임을 알 수 있다.

HACKERS PRACTICE 🎧 T4_S1_1_Practice

Listen to each academic talk and fill in the blanks. Then choose the best answer for the question. (You will hear each talk twice.)

01

Let's _____ _____. Enzymes are proteins that act as biological catalysts. In other words, they _____ _____ _____ within all living organisms. Essentially, what they do is _____ of a chemical reaction. Now, to help you understand what an enzyme does, I'd like to look a little more closely into the actual _____ _____.

What is the talk mainly about?

Ⓐ The mechanism of enzymatic processes
Ⓑ The discovery of enzyme functions
Ⓒ Applications of enzymes in industry
Ⓓ Different types of biological substances

02

A lot of the traditional arts by Native North Americans _____ _____ over the centuries by European travelers. These artworks were also _____ the public's taste in art. Originally, they were produced in a completely different cultural context. In some cases, native people gave a blanket or piece of pottery qualities that weren't related to _____. And some groups produced items that revealed ____ _____.

What is the topic of the talk?

Ⓐ Cultural changes in native communities
Ⓑ Native American production techniques
Ⓒ Recontextualization of indigenous art
Ⓓ Functional values of native crafts

03

I'm going to focus on _____
_____. Actually, there are _____
_____ about it. Some people argue that the Moon _____ Earth, while others believe it formed elsewhere and was later captured by Earth's gravity. In recent decades, the theory that the Moon formed from debris produced _____ between Earth and another body has gained wide acceptance.

What is the main topic of the talk?

Ⓐ The physical properties of the Moon
Ⓑ The impact of Moon research on planetary science
Ⓒ Findings from recent Moon missions
Ⓓ Different theories about the Moon's formation

04

Today, we're discussing _____
_____. You might wonder, if ancient volcanoes brought diamonds to the surface, why can't _____ do the same?
Diamonds form 150 kilometers below Earth's surface _____.
Ancient volcanic eruptions originated from these depths, but _____ shallow magma chambers within the crust, at depths less than 30 kilometers. This explains why diamond mining focuses on ancient formations rather than _____.

What is the topic of the talk?

Ⓐ Depth differences between crustal layers
Ⓑ Volcanic processes and diamond formation
Ⓒ Modern diamond mining techniques
Ⓓ The timeline of Earth's volcanic evolution

HACKERS TEST 🎧 T4_S1_1_Test

[01-04] Listen to a talk in a psychology class.

01 What is the main topic of the talk?

Ⓐ The limitations of scientific research
Ⓑ Exceptional abilities in young children
Ⓒ Ways psychologists gather information
Ⓓ The history of psychological observation

02 Why does the speaker mention the V-pattern?

Ⓐ To illustrate an example of naturalistic observation
Ⓑ To explain why birds are ideal research subjects
Ⓒ To compare bird behavior with human behavior
Ⓓ To introduce the limitations of observing in nature

03 According to the speaker, what is a problem with using case studies?

Ⓐ They are more expensive than other research methods.
Ⓑ The researchers may have difficulty seeing subjects clearly.
Ⓒ The results are difficult to apply to the general population.
Ⓓ They can only be conducted in laboratory settings.

04 What will the speaker most likely discuss next?

Ⓐ Case studies of individuals with exceptional abilities
Ⓑ Alternative research approaches not yet mentioned
Ⓒ Modern technology used in observational studies
Ⓓ Notable results from each research methodology

[05-08] Listen to a talk in an environmental science class.

05 What is the talk mainly about?

Ⓐ Various industrial uses of activated charcoal
Ⓑ Archaeological discoveries related to fuel sources
Ⓒ Chemical reactions involved in charcoal activation
Ⓓ Applications of charcoal throughout human history

06 Why does the speaker mention wood?

Ⓐ To describe the process of converting wood into charcoal
Ⓑ To point out the weight-to-heat ratio advantage of charcoal
Ⓒ To discuss the sustainability issues of traditional fuel sources
Ⓓ To examine the historical shift from one fuel source to another

07 What does the speaker mention as a way that activated charcoal helps in battlefield conditions?

Ⓐ By creating smoke signals for communication
Ⓑ By allowing for lightweight fuel transportation
Ⓒ By offering protection against poisonous gases
Ⓓ By providing camouflage through its dark color

08 What will the speaker discuss next?

Ⓐ The potential negative effects of charcoal usage
Ⓑ The environmental benefits of activated charcoal
Ⓒ The most efficient methods of charcoal activation
Ⓓ The archaeological evidence for prehistoric charcoal use

HACKERS TEST

[09-12] Listen to a talk in an art class.

09 What is the topic of the talk?

Ⓐ The role of natural materials in landscape-based art
Ⓑ A history of postmodernism in European art
Ⓒ Famous techniques used by postmodern artists
Ⓓ Two distinct forms of postmodern artistic practice

10 Why does the speaker mention the desert or the forest?

Ⓐ To illustrate the typical settings for earth art
Ⓑ To compare urban and natural artistic settings
Ⓒ To describe where art materials are sourced from
Ⓓ To explain why some art is inaccessible to the public

11 Why does the speaker mention the backdrop?

Ⓐ To demonstrate the importance of lighting in art
Ⓑ To show how site-specific art considers the site's context
Ⓒ To explain painting techniques in postmodern art
Ⓓ To contrast with the background elements in sculpture

12 What will the speaker most likely discuss next?

Ⓐ The artistic techniques of Robert Smithson
Ⓑ Famous earth art installations around the world
Ⓒ Lawrence Weiner's artistic techniques and works
Ⓓ A comparison between Smithson and other earth artists

[13-16] Listen to a talk in a literature class.

13 What aspect of Romantic poetry is the talk mainly about?

Ⓐ The biographical details of major Romantic poets
Ⓑ The historical context of the Romantic period
Ⓒ The influence of Romantic poetry on other art forms
Ⓓ The way Romantic poets viewed nature

14 How does the speaker explain the characteristics of Romantic poets?

Ⓐ By analyzing poems in chronological order
Ⓑ By comparing Romantic poetry to an earlier tradition
Ⓒ By focusing on the life experiences of individual poets
Ⓓ By examining the political influences on Romantic poetry

15 Why does the speaker mention *The Rime of the Ancient Mariner*?

Ⓐ To demonstrate how Romantic poets used religious themes
Ⓑ To highlight Coleridge's mastery of narrative poetry
Ⓒ To illustrate how nature imagery explored deeper themes
Ⓓ To show how popular sea imagery was in Romantic literature

16 According to the speaker, why did Romantic poets prioritize imagination over reason?

Ⓐ They felt intuitive insight could reveal profound truths.
Ⓑ They believed rational approaches ignored human feelings.
Ⓒ They thought logical analysis restricted poetic inspiration.
Ⓓ They wanted to emphasize personal experience over scholarship.

Answers p.536

2. Discuss Next Questions

Overview

화자가 강의에서 다음에 다룰 내용을 묻는 문제 유형이다. 매 시험 1~2문제가 출제되며, 강의의 마지막 문제로 자주 출제된다.

Types of Questions

주로 discuss next라는 표현을 포함한 형태로 출제된다.

Discuss Next

What will the speaker discuss next?

What will the speaker most likely discuss next?

What aspect of renewable energy will the speaker discuss next?

Hackers Strategy

1 다음에 다룰 내용은 강의의 마지막 부분에서 들을 수 있다.

Discuss Next 문제는 강의에서 다음에 다룰 내용을 묻기 때문에, 정답의 단서는 대부분 강의의 마지막 부분에 언급된다. 따라서, 마지막까지 강의를 집중해서 잘 들어야 한다.

2 다음에 다룰 내용을 나타내는 표현에 귀를 기울인다.

Next, Let's turn to ~, Let's now examine ~, This leads us to ~와 같은 표현이 포함된 문장을 들으면 Discuss Next 문제가 출제될 것을 예상할 수 있으며, 주로 해당 표현들 뒤에서 정답의 단서를 들을 수 있다.

3 자주 나오는 오답 유형에 주의한다.

강의에서 언급된 단어를 포함하고 있지만 내용이 틀린 오답이나 강의에서 언급된 사실과 전혀 관련이 없는 오답이 자주 등장한다. 특히, 강의에서 중점적으로 다뤘던 내용이 오답으로 종종 등장하므로, 헷갈리지 않도록 주의한다.

Example 🎧 T4_S1_2_Example

Script

The American labor movement arose because of inequality between employers and employees. Workers wanted more control over their hours and compensation. The first to strike were printers, followed by cabinetmakers and carpenters, leading to various labor unions. Unlike Western European countries where the government regulated wages, American unions believed workers and employers should negotiate directly. This difference meant American workers often had to struggle—sometimes risking their lives—to achieve basic rights like the eight-hour workday and minimum wage. Let's now examine what these workers' struggles actually involved.

What will the speaker most likely discuss next?

Ⓐ Specific examples of conflicts during labor disputes
Ⓑ Influence of European labor movements on American unions
Ⓒ The role of the government in modern labor negotiations
Ⓓ Biographical accounts of prominent labor leaders

정답 Ⓐ

해설 화자가 다음에 다룰 내용을 묻는 문제이므로, 강의 마지막 부분에서 정답의 단서를 찾을 수 있다. 화자가 "Let's now examine what these workers' struggles actually involved."라며 근로자들의 투쟁이 실제로 무엇을 포함했는지 살펴보자고 했으므로 Ⓐ가 정답임을 알 수 있다.

HACKERS PRACTICE 🎧 T4_S1_2_Practice

Listen to each academic talk and fill in the blanks. Then choose the best answer for the question. (You will hear each talk twice.)

01

While quilting originated in Egypt and Mongolia, European colonists _____ _____ America in the 1600s. The real transformation occurred in the 1800s when American textile mills _____ _____, high-quality fabrics. Revolutionary printing methods and synthetic dyes created unprecedented color palettes, inspiring quilters to _____ _____. This combination of industrial innovation and domestic creativity established quilting as a truly American art form. Next, we will explore _____ _____ with American pioneers and evolved into distinct regional styles.

What aspect of American quilting will the speaker discuss next?

Ⓐ How it influenced textile manufacturing processes
Ⓑ How it developed different regional characteristics
Ⓒ How it competed with European quilting traditions
Ⓓ How it declined after the Industrial Revolution

02

Today, we're _____ _____ and their vulnerability. Charles Elton introduced this concept in 1927, describing energy flow from plants to herbivores to carnivores. Remove one link, and _____ _____. Consider sea turtles: these coastal animals lay eggs containing fluids that nourish dune vegetation, preventing erosion. When conservationists _____ _____, vegetation died, coastlines eroded, and marine animals disappeared. This demonstrates a concept called ecological interconnectedness. Let's take a closer look at the cases of _____.

What will the speaker most likely discuss next?

Ⓐ Climate change effects on global food chains
Ⓑ Charles Elton's other contributions to ecology
Ⓒ Detailed analysis of predator-prey relationships
Ⓓ Specific examples of ecological interconnectedness

03

Alright, I want to _____ _____ about the Great Depression. Most think it was simply free market's failure, but _____ _____ a crucial role. US authorities lowered interest rates and increased money supply in the 1920s, _____ _____. This easy money led to poor investment decisions and unstable businesses that inevitably collapsed, triggering _____ and economic hardship. Then, why did the government make such mistakes back then? Let's explore ____ _____.

What will the speaker discuss next?

Ⓐ Labor union responses to economic hardship
Ⓑ Recovery timeline and restoration efforts
Ⓒ Rationale behind authorities' policy decisions
Ⓓ International trade impacts during the period

04

Today, we'll explore one of humanity's oldest meteorological tools, which is the weathervane. Archaeological evidence _____ _____ the first century BC, with the famous Tower of Winds in Athens featuring a spectacular bronze Triton statue holding a directional wand. This was an elaborate representation demonstrating the _____ _____ in ancient societies. Before modern forecasting existed, people worldwide relied on these devices _____ _____. These were crucial for agricultural success. Now, let's take a look at _____ the weather using a weathervane.

What will the speaker most likely discuss next?

Ⓐ Weather prediction methods using weathervanes
Ⓑ Historical development of weather science
Ⓒ Materials used in early meteorological equipment
Ⓓ Social impact of weather prediction tools

Answers p.540

HACKERS TEST

[01-04] Listen to a talk in a biology class.

01 What is the talk mainly about?

Ⓐ The evolutionary advantages of pouches
Ⓑ Different reproductive strategies in mammals
Ⓒ The nurturing behaviors of female marsupials
Ⓓ The importance of placentas in animal reproduction

02 What does the speaker imply about baby marsupials?

Ⓐ It develops faster than placental mammals.
Ⓑ It doesn't return after leaving the pouch.
Ⓒ It is born in a highly underdeveloped state.
Ⓓ It doesn't need the mother's milk to survive.

03 According to the speaker, why can using the term "placental mammals" be misleading?

Ⓐ The placenta is not unique to non-marsupial mammals.
Ⓑ Placental animals can also have pouches like marsupials.
Ⓒ The term focuses too much on one aspect of reproduction.
Ⓓ Both animal groups rely equally on placentas for development.

04 What will the speaker most likely discuss next?

Ⓐ Specific examples of placental mammals
Ⓑ The impact of climate change on mammals
Ⓒ Factors explaining the divergence in reproductive strategies
Ⓓ Common misconceptions about marsupial reproduction

[05-08] Listen to a talk in a music class.

05 What is the main topic of the talk?

  Ⓐ The distinctive elements of musical Impressionism
  Ⓑ The relationship between visual and musical art forms
  Ⓒ The evolution of chord progressions in classical music
  Ⓓ The revolutionary compositional techniques in music history

06 What does the speaker indicate about Debussy?

  Ⓐ He deliberately rejected all traditional musical principles.
  Ⓑ He was primarily influenced by Romantic composers.
  Ⓒ He was criticized for his unconventional techniques.
  Ⓓ He created a sense of floating using whole-tone scales.

07 Why does the speaker mention parallel chords?

  Ⓐ To highlight an unconventional Impressionist approach
  Ⓑ To explain why later composers abandoned these techniques
  Ⓒ To emphasize why Impressionist music was difficult to perform
  Ⓓ To demonstrate how modern music evolved from Impressionism

08 What will the speaker most likely discuss next?

  Ⓐ The legacy of Impressionism in contemporary music
  Ⓑ The key features and historical context of Neoclassicism
  Ⓒ The biographical details of Neoclassical composers
  Ⓓ The rapid decline of the Impressionist movement

HACKERS TEST

[09-12] Listen to a talk in a business management class.

09 What is the talk mainly about?

   Ⓐ The psychology behind customer disappointment
   Ⓑ A counterintuitive concept in customer satisfaction
   Ⓒ The influence of advertising on customer experience
   Ⓓ Service failures and their impact on business reputation

10 Why does the speaker mention her daughter?

   Ⓐ To show the limitations of the service recovery paradox
   Ⓑ To highlight the stress caused by technology failures
   Ⓒ To present a case of effective problem resolution
   Ⓓ To criticize the company's initial product quality

11 According to the speaker, why does the service recovery paradox work?

   Ⓐ Companies exceed customer expectations when resolving issues.
   Ⓑ Manufacturers shift customers' focus away from the original issue.
   Ⓒ Defective products are replaced with better-quality alternatives.
   Ⓓ Companies convince customers that the problem was an isolated incident.

12 What will the speaker most likely discuss next?

   Ⓐ Long-term consequences of service failures
   Ⓑ Scientific studies about service recovery constraints
   Ⓒ Strategies for rebuilding damaged business reputations
   Ⓓ Companies with successful crisis management approaches

[13-16] Listen to a talk in a physics class.

13 What is the talk mainly about?

  Ⓐ How noise affects human perception
  Ⓑ Harmful effects of environmental noise
  Ⓒ Different types and perceptions of noise
  Ⓓ Physical classification criteria of noise

14 What does the speaker say about white noise?

  Ⓐ It should be avoided during sleep hours.
  Ⓑ It is similar to the sound of busy street traffic.
  Ⓒ It is too complex for most people to recognize.
  Ⓓ It contains all audible frequencies simultaneously.

15 Why does the speaker mention white light?

  Ⓐ To visualize the concept of combined frequencies
  Ⓑ To introduce a similar study on sensory perception
  Ⓒ To distinguish between natural and artificial light sources
  Ⓓ To explain why white noise appears white in spectral displays

16 What will the speaker most likely discuss next?

  Ⓐ Health impacts of different noise types
  Ⓑ Audio demonstrations of blue and pink noise
  Ⓒ Research on noise sensitivity variations in humans
  Ⓓ Cultural perceptions of pleasant and unpleasant sounds

Answers p.541

3. Detail Questions

Overview

강의를 통해 알 수 있는 다양한 세부 사실을 묻는 문제 유형이다. 질문에서 묻는 내용과 질문 형태가 매우 다양하다. 특히 강의에서는 화자가 언급하지 않은 내용을 묻는 문제도 출제되므로, 시험에 출제될 수 있는 다양한 Detail 문제들을 알아 두는 것이 중요하다. 매 시험 4~5문제가 출제되어 출제 비율도 상당히 높다.

Types of Questions

Detail 문제는 세부적으로 묻고자 하는 내용에 따라 다양한 형태로 출제된다. say about, point라는 표현을 포함한 형태로 출제되어 특정 대상에 대해 화자가 언급한 사항을 묻거나, NOT이나 EXCEPT라는 표현이 포함되어 화자가 언급하지 않은 내용을 묻는다. how라는 표현을 포함한 형태로 출제되어 방법을 묻거나, 그 외에도 강의 안의 세부 사항에 대해 묻는 다양한 문제가 출제되기도 한다.

Mention

What does the speaker say about cultural relativism?

What point does the speaker make about improvisation?

What does the speaker point out about a malaria-carrying mosquito?

Not Mentioned

What is NOT mentioned as an example of digital art?

According to the speaker, the research contributed to all of the following EXCEPT

Method

According to the talk, how do economists measure income inequality?

Etc.

What is an important feature of volcanic eruptions?

According to the speaker, what is a central concern of comparative linguists?

Hackers Strategy

1 화자가 주요한 개념과 관련하여 언급하는 사실들을 Note-taking한다.

화자가 강의에서 다루는 주요한 개념에 대해 몇 가지 사실을 설명하는 경우에는 이에 대한 문제가 출제될 확률이 높으므로, 주요한 내용을 Note-taking해두는 것이 중요하다. 특히, TASK 4에서는 강의에 언급되지 않은 내용을 묻는 문제도 출제되므로 강의에 언급된 세부 사항을 Note-taking하는 것이 중요하다.

2 화자가 한 말을 paraphrasing한 것을 정답으로 고른다.

강의에서 출제되는 Detail 문제의 정답에서는 화자가 했던 말을 그대로 인용하기보다 다른 표현으로 바꾸어 쓰는 경우가 많다.

3 자주 나오는 오답 유형에 주의한다.

강의에서 언급된 단어를 포함하고 있지만 내용이 틀린 오답이나 강의에서 언급된 사실과 전혀 관련이 없는 오답이 자주 등장한다. 특히, 이미 알고 있는 사실이더라도 강의에 언급되지 않은 내용을 정답으로 고르지 않도록 주의한다.

Example 🎧 T4_S1_3_Example

Script

Let's talk about purple loosestrife, scientifically known as *Lythrum salicaria*. This invasive plant has become an ecological concern in America, outcompeting native vegetation and disrupting wetland ecosystems. So how did it get there? It was probably in the early 1800s when purple loosestrife was brought over to America from Europe. A couple of researchers identified it in the 1830s as a "native" plant, although now we know that's not true. In any case, the plant is known to have arrived with rocks or water in the lower part of the ship, which were used to stabilize ships. Those ships sailed from Northern Europe, which was home to major export centers for trade with America.

According to the talk, how did purple loosestrife get to America?

Ⓐ By being imported as an ornamental plant
Ⓑ By naturally migrating across the Atlantic
Ⓒ By being brought over by American botanists
Ⓓ By being carried in the water at the base of ships

정답 Ⓓ

해설 purple loosestrife(털부처꽃)가 아메리카 대륙에 어떻게 들어왔는지를 묻는 문제이므로, purple loosestrife와 관련하여 화자가 강의에서 언급한 사실에서 정답의 단서를 찾을 수 있다. 화자가 "the plant is known to have arrived with rocks or water in the lower part of the ship"이라며 배 아래 부분의 돌이나 물과 함께 섞여 도착한 것으로 알려져 있다고 했으므로 Ⓓ가 정답임을 알 수 있다.

HACKERS PRACTICE 🎧 T4_S1_3_Practice

Listen to each academic talk and fill in the blanks. Then choose the best answer for the question. (You will hear each talk twice.)

01

Today, we'll discuss insomnia, _____ _____ or staying asleep. There are two types: acute and chronic.
Acute insomnia, which is caused by _____ _____, lasts only a few days and typically resolves on its own. On the other hand, chronic insomnia occurs at least three nights a week for over three months. Various physical and psychological factors _____ _____.
Now, treatment for insomnia _____ _____. This includes consistent bedtimes, _____, limiting caffeine, and maintaining cool, dark sleeping environments without distractions.

What is NOT mentioned as a treatment for insomnia?

Ⓐ Strenuous exercise
Ⓑ Caffeine restriction
Ⓒ Consistent bedtimes
Ⓓ Temperature control

02

The _____ is of great interest to scientists. Out of the past 1,150 years, the Sun has been _____ _____ the last sixty. With the increase in sunspots, the Earth has been getting warmer. This information suggests that changes in solar activity _____ _____. In fact, historical data and climate records support the idea that _____ _____ have played a role in long-term climate changes.

What does the speaker say about solar activity?

Ⓐ It peaked approximately 1,150 years ago.
Ⓑ It follows predictable cycles every sixty years.
Ⓒ It has been particularly intense in recent decades.
Ⓓ It has minimal impact on global weather patterns.

03

Bubonic plague is _____ _____. During the reign of the Roman Emperor Justinian, about 50% of the Mediterranean population died from the plague. This clearly shows that the plague was _____ _____ disease. Improved hygiene and quarantine measures have helped control it, but _____ _____ in parts of Asia, such as India, where around 5,000 cases were reported in 1994.

According to the speaker, what is a key characteristic of bubonic plague?

Ⓐ Slow progression over many years
Ⓑ Resistance to modern quarantine measures
Ⓒ Deadly infection affecting only children
Ⓓ Continued presence in certain regions

04

Absolute dating is a method that establishes _____ or event in terms of calendar years. It often relies on the decay of radioactive isotopes, such as carbon-14 and uranium-238, _____ _____. For example, geologists may find three layers of different types of rock. Determining _____ _____ is straightforward: the deepest layer is the oldest, the middle layer is younger, and the uppermost layer is the youngest. However, if a piece of pottery is found in the middle layer and the geologists want to know exactly which period it belongs to, absolute dating can be used to _____.

According to the talk, how do scientists determine the precise age of an object?

Ⓐ By comparing it to surrounding rock layers
Ⓑ By analyzing the decay of radioactive isotopes
Ⓒ By examining its physical appearance
Ⓓ By characterizing its mineral composition

Answers p.545

HACKERS TEST

[01-04] Listen to a talk on a podcast about sociology.

01 What is the main topic of the talk?

Ⓐ The rising costs of college education
Ⓑ Financial aid programs for low-income students
Ⓒ The relationship between education and social mobility
Ⓓ Hidden expenses at higher educational institutions

02 What point does the speaker make about recent research on education?

Ⓐ It suggests that the link between education and social mobility is complicated.
Ⓑ It shows that financial barriers have been completely eliminated.
Ⓒ It reveals that wealthy families have no educational advantages.
Ⓓ It proves that education no longer provides social mobility opportunities.

03 What does the speaker say about students from affluent families?

Ⓐ They depend on mentoring programs for academic success.
Ⓑ They have advantages that strengthen college applications.
Ⓒ They focus more on career training than academic preparation.
Ⓓ They tend to underestimate the role of education in social mobility.

04 What will the speaker discuss next?

Ⓐ Research findings on educational inequality
Ⓑ Career counseling strategies for disadvantaged students
Ⓒ International comparisons of education systems
Ⓓ Examples of effective educational support programs

[05-08] Listen to a talk in an anthropology class.

05 What is the main topic of the talk?

Ⓐ The role of play in human culture and civilization
Ⓑ The distinction between work and leisure activities
Ⓒ The significance of rule-following in social contexts
Ⓓ The relationship between games and legal systems

06 Why does the speaker mention hide-and-seek?

Ⓐ To suggest how culture influences game selection
Ⓑ To demonstrate the universal nature of children's play
Ⓒ To show that games teach important social behavior
Ⓓ To argue that rules are unnecessary in child development

07 What is NOT mentioned as a factor that play can shape?

Ⓐ Military conflict
Ⓑ Legal institutions
Ⓒ Social organization
Ⓓ Essential survival skills

08 Why does the speaker mention ordinary life?

Ⓐ To contrast adults' and children's games
Ⓑ To demonstrate that play transcends necessity
Ⓒ To highlight the seriousness of cultural institutions
Ⓓ To explain why games require structured rules

HACKERS TEST

[09-12] Listen to a talk in an astronomy class.

09 What is the talk mainly about?

Ⓐ Observational techniques for invisible radiation
Ⓑ The properties and importance of high-energy photons
Ⓒ The challenges of conducting astronomical observations
Ⓓ A comparison among different electromagnetic waves

10 What does the speaker imply about gamma rays?

Ⓐ They are primarily artificial rather than natural.
Ⓑ They are easily detected by ground-based instruments.
Ⓒ They have moderate energy levels compared to X-rays.
Ⓓ They emerge from regions with extreme conditions.

11 Why does the speaker mention the Compton Gamma Ray Observatory?

Ⓐ To describe the satellite's orbital characteristics
Ⓑ To discuss the limitations of current instruments
Ⓒ To illustrate solutions for atmospheric interference
Ⓓ To explain the principles of electromagnetic detection

12 According to the speaker, why should gamma rays be studied?

Ⓐ They offer information about planetary atmospheres.
Ⓑ They provide insights into Earth's geological processes.
Ⓒ They help develop advanced medical imaging techniques.
Ⓓ They reveal information about cosmic expansion processes.

[13-16] Listen to a talk in a biology class.

13 What is the main topic of the talk?

Ⓐ Methods for determining twin types during pregnancy
Ⓑ Formation and characteristics of different twin types
Ⓒ Parental genetic contributions to twin development
Ⓓ Environmental effects on the formation of twins' personalities

14 According to the speaker, what do identical twins actually share?

Ⓐ Their personality development
Ⓑ Their physical appearance
Ⓒ Their gender characteristics
Ⓓ Their environmental adaptations

15 What point does the speaker make about fraternal twins?

Ⓐ They develop from separate eggs and separate sperm cells.
Ⓑ They share a single placenta during development.
Ⓒ They demonstrate the same personality traits.
Ⓓ They are typically more similar than identical twins.

16 What will the speaker discuss next?

Ⓐ Treatment options for twin-specific conditions
Ⓑ Parental genetic factors influencing twin pregnancies
Ⓒ Long-term health outcomes for different twin types
Ⓓ Diagnostic approaches for determining twin type

Answers p.547

4. Intention Questions

Overview

강의에서 화자가 특정 대상을 언급한 의도를 묻는 문제 유형이다. 매 시험 2~3문제가 출제된다.

Types of Questions

Why does ~ mention이라는 표현을 포함한 형태로 출제되며, 화자가 강의에서 언급한 대상을 질문에 제시한다.

Intention

  Why does the professor mention surrealism?
  Why does the speaker mention the size of mammals?

Hackers Strategy

1 화자가 언급하는 주장, 예시, 비교 등에 주목한다.
화자는 주로 강의에서 특정 대상을 언급하면서 본인의 주장을 뒷받침하거나, 예시를 들어주거나, 다른 대상과의 비교를 하는데, 이때 언급된 대상이 질문에 제시되는 경우가 많다. 따라서, 화자의 주장이나 화자가 들어주는 예시, 화자가 다른 대상과 비교하는 내용을 집중해서 들으면, 언급된 대상의 목적을 유추할 수 있다.

2 강의의 맥락 속에서 화자의 말을 이해한다.
화자의 의도를 전체적인 맥락 안에서 파악하는 것이 가장 중요하며, 이를 위해서는 강의에서 언급된 말을 통해 그 사이에 함축된 화자의 의도를 파악해야 한다.

3 자주 나오는 오답 유형에 주의한다.
강의에서 알 수 있는 화자의 의도가 아닌 표면적 의미만을 제시한 오답이나 전후 문맥을 잘못 파악한 오답이 자주 등장한다.

Example
🎧 T4_S1_4_Example

Script

I want to talk about the first theory to propose multiple spatial dimensions, the Kaluza-Klein theory. It attempted to unify gravity and electromagnetic force, but it had to assume the existence of a fourth spatial dimension for the theory to work. Theodor Kaluza introduced the idea that a dimension can be small and invisible. Think of a garden hose. From a distance, the hose appears one-dimensional, but up close we can see that it has an extra, circular dimension. The Kaluza-Klein theory suggests the universe may have other dimensions curled up, like the hose's circular dimension, existing on a very small scale.

Why does the professor mention a garden hose?

Ⓐ To describe the known dimensions of the universe
Ⓑ To give an example of an unseen extra dimension
Ⓒ To clarify how an object can have four dimensions
Ⓓ To compare spatial and temporal dimensions

정답 Ⓑ

해설 교수가 정원 호스를 언급한 의도를 묻는 문제이므로, 해당 대상을 언급하면서 함께 한 말에서 정답의 단서를 찾을 수 있다. 교수가 "From a distance, the hose appears one-dimensional, but up close we can see that it has an extra, circular dimension"이라며 호스가 멀리서 봤을 때는 1차원으로 보이지만 가까이 가면 원형의 추가 차원이 있음을 알 수 있다고 했다. 따라서, Kaluza의 생각인 차원이 작고 보이지 않을 수도 있다는 것의 예시를 주기 위해 정원 호스를 언급한 것이므로 Ⓑ가 정답임을 알 수 있다.

HACKERS PRACTICE 🎧 T4_S1_4_Practice

Listen to each academic talk and fill in the blanks. Then choose the best answer for the question. (You will hear each talk twice.)

01

Originally, coyotes were wild animals with _____. However, as suburban development expanded, some coyote populations began _____ _____. What's interesting is their behavioral shift. These urban coyotes have learned that humans pose little threat, and this has led to _____ _____. They've started hunting during daylight hours and _____ _____. Some even approach children directly, which represents _____ from their traditionally cautious nature.

Why does the speaker mention children?

Ⓐ To describe the natural prey preferences of urban coyotes
Ⓑ To criticize parents for not supervising their children properly
Ⓒ To highlight the unprecedented boldness of urban coyotes
Ⓓ To propose educational programs about wildlife encounters

02

Today, let's examine the _____ _____ underlying the Big Bang theory. Many people believe the Big Bang occurred at _____. But scientists actually assume the universe is infinite and has no boundaries or edges. This means the Big Bang occurred _____ _____. That is, what's expanding isn't the universe itself, but the space-time continuum within it. Additionally, the Big Bang theory relies on Einstein's theory of relativity, which describes _____ _____ rather than absolute. This not only explains gravitational interactions between all matter in our universe but also serves as _____ _____ the Big Bang theory itself.

Why does the professor mention Einstein's theory of relativity?

Ⓐ To illustrate how gravity affects cosmic expansion
Ⓑ To demonstrate that time flows at different rates
Ⓒ To prove that the universe started from a single point
Ⓓ To provide scientific basis for the Big Bang theory

03

Scientists create climate models using historical data and computer simulations to _____ _____. A fascinating case involves research on _____ _____. Climate scientist Lonnie Thompson analyzed thousands of samples worldwide and discovered evidence of _____ _____ approximately 5,200 years ago. Remarkably, he claims that current climate patterns _____ _____, suggesting we're approaching a similar dramatic change.

Why does the professor mention ice cores?

Ⓐ To suggest alternative research methodologies
Ⓑ To show the cyclical nature of climate patterns
Ⓒ To challenge existing climate change theories
Ⓓ To prove that climate models are unreliable

04

When psychologists first began mapping the brain's emotional circuits, they discovered fascinating connections between our _____ _____. They found that some people show heightened activity in the amygdala, the brain's alarm center, making them _____ _____. Are these differences genetic or learned? Current research suggests that _____. People with overactivated fear circuits often have family histories of anxiety, which indicates _____ _____. However, environmental experiences also _____ _____.

Why does the speaker mention environmental experiences?

Ⓐ To explain the factors that shape fear responses
Ⓑ To prove that environmental factors outweigh genetic factors
Ⓒ To propose new directions for psychological research
Ⓓ To challenge traditional views on anxiety disorders

Answers p.551

HACKERS TEST 🎧 T4_S1_4_Test

[01-04] Listen to a talk in a biology class.

01 What is the talk mainly about?

Ⓐ Scientific research methods in marine biology
Ⓑ The significance of scientists' discovery in 1977
Ⓒ A unique species with remarkable survival adaptations
Ⓓ The relationship between bacteria and marine animals

02 Why does the speaker mention the baby worms?

Ⓐ To explain how tubeworms reproduce in harsh environments
Ⓑ To introduce the concept of metamorphosis in marine life
Ⓒ To demonstrate the feeding habits of young tubeworms
Ⓓ To contrast mobility between life stages

03 What does the speaker imply about the tubeworm?

Ⓐ It can communicate with other tubeworms in its vicinity.
Ⓑ It has survived despite lacking basic anatomical features.
Ⓒ It has evolved differently from other deep-sea creatures.
Ⓓ It is the most recently discovered species at hydrothermal vents.

04 What will the speaker most likely discuss next?

Ⓐ The mechanism of bacterial entry into tubeworms
Ⓑ Scientific research techniques for studying deep-sea life
Ⓒ The classification of bacterial species found in tubeworms
Ⓓ Reasons why tubeworms lack mouths and digestive systems

[05-08] Listen to a talk in a sociology class.

05 What is the main topic of the talk?

Ⓐ The evolution of research methods in sociology
Ⓑ The formative experiences of post-war generations
Ⓒ The challenges in distinguishing age-related behaviors
Ⓓ The significance of shared experiences within age groups

06 Why does the speaker discuss the Baby Boomer cohort?

Ⓐ To criticize their response to advancements in technology
Ⓑ To provide a timeline for the development of cohort analysis
Ⓒ To present a concrete example of a cohort group
Ⓓ To compare the Baby Boomer cohort with other groups

07 What can a cohort analysis contribute to sociology?

Ⓐ Categorization of cultural differences between societies
Ⓑ Explanation of behavioral differences between generations
Ⓒ Prediction of future technological adoption trends in society
Ⓓ Recognition of universal behavioral patterns across all age groups

08 What will the speaker discuss next?

Ⓐ The limitations of traditional cohort analysis
Ⓑ Examples of digital technology use across generations
Ⓒ Professional viewpoints on generational behavior patterns
Ⓓ The methodology of distinguishing between different effects

HACKERS TEST

[09-12] Listen to a talk in a psychology class.

09 What is the talk mainly about?

  Ⓐ The psychological mechanism behind the Barnum effect
  Ⓑ The psychological effects of positive and negative feedback
  Ⓒ The connection between horoscopes and self-identity
  Ⓓ The manipulation techniques used in fortune-telling

10 What does the speaker say about P.T. Barnum?

  Ⓐ He was the creator of personality tests used in modern psychology.
  Ⓑ He established the psychological principle of self-confirmation bias.
  Ⓒ He was famous for his ability to connect with general audiences.
  Ⓓ He collaborated with early psychologists on personality studies.

11 Why does the speaker mention psychologists?

  Ⓐ To introduce controversial views in personality psychology
  Ⓑ To suggest better approaches to understanding personality
  Ⓒ To explain why personality tests remain popular despite criticism
  Ⓓ To provide evidence about the effectiveness of the Barnum effect

12 What will the speaker most likely discuss next?

  Ⓐ Advanced psychological research on personality traits
  Ⓑ The potentially harmful impacts of the Barnum effect
  Ⓒ The evolution of psychological testing methods
  Ⓓ Examples of famous personality psychologists

[13-16] Listen to a talk in a geology class.

13 What is the main topic of the talk?

Ⓐ The role of microorganisms in soil formation
Ⓑ The importance of parent material in soil formation
Ⓒ The relationship between water and soil formation
Ⓓ The process of soil development and its components

14 What does the speaker say about the two main types of weathering?

Ⓐ They occur simultaneously in most environments.
Ⓑ They create soil through distinct breakdown processes.
Ⓒ Physical weathering primarily affects limestone and chalk.
Ⓓ Chemical weathering is more common in desert environments.

15 Why does the speaker mention the Makgadikgadi Pans?

Ⓐ To contrast physical and chemical weathering processes
Ⓑ To explain why calcium and magnesium improve soil fertility
Ⓒ To provide evidence of long-term environmental effects on soil
Ⓓ To demonstrate how organic matter forms in extreme conditions

16 What is NOT mentioned as a category of organic matter?

Ⓐ Slow
Ⓑ Active
Ⓒ Soluble
Ⓓ Passive

Answers p.552

5. Organization Questions

Overview

강의에서 화자가 정보를 어떻게 구성하고 전개하는지를 묻는 문제 유형이다. 강의 내용이 서로 어떤 구조로 연결되어 있는지를 묻는 Organization 문제와 표에 나타난 여러 가지 사실들 간의 연관성을 종합적으로 이해해야 하는 List/Matching/Ordering 문제가 출제된다. 매 시험 0~1문제가 출제되어, 출제 빈도는 낮은 편이다.

Types of Questions

Organization 문제는 How does the speaker라는 표현을 포함한 형태로 출제되며, List/Matching/Ordering 문제에는 질문과 표가 함께 등장하여 표 안의 내용을 채우는 형태로 출제된다.

Organization

How does the speaker introduce the concept of Impressionism?

How does the speaker explain the formation of galaxies?

How does the speaker develop the talk about political campaign strategies?

How does the speaker organize the talk?

List

In the talk, the speaker describes ~. Indicate whether each of the following is ~.

Click in the correct box for each phrase.

	Included (or Yes)	Not included (or No)
Statement A		
Statement B		
Statement C		

Matching

Indicate for each example what type of ~.

Click in the correct box.

	Type A	Type B	Type C
Ex 1			
Ex 2			
Ex 3			

Ordering

The speaker explains the steps in the process of ~. Put these steps in order.

Drag each sentence to the space where it belongs.

Step 1	
Step 2	
Step 3	
Step 4	

- process ex 1
- process ex 2
- process ex 3
- process ex 4

(■ process ex 5)

*선택지의 개수가 정답에 이용될 항목의 개수보다 하나 더 많은 경우가 있다.

Hackers Strategy

1 강의에서 주어지는 정보들 간의 관계를 알려주는 표시어들을 놓치지 않고 듣는다.

강의의 정보들이 구조적으로 혹은 내용상 서로 어떤 관계를 지니는가를 알려주는 표시어들이 있으며, 이러한 표시어를 통해 정보들 간의 관계가 비교, 대조, 유형별로 분류된 관계, 순차적인 관계, 예시 및 열거인지 확인할 수 있다.

비교의 방식에서 자주 쓰이는 표시어

faster/smaller than	These newly found stars were spinning several times **faster than** the sun.
in comparison to	Also, ocean currents are constant and predictable **in comparison to** wind.
likewise	The squid benefit from the Vibrio fischeri when these bacteria luminesce. **Likewise**, the Vibrio fischeri benefit from the squid by consuming food particles the squid supply.
similar(ly) to	The coelacanth's sensory organ functions **similarly to** those in sharks that use an electroreceptor to find prey buried in the sea floor.

대조의 방식에서 자주 쓰이는 표시어

different from	Mammals are **different from** reptiles in their blood temperature regulation methods.
on the other hand	So, these birds have evolved a slender beak to catch their prey most efficiently. **On the other hand**, birds of prey, such as falcons and hawks, have bills that are short and hooked.
whereas	The rural sociologist Ashby conducted research in which she argued that farmers in one locality adopted technological innovations **whereas** similar populations in other areas did not.

유형별로 분류하여 설명하는 방식에서 자주 쓰이는 표시어

There are two types of	**There are two types of** architecture I want to discuss today . . . Victorian and Elizabethan.
can classify	We **can classify** Ancient Greek sculpture into four distinct periods.

순차적인 관계를 설명하는 방식에서 자주 쓰이는 표시어

and then	Human beings had been killing the elk, **and then** the gray wolf, finding no elk to subsist on, turned to other sources of food.
before that	So the government put planks on dirt roads to improve them, but **before that**, people had to put up with a lot of mud and dust when they traveled.
subsequently	The chemically treated and filtered water is **subsequently** degasified and disinfected.

예시 및 열거의 방식에서 자주 쓰이는 표시어

for example	**For example**, the fact that thousands of pieces of jewelry were found buried at these gravesites tells us that these tribes engaged in trade.
in this case	**In this case**, an embankment dam would be more appropriate because the valley is wide.
such as	Simple designs **such as** triangles, zigzags, and dots are used in Indian pottery to represent sacred beliefs.

2 강의 내용이 특정한 전개 방식으로 설명될 때는 각 전개 방식에 따른 문제 유형을 예상해보고 그에 맞게 Note-taking한다.

강의 내용이 비교, 대조, 유형별 설명, 순차적인 설명, 예시 등의 특정한 전개 방식으로 설명될 때는 각 전개 방식에 따라 어떤 문제가 출제될 것인지를 예상해볼 수 있다. 전개 방식을 파악하고 문제를 예상했다면 강의를 들으면서 각 전개 구조에 맞도록 Note-taking해두는 것이 효과적이다.

Example

🎧 T4_S1_5_Example

Script

In the early 20th century, photography emerged as a legitimate fine art form through movements like Pictorialism. The pictorialists formed a group known as Photo-Secession, founded in 1902 by Alfred Stieglitz. Clarence White, who was also a member, became the movement's leader after Stieglitz rejected Pictorialism. Stieglitz changed his mind and came to favor Straight Photography, the exact opposite of Pictorialism. Straight Photography focuses on the subject rather than on methods or equipment used for effects. On the other hand, Pictorialism emphasizes the purely photographic or scenic qualities, which Clarence White strongly supported. With Pictorialism, the focus was not on the subject but on how the photographer presented and manipulated the subject.

How does the speaker introduce Clarence White's ideas about picture-taking?

Ⓐ By contrasting them with those of Stieglitz
Ⓑ By providing examples of pictures taken by White
Ⓒ By giving details of White's life as a photographer and artist
Ⓓ By explaining how and why Photo-Secession was established

정답 Ⓐ

해설 화자가 사진 촬영에 대한 Clarence White의 의견을 어떻게 소개하는지를 묻는 문제이므로, 해당 정보와 함께 쓰인 표시어에서 정답의 단서를 찾을 수 있다. 화자가 Stieglitz는 픽토리얼리즘과 반대인 스트레이트 사진을 지지하게 되었다며 순수 사진술에 대한 설명을 하고, "On the other hand" 뒤에 Clarence White가 지지한 픽토리얼리즘에 대해 설명했다. 따라서, Clarence White의 의견을 Stieglitz의 의견과 대조하면서 소개했으므로 Ⓐ가 정답임을 알 수 있다.

HACKERS PRACTICE 🎧 T4_S1_5_Practice

Listen to each academic talk and fill in the blanks. Then choose the best answer for the question. (You will hear each talk twice.)

01

We are considering _____, _____, comets and asteroids, which can be hard to distinguish with the naked eye. _____, we look at their size, composition, and orbits. Comets are usually a few kilometers to tens of kilometers across and may show a bright head and a _____ _____. Asteroids range from pebble-sized to about one thousand kilometers in diameter. Asteroids _____ _____, while comets are mostly ice, dust, carbon dioxide, and methane. Comets follow highly elliptical orbits, moving in and out of _____. Most asteroids remain within the solar system, primarily in the asteroid belt between Jupiter and Mars.

How does the speaker describe the two types of celestial bodies?

Ⓐ By contrasting them with other celestial bodies
Ⓑ By explaining how they were discovered
Ⓒ By comparing them according to a set of criteria
Ⓓ By presenting theories on their formation

02

Amartya Sen has been a _____ _____ because of their role in man-made famines. His work showed empirically that famines are due to the _____ _____—for example, when traders hoard food for speculation and profit—rather than to inadequate supplies. As a result, Amartya Sen emphasized entitlement—that is, access to _____—over food availability alone, as a strategy to address poverty and famine.

How does the speaker clarify the maldistribution of food?

Ⓐ By giving an example of maldistribution
Ⓑ By analyzing statistical data on global food production
Ⓒ By comparing urban and rural food access patterns
Ⓓ By discussing environmental factors that affect food supply

03

There are _____: red muscle and white muscle. Red muscle fibers _____ myoglobin, which stores and delivers oxygen within muscle tissue. These muscles _____ and use oxygen to release energy. Red muscle fibers are _____. White muscle fibers, on the other hand, contract rapidly _____. White muscle fibers rely on anaerobic pathways and glycolytic enzymes to release energy without oxygen, _____ _____ to deplete more quickly.

Indicate which muscle type the following phrases are a description of.

Click in the correct box.

	Red muscle	White muscle
Does not tire easily		
Relies on glycolytic enzymes		
Releases energy quickly		
Contracts slowly		

04

Today we'll examine how different people _____. Research reveals that "baby talk" follows _____ the speaker's relationship to the child. Mothers use well-structured, short sentences, _____ _____ for body parts and bodily functions, such as "poo." Fathers employ _____ with a broader vocabulary than mothers do. _____ _____, such as neighbors and visitors, use simplified, higher-pitched speech. These variations _____ _____ in early language development.

Indicate for each individual the characteristic manner in which they converse with babies.

Click in the correct box.

	Mother	Father	Neighbors/ Visitors
Bigger words			
Special language			
Higher-pitched speech			

Answers p.556

HACKERS TEST 🎧 T4_S1_5_Test

[01-04] Listen to a talk in a linguistics class.

01 How is the talk mainly organized?

　Ⓐ It presents both supporting and opposing opinions about the theory.
　Ⓑ It describes the information chronologically from childhood to adulthood.
　Ⓒ It traces the evolution of the hypothesis since its creation.
　Ⓓ It contrasts first and second language acquisition processes.

02 What does the speaker say about brain plasticity?

　Ⓐ It increases significantly during adolescence.
　Ⓑ It allows the brain to reorganize neural pathways.
　Ⓒ It shows why formal instruction is essential for language acquisition.
　Ⓓ It affects reading skills more than speaking abilities.

03 Why does the speaker mention feral children?

　Ⓐ To compare animal and human language acquisition
　Ⓑ To challenge traditional views on language development
　Ⓒ To demonstrate difficulties in delayed language exposure
　Ⓓ To suggest an example of successful late language acquisition

04 What do critics of the hypothesis emphasize?

　Ⓐ The neurological changes occurring during maturation
　Ⓑ The appropriate learning environments for language acquisition
　Ⓒ The reduced neural connection formation in adults
　Ⓓ The biological constraints on adult language learning

[05-08] Listen to a talk in an environmental science class.

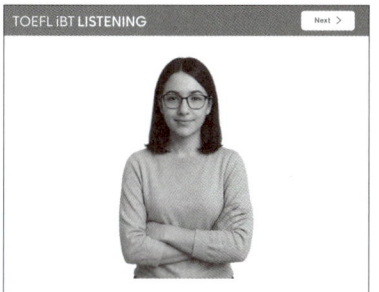

05 How does the speaker explain ecosystem services?

Ⓐ By providing examples of specific ecosystems
Ⓑ By organizing them into distinct categories
Ⓒ By contrasting them with artificial services
Ⓓ By examining their scientific mechanisms

06 What is NOT mentioned as an element of regulating services?

Ⓐ Water purification
Ⓑ Climate regulation
Ⓒ Nutrient cycling
Ⓓ Disease control

07 According to the speaker, how do human activities threaten ecosystem services?

Ⓐ By decreasing species diversity
Ⓑ By reducing government funding
Ⓒ By developing artificial alternatives
Ⓓ By creating inadequate wildlife corridors

08 What will the speaker discuss next?

Ⓐ Detailed classification of ecosystem types
Ⓑ Scientific methods for measuring biodiversity
Ⓒ Cultural significance of natural landscapes
Ⓓ Specific conservation and restoration approaches

HACKERS TEST

[09-12] Listen to a talk in a chemistry class.

09 What is the main topic of the talk?

Ⓐ The chemical composition of urban air
Ⓑ The types and roles of chemical catalysts
Ⓒ Chemical reaction mechanisms in laboratory settings
Ⓓ Industrial applications of iron-based catalytic systems

10 What does the speaker say about heterogeneous catalysts?

Ⓐ They are typically found dissolved in liquid reaction mixtures.
Ⓑ They require the same energy levels as homogeneous systems.
Ⓒ They exist in different phases from the reacting substances.
Ⓓ They work exclusively with combinations of nitrogen and hydrogen.

11 How does the speaker introduce the industrial importance of catalysis?

Ⓐ By providing a statistical figure about its prevalence
Ⓑ By demonstrating the Haber-Bosch process for ammonia production
Ⓒ By discussing phase differences in catalytic systems
Ⓓ By comparing the effectiveness of homogeneous and heterogeneous catalysts

12 According to the talk, how do catalytic converters contribute to environmental protection?

Ⓐ By reducing the energy requirements for chemical reactions
Ⓑ By providing homogeneous catalyst systems for emission control
Ⓒ By increasing the efficiency of fertilizer production processes
Ⓓ By transforming toxic exhaust emissions into safer compounds

[13-16] Listen to a talk in a history class.

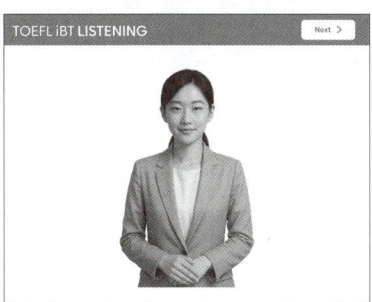

13 What is the main topic of the talk?

Ⓐ The architectural wonders of ancient Babylon
Ⓑ The rise and fall of the Neo-Babylonian Empire
Ⓒ The historical significance of Mesopotamian empires
Ⓓ The Assyrian-Babylonian religious conflicts

14 Why does the speaker mention Nabonidus?

Ⓐ To show how his policies weakened Babylonia internally
Ⓑ To explain his role in Babylonia's independence
Ⓒ To showcase his victories over Persia
Ⓓ To describe how he strengthened Babylonia's defenses

15 What will the speaker discuss next?

Ⓐ The decline of Persian influence in Mesopotamia
Ⓑ The reconstruction of Babylon under new leadership
Ⓒ The destruction of Babylon's famous monuments
Ⓓ The effects of Persian rule on Mesopotamian society

16 The speaker explains the steps in the development of the Neo-Babylonian Empire. Put these steps in order.

Drag each sentence to the space where it belongs.

Step 1	
Step 2	
Step 3	
Step 4	

- The Hanging Gardens and the Ishtar Gate were built.
- A revolt established Babylonia's independence from Assyrian rule.
- Neo-Babylonia faced instability and weak rulers.
- The Old Babylonian Empire fell to invaders.

Answers p.557

6. Inference Questions

Overview

강의에서 직접적으로 언급되지 않았으나 강의 내용을 통해 논리적으로 추론할 수 있는 사실을 묻는 문제이다. 매 시험 1~2문제가 출제된다.

Types of Questions

inferred, concluded라는 표현을 포함한 형태로 출제되어 강의에 언급된 대상에 대해 추론할 수 있는 바를 묻거나, imply, indicate라는 표현을 포함한 형태로 출제되어 언급된 대상에 대해 화자가 암시하는 바를 묻기도 한다.

Inference

What can be inferred about voting patterns?
What can be concluded about art critics' influence on public opinion?

Implication

What does the speaker imply about solar panels?
What does the speaker indicate about the effectiveness of online education?
What is implied about language preservation efforts in indigenous communities?
The speaker implies that viewing older technology as completely obsolete is an example of what?

Hackers Strategy

1 화자가 언급하는 내용의 결론을 생각한다.
강의에서 화자가 언급하는 말을 그대로만 받아들이지 말고, 결론적으로 화자가 말하고자 하는 바가 무엇인지를 염두에 두어야 한다.

2 화자가 암시하는 바를 paraphrasing한 것을 정답으로 고른다.
화자가 직접적으로 말하지는 않았으나, 화자가 한 말을 통해 간접적으로 알 수 있는 사실이 있다. 이렇듯 화자의 말에 함축된 의미를 바르게 paraphrasing한 것이 정답이 된다. 특히, 강의에서 화자가 반복해서 한 말을 통해서 화자의 말이나 행동에 대한 근거를 찾는다.

3 자주 나오는 오답 유형에 주의한다.
강의에서 언급된 단어를 포함하고 있지만 내용이 틀린 오답, 강의에서 언급되지 않은 오답, 충분한 근거 없이 확대해서 해석한 오답이 자주 등장한다. 특히, Inference 문제는 높은 수준의 추리력이나 논리력을 요구하지 않으므로, 반드시 화자의 말 안에서 근거를 찾도록 한다.

Example
T4_S1_6_Example

Script

Today we're going to discuss deflation. While inflation refers to a general rise in prices, deflation is a persistent decrease in the level of consumer prices. You might think that falling prices would be good for consumers, but deflation is far more complex and potentially dangerous than many people realize. When prices go down, producers have no choice but to produce more in order to make the same amount of profits. So the market's flooded, the prices go down even more, the producer makes even less money.

What does the speaker imply about deflation?

(A) It is easier to control than inflation.
(B) It is primarily affected by international trade relationships.
(C) It causes the value of products to decrease.
(D) It benefits consumers more than it harms producers.

정답 ⓒ

해설 화자가 디플레이션에 대해 암시하는 것을 묻는 문제이므로, 해당 대상에 대해 언급된 말에서 정답의 단서를 찾을 수 있다. 화자가 "deflation is ~ decrease in the level of consumer prices"라며 디플레이션은 소비자 가격이 떨어지는 현상이라고 했고, 화자의 설명에서 디플레이션이 일어나면 상품의 가격이 하락하는 상태에서 상품의 생산량은 계속 증가하여 결국 상품 가치가 떨어진다는 것을 추론할 수 있으므로 ⓒ가 정답임을 알 수 있다.

HACKERS PRACTICE 🎧 T4_S1_6_Practice

Listen to each academic talk and fill in the blanks. Then choose the best answer for the question. (You will hear each talk twice.)

01

Let's talk about one of nature's most underrated creatures, the earthworm. They are, in fact, like _____. When they tunnel through compacted soil, they're _____. This creates pathways for air and water circulation, which is crucial for _____ and soil health. Here's a fascinating statistic. Researchers found that on just one acre of cultivated land, earthworms deposit about 16,000 pounds of _____ annually, sometimes up to 30,000 pounds! These castings _____ like nitrogen, calcium, and phosphorus.

What can be inferred about earthworms in agriculture?

Ⓐ They require careful monitoring by agricultural experts.
Ⓑ They consume too much organic matter from the soil.
Ⓒ They reduce the need for water in agricultural systems.
Ⓓ They naturally improve soil conditions for plant growth.

02

Sunspots are relatively cool, darkish spots ____ _____ on the Sun's surface. Between 1645 and 1715, _____ _____ very little, or even zero, sunspot activity. Sunspots _____ during those years. In relation to this, the English astronomer Edward Walter Maunder observed that temperatures fell _____ _____ that the world, particularly Europe, appeared to have undergone a Little Ice Age. Consequently, scientists speculated that there might be an association between the Earth's climate and _____ _____ on the Sun's surface.

What can be concluded about sunspots?

Ⓐ They seem to appear only during winter months.
Ⓑ They may be associated with lower temperatures around the world.
Ⓒ They increase in size during cold periods.
Ⓓ They might disappear permanently after a certain period.

03

The ancient Egyptians used _____ _____, especially when the Nile floods destroyed boundaries. They applied these _____.
Meanwhile, the Greeks advanced further. Greek mapmakers began creating more systematic and scientific maps _____ _____ of a spherical Earth.
By the seventeenth century, mapmakers _____. While calculating latitude became easier with the sextant, _____ problematic. It was not until the 1884 Washington conference that the Greenwich Meridian was established as zero longitude, _____ _____.

What does the speaker imply about the 1884 Washington conference?

Ⓐ It was organized by the astronomers at the Greenwich Observatory.
Ⓑ It established new techniques for measuring latitude.
Ⓒ It addressed a long-standing problem in mapping.
Ⓓ It introduced the concept of mapping based on a spherical Earth.

04

Today we'll examine dowsing rods, _____ _____ that generates considerable debate in scientific circles. These Y-shaped tools, made of wood or metal, are _____ underground water, minerals, or even missing persons. Dowsers hold the rods close to their bodies and believe they _____ _____. Despite some reported successes, scientific testing has _____ _____. For instance, in one experiment, a dowser _____ _____ which beaker contained water across multiple trials. Nevertheless, the practice remains _____.

What is implied about the reported successes of dowsing?

Ⓐ They appear to contradict systematic experimental evidence.
Ⓑ They demonstrate the importance of cultural preservation.
Ⓒ They establish dowsing as a legitimate scientific practice.
Ⓓ They suggest that dowsing is more reliable than expected.

Answers p.561

HACKERS TEST 🎧 T4_S1_6_Test

[01-04] Listen to a talk in an archaeology class.

01 What is the talk mainly about?

Ⓐ The toolmaking techniques of Neanderthals
Ⓑ The study of pollen and other microscopic particles
Ⓒ The research methods in prehistoric archaeology
Ⓓ The comparison between different dating methods

02 What does the speaker imply about pollen?

Ⓐ It provides more accurate dating than other methods.
Ⓑ It can only be found in specific geographical regions.
Ⓒ It offers limited insight into ancient human activities.
Ⓓ It remains intact for extraordinarily long periods.

03 Why does the speaker mention Belize?

Ⓐ To compare different archaeological excavation methods
Ⓑ To explain the dating techniques used in Central America
Ⓒ To exemplify how palynology shows human settlement patterns
Ⓓ To describe the challenges of working in tropical archaeological sites

04 What will the speaker discuss next?

Ⓐ Advanced dating techniques for archaeological artifacts
Ⓑ Procedures for collecting and studying pollen specimens
Ⓒ Case studies from additional archaeological excavations
Ⓓ Environmental reconstruction of other ancient civilizations

[05-08] Listen to a talk in an economics class.

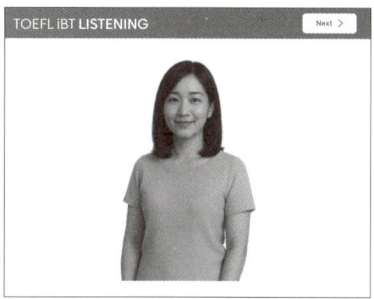

05 What is the main topic of the talk?

Ⓐ The evolution of luxury goods marketing strategies
Ⓑ General methods businesses use to reduce costs during recessions
Ⓒ An economic phenomenon observed during recessions
Ⓓ The psychological impact of financial stress on consumer emotions

06 What does the speaker imply about the Lipstick Effect?

Ⓐ It reflects poor financial management by consumers during recessions.
Ⓑ It provides insights into business strategy during economic downturns.
Ⓒ It was primarily observed among younger consumers.
Ⓓ It only applies to the cosmetics industry.

07 According to the talk, how might the Lipstick Effect help people during economic downturns?

Ⓐ By participating in consumer trends despite a recession
Ⓑ By reducing impulse purchases of more expensive items
Ⓒ By preserving a feeling of stability and emotional well-being
Ⓓ By developing stronger brand loyalty to specific companies

08 What will the speaker most likely discuss next?

Ⓐ Examples of the Lipstick Effect in various industries
Ⓑ Alternative theories about consumer spending habits
Ⓒ Market research methods for measuring the Lipstick Effect
Ⓓ Changes in advertising strategies during economic downturns

HACKERS TEST

[09-12] Listen to a talk on a podcast about music.

09 What is the main topic of the talk?

Ⓐ Differences between the sounds of the clarinet and the oboe
Ⓑ Common misconceptions about the classification of the saxophone
Ⓒ The invention of reed instruments
Ⓓ The manufacturing process for saxophone components

10 What does the speaker imply about Adolphe Sax?

Ⓐ He was primarily known for his clarinet performances.
Ⓑ He worked exclusively with Belgian instrument manufacturers.
Ⓒ He focused on improving the durability of musical instruments.
Ⓓ He developed an innovative approach to instrument construction.

11 Why does the speaker mention the clarinet mouthpiece?

Ⓐ To describe the visual appearance of saxophone components
Ⓑ To explain why saxophones are easier to play than clarinets
Ⓒ To clarify why the saxophone is classified as a woodwind
Ⓓ To compare the cost of different instrument parts

12 Why does the speaker mention an oboe?

Ⓐ To describe what the saxophone sounds like.
Ⓑ To contrast the oboe's playing techniques with those of the saxophone
Ⓒ To explain why oboes are preferred in classical orchestras
Ⓓ To discuss the range limitations of different wind instruments

[13-16] Listen to a talk in a literature class.

13 What is the main purpose of the talk?

ⓐ To analyze Mary Shelley's writing techniques
ⓑ To explore a genre of classical literature
ⓒ To discuss the symbolism used in Gothic architecture
ⓓ To illustrate the evolution of horror fiction

14 According to the speaker, how does Gothic literature create a sense of foreboding?

ⓐ By using direct and explicit explanations
ⓑ By including scientific explanations
ⓒ By contrasting light and shadow imagery
ⓓ By using ambiguous and unsettling imagery

15 What does the speaker point out about Gothic novels' narrative techniques?

ⓐ They rely heavily on realistic descriptions.
ⓑ They use straightforward chronological structures.
ⓒ They often feature unreliable narrators.
ⓓ They focus primarily on dialogue between characters.

16 What can be concluded about Gothic literature's influence?

ⓐ It was quickly replaced by modern literary styles.
ⓑ It reflects enduring human fears and desires.
ⓒ It discourages the exploration of emotional depth.
ⓓ It incorporated rationalist values into its works.

Answers p.563

무료 토플자료·유학정보 공유
goHackers.com

Section II
Academic Topics

Section II에서는 TASK 4에 자주 출제되는 주제들을 중심으로 각 세부 단원을 구성하였다. TOEFL에는 실제 대학 강의에서 다루어지는 다양한 학문 분야들이 출제되는데, 크게 인문학, 예술, 사회과학, 물리과학, 생명과학으로 나누어 볼 수 있다.

TASK 4의 Academic Topics에는 다음의 5가지가 있다.

1. Humanities
2. Arts
3. Social Science
4. Physical Science
5. Life Science

1. Humanities

인문학은 인간의 문화, 역사, 언어, 사상을 탐구하는 학문 영역으로, 크게 역사, 문학, 언어학, 철학의 네 가지 주제로 나누어 볼 수 있다. TOEFL에서는 역사적 사건과 그 영향, 문학 작품의 분석과 문예 사조, 언어학의 다양한 이론과 언어 습득 과정, 그리고 철학적 사상과 개념들이 주로 다뤄진다.

■ History (역사)

인간이 살아온 모습과 인간의 행위로 일어난 사실 및 그 사실에 대한 기록을 말한다. TOEFL에서는 세계의 역사가 주로 다루어지며, 시대는 크게 고대, 중세, 근대로 나누어 볼 수 있다.

고대 (인류문명의 시작 ~ 로마제국의 멸망) 500 BC ~ AD 400	• 고대 로마(Ancient Rome): 기원전 8세기 중엽 티베르강 유역에서 라틴인이 건국한 제국으로 지중해(Mediterranean Sea)의 패권을 장악했다. 왕과 귀족이 함께 통치하는 공화정 제도가 있었으며 토목·의학·과학·법률 등 실용적인 문화가 발달했다. 많은 군인황제가 출현하고 이민족의 침입, 인구감소 등의 사회혼란으로 인해 동·서 로마로 분열되었다. 476년 게르만 족(Germanic peoples)의 침입으로 서로마가 멸망하면서 로마제국이 무너지고 게르만족이 유럽을 장악했다.
중세 (로마제국 멸망 이후 ~ 르네상스) AD 400 ~ 16C	• 르네상스(Renaissance): 14세기와 16세기 사이에 이탈리아에서 시작된 문화운동이다. 학문 또는 예술의 재생·부활을 목적으로 고대 그리스·로마의 인간중심 문화를 부흥시키는 것에 중점을 두었다. 사상·문학·미술·건축 등 다방면에 걸친 변화가 일어났으며 신 중심이었던 중세 예술을 인간 중심으로 전환시켜 현실을 바탕으로 한 표현이 발전했다.
근대 (르네상스 이후 ~ 제2차 세계대전) 16C ~ 1945	• 계몽주의(Enlightenment): 17, 18세기에 유럽에서 일어난 사회개혁운동으로, 이성의 힘을 중시했으며 기존의 봉건사상을 타파하고 사회를 개혁하는 데 목적을 둔 사상운동이다. 루소(Rousseau), 칸트(Kant) 등을 계몽주의에 큰 영향을 끼친 지식인들로 꼽을 수 있다. 커피하우스(coffee house)는 이러한 계몽주의의 확산에 큰 영향을 준 것으로 이야기되는데, 여러 지식인들이 모여 자유롭고 합리적인 토론을 하는 것을 가능하게 한 장소였을 뿐만 아니라 일반 대중들도 정치·철학적 현안에 대한 전문가적인 견해를 듣거나, 활자 매체를 접할 수 있는 장소였기 때문이다. • 산업혁명(Industrial Revolution): 18세기 중엽 영국에서 시작된 기술혁신과 이에 따라 일어난 사회·경제 구조의 대변화를 의미한다. 제임스 와트(James Watt)가 발명한 증기기관(steam engine)으로 인해 새로운 에너지원이 등장했다. 이는 산업혁명의 직접적인 원동력이라 할 수 있다.

Literature (문학)

언어에 기반을 둔 예술 작품을 다루는 학문을 말한다. TOEFL에서는 시대별 문예 사조의 흐름과 특징이나 구체적인 문학 장르와 관련된 강의가 주로 출제된다.

1. Literary Thoughts (문예사조)

Classicism (고전주의)	고전주의는 르네상스(Renaissance) 시대의 고대 그리스·로마 고전 연구에서 시작되었으며 17세기 당시 인간의 이성을 존중하는 경향에 부합하였다. 문학은 이성에 입각해야 하며 문학에서 묘사하는 세계는 도덕적이야 한다는 이념을 바탕으로 한다. 프랑스의 희곡(drama) 문학에서 전형적인 형태로 발전하였고 장편 서사시(epic)와 비극(tragedy) 작품들이 많이 등장했다.
Romanticism (낭만주의)	낭만주의는 18세기 말에서 19세기 중엽 사이에 유럽에서 민족정신의 각성과 함께 발생했다. 그리스·로마의 고전으로부터 눈을 돌려 각 나라의 과거에서 새로운 문화의 원천을 찾고 인간성을 회복하려는 기운이 일어난 것이다. 1789년 발발한 프랑스 혁명 또한 인간 이성의 불합리함을 발견해 낭만주의 사조를 촉발하는 계기가 되었다.
Realism (사실주의)	사실주의는 객관적 사물을 있는 그대로 정확하게 재현하는 것을 목표로 하며, 19세기의 과학존중 사상 및 실증주의와 결합하여 발달하였다. 시민사회(civil society)가 일찍 발달한 영국에서는 사실주의 문학의 발달도 빨랐으며 이후 디킨스(Dickens)와 엘리엇(Eliot)에 의해 계승되었다.
Naturalism (자연주의)	자연주의는 유럽의 사실주의를 계승하여 자연의 틀 속에서 인간을 보는 관점에 바탕을 두고 있다. 작가의 태도는 자연과 학자의 연장선 상에 있으며 인간을 자연의 일부로서 본능과 생리에 의해 지배되는 나약하고 단순한 존재로 여긴다.

2. Literary Genres (문학 장르)

Poetry (시)	산문(prose)과 구별되어 리듬(rhythm)과 운율(meter)을 가진 간결한 언어로 표현된 글을 말한다. 시는 주제와 형식에 따라 세 종류로 구분할 수 있다. 서사시(epic poem)는 영웅의 업적을 찬양하고 국가적으로 중요한 의미가 있는 주제를 다루는 시이며, 서정시(lyric poem)는 개인의 감정을 주제로 삼고, 마지막으로 극시(dramaticpoem)는 운문으로 이루어진 희곡을 뜻한다.
Drama (희곡)	희곡은 고대 그리스 시대에 50명의 합창단이 디오니소스(Dionysus) 제단 주위에서 부르던 찬가에서 유래되었으며 희극과 비극으로 나누어진다. 비극에 비해 희극은 더 늦게 발달하였는데 희극의 주제는 주로 정치와 전쟁이었다. 이 시대의 주요한 극작가로는 아에스킬로스(Aeschylus), 소포클레스(Sophocles), 유리피데스(Euripides) 등이 있다.
Memoir & Autobiography (자서전)	둘 다 자서전이라는 뜻으로 한 사람의 일생에 대해 기술한다는 측면에서 비슷하지만 memoir는 일생에 있었던 특정한 사건이 중심이 되고 autobiography는 일생을 모두 기술한다는 측면에서 차이가 있다. Memoir의 경우 전통적인 형식에서는 정치·사회적 내용이 주로 주제가 되었던 것에 반해 최근에는 좀 더 개인적인 이야기가 주제가 되는 추세이다. Memoir는 전적으로 작가 자신의 관점으로 사건을 해석하기 때문에 소설과 구분하기가 어렵다.

■ Linguistics (언어학)

인간의 언어를 연구하는 학문이다. TOEFL에서는 언어학의 분야, 언어와 의사소통의 차이, 언어 습득 등과 관련된 강의가 주로 출제된다.

1. Fields of Linguistics (언어학의 분야)

Phonetics (음성학)	음성학은 언어의 음성적 특성인 발음과 억양을 연구한다. 언어음성은 크게 세 단계를 거쳐 전달된다. 1단계는 화자가 여러 발음기관(speech organs)을 움직여서 소리를 내는 과정이며, 그 단계를 통해 나온 소리가 음파(sound waves)로서 듣는 사람의 귀에 도달하는 과정이 2단계이다. 3단계는 음파가 고막(eardrum)을 진동시켜 소리를 인식하게 되는 과정이다. 이 각각의 단계에 따라 음성학의 연구주제와 연구방법이 달라진다.
Phonology (음운론)	음운론은 일련의 언어음성이 특정 언어에서 수행하는 기능에 초점을 둔다. 한 언어에서 서로 다른 소리가 서로 다른 의미를 가질 수 있게 하는 요소나, 음색(tone color)이나 발음의 차이 등에 따라 물리적으로 서로 다른 소리가 동일한 의미를 가질 수 있게 해주는 요소에 대해 연구한다.
Morphology (형태론)	형태론은 단어를 형태소(morpheme) 단위로 나누어 그 구조를 분석한다. 형태소는 의미를 가지는 언어의 최소 단위를 뜻한다. 'singers'라는 단어를 형태론적으로 분석해보면, 먼저 어근(root)으로서 행위를 나타내는 'sing', 행위의 수행자를 나타내는 접미어(suffix) '-er', 복수형을 나타내는 접미어 '-s'로 나눌 수 있다.

2. Language & Communication (언어와 의사소통)

동물의 의사소통과 구분되는 언어의 특징	인간의 언어(language)는 동물의 의사소통(communication)과 몇 가지 면에서 분명히 구별된다. 우선 동물의 의사소통은 본능적(instinct)인 데 반해 언어는 배워야만 구사할 수 있는 것이다. 또한 언어에는 문법(grammar)이 있다. 프레리도그(prairie dog)와 같은 일부 동물도 음의 높낮이(pitch)에 따라 다른 품사를 나타내는 등 일부 문법적인 의사소통 수단을 가지는 것으로 알려져 있다. 하지만 인간의 언어는 단순히 단어의 품사를 구분하는 것에서 나아가 문장을 절로, 단어로, 음절로, 그리고 음소로 나누는 등 훨씬 세부적인 구분이 가능하다. 이런 분리성(discreteness)이 동물의 의사소통과 구분되는 언어의 또 다른 특성이다. 이런 개별 구성 요소(individual units)로 나누어지는 언어의 특성에서 오는 또 다른 특성은 생산성(productivity), 즉 나누어진 개별 구성요소를 이용해 새로운 문장을 창조적으로 만들어낼 수 있다는 것이다. 마지막으로 동물의 의사소통은 현재 그 자리에서 발생하는 일을 전달하는 기능밖에 없는 데 반해 인간의 언어는 과거나 미래, 상상 속의 일도 전달할 수 있다.
Gricean Maxims (그라이스의 대화격률)	언어철학자인 폴 그라이스(Paul Grice)가 효율적인 대화에 필요한 네 가지 원칙을 정리한 것이다. 그라이스의 대화격률은 '진실만을 말하라'는 질의 격률(maxim of quality), 쓸데없는 정보를 제외하고 '필요한 만큼만 말하라'는 양의 격률(maxim of quantity), '대화의 주제와 관련 있는 말만 하라'는 관련성의 격률(maxim of relevance), 그리고 '분명하고 조리 있게 말하라'는 태도의 격률(maxim of manner)로 이루어져 있다.

3. Language Acquisition (언어습득)

Critical Period Hypothesis (결정적 시기론)	유아기의 언어습득에서 가장 중요한 시기(critical period)를 놓치면 이후의 언어능력이 발달하기 힘들다. **언어습득의 다양한 이론** 아이가 언어를 습득하는 방법과 원리에 대한 세 가지 이론이 있다. 첫째, 행동주의 이론(behaviorism)은 아기가 주변 어른들의 말투를 흉내 내면서 언어를 습득한다는 이론이다. 둘째, 생득주의 이론(innatism)은 인간은 태어나면서 이미 언어획득장치(Language Acquisition Device)를 가지고 있으므로 특별한 훈련 없이 외부의 언어자극을 스스로 분석하여 학습한다는 이론이다. 마지막으로 인지적 상호작용 이론(cognitive theory)이 있다. 이를 주장한 Piaget는 언어 발달이 인지발달과 밀접하게 연관되어 있다고 설명했다. 언어는 유아의 사고를 표현하는 수단으로 발달한다는 것이다.
Language Acquisition vs. Learning (언어습득과 학습)	인위적으로 배우게 되는 학습과 달리 자연스럽게 언어를 습득하기 위해서는 언어를 접하게 되는 시기와 동기가 중요하다. **mother tongue vs. foreign language (모국어와 외국어)** 모국어 습득과 외국어 학습에는 여러 차이가 있다. 모국어는 생활과 직결되어 상대방과의 자연스러운 만남을 통해 무의식적으로 익히게 되지만 외국어는 인위적으로 정해진 대상과 이야기함으로써 의식적으로 학습한다. 또한 외국어는 인위적인 환경에서 언어 자체가 아닌 언어구조를 학습해야 한다.

■ Philosophy (철학)

인간의 존재, 지식, 가치, 이성 등 근본적인 문제를 탐구하는 학문이다. TOEFL에서는 다양한 철학 학파와 관련된 강의가 주로 출제된다.

Pragmatism (실용주의)	실용주의는 19세기 후반 미국에서 시작된 철학 사조로, 윌리엄 제임스(William James), 찰스 샌더스 퍼스(Charles Sanders Peirce), 존 듀이(John Dewey) 등이 주요 사상가이다. 실용주의는 진리의 가치를 그것의 실용적 결과나 유용성으로 판단한다는 입장을 취한다. 즉, 어떤 믿음이나 이론이 실제 삶에서 성공적으로 작동하고 유익한 결과를 가져온다면 그것이 참된 것이라고 본다. 이는 추상적이고 절대적인 진리보다는 구체적이고 경험적인 효과를 중시하는 관점이다.
Rationalism (합리주의)	합리주의는 지식의 근원을 감각 경험보다는 이성에서 찾는 철학적 입장이다. 데카르트, 스피노자(Spinoza), 라이프니츠(Leibniz) 등이 대표적인 합리주의 철학자들이다. 이들은 수학적 방법을 철학에 적용하여 확실하고 명증한 지식을 얻을 수 있다고 믿었으며, 선천적 관념의 존재를 주장하였다.
Empiricism (경험주의)	경험주의는 모든 지식이 감각 경험에서 비롯된다고 보는 철학적 관점이다. 존 로크(John Locke), 조지 버클리(George Berkeley), 데이비드 흄(David Hume) 등이 주요 인물이며, 이들은 인간의 정신을 백지상태(tabula rasa)로 보고 경험을 통해 지식이 축적된다고 주장하였다.

HACKERS TEST 🎧 T4_S2_1_Test

[01-04] Listen to a talk in a philosophy class.

01 What is the main topic of the talk?

Ⓐ The historical development of moral philosophy
Ⓑ The relationship between happiness and morality
Ⓒ The practical applications of utilitarianism
Ⓓ The comparison between two utilitarian philosophers

02 What does the speaker say about the hedonistic calculus?

Ⓐ It was rejected by most philosophers of Bentham's time.
Ⓑ It provided a systematic method for evaluating pleasures.
Ⓒ It was revolutionary in its recognition of qualitative differences.
Ⓓ It required extensive training to implement in real-world situations.

03 Why does the speaker mention a pig?

Ⓐ To contrast different levels of satisfaction and fulfillment
Ⓑ To show that animals can experience genuine happiness
Ⓒ To suggest that simple pleasures are often more authentic
Ⓓ To explain why physical pleasures should be completely avoided

04 What will the speaker discuss next?

Ⓐ Biographical details about Bentham and Mill
Ⓑ Detailed explanations of the hedonic calculus
Ⓒ Contemporary applications of utilitarian principles
Ⓓ The evolution of utilitarian thought after Mill

[05-08] Listen to a talk in a literature class.

05 How does the speaker introduce the stream-of-consciousness technique?

Ⓐ By conducting a comparative literature analysis
Ⓑ By presenting examples to demonstrate the method
Ⓒ By explaining its historical development
Ⓓ By showing how it affects character development

06 According to the speaker, how does Molly Bloom's soliloquy demonstrate the stream-of-consciousness technique?

Ⓐ By providing comprehensive character backgrounds
Ⓑ By following logical thought sequences carefully
Ⓒ By organizing memories in chronological order
Ⓓ By showing the random and associative nature of thought

07 Why does the speaker mention third-person narration?

Ⓐ To suggest hybrid approaches that combine both methods
Ⓑ To demonstrate its effectiveness in character development
Ⓒ To show its inability to capture psychological complexity
Ⓓ To show its compatibility with modern techniques

08 What will the speaker most likely discuss next?

Ⓐ Modern fiction employing this technique
Ⓑ Joyce's influence on contemporary literature
Ⓒ Academic debates about literary techniques
Ⓓ Psychological theories behind human consciousness

HACKERS TEST

[09-12] Listen to a talk in a history class.

09 What aspect of coffeehouses is the talk mainly about?

Ⓐ The architectural evolution of public gathering spaces
Ⓑ The evolution of coffee consumption habits
Ⓒ The technical innovations in coffee roasting and brewing
Ⓓ The role as centers for rational discourse and learning

10 Why does the speaker mention taverns?

Ⓐ To indicate the comparative advantages of coffeehouses
Ⓑ To compare the customer demographics of the two establishments
Ⓒ To identify the primary competitors of coffeehouses
Ⓓ To describe the historical origins of public gathering places

11 How did coffeehouses come to be known as "penny universities"?

Ⓐ By establishing partnerships with nearby universities
Ⓑ By offering inexpensive access to scholarly conversations
Ⓒ By organizing formal debates between competing scholars
Ⓓ By collecting fees to fund educational scholarships

12 What amplified coffeehouses' impact in the late 17th century?

Ⓐ The increased availability of imported reading materials
Ⓑ The spread of coffeehouses across Europe
Ⓒ The circulation of diverse and uncensored reading materials
Ⓓ The government's support for educational initiatives

[13-16] Listen to a talk in a literature class.

13 According to the speaker, the works of the classical period emphasized all of the following EXCEPT

Ⓐ ethical guidance
Ⓑ aesthetic brilliance
Ⓒ romantic relationships
Ⓓ enduring themes

14 According to the speaker, what characterized classical literature?

Ⓐ Its emphasis on individual psychological experiences
Ⓑ Its observance of particular structures and rules
Ⓒ Its rejection of traditional narrative structures
Ⓓ Its focus on regional dialects and customs

15 Why does the speaker mention the Renaissance?

Ⓐ To illustrate the revival of classical principles
Ⓑ To identify the pinnacle of classical writing
Ⓒ To contrast medieval and classical literature
Ⓓ To describe the decline of classical literary influence

16 What will the speaker discuss next?

Ⓐ The decline of the neoclassical movement
Ⓑ Examples of using classical works in education
Ⓒ The influence of Homer on later writers
Ⓓ Modern instances of classical influence

HACKERS TEST

[17-20] Listen to a talk in a history class.

17 What is the main topic of the talk?

  Ⓐ The origins of modern labor union movements
  Ⓑ Conflicts between skilled craftsmen and new technology
  Ⓒ Social reforms during the Industrial Revolution
  Ⓓ Government policies toward labor movements in Britain

18 Why does the speaker mention power looms?

  Ⓐ To describe the most advanced technology of the period
  Ⓑ To illustrate the working conditions in early factories
  Ⓒ To explain what motivated the workers' destructive actions
  Ⓓ To highlight the superior quality of machine-made products

19 What does the speaker say about the Luddites?

  Ⓐ They successfully prevented factory mechanization.
  Ⓑ They focused on improving working conditions.
  Ⓒ They advocated for gradual technological change.
  Ⓓ They were primarily concerned about losing their jobs.

20 What will the speaker most likely discuss next?

  Ⓐ Automation concerns influencing today's labor movements
  Ⓑ The transportation of convicted Luddites to Australia
  Ⓒ Alternative employment opportunities for displaced workers
  Ⓓ The spread of similar movements to other countries

[21-24] Listen to a talk in a linguistics class.

21 What is the talk mainly about?

Ⓐ The cognitive advantages of speaking multiple languages
Ⓑ The historical origins of the Sapir-Whorf hypothesis
Ⓒ The practical applications of linguistic research
Ⓓ The influence of linguistic structures on human thinking

22 What does the speaker say about Aboriginal Australian speakers?

Ⓐ They possess unique color perception.
Ⓑ They demonstrate remarkable spatial perception skills.
Ⓒ They preserve ancient linguistic traditions more effectively.
Ⓓ They developed their languages through cultural isolation.

23 What can be inferred about the Sapir-Whorf hypothesis?

Ⓐ It continues to generate debate among researchers.
Ⓑ It was originally intended for educational applications.
Ⓒ It challenges traditional views of universal grammar.
Ⓓ It has limited relevance to contemporary linguistics.

24 What will the speaker discuss next?

Ⓐ The role of culture in shaping linguistic structures
Ⓑ The relationship between language and thought
Ⓒ The cognitive effects of speaking multiple languages
Ⓓ The connection between memory and linguistic diversity

Answers p.567

2. Arts

예술은 인간의 감정과 사상을 시각, 청각, 공연 매체로 창조적으로 표현하는 활동을 다루는 영역으로, 크게 음악, 미술, 영화, 사진, 건축의 다섯 가지 주제로 나누어 볼 수 있다. 음악사와 장르별 특성, 미술 사조의 발전과 작품 분석, 영화와 사진의 예술적 기법, 건축 양식의 변화와 의미 등이 핵심 주제로 등장하며, 특히 TOEFL에 출제되는 예술 강의는 단순한 작품 감상을 넘어서 예술 작품이 탄생한 사회적 배경, 예술가의 의도와 기법, 그리고 예술이 사회에 미치는 영향을 종합적으로 분석한다.

■ Music (음악)

소리를 소재로 하여 박자(time)·선율(melody)·화성(harmony)·음색(timbre) 등을 일정한 법칙과 형식으로 조합하여 사상과 감정을 표현하는 예술이다. TOEFL에서는 다양한 음악의 장르와 그 경향, 그리고 악기와 관련된 강의가 주로 출제된다.

1. Music Genres & Trends (음악의 장르와 경향)

Classical Music (클래식 음악)	로마시민 중 최상류층을 가리키는 클라시쿠스(Classicus)라는 말에서 유래되었으며 '잘 정돈된, 품위 있는'의 의미를 갖고 있다. 이 말을 따서 예술상의 최고 걸작을 고전(classic)이라 부르게 되었다. 바흐가 사망한 1750년부터 베토벤이 사망한 1827년까지의 기간 동안 활동한 음악가들이 만든 작품들을 클래식이라 할 수 있다. 모차르트(Mozart), 하이든(Haydn), 베토벤(Beethoven) 등이 대표적인 음악가이다.
Romantic Music (낭만주의 음악)	낭만주의 음악은 고전주의 이후, 약 1820년대에서 1900년대 초반까지 창조된 음악 장르이다. 19세기에 유럽과 근대 국가에서 산업혁명이 일어났고 악기들은 산업 혁명의 기술 발전에 힘입어 더욱 자유로운 성량 및 음정 표현이 가능하도록 개량되었다. 호른, 트럼펫 등의 금관 악기에는 소리의 질을 높여주는 밸브가 부착되었고, 이러한 발전은 더욱 다양하고 풍부한 색채의 음향을 창출해낼 수 있도록 하였다. 연주 기술에서도 반음과 불협화음을 사용하는 다양한 기법이 등장했다. 낭만주의 음악의 대표적인 음악가는 베토벤, 쇼팽, 슈베르트, 브람스, 차이코프스키 등이다.
Opera (오페라)	중세 이탈리아에서 시작된 오페라는 인문주의자라고 불리는 예술가들의 집단에 의해 만들어졌다. 인문주의자들은 노래와 이야기가 섞인 고대 그리스의 연극을 상기시키는 예술 형태를 만들어내고자 했다. 오페라는 크게 두 부분으로 구성되어 있는데 이는 recitative(줄거리를 발전시키기 위해 평소 대화할 때와 비슷한 느낌으로 부르는 노래)와 aria(등장인물의 감정을 표현하기 위해 악기를 포함한 강렬한 노래)이다. 1670년대 프랑스에서는 tragédie en musique라는 새로운 형태의 오페라가 만들어졌고, 18세기에는 opera serie라는 이탈리아 스타일의 오페라가 영국에 소개되었다.

Jazz (재즈)	19세기 말 아프리카에서 미국으로 팔려온 흑인 노예들의 민속 음악과 미국 본토 백인의 유럽음악의 결합으로 생겨났다.

ragtime (래그타임)
1910년대에 들어서부터 재즈라는 명칭을 사용하기 시작했으며 그 이전에는 일반적으로 래그타임(ragtime)이라고 불렸다. 이는 'Ragged Time'에서 유래한 것으로 음표를 박자보다 조금 앞이나 뒤에 놓음으로써 멜로디가 박자와 박자 사이에 떠 있는 것처럼 느껴지도록 하는 Ragged 기법과 관련되어 있다. 왼손은 정확한 박자를 짚지만, 오른손은 당김음인 분절법(syncopation)을 사용하여 리듬이 어긋나 있는 것이 래그타임의 특징이다. 스콧 조플린(Scott Joplin)과 젤리 롤 모턴(Jelly Roll Morton) 등이 래그타임의 대표적인 음악가이며, 조플린의 <Maple Leaf Rag>는 래그타임 음악 중 가장 잘 알려진 곡일 것이다.

Regina Carter (레지나 카터)
1966년, 미시건 주의 디트로이트에서 태어난 레지나 카터는 미국의 가장 창조적인 예술가 중 한 명이다. 그녀는 클래식 바이올리니스트로 시작했지만 프랑스 출신의 재즈 바이올리니스트 스테란 그래펠리의 연주를 듣고 자유로운 재즈 연주에 매료되어 재즈 바이올리니스트로 전환하게 된다. 그 후, 그녀는 여성 재즈 5인조 Straight Ahead로 이름을 알렸고, Berklee College of Music을 포함한 여러 기관에서 학생들을 가르쳤다.

avant-garde music (아방가르드 음악)
예술에서 아방가르드는 이제까지의 예술 개념을 변화시킬 수 있는 혁명적인 예술 경향을 뜻한다. 아방가르드 음악은 소리에 자발적이며 자유로운 생동감을 주기 위해 음조(pitch)·리듬·형식 등의 요소를 미리 정하지 않고 연주자의 임의성(voluntariness)에 맡긴다.

John Cage (존 케이지)
미국 출신의 우연성 음악(chance operation)의 대표 음악가이다. 그의 <4분 33초>라는 작품은 연주 중에 이 시간만큼 일부러 아무런 연주를 하지 않음으로써 청중에게 들리는 우연적 음향을 표현했다. 이는 작곡가나 연주가에 의해 제시된 음악적 재료를 어떤 법칙이나 제약 없이 전달하기 위한 행위 예술이었다.

2. Musical Instruments (악기)

Musical Instrument Classification (악기 분류)	소리를 내어 음악을 이루는 요소가 되는 기구들은 모두 악기라 할 수 있다. 하나의 분류 기준으로는 다양한 악기의 성격을 제대로 반영하기 힘들기 때문에 악기의 재료·모양·연주형태·연주법 등의 여러 기준으로 분류하고 있다. 일반적으로는 연주기법을 기준으로 악기를 구분한다. 현악기(string instruments)는 줄을 활로 켜거나 손으로 뜯어서 소리 내는 악기이며 바이올린·첼로·기타 등이 있다. 관악기(wind instruments)는 입으로 불어서 소리 내는 관 모양의 악기로 재료에 따라 목관악기·금관악기로 나뉜다. 타악기(percussion instruments)는 치거나, 흔들거나, 두드려서 소리 내는 모든 악기들을 말하며 가락을 연주할 수 있는 것과 단순히 리듬이나 효과만을 낼 수 있는 악기로 나누어진다. 피아노와 오르간은 건반악기(keyed instruments)에 속한다.
Piano (피아노)	하프시코드(harpsichord)를 제작한 바르톨로메오 크리스토포리(Bartolomeo Cristofori)가 1698년에 새로운 건반 악기를 만들기 시작했다. 당시 하프시코드는 음량 조절이 불가능해 대중적인 인기를 얻지 못했고, 그래서 그는 음량 조절이 가능한 악기를 만들고 싶어 했다. 1709년에 새로운 악기가 완성되었고, 이 악기의 이름은 '피아노와 포르테가 되는 챔발로'(gravicembalo col piano e forte)였다. 그 후, 이것의 이름은 피아노포르테(pianoforte)로 바뀌었고, 그리고는 piano(피아노)란 이름으로 불리게 되었다.

Art (미술)

인간의 미적 감각을 형상화시키는 창조 활동과 그 결과물인 작품을 다루는 분야이다. TOEFL에서는 다양한 미술 양식에 대해 탐구하며 대표 작품에 대해 소개하는 강의가 주로 출제된다.

Prehistoric Art (선사 시대 미술)	선사 시대에는 주로 실용적인 그림이나 다산을 비는 그림 등 무언가를 바라는 그림이 많았다. 선사 시대 미술 작품은 주로 동굴 벽에서 발견되었다.
Greek Art (그리스 미술)	그리스 미술은 아테네 지역을 중심으로 로마의 지배를 받기 전까지 대표적이었던 미술 양식이다. 이집트 조각의 전면성과 부동성, 그리고 이집트적인 비례가 사용되었던 것으로 미루어 그리스 조각은 고대 이집트의 영향을 받았음을 알 수 있다. 하지만 이집트의 조각들과 달리 이 조각들은 두 팔과 몸통 사이, 다리 사이에 무게를 지탱하는 돌 구조물이 없었다. 또한 그리스 미술은 인체를 정확히 묘사하는 것에 중점을 두었다.
Gothic Art (고딕 미술)	중세 미술(Medieval Art)의 특징은 일반 시민들에게 성경의 내용을 전달하려 했다는 것이다. 그리하여 중세 시대의 예술과 신과 만나는 장소인 성당(cathedral)은 웅장하고 화려해졌다. 고딕 미술은 중세 시대의 미술 양식이다. 고딕 미술은 중세 후기에 영국, 독일, 프랑스 등 여러 나라에 전파되어 유럽을 하나의 예술양식으로 통합시켰다. 고딕 미술 시대에는 염료의 발달로 화려한 색을 많이 사용하기 시작했다. 특히 고딕양식으로 건축된 성당은 스테인드 글라스를 이용해 장식한 거대한 창이 특징으로, 첨탑양식과 인물의 자연스러운 표현에 중점을 두었다.
Renaissance Art (르네상스 미술)	르네상스 미술은 14~16세기 서유럽에서 일어난 문화 운동이다. 르네상스 문화는 이탈리아를 중심으로 발전하여 전 유럽으로 퍼져 나갔다. 이 시기에 교회는 신 중심에서 인간을 위한 것으로 변했고, 미술은 인간 중심의 아름다움을 추구하고자 했다. 르네상스 대표 예술가로는 보티첼리, 도나텔로, 미켈란젤로 등이 있다. 르네상스 시대에 예술품을 복원하는 데는 미적 가치에 비중을 두느냐, 원상태를 유지하는 것에 비중을 두느냐에 따라 두 가지 방법이 있었다. 미적 가치를 추구하는 예술가들은 예술품들을 복원하기 위해 새로운 재료나, 심지어 다른 예술품의 조각들을 사용했고, 그 결과 최초 예술품과는 아주 다른, 새로운 예술품들이 만들어졌다. 원상태를 유지하는 것에 비중을 둔 예술가들은 최초 예술품과 거리가 멀어지는 것을 싫어했고, 그들의 복원 방법은 최초 예술품에서 떨어진 조각들을 다시 붙이는 것에 머물렀다.
Baroque Art (바로크 미술)	17세기 초부터 18세기 전반에 걸쳐 이탈리아를 중심으로 유럽의 여러 가톨릭 국가에서 발전한 미술 양식이다. 바로크 미술은 가톨릭 국가의 종교미술에 새로운 힘을 불어넣었으며 회화의 새로운 기법들과 주제를 다루기 시작했다. 명암(shading)의 강한 대비를 이용하여 세속적이고 현세적인 주제를 다루었고 원근법(perspective)이 등장했다. 바로크 미술은 비고전적·동적·불규칙적·과장적인 특징을 지닌다. 바로크 양식의 대표적인 조각가이자 건축가는 베르니니(Bernini)이다.
Naturalism (자연주의)	19세기의 자연주의는 예술, 철학, 과학에서 나타난 사실주의 운동이자 사실적으로 물체를 묘사하는 데 중점을 둔 예술형태이다. 자연주의 작품의 예로는 미국 화가인 윌리엄 블리스 베이커(William Bliss Baker)의 풍경화, 구스타브 플로베르(Gustave Flaubert)의 <Madame Bovary>가 있다.
Impressionism (인상파)	인상파는 19세기 후반 프랑스를 중심으로 발전했다. 자연을 하나의 색채 현상으로 보고, 빛과 함께 시시각각 움직이는 색채의 미묘한 변화 속에서 자연을 묘사하는 것에 중점을 두었다. 반 고흐(Van Gogh)·모네(Monet)·르누아르(Renoir) 등이 대표적인 인상파 화가이다. 그들은 빛에 의해 변하는 자연의 순간적인 모습을 표현하기 위해 다양한 새로운 기법을 연구했다.

■ Film (영화)

연속 촬영으로 필름에 기록한 화상을 스크린에 투영하여 움직이는 영상을 보여주는 장치, 또는 그것으로 만들어지는 작품을 말하며, motion picture, movie, cinema 등의 용어가 함께 쓰인다. TOEFL에서는 영화의 역사나 영화 기술과 관련된 강의가 주로 출제된다.

1. History of Film (영화의 역사)

Invention of Film (영화의 발명)	물체의 움직임을 포착하여 재현하고자 하는 인간의 시도는 고대부터 시작되었다. 약 2~3만 년 전에 그려진 다리가 8개인 황소 동굴벽화가 에스파냐에서 발견되었다. **Eadweard Muybridge (이드위어드 머이브릿지)** 영국의 사진작가 이드위어드 머이브릿지(Eadweard Muybridge)는 1878년에 말이 뛸 때 네 발이 모두 땅에서 떨어지는지 확인해달라는 부탁을 받아, 달리는 말의 사진 12장을 1/1000초 간격으로 찍는 데 성공했고 네 발이 모두 땅에서 떨어지는 것을 알아냈다. 그 후 머이브릿지는 움직임을 재현하고 싶어 했고, 1879년에 유리 원반에 사진을 그려 넣어 이 판을 회전시키는 방법으로 연속적인 동작을 재생했다. 주프락시스코프(zoopraxiscope)라 불리는 이 기계는 활동사진 영사기의 시초로, 에디슨(Edison)이 사물의 움직임을 볼 수 있는 영사기인 키네토스코프(kinetoscope)를 발명하기 15년 전에 발명된 것이다.
The First Movie Theater (최초의 영화관)	1900년대 초 니켈로디언이 등장하기 전까지는 영화만을 전문적으로 상영하는 영화관이 없었다. 니켈로디언은 영화의 보급과 영화관의 발전에 큰 영향을 준 최초의 영화관이었다. **nickelodeon (니켈로디언)** 니켈로디언(nickelodeon)은 입장료가 5센트이기 때문에 5센트 동전인 니켈(nickel)을 따서 이름이 붙여졌다. 1905년에 최초로 지어져 하루에 15~20분의 영화 수 편을 상영했고 5센트만 내면 영화를 볼 수 있었기 때문에 매우 인기를 얻었다. 하지만 1907년을 전후로 더 길고 짜임새 있는 영화들이 등장했고 이런 영화들을 상영하는 더 큰 규모의 영화관들이 지어지면서 인기가 떨어지게 되었다.
1920s~30s Film (1920~1930년대의 영화)	세계 영화사에서 1920년대와 1930년대는 영화가 예술적 매체로 인정 받을 수 있는 작품들이 나타나고 영화의 수용이 대폭 증가된 시기였다. 1920년대 후반에 사운드를 가진 영화가 미국에서 등장한 것이 영화발전의 원동력이 되었다. **The Wizard of Oz (오즈의 마법사)** 1930년대 대공황 시기에는 사람들이 어려움을 잊고 즐길 수 있는 밝은 내용과 교훈적인 메시지를 가진 뮤지컬 영화가 많이 만들어졌다. 그 대표적인 영화가 1939년에 개봉한 <오즈의 마법사>이다. 고난을 이겨내면서 집으로 돌아가는 주인공 도로시와 주인공을 돕는 주변 등장인물들의 모습을 통해 미국의 전통적인 가치를 살리려는 노력이 깃든 작품이다.

2. Technology of Film (영화 기술)

Silent Film & Sound Pictures (무성영화와 유성영화)	무성영화는 음향을 수반하지 않는 영화이며 1927년 미국에서 최초의 유성영화 <Jazz Singer>가 만들어졌다. 초기 무성영화는 부자연스러운 특징이 있었으나 피아노나 다른 악기들의 반주를 배경음악으로 사용하게 되면서 점차 자연스러워졌다. 행동과 몸짓, 표정만으로 영화의 내용을 전달해야 했기 때문에 배우들은 다소 과장하여 연기하는 경향이 있었다. 따라서 무성영화 시대의 배우가 연극을 하거나 유성영화에 출연할 때에는 과장된 연기 때문에 문제가 발생했다. 유성영화 시대가 시작되면서 음향 기술은 점차적으로 발달하여 현재에는 digital sound를 이용하고 있다. 음향 편집 과정에서 이미지와 사운드가 동시에 일어난 것처럼 하는 것을 synchronous sound라고 하며 시간적 차이를 염두에 두고 음향이 삽입되는 것을 non-synchronous sound라고 한다. 이는 대사뿐만 아니라 배경음악까지도 포함하는 개념이다.

Photography (사진)

태양광·전자선 등이 필름 위에 피사체의 영상을 찍어내는 것을 말하는데 과학기술과 예술의 특성을 모두 가지고 있다. TOEFL에서는 사진술의 발달과 사진의 사조와 관련된 강의가 주로 출제된다.

1. History of Photography (사진의 역사)

Invention of Photography (사진술의 발명)	사진술 발명의 관건은 움직이는 이미지의 고정된 화상을 어떻게 얻어낼 수 있는가였으며, 많은 사람들이 이를 성공시키기 위해 노력했다. **heliography (헬리오그래피)** 헬리오그래피는 1826년 프랑스의 니엡스(Niepce)가 발명한 사진술로, 아스팔트 건판과 카메라 옵스큐라를 사용했다. 니엡스는 아스팔트 건판을 카메라 옵스큐라의 상이 맺히는 면에 설치한 후 오랜 시간 빛에 노출시켜 인쇄판을 얻었다. 그러나 니엡스는 자신의 사진술이 미완성이라고 생각하여 헬리오그래피의 제작과정을 공표하지 않았고, 따라서 세계 최초의 사진 발명가로 공식적인 인정을 받지는 못했다. **daguerreotype (다게레오타입)** 다게레오타입은 1837년 프랑스 화가 다게르(Daguerre)가 발명한 사진술로, 은판사진법이라고도 한다. 연마한 은판 표면에 요오드화은의 빛에 의해 변하기 쉬운 성질을 지닌 감광막(photosensitive film)을 만들어 30여분 동안 노출한 후 수은 증기로 현상하는 방법으로, 최초의 성공적인 사진술이다. 다게르가 발명한 은판사진은 1839년 프랑스의 과학 아카데미에서 정식 발명품으로 인정받았다. **calotype (캘로타입)** 캘로타입은 1835년 영국의 의사 겸 과학자 탈보트(Talbot)가 발명한 사진술로, 금속판을 사용한 다게레오타입과는 달리 종이에 인화하는 방법이었다. 캘로타입은 1839년 1월 7일 발표된 다게레오타입보다 며칠 늦은 1839년 1월 25일 발표되었기 때문에 최초의 사진술로는 인정받지 못하였다. 한번에 한 장의 사진만 찍어낼 수 있는 다게레오타입과 달리 캘로타입은 복제가 가능했지만, 당시에 종이의 질이 좋지 않아 세부적인 묘사가 어려웠기 때문에 다게레오타입에 비해 대중의 인기는 얻지 못했다.
Camera (카메라)	카메라는 물체의 상을 렌즈를 통해 감광재료(필름)에 맺히게 하여 사진을 찍는 도구이다. 카메라 옵스큐라에서 시작된 이후 기술이 발전해 점점 더 좋은 화질의 사진을 얻을 수 있게 되었다. **camera obscura (카메라 옵스큐라)** 카메라 옵스큐라는 사진기의 기원으로, 라틴어로 '어두운 방'이라는 뜻이다. 이것은 카메라 상자 안쪽에 광선의 초점을 맞추기 위한 렌즈나 핀홀을 갖춘 셔터가 없는 초기 형태의 카메라이다. 1589년에는 이탈리아의 포르타(Porta)가 큰 상자에 반사경과 볼록렌즈(convex lens)를 붙여 상을 비추는 장치를 만들어냈으며, 1685년 독일 수도승 요한 찬(Johann Zahn)이 그림을 그리는 도구로 만든 휴대용 카메라 옵스큐라가 훗날 박스 카메라의 원형이라 할 수 있다. **pinhole camera (핀홀 카메라)** 핀홀 카메라는 렌즈 대신 바늘 구멍(pinhole)을 이용해 사진을 찍는 카메라이다. 내부를 검게 칠한 통의 한쪽 면에 작은 구멍을 내고 반대쪽 면에 필름을 장치하도록 되어 있다. 렌즈를 사용하는 카메라와 달리 근거리에서 원거리까지 모두 초점이 맞는다는 특징이 있다. 그러나 구멍을 통해 들어오는 빛의 양이 적기 때문에 장시간 노출(exposure)이 필요하며 움직이는 물체의 촬영에는 적합하지 않다. 구멍을 크게 하면 노출시간은 줄어드나 영상이 선명하지 않고 흐려진다.

2. Trends in Photography (사진의 사조)

naturalistic photography (자연주의적 사진)	자연주의적 사진은 19세기 말과 20세기 초에 유럽 전반에서 유행하던 아카데믹한 회화양식을 모방한 사진술에 반대하는 운동이다. 1889년 영국의 피터 헨리 에머슨(Peter Henry Emerson)에 의해 시작되었으며 눈에 보이는 그대로의 영상을 얻는 것을 목적으로 한다. 망막(retina)에 비치는 것처럼 대상을 충실하게 기록하기 위해서는 렌즈의 가장자리를 아웃 포커스(out of focus) 시켜야 한다고 주장했다. 아웃 포커스란 초점을 정확하게 맞추지 않고 흐려 보이도록 하는 기법이다.

■ Architecture (건축)

인간의 생활을 보조하기 위해 여러 가지 용도의 구축물을 세우는 공간 예술이다. TOEFL에서는 건축의 역사와 시대별 다양한 건축 양식과 관련된 강의가 주로 출제된다.

Prehistoric Times (선사시대)	신석기 시대의 움집	인류의 역사가 시작되면서부터 인간은 자연적인 환경인 온도·습도·비·눈·바람으로부터 자신을 보호하기 위한 방법을 찾기 시작했다. 구석기 시대(Old Stone Age)에는 유랑생활의 영향으로 동굴에서 살았으며 농경으로 인해 정착생활을 시작한 신석기 시대(New Stone Age)에는 물가에 움집(dugout hut)을 짓고 마을을 형성하였다.
Ancient Times (고대)	**ancient housing (고대의 주택)** 로마의 귀족 주택	가장 오래된 주택은 이집트의 유적에서 발견된다. 흙벽돌을 쌓고 그 위에 마른 풀을 엮어 얹어 천장을 만들었다. 로마 시대의 주택은 석재와 벽돌을 재료로 사용했다. 귀족의 주택은 거실·식당·욕실·침실·객실 등으로 호화스럽게 구성되었으며 실외에 화려한 정원 또한 조성되어 있었다. 그러나 지방에서는 여전히 나뭇가지와 흙을 재료로 한 주택이 일반적이었다.
	ancient theater (고대의 극장) 연극 관람은 고대 그리스 문화에서 매우 중요한 부분이어서 헬레니즘 시대가 되자 모든 마을이 극장을 소유하고 있을 정도였다. 고대 그리스의 극장은 오케스트라(orchestra), 스케네(skene), 테아트론(theatron) 3가지의 주요 부분으로 구성되었는데, 오케스트라는 연극이 상연되는 무대로 반원 모양이었다. 분장실의 역할을 한 스케네(skene)는 오케스트라 뒤에서 관객들을 향해 있는 직사각형의 건물이었으며, 스케네의 평평한 지붕은 연극 중 신(god)이 등장하는 장소로 종종 쓰였다. 관객석은 테아트론(theatron)이라 불리며 오케스트라 주위에 반원형으로 배열되어 뒤로 갈수록 높아지도록 지어졌다. 테아트론의 이러한 구조는 가장 멀리 앉은 사람도 배우들이 하는 말을 들을 수 있도록 하는 뛰어난 음향효과를 자아냈다.	
Medieval Times (중세)	중세 서양의 빈번했던 전쟁과 절도행위는 건축형식에도 영향을 미쳤다. 귀족계급들은 주택을 지을 때 침입에 대비하여 돌 등의 재료로 두꺼운 외벽을 만들고, 창문을 작게 만들었다. 도시의 주위에는 성벽을 쌓았으며, 성벽 안의 한정된 공간에서 주택들은 성 중심에 위치한 시장 주변으로 둥글게 배치되어 있었다.	

HACKERS TEST 🎧 T4_S2_2_Test

[01-04] Listen to a talk in a film class.

01 What is the main topic of the talk?

Ⓐ The technical equipment used by boom operators
Ⓑ The evolution of film sound recording methods
Ⓒ Methods for capturing and processing film dialogue
Ⓓ Different microphone types in professional filmmaking

02 What is NOT mentioned as a key element of a complete movie soundtrack?

Ⓐ Audio effects
Ⓑ Sound balancing
Ⓒ Music
Ⓓ Spoken lines

03 According to the speaker, what is a problem with hiding microphones on actors' clothing?

Ⓐ It makes actors feel uncomfortable during filming.
Ⓑ It requires actors to wear specific types of clothing.
Ⓒ It creates shadows that are visible in the camera frame.
Ⓓ It captures unwanted noises that disrupt the clarity of dialogue.

04 What will the speaker most likely discuss next?

Ⓐ Digital tools for audio post-production
Ⓑ Software-based volume normalization
Ⓒ Evaluation criteria for the practical exam
Ⓓ Advanced sound mixing techniques

[05-08] Listen to a talk in an architecture class.

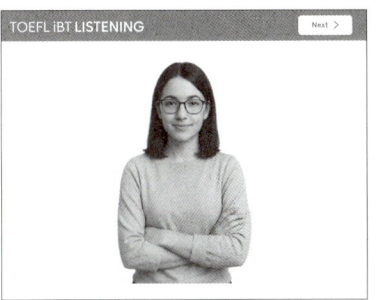

05 What is the talk mainly about?

   Ⓐ The architectural elements of Greek theaters
   Ⓑ The building materials used in ancient Greece
   Ⓒ The gods and mythology in Greek theater
   Ⓓ The cultural importance of theater in ancient Greece

06 Why does the speaker mention the Hellenistic period?

   Ⓐ To compare different architectural periods
   Ⓑ To emphasize the cultural shift in Greek society
   Ⓒ To demonstrate how common theaters had become
   Ⓓ To explain when theater architecture was standardized

07 What is NOT mentioned as one of the three main parts of ancient Greek theater?

   Ⓐ Chorus
   Ⓑ Orchestra
   Ⓒ Seating area
   Ⓓ Backdrop building

08 What will the speaker most likely discuss next?

   Ⓐ The acoustic research methods used by scientists
   Ⓑ The evolution of theatrical performances over time
   Ⓒ The influence of Greek theater on Roman architecture
   Ⓓ The comparison of ancient and contemporary theaters

HACKERS TEST

[09-12] Listen to a talk in an art class.

09 What is the main topic of the talk?

Ⓐ The technical challenges of producing blue pigments
Ⓑ The chemical composition of ancient pigments
Ⓒ The chronological development of blue pigments
Ⓓ The comparison between natural and synthetic colors

10 Why does the speaker mention Afghanistan?

Ⓐ To show the geographic origin of lapis lazuli
Ⓑ To describe the transportation methods of the time
Ⓒ To illustrate the dangers of ancient mining operations
Ⓓ To compare different mining techniques across cultures

11 According to the speaker, what was a problem with lapis lazuli?

Ⓐ It was used only for royal artwork.
Ⓑ It was costly and dangerous to import.
Ⓒ It was difficult to extract from the rock.
Ⓓ It faded quickly when exposed to sunlight.

12 What does the speaker say about Egyptian blue?

Ⓐ It was more durable than modern blue paints.
Ⓑ It was used exclusively for religious purposes.
Ⓒ It was the first artificially produced blue pigment.
Ⓓ Its production method was rediscovered in modern times.

[13-16] Listen to a talk in an architecture class.

13 What is the purpose of the talk?

Ⓐ To promote Gothic Revival buildings for tourism
Ⓑ To criticize modern interpretations of medieval designs
Ⓒ To encourage preservation of authentic Gothic buildings
Ⓓ To illustrate cultural differences in architectural adaptation

14 What is implied about European Gothic architecture?

Ⓐ It integrated architectural form with a religious purpose.
Ⓑ It focused on creating comfortable living spaces for nobles.
Ⓒ It was built primarily to showcase technical construction skills.
Ⓓ It prioritized ornamental features over structural integrity.

15 What is NOT mentioned as a characteristic of Notre Dame Cathedral's Gothic style?

Ⓐ Elaborate ornamentation
Ⓑ Grid-like facade pattern
Ⓒ Narrow windows
Ⓓ Flying buttresses

16 What will the speaker most likely discuss next?

Ⓐ Biographical information about Gothic Revival architects
Ⓑ Additional examples of culturally transformed architectural styles
Ⓒ Technical specifications of Gothic structural elements
Ⓓ Restoration projects for European Gothic cathedrals

HACKERS TEST

[17-20] Listen to a talk in a music class.

17 What is the main topic of the talk?

  Ⓐ The development of instrumental music in Europe
  Ⓑ The influence of Johann Sebastian Bach on modern music
  Ⓒ The comparison between Renaissance and the Classical period
  Ⓓ The period of dramatic musical transformation in Europe

18 Why does the speaker mention churches and royal courts?

  Ⓐ To show how performance locations influenced musical style
  Ⓑ To highlight the religious themes in Baroque compositions
  Ⓒ To compare different acoustic environments for performances
  Ⓓ To explain the patronage system for Baroque composers

19 According to the speaker, what is basso continuo?

  Ⓐ A performance style emphasizing dramatic musical contrasts
  Ⓑ A method for transitioning between major and minor keys
  Ⓒ A continuous bass line that provides harmonic support
  Ⓓ An instrumental ensemble featuring violin-family instruments

20 What is NOT mentioned as a musical form established during the Baroque period?

  Ⓐ Fugue
  Ⓑ Symphony
  Ⓒ Sonata
  Ⓓ Suite

[21-24] Listen to a talk in a photography class.

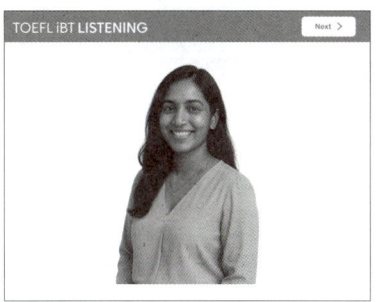

21 What point does the speaker make about the camera obscura?

Ⓐ It is literally translated as "bright room" in Latin.
Ⓑ It projects an inverted image onto the opposite wall.
Ⓒ It requires sophisticated technology to function.
Ⓓ It was invented by medieval scholars for scientific research.

22 What can be inferred about the historical significance of the camera obscura?

Ⓐ It was considered a form of magic rather than science.
Ⓑ It contributed to the development of art and science.
Ⓒ It represented the peak of ancient technological achievement.
Ⓓ It improved medieval scholars' understanding of the human body.

23 Why does the speaker mention the human eye?

Ⓐ To describe the biological basis of image formation
Ⓑ To explain why cameras were unnecessary before modern times
Ⓒ To highlight why Ibn al-Haytham focused on optical research
Ⓓ To compare ancient and modern understanding of optics

24 What will the speaker most likely discuss next?

Ⓐ Modern applications of the camera obscura in contemporary art
Ⓑ The decline in the use of the camera obscura in modern times
Ⓒ The historical progression from observation to image capture
Ⓓ A detailed analysis of the behavior of light rays in optical systems

Answers p.573

3. Social Science

사회과학은 인간 사회의 구조와 행동 양식을 과학적으로 연구하는 분야로, 크게 경제학, 경영학, 사회학, 인류학, 고고학의 여섯 가지 주제로 나누어 볼 수 있다. 경제학의 이론과 시장 메커니즘, 현대 비즈니스와 경영 전략, 심리학의 다양한 요소, 사회학의 사회 현상 해석, 인류학과 고고학의 문화 탐구가 주요 주제이다. 특히, TOEFL의 사회과학 강의는 이론적 개념을 실제 사례에 적용하여 설명하는 경우가 많다.

■ Economics (경제학)

인간이 자신의 욕구를 가장 효율적으로 충족시키기 위해 제한된 유·무형의 재화를 가지고 어떤 선택을 하는지에 대해 주로 연구하는 사회과학 분야의 학문이다. TOEFL에서는 경제와 관련된 다양한 개념을 소개하는 강의가 주로 출제된다.

Absolute Advantage (절대우위)	어떤 재화에 대해 이를 생산하는 데 필요한 비용이 한 나라가 다른 나라보다 낮을 때, 그 나라는 이 재화의 생산에 있어 절대우위에 있다고 한다. 예를 들어, 밀을 생산하는 데 있어 A 나라가 B 나라보다 같은 단위를 생산하는 데 들어가는 비용이 낮다면 A 나라는 밀 생산에서 절대우위에 있게 된다. 두 국가 사이에 절대우위를 가지는 재화의 종류가 다를 경우 각 국가가 절대우위에 있는 재화의 생산에 집중하여 서로 교환함으로써 그렇지 않은 경우보다 더 많은 재화를 얻을 수 있다.
Comparative Advantage (비교우위)	어떤 재화에 대해 이를 생산하는 데 필요한 비용이 한 나라가 다른 나라보다 상대적으로 낮을 때, 즉 그 재화의 생산에 대한 기회비용이 다른 나라보다 낮을 때 그 나라는 이 재화의 생산에 있어 비교우위에 있다고 한다. 예를 들어, A 나라가 밀과 커피 두 재화 모두에 대해 절대우위에 있다고 하더라도, A 나라의 밀 생산에 대한 기회비용이 B 나라보다 작고, B 나라의 커피 생산에 대한 기회비용이 A 나라보다 작다면, A 나라와 B 나라는 각각 밀과 커피의 생산에 있어 비교우위에 있게 된다. 이 경우에도 각 국가가 비교우위를 가지는 재화의 생산에 집중하여 서로 교환함으로써 그렇지 않은 경우보다 더 많은 재화를 얻을 수 있다.
Opportunity Cost (기회비용)	제한된 자원을 가지고 한 재화를 생산하기 위해서는 다른 재화의 생산을 포기해야 하는데, 이때 생산하지 않은 재화를 생산했을 경우 얻을 수 있었을 이익을 기회비용이라고 한다. 예를 들어, A 나라가 정해진 단위의 자원을 투입했을 때 밀 2톤 또는 커피 1톤을 생산할 수 있다고 한다면, A 나라의 밀 1톤을 생산하기 위한 기회비용은 커피 0.5톤이고 커피 1톤을 생산하기 위한 기회비용은 밀 2톤이다.

Business Management (경영학)

기업의 효율적인 운영을 위해 기업의 조직과 관리 및 운영에 대해 과학적으로 연구하는 학문이다. TOEFL에서는 경영학과 관련된 다양한 개념을 소개하거나 마케팅과 관련된 강의가 주로 출제된다.

1. 경영학 기초 개념

Financial Management (재무 관리)	기업의 경영활동에 필요한 자금을 조달하고 전반적인 자금 운용을 효율적으로 관리하는 활동을 말한다. 단순한 이익의 극대화에 국한되지 않고 기업가치를 높여 주주의 부를 극대화하는 것을 목적으로 한다.
Production Management (생산 관리)	주로 제조업에서 생산활동을 계획·조직·통제하는 전반적인 활동을 말한다. 제품과 서비스의 생산을 효과적이고 효율적으로 관리하여 생산성을 극대화하는 것을 목적으로 한다.
Marketing (마케팅)	소비자에게 재화와 서비스를 유통하는 전 과정에 걸친 활동을 말한다. 소비자에게 최대의 만족을 주고 생산목적을 가장 효율적으로 달성하는 것을 목적으로 하며 상품 및 서비스의 개발, 가격결정, 광고, 유통 등이 포함된다.
Human Resources Management (인적 자원 관리)	인력의 확보·개발·활용에 관한 계획적이고 조직적인 관리활동을 말한다. 조직의 목표와 개인의 목표가 조화를 이루도록 하여 기업의 목표를 이루기 위한 인적 자원을 확보하고 그들이 최대한의 역량을 발휘하도록 하는 것을 목적으로 한다.

2. Marketing (마케팅)

4Ms of Marketing (마케팅의 4M)	성공적인 마케팅 전략을 위해 고려해야 할 4가지 요소, 시장(market), 돈(money), 메시지(message), 매체(media)를 마케팅의 4M이라고 한다. 구체적으로 4M이란 첫째, 상품을 판매하고자 하는 대상인 표적 시장(target market)을 정확히 파악해야 한다는 것이며 둘째, 효율적인 방법으로 돈(money)을 투자해야 한다는 것이다. 또한 셋째, 마케팅 수단을 선택할 때 이것이 지니는 의미나 메시지(message)를 고려해야 하며 넷째, 표적 시장에 따라 효과적으로 메시지를 전달할 수 있는 매체(media)를 선택해야 한다는 것을 의미한다.
Market Segmentation (시장 세분화)	시장 세분화란 소비자를 특정 기준에 따라 나누고 각 소비자 층에 따라 시장을 구분하여 집중적으로 마케팅 전략을 펴는 것이다. 이는 소비자의 필요와 욕구를 정확하게 충족시키고 변화하는 시장수요에 능동적으로 대처하기 위한 것이다. 지리적 기준, 연령과 성별 및 직업 등의 인구통계학적 기준, 라이프스타일과 개성 등의 사회심리학적 기준, 상품 또는 서비스의 사용량과 상표충성도 등을 포함하는 행동분석적 기준을 적용하여 시장을 세분화할 수 있다.
Crisis Management (위기 관리)	위기 관리는 문제가 발생했을 경우 회사 전체가 관여하는 조직적인 접근 방법이다. 예를 들어, 제품에 문제가 있는 것으로 드러날 경우 회사는 해당 문제에 대해서 대중들에게 사과(apology)를 하고, 문제가 있는 제품들을 리콜(recall)한다. 이로써 대중들에게 회사가 자신들의 이익보다 소비자의 안전을 우선시한다는 인식을 준다. 또한 이에 그치지 않고 같은 문제가 다시 발생하지 않도록 제품의 품질관리 조사(quality control check)를 실시하고 방침을 수정하며 대외 홍보(Public Relations)팀이 이를 소비자에게 공식 성명을 통해 알린다. 그리고 소비자가 제품을 다시 구매하도록 특별한 판매 촉진(special promotion)을 실행하여 문제가 발생하기 전의 이익과 명성을 회복할 수 있도록 노력한다. **service recovery paradox (서비스 회복의 역설)** 서비스 회복의 역설이란, 기업이 고객의 문제를 매우 잘 처리하여 애초에 문제가 없었을 경우보다 고객의 만족도와 충성도(loyalty)가 더 높아진 경우를 말한다. 이는 고객들이 그들을 만족시키기 위해 기업이 특별한 관심과 노력을 들였으며 앞으로도 그렇게 할 것이라고 느끼기 때문에 가능하다.

Psychology (심리학)

인간 혹은 동물의 행동과 정신 활동을 연구하는 학문이다. TOEFL에서는 심리학적 요인이나 다양한 심리학 실험과 관련된 강의가 주로 출제된다.

1. Psychological Elements (심리학적 요소)

Memory (기억)

인간은 기억 능력 덕분에 경험하거나 생각한 것을 일정 시간이 지난 후에도 재구성할 수 있다.

short-term memory & long-term memory (단기기억과 장기기억)

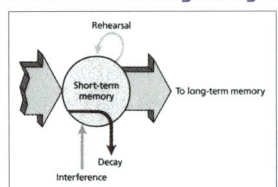

기억은 단기기억과 장기기억 두 종류로 구분할 수 있다. 단기기억은 몇십 초의 짧은 시간 동안 뇌에 저장되었다가 소멸하며, 장기기억은 매우 오랜 기간 동안 뇌의 기억장치에 저장된다. 단기기억 용량은 사람의 경우 평균 7개의 숫자나 문자 정도이고, 단기 기억장치가 가득 차 있는 상태에서 새로운 정보가 유입되면 원래의 정보가 새로운 정보로 치환된다. 단기기억이 반복되어 형성되는 장기기억의 경우, 정보는 비교적 오랫동안 유지되며 용량에도 제한이 없다.

Needs (욕구)

생명을 유지하고 생활을 영위하기 위해 신체적·정신적 부족 상태를 채우려는 심리를 의미한다.

hierarchy of needs (욕구계층이론)

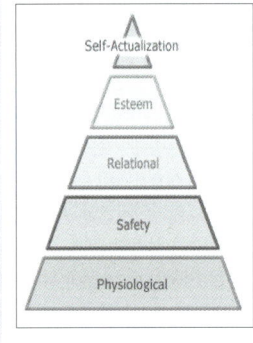

미국의 심리학자 매슬로우(Maslow)는 욕구계층이론을 통해 인간의 욕구는 타고난 것이며 행동의 동기라고 정의했다. 인간의 욕구는 강도와 중요성에 따라 5단계로 구분되며 하위 단계의 욕구가 충족되어야 그 다음 단계의 욕구가 발생한다. 1단계는 생리적 욕구(physiological needs)로 의식주, 종족보존 등과 관련된다. 2단계는 안전에 대한 욕구(safety needs)로 추위·질병·위험으로부터 자신을 보호하려는 욕구이다. 3단계는 애정과 소속에 대한 욕구(love and belongingness needs)로 가정을 이루거나 친구를 사귀는 등 단체에 소속되어 애정을 주거나 받고자 하는 욕구이다. 4단계는 자기존중의 욕구(self-esteem needs)로 명예나 권력을 누리려는 욕구이다. 5단계인 자아실현의 욕구(self-actualization needs)는 자신의 재능과 잠재력을 발휘하려는 최고 수준의 욕구이다.

Personality (성격)

지능과 함께 개인을 특징짓는 요소로서, 한 개인의 지속적이며 일관된 행동 양식을 말한다.

character formation (성격 형성)

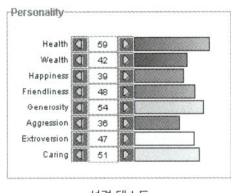

성격 테스트

성격 형성에 영향을 미치는 요소는 다양하다. 기본적으로 선천적·유전적 요인을 토대로 나이, 문화적 환경, 성별, 교육과 경험의 정도, 사회적 위치 등 여러 변수들이 작용하여 개개인의 고유한 성격이 형성된다. 이러한 요인들에 의해 형성되는 성격은 감정(emotion)의 강약, 외향성(extroversion), 개방성(openness), 친밀성(agreeableness), 성실성(conscientiousness) 등의 요소들이 결합해 표출된다.

Feelings (감정)

어떤 행동을 할 때 생리적, 심리적 원인으로 인해 발생하는 주관적 동요를 감정이라 한다.

감정의 종류

프로이드

희로애락의 감정은 비교적 격렬하고 폭발적으로 표출되지만 오래 지속되지 않는다. 이에 비해서 걱정, 불안은 표현이 억제되지만 비교적 오래 지속되는 경향이 있다. 이 밖에도 유머, 행복, 존경 등과 같이 가치의식(value consciousness)이 가해진 안정적이고 지속적인 감정도 있다. 한편, 프로이드(Freud)는 사랑과 미움, 복종과 반항, 쾌락과 고통 등 상반된 감정이 동시에 존재하는 것을 양향성(ambivalence)이라고 하였다. 양향성은 복잡한 감정의 심리적 특성을 잘 반영하고 있다.

2. Psychological Experiments (심리학 실험)

Marshmallow Test (마시멜로 실험)	월터 미셸(Walter Mischel)이 1972년에 실시한 마시멜로 실험은 지연 만족(delayed gratification)과 자기 통제 능력을 연구한 대표적인 실험이다. 이 실험에서는 4-6세 아이들에게 마시멜로 하나를 주고, 연구자가 돌아올 때까지 기다리면 마시멜로를 하나 더 받을 수 있다고 말했다. 약 15분 후 돌아온 연구자는 기다린 아이들에게 약속대로 추가 마시멜로를 주었다. 장기 추적 연구 결과, 기다릴 수 있었던 아이들이 성인이 되어서도 더 높은 학업 성취도, 더 나은 건강 상태, 낮은 비만율을 보였다. 이 실험은 자기 통제 능력이 인생 전반의 성공에 미치는 영향을 보여주는 중요한 연구로 여겨진다. 그러나 최근 연구들은 사회경제적 배경, 신뢰도 등 다른 요인들도 결과에 영향을 미칠 수 있음을 지적하고 있다.
Strange Situation Test (낯선 상황 실험)	미국의 발달심리학자인 매리 에인스워스(Mary Ainsworth)는 일련의 낯선 상황을 조성하는 실험을 고안했다. 실험의 요지는 보호자의 참석 여부에 따라 낯선 이에게 보이는 반응 차이와 보호자가 떠났다가 다시 돌아올 때의 반응을 관찰, 분류하여 유아들의 애착형성 유형을 구분하는 것이다. 심리학자들은 이 실험에 근거해 유아의 애착유형을 긍정적인 것과 부정적인 것으로 나누고, 또 부정적인 유형을 회피형과 양면형으로 나눴다. 우선 긍정적인 애착유형인 안정 애착(secure attachment)을 가지는 유아는 보호자 참석 시 거리낌 없이 방안을 돌아다니고 낯선 사람과도 무리 없이 교류한다. 하지만 보호자가 자리를 뜨면 눈에 띄게 동요하는 모습을 보이며, 보호자가 돌아왔을 때 매우 행복한 듯한 반응을 보인다. 부정적인 애착유형 중, 회피 애착(avoidant attachment)을 가지는 유아는 실험이 진행되는 동안 감정의 변화를 거의 보이지 않는다. 보호자의 참석 여부에 상관없이 장난감 등 자기의 관심사에만 집중하며 보호자와 낯선 사람 모두에게 일정한 감정적 거리를 유지한다. 다른 하나의 부정적 애착유형인 양면 애착(ambivalent attachment)은 실험 내내 보호자의 곁에 머무는 행동을 보인다. 보호자가 자리를 뜨면 굉장한 스트레스를 표출하다가 보호자가 다시 돌아오면 물리적으로 가까운 거리에 머문다. 특이한 점은 비록 물리적으로 근접한 곳에 머물긴 하지만 보호자와 감정적인 교류를 거부하고 보호자가 달래주려고 해도 이에 대해 반응을 보이지 않는다는 것이다.

■ Sociology (사회학)

인간 사회의 구조, 기능, 변동을 체계적으로 연구하는 학문이다. TOEFL에서는 사회학과 관련된 다양한 개념에 대해 설명하는 강의가 주로 출제된다.

Social Capital (사회 자본)	사회 자본은 개인이나 집단이 사회적 네트워크와 관계를 통해 얻을 수 있는 자원을 의미한다. 신뢰, 상호 협력, 공유된 가치와 규범 등이 사회 자본의 구성 요소이다. 사회 자본은 결속형 사회 자본(bonding social capital)과 연결형 사회 자본(bridging social capital)으로 구분되며, 전자는 동질적인 집단 내의 강한 유대를, 후자는 서로 다른 집단 간의 약한 유대를 의미한다. 사회 자본이 높은 지역 사회는 범죄율 감소, 재해 대응 능력 향상, 주민 건강 증진 등의 긍정적 효과를 보이지만, 과도한 결속은 외부인 배제나 집단 사고를 야기할 수 있다.
Cohort (코호트)	코호트는 특정 시기에 공통된 경험을 공유하는 개인들의 집단을 의미한다. 사회학에서 코호트는 주로 출생 코호트(birth cohort)를 가리키며, 같은 시기에 태어나 유사한 역사적 사건과 사회적 변화를 경험한 세대를 지칭한다. 예를 들어, 베이비붐 세대(1946-1964년생), 밀레니얼 세대(1981-1996년생) 등이 대표적인 코호트이다. 코호트 분석을 통해 사회학자들은 세대 간 차이, 사회 변동의 영향, 생애 주기에 따른 행동 패턴 등을 연구한다. 코호트 효과(cohort effect)는 특정 세대가 공유하는 독특한 특성이나 행동 양식이 생애 전반에 걸쳐 지속되는 현상을 설명한다.
Cultural Relativism (문화 상대주의)	문화 상대주의는 각 문화를 그 문화 자체의 맥락에서 이해하고 평가해야 한다는 관점이다. 이는 자문화 중심주의(ethnocentrism)와 대비되는 개념으로, 다른 문화를 자신의 문화 기준으로 판단하는 것을 지양한다. 문화 상대주의는 문화의 다양성을 인정하고 존중하는 태도를 강조하지만, 보편적 인권과의 균형을 맞추는 것이 중요한 과제이다.

■ Anthropology (인류학)

생물학적인 인류의 특징 및 의식주·사회구조·종교·예술 등 다른 동물에서 찾아볼 수 없는 인류 특유의 생활방식인 문화를 연구하는 학문이다. TOEFL에서는 인류의 특징과 인류의 다양한 문명과 관련된 강의가 주로 출제된다.

1. Features of Humans (인류의 특징)
인류가 유인원과 구별되는 특징은 직립보행을 할 수 있다는 점과 창조적이고 추상적인 사고능력(creative and abstract thinking)을 통해 도구와 불, 언어를 사용한다는 것이다.

인류의 직립보행	인류는 약 250만 년 전에 등장한 오스트랄로피테쿠스 때부터 직립보행을 시작했다. 두 발로 서서 걷게 되면서 인류의 뇌의 크기가 커졌고 손이 자유로워져 도구 사용이 가능해졌다. 또한 시야가 넓어져 전반적인 생활 능력이 향상되었다.
인류의 불과 언어 사용	약 50만 년 전 인류가 처음으로 불을 사용하게 되면서 음식을 익혀 먹을 수 있게 되고 토기(earth vessel)가 발명되어 생활 능력이 향상되었다. 언어가 발생하면서 인간의 창조적이고 추상적인 사고능력이 시작되었다. 인류학자들은 원시인들(primitives)의 두개골(skull)과 턱뼈에 붙어있는 뇌와 혀를 잇는 신경 근육을 연구한 결과, 인류가 처음으로 언어를 사용하기 시작한 때를 약 40만 년 전으로 추측하고 있다. 이는 원인류의 뇌가 현생인류의 뇌의 크기와 비슷해지는 시기와 일치한다.

2. Civilization (문명)
인류가 이룩한 물질적·사회적인 발전을 문명이라고 하며 도시적 요소, 사회계층분화, 고도의 기술 등을 특징으로 하는 문화 복합체를 의미한다.

Mayan Civilization (마야문명)	마야문명은 기원전 2500년경 지금의 멕시코 및 과테말라 지역을 중심으로 번성한 고대문명(ancient civilization)이다. 다른 문명들과는 달리 인간이 살기에 부적합한 열대 밀림에 위치하였으며 수많은 부족으로 구성된 도시국가(city-state) 형태였다. 사회적 지위가 엄격하게 구분되는 계급사회였으며 통화(currency)를 사용하여 교역을 하기도 했다. 점성술(astrology)·역법(the calendar)·수학·미술·공예 등이 발달하였으며 상형문자의 일종인 신성문자와 숫자를 사용하여 그들만의 독특한 문화를 이룩하였다. 마야문명은 고전기와 신마야기로 나뉘는데 고전기 마야문명이 갑자기 멸망한 이유에 대해서는 노예의 반란, 다른 민족의 침입, 천재지변, 화전 농업(fire agriculture), 문화에 따른 이동 등 다양한 의견으로 논란이 많다.
Cretan Civilization (크레타문명)	크레타문명은 기원전 2500년경 지중해 동부 에게 해(Aegean sea)의 크레타(Crete) 섬을 중심으로 번영한 고대문명이다. 수도 크노소스(Cnossos)를 중심으로 최초로 섬 전체를 지배한 미노스(Minos) 왕의 이름에서 유래되어 미노아문명(Minoan civilization)이라고도 한다. 크레타 섬은 다른 섬들보다 면적이 넓고 평야가 많아서 문명 발생에 좋은 환경이었으며 오리엔트(Orient) 세계, 특히 이집트로부터 많은 영향을 받았다. 미노스 왕 이후 정치·군사·예술 등이 급속도로 발전하였으며 동부 지중해 지역의 교역을 독점했다. 크레타인의 개방적이고 현대적인 감각을 바탕으로 사실적이며 화려한 문화가 발전했다.
Andean Civilization (안데스문명)	안데스문명은 기원전 1000년경 남아메리카 안데스 지역에 번영한 고대문명이다. 도시문화가 형성된 이후 도시의 규모가 커지면서 군사적 힘이 강해졌다. 대표적인 부족으로는 잉카(Inca) 족이 있는데, 지금의 페루지역인 남부 산악지대에 본거지를 뒀으며 15세기 중엽 잉카제국을 건설했다. 잉카제국의 사회에서는 절대군주인 잉카를 받들고, 지배층과 평민으로 나뉘는 계층사회를 형성하여 중앙집권적 전제정치를 시행하였다. 그러나 평민을 위한 사회보장이 완비되어 있었다는 특징이 있다.

Archaeology (고고학)

인간이 남긴 유적·유물의 특징과 관계를 밝혀 과거의 문화·역사 및 생활방법을 연구하는 학문이다. TOEFL에서는 선사시대의 각 시대 특징이나 고고학의 연구 방법과 관련된 강의가 주로 출제된다.

1. Prehistoric Age (선사시대)

인류의 발달과정은 도구를 만드는 방법을 기준으로 구분할 수 있다. 석기, 청동기, 철기를 사용하던 시대로 나누어지며 도구의 특성에 따라 생활방식과 사회상이 다르게 나타난다.

Old Stone Age (구석기 시대)	구석기 시대는 돌을 깨뜨려 도구를 만들어 쓰던 시대이며 기원전 10,000년경에 신석기가 시작되기 전까지 이어진 가장 오래된 문화 발달시기이다. 대표적인 유물로는 주먹도끼(hand ax), 동물의 뼈를 이용한 조각품, 사냥 장면이나 동물을 그린 동굴벽화 등이 있다. 이들을 통해 구석기인들의 수렵(hunting), 채취(gathering), 생활방식과 주술이 가미된 예술 표현 방식 등을 알 수 있다.
New Stone Age (신석기 시대)	신석기 시대는 돌을 갈아서 도구를 만들던 시대이다. 혈연을 중심으로 마을을 형성하여 정착생활을 하면서 문명형성의 기틀이 마련되었다. 기술이 진보하여 식량 생산이 가능해졌으며 식량을 저장하거나 익혀 먹기 위한 토기가 발명되었다. 신석기인들의 신앙으로는 어떤 특정한 동물을 자기 씨족(clan)의 수호신으로 생각하여 숭배하는 토테미즘(totemism)과 우주 만물에 영혼이 있다고 믿는 애니미즘(animism)이 있다. 또한 시체를 매장할 때 죽은 사람이 생전에 아끼던 물건을 함께 묻는 풍습을 통해 사후세계에 대한 믿음을 알 수 있다.
Bronze Age (청동기 시대)	청동기 시대에는 청동으로 만든 도구를 사용하기 시작하여 사회와 경제가 급격히 발전하였다. 농사가 발달하면서 평등했던 부족사회(tribal society)가 무너지고 사유 재산(private property)이 축적되면서 계급이 발생했다. 예술에서 비약적인 진보가 나타났는데 이는 당시의 종교와 정치를 반영하고 있다. 바위에 동물이나 기하학적 무늬를 그린 그림, 흙으로 빚은 동물이나 사람 모양의 토우 등을 통해 사냥의 번성과 농사의 풍요를 빌었다. 당시 제사장이나 군장들이 사용했던 칼·거울·방패 등에서 발견되는 화려한 장식과 무늬는 청동기인들의 미의식을 보여준다.
Iron Age (철기 시대)	철기 시대는 무기나 생산도구의 재료로 철을 사용하게 된 시대를 가리킨다. 청동은 원료를 채취하는 곳이 한정되어 값이 비쌌기 때문에 주로 왕이나 귀족들만이 소유했다. 그러나 철은 비교적 얻기 쉬워서 무기나 농기구 등을 대량으로 만들 수 있었다. 철로 만든 무기와 전쟁도구는 전투력 강화에 유용했으며 쇠도끼·괭이·쟁기 등은 농업 생산력을 증대시켰다. 철 생산지가 늘어나면서 지역 간 물자 교류가 활발해졌다.

2. Method of Study (연구 방법)

Radiocarbon Dating (방사성 탄소 연대 측정법)	화석의 연대를 측정하는 데 많이 쓰이는 방법으로 모든 살아있는 생물체가 방사성 동위 원소(radioisotope)인 탄소($C14$)를 일정하게 유지하다가 죽은 후부터는 $C14$가 보충되지 않아 감소한다는 원리에 바탕을 두고 있다. 남아있는 $C14$의 양을 측정하여 그 생물체가 죽은 연대를 알아내는 방법이다.
Ground Penetrating Radar (GPR)	고주파의 신호를 토양에 방사시켜 목표물에 반사하여 되돌아온 신호를 분석함으로써 목표물에 대한 정보를 알아 내는 방법이다. 땅을 파서 유적을 발굴하는 기존의 방법은 유물을 많이 손상시키는 문제점이 있으나 GPR은 물리적 충격을 가하지 않고도 유적을 탐사할 수 있는 장점이 있다.

HACKERS TEST

[01-04] Listen to a talk in an anthropology class.

01 What is the main topic of the talk?

Ⓐ Population growth in ancient Maya cities
Ⓑ Archaeological methods for studying ruins
Ⓒ Construction techniques for Maya monuments
Ⓓ The sudden abandonment of Maya urban centers

02 According to the talk, how did scientists discover ancient weather patterns?

Ⓐ By examining ocean sediment samples
Ⓑ By comparing different archaeological theories
Ⓒ By calculating population changes over centuries
Ⓓ By examining the growth patterns of ancient trees

03 What is NOT mentioned as a period of drought in the Maya civilization?

Ⓐ AD 810
Ⓑ AD 860
Ⓒ AD 900
Ⓓ AD 910

04 What will the speaker most likely discuss next?

Ⓐ The archaeological excavation techniques used at Maya sites
Ⓑ The implications for modern resource conservation
Ⓒ The influence of Maya culture on modern Mexico
Ⓓ Examples of other collapsed civilizations

[05-08] Listen to a talk in a psychology class.

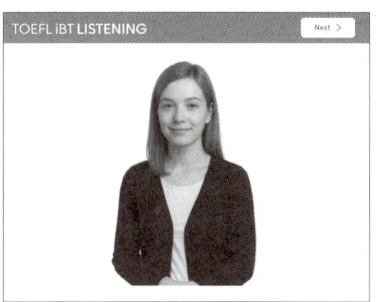

05 What is the talk mainly about?

Ⓐ A study of delayed gratification and its result
Ⓑ The correlation between success and dietary habits
Ⓒ A comparison of different parenting styles and outcomes
Ⓓ Criticism of traditional psychological theories in modern research

06 What does the speaker say about the Marshmallow experiment?

Ⓐ The results were compared across different age groups.
Ⓑ The researchers provided toys to help children resist temptation.
Ⓒ The study connected early self-control abilities to later success in life.
Ⓓ The methodology was criticized for being too complex.

07 Why does the speaker mention behavioral economics?

Ⓐ To highlight contradictions in the Marshmallow experiment
Ⓑ To illustrate how emotional factors influence decision-making
Ⓒ To demonstrate how other fields have misinterpreted the study
Ⓓ To argue that children make better economic decisions than adults

08 What will the speaker most likely discuss next?

Ⓐ Neurological basis for delayed gratification
Ⓑ Alternative rewards used in similar experiments
Ⓒ Critical perspectives on the Marshmallow experiment
Ⓓ Expansion of the experiment to adult participants

HACKERS TEST

[09-12] Listen to a talk in an economics class.

09 What is the main topic of the talk?

Ⓐ Cultural symbolism in business
Ⓑ Limitations of traditional marketing
Ⓒ Marketing through artistic elements
Ⓓ Economic impact of art sponsorship

10 What can a company gain from art-based marketing?

Ⓐ Immediate increase in market share
Ⓑ Simplified product design requirements
Ⓒ Elimination of competition in the marketplace
Ⓓ Deeper emotional connections with consumers

11 Why does the speaker mention luxury fashion houses?

Ⓐ To demonstrate strategic artistic partnerships
Ⓑ To describe their manufacturing techniques
Ⓒ To emphasize their declining influence
Ⓓ To criticize their excessive spending

12 What is NOT mentioned as a company effort for art-based marketing?

Ⓐ Limited-edition artistic designs
Ⓑ Collaboration with artists
Ⓒ Strategic positioning in cultural contexts
Ⓓ Investment in digital marketing campaigns

[13-16] Listen to a talk in a business management class.

13 What is the talk mainly about?

Ⓐ Motivational issues in the modern workplace
Ⓑ The evolution of team coordination strategies
Ⓒ The relationship between team size and productivity
Ⓓ The development of modern management techniques

14 Why does the speaker mention the rope-pulling task?

Ⓐ To demonstrate the limitations of early scientific research
Ⓑ To introduce the historical context of industrial psychology
Ⓒ To compare different methods of measuring team strength
Ⓓ To exemplify how individual effort decreases in group settings

15 According to the speaker, why do coordination losses occur?

Ⓐ Team members develop competing approaches to the same task.
Ⓑ Synchronization becomes more difficult as team size increases.
Ⓒ Leaders fail to provide clear direction in multi-person tasks.
Ⓓ Groups tend to work at the pace of the fastest member.

16 What will the speaker most likely discuss next?

Ⓐ A management approach that assigns clear accountability
Ⓑ Ways to measure individual productivity in group settings
Ⓒ Further research extending Ringelmann's original findings
Ⓓ Examples of coordination losses in large teams

HACKERS TEST

[17-20] Listen to a talk in an archaeology class.

17 What is the main topic of the talk?

Ⓐ The archaeological discoveries at Nineveh
Ⓑ The Assyrian record-keeping and archival systems
Ⓒ The development of record-keeping in ancient civilizations
Ⓓ The historical importance of Nineveh's royal archives

18 Why does the speaker mention King Ashurbanipal?

Ⓐ To distinguish between Assyrian and Babylonian record-keeping
Ⓑ To present evidence of the scribal profession's importance
Ⓒ To emphasize the diverse subjects covered in his library
Ⓓ To illustrate the political power of Assyrian rulers

19 What does the speaker say about Assyrian scribes?

Ⓐ They were primarily recruited from noble families.
Ⓑ They were responsible for translating foreign languages.
Ⓒ They operated within specialized spaces in important buildings.
Ⓓ They used various writing systems for different purposes.

20 What will the speaker most likely discuss next?

Ⓐ The specific contents of major Assyrian literary works
Ⓑ The technological advancements in clay tablet production
Ⓒ Similar writing systems in neighboring civilizations
Ⓓ The influence of Assyrian record-keeping systems on later societies

[21-24] Listen to a talk on a podcast about economics.

21 What is the main topic of the talk?

- Ⓐ The trade-offs involved in making choices
- Ⓑ The consequences of poor decision-making
- Ⓒ The importance of time management for students
- Ⓓ The benefits of making smarter decisions

22 What does the speaker say about her experience last weekend?

- Ⓐ She couldn't submit her project because of the concert.
- Ⓑ She prioritized seeing her favorite band over schoolwork.
- Ⓒ She was disappointed by her favorite band's performance.
- Ⓓ She worked on her project during the concert intermission.

23 What point does the speaker make about opportunity cost?

- Ⓐ They can be calculated precisely using economic formulas.
- Ⓑ They help people avoid making difficult decisions.
- Ⓒ They can be eliminated through careful time management.
- Ⓓ They reflect the value of the foregone alternative.

24 Why does the speaker mention computers?

- Ⓐ To explain why cars cost more than computers
- Ⓑ To compare opportunity costs between industries
- Ⓒ To argue that countries should focus on technology
- Ⓓ To demonstrate opportunity cost in resource allocation

Answers p.578

4. Physical Science

물리과학은 자연 세계의 기본 법칙과 물질의 성질을 탐구하는 학문으로, 크게 천문학, 지구과학, 지질학, 기상학, 공학, 물리학, 화학의 일곱 가지 주제로 나누어 볼 수 있다. 천문학의 우주 현상과 천체 운동, 지구과학의 지구 시스템과 기후 변화, 지질학의 지구 역사와 구조, 기상학의 대기 현상, 공학의 기술 혁신과 응용, 물리학의 기본 원리와 법칙, 그리고 화학의 분자 구조와 반응 메커니즘이 다뤄진다. TOEFL의 물리과학 강의는 복잡한 과학적 개념을 논리적으로 설명하고, 실험과 관찰을 통한 과학적 방법론을 강조한다.

■ Astronomy (천문학)

우주 전체와 우주 안에 있는 여러 천체의 기원, 진화, 구조, 거리, 운동 등을 연구하는 학문이다. TOEFL에서는 행성과 천체와 관련된 강의가 주로 출제된다.

1. Major Planets (대행성)

Terrestrial Planets (지구형 행성)	크기가 작고 밀도가 높으며 주로 금속(metal)이나 암석(rock)으로 이루어져 있다. 태양계의 안쪽에 위치하는 수성(Mercury), 금성(Venus), 지구(Earth), 화성(Mars)이 이에 속한다.
Jovian Planets (목성형 행성)	크기가 크고 밀도가 낮으며 가스나 얼음이 주성분이다. 바깥쪽에 위치하는 목성(Jupiter), 토성(Saturn), 천왕성(Uranus), 해왕성(Neptune)이 이에 속한다.

2. Minor Celestial Bodies (작은 천체들)

Pluto (명왕성)	비교적 최근까지 행성으로 분류되었으나 태양계의 다른 행성과 비교해 17도 기울어진 궤도를 공전하고 얼음으로 이루어져 있어 행성(planet)이라기 보다는 혜성(comet)으로 분류해야 한다는 의견과, 위성을 갖고 있고 혜성보다는 훨씬 크기가 커서 행성으로 분류해야 한다는 의견이 대립해왔다. 이후 위성을 가진 큰 혜성과 해왕성 바깥에 명왕성과 비슷한 특성을 가지는 얼음과 운석으로 된 천체들의 집합체인 카이퍼 벨트(Kuiper Belt)가 발견되어 결국 2006년에 대행성 지위를 박탈당하고 왜소행성(dwarf planet)으로 다시 분류되었다.
Asteroid (소행성)	주로 화성과 목성의 공전궤도 사이에서 태양의 둘레를 돌고 있는 작은 떠돌이별들을 가리킨다. 이들이 모여 소행성대(asteroid belt)를 이룬다.
Comet (혜성)	혜성은 타원이나 포물선 궤도를 따라 태양 둘레를 도는 긴 꼬리를 가진 천체이다. 먼지와 얼음으로 구성된 혜성의 핵이 태양의 열로 조금씩 녹아 코마(coma)라고 하는 대기를 형성하여 밝게 빛난다. 이온 상태인 코마 안의 가스와 혜성에서 나온 먼지는 태양풍에 날려 태양의 반대 방향으로 긴 꼬리를 만든다.

■ Earth Science (지구과학)

지구의 물리적 구조와 현상을 종합적으로 연구하는 학문이다. TOEFL에서는 판구조론, 암석의 형성 과정, 빙하 작용과 관련된 강의가 주로 출제된다.

Plate Tectonics (판구조론)	판구조론은 지구의 표면이 여러 개의 거대한 판으로 구성되어 있으며, 이들이 맨틀 대류에 의해 움직인다는 이론이다. 판의 경계에서는 지진, 화산 활동, 산맥 형성 등 다양한 지질 현상이 발생한다. 발산 경계에서는 새로운 해양 지각이 생성되고, 수렴 경계에서는 판이 충돌하거나 한 판이 다른 판 아래로 섭입한다. 변환 경계에서는 판들이 옆으로 미끄러지면서 지진을 발생시킨다.
Rock Cycle (암석 순환)	암석 순환은 지구상의 암석이 화성암, 퇴적암, 변성암 사이를 순환하는 과정을 설명하는 개념이다. 마그마가 냉각되어 화성암이 되고, 풍화와 침식을 통해 생성된 퇴적물이 퇴적암을 형성한다. 기존 암석이 열과 압력을 받으면 변성암이 되며, 극도의 열에 의해 다시 마그마로 녹을 수 있다. 이 순환 과정은 수백만 년에 걸쳐 일어난다.
Glacial Processes (빙하 작용)	빙하는 지표면을 침식하고 퇴적시키는 강력한 지질 작용력이다. 빙하의 움직임은 U자형 계곡, 피오르드(fjord), 모레인 등 특징적인 지형을 만들어낸다. 피오르드는 빙하가 바다로 흘러드는 계곡을 깊게 파낸 후, 빙하가 후퇴하면서 바닷물이 들어와 형성된 좁고 깊은 만이다. 노르웨이의 게이랑에르 피오르드나 뉴질랜드의 밀포드 사운드가 대표적인 예이다. 피오르드는 일반적으로 가파른 절벽으로 둘러싸여 있으며, 빙하 작용의 강력함을 보여주는 지형적 증거이다.

■ Geology (지질학)

지각의 조성·성질·구조·역사 등을 연구하는 학문이다. TOEFL에서는 다양한 암석의 종류와 관련된 강의가 주로 출제된다.

Types of Rocks (암석의 종류)	암석은 지각(crust)과 상부 맨틀(mantle)을 구성하는 물질이며 광물의 집합체이다. 암석은 생성되는 조건에 따라 퇴적암(sedimentary rock), 화성암(igneous rock), 변성암(metamorphic rock)으로 나누어진다. 퇴적암은 물질이 퇴적해 형성되므로 주로 해저에서 생성된다. 화성암은 지구 내부의 마그마가 굳어서 형성된다. 마그마가 땅속 깊은 곳에서 서서히 식으면 큰 입자를 가지게 되는데 이를 화강암(granite)이라고 한다. 반면, 지표 근처에서 급속히 냉각되어 작은 입자를 가지는 암석을 현무암(basalt)이라고 한다. 퇴적암과 화성암이 온도와 압력의 영향을 받아 광물의 조성과 조직이 변화한 것을 변성암이라 한다.
Hoodoo (후두)	후두는 침식작용으로 기둥처럼 생긴 바위를 말한다. 성분이 일정하지 않은 퇴적암이 침식되어 만들어지기 때문에 암석 부분부분의 침식속도가 일정하지 않아 울퉁불퉁 기괴한 모양을 하고 있으며 건조한 지역에 주로 형성된다.
Zircon (지르콘)	무색·회색·황갈색·적색·청색 등 여러 가지 색깔을 띠는 광택이 있는 결정체이다. 40여억 년 전의 지르콘에서 생명체와 관련된 탄소와 미네랄이 발견되면서 태고의 지구가 과학자들이 예상했던 것보다 훨씬 빠른 속도로 식었거나, 혹은 아예 화염이 아니라 얼음으로 뒤덮여 있었을 가능성이 제기되었다.
Petroleum (석유)	석유는 논란의 여지는 있으나 일반적으로 플랑크톤류의 바다생물이 오랜 기간 높은 압력과 열을 받아 생성되었다고 설명된다. 석유는 중동지역에서 주로 발견되는데, 'oil pool'은 웅덩이의 모습이 아니라 암석 사이사이의 틈에 끼어있는 형태인 석유층을 비유적으로 가리키는 말이다.

Meteorology (기상학)

기상이변을 포함한 날씨와 기후뿐만 아니라 대기 중의 물리·화학적 현상을 연구하는 학문이다. TOEFL에서는 기후의 변화 과정과 관련된 강의가 주로 출제된다.

Glacial and Interglacial Period (빙하기와 간빙기)	빙하시대(ice age)는 지구 전체의 기온이 매우 낮게 떨어진 채로 오랫동안 유지되어 남북극의 빙하와 높은 산악 지대의 빙하가 확장되는 시기로 정의되며, 빙하시대 내에서도 더 추운 시기인 빙하기(glacial period)와 덜 추운 시기인 간빙기(interglacial period)가 존재한다. 현재까지 지구에는 총 4번의 빙하기가 있었으며, 최근 수 백만 년 동안의 빙하기와 간빙기의 주기는 약 40,000년이었다.
Milankovitch Theory (밀란코비치 이론)	세르비아의 천문학자인 밀루틴 밀란코비치(Milutin Milankovitch)는 지구의 자전·공전궤도 상의 여러 특징이 복합적으로 작용하여 빙하기와 간빙기에 영향을 준다고 주장했으며, 이에 따른 기후 변화의 주기를 설명했다. **Orbital eccentricity (공전궤도 이심률)** 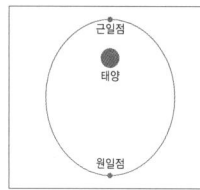지구의 공전궤도는 약 10만년을 주기로 원 모양과 타원 모양으로 형태가 바뀐다. 지구가 태양에서 가장 가까운 지점을 근일점(perihelion), 가장 먼 지점을 원일점(aphelion)이라고 하는데, 지구의 궤도가 타원형일 때 근일점과 원일점에서의 지구가 받는 태양 복사량의 차이가 지구의 궤도가 원형일 때 받는 복사량의 차이보다 크다. 따라서 지구의 궤도가 타원형일 때 원일점과 근일점의 온도 차이도 크다. **Axial precession (세차운동)** 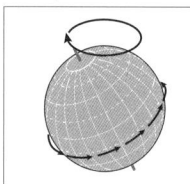세차운동은 지구가 자전함에 따라 마치 팽이의 축이 흔들거리듯이 지구의 자전축도 회전하는 것을 의미하며, 지구 자전축의 회전 주기는 26,000년이다. 지구 자전축은 약 23.5° 기울어져 있는데, 따라서 회전하면서 방향이 바뀌게 되고, 지구 자전축의 방향이 변화하면 북반구와 남반구의 계절이 시작하는 시기에 영향을 미친다. **Axial tilt, Obliquity (자전축 경사)** 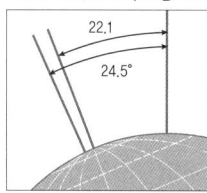지구의 자전축은 회전할 뿐만 아니라 기울기도 변한다. 지구 자전축의 기울기는 약 40,000 년 주기에 따라 22.1도에서 24.5도까지 변화한다. 지구 자전축의 기울기가 클수록 여름과 겨울에 받는 태양 복사량의 차이가 커져 두 계절의 기온 차이가 커지며, 기울기가 작을수록 여름과 겨울의 기온 차이가 작아진다.

■ Engineering (공학)

주로 인간 생활에 필요한 물품을 생산·가공하는 활동을 연구하는 응용과학이다. TOEFL에서는 기계공학, 화학공학, 컴퓨터공학, 유전공학과 같이 공학의 다양한 학문 분야와 관련된 강의가 주로 출제된다.

1. Mechanical Engineering (기계공학)

기계공학은 기계 및 관련 설비의 설계·제작·이용·운전 등에 관한 기초적·응용적 분야를 연구하며 재료를 다루는 재료 역학, 외력과 운동에 의해 생기는 속도와 가속도 등을 다루는 기체역학과 같은 기초분야를 포함한다.

Bicycle (자전거)	최초의 자전거는 running machine이라고 불렸으며, 핸들과 안장, 앞바퀴와 뒷바퀴가 있었으나 페달(pedal)과 브레이크(break)가 없었고 매우 무거웠다. 이후 등장한 penny-farthing은 새로운 금속 합금(metal alloy)을 사용해 무게가 가벼워졌지만, 페달이 부착되어 있는 앞바퀴가 커야 빨리 갈 수 있었기 때문에 매우 큰 앞바퀴가 있었으며, 이로 인해 탑승자가 떨어져서 부상을 당할 위험이 컸다. 그 후 오늘날의 자전거와 같은 형태의 체인(chain)과 기어(gear)를 사용한 safety bicycle이 등장했다. Safety bicycle에서는 페달이 체인을 통해 기어를 돌리고 기어가 뒷바퀴를 돌리게 되어 있었다. 따라서 속도는 바퀴의 크기가 아닌 기어의 크기에 영향을 받게 되었으며, 기계적 확대율(mechanical advantage)이 적용되어 보다 적은 힘으로 빨리 이동할 수 있게 되었다.
Airplane (비행기)	비행기는 3개의 축-pitch, roll, yaw-을 중심으로 조종(three-axis control)된다. pitch는 비행기의 기수의 상하 운동을 조종하는 것이고 roll은 비행기의 동체를 축으로 양 날개를 좌우로 기울이는 것을 말한다. 마지막으로 yaw는 비행기 동체를 수평으로 유지한 채 기수를 좌우로 움직이는 것을 말한다. 이 조종원리를 처음으로 실제 비행에 적용시켜 성공한 인물은 라이트형제(Wright brothers)인데, 라이트형제는 이 외에도 가벼운 알루미늄 엔진, 비행기용 프로펠러 등을 장착하여 사상 처음으로 동력비행을 성공시키기도 했다.

2. Chemical Engineering (화학공학)

화학공학은 화학제품의 제조공정을 효율화하기 위한 공정에 대해 연구한다. 화학공업은 여러 원료물질을 혼합하여 가열하거나, 촉매(catalyst)와 접촉시키는 방법 등으로 화학반응(chemical reaction)을 일으켜 제품을 생산한다. 이러한 공정은 제철공업, 식품공업, 의학 분야 등에서 응용되고 있다. 특히 석유나 천연가스를 원료로 하여 연료 이외의 용도로 사용되는 석유화학제품을 만드는 석유화학산업(petrochemical industry)이 가장 발달되어 있다.

3. Computer Engineering (컴퓨터공학)

컴퓨터공학은 컴퓨터 시스템과 관련된 여러 기술을 개발하여 각 분야에 응용하는 공학이다. 컴퓨터 시스템의 구조와 운영 및 네트워크 등을 다루는 시스템 분야와 프로그래밍 언어와 소프트웨어 개발을 다루는 소프트웨어 분야, 데이터베이스 등 컴퓨터의 다양한 응용을 다루는 응용 분야로 나누어진다. 정보화 시대를 주도하는 첨단 학문으로서 현대의 거의 모든 산업이 컴퓨터와 관련되어 있기 때문에 수요가 많고 앞으로 비약적인 발전이 기대되는 분야이기도 하다.

4. Genetic Engineering (유전공학)

유전공학은 생물의 유전자(gene)를 인공적으로 가공하여 인간에게 필요한 물질을 대량으로 얻는 기술을 연구한다. 이 분야에서는 DNA 재조합 기술(DNA recombinant technology), 세포융합기술(cell fusion technology)에 대한 연구가 활발히 진행되고 있다. 이러한 기술의 발전은 인간이 직면한 에너지·식량·의료 문제 등에 대한 해결책이 될 것으로 기대되고 있다.

Physics (물리학)

자연현상을 지배하는 기본법칙을 규명하는 학문으로서 물체의 운동이나 구조·열·빛·전기·신소재 등 다양한 분야를 연구한다. TOEFL에서는 물리학의 기초가 되는 법칙들의 원리나 이를 실생활에 적용하는 내용의 강의가 주로 출제된다.

1. Force & Motion (힘과 운동)

Force (힘)	힘은 정지하고 있는 물체를 움직이고, 움직이는 물체의 속도나 방향을 바꾼다. **gravity (중력)** 우주상의 모든 물체 사이에는 서로 끌어당기는 힘인 만유인력(universal gravitation)이 작용한다. 물체와 지구 사이에 작용하는 중력이 그 예이다. 무중력(weightless) 상태에서 인간은 다양한 신체적 변화를 겪게 된다. 균형감각을 유지하는 반고리관이 제대로 기능하지 못하여 위치감각을 잃게 되고, 관절 사이의 간격이 넓어져서 키가 커진다.
Motion (운동)	운동은 일정한 기준점(control point)에 대해 물체의 위치가 변화하는 현상을 뜻한다. **Newton's law of motion (뉴턴의 운동법칙)** 운동을 지배하는 자연법칙은 수없이 많으나 그 기본이 되는 것은 뉴턴의 운동법칙이다. 제1법칙(Newton's first law)은 관성의 법칙(law of inertia)으로, 외부로부터 힘의 작용이 없으면 물체는 정지한 채로 있거나 등속도 운동(uniform motion)을 계속한다는 것이다. 제2법칙은 물체에 힘이 작용했을 때 물체는 그 힘에 비례하는 가속도(acceleration)를 가진다는 법칙이다. 제3법칙은 작용-반작용(action-reaction)의 법칙이라고도 하며 두 물체의 상호작용(interaction), 즉, 한쪽 물체가 받는 힘과 다른 쪽 물체가 받는 힘은 크기가 같고 방향이 반대임을 나타낸다. **conservation of momentum (운동량 보존의 법칙)** 전체 운동량은 에너지와 마찬가지로 외부작용이 없는 한 언제까지나 보존된다는 것이 운동량 보존의 법칙이다. 물체의 운동량(momentum)은 물체에 작용하는 힘인 질량(mass)과 속도(velocity)에 비례한다. 힘이 물체의 운동량을 변화시키는 원인이므로, 외부에서 힘이 작용하지 않는 한 물체의 운동량은 변하지 않는다는 원리이다.

2. Light, Sound, Heat (빛, 소리, 열)

Light (빛)	일반적으로 전자기파 중에서 사람의 눈에 보이는 범위의 파장을 가진 가시광선(visible rays)을 빛이라고 하며, 넓은 의미로는 자외선(ultraviolet rays)과 적외선(infrared rays)을 포함한다.
Sound (소리)	소리는 물체의 진동이나 기체의 흐름으로 발생하는 파동의 한 가지로, 소리의 세기는 데시벨(decibel)로 나타내며 주파수(frequency)가 높을수록 높은 음이다. **noise (소음)** 일반적으로 소음은 불쾌하고 좋지 않은 영향을 미치는 소리로 알려져 있으며 실제로 80데시벨(decibel)을 넘어가면 사람에게 해롭다고 알려져 있다. 하지만 일부 소음은 긍정적인 효과를 준다. 들을 수 있는 모든 주파수를 포함하는 임의적 소음(random noise) 중 하나인 백색 소음(white noise)은 다른 소리를 차단하므로, 진정 및 수면을 돕는다. 다른 임의적 소음으로는 가장 낮은 분홍색 소음(pink noise)과 분홍색 소음보다는 조금 더 높은 음을 가지는 파란색 소음(blue noise)이 있다.
Heat (열)	열은 물체의 온도를 높이고 고체, 액체, 기체의 상태를 변화시키는 에너지이다.

Chemistry (화학)

물질의 성질·조성·구조 및 그 변화를 연구하는 학문이다. TOEFL에서는 여러 화학반응이나 일상생활에서의 적용을 설명하는 강의가 주로 출제된다.

1. Matter (물질)

Solid (고체)	금속이나 광물과 같이 일정한 형태와 부피를 가지고 있는 물체를 말한다. 고체는 원자(atom) 또는 분자 (molecule) 사이의 강한 인력(attraction) 때문에 유동성(liquidity)이 없다. coal (석탄) 석탄은 지질시대의 식물이 퇴적되고 매몰된 후 높은 온도와 압력을 받아 변질된 암석이다. 주로 탄소로 구성되어 있고 수 소와 산소를 포함하고 있다. 산업혁명 이후 에너지원으로서의 석탄의 이용이 비약적으로 증대하였다. 또한 석탄을 가공하여 얻는 여러 물질은 많은 화학공업의 원료로 사용되고 있다.
Liquid (액체)	물·기름과 같이 일정한 형태는 갖지 않되 일정한 부피는 갖는 상태이며 기온·압력의 조건에 따라 기체나 고체로 변할 수 있다
Gas (기체)	일정한 형태나 부피를 가지지 않으며 입자(particle)들의 운동이 가장 활발한 상태이다. 액체가 기체로 변하는 것을 기화(evaporation), 고체가 기체로 변하는 것을 승화(sublimation)라고 한다.
Molecular Arrangement (분자 배열)	원자나 분자의 배열 방식에 따라 물질은 다른 성질을 가진다. 흑연과 다이아몬드의 경우 둘 다 탄소 원자로만 이루어져 있지만 어떻게 배열되느냐에 따라 흑연이 되기도 하고 다이아몬드가 되기도 한다. 또한 또 다른 특정한 모양으로 탄소 원자가 배열되면 C60(buckyball)이라는 물질이 되는데, C60은 탄소 원자 60개가 축구공 모양으로 배열된 지름 1나노미터의 물질로 의학적 용도 등 다양한 곳에 쓰일 수 있다. C60과 비슷하게 역시 탄소만으로 이루어진 다른 물질로는 나노튜브(nanotube)가 있다.

2. Energy (에너지)

Fossil Fuel Energy (화석에너지)	석탄·석유·천연가스와 같이 지하에 묻힌 동식물의 유해가 오랜 세월에 걸쳐 화석화되어 형성된 연료를 화석연료라 하며 이것에 의해 얻어진 에너지를 화석에너지라고 한다. crude oil refining process (원유 정제법) 원유를 정제하여 석유(petroleum)를 얻는 방법에는 두 가지가 있다. 증류(distillation)는 혼합물인 액체를 가열하여 얻은 기체를 액화(condensation)시켜 각각의 순수한 성분으로 분리시키는 것으로 고대 때부터 사용하던 방법이다. 열을 가하여 분리하는 열분해(cracking)는 증류보다 많은 양의 휘발유(gasoline)와 플라스틱(plastic) 등의 부산물을 얻을 수 있다.
Nuclear Energy (핵에너지)	원자핵(atomic nucleus) 변환(conversion)을 통해 방출되는 방사선(radioactive ray) 에너지를 이용하는 것을 말한다. 화석에너지의 대체에너지(alternative energy)로 사용되며 의료, 공업, 식품 등 다양한 분야에 이용할 수 있다.

HACKERS TEST 🎧 T4_S2_4_Test

[01-04] Listen to a talk in an engineering class.

01 What is the talk mainly about?

Ⓐ The popularity of bicycles in the 1800s
Ⓑ The safety concerns of 19th-century vehicles
Ⓒ The gradual improvement of bicycle technology
Ⓓ The invention of the modern bicycle in Germany

02 What does the speaker say about the "running machine" from 1818?

Ⓐ It was made entirely of iron.
Ⓑ It weighed approximately 100 pounds.
Ⓒ It was invented in early 19th-century France.
Ⓓ It required riders to propel themselves with their feet.

03 According to the speaker, what was a problem with the "penny-farthing"?

Ⓐ The pedals were too difficult to operate.
Ⓑ Riders had to sit at a dangerous height.
Ⓒ It was too heavy for most riders to handle.
Ⓓ One pedal rotation moved it less than five feet.

04 What will the speaker most likely discuss next?

Ⓐ The cost of bicycles in the 1800s
Ⓑ A comparison with motorized vehicles
Ⓒ The mechanics of the chain drive system
Ⓓ The modern bicycle manufacturing industry

[05-08] Listen to a talk in an astronomy class.

05 What is the main topic of the talk?

Ⓐ The orbits of small moons around Saturn
Ⓑ The unique features of Saturn's ring system
Ⓒ The differences between rocky and icy rings
Ⓓ A comparison of ring systems across planets

06 What does the speaker say about planetary rings?

Ⓐ They are composed entirely of solid materials.
Ⓑ They are visible only through powerful telescopes.
Ⓒ They were discovered simultaneously in 1610.
Ⓓ They can be found around multiple planets.

07 Why does the speaker mention Maxwell?

Ⓐ To support the theory that rings are composed of particles
Ⓑ To introduce the concept of orbital mechanics
Ⓒ To explain who first discovered Saturn's rings
Ⓓ To compare different astronomical theories

08 What will the speaker most likely discuss next?

Ⓐ The rings of Jupiter and Neptune
Ⓑ The formation process of planetary rings
Ⓒ The atmospheric conditions near Saturn
Ⓓ The elements and composition of the rings

HACKERS TEST

[09-12] Listen to a talk in a geology class.

09 What is the talk mainly about?

Ⓐ The role of crystallization in forming Earth's crust
Ⓑ The environmental factors affecting mineral formation
Ⓒ The significance of fossils in understanding prehistoric life
Ⓓ The classification of Earth materials based on their origin

10 According to the speaker, what is true about inorganic minerals?

Ⓐ They require biological processes to form over time.
Ⓑ They contain fossilized remains of ancient organisms.
Ⓒ They form through crystallization from molten rock.
Ⓓ They are often overlooked in common mineral studies.

11 What does the speaker say about amber?

Ⓐ It forms primarily from coal under pressure.
Ⓑ It is not considered a mineral in the strict sense.
Ⓒ It forms when plant material decomposes completely.
Ⓓ It is primarily composed of inorganic compounds.

12 Why does the speaker mention tectonic movements?

Ⓐ To illustrate a geological process that inorganic minerals can reveal
Ⓑ To demonstrate the decomposition process of plant matter
Ⓒ To explain how ancient environments changed over time
Ⓓ To show how biological materials become fossilized

[13-16] Listen to a talk in an earth science class.

13 What is the topic of the talk?

   Ⓐ The impact of ice ages on various landscapes
   Ⓑ The origin and notable aspects of dramatic coastal inlets
   Ⓒ The environmental challenges to the preservation of fjords
   Ⓓ The geological differences between fjords and other valleys

14 What does the speaker say about glaciers?

   Ⓐ They only formed under specific climate conditions in Norway.
   Ⓑ They contributed to rising sea levels in modern times.
   Ⓒ They widened and deepened valleys as they moved.
   Ⓓ They moved too slowly to cause significant erosion.

15 What feature of fjords does the speaker say contributes to unique ecosystems?

   Ⓐ The geological composition of the rocks
   Ⓑ The layering effect of river water over seawater
   Ⓒ The nutrient-rich sediment from glacial deposits
   Ⓓ The coexistence of marine and freshwater currents

16 What will the speaker most likely discuss next?

   Ⓐ Environmental threats to fjord ecosystems
   Ⓑ Recreational activities popular in fjord regions
   Ⓒ Scientific methods for measuring fjord depths
   Ⓓ Prominent examples of fjords around the world

HACKERS TEST

[17-20] Listen to a talk on a podcast about physics.

17 What is the talk mainly about?

  Ⓐ The practical applications of GPS technology
  Ⓑ The revolutionary concept of spacetime in physics
  Ⓒ The visual beauty of the stars in the night sky
  Ⓓ The relationship between astronomy and everyday life

18 Why does the speaker mention a bowling ball?

  Ⓐ To criticize outdated models of the universe
  Ⓑ To emphasize the complexity of Einstein's calculations
  Ⓒ To compare the Sun's effect on spacetime to a trampoline
  Ⓓ To highlight the mathematical principles behind relativity

19 What does the speaker say about time?

  Ⓐ It remains constant regardless of an object's speed.
  Ⓑ It helps scientists calculate exact positions on maps.
  Ⓒ It flows at different rates depending on motion and gravity.
  Ⓓ It explains why stars appear differently when observed from space.

20 Why does the speaker mention GPS satellites?

  Ⓐ To criticize the limitations of current navigation technology
  Ⓑ To demonstrate how the theory of relativity applies to daily life
  Ⓒ To explain how massive objects affect spacetime
  Ⓓ To compare Einstein's predictions with modern discoveries

[21-24] Listen to a talk in a chemistry class.

21 What is the talk mainly about?

Ⓐ The industrial applications of graphite and diamonds
Ⓑ Carbon allotropes and their unique characteristics
Ⓒ Methods for identifying different carbon-based substances
Ⓓ The process of converting graphite into diamond form

22 What does the speaker say about graphite?

Ⓐ It serves as an electrical insulator in most applications.
Ⓑ It forms a three-dimensional lattice of carbon atoms.
Ⓒ It conducts electricity due to its extra electrons.
Ⓓ It requires extreme temperatures for natural formation.

23 What is NOT mentioned as a characteristic of the HPHT method?

Ⓐ It uses graphite as the starting material.
Ⓑ It utilizes extremely high-pressure conditions.
Ⓒ It operates at temperatures exceeding 1000°C.
Ⓓ It produces diamonds faster than the CVD method.

24 What will the speaker most likely discuss next?

Ⓐ Further exploration of the two diamond creation methods
Ⓑ The economic advantages of artificial diamond production
Ⓒ Other carbon allotropes beyond graphite and diamonds
Ⓓ Environmental impacts of synthetic diamond manufacturing

Answers p.584

# 5. Life Science

생명과학은 생명체의 구조, 기능, 진화를 연구하는 분야로, 크게 생물학, 환경과학, 생리학의 세 가지 주제로 나누어 볼 수 있다. 생물학의 생명 과정이나 다양한 동식물에 대한 특징, 환경과학의 생태계 상호작용과 보존, 그리고 생리학의 생물체 기능과 적응 메커니즘이 핵심 주제이다. TOEFL의 생명과학 강의는 미시적 세포 단위부터 거시적 생태계까지 다양한 층위에서 생명 현상을 탐구한다.

■ Biology (생물학)

생물체 전반의 구조와 기능을 과학적으로 연구하는 학문이다. 학문 분야가 상당히 넓으며, TOEFL에서는 주로 식물학 또는 동물학에 대한 내용이 출제된다.

1. Botany (식물학)

Plant Organ (식물의 기관)	식물세포는 얇은 막인 세포벽(cell wall)으로 둘러싸여 있다. **물과 무기양분(mineral)의 이동** 뿌리(root)로부터 흡수된 물과 무기양분은 줄기(stem)를 따라 식물 곳곳으로 운반된다. 줄기의 관다발(vascular bundle)이 통로 역할을 한다. 관다발이 있는 대부분의 종자식물(seed plant)과는 달리 이끼류(moss)와 해조류(algae)는 뿌리가 없어 세포가 흡수작용을 대신한다. **잎(leaf)의 기능** 잎은 에너지를 만드는 작용인 광합성(photosynthesis)을 주기능으로 한다. 식충식물(insectivorous plant) 중에서 Venus Flytrap의 잎은 곤충을 잡는 덫의 역할을 하기도 한다. Venus Flytrap의 잎에는 감각모가 있어서 벌레가 앉으면 순식간에 잎을 닫고 소화액을 내보내 벌레를 죽여서 영양분을 흡수한다.
Metabolism (물질대사)	식물이 생명을 유지하기 위해 흡수한 물질을 에너지로 바꾸고 이때 생긴 노폐물을 외부로 배출하는 과정이다. **photosynthesis (광합성)** 광합성이란 태양의 빛 에너지를 이산화탄소(CO_2), 물(H_2O)을 매개로 하여 유기물인 화학 에너지로 바꿔 저장하는 활동으로, 광합성에 필요한 요소를 포함하고 있는 잎의 엽록체(chloroplast)에서 일어난다. 그 중 엽록소(chlorophyll)는 빛 에너지를 포착하는 기능을 한다.

2. Zoology (동물학)

Fish (어류)

물속에서 아가미(gills)로 호흡하는 척추동물(vertebrate)이다. 비늘(scale)을 가지며 지느러미(fin)로 몸의 평형을 유지한다. 수중생활을 하더라도 폐로 호흡하는 고래나 무척추동물인 오징어·조개 등은 어류에 속하지 않는다.

번식(breeding) 방법
난생인 대부분의 어류는 체외수정을 하지만 상어처럼 성어(full-grown fish)를 낳는 어류는 체내수정을 한다. 일반적으로 알이 부화하면 치어(young fish)가 되고 이어서 성어로 성장하는 변태과정을 거친다.

salmon (연어)
연어는 산란을 위해 바다에서 다시 강을 거슬러 올라오는 귀소본능(homing instinct)이 있다. 연어가 태어난 강을 기억하고 찾아가는 방법에 대해 후각을 이용하여 태어난 강을 기억한다는 이론과 태양의 위치변화를 지표로 삼아 이동한다는 이론이 있다.

Amphibian (양서류)

개구리처럼 어릴 때는 아가미로 호흡하며 수중생활을 하고, 성장한 후에는 폐로 호흡하며 육지 생활을 하는 동물이다. 축축한 피부를 가지고 있고 못이나 개울 주변의 습한 곳에서 서식한다.

hibernation (동면)
양서류는 변온동물이기 때문에 겨울이 되면 생활작용이 매우 느려져 동면한다. 이 기간에는 피부로만 호흡하며, 먹이를 전혀 먹지 않고 동면하기 전에 섭취한 영양분을 서서히 소비한다. 동면(hibernation)과 휴면(dormancy)은 겨울 수면을 뜻하는 것으로 비슷하다고 생각할 수 있지만, 동면은 동물들이 겨울철 추위와 식량 부족을 이겨내기 위해 하는 수면이고 휴면은 생물체가 자라고 발달하기 위해 잠시 육체적인 활동을 멈추는 것을 뜻한다. 깊은 동면을 하는 동물로는 뱀과 다람쥐가 있고, 두꺼비(toad)는 산란 후 다시 땅속에 들어가 춘면(sleep in spring)을 하기도 한다.

Bird (조류)

깃털과 날개가 있으며 알을 낳는 척추동물이다.

migratory bird (철새)
기후변화나 먹이를 따라 이동하는 조류를 철새라고 한다. 이동 시기에 따라 낮에 이동하는 주행성(diurnal), 밤에 이동하는 야행성(nocturnal)으로 나뉜다. 주행성 철새는 생체시계에 의하여 시각을 알고 태양의 방위를 관찰하여 이동 방향을 결정한다. 야행성 철새는 특정 별자리의 위치를 이용하여 이동한다는 학설이 있다.

Mammal (포유류)

젖으로 새끼를 양육하는 척추동물이다.

marsupial (유대류)
유대류는 발육이 불완전한 상태로 태어난 새끼를 어미의 배에 넣고 키우는 습성을 가진 포유류이다. 캥거루나 코알라가 대표적인 예이며 호주와 아메리카에 주로 서식한다.

bat (박쥐)
날아다니는 유일한 포유류인 박쥐는 주로 동굴에서 서식한다. 야행성이며 동면을 하는 특성이 있다. 초음파를 발사하여 반사되는 신호를 분석하여 물체의 존재를 측정하는 능력인 반향정위(echolocation)를 지니고 있다. 또한 초음파를 통해 동굴 바깥의 기후를 예측하여 곤충이 활동하기 좋은 따뜻한 온도일 때 먹이를 잡으러 나간다.

Environmental Science (환경과학)

인간의 활동이 야기하는 여러 가지 환경 문제에 과학적으로 접근하여 해결 방안을 탐구하는 응용과학의 한 분야이다. TOEFL에서는 생태계 및 기후변화와 관련된 강의가 주로 출제된다.

1. Ecosystem (생태계)

Food Chain (먹이사슬)	생태계는 생산자(녹색식물) → 1차 소비자(herbivore) → 2차 소비자(carnivore) → 3차 소비자의 먹이연쇄를 이룬다. **cycle (순환)** 먹이연쇄는 단방향으로 진행되는 게 아니라 순환의 과정을 거친다. 동식물의 죽은 몸체는 세균, 즉 분해자(decomposer)에 의해 분해되고, 그 결과물인 무기물(mineral)이 다시 1차 소비자인 식물로 흡수되는 과정을 통해 순환되는 것이다. 실제 자연계의 먹이연쇄는 먹이그물(food web)의 형태로 여러 개의 먹이사슬이 서로 얽혀 있는 구조이다. **biological concentration (생물농축)** 생물농축은 1차 소비자가 흡수한 오염물질이 먹이그물을 따라 2차, 3차 소비자로 농축되어가는 현상을 말한다. 수은(mercury), 납(lead)과 같은 중금속이나 살충제(pesticide) 등의 일부 독성물질은 체내에서 분해되지 않고 농축되어 생물이나 사람에게 심각한 질병을 일으킨다.
Endangered Species (멸종위기 동물)	먹이사슬(food chain)을 구성하는 종(species) 중 한 종류의 개체 수에 급격한 변화가 생기면 사슬 내의 다른 동물들의 생존에도 영향을 미치며, 나아가 생태계 전체에 위기를 불러올 수 있다. 따라서 멸종 위기에 처한 동물을 보호하기 위한 노력이 필요하다. **자연 보호주의자(conservationist)들의 자연보호 방법** 기존에는 멸종위기 동물을 포획하여 수를 늘린 후 야생으로 되돌려 보내는 방법이 일반적이었다. 하지만 야생 상태에서는 먹이와 활동공간의 부족으로 멸종동물의 개체 수가 더 이상 증가하지 못하는 문제점이 있기 때문에 자연 보호주의자들은 야생동물이 서식할 수 있는 공간을 따로 마련하고 풍부한 식량자원을 공급하는 방향으로 정책을 바꾸고 있다.

2. Climate Change (기후변화)

기후가 오랜 기간에 걸쳐 점차 변화하는 것을 말하는데, 특히 20세기 이후 지구의 평균기온이 점차 상승하고 있는 것을 가리킨다.

Urban Heat Island (열섬 현상)	도시의 기온이 인공적인 열이나 대기오염의 영향으로 교외보다 높아지는 현상이다. 공장 등에서 뿜어내는 인공열에 의한 대기오염과 빛을 흡수한 후 적외선의 형태로 다시 외부로 내보내는 아스팔트·콘크리트 등의 각종 인공 시설물의 증가, 그리고 태양열을 흡수하고 그늘을 만드는 각종 식물의 감소가 주 원인이다. 기온이 높아지면 압력이 낮아져 주변의 찬 공기가 모이고 아래의 더운 공기는 상승하게 되는데, 이때 찬 공기와 더운 공기가 만난 후 응축되면 비구름이 생성된다. 이 때문에 도시에서 상대적으로 소나기가 자주 내리게 된다.
Greenhouse Effect (온실효과)	대기 중의 수증기나 이산화탄소(carbon dioxide)가 온실 역할을 하여 지구 표면의 온도를 높게 유지하는 현상이다. 예방하기 위해서는 온실효과의 주 원인인 대기 중의 이산화탄소 양을 줄이는 것이 중요하다. 석탄·석유 등 화석연료(fossil fuel)의 사용을 줄이거나 이산화탄소를 흡수하고 산소를 방출하는 녹지를 늘리는 지구공학적 작용(geo-engineering)을 이용하는 방법이 있다. 바다에 철분(iron)을 투입하여 이산화탄소를 흡수하는 식물성 플랑크톤을 대량으로 증식시키는 방법도 있지만 부영양화를 일으킬 위험이 있다.

Physiology (생리학)

동·식물의 기능을 중심으로 그 기능이 나타나는 과정과 원인을 과학적으로 분석하는 학문이다. 생물학(Biology)의 한 분야이며 해부학(Anatomy)·세포학(Cytology)과 밀접하게 관련되어 있다. TOEFL에서는 뇌, 호르몬, DNA와 같이 인체를 구성하는 기관의 특징과 역할과 관련된 강의가 주로 출제된다.

1. Brain (뇌)

신경계를 조절하여 인체를 관리하는 기능을 한다. 뇌의 작용은 매우 활발하고 정교하며 뇌의 각 부분들이 인체 기관을 분담하여 조절한다.

MRI (Magnetic Resonance Imaging)	MRI는 인체를 구성하는 물질의 자기적 성질을 측정하여 컴퓨터를 통해 재구성하고 영상화(visualization)하는 기술이다. 뇌의 구성과 작용을 연구할 때 유용하게 쓰인다. 뇌의 기능을 알아보기 위한 일반적인 방법은 뇌혈관(blood vessel)의 혈액 흐름을 조사하는 것이다. 예를 들어 언어 활동을 할 때 뇌의 특정 부분에 혈류가 형성되는 것을 알 수 있다. 이를 통해 두 언어를 구사하는 사람(bilingual)이 두 언어를 사용할 때 활동하는 뇌의 부위가 같음이 밝혀졌다. 자극이 주어질 때 활성화(activation)되는 뇌 혈류를 추적하기 위해 기존에는 방사성 동위원소(radioisotope)를 이용하였으나 인체에 해를 끼치는 단점이 있었다. MRI는 인체에 무해하며 3차원 영상을 얻을 수 있다는 장점이 있으나 비용이 비싸고 검사시간이 오래 걸리는 단점이 있다.
Brain wave (뇌파)	뇌파를 통해 뇌 기능과 활동상태를 알 수 있는데 전기적으로 측정한 뇌파를 EEG (Electroencephalogram) 또는 뇌파도라고 한다. 뇌파의 진폭(amplitude)과 주파수(frequency)를 분석하여 수면을 총 4단계로 구분한다. 졸리기 시작하는 1단계에서는 세타 활동(theta activity)이 나타나며 2단계는 진폭이 급격히 커지는 K 복합 (K-complex)이 나타난다. 깊은 수면 상태인 3단계에서는 느리게 움직이는 델타 활동 (delta activity)이 일어나고 4단계는 REM수면이라고도 하는 꿈을 꾸게 되는 단계이다.

2. Hormone (호르몬)

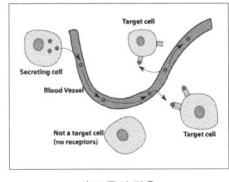

호르몬의 작용

땀(sweat), 침(saliva), 소화액(digestive fluid)처럼 몸 밖으로 분비되는 물질과는 달리 호르몬은 내분비선(gland)에서 형성되어 혈액을 따라 이동한다. 호르몬은 인체가 변화하는 환경에 적응하도록 신체 각 부분의 기능을 적절히 조절하기 위한 명령을 전달한다. 소량으로 생리작용(physiological function)을 조절하며 분비(secretion)량에 이상이 생기면 결핍증(deficiency disease)이나 과다증을 유발한다.

3. DNA

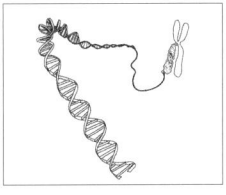

DNA는 생명체의 유전 형질(genetic character)을 기록한 일종의 기록 저장소라고 할 수 있다. 단백질(protein)을 합성할 수 있는 의미 있는 DNA 서열이 유전자 (gene)이며, 게놈(genome)은 어떤 생물체의 전체 DNA를 의미한다. 염색체 (chromosome)는 세포의 핵(nucleus) 속에서 DNA가 존재하는 형태를 말한다. 최근 유전자 진단 방법인 PCR(Polymerase Chain Reaction)이 개발되어 정확하고 쉬운 DNA 복제(DNA replication)가 가능해져서 다양한 분야에 응용되고 있다.

HACKERS TEST T4_S2_5_Test

[01-04] Listen to a talk in a biology class.

01 What is the talk mainly about?

Ⓐ The protective mechanisms of butterfly chrysalises
Ⓑ The complete developmental process of butterflies
Ⓒ The vulnerability of butterflies during different life stages
Ⓓ The adaptive strategies of butterflies in various environments

02 Why does the speaker mention the number of eggs?

Ⓐ To calculate the survival rate of butterfly populations
Ⓑ To identify which butterfly species lay the most eggs
Ⓒ To show how climate influences reproductive adaptations
Ⓓ To explain why egg counting is important for researchers

03 According to the speaker, why is it important for female butterflies to select the right plants?

Ⓐ Plants determine the duration of each developmental stage.
Ⓑ Scented plants attract more male butterflies for future mating.
Ⓒ Inappropriate plant selection could lead to larval mortality.
Ⓓ The chemical composition of plants affects a butterfly's final coloration.

04 What does the speaker say about larvae?

Ⓐ They hibernate during cold weather to conserve energy.
Ⓑ They stop eating before entering the pupal stage.
Ⓒ They spin protective silk coverings each night.
Ⓓ They can survive in various temperature conditions.

[05-08] Listen to a talk in an environmental science class.

05 What is the main topic of the talk?

Ⓐ Solutions to environmental issues
Ⓑ Human impact on the environment
Ⓒ Factors contributing to climate change
Ⓓ Scientific disagreements about pollution

06 What does the speaker say about deforestation?

Ⓐ It is less harmful than burning fossil fuels.
Ⓑ It contributes to natural warming and cooling cycles.
Ⓒ It primarily affects oxygen production rather than CO_2 absorption.
Ⓓ It has destroyed about half of the world's rainforests in four decades.

07 Why does the speaker mention the Ice Age?

Ⓐ To highlight differences between natural and human impacts
Ⓑ To demonstrate that Earth experiences natural climate variations
Ⓒ To prove deforestation wasn't a factor in prehistoric times
Ⓓ To emphasize the effects of human activity on climate

08 Why does the speaker mention the scientific community?

Ⓐ To recommend specific research directions
Ⓑ To challenge mainstream climate change theories
Ⓒ To promote collaboration between research groups
Ⓓ To indicate that multiple perspectives exist on climate change causation

HACKERS TEST

[09-12] Listen to a talk in a biology class.

09 What is the talk mainly about?

  Ⓐ Various fish species and their unique characteristics
  Ⓑ Survival strategies of freshwater and saltwater fish
  Ⓒ The physical capabilities of various fish species
  Ⓓ Explanations of why fish leap out of the water

10 What does the speaker say about the silver arowana?

  Ⓐ It straightens its body rapidly to generate thrust.
  Ⓑ It jumps to overcome obstacles during migration.
  Ⓒ It uses jumping as a form of courtship communication.
  Ⓓ It contorts its body to escape from underwater predators.

11 What is NOT mentioned as an effect of fish jumping?

  Ⓐ Escaping from predators
  Ⓑ Overcoming physical barriers
  Ⓒ Communicating with other fish
  Ⓓ Regulating body temperature

12 What will the speaker most likely discuss next?

  Ⓐ Additional examples of jumping fish species
  Ⓑ The reproductive strategies of migratory fish
  Ⓒ The physical processes that enable fish jumping
  Ⓓ The ecological importance of fish jumping behavior

[13-16] Listen to a talk in a physiology class.

13 What is the main topic of the talk?

Ⓐ The discovery of brain wave patterns
Ⓑ The medical applications of EEG technology
Ⓒ The progression through various sleep stages
Ⓓ The relationship between meditation and sleep

14 What does the speaker say about theta waves?

Ⓐ They only appear during REM sleep.
Ⓑ They characterize the first two stages of sleep.
Ⓒ They are the largest waves produced by the brain.
Ⓓ They occur when people are fully awake and alert.

15 Why does the speaker mention muscle jerks?

Ⓐ To warn about the dangers of interrupted sleep
Ⓑ To demonstrate how muscles relax in deep sleep
Ⓒ To give a recognizable example of stage-one sleep
Ⓓ To explain why some people have trouble falling asleep

16 What will the speaker most likely discuss next?

Ⓐ The truth about dreams and restful sleep
Ⓑ The therapeutic uses of dream analysis
Ⓒ The health consequences of poor sleep
Ⓓ The techniques for improving sleep quality

HACKERS TEST

[17-20] Listen to a talk in an environmental science class.

17 What is the talk mainly about?

Ⓐ The declining availability of traditional energy sources
Ⓑ Environmental problems caused by energy consumption
Ⓒ The future depletion of non-renewable energy sources
Ⓓ The advantages and disadvantages of different fuel types

18 Why does the speaker mention ethanol?

Ⓐ To introduce a fuel made from recently living organisms
Ⓑ To emphasize the cost differences between fuel types
Ⓒ To challenge assumptions about renewable energy
Ⓓ To criticize inefficient energy alternatives

19 According to the speaker, what is a problem with biofuels?

Ⓐ They cannot be used in existing vehicle engines.
Ⓑ They release more carbon dioxide than fossil fuels.
Ⓒ They consume a significant amount of energy during their production.
Ⓓ They can't be produced in sufficient quantities to meet global demand.

20 What will the speaker most likely discuss next?

Ⓐ A comparison of energy policies across different countries
Ⓑ A comprehensive ecological assessment of biofuel alternatives
Ⓒ Future projections of energy consumption
Ⓓ Technological innovations in fuel efficiency

[21-24] Listen to a talk in a biology class.

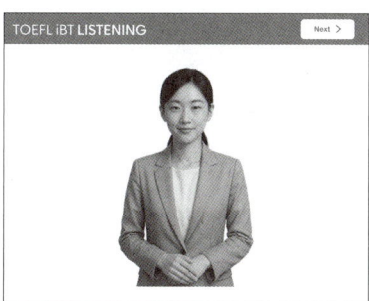

21 What is the main topic of the talk?

   Ⓐ The temperature tolerance of ocean animals
   Ⓑ The protective environment for marine algae
   Ⓒ Mutualistic relationships in coral ecosystems
   Ⓓ The limestone structures formed by marine animals

22 What does the speaker say about the zooxanthellae?

   Ⓐ They form colonies outside of coral tissue.
   Ⓑ They reside within coral tissue.
   Ⓒ They weaken coral under normal conditions.
   Ⓓ They consume essential nutrients from water.

23 According to the speaker, why is coral bleaching a problem?

   Ⓐ The algae multiply too rapidly inside the coral.
   Ⓑ The coral tissues produce harmful substances.
   Ⓒ The ocean temperature drops below tolerance levels.
   Ⓓ The coral suffers from food deprivation and weakness.

24 What will the speaker most likely discuss next?

   Ⓐ Sugar production in marine plants
   Ⓑ The measurement of ocean temperatures
   Ⓒ Conservation efforts for coral ecosystems
   Ⓓ The diving techniques used by marine researchers

Answers p.590

**Hackers
Updated TOEFL
LISTENING**

ACTUAL TEST

**ACTUAL TEST 1
ACTUAL TEST 2**

ACTUAL TEST 1

◀ 음성 바로 듣기

🎧 AT1

TOEFL iBT LISTENING Begin >

Module 1

During the test, the clock will show you how much time you have to finish each question.

You can use **Next** to move to the next question.

You WILL NOT be able to go back to previous questions.

The first task is **Listen and Choose a Response**. In this task, you will listen to a sentence or question. You will then read four sentences and choose the option that is the best response.

TOEFL iBT LISTENING Questions 01~04 of 20

Choose the best response.

01
Ⓐ Let me wrap up this email first.
Ⓑ Yes, the project was a success.
Ⓒ I really like the setup in here.
Ⓓ No, further from the screen.

02
Ⓐ Who can reserve it?
Ⓑ Either room is available.
Ⓒ Yes, I should.
Ⓓ It's already booked by someone else.

03
Ⓐ It opens at 9 A.M.
Ⓑ I believe it's in the main lobby.
Ⓒ You should bring your ID to register.
Ⓓ I'm thinking about joining next month.

04
Ⓐ So am I.
Ⓑ I recommend a microwave.
Ⓒ It blends in well.
Ⓓ Oh, I didn't expect that.

Choose the best response.

05 Ⓐ They provided a broad agenda.
　　Ⓑ It's at 10 o'clock.
　　Ⓒ The executives will be there.
　　Ⓓ Keep me posted.

06 Ⓐ We're all set to go.
　　Ⓑ No need to try explaining that.
　　Ⓒ I've actually already tried it out.
　　Ⓓ Take a look at the sales projections.

07 Ⓐ It depends mainly on the professor's teaching schedule.
　　Ⓑ Twelve classrooms on each floor of the building.
　　Ⓒ Beginning right at the end of August this year.
　　Ⓓ Covering various topics divided into four modules.

08 Ⓐ Several errors in the old employee manual, actually.
　　Ⓑ The training room was used earlier this morning.
　　Ⓒ In the storage facility until they can be recycled.
　　Ⓓ George is collecting them from the print shop tomorrow.

[09-10] Listen to a conversation.

09 What event are the speakers discussing?

Ⓐ A company merger
Ⓑ A product launch
Ⓒ An employee promotion
Ⓓ A departmental meeting

10 What does the woman think about the layoffs?

Ⓐ They are unfortunate but inevitable.
Ⓑ They will not be implemented.
Ⓒ They will occur at the same time as the staff relocations.
Ⓓ They are planned for specific departments only.

[11-12] Listen to a conversation.

11 Why can't the man keep the dinner reservation?

Ⓐ He forgot to confirm the booking.
Ⓑ He was informed of an emergency closure.
Ⓒ He learned of the clients' schedule change.
Ⓓ He has a plumbing problem at home.

12 What does the man suggest the woman do?

Ⓐ Search for other restaurants
Ⓑ Have dinner with him
Ⓒ Cancel the client meeting
Ⓓ Visit alternative venues ahead of time

[13-14] Listen to an announcement at a university event.

13 What is the main topic of the announcement?

  Ⓐ An upcoming deadline
  Ⓑ A new performance venue
  Ⓒ A course enrollment process
  Ⓓ A student ID policy change

14 What are students advised to bring?

  Ⓐ A registration fee
  Ⓑ An identification card
  Ⓒ A performance reel
  Ⓓ A letter of support

[15-16] Listen to an announcement on the school radio.

15 What is the main purpose of the announcement?

  Ⓐ To describe a new resource at the school library
  Ⓑ To promote effective time management strategies
  Ⓒ To explain conference room booking procedures
  Ⓓ To provide information about an upcoming event

16 What are students encouraged to do according to the announcement?

  Ⓐ Discuss the event with others
  Ⓑ Arrive early to secure a seat
  Ⓒ Come prepared with a plan
  Ⓓ Write down a list of questions

[17-20] Listen to a talk in an archaeology class.

17 What is the main topic of the talk?

Ⓐ The inadequacy of traditional methods used to study history
Ⓑ Strengths and weaknesses of experimental archaeology
Ⓒ Difficulties associated with reconstructing Iron Age buildings
Ⓓ Differences between experimental and traditional archaeology

18 What can researchers learn about from constructing Iron Age houses?

Ⓐ Cutting tools
Ⓑ Navigation methods
Ⓒ Flint-knapping techniques
Ⓓ Insulation properties

19 Why does the speaker mention the cultural context of a past era?

Ⓐ To highlight a shortcoming of experimental archaeology
Ⓑ To illustrate the importance of culture in guiding past societies
Ⓒ To explain how knowledge was transmitted across generations
Ⓓ To suggest that contemporary knowledge facilitates understanding the past

20 What aspect of experimental archaeology will the speaker discuss next?

Ⓐ Its development history
Ⓑ Challenges expected in experimental projects
Ⓒ How modern technology is integrated with traditional methods
Ⓓ Methods of training experimental archaeologists

End of Module 1

The first module of the Listening Section is now complete.
Module 2 will begin next.

TOEFL iBT LISTENING

Module 2

During the test, the clock will show you how much time you have to finish each question.

You can use **Next** to move to the next question.

You WILL NOT be able to go back to previous questions.

Choose the best response.

01 Ⓐ Have you seen the report?
　　Ⓑ Should we join the discussion?
　　Ⓒ Tomorrow morning.
　　Ⓓ The best financial plan.

02 Ⓐ No, it's this Friday.
　　Ⓑ No, I don't have time.
　　Ⓒ Yes, I could.
　　Ⓓ Yes, that's reasonable.

03 Ⓐ Last Friday.
　　Ⓑ The auditorium on campus.
　　Ⓒ Can you join next time?
　　Ⓓ As a matter of fact, it was canceled.

[04-05] Listen to a conversation.

04 What are the speakers mainly discussing?

Ⓐ A hotel room's condition
Ⓑ An unfulfilled guest request
Ⓒ A malfunctioning telephone system
Ⓓ A missed welcoming event

05 What does the woman offer to do?

Ⓐ Request that an event be rescheduled
Ⓑ Train a new staff member
Ⓒ Provide the man with a meal
Ⓓ Arrange a service for the man

[06-07] Listen to a conversation.

06 Why does the man say "My mind's all over the place"?

Ⓐ He is not sure how to contact Miranda.
Ⓑ He is handling too many things at once.
Ⓒ He is unaware of where his bag is.
Ⓓ He is thinking about where Miranda could be.

07 What does the woman encourage the man to do?

Ⓐ Take a break to relax
Ⓑ Check if his bag is in his desk
Ⓒ Send Miranda an email
Ⓓ Have some coffee with her

[08-11] Listen to a talk in a psychology class.

08 What is the main topic of the talk?

Ⓐ Reasons for poor academic performance
Ⓑ Causes and effects of stereotype threat
Ⓒ Impacts of testing on student learning
Ⓓ Stereotypes prevalent in academic settings

09 Why does the speaker discuss a study from 2021?

Ⓐ To illustrate the far-reaching consequences of stereotype threat on society
Ⓑ To suggest that stereotype threat can result from perceptions about any aspect of identity
Ⓒ To demonstrate how research methodologies have changed since the 1990s
Ⓓ To argue that there is a correlation between race and socioeconomic background

10 According to the speaker, stereotype threat can lead to all of the following EXCEPT

Ⓐ decreased academic concentration
Ⓑ doubts about personal abilities
Ⓒ impaired cognitive development
Ⓓ the fulfillment of feared stereotypes

11 What can be concluded about the impact of "belonging uncertainty" on individuals?

Ⓐ It enhances their ability to deal with stress.
Ⓑ It relieves them of the pressure to fit in.
Ⓒ It redirects their mental energy.
Ⓓ It reinforces their sense of identity.

[12-15] Listen to a talk in a meteorology class.

12 What is the talk mainly about?

　Ⓐ How temperature differences are measured
　Ⓑ Higher temperatures in cities compared to rural areas
　Ⓒ The relationship between solar radiation and urban materials
　Ⓓ The cause of climate change in cities

13 According to the speaker, how do scientists study urban temperature differences?

　Ⓐ By analyzing greenhouse gas emissions in urban areas
　Ⓑ By measuring solar radiation absorption in different materials
　Ⓒ By comparing weather data collected from different locations
　Ⓓ By tracking patterns of cooling system usage

14 Why does the speaker mention air conditioning?

　Ⓐ To explain how cities measure their energy consumption
　Ⓑ To compare energy usage between cities and rural areas
　Ⓒ To emphasize the vulnerability of public health in cities
　Ⓓ To describe how the urban heat island effect impacts energy consumption

15 What will the speaker most likely discuss next?

　Ⓐ Some typical patterns of heat islands in cities
　Ⓑ Major elements that influence heat island intensity
　Ⓒ Cases of extreme heat events in urban areas
　Ⓓ Differences between heat islands in various climate zones

End of Module 2

The Listening Section is now complete.

무료 토플자료·유학정보 공유
goHackers.com

ACTUAL TEST 2

AT2

TOEFL iBT **LISTENING**

Begin >

Module 1

During the test, the clock will show you how much time you have to finish each question.

You can use **Next** to move to the next question.

You WILL NOT be able to go back to previous questions.

The first task is **Listen and Choose a Response**. In this task, you will listen to a sentence or question. You will then read four sentences and choose the option that is the best response.

Choose the best response.

01
Ⓐ They can use the visitor parking lot.
Ⓑ We'll discuss the goals of the visit.
Ⓒ How many people are supposed to come?
Ⓓ From our most recently opened branch.

02
Ⓐ The HR department is in charge of hiring.
Ⓑ Only for full-time staff.
Ⓒ Claims must be filed promptly.
Ⓓ Yes, it provides paid time off.

03
Ⓐ In front of City Hall.
Ⓑ They're really colorful.
Ⓒ At 9 P.M.
Ⓓ To celebrate the holiday.

04
Ⓐ Which part is hard for you to understand?
Ⓑ You're quite skilled.
Ⓒ The software needs an update.
Ⓓ That works fine for me.

Choose the best response.

05 Ⓐ It was developed online last year.
Ⓑ Yes, training is mandatory for all staff.
Ⓒ No, the materials aren't very informative.
Ⓓ Log in with your employee ID and the password we emailed you.

06 Ⓐ Employees are evaluated once a year.
Ⓑ It was a long time coming.
Ⓒ The promotion helped boost sales.
Ⓓ I do not like my current schedule.

07 Ⓐ This Saturday.
Ⓑ Are you up for some running?
Ⓒ Next to the golf course.
Ⓓ Keep the door open.

08 Ⓐ It starts at 8 in the morning.
Ⓑ The schedule should say.
Ⓒ We need to shift our focus.
Ⓓ Terry called in sick today.

Choose the best response.

09 Ⓐ Yes, that's why I hate downtown.
Ⓑ I'll be on vacation next month.
Ⓒ I usually take off around 6 on Fridays.
Ⓓ Then, how about Saturday instead?

10 Ⓐ We're getting close.
Ⓑ The one next to you.
Ⓒ Of course not.
Ⓓ That's not mine.

[11-12] Listen to a conversation.

11 Why does the man suggest pushing back the presentation?

Ⓐ The conference room is unavailable until later.
Ⓑ He scheduled the presentation too early.
Ⓒ He prefers a small room on the second floor.
Ⓓ The presentation slides are not ready.

12 What will the woman do next?

Ⓐ Book a different room
Ⓑ Inform others about a new location
Ⓒ Postpone a meeting time
Ⓓ Complete some presentation materials

[13-14] Listen to a conversation.

13 What does the man offer to do?

Ⓐ Create digital advertisements
Ⓑ Plan a product launch event
Ⓒ Design print materials
Ⓓ Share a way to lower expenses

14 Why does the man mention digital ads?

Ⓐ To propose increasing the overall marketing budget
Ⓑ To explain why print ads are preferable
Ⓒ To highlight his expertise in the marketing field
Ⓓ To suggest a more affordable alternative

[15-16] Listen to a conversation.

15 What does the man assure the woman about?

Ⓐ That the produce will be organic
Ⓑ That shopping won't be a problem if it rains
Ⓒ That 9:00 AM is a good time to go
Ⓓ That the location will be easy to find

16 Where are the speakers meeting?

Ⓐ At the plaza
Ⓑ At the library
Ⓒ At a bakery
Ⓓ At a flower shop

[17-18] Listen to an announcement in a classroom.

17 What is the main topic of the announcement?

Ⓐ Additional guest speaker recruitment
Ⓑ Changes made to a course schedule
Ⓒ Review procedures for a syllabus
Ⓓ How to prepare for class discussions

18 Why does the speaker mention the announcements section?

Ⓐ To encourage students to take another course
Ⓑ To inform students about online materials
Ⓒ To help students find updated information
Ⓓ To give students new assignments

[19-20] Listen to an announcement at a student meeting.

19 Which of the following is true about the peer tutoring program?

Ⓐ Each tutoring session time varies depending on the subject.
Ⓑ Only students with a GPA of under 3.5 can request tutoring help.
Ⓒ Participating students are charged an enrollment fee.
Ⓓ The program was offered in just one type of format last year.

20 What does the speaker hope the listeners will do?

Ⓐ Take a practice test
Ⓑ Purchase study materials
Ⓒ Reserve a tutoring session
Ⓓ Select a certified tutor

[21-24] Listen to a talk on a podcast about psychology.

21 What is the topic of the talk?

Ⓐ How memory affects our daily activities
Ⓑ Three types of cognitive load
Ⓒ The importance of working memory capacity
Ⓓ How to improve concentration skills

22 According the speaker, what is intrinsic load?

Ⓐ Information that exceeds what can be processed
Ⓑ Irrelevant details that make it hard to concentrate
Ⓒ The cognitive power needed to complete a task
Ⓓ Energy dedicated to processing new information

23 Why does the speaker mention studying with loud music playing in the background?

Ⓐ To suggest that studying while distracted is common
Ⓑ To provide an example of cognitive load caused by external influences
Ⓒ To explain how poor study habits develop
Ⓓ To emphasize the importance of smart instructional design

24 What does the speaker say about germane load?

Ⓐ It occurs when intrinsic and extraneous loads are high.
Ⓑ It should be minimized for better learning.
Ⓒ It creates mental fatigue and stress.
Ⓓ It helps create understanding and memories.

[25-28] Listen to a talk in an art class.

25 Why does the professor mention a hobbyhorse at the beginning of the talk?

Ⓐ To explain the possible origin of a name
Ⓑ To describe a symbol frequently used in art
Ⓒ To suggest traditions represented outdated values
Ⓓ To show how artists embraced childishness and randomness

26 According to the speaker, what is a key characteristic of Dadaism?

Ⓐ The creation of aesthetically beautiful compositions
Ⓑ Adherence to established artistic conventions
Ⓒ The use of shocking and unconventional methods
Ⓓ A focus on depicting global war and conflict

27 The speaker implies that Duchamp's submission of "Fountain" as an artwork is an example of what?

Ⓐ Traditional sculptural techniques
Ⓑ Technical mastery in a three-dimensional work
Ⓒ Religious symbolism in modern art
Ⓓ Subversion of basic beliefs about art

28 What can be inferred about later avant-garde movements?

Ⓐ They returned to creating beautiful objects.
Ⓑ They built on concepts introduced by Dadaism.
Ⓒ They influenced Dadaists to explore the meaning of art.
Ⓓ They were not as relevant as Dadaism.

End of Module 1

The first module of the Listening Section is now complete.
Module 2 will begin next.

TOEFL iBT LISTENING

Module 2

During the test, the clock will show you how much time you have to finish each question.

You can use **Next** to move to the next question.

You WILL NOT be able to go back to previous questions.

Choose the best response.

01 Ⓐ Where exactly can I get it from?
Ⓑ I'll take part in the authorization process.
Ⓒ You need to complete some paperwork.
Ⓓ And what form should I submit?

02 Ⓐ I doubt whether it will work.
Ⓑ Yes, I remembered my umbrella.
Ⓒ The local news.
Ⓓ I'll do that now.

03 Ⓐ We're asking for a good price.
Ⓑ They've got lots of other options to see.
Ⓒ That puts the matter into perspective.
Ⓓ More people are coming to take a look.

[04-05] Listen to a conversation.

04 What aspect of the visa application does the woman talk about?

Ⓐ The unclear instructions
Ⓑ The accompanying paperwork
Ⓒ The high processing cost
Ⓓ The approval waiting period

05 What does the man say about the International Student Office?

Ⓐ They rejected his application.
Ⓑ They required him to make an appointment.
Ⓒ He went to them for help with his application.
Ⓓ Assistance from them was difficult to obtain.

[06-07] Listen to a conversation.

06 What is the woman's problem with the fitness center?

Ⓐ It is located too far from her home.
Ⓑ It does not offer a variety of classes.
Ⓒ It lacks sufficient parking space.
Ⓓ It charges too much for membership.

07 What about the fitness center impresses the man?

Ⓐ Its hours are convenient.
Ⓑ Its equipment is excellent.
Ⓒ Personal trainers are available.
Ⓓ It collaborates with other businesses.

[08-11] Listen to a talk in a biology class.

08 What is the talk mainly about?

   Ⓐ How different species share common ancestors
   Ⓑ The role of environmental factors in animal behavior
   Ⓒ Examples of similar traits developing independently in unrelated species
   Ⓓ Methods by which species survive environmental pressures

09 According to the speaker, what causes dolphins and bats to use sound waves for navigation and hunting?

   Ⓐ Shared evolutionary ancestry
   Ⓑ Limited environmental visibility
   Ⓒ Similar brain structures
   Ⓓ Comparable social structures

10 What does the speaker point out about bird wings?

   Ⓐ They are more efficient than insect wings.
   Ⓑ They have the same structure as that of insects.
   Ⓒ They evolved from changes in arm bones.
   Ⓓ They move independent of each other in flight.

11 What does the speaker imply about environmental pressures?

   Ⓐ They can produce similar evolutionary outcomes in different species.
   Ⓑ They affect plants more significantly than animals.
   Ⓒ They are the primary cause of species evolution.
   Ⓓ They can be reduced with predictable solutions.

[12-15] Listen to a talk in an economics class.

12 What is the main topic of the talk?

  Ⓐ Benefits of cutting corporate tax rates
  Ⓑ Reasons trickle-down economics fails
  Ⓒ Successful pro-growth strategies
  Ⓓ Factors influencing economic growth

13 According to the speaker, what is a problem with tax breaks for corporations and the wealthy?

  Ⓐ They encourage individuals to spend more than they save.
  Ⓑ They can increase wealth disparity in society.
  Ⓒ They lead to the creation of more jobs than the economy can handle.
  Ⓓ They are not always reported to the general public.

14 Why does the speaker mention stock buybacks?

  Ⓐ To illustrate that corporate tax breaks may not help workers
  Ⓑ To highlight an efficient way for corporations to boost earnings
  Ⓒ To demonstrate how corporations could create jobs but do not
  Ⓓ To show how corporations encourage consumer spending

15 What will the speaker most likely discuss next?

  Ⓐ The positive effects of wealth distribution on growth
  Ⓑ Debates sparked by trickle-down economics
  Ⓒ The potential outcomes of different tax structures
  Ⓓ Viewpoints that have shaped tax policy discourse

End of Module 2

The Listening Section is now complete.

무료 토플자료·유학정보 공유
goHackers.com

무료 토플자료·유학정보 공유
goHackers.com

Hackers Updated TOEFL LISTENING

TASK별 실전 필수 어휘

DAY 01　TASK 1 실전 필수 어휘
DAY 02　TASK 1 실전 필수 어휘
DAY 03　TASK 1 실전 필수 어휘
DAY 04　TASK 1 실전 필수 어휘
DAY 05　TASK 2 실전 필수 어휘
DAY 06　TASK 2 실전 필수 어휘
DAY 07　TASK 2 실전 필수 어휘
DAY 08　TASK 2 실전 필수 어휘
DAY 09　TASK 3 실전 필수 어휘
DAY 10　TASK 3 실전 필수 어휘
DAY 11　TASK 3 실전 필수 어휘
DAY 12　TASK 3 실전 필수 어휘
DAY 13　TASK 4 실전 필수 어휘
DAY 14　TASK 4 실전 필수 어휘
DAY 15　TASK 4 실전 필수 어휘
DAY 16　TASK 4 실전 필수 어휘
DAY 17　TASK 4 실전 필수 어휘
DAY 18　TASK 4 실전 필수 어휘
DAY 19　TASK 4 실전 필수 어휘
DAY 20　TASK 4 실전 필수 어휘

Day 01 — TASK 1 실전 필수 어휘

☑ TASK 1을 위해 필수적으로 알아야 할 어휘들이므로, 확실히 암기해 둡니다.

🎧 DAY01

☐ a stack of	많은		☐ attractive [ətræktiv]	매력적인
☐ a ton of	매우 많은		☐ automatic [ɔ̀:təmǽtik]	자동의
☐ a variety of	다양한		☐ avoid [əvɔ́id]	피하다
☐ absent [ǽbsənt]	결석한		☐ awake [əwéik]	깨어있는
☐ absentminded [ǽbsəntmàindid]	방심 상태의		☐ awfully [ɔ́:fəli]	대단히
☐ absolutely [ǽbsəlú:tli]	절대적으로		☐ back and forth	반복적으로, 앞뒤로
☐ absorbed in	~에 몰두한		☐ back on one's feet	회복하여
☐ accept [əksépt]	받아들이다		☐ banquet [bǽŋkwit]	만찬
☐ access [ǽkses]	접속하다		☐ basically [béisikəli]	기본적으로
☐ account [əkáunt]	계정, 계좌		☐ be acquainted with	~을 알고 있다
☐ acquaintance [əkwéintəns]	아는 사람, 지인		☐ be all set to	~할 준비가 끝나다
☐ active [ǽktiv]	활동적인		☐ be aware of	~을 알고 있다
☐ add up	계산이 맞다		☐ be closed all day	종일 휴무이다
☐ admit [ədmít]	인정하다		☐ be familiar with	~에 익숙하다
☐ afford [əfɔ́:rd]	감당하다, ~을 살 여유가 있다		☐ be far off the mark	동떨어진 얘기를 하다
☐ after all	결국		☐ be in over one's head	능력이 미치지 못하다
☐ afterward [ǽftərwərd]	후에, 나중에		☐ be on one's way	오는 중이다
☐ ahead of time	일찍, 먼저		☐ be responsible for	책임지다
☐ alphabetical [ælfəbétikl]	알파벳순의		☐ be scheduled for	예정되어 있다
☐ amazingly [əméiziŋli]	놀랍게도		☐ be through with	끝내다, 마치다
☐ apologize [əpálədʒàiz]	사과하다		☐ be tied up	바쁘다
☐ appearance [əpíərəns]	외모		☐ be willing to	기꺼이 ~하다
☐ appointment [əpɔ́intmənt]	약속		☐ behind the scenes	뒤에서 조용히 일하다
☐ as a matter of fact	실은, 사실상		☐ belong to	~의 소유이다, ~에 속하다
☐ assist [əsíst]	돕다		☐ big deal	대단한 것, 큰일
☐ at a loss	당황하여		☐ borrow [bá:rou]	빌리다, 차용하다
☐ at best	기껏해야		☐ boss around	이래라저래라 하다
☐ at ease	여유 있게, 안심하고		☐ bother [bá:ðər]	성가신 일; 귀찮게 하다
☐ at first	처음에는		☐ bound to	~하게 마련인
☐ attend [əténd]	참석하다		☐ brand-new	신품의, 새로운

Day 02 — TASK 1 실전 필수 어휘

☑ TASK 1을 위해 필수적으로 알아야 할 어휘들이므로, 확실히 암기해 둡니다. 🎧 DAY02

☐ break [breik]	휴식 시간		☐ convenient [kənví:njənt]	편리한
☐ break a promise	약속을 어기다		☐ convince [kənvíns]	납득시키다
☐ bring along	가지고 가다		☐ crowded [kráudid]	붐비는, 혼잡한
☐ bring someone up to speed	최신 상황을 알려주다		☐ cut out to be	~에 적임이다, 어울리다
☐ bump into	우연히 만나다		☐ daily [déili]	매일의
☐ burn up	약 올리다		☐ definitely [défənitli]	분명히
☐ busy [bízi]	바쁜		☐ deliver [dilívər]	배송하다
☐ by accident	우연히, 실수로		☐ depend on	~에 달려 있다
☐ by coincidence	우연히		☐ deserve [dizə́:rv]	~할 자격이 있다
☐ call on	방문하다		☐ detailed [dí:teild]	상세한
☐ calm down	진정시키다		☐ disappointing [dìsəpɔ́intiŋ]	실망스러운
☐ carefree [kέərfrì:]	근심이 없는		☐ distracted [distrǽktid]	마음이 산란한
☐ challenging [tʃǽlindʒiŋ]	도전적인, 힘든		☐ doable [dú:əbl]	가능한
☐ charge [tʃɑːrdʒ]	청구하다		☐ double-sided	양면의
☐ charming [tʃɑ́:rmiŋ]	멋진, 매력적인		☐ down pat	완전히 이해하다
☐ clear up	날씨가 맑아지다, 처리하다		☐ doze off	깜빡 졸다
☐ clueless [klú:lis]	모르는		☐ dragged out	기진맥진하여
☐ clumsy [klʌ́mzi]	서투른		☐ drop by	잠깐 들르다
☐ come across	우연히 발견하다		☐ drop something off	맡기다, 전달하다
☐ come along	따라가다		☐ drowsy [dráuzi]	졸리는
☐ come down with	~의 병에 걸리다		☐ dull [dʌl]	지루한
☐ come in	도착하다		☐ dumb [dʌm]	어리석은
☐ come out	나오다		☐ eager [íːgər]	열렬한, 간절히 원하는
☐ comfortable [kʌ́mfərtəbl]	편안한		☐ effective [iféktiv]	효과적인
☐ complain [kəmpléin]	불평하다		☐ exceed [iksí:d]	초과하다
☐ compliment [kɑ́:mpləmənt]	칭찬		☐ exhausted [igzɔ́:stid]	지친
☐ conduct [kəndʌ́kt]	실시하다		☐ expedite [ékspədàit]	신속히 처리하다
☐ conference [kɑ́nfərəns]	회의		☐ expensive [ikspénsiv]	비싼
☐ confident [kɑ́nfədənt]	자신감 있는		☐ extend [iksténd]	연장하다
☐ congratulate [kəngrǽtʃulèit]	축하하다		☐ extremely [ikstrí:mli]	매우

Day 03 — TASK 1 실전 필수 어휘

☑ TASK 1을 위해 필수적으로 알아야 할 어휘들이므로, 확실히 암기해 둡니다.

🎧 DAY03

☐ fairly [féərli]	꽤	
☐ foolish [fúːliʃ]	바보 같은	
☐ for starters	우선	
☐ frankly [frǽŋkli]	솔직히 말해서	
☐ frustrated [frʌ́streitid]	좌절한	
☐ frustrating [frʌ́streitiŋ]	좌절감을 주는, 답답한	
☐ genuinely [dʒénjuinli]	정말로	
☐ get along	사이좋게 지내다	
☐ get back to someone	다시 연락하다	
☐ get in touch with	연락하다	
☐ get one's hopes up	기대하다	
☐ get someone right	~의 말을 제대로 이해하다	
☐ get used to	~에 익숙해지다	
☐ give a hand	도와주다, 박수를 보내다	
☐ give a hoot	관심을 가지다	
☐ give it a try	시도하다	
☐ go out of one's way	굳이 ~하다	
☐ hands are tied	마음대로 못하다	
☐ hang on	기다리다	
☐ happen to	우연히 ~하게되다	
☐ hardly [háːrdli]	거의 ~ 않다	
☐ hassle [hǽsl]	골치 아픈 일	
☐ have what it takes	필요한 자질을 갖추다	
☐ hear from	~와 연락하다, ~로부터 소식이 있다	
☐ hear of	~에 대해 알다, 친숙하다	
☐ hear out	끝까지 듣다	
☐ hectic [héktik]	바쁜	
☐ hesitate [hézətèit]	주저하다	
☐ hold on	기다리다	
☐ hold still	움직이지 않다	

☐ identify [aidéntəfài]	식별하다
☐ immediately [imíːdiətli]	곧
☐ in a heartbeat	곧장, 두 말 없이
☐ in a nutshell	간단히 말해서
☐ in effect	시행 중인
☐ in no time	곧
☐ in some way	어떤 식으로든
☐ in the dark	아무것도 모르는
☐ incredible [inkrédəbl]	놀라운
☐ itchy [ítʃi]	가려운
☐ just about everything	거의 모두 다
☐ keep in mind	유념하다
☐ keep on	계속하다
☐ lame [leim]	서투른, 궁색한
☐ later on	나중에
☐ let down	실망시키다
☐ lifesaver [láifsèivər]	구원자
☐ look forward to	기대하다
☐ look something up	찾아보다
☐ major in	전공하다
☐ make a mess	어지럽히다
☐ make it on time	제시간에 맞추다
☐ make the effort	애쓰다
☐ make up one's mind	결심하다
☐ mess up	망치다, 엉망으로 만들다
☐ mixed up	혼란스러운
☐ nearby [nìərbái]	가까운
☐ need a hand	도움을 필요로 하다
☐ nonsense [náːnsens]	어리석은 생각
☐ official [əfíʃəl]	공식적인

Day 04   TASK 1 실전 필수 어휘

☑ TASK 1을 위해 필수적으로 알아야 할 어휘들이므로, 확실히 암기해 둡니다.

☐ on one's own	스스로
☐ on second thought	재고한 후에
☐ on the tip of one's tongue	말이 혀끝에서 도는
☐ overdue [òuvərdjú:]	기한이 지난
☐ oversleep [òuvərslí:p]	늦잠 자다
☐ pass something along	전달하다
☐ pick on	괴롭히다, 비난하다
☐ pick something up	수령하다, 찾아가다
☐ picky [píki]	까다로운
☐ post [poust]	게시하다, (기둥·벽에) 붙이다
☐ postpone [poustpóun]	연기하다
☐ present [préznt]	발표하다
☐ pushover [púʃòuvər]	손쉬운 일
☐ put something up for sale	매물로 내놓다
☐ put up with	견디다
☐ relocate [rì:loukéit]	이전하다
☐ represent [rèprizént]	대표하다
☐ reschedule [rì:skédʒu:l]	일정을 변경하다
☐ reservation [rèzərvéiʃən]	예약
☐ rough [rʌf]	힘든
☐ rub it in	몰아세우다, 상기시키다
☐ rude [ru:d]	무례한
☐ run longer than expected	예상보다 오래 걸리다
☐ see one's point	~의 말뜻을 알다, 이해하다
☐ select [silékt]	선정하다
☐ ship [ʃip]	배송하다
☐ short on cash	돈이 부족한
☐ short on time	시간이 모자라는
☐ shout [ʃaut]	소리 지르다
☐ show off	자랑하다
☐ show up	나타나다
☐ be sick and tired of	~에 진절머리가 나다
☐ stay away from	~을 멀리하다
☐ stay on track	계획대로 진행되다
☐ stay up	자지 않고 있다
☐ stock [stɑk]	비치하다
☐ submit [səbmít]	제출하다
☐ subscription [səbskrípʃən]	구독
☐ take a chance	모험을 하다
☐ take a day off	하루 쉬다
☐ take a raincheck	약속을 후일로 미루다
☐ take care of	~을 처리하다
☐ take one's time	천천히 하다
☐ terrific [tərífik]	멋진
☐ timely [táimli]	시의적절한
☐ to be honest	솔직히
☐ to tell the truth	솔직히 말하자면
☐ truly [trú:li]	진실로
☐ turn down	거절하다, 소리를 줄이다
☐ under the weather	몸이 좋지 않은
☐ unfortunate [ʌnfɔ́:rtʃənət]	유감스러운
☐ unfortunately [ənfɔ́:rtʃənətli]	안타깝게도, 불행히도
☐ up to now	지금까지
☐ upset [ʌpsét]	속상한, 근심되는
☐ verify [vérəfài]	확인하다
☐ weird [wiərd]	이상한
☐ wet blanket	흥을 깨는 사람
☐ wind down	긴장을 풀다
☐ wonder [wʌ́ndər]	궁금해하다
☐ worth a try	시도할 만한 가치가 있는

Day 05   TASK 2 실전 필수 어휘

☑ TASK 2를 위해 필수적으로 알아야 할 어휘들이므로, 확실히 암기해 둡니다.

🎧 DAY05

☐ a few extra	여분의	
☐ access card	출입카드	
☐ accommodation [əkɑ̀mədéiʃən]	숙소, 숙박 시설	
☐ accomplish [əkɑ́mpliʃ]	성취하다	
☐ accountant [əkáuntənt]	회계사	
☐ act up	제 기능을 못하다	
☐ adjust [ədʒʌ́st]	적응하다	
☐ admirer [ədmáiərər]	팬, 찬양자	
☐ advertise [ǽdvərtàiz]	광고하다	
☐ affordable [əfɔ́:rdəbl]	가격이 알맞은	
☐ aim [eim]	목표 삼다	
☐ aisle [ail]	복도, 통로	
☐ allergic [əlɚ́:rdʒik]	알레르기의	
☐ all-time	사상 최고의/최저의	
☐ along the lines of	~와 같은 종류의	
☐ amenities [əménətis]	편의시설	
☐ anticipate [æntísəpèit]	예상하다	
☐ anxiety [æŋzáiəti]	불안	
☐ apparently [əpǽrəntli]	겉보기에, 듣자 하니	
☐ appropriate [əpróupriət]	적당한	
☐ arrange [əréindʒ]	조정하다, 세우다	
☐ arrive early	일찍 도착하다	
☐ aside from	외에도	
☐ assume [əsú:m]	가정하다, 추정하다	
☐ astonishing [əstɑ́niʃiŋ]	놀라운	
☐ at most	많아야	
☐ at one's fingertips	당장 이용할 수 있는	
☐ award recipient	수상자	
☐ backfire [bǽkfair]	역효과; 역효과를 내다	
☐ back-to-back	연이은	

☐ barely [bɛ́ərli]	거의 ~ 않다	
☐ be at odds with	~와 사이가 좋지 않다	
☐ be conscious of	~을 의식하다	
☐ be in luck	운이 좋다	
☐ be similar to	~과 비슷하다	
☐ be supposed to	~하기로 되어있다	
☐ be torn between	양자택일을 망설이다	
☐ be unable to	~을 할 수 없다	
☐ bizarre [bizɑ́:r]	별난	
☐ blanket [blǽŋkit]	담요	
☐ board [bɔ:rd]	이사회	
☐ bottom line	요지, 핵심	
☐ burn out	번아웃되다	
☐ business trip	출장	
☐ buzz [bʌz]	이야기, 소문, 웅성거림	
☐ by any chance	혹시	
☐ call a plumber	배관공을 부르다	
☐ cardio [kɑ́:rdiou]	유산소 운동	
☐ catch up	따라잡다	
☐ catering company	출장연회 업체	
☐ change bus lines	버스를 갈아타다	
☐ change one's clothes	옷을 갈아입다	
☐ check availability	사용 가능 여부를 확인하다	
☐ check out	계산하다, 알아보다	
☐ club activities	동아리 활동	
☐ club constitution	동아리 회칙	
☐ club newsletter	동아리 소식지	
☐ collaborate [kəlǽbərèit]	협업하다	
☐ community service	지역사회 봉사활동	
☐ commute time	통근 시간, 통학 시간	

Day 06 TASK 2 실전 필수 어휘

☑ TASK 2를 위해 필수적으로 알아야 할 어휘들이므로, 확실히 암기해 둡니다. ♪ DAY06

□ company retreat	회사 야유회	□ flexible [fléksəbl]	융통성 있는, 유연한
□ computer lab	컴퓨터실	□ forget one's head	정신이 없다
□ conference call	전화 회의	□ freeze [fri:z]	멈추다
□ cozy [kóuzi]	아늑한	□ get a good spot	좋은 자리를 잡다
□ craft fair	공예품 박람회	□ get back into	~을 다시 시작하다
□ customer feedback	고객 의견	□ get in shape	몸을 만들다
□ daily special	일일 특선 요리	□ get ready	준비하다
□ data collection	데이터 수집	□ give someone a call	전화하다
□ decide between	둘 중에서 결정하다	□ go shopping	쇼핑을 가다
□ decidedly [disáididli]	명백히	□ go with	고르다, 선택하다
□ decline [dikláin]	거절하다	□ gradually [grǽdʒuəli]	점진적으로
□ demonstration [dèmənstréiʃən]	시연	□ handmade [hǽndmeid]	수제의
□ diagnose [dáiəgnòus]	진단하다	□ handout [hǽndáut]	인쇄물, 유인물
□ discover [diskʌ́vər]	발견하다	□ hands-on	실습의, 직접 해보는
□ diverse [dáivə:rs]	다양한	□ have space	자리가 남아 있다
□ double-check	재확인하다	□ have trouble with	~에 어려움을 겪다
□ downtown [dàuntáun]	도심	□ head down to	~로 내려가다
□ earn [ə:rn]	획득하다, 얻다	□ healthy [hélθi]	건강한
□ emergency procedures	비상 절차	□ heavy workload	과도한 업무량
□ emphasize [émfəsàiz]	강조하다	□ help out	도와주다
□ employee [implɔiíː]	고용인, 피고용자	□ hire a professional	전문가를 고용하다
□ equipment [ikwípmənt]	장비	□ hiring process	채용 과정
□ exhibit [igzíbit]	전시	□ host [houst]	주최자; 주최하다
□ expand [ikspǽnd]	확장하다	□ hours of operation	운영 시간
□ explore all the stalls	모든 가판대를 둘러보다	□ housing office	주거 관리 사무실
□ facility hours	운영 시간	□ illustrate [íləstrèit]	보여주다
□ fascinating [fǽsənèitiŋ]	흥미로운, 매력적인	□ implement [ímpləmènt]	도입하다, 시행하다
□ fiddle [fídl]	(세부사항을) 조작하다	□ in demand	수요가 많은
□ finalize [fáinəlàiz]	마무리 짓다	□ in the meantime	그동안
□ flat tire	바람 빠진 타이어	□ in the middle of	~을 하는 중인

Day 07   TASK 2 실전 필수 어휘

✅ TASK 2를 위해 필수적으로 알아야 할 어휘들이므로, 확실히 암기해 둡니다.

🎧 DAY07

☐ indicate [índikèit]	나타내다
☐ instructor [instrʌ́ktər]	전임 강사
☐ intense [inténs]	강도 높은
☐ keep an eye out	눈여겨보다
☐ keep dropping	자꾸 끊기다
☐ leadership position	임원직
☐ lend [lend]	빌려주다
☐ light [lait]	가벼운
☐ lost and found	분실물 보관소
☐ love [lʌv]	매우 좋아하다
☐ maintenance request	수리 요청
☐ make arrangements	준비하다, 주선하다
☐ make it to	~에 이르다, 도착하다
☐ make sure to	반드시 ~하다
☐ manage to	~을 해내다
☐ manageable [mǽnidʒəbl]	감당할 수 있는
☐ mission [míʃən]	임무
☐ mix up	뒤섞다, 혼동하다
☐ motivate [móutəvèit]	동기를 주다, 자극하다
☐ move in	이사를 들어오다
☐ move into	이사 들어가다
☐ narrow down	좁히다, 후보를 추려내다
☐ need attention	주목할 필요가 있다
☐ neighbor [néibər]	이웃
☐ not until	~까지는 아니다
☐ obligation [àbləgéiʃən]	의무, 책무
☐ office hours	면담 시간
☐ on a budget	한정된 예산으로
☐ on the go	이동 중인
☐ out of order	고장 난
☐ out of stock	재고가 떨어진
☐ overdo [òuvərdú:]	과장하다, 도를 넘다
☐ pace oneself	페이스를 조절하다
☐ parking permit	주차 허가증
☐ part-time position	아르바이트 자리
☐ performance evaluation	성과 평가
☐ pick up	사다, 구매하다
☐ plenty of	많은
☐ policy [páləsi]	정책
☐ portable [pɔ́:rtəbl]	휴대가 쉬운
☐ prefer [prifə́:r]	선호하다
☐ print [print]	인쇄하다
☐ printing service	인쇄 서비스
☐ prioritize [pràiɔ́:rətàiz]	우선순위를 매기다
☐ produce [prədjú:s]	생산하다; 생산물
☐ product description	제품 설명
☐ product launch event	제품 출시 행사
☐ productive [prədʌ́ktiv]	생산적인
☐ properly [prápərli]	제대로
☐ quarterly report	분기 보고서
☐ reception [risépʃən]	연회
☐ recommendation [rèkəmendéiʃən]	추천
☐ recruit [rikrú:t]	채용하다, 모집하다
☐ relevant [réləvənt]	관련 있는
☐ relief [rilí:f]	안심, 경감
☐ repair estimate	수리 견적
☐ repair shop	수리점
☐ repel [ripél]	쫓아내다, 떨쳐 버리다
☐ replace [ripléis]	대체하다
☐ replacement part	교체 부품

Day 08   TASK 2 실전 필수 어휘

☑ TASK 2를 위해 필수적으로 알아야 할 어휘들이므로, 확실히 암기해 둡니다.

🎧 DAY08

☐ research assistant	연구 조교		☐ suit [suːt]	~에게 어울리다, 적합하다
☐ reserve [rizə́ːrv]	예약하다		☐ swing by	잠깐 들르다
☐ resource [riːsɔ́ːrs]	자료		☐ take up	시작하다
☐ restart [ristɑ́ːrt]	재시작하다		☐ teaching assistant	조교
☐ return [ritə́ːrn]	반납하다		☐ technical support	기술 지원팀
☐ review [rivjúː]	평론		☐ technician [teknίʃən]	기술자
☐ routine [ruːtíːn]	규칙적인 습관		☐ tedious [tíːdiəs]	지루한
☐ run a virus scan	바이러스 검사를 실행하다		☐ training workshop	교육 워크숍
☐ run late	늦어지다		☐ transfer [trænsfə́ːr]	환승하다
☐ safety training	안전교육		☐ trend [trend]	동향
☐ sales figures	판매 수치		☐ troubleshoot [trʌ́bljúːt]	문제를 해결하다
☐ satisfy [sǽtisfài]	만족시키다		☐ unique [juːníːk]	독특한, 유일한
☐ season [síːzn]	양념하다		☐ unrealistic [ʌ̀nriːəlístik]	비현실적인
☐ security office	보안실		☐ unusual [ʌnjúːʒuəl]	독특한
☐ set up	~을 준비하다, 설정하다		☐ urgent [ə́ːrdʒənt]	긴급한, 절박한
☐ shortly [ʃɔ́ːrtli]	곧		☐ vacant [véikənt]	텅 빈, 생각이 없는
☐ shut down	멈추다		☐ vague [veig]	막연한, 모호한
☐ sidetrack [sàidtrǽk]	딴 길로 빠지다, (일을) 회피하다		☐ vanity [vǽnəti]	허영심
☐ sign up	가입하다		☐ vegetarian options	채식 메뉴
☐ slog [slag]	고된 일, 힘든 일		☐ vendor [véndər]	판매업체, 판매상
☐ social events	친목 행사		☐ ventilate [véntəleit]	환기하다
☐ soggy [sági]	흠뻑 젖은		☐ wag [wæg]	흔들다, 흔들리다
☐ speedy [spíːdi]	빠른		☐ walk someone through	자세히 설명하다
☐ split the fare	요금을 나눠내다		☐ warranty coverage	보증 범위
☐ sporting goods store	운동용품점		☐ well-known	잘 알려진
☐ starve [stɑːrv]	굶주리다		☐ wind up	해산하다, 그만두다
☐ stock up on	~을 많이 사다		☐ work out	운동하다, 일을 해결해내다
☐ stop by	가는 길에 들르다		☐ workflow process	업무 프로세스
☐ strategy [strǽtədʒi]	전략, 계획		☐ worn out	지친, 닳은
☐ student employment	학생 고용		☐ wrap up	마무리 짓다

Day 09 — TASK 3 실전 필수 어휘

☑ TASK 3를 위해 필수적으로 알아야 할 어휘들이므로, 확실히 암기해 둡니다.

🎧 DAY09

☐ abbreviated [əbríːvièitid]	단축된, 간결하게 한	
☐ accommodate [əkάːmədèit]	수용하다	
☐ accordingly [əkɔ́ːrdiŋli]	그에 맞춰	
☐ accuracy [ǽkjurəsi]	정확성	
☐ accurately [ǽkjurətli]	정확히	
☐ achievement [ətʃíːvmənt]	성과, 업적	
☐ adequately [ǽdikwətli]	충분히	
☐ adhere to	~을 준수하다	
☐ administration [ədmìnistréiʃən]	행정부	
☐ administrative [ədmínistrèitiv]	행정상의	
☐ admission [ədmíʃən]	입학	
☐ advanced [ədvǽnst]	첨단의, 진보한	
☐ advancement [ədvǽnsmənt]	발전	
☐ adviser [ədváizər]	지도 교수	
☐ agency [éidʒənsi]	기관	
☐ agenda [ədʒéndə]	의제	
☐ aid [eid]	지원	
☐ allot [əlάːt]	할당하다	
☐ alternate [ɔ́ltərnèit]	대체의	
☐ alternative [ɔːltə́ːrnətiv]	대안, 다른 방도	
☐ annex [ǽneks]	별관, 부가물	
☐ announce [ənáuns]	발표하다	
☐ announcement [ənáunsmənt]	공지, 발표	
☐ annual [ǽnjuəl]	연간의	
☐ applicable [ǽpləkəbl]	적용할 수 있는	
☐ appointed [əpɔ́intid]	지정된	
☐ appreciate [əpríːʃièit]	감사하다	
☐ apprise [əpráiz]	통지하다	
☐ approve [əprúːv]	찬성하다, 승인하다	
☐ around the corner	코앞에 와 있는	

☐ as soon as possible	가능한 한 빨리
☐ as usual	늘 그렇듯이
☐ assign [əsáin]	할당하다, (과제 등을) 내주다
☐ assignment [əsáinmənt]	과제, 숙제
☐ at least	적어도
☐ attendance [əténdəns]	출석
☐ audit [ɔ́ːdit]	청강하다
☐ auditorium [ɔ̀ːditɔ́ːriəm]	강당
☐ authority [əθɔ́ːrəti]	권한
☐ authorization [ɔ̀ːθərizéiʃən]	허가, 인정
☐ available [əvéiləbl]	이용 가능한
☐ award-winning	상을 받은
☐ awareness material	교육 자료, 홍보 자료
☐ bachelor's degree	학사학위
☐ be about to	막 ~하려 하다
☐ be closed for repairs	보수 공사로 폐쇄되다
☐ be concerned with	~에 관여하다
☐ be counted toward	~에 포함되다
☐ be cut out for	~에 자질이 있다
☐ be dedicated to	~에 헌신하다
☐ be done with	~을 마치다, 끝내다
☐ be due to	~할 예정이다
☐ be equipped with	~을 갖추다
☐ be excited to announce	~을 발표하게 되어 기쁘다
☐ be likely to	~할 것 같다
☐ be obligated to	~할 의무가 있다
☐ be paired with	짝지어지다
☐ be recognized for	~으로 인정받다
☐ be subject to	~의 대상이 되다
☐ be sure to	반드시 ~하세요

Day 10 — TASK 3 실전 필수 어휘

TASK 3를 위해 필수적으로 알아야 할 어휘들이므로, 확실히 암기해 둡니다.

☐ behind schedule	예정보다 늦은		☐ don't miss out on	~을 놓치지 마세요
☐ bring up	(문제 등을) 언급하다		☐ donation [dounéiʃən]	기부
☐ broken [bróukən]	파손된		☐ door prize	경품
☐ bulletin board	게시판		☐ dormitory [dɔ́ːrmətɔ̀ːri]	기숙사
☐ call a meeting	회의를 소집하다		☐ drop out	학교를 중퇴하다
☐ call off	~을 취소하다		☐ due to	~ 때문에
☐ candidate [kǽndidèit]	후보자, 지원자		☐ elective [iléktiv]	선택 과목
☐ ceiling [síːliŋ]	천장		☐ eligibility [èlidʒəbíləti]	자격, 적격
☐ celebrate [séləbrèit]	기념하다		☐ eligible [élidʒəbl]	자격이 있는
☐ charity auction	자선 경매		☐ encourage [inkə́ːridʒ]	권장하다, 격려하다
☐ citation [saitéiʃən]	인용		☐ enroll [inróul]	등록하다
☐ closure [klóuʒər]	폐쇄		☐ enrollment [inróulmənt]	등록
☐ come up with	~을 제안하다		☐ entry [éntri]	참가자, 출품작
☐ committee [kəmíti]	위원회		☐ expert [ékspəːrt]	전문가
☐ competition [kàmpətíʃən]	대회		☐ explore [iksplɔ́ːr]	탐색하다
☐ complimentary [kámpləméntəri]	무료 제공의, 칭찬하는		☐ extracurricular [èkstrəkəríkjələr]	과외의
☐ compulsory [kəmpʌ́lsəri]	필수의		☐ facilitate [fəsílətèit]	촉진하다, 용이하게 하다
☐ consider [kənsídər]	고려하다		☐ faculty [fǽkəlti]	교직원
☐ contribute to	~에 공헌을 하다		☐ feature [fíːtʃər]	특성; 특색을 이루다
☐ count on	~에 기대다, 의지하다		☐ feel free to	자유롭게 ~하다
☐ criteria [kraitíriə]	기준		☐ festival booth	축제 부스
☐ curriculum [kəríkjuləm]	교과과정		☐ figure out	알아내다
☐ deadline [dédlàin]	마감일		☐ fill out	작성하다
☐ dean [diːn]	학장		☐ finalist [fáinəlist]	결선 진출자
☐ degree [digríː]	학위		☐ formal [fɔ́ːrməl]	공식적인
☐ department [dipáːrtmənt]	학부, 학과		☐ freshman [fréʃmən]	신입생
☐ designate [dézignèit]	지정하다		☐ fulfill [fulfíl]	이수하다, 충족시키다
☐ diploma [diplóumə]	졸업증서		☐ funding [fʌ́ndiŋ]	자금, 기금
☐ disallow [dìsəláu]	~을 못하게 하다		☐ fundraising event	모금 행사
☐ dismiss [dismís]	해산하다		☐ fun-filled	즐거움이 가득한

Day 11 — TASK 3 실전 필수 어휘

☑ TASK 3를 위해 필수적으로 알아야 할 어휘들이므로, 확실히 암기해 둡니다.

🎧 DAY11

☐ gain insight into	~에 대한 통찰력을 얻다	
☐ general audience	일반 청중	
☐ get started	시작하다	
☐ get a move on	서두르다	
☐ get down to	~에 착수하다	
☐ get together	모이다	
☐ gifted [gíftid]	뛰어난 지능을 가진	
☐ give back	환원하다	
☐ give instructions	설명하다	
☐ go into effect	시행되다	
☐ go over	살펴보다	
☐ grade [greid]	성적을 매기다; 평점	
☐ graduation [grædʒuéiʃən]	졸업	
☐ grant [grænt]	수여하다, 보조금	
☐ guest lecture	초청 강연	
☐ guest speaker	초청 연사	
☐ guideline [gáidlàin]	지침, 안내	
☐ gymnasium [dʒimnéiziəm]	체육관	
☐ hand in	제출하다	
☐ hand out	나눠주다	
☐ head out	출발하다	
☐ highly recommend	적극 권하다	
☐ impact [ímpækt]	충돌, 충격, 효과, 영향	
☐ in charge of	~을 담당하는	
☐ in honor of	~를 기리기 위해	
☐ in terms of	~의 측면에서 보면	
☐ in the area of	~의 분야에서	
☐ in time	제시간에	
☐ incoming [ínkʌ̀miŋ]	들어오는	
☐ inconvenience [ìnkənvíːnjəns]	불편	

☐ indent [indént]	들여 쓰다	
☐ inform A of B	A에게 B를 알리다	
☐ initiative [iníʃiətiv]	계획	
☐ instead of	~ 대신에	
☐ introductory [ìntrədʌ́ktəri]	입문적인	
☐ invite [inváit]	초대하다	
☐ it's important to	~하는 것이 중요하다	
☐ job fair	취업 박람회	
☐ join in	~에 참여하다	
☐ judge [dʒʌdʒ]	심사위원	
☐ junior [dʒúːnjər]	3학년생	
☐ keep up with	~에 뒤처지지 않다	
☐ laboratory [lǽbərətɔ̀ːri]	실험실	
☐ librarian [laibréəriən]	사서	
☐ limited seating	좌석 제한	
☐ look over	~을 검토하다	
☐ major [méidʒər]	전공	
☐ make a difference	변화를 만들다	
☐ make our way to	~로 함께 가다	
☐ make sure that	~을 확실히 하다	
☐ make up for	~을 만회하다	
☐ mandatory [mǽndətɔ̀ːri]	의무적인	
☐ matriculation [mətrìkjuléiʃən]	(대학) 입학 허가	
☐ navigate [nǽvəgèit]	헤쳐 나가다, 길을 찾다	
☐ observe [əbzə́ːrv]	준수하다, 관찰하다	
☐ officially [əfíʃəli]	공식적으로	
☐ on site	현장에서	
☐ permission [pərmíʃən]	허가	
☐ pipe [paip]	배관	
☐ popularity [pɑ̀pjulǽrəti]	인기	

Day 12 — TASK 3 실전 필수 어휘

TASK 3를 위해 필수적으로 알아야 할 어휘들이므로, 확실히 암기해 둡니다.

DAY12

practice [præktis]	연습하다	specialize [spéʃəlàiz]	전공하다
prepare [pripέər]	준비하다	speech [spi:tʃ]	연설
prerequisite [pri:rékwəzit]	필수 과목	student lounge	학생 라운지
present an award	상을 수여하다	studious [stjú:diəs]	면학에 힘쓰는, 학문적인
priority [praiɔ́:rəti]	우선권	study abroad program	유학 프로그램
proceeds [próusi:dz]	수익금	submission [səbmíʃən]	제출
proposal [prəpóuzəl]	제안	supervision [sù:pərvíʒən]	감독
Q&A session	질의응답 시간	support [səpɔ́:rt]	지원
qualification [kwὰ:ləfikéiʃən]	자격	syllabus [síləbəs]	강의 계획표
qualify [kwάləfài]	자격을 얻다	take a moment to	~할 시간을 잠시 내다
questionnaire [kwèstʃənέər]	설문지	take advantage of	~을 이용하다
raise funds for	~을 위한 기금을 모으다	take note of	유의하다
reach out	연락하다	take place	개최되다
register [rédʒistər]	등록하다, 신청하다	take steps	조치를 취하다
remind A of B	A에게 B를 다시 알려주다	take the floor	발표하다, 발언하다
reminder [rimáindər]	상기시키는 것	tardy [tά:rdi]	지각한, 늦은
renowned [rináund]	유명한, 명성 있는	theme [θi:m]	주제
requirement [rikwáiərmənt]	필수 요건, 필수 사항	tuition [tju:íʃən]	수업료
résumé [rézumèi]	이력서	turn in	제출하다
revision [rivíʒən]	수정	tutor [tjú:tər]	튜터; 지도하다
scholarship [skάlərʃip]	장학금	upcoming [ʌ́pkὰmiŋ]	다가오는
secure a seat	좌석을 확보하다	urge [ə:rdʒ]	촉구하다, 주장하다
secure a spot	자리를 맡다	vacancy [véikənsi]	공석, 결원
semester [siméstər]	학기	valedictorian [vὰlidiktɔ́:riən]	졸업생 대표
senior [sí:njər]	4학년생	valid [vǽlid]	유효한
share details	세부 사항을 공유하다	venue [vénju:]	장소
showcase [ʃóukèis]	선보이다	verification [vèrəfəkéiʃən]	확인, 증명
shuttle [ʃʌ́tl]	셔틀버스	volunteer [vὰ:ləntíər]	자원봉사하다
sign-up sheet	참가 신청서	weekly [wí:kli]	매주의, 주 1회의
sophomore [sά:fəmɔ:r]	2학년생	wing [wiŋ]	(건물의) 별관, 부속건물

Day 13 — TASK 4 실전 필수 어휘

음성 바로 듣기 ▶

☑ TASK 4를 위해 필수적으로 알아야 할 어휘들이므로, 확실히 암기해 둡니다.

🎧 DAY13

□ a flock of	한 떼		□ alternate with	~와 교대하다
□ a mass of	다량의		□ altitude [ǽltətjúːd]	고도, 높이
□ a wide variety of	다양한		□ amass [əmǽs]	쌓다, 모으다
□ abbey [ǽbi]	수도원, 대수도원		□ ambiguous [æmbíɡjuəs]	모호한
□ aborted [əbɔ́ːrtid]	유산된, 발육 부전의		□ analogous [ənǽləɡəs]	유사한
□ abreast [əbrést]	나란히, ~와 병행하여		□ analogy [ənǽlədʒi]	비유
□ absolute [ǽbsəlùːt]	절대적인		□ analyze [ǽnəlàiz]	분석하다
□ absorb [æbsɔ́ːrb]	흡수하다		□ ancestor [ǽnsestər]	조상
□ abundant [əbʌ́ndənt]	풍족한, 많은		□ anomaly [ənɑ́məli]	이상 현상
□ acclimate [əkláimət]	순응하다		□ appease [əpíːz]	달래다, 진정시키다
□ accompany [əkʌ́mpəni]	수반하다		□ approximate [əprɑ́ksəmət]	대략의
□ account for	~의 원인이 되다		□ arbitrate [ɑ́ːrbitrèit]	중재하다
□ accumulate [əkjúːmjulèit]	축적하다		□ arctic [ɑ́ːrktik]	북극의
□ acid [ǽsid]	산, 산성		□ aristocratic [ərìstəkrǽtik]	귀족적인, 귀족의
□ acoustic [əkúːstik]	청각의		□ articulate [ɑːrtíkjulət]	명료한
□ acquit [əkwít]	무죄로 하다		□ artificial [ὰːrtəfíʃəl]	인위적인
□ acute [əkjúːt]	급성의, 심한		□ artistic [ɑːrtístik]	예술적인
□ adapt [ədǽpt]	적응하다		□ as to	~에 관하여
□ adhere [ədhíər]	붙다		□ aspect [ǽspekt]	양상, 측면
□ adjacent [ədʒéisnt]	이웃의, 인접한		□ assemble [əsémbl]	부품을 조립하다
□ adopt [ədɑ́pt]	채택하다		□ associate [əsóusièit]	관련시키다
□ adversity [ædvə́ːrsəti]	역경		□ assumption [əsʌ́mpʃən]	가정
□ advocate [ǽdvəkèit]	옹호하다		□ asymmetrical [èisəmétrikəl]	비대칭의
□ aerodynamic [ὲəroudainǽmik]	공기역학의		□ at the expense of	~를 희생하여
□ aesthetics [esθétiks]	미학		□ atmospheric [ὰtməsférik]	대기의
□ affirm [əfə́ːrm]	단언하다		□ atom [ǽtəm]	원자
□ affix [əfíks]	부착시키다		□ attraction [ətrǽkʃən]	인력, 끌림
□ agricultural [ǽɡrəkʌ́ltʃərəl]	농업의		□ authentic [əːθéntik]	진짜의
□ algae [ǽldʒiː]	조류		□ avant-garde	전위적인
□ alleviate [əlíːvièit]	완화하다		□ average [ǽvəridʒ]	평균

Day 14   TASK 4 실전 필수 어휘

☑ TASK 4를 위해 필수적으로 알아야 할 어휘들이므로, 확실히 암기해 둡니다.   🎧 DAY14

☐ ban [bæn]	금지 조치	
☐ batter [bǽtər]	강타하다	
☐ be comprised of	~로 구성되다	
☐ behavioral [bihéivjərəl]	행동의	
☐ beneficial [bènəfíʃəl]	이로운, 유익한	
☐ bias [báiəs]	편향	
☐ biodiversity [bàioudivə́:rsəti]	생물의 다양성	
☐ biography [baiágrəfi]	전기, 일대기	
☐ biological [bàiəládʒikəl]	생물학적인	
☐ boisterous [bɔ́istərəs]	떠들썩한, 야단법석인	
☐ break down into pieces	분해하다	
☐ broad [brɔːd]	넓은	
☐ buildup [bíldʌp]	증가, 증대	
☐ by means of	~을 통해	
☐ capacity [kəpǽsəti]	용량	
☐ capitalize [kǽpitəlàiz]	자본화하다, 이용하다	
☐ capture [kǽptʃər]	(마음·관심을) 사로잡다	
☐ carnivorous [kɑːrnívərəs]	육식성의	
☐ carve out	새기다, 조각하다	
☐ case study	사례 연구	
☐ catalyst [kǽtəlist]	촉매	
☐ categorize [kǽtəgəràiz]	분류하다	
☐ caterpillar [kǽtərpìlər]	애벌레, 유충	
☐ cathedral [kəθíːdrəl]	성당	
☐ cattle [kǽtl]	소, 가축	
☐ cementation [sìːməntéiʃən]	접합, 교착	
☐ centralize [séntrəlàiz]	집중하다	
☐ chaos [kéiɑs]	무질서, 혼돈	
☐ choreography [kɔ̀ːriágrəfi]	안무, 무용술	
☐ chronic [kránik]	만성의	
☐ cinematic [sìnəmǽtik]	영화의
☐ circular [sə́ːrkjulər]	원형의, 순환성의
☐ circulate [sə́ːrkjəleit]	순환하다
☐ claim [kleim]	주장하다
☐ classify [klǽsəfài]	분류하다
☐ climate [kláimit]	분위기, 기후
☐ cognition [kɑgníʃən]	인지
☐ cognitive [kágnətiv]	인식의
☐ collapse [kəlǽps]	폭락하다, 무너지다
☐ collide [kəláid]	충돌하다
☐ combat [káːmbæt]	억제하다, 맞서 싸우다
☐ combination [kàmbənéiʃən]	합성, 조합, 결합, 배합
☐ combine [kəmbáin]	결합하다, 합치다
☐ comedy [kámidi]	희극
☐ commemorate [kəmémərèit]	기념하다
☐ commercial [kəmə́ːrʃəl]	상업의, 영리적인
☐ commission [kəmíʃən]	의뢰하다, 주문하다
☐ commit [kəmít]	자행하다, 범하다
☐ commodity [kəmádəti]	상품
☐ compact [kəmpǽkt]	압축하다
☐ compensate [kámpənsèit]	보상하다, 보정하다
☐ compile [kəmpáil]	모으다
☐ complement [kámpləmənt]	보완하다, 보충하다
☐ complex [kəmpléks]	복잡한, 복합의
☐ component [kəmpóunənt]	구성 요소
☐ compose [kəmpóuz]	작곡하다
☐ composition [kàmpəzíʃən]	구성
☐ compound [kəmpáund]	합성의, 화합물
☐ concept [kánsept]	개념
☐ conclude [kənklúːd]	완료하다, 결론을 내다

TASK별 실전 필수 어휘   **397**

Day 15   TASK 4 실전 필수 어휘

TASK 4를 위해 필수적으로 알아야 할 어휘들이므로, 확실히 암기해 둡니다.

DAY15

☐ condensation [kàndenséiʃən]	액화, 응결
☐ condense [kəndéns]	농축하다
☐ conductor [kəndʌ́ktər]	전도체
☐ confine [kánfain]	제한하다
☐ conflict [kánflikt]	마찰, 충돌
☐ conquest [káːŋkwest]	정복
☐ consequence [kánsəkwèns]	결과
☐ consequently [kánsəkwèntli]	따라서
☐ consist of	~로 구성되다
☐ consistent [kənsístənt]	일관된
☐ constituent [kənstítʃuənt]	성분, 구성 요소
☐ consumer [kənsúːmər]	소비자
☐ consumption [kənsʌ́mpʃən]	소비
☐ contain [kəntéin]	포함하다
☐ contamination [kəntæ̀mənéiʃən]	오염
☐ context [káːntekst]	환경, 정황
☐ contour [kántuər]	윤곽을 그리다
☐ contract [kántrækt]	계약, 수축하다
☐ contradiction [kàntrədíkʃən]	상충, 모순
☐ contribute [kəntríbjuːt]	기여하다, 기부하다
☐ controlled [kəntróuld]	통제된
☐ controversial [kàntrəvə́ːrʃəl]	논란이 되는
☐ convection [kənvékʃən]	열이나 공기의 대류
☐ convention [kənvénʃən]	회의
☐ conventional [kənvénʃənl]	전통적인
☐ convert [kənvə́ːrt]	전환하다
☐ convey [kənvéi]	운반하다
☐ cooperative [kouá:pərətiv]	공동, 협력의
☐ copyright [káːpirait]	저작권
☐ cornerstone [kɔ́ːrnərstòun]	초석, 기초
☐ correlation [kɔ̀ːrəléiʃən]	상관성
☐ corresponding [kɔ̀ːrispándiŋ]	일치하는, 대응하는
☐ cortex [kɔ́ːrteks]	대뇌피질
☐ courtship [kɔ́ːrtʃip]	짝짓기
☐ coverage [kʌ́vəridʒ]	적용 범위
☐ crime [kraim]	죄, 범죄
☐ criminal [kríminl]	범인
☐ crisis [kráisis]	위기
☐ critical [krítikəl]	중요한, 비판적인
☐ crystallize [krístəlàiz]	결정시키다, 구체화하다
☐ cultivate [kʌ́ltəvèit]	경작하다
☐ currency [kə́ːrənsi]	통화
☐ current [kə́ːrənt]	현재의, 물결
☐ cut across	~에 널리 미치다
☐ cut one's losses	손실을 줄이다
☐ debate [dibéit]	토론하다
☐ decade [dékeid]	10년
☐ decision-making	의사결정 과정
☐ declare [dikléər]	선언하다
☐ decompose [dìːkəmpóuz]	분해되다
☐ decorative [dékərətiv]	장식적인
☐ decrease [dikríːs]	감소시키다
☐ dedication [dèdikéiʃən]	헌신
☐ deduce [didjúːs]	추론하다
☐ deficient [difíʃənt]	부족한
☐ definition [dèfəníʃən]	정의
☐ deforest [diːfɔ́ːrist]	벌채하다
☐ degrade [digréid]	퇴화시키다
☐ deliberate [dilíbərət]	신중한
☐ deliberately [dilíbərətli]	고의로

Day 16 TASK 4 실전 필수 어휘

☑ TASK 4를 위해 필수적으로 알아야 할 어휘들이므로, 확실히 암기해 둡니다.

🎧 DAY16

☐ demand [diménd]	수요
☐ democratic [dèməkrǽtik]	민주적인
☐ demonstrate [démənstrèit]	보여주다
☐ density [dénsəti]	밀도
☐ depict [dipíkt]	그리다, 묘사하다
☐ deplete [diplí:t]	고갈시키다
☐ deposit [dipázit]	퇴적물; 쌓다
☐ depression [dipréʃən]	불경기, 우울증
☐ derive [diráiv]	얻다, 유래하다
☐ describe [diskráib]	기술하다
☐ descriptive [diskríptiv]	설명적인
☐ designation [dèzignéiʃən]	명칭
☐ despite [dispáit]	~에도 불구하고
☐ destroy [distrɔ́i]	파괴하다
☐ destructive [distrʌ́ktiv]	파괴적인
☐ detection [ditékʃən]	감지
☐ deteriorate [ditíəriərèit]	악화되다, 악화시키다
☐ determine [ditə́rmin]	결정하다
☐ devastation [dèvəstéiʃən]	대참사
☐ devise [diváiz]	고안하다
☐ devote [divóut]	헌신하다
☐ diameter [daiǽmətər]	지름
☐ digest [daidʒést]	소화하다
☐ dignity [dígnəti]	위엄
☐ dilation [dìléiʃən]	팽창, 확장
☐ dimension [diménʃən]	차원
☐ direction [dirékʃən]	방향
☐ disorder [disɔ́rdər]	무질서, 혼란, 장애
☐ disruptive [disrʌ́ptiv]	파괴적인
☐ dissolve [dizá:lv]	녹다
☐ distance [dístəns]	거리
☐ distinction [distíŋkʃən]	구별
☐ distinctive [distíŋktiv]	독특한
☐ distinguish [distíŋgwiʃ]	구별하다
☐ distribute [distríbju:t]	배포하다
☐ divergent [daivə́:rdʒənt]	다른
☐ diversity [daivə́:rsəti]	다양성
☐ divide [diváid]	나누다
☐ divine [diváin]	알아 맞추다, 신의
☐ domain [douméin]	영역
☐ domestic [dəméstik]	국내의
☐ dominant [dámənənt]	지배적인
☐ dramatic [drəmǽtik]	극적인
☐ drastic [drǽstik]	급격한
☐ drift [drift]	표류하다, 떠돌다
☐ durable [djúərəbl]	튼튼한, 잘 견디는
☐ ecological [ìkəláːdʒikəl]	생태학적인
☐ ecosystem [ì:kousístəm]	생태계
☐ efficiency [ifíʃənsi]	효율
☐ effortless [éfərtlis]	쉬운, 노력이 필요 없는
☐ eject [idʒékt]	방출하다
☐ elastic [ilǽstik]	탄력 있는
☐ electrical [iléktrikəl]	전기의
☐ electronic [ìlektrá:nik]	전자의
☐ element [éləmənt]	요소, 원소, 성분
☐ elevate [éləvèit]	높이다
☐ elicit [ilísit]	도출하다, 이끌어 내다
☐ eliminate [ilímənèit]	제거하다
☐ elliptical [ilíptikəl]	타원의
☐ embed [imbéd]	끼워 넣다, 박아 넣다

Day 17   TASK 4 실전 필수 어휘

☑ TASK 4를 위해 필수적으로 알아야 할 어휘들이므로, 확실히 암기해 둡니다.

🎧 DAY17

☐ embellish [imbéliʃ]	미화하다, 장식하다
☐ emerge [imə́:rdʒ]	생기다, 나타나다
☐ emit [imít]	내뿜다, 방사하다
☐ empirical [impírikəl]	경험적인
☐ emulate [émjulèit]	모방하다
☐ enact [inǽkt]	제정하다
☐ endangered [indéindʒərd]	멸종 위기에 처한
☐ endeavor [indévər]	시도, 노력
☐ engage in	참가하다
☐ engineering [èndʒəníəriŋ]	공학
☐ enhance [inhǽns]	높이다
☐ enlargement [inlá:rdʒmənt]	확대
☐ enslave [insléiv]	노예로 만들다
☐ entail [intéil]	수반하다
☐ enterprise [éntərpràiz]	기업
☐ environment [inváiərənmənt]	환경
☐ enzyme [énzaim]	효소
☐ equator [ikwéitər]	적도
☐ equivalent [ikwívələnt]	같은, 동등한
☐ erect [irékt]	세우다
☐ erode [iróud]	침식하다
☐ erupt [irʌ́pt]	분출하다
☐ escalate [éskəlèit]	확대하다
☐ essential [isénʃəl]	필수적인
☐ estate [istéit]	사유지
☐ estimate [éstəmèit]	추산하다
☐ evaporate [ivǽpərèit]	증발하다
☐ evidence [évədəns]	증거
☐ evident [évədənt]	명백한
☐ evolution [èvəlú:ʃən]	진화
☐ evolve [iválv]	진화시키다
☐ exacerbate [igzǽsərbèit]	악화시키다
☐ examine [igzǽmin]	검토하다
☐ excavate [ékskəvèit]	발굴하다
☐ exceptional [iksépʃənl]	예외적인
☐ excessive [iksésiv]	지나친
☐ exclusion [iksklú:ʒən]	배제
☐ exclusively [iksklú:sivli]	오로지
☐ excrete [ikskrí:t]	배설하다
☐ exhaust [igzɔ́:st]	고갈시키다
☐ expansion [ikspǽnʃən]	팽창
☐ expedition [èkspədíʃən]	원정
☐ expend [ikspénd]	소비하다
☐ experiment [ikspérəmənt]	실험
☐ expertise [èkspərtí:z]	전문적 지식
☐ explicit [iksplísit]	명백한
☐ exploit [iksplɔ́it]	활용하다
☐ explosive [iksplóusiv]	폭발적인
☐ expose [ikspóuz]	노출하다
☐ external [ekstə́:rnəl]	외부의
☐ extinct [ikstíŋkt]	멸종된
☐ extract [ikstrǽkt]	추출하다
☐ extraneous [ikstréiniəs]	외래의, 관련 없는
☐ extreme [ikstrí:m]	극도의
☐ fabricate [fǽbrikèit]	꾸며내다
☐ façade [fəsá:d]	건물의 외관
☐ factor in	~을 요인으로 포함하다
☐ fame [feim]	명성
☐ favor [féivər]	지지하다
☐ fertilize [fə́:rtəlàiz]	수정시키다, 비료를 주다

Day 18   TASK 4 실전 필수 어휘

☑ TASK 4를 위해 필수적으로 알아야 할 어휘들이므로, 확실히 암기해 둡니다.

🎧 DAY18

☐ fetal [fí:tl]	태아의, 태아 단계의		☐ generalization [dʒènərəlizéiʃən]	일반화, 보편화
☐ fictional [fíkʃənəl]	허구의		☐ generate [dʒénərèit]	발생시키다
☐ filter [fíltər]	여과기; 여과하다		☐ generosity [dʒènərá:səti]	관대함
☐ financial [fainǽnʃəl]	재정의		☐ genetic [dʒənétik]	유전자의
☐ firmly [fə́:rmli]	확고히		☐ geometric [dʒì:əmétrik]	기하학적인
☐ fixed [fikst]	고정된		☐ glorify [gló:rəfài]	미화하다
☐ flammable [flǽməbl]	가연성의		☐ grave [greiv]	중대한
☐ flatten [flǽtn]	평평하게 하다		☐ gravity [grǽvəti]	중력
☐ flex [fleks]	구부리다		☐ greenhouse [grí:nhàus]	온실
☐ float [flout]	떠다니다		☐ grievance [grí:vəns]	불만, 고충
☐ flood [flʌd]	범람하다		☐ habitat [hǽbitæt]	서식지
☐ flourish [flə́:riʃ]	번성하다		☐ harsh [hɑ:rʃ]	가혹한, 엄격한
☐ fluid [flú:id]	액체		☐ hazardous [hǽzərdəs]	위험한
☐ forage [fó:ridʒ]	먹이를 찾다		☐ hence [hens]	따라서
☐ forecast [fó:rkæst]	예보하다		☐ heritage [héritidʒ]	유산
☐ foresee [fɔ:rsí:]	예견하다, 예측하다		☐ hibernation [hàibərnéiʃən]	동면, 겨울잠
☐ formality [fɔ:rmǽləti]	형식, 절차		☐ historical [histɔ́:rikəl]	역사의
☐ formation [fɔ:rméiʃən]	형성, 생성		☐ hollow [hálou]	속이 빈
☐ formulate [fɔ́:rmjulèit]	만들다, 공식화하다		☐ homage [hámidʒ]	경의
☐ foundation [faundéiʃən]	토대		☐ horizontal [hɔ̀:rəzá:ntl]	수평의
☐ fragmentation [frægməntéiʃən]	분절화		☐ horticulture [hɔ́:rtəkʌ̀ltʃər]	원예
☐ frame [freim]	틀, 만들다		☐ human rights	인권
☐ fraud [frɔ:d]	사기		☐ hypothesis [haipá:θəsis]	가설, 가정
☐ frequency [frí:kwənsi]	주파수		☐ identical [aidéntikəl]	똑같은
☐ friction [fríkʃən]	마찰		☐ identity [aidéntəti]	정체성
☐ function [fʌ́ŋkʃən]	기능, 작용하다		☐ ideology [àidiá:lədʒi]	이념
☐ fundamental [fʌ̀ndəméntl]	근본적인		☐ illustrative [ilʌ́strətiv]	설명하는, 예증적인
☐ fungi [fʌ́ndʒai]	버섯, 균류		☐ imaginary [imǽdʒəneri]	상상의
☐ furnace [fə́:rnis]	용광로		☐ imitate [ímətèit]	모방하다
☐ galaxy [gǽləksi]	은하		☐ immense [iméns]	거대한

Day 19 TASK 4 실전 필수 어휘

☑ TASK 4를 위해 필수적으로 알아야 할 어휘들이므로, 확실히 암기해 둡니다.

🎧 DAY19

□	impersonal [impə́ːrsənl]	비인간적인
□	implication [ìmplikéiʃən]	함축
□	implicit [implísit]	암묵적인, 암시적인
□	impose [impóuz]	부과하다
□	impressionism [impréʃənìzm]	인상주의
□	improvisation [impràvəzéiʃən]	즉흥 연주
□	impulse [ímpʌls]	자극
□	impurity [impjúərəti]	불순물
□	in conjunction with	~와 병행하여
□	in large quantities	다량으로
□	in light of	~의 관점에서
□	in point	적절한
□	in regard to	~에 관하여
□	inaccessible [inəksésəbl]	도달하기 어려운
□	inanimate [inǽnəmət]	생명이 없는
□	incident [ínsidənt]	사건
□	incorporate [inkɔ́ːrpərèit]	통합하다, 포함하다
□	incubate [ínkjubèit]	(인공) 부화하다
□	independent [ìndipéndənt]	독립적인
□	in-depth	상세한
□	indicative [indíkətiv]	지시하는, 표시하는
□	indigenous [indídʒənəs]	고유한
□	indisputable [ìndispjúːtəbl]	이의를 제기할 수 없는
□	inevitable [inévətəbl]	피할 수 없는
□	infamous [ínfəməs]	악명 높은
□	infant [ínfənt]	유아; 유아의
□	infect [infékt]	감염시키다
□	infinite [ínfənət]	무한한
□	infinitesimal [ìnfinitésəməl]	극미한
□	inflame [infléim]	자극하다
□	inflict [inflíkt]	주다, 가하다
□	influence [ínfluəns]	영향
□	influential [ìnfluénʃəl]	영향력 있는
□	ingenious [indʒíːnjəs]	재치 있는, 영리한
□	ingest [indʒést]	섭취하다
□	inhabit [inhǽbit]	서식하다
□	inherent [inhérənt]	타고난
□	innate [inéit]	선천적인
□	innovative [ínəvèitiv]	혁신적인
□	input [ínpùt]	입력하다; 투입
□	insight [ínsàit]	통찰력
□	insignificant [ìnsignífikənt]	하찮은
□	inspire [inspáiər]	영감을 주다
□	institution [ìnstitúːʃən]	기관
□	instrumental [ìnstrəméntl]	도움이 되는
□	insulate [ínsəlèit]	단열하다
□	integrate [íntəgrèit]	통합하다
□	interact [ìntərǽkt]	상호작용하다
□	intermediate [ìntərmíːdiət]	중간의
□	internal [intə́ːrnl]	내부의, 체내의
□	interpersonal [ìntərpə́ːrsənəl]	대인 관계의
□	interpret [intə́ːrprit]	해석하다, 통역하다
□	intervene [ìntərvíːn]	끼어들다, 개입하다
□	intricate [íntrikət]	복잡한
□	intriguing [intríːgiŋ]	흥미를 자아내는
□	invaluable [invǽljuəbl]	매우 귀중한
□	invasion [invéiʒən]	침해, 침입
□	invent [invént]	발명하다
□	investigate [invéstəgèit]	조사하다
□	invoke [invóuk]	기원하다, 호소하다

Day 20   TASK 4 실전 필수 어휘

☑ TASK 4를 위해 필수적으로 알아야 할 어휘들이므로, 확실히 암기해 둡니다.

☐	involuntary [inváləntèri]	비자발적인	☐	stimulus [stímjuləs]	자극
☐	involve [inválv]	수반하다, 관련시키다	☐	sustainable [səstéinəbl]	지속 가능한
☐	irregular [irégjulər]	불규칙한, 고르지 못한	☐	symbolic [simbálik]	상징적인, 표상하는
☐	irritable [írətəbl]	예민한, 짜증을 잘 내는	☐	typical [típikəl]	일반적인
☐	issue [íʃuː]	발행하다, 판	☐	ultimate [ʌ́ltəmət]	궁극적인, 최종적인
☐	jeopardize [dʒépərdàiz]	위태롭게 하다	☐	underestimate [ʌ̀ndəréstəmeit]	과소평가하다
☐	juggle [dʒʌ́gl]	동시에 처리하다	☐	undergo [ʌ̀ndərgóu]	겪다, 경험하다
☐	lift a ban	금지를 해제하다	☐	underlying [ʌ̀ndərlàiiŋ]	근원적인, 밑에 있는
☐	luxurious [lʌgʒúəriəs]	호화로운	☐	uniform [júːnəfɔ̀ːrm]	균일한
☐	legacy [légəsi]	유산	☐	universal [jùːnəvə́ːrsəl]	보편적인
☐	likelihood [láiklihùd]	가능성	☐	urban [ə́ːrbən]	도시의
☐	manipulate [mənípjulèit]	조작하다	☐	utilize [júːtəlàiz]	이용하다
☐	mitigate [mítəgèit]	완화하다	☐	vanish [vǽniʃ]	사라지다
☐	modify [mádəfài]	변경하다, 조절하다	☐	ventilation [vèntəléiʃən]	환기, 환기 장치
☐	negotiate [nigóuʃièit]	협상하다	☐	verbal [və́ːrbəl]	언어의, 말로 나타낸
☐	objective [əbdʒéktiv]	객관적인	☐	vertical [və́ːrtikəl]	수직의
☐	optimism [ɑ́ːptəmìzm]	낙관주의	☐	vibrate [váibreit]	진동하다
☐	overestimate [òuvəréstəmèit]	과대평가하다	☐	violent [váiələnt]	폭력적인, 격렬한
☐	prohibit [prəhíbit]	금지하다	☐	visualize [víʒuəlaiz]	구체화하다
☐	protect [prətékt]	보호하다	☐	vital [váitl]	매우 중요한
☐	quantity [kwántəti]	양, 수량	☐	voluntary [váːləntèri]	자발적인
☐	rationalize [rǽʃənəlàiz]	합리화하다	☐	vulnerable [vʌ́lnərəbl]	영향 받기 쉬운, 약한
☐	recover [rikʌ́vər]	회복하다	☐	wage [weidʒ]	임금; (전쟁·캠페인을) 벌이다
☐	replicate [réplikèit]	복제하다, 재현하다	☐	weaken [wíːkən]	약화시키다
☐	reputation [rèpjutéiʃən]	명성, 평판	☐	well-rounded	다재다능한, 만능의
☐	revive [riváiv]	부흥시키다	☐	whereas [wɛ̀əræz]	~에 반하여
☐	rotate [róuteit]	회전하다	☐	wholesale [hóulsèil]	도매의, 대대적인
☐	soothe [suːð]	달래다	☐	with respect to	~에 대한
☐	stable [stéibəl]	안정된	☐	withstand [wiθstǽnd]	견디다, 저항하다
☐	stare at	응시하다	☐	yield [jiːld]	산출하다, 낳다; 수확량

**Hackers
Updated TOEFL
LISTENING**

미국식 영어와
영국식 영어의
차이

미국식 영어와 영국식 영어의 차이

Hackers Updated TOEFL LISTENING

iBT TOEFL 리스닝에서는 미국식 발음 뿐만 아니라 영국, 호주 또는 뉴질랜드식 발음도 등장한다. 그동안 미국식 영어에 많이 노출되어 있던 한국 학습자들에게 타 영어권 국가의 발음은 낯설고 어렵게 느껴질 수 있으므로, 기본적인 차이점을 숙지하고 각 영어권 국가의 발음을 비교하며 듣는 연습을 하는 것이 좋다. 호주와 뉴질랜드식 영어는 영국식 영어와 유사하기 때문에 크게 미국식 영어와 영국식 영어를 비교해서 알아두면 된다.

발음의 차이

미국식 영어와 영국식 영어는 발음에서뿐만 아니라 어휘와 철자에서도 차이가 있다. 미국식 영어와 영국식 영어의 발음, 어휘, 철자에 어떤 차이점이 있는지 알아두도록 한다. 전반적으로 미국식 영어는 영국식 영어에 비해 목소리 톤이 높고 부드럽게 들린다. 영국식 영어는 철자에 가까운 발음(spelling pronunciation)을 하며, 억양 변화가 많고 모음을 짧게 발음하기 때문에 상대적으로 빠르게 들린다.

1. 자음

1 끝소리 /r/

미국식 영어에서는 모음 뒤의 [r]음을 항상 발음한다. 반면 영국식 영어에서는 첫소리 [r]을 제외한 끝소리 [r]은 탈락되는 경우가 대부분이다.

	together	here	turn	burn
미국	[təgéðər]	[hiər]	[təːrn]	[bəːrn]
영국	[təgéðə]	[hiə]	[təːn]	[bəːn]

2 모음 사이에 오는 /t/

미국식 영어에서는 모음과 모음 사이에 오는 /t/는 부드럽게 굴려서 [d]와 [r]의 중간 소리로 발음하지만 영국식 영어에서는 [t]소리 그대로 발음한다.

	total	item	later	automatic
미국	[tóud*l]	[áid*əm]	[léid*ər]	[ɔːd*əmǽd*ik]
영국	[tóutl]	[áitəm]	[léitə]	[ɔːtəmǽtik]

변화된 [t]를 편의상 [d]로 표기하였으나, 정확한 [d]발음과는 다른 [d]와 [r]의 중간 소리입니다.

2. 모음

1 /ɑ/

미국식 영어에서는 [æ]로 발음되지만 영국식 영어에서는 [ɑ]로 발음된다.

	pass	half	class	after
미국	[pæs]	[hæːf]	[klæs]	[ǽftər]
영국	[pɑːs]	[hɑːf]	[klɑːs]	[ɑːftə]

2 /i/

특정 단어의 경우 미국식 영어에서는 [i]로 발음되지만 영국식 영어에서는 [ai]로 발음된다.

	either	neither	direction	organization
미국	[iːðər]	[niːðər]	[dirékʃən]	[ɔːrgənizéiʃən]
영국	[áiðə]	[náiðə]	[dairékʃən]	[ɔːrgənaizéiʃən]

3 /o/

특정 단어의 경우 미국식 영어에서는 [ɑ]로 발음되지만 영국식 영어에서는 [ɔ]로 발음된다.

	not	shop	stop	copy
미국	[nɑːt]	[ʃɑːp]	[stɑːp]	[kɑ́pi]
영국	[nɔːt]	[ʃɔːp]	[stɔp]	[kɔ́pi]

4 /u/

미국식 영어에서는 주로 [u] '우'로 발음되는 반면 영국식 영어에서는 [ju] '유'로 발음된다.

	tune	news	student	opportunity
미국	[tuːn]	[nuːz]	[stúːdnt]	[àpərtúːnəti]
영국	[tjuːn]	[njuːz]	[stjúːdnt]	[ɔ̀pərjúːnəti]

3. 중요한 음운 현상

1 모음 사이에 /nt/가 오는 경우

/nt/가 두 모음 사이에 오면, 미국식 영어에서는 [t]소리가 생략되는 반면 영국식 영어에서는 [t]발음이 살아 있다.

	twenty	interview	entertainment	interchange
미국	[twéni]	[ínərvjùː]	[ènərtéinmənt]	[ìnərtʃéindʒ]
영국	[twénti]	[íntərvjùː]	[èntərtéinmənt]	[ìntərtʃéindʒ]

2 [tn], [tli] 발음으로 끝나는 경우

[tn]으로 끝나는 경우, 미국식 영어에서는 [t]소리를 발음하지 않고 한번 숨을 멈추었다가 [n]의 끝소리를 거의 '응' 혹은 '은'으로 발음한다. [tli]로 끝나는 경우에도 미국식 영어에서는 [t]를 발음하지 않고 한번 숨을 멈추었다가 [li]만 발음한다. 반면 영국에서는 [t]를 그대로 살려 강하게 발음한다.

	cotton	fountain	absolutely	diligently
미국	카ㅌ은	파운(ㅌ)은	앱솔루ㅌ리	딜리전(ㅌ)리
영국	[kɔ́tn]	[fáuntən]	[æ̀bsəlúːtli]	[dílədʒəntli]

3 /rt/

미국식 영어에서는 [t]발음을 생략하지만 영국식 영어에서는 [t]를 그대로 발음한다.

	artist	quarter	portable	reporter
미국	아r리스트	쿠어r러	포어r러블	뤼포어r러
영국	[áːtist]	[kwɔ́ːtə]	[pɔ́ːtəbl]	[ripɔ́ːtə]

4. 강세

미국식 영어에서는 뒤에 오는 반면 영국식 영어에서는 앞에 오는 경우가 있다.

	garage	baton	debris
미국	[gərɑ́:ʒ]	[bətɑ́n]	[dəbríː]
영국	[gǽrɑːʒ]	[bǽtɔn]	[débriː]

5. 마지막 음절의 모음

미국식 영어는 발음하는 반면 영국식 영어는 생략하는 경우가 있다.

	secretary	territory	conservatory	preparatory
미국	[sékrətèri]	[térətɔ̀:ri]	[kənsé:rvətɔ̀:ri]	[pripǽrətɔ̀:ri]
영국	[sékrətəri]	[térətəri]	[kənsé:rvətəri]	[pripǽrətəri]

어휘의 차이

발음에 비해 미국식 영어와 영국식 영어에서 사용하는 어휘의 의미가 다른 경우는 많지 않으나 꼭 구분해야 할 몇 가지 단어들이 있으므로 알아두도록 한다.

1. 동일한 개념, 다른 어휘

	미국	영국
수도꼭지	faucet	tap
지폐	bill	note
화장실	restroom	toilet
변호사	attorney, lawyer	solicitor
옥수수	corn	maize
승강기	elevator	lift
1층, 2층	first floor, second floor	ground floor, first floor
짐(화물)	baggage	luggage
자동차	automobile	motorcar
매표소	ticket office	booking office
영화	movies	films
아파트	apartment	flat
대학교 1학년	freshman	first-year student
대학교 2학년	sophomore	second-year student
대학교 3학년	junior	third-year student
대학교 4학년	senior	fourth-year student

2. 동일한 어휘, 다른 개념

	미국	영국
football	미식 축구	축구
vest	조끼	속옷
student	초, 중, 고, 대학생 모두를 지칭	대학생만을 지칭(초, 중, 고 학생은 pupil)
public school	공립학교	사립중등학교
merchant	소매 상인	도매상, 무역상
continent	북미 대륙	유럽 대륙
faculty	교수진	학부
pocketbook	핸드백	수첩
subway	지하철	지하도
holiday	공휴일	휴가
billion	10억	1조

철자의 차이

미국식 영어와 영국식 영어에서 같은 개념, 같은 어휘로 쓰이나 철자가 조금씩 다른 경우가 있으므로 이를 알아두도록 한다.

미국	영국
color	colour
honor	honour
favorite	favourite
neighbor	neighbour
center	centre
theater	theatre
gray	grey
organize	organise
realize	realise
memorize	memorise
disk	disc
check	cheque
defense	defence
jewelry	jewellery
airplane	aeroplane

MEMO

MEMO

MEMO

기본에서 실전까지 NEW 토플 리스닝 완벽 대비

HACKERS
Updated
TOEFL
LISTENING

개정 6판 4쇄 발행 2026년 2월 2일
개정 6판 1쇄 발행 2025년 11월 7일

지은이	David Cho	언어학 박사, 前 UCLA 교수, 해커스 어학연구소 공저
펴낸곳	(주)해커스 어학연구소
펴낸이	해커스 어학연구소 출판팀

주소	서울특별시 서초구 강남대로61길 23 (주)해커스 어학연구소
고객센터	02-537-5000
교재 관련 문의	publishing@hackers.com
동영상강의	HackersIngang.com

ISBN	978-89-6542-655-4 (13740)
Serial Number	06-04-01

저작권자 ⓒ 2025, David Cho, 해커스 어학연구소
이 책 및 음성파일의 모든 내용, 이미지, 디자인, 편집 형태에 대한 저작권은 저자에게 있습니다.
서면에 의한 저자와 출판사의 허락 없이 내용의 일부 혹은 전부를 인용, 발췌하거나 복제, 배포할 수 없습니다.

외국어인강 1위,
해커스인강(HackersIngang.com)
해커스인강

- 실전 감각을 극대화하는 **iBT 리스닝 실전모의고사**
- 효과적인 리스닝 학습을 돕는 **교재 MP3 · 단어암기 MP3**
- 청취력 향상을 위한 **쉐도잉 프로그램**
- 해커스 토플 스타강사의 **본 교재 인강**

전세계 유학정보의 중심,
고우해커스(goHackers.com)
고우해커스

- **토플 보카 외우기, 토플 스피킹/라이팅 첨삭 게시판** 등 무료 학습 콘텐츠
- 고득점을 위한 **토플 공부전략 강의**
- **국가별 대학 및 전공별 정보, 유학 Q&A 게시판** 등 다양한 유학정보

[외국어인강 1위] 헤럴드 선정 2018 대학생 선호브랜드 대상 '대학생이 선정한 외국어인강' 부문 1위

전세계 유학정보의 중심
고우해커스

goHackers.com

HACKERS
Updated
TOEFL
LISTENING

정답·스크립트·해석·정답단서

**2026년 1월 21일
NEW TOEFL
완벽 대비**

해커스 어학연구소

HACKERS
Updated TOEFL
LISTENING

정답·스크립트·해석·정답단서

DIAGNOSTIC TEST

p.21

```
01 Ⓑ    02 Ⓒ    03 Ⓐ    04 Ⓒ    05 Ⓑ
06 Ⓒ    07 Ⓓ    08 Ⓑ    09 Ⓐ    10 Ⓒ
11 Ⓒ    12 Ⓑ    13 Ⓒ    14 Ⓓ    15 Ⓑ
16 Ⓐ    17 Ⓓ    18 Ⓐ    19 Ⓒ    20 Ⓑ
```

※ 각 문제의 음성을 읽는 성우의 국적은 다음과 같이 표시되어 있습니다.
미국: Am   영국: En   호주: Au   뉴질랜드: Nz

01 Who Question 🔊 Am

Who is in charge of the marketing campaign?

Ⓐ Sandra does.
✓ I have no idea.
Ⓒ It needs improvement.
Ⓓ After about a week or two.

in charge of ~을 담당하는
improvement [imprúːvmənt] 개선, 향상

마케팅 캠페인은 누가 담당해요?
Ⓐ Sandra가 해요.
✓ 전혀 모르겠어요.
Ⓒ 그것은 개선이 필요해요.
Ⓓ 대략 일주일이나 이주 후예요.

02 Alternative Question 🔊 Nz

Would you prefer a window or an aisle seat?

Ⓐ I'll check under my seat.
Ⓑ It's near the front of the plane.
✓ Anywhere but the middle is fine.
Ⓓ In the overhead compartment.

aisle [ail] 복도, 통로   overhead compartment 짐칸

당신은 창가 좌석을 선호하나요, 복도 좌석을 선호하나요?
Ⓐ 제 좌석 아래를 확인할게요.
Ⓑ 비행기 앞쪽 근처에 있어요.
✓ 가운데만 아니면 어디든 괜찮아요.
Ⓓ 짐칸 안에요.

03 Auxiliary Verb Question 🔊 En

Did you receive my email about the project deadline?

✓ I haven't checked my inbox since yesterday.
Ⓑ Yes, the project is quite challenging.
Ⓒ Do you need it now?
Ⓓ Very important.

deadline [dédlàin] 마감일   inbox [ínbɑːks] 받은 편지함
challenging [tʃǽlindʒiŋ] 힘드는, 도전적인

프로젝트 마감일에 관한 제 이메일을 받으셨나요?
✓ 어제 이후로 받은 편지함을 확인하지 않았어요.
Ⓑ 네, 그 프로젝트는 꽤 힘들어요.
Ⓒ 지금 그것이 필요하세요?
Ⓓ 매우 중요해요.

04 When Question 🔊 Am

When is the fire drill?

Ⓐ She was recently fired.
Ⓑ We need to be prepared.
✓ Any time now.
Ⓓ Inside the whole building.

fire drill 화재 대피 훈련   fire [faiər] 해고하다

화재 대피 훈련은 언제인가요?
Ⓐ 그녀는 최근 해고되었어요.
Ⓑ 저희는 준비가 되어있어야 해요.
✓ 이제 곧이에요.
Ⓓ 건물 전체 내부에서요.

05 Informative Statement 🔊 En

I'm going to apply to be an exchange student.

Ⓐ The committee meets on Thursday.
✓ I'm thinking about doing that, too.
Ⓒ Next semester.
Ⓓ A school in Spain.

apply [əplái] 지원하다, 신청하다   exchange student 교환학생
committee [kəmíti] 위원회

저는 교환학생이 되기 위해 지원하려고 해요.
Ⓐ 위원회는 목요일에 모여요.
✓ 저도 그걸 하려고 생각 중이에요.
Ⓒ 다음 학기에요.
Ⓓ 스페인에 있는 학교요.

06 Where Question 🔊 Am

Where can I pick up my grocery order?

Ⓐ The store closes at 9 P.M.
Ⓑ They offer delivery now, too.
✓ You should get a text message with instructions.
Ⓓ Business has really picked up.

pick up 수령하다, 회복되다   order [ɔ́ːrdər] 주문
instructions [instrʌ́kʃəns] 안내, 지시사항

제 식료품 주문은 어디에서 수령할 수 있나요?
Ⓐ 그 가게는 오후 9시에 문을 닫아요.
Ⓑ 그들은 이제 배송도 제공해요.
✓ⓒ 안내가 담긴 문자 메시지를 받게 될 거예요.
Ⓓ 사업체가 회복되었어요.

07 Be Verb Question
🎧 Au

Are you comfortable with the decision?

Ⓐ No, it's very comfortable.
Ⓑ They settled on it.
Ⓒ I decided against going.
✓Ⓓ It was out of my hands.

decision[disíʒən] 결정 settle[sétl] 합의하다
decide against ~하지 않기로 결정하다
out of one's hands ~의 관할 밖인

당신은 그 결정이 괜찮으신가요?
Ⓐ 아니요, 그것은 아주 편안해요.
Ⓑ 그들이 그것으로 합의했어요.
Ⓒ 저는 가지 않기로 결정했어요.
✓Ⓓ 그것은 제 관할 밖이었어요.

08 Be Verb Question
🎧 Am

Isn't a vegetarian menu available here?

Ⓐ Yes, the chicken is the best here.
✓Ⓑ Let me call the waiter over to ask.
Ⓒ This restaurant opened last month.
Ⓓ I don't think I'm hungry.

vegetarian menu 채식 메뉴

이곳은 채식 메뉴가 제공되지 않나요?
Ⓐ 네, 이곳의 치킨이 최고예요.
✓Ⓑ 제가 웨이터를 불러서 물어볼게요.
Ⓒ 이 식당은 지난달에 문을 열었어요.
Ⓓ 저는 배고픈 것 같지 않아요.

[09-10]
🎧 M-En W-Au

Listen to a conversation.

M Are you ready for the big get-together at Sarah's house this weekend?
W Of course! ⁰⁹**Nothing beats a backyard cookout with friends.** I heard there will be live music, too.
M That sounds great! ⁰⁹**I love a good barbecue.** What time does it start again?
W It starts at 2 P.M. on Saturday. ¹⁰**I'm bringing my famous potato salad.**
M Perfect! I'll bring some drinks and see you there.

get-together 모임, 파티
cookout[kúkàut] 요리 모임, 야외 파티

대화를 들으시오.
M 이번 주말 Sarah 집에서 있을 모임 준비는 다 됐나요?
W 물론이죠! ⁰⁹친구들과 함께하는 뒷마당 요리 모임보다 좋은 건 없어요. 라이브 음악도 있을 거라고 들었어요.
M 정말 좋네요! ⁰⁹저는 맛있는 바베큐를 좋아해요. 몇 시에 시작한다고 했죠?
W 토요일 오후 2시에 시작해요. ¹⁰저는 제 유명한 감자 샐러드를 가져갈 거예요.
M 완벽해요! 저는 음료수를 좀 가져가서 거기서 뵙겠어요.

09 Main Topic Question

화자들은 어떤 행사에 대해 이야기하고 있는가?
✓Ⓐ 바베큐 파티
Ⓑ 저녁 식사 예약
Ⓒ 요리 수업
Ⓓ 레스토랑 개업

어휘 reservation[rèzərvéiʃən] 예약 opening[óupəniŋ] 개업

10 Detail Question

여자는 행사에 무엇을 가져갈 계획인가?
Ⓐ 음향 장비
Ⓑ 음료수
✓Ⓒ 그녀의 감자 샐러드
Ⓓ 바베큐 재료

어휘 equipment[ikwípmənt] 장비 beverage[bévəridʒ] 음료수
ingredient[ingrí:diənt] 재료

[11-12]
🎧 W-En M-Nz

Listen to a conversation.

W I'm torn between taking the bus and driving to campus every day. What do you think would work best?
M It really depends on your priorities. ¹¹**If you want to cut back on expenses, public transportation is definitely the way to go, especially considering the cost of gas.**
W I guess that makes sense. However, ¹²**I'm concerned about the time factor. Wouldn't driving shorten my commute?**
M Fair enough.

torn between ~ 사이에서 고민인 depend on ~에 달려 있다
priority[praiɔ́:rəti] 우선순위 cut back on ~을 줄이다
expense[ikspéns] 비용 public transportation 대중교통
shorten[ʃɔ́:rtn] 줄이다

대화를 들으시오.
W 매일 캠퍼스에 버스를 타고 가는 것과 운전해서 가는 것 사이에서 고민이에요. 무엇이 가장 좋을 것 같다고 생각하세요?
M 당신의 우선순위에 달려 있어요. ¹¹비용을 줄이고 싶으시다면, 특히 기름값을 고려할 때 대중교통이 확실히 좋은 방법이에요.
W 일리가 있는 것 같네요. 하지만, ¹²시간 요소에 대해 걱정이 되어요. 운전하는 것이 통근 시간을 줄이지 않을까요?

M 맞는 말이에요.

11 Detail Question
남자는 대중교통 이용에 대한 자신의 제안에 대해 어떤 이유를 제시하는가?
Ⓐ 더 편리하다.
Ⓑ 혼잡한 시간대 동안 시간을 절약한다.
☑ 돈을 절약하는 데 도움이 된다.
Ⓓ 환경에 더 좋다.

어휘 convenient [kənvíːnjənt] 편리한
　　 environment [inváiərənmənt] 환경

12 Detail Question
여자는 캠퍼스에 운전해서 가는 것에 대해 무엇을 말하는가?
Ⓐ 통근을 더 스트레스 받게 만들 것이다.
☑ 이동 시간을 줄일 것이다.
Ⓒ 그녀의 일정에 더 잘 맞을 것이다.
Ⓓ 지각하는 것을 방지할 것이다.

어휘 travel time 이동 시간   prevent [privént] 방지하다

[13-14]   Au
Listen to an announcement at a university club meeting.

Thanks for joining the photography club's weekly gathering! ¹³Before we begin, I'd like to inform you about our upcoming exhibition. We're accepting submissions on the theme of urban landscapes, and ¹⁴all photos must be uploaded to our website by next Friday for review. Best wishes to all participants!

weekly [wíːkli] 매주의   exhibition [èksəbíʃən] 전시회
submission [səbmíʃən] 출품작, 제출

대학교 동아리 회의에서의 공지를 들으시오.
사진 동아리의 주간 모임에 참여해 주셔서 감사합니다! ¹³시작하기 전에, 우리의 다가오는 전시회에 대해 알려드리고 싶습니다. 우리는 도시 풍경이라는 주제로 출품작을 받고 있으며, ¹⁴모든 사진은 검토를 위해 다음 주 금요일까지 우리 웹사이트에 업로드되어야 합니다. 모든 참가자들에게 행운을 빕니다!

13 Main Topic Question
공지의 주요 주제는 무엇인가?
Ⓐ 초청 강연
Ⓑ 주간 일정
☑ 사진 전시회
Ⓓ 다가오는 워크숍

14 To Do Question
공지에 따르면 학생들은 무엇을 해야 하는가?
☑ 마감일까지 작품을 제출한다.
Ⓑ 다음 워크숍에 참석한다.
Ⓒ 온라인으로 사진에 투표한다.
Ⓓ 사진을 전시하기 위해 신청한다.

어휘 entry [éntri] 작품, 입장   sign up 신청하다
　　 display [displéi] 전시하다

[15-16]   Nz
Listen to an announcement at a school event.

Attention school career fair attendees. ¹⁵We'd like to introduce an exciting opportunity for students interested in summer internships. Local businesses are offering paid internship positions in the fields of marketing, technology, and healthcare. These positions provide valuable work experience and potential college recommendation letters. To apply, ¹⁶please bring your résumé along with a completed internship application form to the guidance counselor's office by this Friday.

career fair 진로 박람회   attendee [ətèndíː] 참석자
opportunity [ɑ̀pərtjúːnəti] 기회   local [lóukəl] 지역의
potential [pəténʃəl] 잠재적   recommendation letter 추천서
along with ~과 함께

학교 행사에서의 공지를 들으시오.
학교 진로 박람회 참석자 여러분 주목해주세요. ¹⁵우리는 여름 인턴십에 관심이 있는 학생들을 위한 흥미로운 기회를 소개하고 싶습니다. 지역 사업체들이 마케팅, 기술, 그리고 의료 분야에서 유급 인턴십 자리를 제공할 것입니다. 이러한 일자리들은 귀중한 업무 경험과 잠재적인 대학 추천서를 제공합니다. 지원하기 위해서는, 이번 주 금요일까지 ¹⁶완성된 인턴십 지원서와 함께 당신의 이력서를 진로 상담교사 사무실로 가져와 주세요.

15 Main Purpose Question
공지의 주요 목적은 무엇인가?
Ⓐ 진로 상담교사들을 소개하기 위해
☑ 인턴십 기회들을 홍보하기 위해
Ⓒ 진로 박람회 일정을 공지하기 위해
Ⓓ 대학 지원 절차를 설명하기 위해

어휘 promote [prəmóut] 홍보하다   job fair 진로 박람회
　　 procedure [prəsíːdʒər] 절차, 방법

16 Detail Question
이번 주 금요일까지 지원하기 위해 학생들이 제출해야 하는 것은 무엇인가?
☑ 이력서와 인턴십 지원서
Ⓑ 대학 성적증명서와 시험 점수
Ⓒ 교수들의 추천서
Ⓓ 학업 프로젝트의 포트폴리오

어휘 transcript [trǽnskript] 성적증명서

[17-20]   Am
Listen to a talk in an economics class.

Today, we're going to discuss the concept of network effects. ¹⁷Network effects happen when the value of a product or service increases as more people use it. **This phenomenon plays a crucial role in modern markets, especially in the technology and communication sectors.** The basic idea is that each additional user adds value not just for themselves but for all existing users in the network. [18]**A classic example is digital communication services, like social media platforms and messaging apps.** The more people who join a platform, the more valuable it becomes because you can connect with more people. Companies often leverage network effects by offering free or low-cost access at first to build a user base quickly. Once they reach a critical mass of users, the network becomes self-reinforcing as new users are attracted by the large existing community. [19]**However, network effects can make it difficult for new competitors to break into established markets.** Users may be reluctant to switch to a new platform even if it's technically better, simply because fewer people are using it. [20]**Next, we'll look at how companies strategically manage these network effects, and then we'll discuss regulations to prevent monopolistic behavior in network-driven industries.**

concept[kánsept] 개념   value[vǽlju:] 가치
phenomenon[finámənàn] 현상   crucial[krú:ʃəl] 중요한, 중대한
leverage[lévəridʒ] 활용하다   self-reinforcing 자체 강화되는
competitor[kəmpétətər] 경쟁자   break into ~에 진입하다
be reluctant to ~하는 것을 꺼리다   regulation[règjuléiʃən] 규제

경제학 강의를 들으시오.

오늘 우리는 네트워크 효과의 개념에 대해 논의하겠습니다. [17]네트워크 효과는 더 많은 사람들이 제품이나 서비스를 사용하면서 그 가치가 증가할 때 발생합니다. 이 현상은 현대 시장, 특히 기술과 통신 부문에서 중요한 역할을 합니다. 기본적인 개념은 각각의 추가 사용자가 자신뿐만 아니라 네트워크의 모든 기존 사용자들에게 가치를 더한다는 것입니다. [18]전형적인 예는 소셜 미디어 플랫폼과 메시징 앱과 같은 디지털 통신 서비스입니다. 플랫폼에 참여하는 사람이 많을수록, 더 많은 사람들과 연결할 수 있기 때문에 그것은 더 가치 있어집니다. 기업들은 처음에는 사용자 기반을 빨리 구축하기 위해 무료 또는 저비용 접근을 제공함으로써 네트워크 효과를 활용하는 경우가 많습니다. 일단 사용자의 임계량에 도달하면, 새로운 사용자들이 큰 기존 커뮤니티에 끌려오면서 네트워크는 자체 강화됩니다. [19]하지만, 네트워크 효과는 새로운 경쟁자들이 기존 시장에 진입하기 어렵게 만들 수 있습니다. 사용자들은 기술적으로 더 우수하다 하더라도, 단순히 더 적은 사람들이 사용하고 있다는 이유로 새로운 플랫폼으로 전환하는 것을 꺼릴 수 있습니다. [20]다음에는, 기업들이 이러한 네트워크 효과를 전략적으로 어떻게 관리하는지 살펴볼 것이고, 그 뒤에 네트워크 중심 산업에서 독점적 행동을 방지하기 위한 규제에 대해 논의하겠습니다.

17 Main Topic Question
강의의 주요 주제는 무엇인가?
Ⓐ 기술 시장이 직면한 과제들
Ⓑ 통신 네트워크와 전화 시스템의 역사
Ⓒ 소셜 미디어 시장을 발전시킬 아이디어
✓ⒹⒹ 기술과 통신 부문의 시장 현상

어휘 face[feis] 직면하다

18 Intention Question
화자는 왜 소셜 미디어 플랫폼과 메시징 앱을 언급하는가?
✓Ⓐ 네트워크 효과의 영향을 받는 디지털 서비스의 예를 제시하기 위해
Ⓑ 기업들이 초기 비용을 줄이는 방법을 설명하기 위해
Ⓒ 어떤 새로운 서비스들이 시장에서 성공했는지를 확인하기 위해
Ⓓ 통신 기술의 기술적 특징을 설명하기 위해

어휘 initial[iníʃəl] 초기의   feature[fí:tʃər] 특징

19 Detail Question
화자에 따르면, 네트워크 효과로 인해 발생하는 문제는 무엇인가?
Ⓐ 높은 네트워크 접근 비용
Ⓑ 복잡한 플랫폼 인터페이스
✓Ⓒ 진입에 대한 경쟁 장벽
Ⓓ 불충분한 초기 사용자 유치

어휘 complicated[kámpləkèitid] 복잡한
competitive[kəmpétətiv] 경쟁적인

20 Discuss Next Question
화자는 다음에 무엇을 논의할 것인가?
Ⓐ 네트워크 플랫폼 구축의 이점
✓Ⓑ 기업들에 의한 네트워크 효과의 전략적 관리
Ⓒ 통신 네트워크의 기술적 측면
Ⓓ 사람들이 독점적 네트워크에 가입하는 심리적 이유

어휘 aspect[ǽspekt] 측면
psychological[sàikəládʒikəl] 심리적인

TASK 1 | Listen and Choose a Response

Section I. Wh- Questions

1. What & Which Questions

HACKERS PRACTICE p.36

01 Ⓐ 02 Ⓒ 03 Ⓑ 04 Ⓒ 05 Ⓒ
06 Ⓑ 07 Ⓐ 08 Ⓑ 09 Ⓒ 10 Ⓓ

01 What Question Am

What kind of services are available at the gym?

☑ Personal training and group classes.
Ⓑ I go there every morning.
Ⓒ Yes, it stays open all year.
Ⓓ How much is the membership fee?

available[əvéiləbl] 이용 가능한, 시간이 있는
membership fee 회원비

그 체육관에서는 어떤 서비스를 이용할 수 있나요?
☑ 개인 운동과 그룹 수업이요.
Ⓑ 저는 매일 아침 그곳에 가요.
Ⓒ 네, 그곳은 일 년 내내 문을 열어요.
Ⓓ 회원비가 얼마인가요?

02 What Question Au

What is the price of this smartphone?

Ⓐ That's smart thinking.
Ⓑ The warranty lasts three years.
☑ It costs nine hundred dollars.
Ⓓ It has excellent battery life.

smart[smɑːrt] 현명한, 재치 있는
warranty[wɔ́ːrənti] 보증, 품질 보증서

이 스마트폰의 가격이 어떻게 되나요?
Ⓐ 그것은 현명한 생각이에요.
Ⓑ 보증은 3년 동안 지속되어요.
☑ 그것은 900달러예요.
Ⓓ 그것은 훌륭한 배터리 수명을 가지고 있어요.

03 Which Question Am

Which department is hosting the orientation?

Ⓐ On the second floor.
☑ The Human Resources team.
Ⓒ Every new employee must attend.
Ⓓ Sure, I'll send you the schedule.

department[dipɑ́ːrtmənt] 부서, 학과, 학부
Human Resources team 인사팀
employee[impl5ii:] 사원, 종업원
attend[əténd] 참석하다

어떤 부서가 오리엔테이션을 진행하나요?
Ⓐ 2층에서요.
☑ 인사팀이요.
Ⓒ 모든 신입사원은 참석해야 해요.
Ⓓ 물론이죠, 제가 일정표를 보낼게요.

04 What Question En

What time is your doctor's appointment?

Ⓐ Yes, with Dr. Williams.
Ⓑ At the downtown clinic.
☑ It's at 2:30 P.M.
Ⓓ I think I need a new medicine.

doctor's appointment 병원 진료

병원 진료가 몇 시인가요?
Ⓐ 네, Williams 선생님과요.
Ⓑ 시내 병원에서요.
☑ 오후 2시 30분이에요.
Ⓓ 저는 새로운 약이 필요한 것 같아요.

05 Which Question Au

Which of the projects should we prioritize?

Ⓐ Yes, it started last week.
Ⓑ The deadline was extended.
☑ The client presentation.
Ⓓ Let's hire another developer.

prioritize[praiɔ́ːrətàiz] 우선순위를 두다
extend[iksténd] 연장하다 client[kláiənt] 고객

어떤 프로젝트에 우선순위를 둬야 할까요?
Ⓐ 네, 그것은 지난주에 시작했어요.
Ⓑ 기한이 연장되었어요.
☑ 고객 발표요.
Ⓓ 또 다른 개발자를 고용합시다.

06 What Question Am

What do you think of the new club room?

Ⓐ We opened last month.
☑ Was it renovated?
Ⓒ It's pretty old now.
Ⓓ Which club are you joining?

renovate[rénəvèit] 개조하다, 보수하다, ~을 새롭게 하다

새 동아리방에 대해 어떻게 생각하세요?
Ⓐ 저희는 지난달에 열었어요.
Ⓑ 보수가 되었나요? ✓
Ⓒ 그것은 이제 꽤 오래되었어요.
Ⓓ 당신은 어떤 동아리에 가입할 건가요?

07 Which Question En

Which is your preferred delivery option?

Ⓐ Standard shipping is fine. ✓
Ⓑ The package arrives tomorrow.
Ⓒ I ordered it last Tuesday.
Ⓓ There's a delivery fee.

preferred[prifə́:rd] 선호되는, 우선의, 발탁된

당신의 선호되는 배송 옵션은 무엇인가요?
Ⓐ 일반 배송이 괜찮아요. ✓
Ⓑ 그 소포는 내일 도착해요.
Ⓒ 저는 그것을 지난주 화요일에 주문했어요.
Ⓓ 배송비가 있어요.

08 Which Question Nz

Which of the candidates has the most experience?

Ⓐ The interviews started at noon.
Ⓑ I'll have to check their résumés. ✓
Ⓒ We hired three new employees.
Ⓓ Experience is an important factor.

candidate[kǽndidèit] 후보자, 지원자
résumé[rézumèi] 이력서   hire[haiər] 고용하다

어떤 후보자가 가장 많은 경력이 있나요?
Ⓐ 면접은 정오에 시작했어요.
Ⓑ 그들의 이력서를 확인해야 해요. ✓
Ⓒ 저희는 세 명의 신입사원을 고용했어요.
Ⓓ 경력은 중요한 요소예요.

09 What Question Am

What is causing the unusual noise in the engine?

Ⓐ The traffic is usually bad this time.
Ⓑ No, it's really noisy outside.
Ⓒ I'll have to ask the mechanic. ✓
Ⓓ I just got it serviced last month.

unusual[ʌnjúːʒuəl] 정상이 아닌, 독특한   noisy[nɔ́izi] 시끄러운

엔진에 정상이 아닌 소리를 야기하는 것이 무엇인가요?
Ⓐ 교통은 이 시간에 보통 혼잡해요.
Ⓑ 아니요, 밖은 정말 시끄러워요.
Ⓒ 정비공에게 물어봐야 해요. ✓
Ⓓ 저는 지난달에 막 점검을 받았어요.

10 Which Question En

Which laptop would you recommend?

Ⓐ It has been upgraded.
Ⓑ The warranty expires next week.
Ⓒ Computer prices have increased.
Ⓓ Depends on what you need it for. ✓

expire[ikspáiər] 만료되다

어떤 노트북을 추천하시나요?
Ⓐ 그것은 업그레이드가 되었어요.
Ⓑ 보증이 다음 주에 만료되어요.
Ⓒ 컴퓨터 가격이 올랐어요.
Ⓓ 그것이 무엇을 위해 필요한지에 따라 달렸어요. ✓

HACKERS TEST p.38

01 Ⓓ	02 Ⓐ	03 Ⓐ	04 Ⓒ	05 Ⓓ
06 Ⓓ	07 Ⓑ	08 Ⓑ	09 Ⓐ	10 Ⓑ
11 Ⓒ	12 Ⓒ	13 Ⓐ	14 Ⓐ	15 Ⓓ
16 Ⓒ	17 Ⓓ	18 Ⓐ	19 Ⓑ	20 Ⓐ

01 What Question Am

What time does the museum open on weekends?

Ⓐ It's closed on Mondays.
Ⓑ Tickets are half-price for students.
Ⓒ The special exhibition ends next month.
Ⓓ At 8 A.M., two hours earlier than on weekdays. ✓

exhibition[èksəbíʃən] 전시회, 표출

박물관은 주말에 몇 시에 여나요?
Ⓐ 그것은 월요일에 닫아요.
Ⓑ 표는 학생들에게 반값이에요.
Ⓒ 특별 전시회는 다음 달에 끝나요.
Ⓓ 평일보다 두 시간 더 이른 오전 8시에요. ✓

02 What Question Nz

What type of payment do you accept?

Ⓐ We take credit cards and cash. ✓
Ⓑ The total comes to 45 dollars.
Ⓒ Please sign the receipt.
Ⓓ How much do I need to pay?

receipt[risíːt] 영수증, 수령

어떤 종류의 지불 방식을 받아주시나요?
Ⓐ 저희는 신용카드와 현금을 받아요. ✓
Ⓑ 전체 금액은 45달러예요.
Ⓒ 영수증에 서명을 해주세요.
Ⓓ 제가 얼마를 지불해야 하나요?

03 Which Question

Which document needs the manager's signature?

(A) ✓ The one on top of the pile.
(B) No, it hasn't been signed yet.
(C) The copy machine is out of ink.
(D) The management class starts soon.

signature[sígnətʃər] 서명, 특징 pile[pail] 더미, 쌓아 놓은 것
management[mǽnidʒmənt] 경영, 관리

어떤 서류가 관리자의 서명이 필요한가요?
(A) ✓ 더미 맨 위에 있는 것이요.
(B) 아니요, 아직 서명되지 않았어요.
(C) 복사기에 잉크가 떨어졌어요.
(D) 경영 수업이 곧 시작해요.

04 What Question

What do you think of the company's new policy?

(A) It takes effect next month.
(B) HR sent an email about it.
(C) ✓ I'd say it's reasonable.
(D) The meeting ended earlier than I expected.

policy[pάləsi] 정책, 규정
reasonable[ríːzənəbl] 합리적인, 적당한

회사의 새로운 정책에 대해 어떻게 생각하나요?
(A) 다음 달에 효력이 발생해요.
(B) 인사팀에서 그것에 대한 이메일을 보냈어요.
(C) ✓ 합리적이라고 말하겠어요.
(D) 회의가 제가 예상했던 것보다 일찍 끝났어요.

05 What Question

What is the application fee for this program?

(A) It's non-refundable.
(B) The deadline is next Friday.
(C) You need a recommendation letter.
(D) ✓ I'm not familiar with that detail.

be familiar with ~에 대해 잘 알다, 익숙하다

이 프로그램의 가입비는 얼마인가요?
(A) 그것은 환불이 안 돼요.
(B) 마감일은 다음 주 금요일이에요.
(C) 당신은 추천서가 필요해요.
(D) ✓ 저는 그 세부사항에 대해 잘 모르겠어요.

06 Which Question

Which is the fastest way to get to the downtown campus?

(A) My class starts at 9 A.M. sharp.
(B) The campus tour takes two hours.
(C) Yes, the express train is arriving soon.
(D) ✓ Let me check my GPS app.

sharp[ʃɑːrp] 정각; 날카로운, 급격한

시내 캠퍼스에 가는 가장 빠른 길이 무엇인가요?
(A) 제 수업은 오전 9시 정각에 시작해요.
(B) 캠퍼스 투어는 두 시간이 걸려요.
(C) 네, 급행열차가 곧 도착해요.
(D) ✓ 제 GPS 앱을 확인해 볼게요.

07 What Question

What's included in the tour package?

(A) How many countries have you visited?
(B) ✓ Transportation and guided tours.
(C) I'm planning to travel in June.
(D) The flights are quite expensive.

include[inklúːd] 포함하다   quite[kwait] 꽤, 아주

여행 패키지에는 무엇이 포함되나요?
(A) 몇 개국을 방문해 보셨나요?
(B) ✓ 교통편과 가이드 투어요.
(C) 저는 6월에 여행을 계획하고 있어요.
(D) 항공편이 꽤 비싸요.

08 What Question

What price did the painting sell for?

(A) At the downtown gallery.
(B) ✓ Over ten thousand dollars.
(C) It's an original oil painting.
(D) The auction ended yesterday.

auction[ɔ́ːkʃən] 경매; 경매로 팔다

그 그림이 얼마에 팔렸나요?
(A) 시내 갤러리에서요.
(B) ✓ 만 달러가 넘어요.
(C) 그것은 원본 유화예요.
(D) 경매가 어제 끝났어요.

09 What Question

What time did the package arrive?

(A) ✓ It came just after noon.
(B) The delivery service is reliable.
(C) It's in the mailroom.
(D) Yes, I signed for it.

reliable[riláiəbl] 신뢰할 만한, 확실한

소포가 몇 시에 도착했나요?
(A) ✓ 정오 직후에 왔어요.
(B) 배달 서비스가 신뢰할 만해요.
(C) 그것은 우편실에 있어요.
(D) 네, 제가 서명했어요.

10 Which Question [Am]

Which candidate impressed you the most?

Ⓐ The interview ends at 5 P.M.
☑ Both had excellent qualifications.
Ⓒ No, we still have three more to see.
Ⓓ The position closed yesterday.

qualification [kwɑ̀:ləfikéiʃən] 자격

어느 지원자가 당신에게 가장 감명을 주었나요?
Ⓐ 면접이 오후 5시에 끝나요.
☑ 둘 다 훌륭한 자격을 갖고 있었어요.
Ⓒ 아니요, 아직 세 명을 더 봐야 해요.
Ⓓ 그 직책 모집이 어제 마감됐어요.

11 Which Question [Au]

Which is the correct format for submitting the final report?

Ⓐ I've already submitted my report.
Ⓑ The deadline is next Friday.
☑ The committee prefers PDF files.
Ⓓ Do you need more time to finish?

committee [kəmíti] 위원회

최종 보고서를 제출하는 올바른 형식은 무엇인가요?
Ⓐ 저는 이미 제 보고서를 제출했어요.
Ⓑ 마감일은 다음 주 금요일이에요.
☑ 위원회는 PDF 파일을 선호해요.
Ⓓ 마치는 데 시간이 더 필요하신가요?

12 What Question [Am]

What time does the baseball game start?

Ⓐ The home team is playing well.
Ⓑ Tickets are still available.
☑ It was canceled due to heavy rain.
Ⓓ In the downtown stadium.

야구 경기는 몇 시에 시작하나요?
Ⓐ 홈팀이 잘하고 있어요.
Ⓑ 표가 아직 있어요.
☑ 폭우로 인해 취소되었어요.
Ⓓ 시내 경기장에서요.

13 What Question [Au]

What's the price range for dinner there?

☑ Between 20 and 30 dollars.
Ⓑ The dress code requires business casual attire.
Ⓒ It has been in business for decades.
Ⓓ Reservations are highly recommended.

decade [dékeid] 10년

그곳의 저녁식사 가격대는 어떻게 되나요?
☑ 20달러와 30달러 사이요.
Ⓑ 복장 규정은 비즈니스 캐주얼이에요.
Ⓒ 그곳은 수십 년 동안 영업해 왔어요.
Ⓓ 예약이 강력히 권고됩니다.

14 Which Question [Am]

Which of these reports contains the sales data?

☑ You'll have to ask Jonathan.
Ⓑ We need to update the figures.
Ⓒ No, the marketing team will send it.
Ⓓ This cabinet contains office supplies.

figure [fígjər] 수치, 모습

이 보고서들 중 어느 것이 매출 데이터를 포함하나요?
☑ Jonathan에게 물어봐야 할 거예요.
Ⓑ 수치를 업데이트해야 해요.
Ⓒ 아니요, 마케팅팀에서 그것을 보낼 거예요.
Ⓓ 이 캐비닛에는 사무용품이 들어 있어요.

15 What Question [Nz]

What type of insurance do you offer?

Ⓐ Your insurance will expire next month.
Ⓑ Please fill out the form and wait in the lobby.
Ⓒ How long have you been with your current provider?
☑ We have health and auto plans.

insurance [inʃúərəns] 보험

어떤 종류의 보험을 제공하시나요?
Ⓐ 당신의 보험이 다음 달에 만료될 거예요.
Ⓑ 양식을 작성하고 로비에서 기다려 주세요.
Ⓒ 현재 보험 회사와 얼마나 오래 계약하셨나요?
☑ 저희는 건강 보험과 자동차 보험이 있어요.

16 What Question [Am]

What requirements do I need to meet for the scholarship?

Ⓐ Applications are due next Friday.
Ⓑ The scholarship covers full tuition.
☑ Check the guidelines on the website.
Ⓓ Yes, they require several documents.

scholarship [skɑ́:lərʃip] 장학금   tuition [tju:íʃən] 수업료

장학금을 위해 제가 충족해야 할 요건은 무엇인가요?
Ⓐ 지원서는 다음 주 금요일까지예요.
Ⓑ 장학금이 전체 등록금을 충당해요.
☑ 웹사이트에서 가이드라인을 확인해 보세요.
Ⓓ 네, 여러 문서가 필요해요.

17 What Question ⟨Am⟩

What do you charge for alterations to this pair of jeans?

Ⓐ Our rates are competitive for leather goods.
Ⓑ Would you like to schedule a fitting?
Ⓒ We can have them ready by Friday.
☑ Hemming starts at fifteen dollars.

alteration [ɔ̀:ltəréiʃən] 수선, 변화
competitive [kəmpétətiv] 경쟁적인   hem [hem] 단을 수선하다

이 청바지 수선 비용을 얼마나 받으시나요?
Ⓐ 저희 가죽 제품 요금은 경쟁력이 있어요.
Ⓑ 피팅 일정을 잡으시겠어요?
Ⓒ 금요일까지 준비해 드릴 수 있어요.
☑ 단 수선은 15달러부터 시작해요.

18 What Question ⟨Am⟩

What's the policy on remote work?

☑ It's detailed in the employee handbook.
Ⓑ The Internet connection is quite stable.
Ⓒ Have you seen the remote control?
Ⓓ No, the policy was updated last year.

remote work 원격 근무   detailed [díːteild] 자세한, 상세한
stable [stéibəl] 안정적인

원격 근무에 대한 정책은 무엇인가요?
☑ 직원 핸드북에 자세히 나와 있어요.
Ⓑ 인터넷 연결이 꽤 안정적이에요.
Ⓒ 리모컨을 보셨나요?
Ⓓ 아니요, 정책이 작년에 업데이트되었어요.

19 Which Question ⟨Nz⟩

Which project needs immediate attention?

Ⓐ Please respond to my email immediately.
☑ There are two I'm considering.
Ⓒ I'll be on vacation next week.
Ⓓ The team is working remotely now.

immediate [imíːdiət] 즉각적인, 직접적인

어느 프로젝트가 즉각적인 관심이 필요한가요?
Ⓐ 제 이메일에 즉시 응답해 주세요.
☑ 제가 고려하고 있는 것이 두 개 있어요.
Ⓒ 저는 다음 주에 휴가를 갈 예정이에요.
Ⓓ 팀이 지금 원격으로 작업하고 있어요.

20 What Question ⟨En⟩

What's the membership fee for this streaming service?

☑ Are you asking about monthly or annual rates?
Ⓑ You can watch videos on multiple devices.
Ⓒ Let's streamline the whole process.
Ⓓ New shows are added weekly.

streamline [stríːmlàin] 간소화하다

이 스트리밍 서비스의 회원비는 얼마인가요?
☑ 월간 요금을 물어보시는 건가요, 아니면 연간 요금인가요?
Ⓑ 여러 기기에서 비디오를 시청하실 수 있어요.
Ⓒ 전체 과정을 간소화해 봐요.
Ⓓ 새로운 프로그램이 매주 추가돼요.

2. Who & Where/When Questions

HACKERS PRACTICE   p.42

| 01 Ⓒ | 02 Ⓒ | 03 Ⓓ | 04 Ⓑ | 05 Ⓑ |
| 06 Ⓐ | 07 Ⓒ | 08 Ⓐ | 09 Ⓒ | 10 Ⓐ |

01 Who Question ⟨Am⟩

Who will be speaking at the graduation ceremony?

Ⓐ It begins at 2 P.M.
Ⓑ In the auditorium.
☑ Professor Lee, I think.
Ⓓ Yes, my parents are attending.

auditorium [ɔ̀:ditɔ́:riəm] 강당, 대강의실

졸업식에서 누가 연설할 예정인가요?
Ⓐ 오후 2시에 시작해요.
Ⓑ 강당에서요.
☑ Lee 교수님인 것 같아요.
Ⓓ 네, 제 부모님이 참석하세요.

02 Where Question ⟨En⟩

Where can I find the electronics department?

Ⓐ The newest model was released last week.
Ⓑ Most items have a one-year warranty.
☑ Take the escalator to the third floor.
Ⓓ No, my smartphone is broken.

release [rilíːs] 출시하다, 방출하다

전자제품 매장을 어디서 찾을 수 있나요?
Ⓐ 최신 모델이 지난 주에 출시되었어요.
Ⓑ 대부분의 제품이 1년 보증이 있어요.
☑ 에스컬레이터를 타고 3층으로 가세요.
Ⓓ 아니요, 제 스마트폰이 고장났어요.

03 Who Question

Who should represent us at the meeting?

Ⓐ It will end soon.
Ⓑ The conference room is booked.
Ⓒ We discussed the budget yesterday.
✓ Someone from the marketing department.

book [buk] 예약하다 budget [bʌ́dʒit] 예산

누가 회의에서 우리를 대표해야 하나요?
Ⓐ 그것은 곧 끝날 거예요.
Ⓑ 회의실이 예약되어 있어요.
Ⓒ 우리는 어제 예산에 대해 논의했어요.
✓ 마케팅 부서의 누군가요.

04 Who Question

Who can help me register for classes?

Ⓐ Registration ends this Friday.
✓ I'm unsure, but I can find out.
Ⓒ I'm taking four courses this semester.
Ⓓ No, the classroom is in Building B.

find out 알아보다, 발견하다 semester [siméstər] 학기

누가 제가 수업 등록하는 것을 도와줄 수 있나요?
Ⓐ 등록이 이번 금요일에 끝나요.
✓ 확실하지 않지만, 알아볼 수 있어요.
Ⓒ 저는 이번 학기에 네 과목을 수강해요.
Ⓓ 아니요, 교실은 B동에 있어요.

05 Where Question

Where am I supposed to submit my research proposal?

Ⓐ The deadline is next Friday.
✓ Through the department's online portal.
Ⓒ Dr. Williams wrote the research proposal.
Ⓓ Research methods are covered in chapter five.

proposal [prəpóuzəl] 제안서, 제안

제 연구 제안서를 어디에 제출해야 하나요?
Ⓐ 마감일은 다음 주 금요일이에요.
✓ 부서의 온라인 포털을 통해서요.
Ⓒ Williams 박사님이 연구 제안서를 작성했어요.
Ⓓ 연구 방법은 5장에서 다뤄져요.

06 Who Question

Who is leading the leadership webinar?

✓ The manager usually does.
Ⓑ Yes, she is the new leader.
Ⓒ About project management techniques.
Ⓓ Registration closes this afternoon.

technique [tekníːk] 기법, 기술

누가 리더십 웨비나를 이끌고 있나요?
✓ 관리자가 보통 해요.
Ⓑ 네, 그녀가 새로운 리더예요.
Ⓒ 프로젝트 관리 기법에 대해서요.
Ⓓ 등록이 오늘 오후에 마감돼요.

07 When Question

When does the next train to Chicago depart?

Ⓐ Platform number five.
Ⓑ It takes about three hours.
✓ In 20 minutes.
Ⓓ Tickets are still available.

depart [dipáːrt] 출발하다, 떠나다

시카고행 다음 열차는 언제 출발하나요?
Ⓐ 5번 승강장이요.
Ⓑ 약 3시간 걸려요.
✓ 20분 후에요.
Ⓓ 표가 아직 있어요.

08 Where Question

Where should we hold the company picnic this year?

✓ Magnolia Park has nice facilities.
Ⓑ No more than 30 minutes.
Ⓒ It's scheduled for June 15th.
Ⓓ Yes, we need to order catering.

facility [fəsíləti] 시설, 설비

올해 회사 소풍을 어디서 개최해야 하나요?
✓ Magnolia 공원에 좋은 시설들이 있어요.
Ⓑ 30분 이내로요.
Ⓒ 6월 15일로 예정되어 있어요.
Ⓓ 네, 출장 요리를 주문해야 해요.

09 When Question

When was the last time you visited the art gallery downtown?

Ⓐ The tickets are reasonably priced.
Ⓑ The visitor center is over there.
✓ Actually, I've never been there.
Ⓓ Yes, it's located close to the campus.

시내 미술관에 마지막으로 언제 방문했나요?
Ⓐ 표 가격이 합리적이에요.
Ⓑ 방문자 센터가 저기에 있어요.
✓ 사실, 저는 거기에 가본 적이 없어요.
Ⓓ 네, 캠퍼스 가까이에 위치해 있어요.

10 Who Question　　🔊 Am

Who is going to cook dinner tonight?

- (A) Actually, we're going out to eat. ✓
- (B) Yes, Harry will clean the kitchen.
- (C) I prefer chicken over fish.
- (D) Did you already have dinner?

clean [kli:n] 청소하다; 청결한

오늘 밤 저녁을 누가 요리할 예정인가요?
- (A) 사실, 우리는 외식할 거예요. ✓
- (B) 네, Harry가 부엌을 청소할 거예요.
- (C) 저는 생선보다 닭고기를 선호해요.
- (D) 이미 저녁을 드셨나요?

HACKERS TEST　　p.44

01 (A)	02 (A)	03 (A)	04 (B)	05 (C)
06 (B)	07 (B)	08 (C)	09 (A)	10 (C)
11 (C)	12 (B)	13 (B)	14 (C)	15 (D)
16 (B)	17 (C)	18 (D)	19 (C)	20 (A)

01 Who Question　　🔊 En

Who is organizing the company retreat this year?

- (A) I believe it's the HR department. ✓
- (B) Next month in Colorado.
- (C) The budget was increased.
- (D) You need to register online.

organize [ɔ́:rgənàiz] 조직하다

누가 올해 회사 야유회를 조직하고 있나요?
- (A) 인사부인 것 같아요. ✓
- (B) 다음 달 콜로라도에서요.
- (C) 예산이 늘어났어요.
- (D) 온라인으로 등록해야 해요.

02 Where Question　　🔊 Am

Where did you get that amazing coffee?

- (A) From the new café on Third Street. ✓
- (B) I usually drink tea in the morning.
- (C) It contains special Colombian beans.
- (D) This mug was a birthday gift.

contain [kəntéin] 들어있다, 포함하다, 담다

그 놀라운 커피를 어디서 구했나요?
- (A) 3번가 새 카페에서요. ✓
- (B) 저는 보통 아침에 차를 마셔요.
- (C) 특별한 콜롬비아 원두가 들어 있어요.
- (D) 이 머그컵은 생일 선물이었어요.

03 When Question　　🔊 Au

When will the exam results be available?

- (A) You can check them online tomorrow. ✓
- (B) The test was very difficult.
- (C) We had thirty questions to answer.
- (D) I think I did well on it.

시험 결과가 언제 나올 예정인가요?
- (A) 내일 온라인으로 확인할 수 있어요. ✓
- (B) 시험이 아주 어려웠어요.
- (C) 우리는 30개 문제에 답해야 했어요.
- (D) 저는 잘했다고 생각해요.

04 Who Question　　🔊 En

Who designed the new company logo?

- (A) The logo was unveiled last month.
- (B) We hired an outside firm. ✓
- (C) I prefer the old design.
- (D) It's for our website.

unveil [ənvéil] 공개하다, 밝히다　　firm [fə:rm] 회사, 기업; 단단한

누가 새로운 회사 로고를 디자인했나요?
- (A) 로고가 지난 달에 공개되었어요.
- (B) 외부 회사를 고용했어요. ✓
- (C) 저는 예전 디자인을 선호해요.
- (D) 저의 웹사이트용이에요.

05 Who Question　　🔊 Au

Who is in charge of the international clients?

- (A) The client meeting is at 2 P.M.
- (B) No, from twelve countries.
- (C) Which specific region are you asking about? ✓
- (D) Yes, the presentation was successful.

in charge of ~을 담당하는, ~을 맡고 있는
specific [spisífik] 구체적인, 명확한　　region [rí:dʒən] 지역, 지방

누가 국제 고객들을 담당하고 있나요?
- (A) 고객 회의가 오후 2시에 있어요.
- (B) 아니요, 12개국에서요.
- (C) 어느 구체적인 지역을 물어보시는 건가요? ✓
- (D) 네, 발표가 성공적이었어요.

06 Where Question　　🔊 Am

Where is the new employee orientation being held?

- (A) It starts at 9 A.M. sharp.
- (B) In Conference Room C. ✓
- (C) The training lasts for two days.
- (D) Five new hires are starting today.

last[læst] 계속되다; 마지막의, 지난

신입사원 오리엔테이션이 어디에서 진행되나요?
Ⓐ 오전 9시 정각에 시작해요.
☑ Ⓒ 회의실에서요.
Ⓒ 교육은 이틀 동안 계속돼요.
Ⓓ 다섯 명의 신규 채용자가 오늘 시작해요.

07 Who Question

Who won the photography contest yesterday?

Ⓐ The exhibition closes on Sunday.
☑ I wasn't at the awards ceremony.
Ⓒ I submitted three photos in total.
Ⓓ The prizes will be awarded tomorrow.

submit[səbmít] 제출하다   award[əwɔ́:rd] 수여하다; 상

누가 어제 사진 콘테스트에서 우승했나요?
Ⓐ 전시회가 일요일에 끝나요.
☑ 저는 시상식에 없었어요.
Ⓒ 총 세 장의 사진을 제출했어요.
Ⓓ 상품들이 내일 수여될 예정이에요.

08 When Question

When does the warranty on this appliance expire?

Ⓐ It's in the fridge.
Ⓑ At our new store.
☑ Please wait while I check.
Ⓓ This model has excellent reviews.

appliance[əpláiəns] 가전제품

이 가전제품의 보증이 언제 만료되나요?
Ⓐ 냉장고 안에 있어요.
Ⓑ 저희 새 매장에서요.
☑ 제가 확인하는 동안 기다려 주세요.
Ⓓ 이 모델은 뛰어난 후기들을 받았어요.

09 Who Question

Who is going to lead the community fundraiser?

☑ Michael volunteered.
Ⓑ The goal is to raise 10,000 dollars.
Ⓒ It's scheduled for next Saturday.
Ⓓ We're supporting the local shelter.

fundraiser[fʌ́ndrèizər] 기금 모금, 모금자
volunteer[vɑ̀:ləntíər] 자원하다, 자원봉사자

누가 지역사회 기금 모금을 이끌 예정인가요?
☑ Michael이 자원했어요.
Ⓑ 목표는 1만 달러를 모으는 것이에요.
Ⓒ 다음 토요일로 예정되어 있어요.
Ⓓ 우리는 지역 쉼터를 지원하고 있어요.

10 When Question

When is the deadline for submitting the marketing proposal?

Ⓐ The CEO approved it yesterday.
Ⓑ We need to include the budget analysis.
☑ Let me check with my manager.
Ⓓ I'm working with the design team.

approve[əprú:v] 승인하다, 찬성하다

마케팅 제안서를 제출하는 마감일이 언제인가요?
Ⓐ CEO가 어제 승인했어요.
Ⓑ 예산 분석을 포함해야 해요.
☑ 제 관리자와 확인해 볼게요.
Ⓓ 저는 디자인팀과 작업하고 있어요.

11 Who Question

Who can help me fix my computer issues?

Ⓐ The printer is working fine now.
Ⓑ It took some time to repair the laptop.
☑ I know a great repair shop downtown.
Ⓓ No, I don't need any help.

repair[ripέər] 수리하다, 치료하다; 수리

누가 제 컴퓨터 문제에 대해 도움을 줄 수 있나요?
Ⓐ 프린터가 이제 잘 작동해요.
Ⓑ 노트북을 수리하는 데 시간이 좀 걸렸어요.
☑ 시내에 좋은 수리점을 알고 있어요.
Ⓓ 아니요, 도움이 필요 없어요.

12 Who Question

Who will be the guest lecturer next Monday?

Ⓐ Yes, it's on the website.
☑ The lecture has been canceled.
Ⓒ You should arrive early to get a seat.
Ⓓ The auditorium is near the science building.

lecture[léktʃər] 강의, 강연

다음 월요일에 초청 강연자가 누가 될 예정인가요?
Ⓐ 네, 웹사이트에 있어요.
☑ 강의가 취소되었어요.
Ⓒ 자리를 잡으려면 일찍 도착해야 해요.
Ⓓ 강당이 과학관 근처에 있어요.

13 When Question

When shall we schedule the follow-up meeting?

Ⓐ The first meeting went very well.
☑ Do we need another meeting?
Ⓒ We discussed the project timeline.
Ⓓ The conference room is booked all day.

follow-up 후속의, 뒤이은; 추적

후속 회의 일정을 언제 잡을까요?
Ⓐ 첫 번째 회의가 아주 잘 진행되었어요.
☑ 또 다른 회의가 필요한가요?
Ⓒ 우리는 프로젝트 일정에 대해 논의했어요.
Ⓓ 회의실이 하루 종일 예약되어 있어요.

14 Where Question　　　　　　　　　Am

Where are we gathering for the next club meeting?
Ⓐ Yes, I'm free after 6 P.M.
Ⓑ I don't think so.
☑ Probably the usual place.
Ⓓ The meeting agenda looks good.

gather [gǽðər] 모이다, 수확하다, 추측하다
agenda [ədʒéndə] 안건, 의제

다음 동아리 회의를 위해 어디서 모이나요?
Ⓐ 네, 저는 오후 6시 이후에 시간이 있어요.
Ⓑ 저는 그렇게 생각하지 않아요.
☑ 아마 늘 가는 곳일 거예요.
Ⓓ 회의 안건이 좋아 보여요.

15 Where Question　　　　　　　　　En

Where can we find quiet study spaces during finals week?
Ⓐ It's always crowded there.
Ⓑ Finals begin next Monday.
Ⓒ Group study sessions help most students.
☑ The fourth floor of the library.

crowded [kráudid] 붐비는, 혼잡한

기말고사 주간에 조용한 학습 공간을 어디서 찾을 수 있나요?
Ⓐ 거기는 항상 붐벼요.
Ⓑ 기말고사가 다음 주 월요일에 시작해요.
Ⓒ 그룹 스터디 시간이 대부분의 학생들에게 도움이 돼요.
☑ 도서관 4층이요.

16 Who Question　　　　　　　　　Am

Who would be interested in joining our study group?
Ⓐ The library will be closing soon.
☑ I'm afraid we're at full capacity.
Ⓒ We met twice last week.
Ⓓ I'm interested in economics.

capacity [kəpǽsəti] 정원, 용량

누가 우리 스터디 그룹에 가입하는 데 관심이 있을까요?
Ⓐ 도서관이 곧 문을 닫을 거예요.
☑ 유감스럽게도 우리는 정원이 찼어요.
Ⓒ 우리는 지난주에 두 번 만났어요.
Ⓓ 저는 경제학에 관심이 있어요.

17 Who Question　　　　　　　　　Nz

Who is presenting at the science fair next Friday?
Ⓐ It will start at 1 o'clock.
Ⓑ The exhibits were really innovative.
☑ It hasn't been announced yet.
Ⓓ I'm planning to attend the lectures.

innovative [ínəvèitiv] 혁신적인

누가 다음 금요일 과학 박람회에서 발표할 예정인가요?
Ⓐ 1시 정각에 시작할 거예요.
Ⓑ 전시물들이 정말 혁신적이었어요.
☑ 아직 발표되지 않았어요.
Ⓓ 강의들에 참석할 계획이에요.

18 Who Question　　　　　　　　　Am

Who is teaching the advanced biology this semester?
Ⓐ In the science building.
Ⓑ Every Tuesday at 2 P.M.
Ⓒ No, Dr. Hayes is not in his office.
☑ I don't know, but I can find out.

이번 학기에 고급 생물학을 누가 가르치나요?
Ⓐ 과학관에서요.
Ⓑ 매주 화요일 오후 2시예요.
Ⓒ 아니요, Hayes 박사님은 사무실에 계시지 않아요.
☑ 모르겠지만, 알아볼 수 있어요.

19 When Question　　　　　　　　　En

When are you going to put the house up for sale?
☑ After we finish the kitchen renovation.
Ⓑ The backyard is quite spacious.
Ⓒ We're using an online listing service.
Ⓓ Property values have increased lately.

spacious [spéiʃəs] 넓은, 널찍한

집을 언제 매물로 내놓을 예정인가요?
☑ 부엌 리모델링을 끝낸 후예요.
Ⓑ 뒤뜰이 꽤 넓어요.
Ⓒ 온라인 매물 서비스를 이용하고 있어요.
Ⓓ 부동산 가치가 최근에 올랐어요.

20 Where Question　　　　　　　　　Au

Where should we hang posters about our club meeting?
☑ The student lounge gets a lot of foot traffic.
Ⓑ Our meeting is next Thursday.
Ⓒ We should order more supplies.

ⓓ The club president approved the design.

hang[hæŋ] 걸다　foot traffic 유동 인구

동아리 회의에 대한 포스터를 어디에 걸어야 할까요?
ⓐ 학생 라운지가 유동 인구가 많아요. ✓
ⓑ 우리 회의는 다음 목요일이에요.
ⓒ 용품을 더 주문해야 해요.
ⓓ 동아리 회장이 디자인을 승인했어요.

ⓒ We offer ten different courses.
ⓓ How about another time?

reschedule[riːskédʒuːl] 일정을 변경하다, 연기하다

강의가 왜 취소되었나요?
ⓐ 수업이 다음 주에 시작해요.
ⓑ 사실, 일정이 변경되었어요. ✓
ⓒ 우리는 10개의 다른 과정을 제공해요.
ⓓ 다른 시간은 어때요?

3. Why & How Questions

HACKERS PRACTICE　p.48

| 01 ⓐ | 02 ⓒ | 03 ⓑ | 04 ⓓ | 05 ⓒ |
| 06 ⓑ | 07 ⓒ | 08 ⓓ | 09 ⓒ | 10 ⓓ |

01 Why Question　Am

Why was the project deadline extended?
ⓐ I had some technical difficulties. ✓
ⓑ The new deadline is next month.
ⓒ I'll work overtime to finish it.
ⓓ Because I finished it early.

overtime[óuvərtaim] 초과 근무

프로젝트 마감일이 왜 연장되었나요?
ⓐ 제가 기술적 어려움을 겪었어요. ✓
ⓑ 새로운 마감일은 다음 달이에요.
ⓒ 저는 그것을 끝내기 위해 초과근무를 할 거예요.
ⓓ 제가 일찍 끝냈기 때문이에요.

02 Why Question　En

Why is the Internet connection so slow today?
ⓐ Sure, you can borrow my phone.
ⓑ We should make fast decisions.
ⓒ Seems like the router needs repairs. ✓
ⓓ I need to send some large files.

오늘 인터넷 연결이 왜 이렇게 느린가요?
ⓐ 물론이죠, 제 전화기를 빌려드릴 수 있어요.
ⓑ 우리는 빠른 결정을 내려야 해요.
ⓒ 라우터가 수리가 필요한 것 같아요. ✓
ⓓ 저는 큰 파일들을 보내야 해요.

03 Why Question　Am

Why did the lecture get canceled?
ⓐ Classes begin next week.
ⓑ Actually, it was rescheduled. ✓

04 Why Question　Au

Why aren't the financial reports ready yet?
ⓐ To the finance department.
ⓑ Yes, I've read through all of them.
ⓒ The quarterly results were positive.
ⓓ Some data needs revision. ✓

quarterly[kwɔ́ːrtərli] 분기의

재무 보고서가 왜 아직 준비되지 않았나요?
ⓐ 재무부로요.
ⓑ 네, 저는 모든 것을 읽어봤어요.
ⓒ 분기 결과가 긍정적이었어요.
ⓓ 일부 데이터가 수정이 필요해요. ✓

05 Why Question　Am

Why didn't you attend the orientation session?
ⓐ It was very informative.
ⓑ The trainer is an expert in the field.
ⓒ I had a conflicting appointment. ✓
ⓓ Yes, it will be offered again.

informative[infɔ́ːrmətiv] 유익한, 교육적인
conflicting[kənflíktiŋ] 겹치는, 상충되는

오리엔테이션 세션에 왜 참석하지 않았나요?
ⓐ 그것은 매우 유익했어요.
ⓑ 교육자는 그 분야의 전문가예요.
ⓒ 겹치는 약속이 있었어요. ✓
ⓓ 네, 다시 제공될 거예요.

06 How Question　En

How can I reserve a study room?
ⓐ Yes, it's a group project.
ⓑ Through the student portal. ✓
ⓒ The study was conducted last month.
ⓓ I finished my project yesterday.

conduct[kəndʌ́kt] 수행하다, 처리하다

학습실을 어떻게 예약할 수 있나요?
ⓐ 네, 그룹 프로젝트예요.
ⓑ 학생 포털을 통해서요. ✓

ⓒ 연구가 지난 달에 수행되었어요.
ⓓ 제가 어제 프로젝트를 끝냈어요.

07 How Question 🎧 Am

How much will it cost to fix my car's air conditioning?

ⓐ The garage closes at 6 P.M.
☑ Between 200 and 250 dollars.
ⓒ I can give you a ride tomorrow.
ⓓ Your warranty expired last month.

garage[gərá:dʒ] 정비소, 차고 give a ride 태워 주다

제 차의 에어컨을 수리하는 데 비용이 얼마나 들까요?
ⓐ 정비소가 오후 6시에 문을 닫아요.
☑ 200달러에서 250달러 사이요.
ⓒ 내일 태워드릴 수 있어요.
ⓓ 당신의 보증이 지난 달에 만료되었어요.

08 How Question 🎧 Au

How often does the campus shuttle run on weekends?

ⓐ Did you take a bus?
ⓑ It's at the main entrance.
ⓒ Let's go jogging this weekend.
☑ Every thirty minutes.

캠퍼스 셔틀이 주말에 얼마나 자주 운행하나요?
ⓐ 버스를 탔나요?
ⓑ 정문에 있어요.
ⓒ 이번 주말에 조깅하러 가요.
☑ 30분마다요.

09 How Question 🎧 Am

How many participants registered for the conference?

ⓐ Registration closes on Friday.
ⓑ You can register online.
☑ So far, almost 100.
ⓓ The venue has limited capacity.

venue[vénju:] 장소

회의에 몇 명의 참가자가 등록했나요?
ⓐ 등록이 금요일에 마감돼요.
ⓑ 온라인으로 등록할 수 있어요.
☑ 지금까지 거의 100명이요.
ⓓ 장소의 수용력이 제한되어 있어요.

10 How Question 🎧 En

How long will the renovation of the student center take?

ⓐ According to the email, last month.
ⓑ The center is located near the library.
ⓒ You need your student ID to enter.
☑ I didn't know it was being renovated.

renovation[rènəvéiʃən] 보수, 수리, 개혁

학생 센터의 보수가 얼마나 걸릴 예정인가요?
ⓐ 이메일에 따르면, 지난 달이에요.
ⓑ 센터가 도서관 근처에 위치해 있어요.
ⓒ 들어가려면 학생증이 필요해요.
☑ 보수가 되고 있는지 몰랐어요.

HACKERS TEST   p.50

01 ⓐ	02 ⓓ	03 ⓐ	04 ⓑ	05 ⓑ
06 ⓐ	07 ⓓ	08 ⓒ	09 ⓒ	10 ⓓ
11 ⓐ	12 ⓒ	13 ⓓ	14 ⓓ	15 ⓑ
16 ⓑ	17 ⓐ	18 ⓒ	19 ⓓ	20 ⓑ

01 How Question 🎧 Au

How do I operate this new coffee machine?

☑ Press the red button to start brewing.
ⓑ The machine was quite expensive.
ⓒ The coffee beans are in the cabinet.
ⓓ The old one broke down.

operate[ápərèit] 작동시키다, 운영하다

이 새 커피 머신을 어떻게 작동시키나요?
☑ 우리기를 시작하려면 빨간 버튼을 누르세요.
ⓑ 머신이 꽤 비쌌어요.
ⓒ 커피 원두가 캐비닛에 있어요.
ⓓ 예전 것이 고장 났어요.

02 Why Question 🎧 Am

Why was the club meeting rescheduled?

ⓐ Yes, the schedule is fixed.
ⓑ Let's join the book club.
ⓒ We used to meet every Thursday.
☑ The original room was unavailable.

used to ~하곤 했다, ~였다
unavailable[ʌ̀nəvéiləbl] 이용할 수 없는

동아리 회의 일정이 왜 변경되었나요?
ⓐ 네, 일정이 확정되어 있어요.
ⓑ 독서 동아리에 가입합시다.

ⓒ 우리는 매주 목요일에 만나곤 했어요.
☑ 원래 방을 이용할 수 없었어요.

03 Why Question   En

Why isn't our food here yet?

☑ The kitchen is busy tonight.
Ⓑ I ordered today's special.
ⓒ The menu has many options.
Ⓓ The restaurant isn't closed yet.

우리 음식이 왜 아직 안 나왔나요?
☑ 주방이 오늘 밤 바빠요.
Ⓑ 오늘의 특선을 주문했어요.
ⓒ 메뉴에 선택지가 많아요.
Ⓓ 레스토랑이 아직 문을 닫지 않았어요.

04 How Question   Nz

How many tickets did you purchase for the concert?

Ⓐ The show starts at 8 P.M.
☑ Four, one for each of us.
ⓒ The venue is downtown.
Ⓓ I prefer classical music.

purchase[pə́ːrtʃəs] 구매하다

콘서트 표를 몇 장 구매했나요?
Ⓐ 공연이 오후 8시에 시작해요.
☑ 네 장, 우리 각각에게 하나씩요.
ⓒ 공연장이 시내에 있어요.
Ⓓ 저는 클래식 음악을 선호해요.

05 Why Question   Am

Why should we consider changing suppliers?

Ⓐ No, their quality declined.
☑ Our current one increased its prices.
ⓒ I'm considering applying for another position.
Ⓓ Deliveries are made weekly.

decline[dikláin] 떨어지다, 쇠퇴하다   apply for ~에 지원하다

공급업체를 바꾸는 것을 왜 고려해야 하나요?
Ⓐ 아니요, 그들의 품질이 떨어졌어요.
☑ 우리 현재 업체가 가격을 올렸어요.
ⓒ 저는 다른 직책에 지원하는 것을 고려하고 있어요.
Ⓓ 배송은 매주 한 번 이루어져요.

06 How Question   En

How often does the farmers market open?

☑ It depends on the season.
Ⓑ The produce is always fresh.
ⓒ I buy organic vegetables there.

Ⓓ It's located near the park.

farmers market 농산물 직판장
depend on ~에 따라 다르다, ~에 달려 있다
organic[ɔːrɡǽnik] 유기농의, 유기체의

농산물 직판장이 얼마나 자주 열리나요?
☑ 계절에 따라 달라요.
Ⓑ 농산물이 항상 신선해요.
ⓒ 거기서 유기농 채소를 사요.
Ⓓ 공원 근처에 위치해 있어요.

07 How Question   Au

How much does the campus parking permit cost?

Ⓐ Park near the humanities building.
Ⓑ The parking lot operates 24 hours.
ⓒ No, I usually take the shuttle bus.
☑ You should ask Mr. Jenson about that.

permit[pərmít] 허가증; 허가하다

캠퍼스 주차 허가증 비용이 얼마나 드나요?
Ⓐ 인문관 근처에 주차하세요.
Ⓑ 주차장은 24시간 운영해요.
ⓒ 아니요, 저는 보통 셔틀버스를 타요.
☑ 그것에 대해서는 Mr. Jenson에게 물어보세요.

08 Why Question   Am

Why is the electricity bill so high this month?

Ⓐ I paid it last week.
Ⓑ The lights are too dim.
☑ That's a mystery to me, too.
Ⓓ It's in the kitchen drawer.

drawer[drɔːr] 서랍

이번 달 전기세가 왜 이렇게 높나요?
Ⓐ 지난주에 지불했어요.
Ⓑ 전등이 너무 어두워요.
☑ 저도 수수께끼예요.
Ⓓ 부엌 서랍 안에 있어요.

09 How Question   En

How long does your company retain client records?

Ⓐ Yes, we have our own policy.
Ⓑ Client meetings are scheduled on Tuesday.
☑ For a maximum of seven years by law.
Ⓓ The file room was recently reorganized.

retain[ritéin] 보관하다, 보유하다
maximum[mǽksəməm] 최대의; 최대

당신의 회사는 고객 기록을 얼마나 오래 보관하나요?
Ⓐ 네, 우리만의 정책이 있어요.

Ⓑ 고객 회의가 화요일에 예정되어 있어요.
☑ 법에 의해 최대 7년간이요.
Ⓓ 파일 보관실이 최근에 재정리되었어요.

10 Why Question 〔Am〕

Why are they renovating the science building?

Ⓐ The construction will finish next month.
Ⓑ Yes, it's the newest building on campus.
Ⓒ Have you seen the architectural plans?
☑ To create additional laboratory space.

architectural [ɑ́ːrkətéktʃərəl] 건축의
laboratory [lǽbərətɔ̀ːri] 실험실

그들이 과학관을 왜 보수하고 있나요?
Ⓐ 건설이 다음 달에 끝날 거예요.
Ⓑ 네, 캠퍼스에서 가장 새로운 건물이에요.
Ⓒ 건축 계획을 보셨나요?
☑ 추가적인 실험실 공간을 만들기 위해서요.

11 Why Question 〔Nz〕

Why didn't you report the server issue?

☑ I thought someone else would handle it.
Ⓑ The problem started last week.
Ⓒ The IT department is down the hall.
Ⓓ Do you know their contact information?

report [ripɔ́ːrt] 보고하다; 보고서
handle [hǽndl] 처리하다, 담당하다, 다루다

서버 문제를 왜 보고하지 않았나요?
☑ 다른 누군가가 처리할 것이라고 생각했어요.
Ⓑ 문제가 지난주에 시작되었어요.
Ⓒ IT 부서는 복도를 따라가면 있어요.
Ⓓ 그들의 연락처 정보를 알고 있나요?

12 Why Question 〔Au〕

Why are customers returning this product?

Ⓐ Some young consumers.
Ⓑ It was launched two months ago.
☑ Let's check the feedback reports.
Ⓓ The marketing campaign was successful.

return [ritə́ːrn] 반품하다, 반납하다
launch [lɔːntʃ] 출시하다, 개시하다, 발사하다

고객들이 이 제품을 왜 반품하고 있나요?
Ⓐ 일부 젊은 소비자들이요.
Ⓑ 그것은 두 달 전에 출시되었어요.
☑ 피드백 보고서를 확인해 봅시다.
Ⓓ 마케팅 캠페인이 성공적이었어요.

13 How Question 〔Am〕

How do you fix a jammed printer?

Ⓐ The print shop is closing soon.
Ⓑ I need to print my essay.
Ⓒ You can save files on the cloud.
☑ It's better to call a professional.

jammed [dʒæmd] 걸린, 고장 난

용지가 걸린 프린터를 어떻게 고치나요?
Ⓐ 인쇄소가 곧 문을 닫아요.
Ⓑ 제 에세이를 인쇄해야 해요.
Ⓒ 클라우드에 파일을 저장할 수 있어요.
☑ 전문가를 부르는 게 낫겠어요.

14 Why Question 〔En〕

Why aren't you attending the meeting today?

Ⓐ No, a week ago.
Ⓑ The presentation is prepared.
Ⓒ The meeting room on the third floor.
☑ Do you mean the budget meeting?

오늘 회의에 왜 참석하지 않나요?
Ⓐ 아니요, 일주일 전에요.
Ⓑ 발표가 준비되어 있어요.
Ⓒ 3층의 회의실이요.
☑ 예산 회의를 말씀하시는 건가요?

15 How Question 〔Am〕

How much does the company spend on employee training?

Ⓐ The training room is reserved.
☑ Approximately 8% of our annual budget.
Ⓒ New employees start next Monday.
Ⓓ The workshop lasts three days.

approximately [əprɑ́ksəmətli] 대략, 약

회사가 직원 교육에 얼마를 지출하나요?
Ⓐ 교육실이 예약되어 있어요.
☑ 연간 예산의 대략 8퍼센트요.
Ⓒ 신규 직원들이 다음 월요일에 시작해요.
Ⓓ 워크숍이 3일간 지속돼요.

16 How Question 〔Nz〕

How often are professors required to hold office hours?

Ⓐ Professor Johnson is in room 302.
☑ The minimum is three hours weekly.
Ⓒ You should email them first.
Ⓓ No, the requirement isn't that strict.

minimum [mínəməm] 최소의; 최소 strict [strikt] 엄격한

교수들은 상담 시간을 얼마나 자주 갖도록 요구받나요?
Ⓐ Johnson 교수님은 302호실에 계세요.
Ⓥ 최소 주 3시간이요.
Ⓒ 먼저 그들에게 이메일을 보내야 해요.
Ⓓ 아니요, 요구사항이 그렇게 엄격하지 않아요.

17 How Question Am

How many guests showed up for the wedding reception?

Ⓐ The ceremony was quite emotional.
Ⓥ It exceeded our expectations.
Ⓒ The venue is located downtown.
Ⓓ We sent invitations three months in advance.

exceed [iksí:d] 초과하다 in advance 미리, 앞서서

결혼식 피로연에 손님이 몇 명이나 나타났나요?
Ⓐ 예식이 꽤 감동적이었어요.
Ⓥ 우리 기대를 초과했어요.
Ⓒ 장소가 시내에 위치해 있어요.
Ⓓ 3개월 전에 미리 초대장을 보냈어요.

18 Why Question En

Why did you cancel the study group meeting?

Ⓐ The library opened an hour ago.
Ⓑ Because I didn't know about it.
Ⓥ Some members asked me to.
Ⓓ I'm sorry that you lost it.

스터디 그룹 모임을 왜 취소했나요?
Ⓐ 도서관은 한 시간 전에 열었어요.
Ⓑ 저는 그것에 대해 몰랐기 때문이에요.
Ⓥ 몇몇 구성원들이 저에게 요청했어요.
Ⓓ 잃어버리셨다니 유감이에요.

19 Why Question Nz

Why do you recommend taking public transportation instead of driving?

Ⓐ The bus station is under renovation.
Ⓑ The parking garage opens quite early.
Ⓒ Because I drive to work every day.
Ⓥ There's a construction project causing traffic delays.

recommend [rèkəménd] 추천하다 parking garage 주차장

운전 대신 대중교통 이용을 왜 추천하나요?
Ⓐ 버스 정류장이 공사 중이에요.
Ⓑ 주차장이 꽤 일찍 열어요.
Ⓒ 제가 매일 차로 출근하기 때문이에요.
Ⓥ 교통 지연을 야기하는 건설 작업이 있어요.

20 Why Question Am

Why is the university implementing a new registration system?

Ⓐ Because it's a newly updated one.
Ⓥ I've been wondering about that myself.
Ⓒ Registration begins next Monday.
Ⓓ It is too late to implement a new policy.

implement [ímpləmènt] 시행하다, 도입하다

대학교가 새로운 등록 시스템을 왜 시행하고 있나요?
Ⓐ 새로 업데이트된 것이기 때문이에요.
Ⓥ 저도 그것에 대해 궁금해하고 있었어요.
Ⓒ 등록이 다음 월요일에 시작해요.
Ⓓ 새로운 정책을 시행하기에는 너무 늦었어요.

Section II. Non Wh- Questions

1. Be/Auxiliary Verb Questions

HACKERS PRACTICE   p.54

01 Ⓑ   02 Ⓒ   03 Ⓑ   04 Ⓐ   05 Ⓒ

01 Auxiliary Verb Question Am

Do you need help with your research project?

Ⓐ The project is due tomorrow.
Ⓥ Yes, I could use some assistance.
Ⓒ Yes, I think I can handle it on my own.
Ⓓ The research lab isn't open now.

assistance [əsístəns] 도움, 지원

연구 프로젝트에 도움이 필요한가요?
Ⓐ 프로젝트가 내일 마감이에요.
Ⓥ 네, 도움이 필요해요.
Ⓒ 네, 혼자서 처리할 수 있다고 생각해요.
Ⓓ 연구실이 지금 열려있지 않아요.

02 Be Verb Question Au

Isn't the bookstore having a sale this week?

Ⓐ I'm looking for some used textbooks.
Ⓑ Yes, they were really expensive.
Ⓥ We should check their website.
Ⓓ It is near the city library.

서점이 이번 주에 할인하고 있지 않나요?
Ⓐ 저는 중고 교재들을 찾고 있어요.
Ⓑ 네, 그것들은 정말 비쌌어요.

☑ 그들의 웹사이트를 확인해봐야겠어요.
Ⓓ 시립 도서관 근처에 있어요.

03 Be Verb Question   🎧 En

Is the assignment due tomorrow?

Ⓐ Yes, it did.
☑ I'm not so sure.
Ⓒ Include at least five sources.
Ⓓ No, you should turn it in tomorrow.

assignment [əsáinmənt] 과제, 숙제   turn in 제출하다

과제가 내일 마감인가요?
Ⓐ 네, 그랬어요.
☑ 확실하지 않아요.
Ⓒ 최소 다섯 개의 출처를 포함하세요.
Ⓓ 아니요, 내일 제출해야 해요.

04 Auxiliary Verb Question   🎧 Am

Does the conference start on Friday?

☑ It begins on Thursday.
Ⓑ The registration fee is 150 dollars.
Ⓒ Yes, it has been canceled.
Ⓓ Are you available on the weekend?

registration fee 등록비

컨퍼런스가 금요일에 시작하나요?
☑ 목요일에 시작해요.
Ⓑ 등록비가 150달러예요.
Ⓒ 네, 취소되었어요.
Ⓓ 주말에 시간이 있나요?

05 Be Verb Question   🎧 En

Were you able to access the online course materials?

Ⓐ No, I downloaded every material.
Ⓑ Our professor required three textbooks.
☑ No, the website was under maintenance.
Ⓓ The library was inaccessible after 10 P.M.

material [mətíəriəl] 자료, 재료, 소재
maintenance [méintənəns] 유지, 관리, 생활비

온라인 강의 자료에 접근할 수 있었나요?
Ⓐ 아니요, 모든 자료를 다운로드했어요.
Ⓑ 우리 교수님은 세 권의 교재를 요구했어요.
☑ 아니요, 웹사이트가 점검 중이었어요.
Ⓓ 도서관은 오후 10시 이후에 접근할 수 없었어요.

HACKERS TEST   p.56

01 Ⓓ	02 Ⓐ	03 Ⓓ	04 Ⓑ	05 Ⓐ
06 Ⓒ	07 Ⓒ	08 Ⓑ	09 Ⓑ	10 Ⓐ
11 Ⓐ	12 Ⓑ	13 Ⓒ	14 Ⓒ	15 Ⓓ
16 Ⓒ	17 Ⓐ	18 Ⓒ	19 Ⓐ	20 Ⓐ

01 Be Verb Question   🎧 Am

Are you planning to attend the guest lecture?

Ⓐ Yes, I'm going on vacation.
Ⓑ Did you check the attendance?
Ⓒ It takes place in the auditorium.
☑ I've already registered online.

attend [əténd] 참석하다   guest lecture 초청 강연
attendance [əténdəns] 출석
auditorium [ɔ̀:ditɔ́:riəm] 강당, 대강의실

초청 강연에 참석할 계획인가요?
Ⓐ 네, 휴가를 갈 거예요.
Ⓑ 출석을 확인했나요?
Ⓒ 그것은 강당에서 열려요.
☑ 이미 온라인으로 등록했어요.

02 Auxiliary Verb Question   🎧 Nz

Should we hire additional staff for the project?

☑ I'd recommend it.
Ⓑ The staff lounge is closed.
Ⓒ Are you applying for the position?
Ⓓ Some additional office supplies.

additional [ədíʃənl] 추가적인   apply for ~에 지원하다
office supply 사무용품

프로젝트를 위해 추가 직원을 고용해야 할까요?
☑ 추천하겠어요.
Ⓑ 직원 휴게실이 문을 닫았어요.
Ⓒ 그 직책에 지원하고 있나요?
Ⓓ 일부 추가 사무용품이요.

03 Be Verb Question   🎧 Am

Were you able to register for all your classes?

Ⓐ The semester ends in June.
Ⓑ The registration desk is downstairs.
Ⓒ I should clear my schedule.
☑ The psychology course was full.

register [rédʒistər] 등록하다; 음역
psychology [saikɑ́:lədʒi] 심리학

모든 수업에 등록할 수 있었나요?
Ⓐ 학기가 6월에 끝나요.
Ⓑ 등록 데스크는 아래층에 있어요.

ⓒ 저는 일정을 비워야 해요.
☑ 심리학 강의가 만석이었어요.

04 Auxiliary Verb Question 🔊 En

Didn't you attend the quarterly budget meeting?

Ⓐ The financial report is ready.
☑ Yes, but I had to leave early.
ⓒ Yes, it's scheduled for tomorrow.
Ⓓ Actually, due to a lack of funding.

quarterly [kwɔ́:rtərli] 분기별, 분기의   lack [læk] 부족, 결핍

분기별 예산 회의에 참석하지 않았나요?
Ⓐ 재무 보고서가 준비되어 있어요.
☑ 네, 하지만 일찍 떠나야 했어요.
ⓒ 네, 내일로 예정되어 있어요.
Ⓓ 사실, 자금 부족 때문이에요.

05 Be Verb Question 🔊 Nz

Is this the first time you've been to this museum?

☑ Yes, I've been looking forward to visiting it.
Ⓑ Yes, the renovation will be finished next month.
ⓒ No, the visitor center is on the ground level.
Ⓓ No, I think the paintings are in the east wing.

look forward to ~을 기대하다   ground level 1층

이 박물관에 오는 것이 처음인가요?
☑ 네, 방문하기를 기대하고 있었어요.
Ⓑ 네, 보수가 다음 달에 완료될 거예요.
ⓒ 아니요, 방문자 센터는 1층에 있어요.
Ⓓ 아니요, 그림들이 동관에 있다고 생각해요.

06 Auxiliary Verb Question 🔊 Am

Do they serve vegetarian options here?

Ⓐ The cafeteria opens at 7 A.M.
Ⓑ I need to return this tray.
☑ Let's ask for the menu.
Ⓓ The new diner downtown.

vegetarian [vèdʒətɛ́əriən] 채식의; 채식주의자

여기서 채식 메뉴를 제공하나요?
Ⓐ 카페테리아가 오전 7시에 열어요.
Ⓑ 이 쟁반을 반납해야 해요.
☑ 메뉴를 요청해 봅시다.
Ⓓ 시내의 새로운 식당이요.

07 Auxiliary Verb Question 🔊 En

Has the professor announced the exam schedule?

Ⓐ The exam will cover many chapters.
Ⓑ You need to bring your student ID.
☑ I haven't heard anything yet.
Ⓓ Are you going to drop the course?

announce [ənáuns] 발표하다, 공지하다

교수님이 시험 일정을 발표했나요?
Ⓐ 시험이 많은 챕터를 다룰 거예요.
Ⓑ 학생증을 가져와야 해요.
☑ 아직 아무것도 듣지 못했어요.
Ⓓ 과정을 수강 취소할 건가요?

08 Auxiliary Verb Question 🔊 Am

Can I use the printer in the library?

Ⓐ Ten copies, please.
☑ What do you need it for?
ⓒ I'm writing a research paper.
Ⓓ Books must be returned by Friday.

research paper 연구 논문

도서관에서 프린터를 사용할 수 있나요?
Ⓐ 열 부 부탁드려요.
☑ 무엇을 위해 필요한가요?
ⓒ 연구 논문을 쓰고 있어요.
Ⓓ 책들은 금요일까지 반납되어야 해요.

09 Auxiliary Verb Question 🔊 En

Don't you think we should reschedule the client meeting?

Ⓐ Customer feedback is always valuable.
☑ Yes, some people can't attend tomorrow.
ⓒ I prepared all the presentation slides.
Ⓓ No, the meeting room is on the fifth floor.

valuable [vǽljuəbl] 가치가 있는, 귀중한

고객 회의 일정을 변경해야 한다고 생각하지 않으세요?
Ⓐ 고객 피드백은 항상 가치가 있어요.
☑ 네, 일부 사람들이 내일 참석할 수 없어요.
ⓒ 모든 발표 슬라이드를 준비했어요.
Ⓓ 아니요, 회의실이 5층에 있어요.

10 Be Verb Question 🔊 Am

Isn't the biology exam scheduled for Friday?

☑ No, it has been moved to Thursday.
Ⓑ No, I didn't study biology in high school.
ⓒ The science building is across from the library.
Ⓓ Dr. Miller is a renowned biologist.

renowned [rináund] 유명한, 저명한

생물학 시험이 금요일로 예정되어 있지 않나요?
☑ 아니요, 목요일로 옮겨졌어요.
Ⓑ 아니요, 고등학교에서 생물학을 공부하지 않았어요.

Ⓒ 과학관은 도서관 맞은편에 있어요.
Ⓓ Miller 박사님은 유명한 생물학자예요

11 Auxiliary Verb Question　　　🔊 Au

Have you visited the new theater yet?

☑ Yes, I went to see a play there.
Ⓑ No, the movie starts at 8:30 tonight.
Ⓒ No, it wasn't as great as I expected.
Ⓓ Yes, I prefer watching films at home.

새 극장에 가봤나요?
☑ 네, 거기에 연극을 보러 갔어요.
Ⓑ 아니요, 영화가 오늘 밤 8시 30분에 시작해요.
Ⓒ 아니요, 기대했던 만큼 훌륭하지 않았어요.
Ⓓ 네, 집에서 영화 보는 걸 선호해요.

12 Be Verb Question　　　🔊 En

So your flight was delayed because of the weather?

Ⓐ The plane is landing soon.
☑ Yes, it was so frustrating.
Ⓒ Luggage weight limit is 23 kilograms.
Ⓓ I'm taking the train instead.

frustrating [frʌ́streitiŋ] 좌절스러운, 답답한

당신의 항공편이 날씨 때문에 지연된 건가요?
Ⓐ 비행기가 곧 착륙해요.
☑ 네, 정말 좌절스러웠어요.
Ⓒ 짐 중량 제한이 23kg예요.
Ⓓ 저는 대신 기차를 탈 거예요.

13 Auxiliary Verb Question　　　🔊 Nz

Does Professor Chen accept late assignments?

Ⓐ I was assigned a different task.
Ⓑ Prepare for the acceptance speech.
☑ Only if you have a valid medical excuse.
Ⓓ The office is closing early today.

valid [vǽlid] 유효한　　excuse [ikskjúːz] 사유; 용서하다

Chen 교수님은 늦은 과제를 받아들이시나요?
Ⓐ 다른 과업을 배정받았어요.
Ⓑ 수상 소감을 준비하세요.
☑ 유효한 의학적 사유가 있는 경우에만요.
Ⓓ 사무실이 오늘 일찍 문을 닫아요.

14 Be Verb Question　　　🔊 Am

Was the client satisfied with our proposal?

Ⓐ The meeting was last week.
Ⓑ I've worked with the client for years.
☑ Actually, some revisions were requested.
Ⓓ The proposal included three price options.

revision [rivíʒən] 수정

고객이 우리 제안서에 만족했나요?
Ⓐ 회의가 지난주에 있었어요.
Ⓑ 저는 그 고객과 수년간 일했어요.
☑ 사실, 일부 수정이 요청되었어요.
Ⓓ 제안서에 세 가지 가격 선택지가 포함되어 있었어요.

15 Auxiliary Verb Question　　　🔊 Au

Did the department approve our funding request?

Ⓐ Someone from the financial department.
Ⓑ When is the department meeting scheduled?
Ⓒ We requested new equipment.
☑ I think they're still reviewing it.

approve [əprúːv] 승인하다, 찬성하다

그 부서가 우리의 자금 지원 요청을 승인했나요?
Ⓐ 재무부에서 온 누군가요.
Ⓑ 부서 회의가 언제 예정되어 있나요?
Ⓒ 우리가 새 장비를 요청했어요.
☑ 아직 검토 중인 것 같아요.

16 Be Verb Question　　　🔊 Am

Isn't this the bus going to the Serenity Park?

Ⓐ No, the park has many facilities.
Ⓑ Yes, the fare is the same for all routes.
☑ No, you are on the wrong one.
Ⓓ Yes, I usually take the subway.

facility [fəsíləti] 시설, 설비

이것이 Serenity 공원으로 가는 버스가 아닌가요?
Ⓐ 아니요, 공원에 많은 시설이 있어요.
Ⓑ 네, 모든 노선의 요금이 같아요.
☑ 아니요, 잘못 탔어요.
Ⓓ 네, 저는 보통 지하철을 타요.

17 Be Verb Question　　　🔊 En

Is there a conference room available for our meeting?

Ⓐ Yes, I'd be happy to help you.
Ⓑ The meeting was informative.
☑ Let's check the reservation system.
Ⓓ I've prepared all the documents.

informative [infɔ́ːrmətiv] 유용한, 유익한

우리 회의를 위해 이용 가능한 회의실이 있나요?
Ⓐ 네, 기꺼이 도와드리겠어요.
Ⓑ 회의가 유용했어요.
☑ 예약 시스템을 확인해 봅시다.

Ⓓ 모든 서류를 준비했어요.

18 Auxiliary Verb Question　🔊 Au

Didn't the company send an email about the policy change?

Ⓐ No, it was sent to all employees.
Ⓑ No, the change begins tomorrow.
✓Ⓒ I don't think I received one.
Ⓓ I prefer phone calls to emails.

policy[páləsi] 정책, 규정

회사가 정책 변경에 대한 이메일을 보내지 않았나요?
Ⓐ 아니요, 모든 직원들에게 보냈어요.
Ⓑ 아니요, 변경이 내일 시작해요.
✓Ⓒ 저는 그것을 받지 못한 것 같아요.
Ⓓ 저는 이메일보다 전화 통화를 선호해요.

19 Auxiliary Verb Question　🔊 Am

Don't you have class in the afternoon?

✓Ⓐ My professor is out this week.
Ⓑ Yes, the classroom is locked.
Ⓒ I already finished my assignment.
Ⓓ The morning courses are always crowded.

오후에 수업이 없나요?
✓Ⓐ 제 교수님이 이번 주에 부재중이에요.
Ⓑ 네, 교실이 잠겨 있어요.
Ⓒ 이미 과제를 끝냈어요.
Ⓓ 오전 강의들은 항상 붐벼요.

20 Auxiliary Verb Question　🔊 En

Did you read the article for tomorrow's discussion?

✓Ⓐ I'm about halfway through it.
Ⓑ The discussion will be held in Room 302.
Ⓒ Peter suggested three scholarly sources.
Ⓓ Reading is my favorite hobby.

scholarly[skάlərli] 학술적인, 전문적인

내일 토론을 위한 기사를 읽었나요?
✓Ⓐ 중간 정도까지 읽었어요.
Ⓑ 토론이 302호실에서 열릴 거예요.
Ⓒ Peter가 세 개의 학술 자료를 제안했어요.
Ⓓ 독서는 제가 가장 좋아하는 취미예요.

2. Tag Questions

HACKERS PRACTICE　p.59

01 Ⓐ　02 Ⓑ　03 Ⓒ　04 Ⓓ　05 Ⓑ

01 Tag Question　🔊 Am

The weather is really nice today, isn't it?

✓Ⓐ Yes, perfect for a walk outside.
Ⓑ What is your favorite season?
Ⓒ Yes, this heat is unbearable.
Ⓓ I'm not sure whether I will attend.

unbearable[ʌnbέərəbəl] 견딜 수 없는, 참기 어려운

오늘 날씨가 정말 좋네요, 그렇지 않나요?
✓Ⓐ 네, 밖에서 산책하기에 완벽해요.
Ⓑ 가장 좋아하는 계절이 무엇인가요?
Ⓒ 네, 이 더위는 견딜 수 없어요.
Ⓓ 저는 참석할지 확실하지 않아요.

02 Tag Question　🔊 En

Ms. Lawson wasn't in the office yesterday, was she?

Ⓐ Her assistant quit last week.
✓Ⓑ She called in sick.
Ⓒ She works late on Tuesdays.
Ⓓ Her office is on the second floor.

assistant[əsístənt] 조수, 보조

Ms. Lawson은 어제 사무실에 없었죠, 그렇죠?
Ⓐ 그녀의 조수가 지난주에 그만뒀어요.
✓Ⓑ 그녀는 병가를 냈어요.
Ⓒ 화요일에 늦게 일해요.
Ⓓ 그녀의 사무실은 2층에 있어요.

03 Tag Question　🔊 Nz

This coffee shop makes the best pastries, doesn't it?

Ⓐ Would you like some iced coffee?
Ⓑ It's open from 9 A.M. to 10 P.M.
✓Ⓒ I haven't had the chance to try them.
Ⓓ How much did you pay for that?

이 커피숍이 가장 좋은 페이스트리를 만들어요, 그렇지 않나요?
Ⓐ 아이스 커피를 드릴까요?
Ⓑ 오전 9시부터 오후 10시까지 열어요.
✓Ⓒ 시도해볼 기회가 없었어요.
Ⓓ 그것에 얼마를 지불했나요?

04 Tag Question 🔊 En

Campus shuttle buses run every 15 minutes, don't they?

Ⓐ The blue line goes downtown.
Ⓑ It is in front of the student center.
Ⓒ No, I missed the last one yesterday.
☑ Yes, but only on the weekdays.

in front of ~ 앞에

캠퍼스 셔틀버스는 15분마다 운행하죠, 그렇지 않나요?
Ⓐ 블루 라인은 시내로 가요.
Ⓑ 학생 센터 앞에 있어요.
Ⓒ 아니요, 어제 마지막 버스를 놓쳤어요.
☑ 네, 하지만 평일에만요.

05 Tag Question 🔊 Am

You submitted your application last week, didn't you?

Ⓐ I am free next weekend.
☑ I needed some more time.
Ⓒ This form is complicated.
Ⓓ Where is the admissions office?

complicated [kámpləkèitid] 복잡한, 뒤얽힌

지난주에 지원서를 제출했죠, 그렇지 않나요?
Ⓐ 다음 주말에 시간이 있어요.
☑ 더 많은 시간이 필요했어요.
Ⓒ 이 양식은 복잡해요.
Ⓓ 입학처가 어디에 있나요?

HACKERS TEST p.60

01 Ⓐ	02 Ⓑ	03 Ⓒ	04 Ⓑ	05 Ⓑ
06 Ⓑ	07 Ⓒ	08 Ⓓ	09 Ⓑ	10 Ⓐ
11 Ⓐ	12 Ⓑ	13 Ⓒ	14 Ⓓ	15 Ⓑ
16 Ⓑ	17 Ⓒ	18 Ⓑ	19 Ⓓ	20 Ⓐ

01 Tag Question 🔊 Au

You've never been to the national museum, have you?

☑ I went there last month.
Ⓑ It's next to City Hall.
Ⓒ No, they close at 5 P.M.
Ⓓ Some art exhibitions.

exhibition [èksəbíʃən] 전시회, 표출

국립 박물관에 한 번도 가본 적이 없죠, 그렇죠?
☑ 지난 달에 거기에 갔어요.
Ⓑ 그것은 시청 옆에 있어요.
Ⓒ 아니요, 오후 5시에 문을 닫아요.
Ⓓ 몇몇 미술 전시회요.

02 Tag Question 🔊 Am

The professors have posted the exam results, haven't they?

Ⓐ The final exam was difficult.
☑ No, they'll be up tomorrow.
Ⓒ No, I couldn't study that much.
Ⓓ The classroom is on the third floor.

교수님들이 시험 결과를 게시했죠, 그렇지 않나요?
Ⓐ 기말시험이 어려웠어요.
☑ 아니요, 내일 올라올 거예요.
Ⓒ 아니요, 그렇게 많이 공부할 수 없었어요.
Ⓓ 교실이 3층에 있어요.

03 Tag Question 🔊 En

You weren't at the orientation meeting, were you?

Ⓐ The meeting will begin at noon.
Ⓑ It lasted about three hours.
☑ I had a doctor's appointment.
Ⓓ The meeting room is empty.

last [læst] 지속되다; 마지막의, 지난

오리엔테이션 모임에 없었죠, 그렇죠?
Ⓐ 모임이 정오에 시작될 거예요.
Ⓑ 대략 3시간 지속되었어요.
☑ 병원 예약이 있었어요.
Ⓓ 회의실이 비어 있어요.

04 Tag Question 🔊 Nz

You finished your research paper early, didn't you?

Ⓐ No, it didn't take that long.
☑ Yes, I submitted it yesterday.
Ⓒ The library has research materials.
Ⓓ Is the deadline going to be extended?

submit [səbmít] 제출하다

연구 논문을 일찍 끝냈죠, 그렇지 않나요?
Ⓐ 아니요, 그렇게 오래 걸리지 않았어요.
☑ 네, 어제 제출했어요.
Ⓒ 도서관에 연구 자료가 있어요.
Ⓓ 마감일이 연장될 건가요?

05 Tag Question

You've seen that new movie at the cinema, haven't you?

Ⓐ Are the tickets sold out?
✓Ⓑ I watched it last weekend.
Ⓒ The cinema is downtown.
Ⓓ I like watching horror movies.

sold out 매진된, 품절의

영화관에서 그 새 영화를 봤죠, 그렇지 않나요?
Ⓐ 표가 매진되었나요?
✓Ⓑ 지난 주말에 봤어요.
Ⓒ 영화관은 시내에 있어요.
Ⓓ 저는 공포 영화 보는 걸 좋아해요.

06 Tag Question

We have class in Room 302, don't we?

Ⓐ The building opens at 8 A.M.
✓Ⓑ I think it's in Room 305 today.
Ⓒ Professor Kim teaches history.
Ⓓ The class started last week.

우리는 302호실에서 수업이 있죠, 그렇지 않나요?
Ⓐ 건물이 오전 8시에 열어요.
✓Ⓑ 오늘은 305호실인 것 같아요.
Ⓒ Kim 교수님이 역사를 가르치세요.
Ⓓ 수업이 지난주에 시작되었어요.

07 Tag Question

That restaurant doesn't take reservations, does it?

Ⓐ The food is quite expensive there.
Ⓑ No, I'm going to order the special.
✓Ⓒ Actually, they started accepting them.
Ⓓ Yes, it's on Main Street.

reservation [rèzərvéiʃən] 예약

그 식당은 예약을 받지 않죠, 그렇죠?
Ⓐ 거기 음식이 꽤 비싸요.
Ⓑ 아니요, 특별 요리를 주문할 거예요.
✓Ⓒ 사실은, 예약을 받기 시작했어요.
Ⓓ 네, Main가에 있어요.

08 Tag Question

The post office is closed on Sundays, isn't it?

Ⓐ Did you see Nina's posting?
Ⓑ I need to mail this package.
Ⓒ I bought a stamp booklet.
✓Ⓓ Yes, we should go tomorrow.

우체국이 일요일에 문을 닫죠, 그렇지 않나요?
Ⓐ Nina의 게시물을 봤나요?
Ⓑ 이 소포를 우편으로 보내야 해요.
Ⓒ 저는 우표첩을 샀어요.
✓Ⓓ 네, 내일 가야겠어요.

09 Tag Question

The library closes at 10 P.M., doesn't it?

Ⓐ You need your student ID card.
Ⓑ I borrowed three books.
✓Ⓒ Actually, it's open until midnight.
Ⓓ The café is on the first floor.

midnight [mídnàit] 자정, 한밤중

도서관이 오후 10시에 문을 닫죠, 그렇지 않나요?
Ⓐ 학생증이 필요해요.
Ⓑ 저는 책 세 권을 빌렸어요.
✓Ⓒ 사실은, 자정까지 열려있어요.
Ⓓ 카페가 1층에 있어요.

10 Tag Question

You've received my report by email, haven't you?

✓Ⓐ Do you mean your expense report?
Ⓑ The Internet is working fine.
Ⓒ Did you have any feedback?
Ⓓ I'll send you a copy now.

expense [ikspéns] 경비, 비용

이메일로 제 보고서를 받았죠, 그렇지 않나요?
✓Ⓐ 경비 보고서를 말씀하시는 건가요?
Ⓑ 인터넷이 잘 작동해요.
Ⓒ 피드백이 있나요?
Ⓓ 한 부를 지금 보낼게요.

11 Tag Question

You haven't registered for next semester yet, have you?

✓Ⓐ I did it online last night.
Ⓑ The semester ends in May.
Ⓒ Registration fees will increase soon.
Ⓓ My advisor is out of town next week.

semester [siméstər] 학기

다음 학기에 아직 등록하지 않았죠, 그렇죠?
✓Ⓐ 어젯밤에 온라인으로 했어요.
Ⓑ 학기가 5월에 끝나요.
Ⓒ 등록비가 곧 오를 거예요.
Ⓓ 제 지도교수님이 다음 주에 외지에 계세요.

12 Tag Question 🔊 Am

The bus leaves at 6:30 P.M., doesn't it?

Ⓐ I'll meet you at the station.
Ⓑ No, it departs at 7 P.M. ✓
Ⓒ The ticket costs five dollars.
Ⓓ I prefer taking the train.

depart [dipá:rt] 출발하다, 떠나다

버스가 오후 6시 30분에 떠나죠, 그렇지 않나요?
Ⓐ 당신을 정거장에서 만날게요.
Ⓑ 아니요, 오후 7시에 출발해요. ✓
Ⓒ 표가 5달러예요.
Ⓓ 저는 기차를 타는 걸 선호해요.

13 Tag Question 🔊 En

That presentation isn't due until next week, is it?

Ⓐ Not everyone was present.
Ⓑ The professor speaks clearly.
Ⓒ We do have more time. ✓
Ⓓ Your slides look great.

present [préznt] 참석하다, 발표하다

그 발표는 다음 주까지 마감이 아니죠, 그렇죠?
Ⓐ 모든 사람이 참석하지는 않았어요.
Ⓑ 교수님은 명확하게 말씀하세요.
Ⓒ 우리에게 시간이 더 있어요. ✓
Ⓓ 당신의 슬라이드가 훌륭해 보여요.

14 Tag Question 🔊 Am

You don't mind giving me a ride, do you?

Ⓐ Where is your car key?
Ⓑ My office is far from here.
Ⓒ Yes, it's in the back seat.
Ⓓ I'm heading that way anyway. ✓

give a ride 태워 주다

저를 태워주는 것을 꺼리지 않으시죠, 그렇죠?
Ⓐ 당신의 자동차 열쇠가 어디에 있나요?
Ⓑ 제 사무실은 여기서 멀어요.
Ⓒ 네, 뒷좌석에 있어요.
Ⓓ 저도 어차피 그쪽으로 가요. ✓

15 Tag Question 🔊 En

The new software update hasn't been installed yet, has it?

Ⓐ IT scheduled it for tomorrow. ✓
Ⓑ The computers are quite new.
Ⓒ I prefer the older version.
Ⓓ Our team needs training.

새 소프트웨어 업데이트가 아직 설치되지 않았죠, 그렇죠?
Ⓐ IT부서가 내일로 예정했어요. ✓
Ⓑ 컴퓨터들이 꽤 새로워요.
Ⓒ 저는 이전 버전을 선호해요.
Ⓓ 우리 팀에게 교육이 필요해요.

16 Tag Question Au

The quarterly report should include last month's data, shouldn't it?

Ⓐ The deadline is next week.
Ⓑ All three months need to be covered. ✓
Ⓒ Did you already email it to me?
Ⓓ The numbers looked promising.

promising [prámisiŋ] 유망한, 전망이 좋은

분기 보고서에 지난 달 데이터가 포함되어야 하죠, 그렇지 않나요?
Ⓐ 마감일이 다음 주예요.
Ⓑ 3개월 모두 다뤄져야 해요. ✓
Ⓒ 이미 제게 이메일로 보냈나요?
Ⓓ 숫자들이 유망해 보였어요.

17 Tag Question 🔊 Am

You've worked with this supplier before, haven't you?

Ⓐ Yes, it's my first time.
Ⓑ The contract expires next month.
Ⓒ Yes, they're very reliable. ✓
Ⓓ Let me contact them tomorrow.

contract [kántrækt] 계약; 수축하다

이 공급업체와 이전에 일해봤죠, 그렇지 않나요?
Ⓐ 네, 처음이에요.
Ⓑ 계약이 다음 달에 만료돼요.
Ⓒ 네, 그들은 매우 믿을 만해요. ✓
Ⓓ 내일 그들에게 연락해 보겠어요.

18 Tag Question 🔊 En

Professor Johnson canceled office hours today, didn't she?

Ⓐ Her office is in Taylor Hall.
Ⓑ No, she's available from 2 to 4. ✓
Ⓒ I need to ask her about the exam.
Ⓓ Why did you cancel it?

available [əvéiləbl] 시간이 있는, 이용 가능한

Johnson 교수님이 오늘 상담 시간을 취소하셨죠, 그렇지 않나요?
Ⓐ 그녀의 사무실은 Taylor Hall에 있어요.
Ⓑ 아니요, 2시부터 4시까지 시간이 있으세요. ✓
Ⓒ 그녀에게 시험에 대해 물어봐야 해요.
Ⓓ 그것을 왜 취소했나요?

19 Tag Question 🔊 Au

That project wasn't as difficult as expected, was it?

Ⓐ The client was quite upset.
Ⓑ When is the deadline?
Ⓒ Nobody expects it.
☑ We finished ahead of schedule.

ahead of ~보다 앞서서, ~보다 빨리

그 프로젝트가 예상했던 만큼 어렵지 않았죠, 그렇죠?
Ⓐ 고객이 꽤 화났어요.
Ⓑ 마감일이 언제인가요?
Ⓒ 아무도 그것을 기대하지 않아요.
☑ 저희는 일정보다 앞서서 끝냈어요.

20 Tag Question 🔊 Am

You've taken Professor Wilson's class before, haven't you?

☑ His lectures are really engaging.
Ⓑ The classroom is in the engineering building.
Ⓒ Registration opens next Monday.
Ⓓ I need to check my schedule.

engaging [ingéidʒiŋ] 흥미로운, 매력적인

Wilson 교수님의 수업을 이전에 수강해봤죠, 그렇지 않나요?
☑ 그분의 강의는 정말로 흥미로워요.
Ⓑ 교실은 공학관에 있어요.
Ⓒ 등록은 다음 주 월요일에 열려요.
Ⓓ 제 일정을 확인해야 해요.

3. Alternative Questions

HACKERS PRACTICE p.63

| 01 Ⓑ | 02 Ⓒ | 03 Ⓓ | 04 Ⓑ | 05 Ⓒ |

01 Alternative Question 🔊 Am

Would you like to join us for dinner or meet up later?

Ⓐ At the department store.
☑ I'll meet you after dinner.
Ⓒ They serve Italian food.
Ⓓ What time is the movie?

meet up 만나다, 놀다

저녁 식사에 합류하시거나 나중에 만날래요?
Ⓐ 백화점에서요.
☑ 저녁 식사 후에 만날게요.
Ⓒ 그들은 이탈리아 음식을 제공해요.
Ⓓ 영화가 몇 시인가요?

02 Alternative Question 🔊 Au

Do you prefer in-person classes or online?

Ⓐ The campus is nearby.
Ⓑ Classes start next week.
☑ I find online more convenient.
Ⓓ The professor is very strict.

nearby [nìərbái] 근처의, 가까운
convenient [kənvíːnjənt] 편리한

대면 수업을 선호하나요, 아니면 온라인을 선호하나요?
Ⓐ 캠퍼스가 근처에 있어요.
Ⓑ 수업이 다음 주에 시작해요.
☑ 온라인이 더 편리하다고 생각해요.
Ⓓ 교수님이 매우 엄격하세요.

03 Alternative Question 🔊 Am

Would you rather take the subway or drive to the conference?

Ⓐ I'll bring the presentation files.
Ⓑ That's my driver's license.
Ⓒ The conference starts at 9 A.M.
☑ I prefer public transportation.

conference [kánfərəns] 회의

회의에 지하철을 타고 가시겠어요, 아니면 운전해서 가시겠어요?
Ⓐ 발표 파일들을 가져올게요.
Ⓑ 그것은 제 운전면허증이에요.
Ⓒ 회의가 오전 9시에 시작해요.
☑ 대중교통을 선호해요.

04 Alternative Question 🔊 En

Do you prefer coffee or tea?

Ⓐ Yes, thank you.
☑ I don't mind.
Ⓒ I think I do.
Ⓓ The café closes at 5 P.M.

커피를 선호하나요, 아니면 차를 선호하나요?
Ⓐ 네, 감사합니다.
☑ 상관없어요.
Ⓒ 그렇다고 생각해요.
Ⓓ 카페가 오후 5시에 문을 닫아요.

05 Alternative Question 🔊 Am

Is the team meeting today or tomorrow?

Ⓐ I'll prepare the agenda.
Ⓑ The room is booked for an hour.

✓ It's been rescheduled to next week.
Ⓓ Let's review what was discussed.

review [rivjú:] 검토하다; 후기

팀 회의가 오늘인가요, 아니면 내일인가요?
Ⓐ 안건을 준비하겠어요.
Ⓑ 방이 한 시간 동안 예약되어 있어요.
✓ 다음 주로 일정이 변경되었어요.
Ⓓ 논의된 것을 검토해 봅시다.

HACKERS TEST

p.64

01 Ⓒ	02 Ⓑ	03 Ⓐ	04 Ⓑ	05 Ⓓ
06 Ⓓ	07 Ⓒ	08 Ⓐ	09 Ⓑ	10 Ⓑ
11 Ⓑ	12 Ⓒ	13 Ⓑ	14 Ⓔ	15 Ⓓ
16 Ⓐ	17 Ⓒ	18 Ⓒ	19 Ⓓ	20 Ⓐ

01 Alternative Question ♪ Nz

Would you rather study at the library or at home?
Ⓐ I usually go on weekends.
Ⓑ The library closes at 9 P.M.
✓ I feel more comfortable at home.
Ⓓ My textbooks are expensive.

comfortable [kʌ́mfərtəbl] 편안한

도서관에서 공부하는 것을 선호하나요, 아니면 집에서 공부하는 것을 선호하나요?
Ⓐ 저는 보통 주말에 가요.
Ⓑ 도서관이 오후 9시에 문을 닫아요.
✓ 집에서 더 편안하게 느껴요.
Ⓓ 제 교재들은 비싸요.

02 Alternative Question ♪ En

Would you prefer working alone or as a team?
Ⓐ The deadline is next Friday.
✓ Teamwork is more efficient.
Ⓒ The report needs revision.
Ⓓ Our manager approved it.

efficient [ifíʃənt] 효율적인, 능률적인

혼자 일하는 것을 선호하나요, 아니면 팀으로 일하는 것을 선호하나요?
Ⓐ 마감일이 다음 주 금요일이에요.
✓ 팀워크가 더 효율적이에요.
Ⓒ 보고서에 수정이 필요해요.
Ⓓ 우리 관리자가 승인했어요.

03 Alternative Question ♪ Am

Would you prefer to meet in my office or yours?
✓ Let's use the conference room instead.
Ⓑ The meeting starts at noon.
Ⓒ I'll bring the presentation slides.
Ⓓ Your report was excellent.

noon [nu:n] 정오

제 사무실에서 만나는 걸 선호하나요, 아니면 당신 사무실에서 만나는 걸 선호하나요?
✓ 대신 회의실을 사용해요.
Ⓑ 회의가 정오에 시작해요.
Ⓒ 발표 슬라이드들을 가져올게요.
Ⓓ 당신의 보고서는 훌륭했어요.

04 Alternative Question ♪ Nz

Would you rather take the bus or walk to campus?
Ⓐ The campus is beautiful.
✓ I'd rather walk when it's nice out.
Ⓒ The bus arrives every ten minutes.
Ⓓ My class has been canceled.

캠퍼스에 버스를 타고 가는 걸 선호하나요, 아니면 걸어가는 걸 선호하나요?
Ⓐ 캠퍼스가 아름다워요.
✓ 날씨가 좋을 때는 걷는 걸 선호해요.
Ⓒ 버스가 10분마다 도착해요.
Ⓓ 제 수업은 취소되었어요.

05 Alternative Question ♪ Am

Shall we take the subway or a taxi to the museum?
Ⓐ The museum opens at 10 A.M.
Ⓑ The exhibit ends next month.
Ⓒ The artwork was interesting.
✓ The subway will be faster.

exhibit [igzíbit] 전시; 보여주다, 설명하다

박물관에 지하철을 타고 갈까요, 아니면 택시를 타고 갈까요?
Ⓐ 박물관은 오전 10시에 열어요.
Ⓑ 전시가 다음 달에 끝나요.
Ⓒ 예술 작품이 흥미로웠어요.
✓ 지하철이 더 빠를 거예요.

06 Alternative Question ♪ En

Would you prefer the window or aisle seat?
Ⓐ The flight is three hours long.
Ⓑ The plane has already departed.
Ⓒ My luggage is overweight.
✓ I always choose the window.

aisle[ail] 통로, 복도
overweight[òùvərwéit] 초과 중량의, 과체중의

창문 좌석을 선호하나요, 아니면 통로 좌석을 선호하나요?
Ⓐ 비행 시간이 3시간이에요.
Ⓑ 비행기는 이미 출발했어요.
Ⓒ 제 짐이 초과 중량이에요.
☑ 저는 항상 창문 좌석을 선택해요.

07 Alternative Question [Nz]

Which club are you more interested in, debate or writing?

Ⓐ We meet on a monthly basis.
Ⓑ Yes, it's written in French.
☑ Neither seems suitable for me.
Ⓓ He's the captain of the debate team.

suitable[súːtəbl] 적합한, 적당한

어느 동아리에 더 관심이 있나요, 토론 동아리인가요, 아니면 글쓰기 동아리인가요?
Ⓐ 우리는 월별로 만나요.
Ⓑ 네, 그것은 프랑스어로 쓰여 있어요.
☑ 둘 다 저에게 적합하지 않은 것 같아요.
Ⓓ 그는 토론 팀의 주장이에요.

08 Alternative Question [En]

Should we order pizza or sandwiches for lunch?

☑ Is there another option?
Ⓑ Yes, I'm allergic to nuts.
Ⓒ Outside the cafeteria.
Ⓓ I didn't eat any lunch.

allergic[ələ́ːrdʒik] 알레르기가 있는

점심으로 피자를 주문할까요, 아니면 샌드위치를 주문할까요?
☑ 다른 선택지가 있나요?
Ⓑ 네, 저는 견과류에 알레르기가 있어요.
Ⓒ 구내식당 밖에요.
Ⓓ 저는 점심 식사를 하지 않았어요.

09 Alternative Question [Am]

Would you rather present your project today or next week?

Ⓐ The projector isn't working.
☑ I need more time to prepare.
Ⓒ Professor Kim graded our papers.
Ⓓ The deadline was yesterday.

grade[greid] 채점하다; 성적, 학년

프로젝트를 오늘 발표하는 걸 선호하나요, 아니면 다음 주에 발표하는 걸 선호하나요?
Ⓐ 프로젝터가 작동하지 않아요.
☑ 저는 준비할 시간이 더 필요해요.
Ⓒ Kim 교수님이 우리 논문을 채점하셨어요.
Ⓓ 마감일이 어제였어요.

10 Alternative Question [Au]

Would you prefer to pay by credit card or cash?

Ⓐ The total is 40 dollars including tax.
☑ Can I use these coupons?
Ⓒ The store closes at 8 P.M.
Ⓓ I need a receipt, please.

receipt[risíːt] 영수증, 수령

신용카드로 지불하는 걸 선호하나요, 아니면 현금으로 지불하는 걸 선호하나요?
Ⓐ 총액이 세금 포함 40달러예요.
☑ 이 쿠폰들을 사용할 수 있나요?
Ⓒ 상점이 오후 8시에 문을 닫아요.
Ⓓ 저는 영수증이 필요해요.

11 Alternative Question [Am]

Do you prefer written exams or oral presentations?

Ⓐ The exam schedule was posted.
☑ I get nervous speaking in public.
Ⓒ No, the exam was very difficult.
Ⓓ The presentation is next week.

oral[ɔ́ːrəl] 구두의 nervous[nə́ːrvəs] 긴장되는, 신경의

필기시험을 선호하나요, 아니면 구두 발표를 선호하나요?
Ⓐ 시험 일정이 게시되었어요.
☑ 공개적으로 말하는 것이 긴장돼요.
Ⓒ 아니요, 시험이 매우 어려웠어요.
Ⓓ 발표가 다음 주예요.

12 Alternative Question [En]

Would you prefer to submit the assignment digitally or in print?

Ⓐ The deadline is next Friday.
Ⓑ I've already completed it.
☑ Digital would be more convenient.
Ⓓ The professor grades fairly.

fairly[fɛ́ərli] 공정하게, 꽤

과제를 디지털로 제출하는 걸 선호하나요, 아니면 인쇄물로 제출하는 걸 선호하나요?
Ⓐ 마감일이 다음 금요일이에요.
Ⓑ 저는 그것을 이미 완료했어요.
☑ 디지털이 더 편리할 것 같아요.
Ⓓ 교수님이 공정하게 채점하세요.

13 Alternative Question　　　🔊 Am

Would you rather have Chinese food or Mexican food for the team dinner?

Ⓐ The meeting starts at noon.
☑ Either option works for me.
Ⓒ I already ate lunch.
Ⓓ The cafeteria is downstairs.

팀 저녁으로 중국 음식을 드시겠어요, 아니면 멕시칸 음식을 드시겠어요?
Ⓐ 회의가 정오에 시작해요.
☑ 어느 선택지든 저에게는 괜찮아요.
Ⓒ 저는 이미 점심 식사를 했어요.
Ⓓ 구내식당은 아래층에 있어요.

14 Alternative Question　　　🔊 Au

Which do you like better, fiction or non-fiction books?

☑ I enjoy reading about real events.
Ⓑ The library closes at 9 P.M.
Ⓒ I haven't read that book yet.
Ⓓ My professor assigned three chapters.

assign[əsáin] 할당하다, (과제 등을) 내주다, 지정하다

어느 것을 더 좋아하나요, 소설인가요 아니면 논픽션 책인가요?
☑ 저는 실제 사건에 대해 읽는 것을 즐겨요.
Ⓑ 도서관이 오후 9시에 문을 닫아요.
Ⓒ 저는 아직 그 책을 읽지 않았어요.
Ⓓ 제 교수님이 세 장을 할당하셨어요.

15 Alternative Question　　　🔊 Am

Shall we sit indoors or outside?

Ⓐ Everything on the menu looks good.
Ⓑ It was difficult to park outside.
Ⓒ Sharon will arrive by five o'clock.
☑ Looks like it's going to rain.

indoors[indɔ́ːrz] 실내에, 집안에서

실내에 앉을까요, 아니면 밖에 앉을까요?
Ⓐ 메뉴의 모든 것이 좋아 보여요.
Ⓑ 밖에 주차하기가 어려웠어요.
Ⓒ Sharon이 5시까지 도착할 거예요.
☑ 비가 올 것 같아 보여요.

16 Alternative Question　　　🔊 En

Would you rather discuss this now or after the meeting?

☑ Let's wait until we're done.
Ⓑ The discussion lasted an hour.
Ⓒ The meeting room is reserved.
Ⓓ I prepared my presentation.

reserve[rizə́ːrv] 예약하다

지금 논의하는 걸 선호하나요, 아니면 회의 후에 논의하는 걸 선호하나요?
☑ 끝날 때까지 기다립시다.
Ⓑ 논의가 한 시간 지속되었어요.
Ⓒ 회의실이 예약되어 있어요.
Ⓓ 저는 제 발표를 준비했어요.

17 Alternative Question　　　🔊 Nz

Do you prefer digital or printed copies of the manual?

Ⓐ We need to fix this computer.
Ⓑ Yes, I would really appreciate it.
☑ Whichever is more convenient for you.
Ⓓ I found the manual quite helpful.

appreciate[əpríːʃièit] 감사하다, 감상하다, 이해하다

사용 설명서의 디지털 사본을 선호하나요, 아니면 인쇄된 사본을 선호하나요?
Ⓐ 저희는 이 컴퓨터를 고쳐야 해요.
Ⓑ 네, 정말로 감사하겠어요.
☑ 어느 것이든 당신이 더 편리한 걸로요.
Ⓓ 저는 그 사용 설명서가 꽤 도움이 된다고 생각했어요.

18 Alternative Question　　　🔊 En

Would you prefer taking notes on paper or on your laptop?

Ⓐ The class lasts two hours.
Ⓑ The professor speaks clearly.
☑ I'm not good with devices.
Ⓓ My laptop is quite new.

take notes on ~에 필기하다, 기록하다

종이에 필기하는 것을 선호하나요, 아니면 노트북에 필기하는 것을 선호하나요?
Ⓐ 수업이 2시간 지속돼요.
Ⓑ 교수님이 명확하게 말씀하세요.
☑ 저는 기기를 잘 다루지 못해요.
Ⓓ 제 노트북은 꽤 새것이에요.

19 Alternative Question　　　🔊 Am

Would you rather email the client or call them directly?

Ⓐ Their office closes at 5 P.M.
Ⓑ Their email address changed.
Ⓒ I sent the document yesterday.
☑ A call would be more personal.

directly[diréktli] 직접

고객에게 이메일을 보내는 걸 선호하나요, 아니면 직접 전화하는 걸 선호하나요?
Ⓐ 그들의 사무실이 오후 5시에 문을 닫아요.
Ⓑ 그들의 이메일 주소가 바뀌었어요.
Ⓒ 어제 문서를 보냈어요.
☑ 전화가 더 개인적일 거예요.

20 Alternative Question 🔊 Nz

Which do you prefer for the weekend, going hiking or visiting a museum?

☑ I want some outdoor activities.
Ⓑ The museum closes at 6 P.M.
Ⓒ That is a high mountain.
Ⓓ Weekend tickets are expensive.

주말에 어느 것을 선호하나요, 하이킹을 가는 것인가요 아니면 박물관을 방문하는 것인가요?
☑ 저는 야외 활동을 원해요.
Ⓑ 박물관이 오후 6시에 문을 닫아요.
Ⓒ 그것은 높은 산이에요.
Ⓓ 주말 표가 비싸요.

4. Suggestion/Offer/Request Questions

HACKERS PRACTICE   p.67

01 Ⓐ   02 Ⓑ   03 Ⓓ   04 Ⓐ   05 Ⓓ

01 Suggestion Question 🔊 Am

Would you like to join our study group?

☑ Sure, when do you meet?
Ⓑ The library closes at 9 P.M.
Ⓒ I studied for three hours.
Ⓓ Yes, these study materials.

material [mətíəriəl] 자료, 재료, 소재

우리 스터디 그룹에 합류하시겠어요?
☑ 물론이죠, 언제 만나나요?
Ⓑ 도서관이 오후 9시에 문을 닫아요.
Ⓒ 저는 3시간 동안 공부했어요.
Ⓓ 네, 이 학습 자료들요.

02 Offer Question 🔊 En

Do you want me to print some extra copies?

Ⓐ The slides look colorful.
☑ That's a great idea.
Ⓒ In the conference room.
Ⓓ Three cups of coffee.

추가 사본을 몇 장 인쇄해 드릴까요?
Ⓐ 슬라이드들이 다채로워 보여요.
☑ 좋은 생각이에요.
Ⓒ 회의실에서요.
Ⓓ 커피 세 잔요.

03 Request Question 🔊 Am

Could you recommend a good café nearby?

Ⓐ The mall opens at 9 A.M.
Ⓑ I prefer tea to coffee.
Ⓒ The cups are in the cabinet.
☑ There is one close to the park.

recommend [rèkəménd] 추천하다

근처에 좋은 카페를 추천해 주실 수 있나요?
Ⓐ 쇼핑몰이 오전 9시에 열어요.
Ⓑ 저는 커피보다 차를 선호해요.
Ⓒ 컵들이 캐비닛에 있어요.
☑ 공원 가까이에 하나 있어요.

04 Request Question 🔊 Au

Would you mind dropping these documents at the front desk?

☑ Not at all, I'm heading that way.
Ⓑ The desk needs to be cleaned.
Ⓒ They were delivered this morning.
Ⓓ Did you drop these on the floor?

drop [drɑːp] 전달하다, 떨어뜨리다; 방울, 감소

이 문서들을 안내 데스크에 전달해 주시겠어요?
☑ 괜찮아요, 저는 그쪽으로 가고 있어요.
Ⓑ 책상이 청소되어야 해요.
Ⓒ 그것들은 오늘 아침에 배달되었어요.
Ⓓ 이것들을 바닥에 떨어뜨렸나요?

05 Offer Question 🔊 En

Would you like me to check your report for errors?

Ⓐ Yesterday at midnight.
Ⓑ It was reported in the news.
Ⓒ The printer is acting up.
☑ I already submitted it.

act up 제 기능을 못하다

당신의 보고서에 오류가 있는지 확인해 드릴까요?
Ⓐ 어제 자정에요.
Ⓑ 그것은 뉴스에서 보도되었어요.
Ⓒ 프린터가 제 기능을 못하고 있어요.
☑ 저는 그것을 이미 제출했어요.

HACKERS TEST

01 ⓑ	02 ⓑ	03 ⓒ	04 ⓓ	05 ⓑ
06 ⓒ	07 ⓒ	08 ⓑ	09 ⓑ	10 ⓑ
11 ⓐ	12 ⓑ	13 ⓑ	14 ⓐ	15 ⓒ
16 ⓑ	17 ⓓ	18 ⓒ	19 ⓑ	20 ⓐ

01 Suggestion Question — Am

How about getting dinner after the meeting?

ⓐ I already ordered lunch.
ⓑ That sounds great to me. ✓
ⓒ The meeting room is too small.
ⓓ Do you have the results?

회의 후에 저녁 식사하는 게 어때요?
ⓐ 저는 이미 점심을 주문했어요.
ⓑ 정말 좋은 것 같아요. ✓
ⓒ 회의실이 너무 작아요.
ⓓ 결과가 있나요?

02 Request Question — Au

Would you turn on the air conditioner?

ⓐ Is the repair shop open now?
ⓑ Sure, it's getting warm in here. ✓
ⓒ The technician took a look at it.
ⓓ The new model is quite reliable.

reliable [riláiəbl] 믿을 만한, 확실한

에어컨을 켜 주시겠어요?
ⓐ 수리점이 지금 열려 있나요?
ⓑ 물론이에요, 여기가 따뜻해지고 있어요. ✓
ⓒ 기술자가 그것을 살펴봤어요.
ⓓ 새 모델은 꽤 믿을 만해요.

03 Request Question — Am

Would you be able to cover my shift tomorrow?

ⓐ You are very diligent.
ⓑ Yes, I'll give him your message.
ⓒ I'm afraid I can't. ✓
ⓓ The schedule was posted yesterday.

diligent [díləd3ənt] 성실한, 부지런한

내일 제 교대 근무를 대신해 주실 수 있을까요?
ⓐ 당신은 매우 성실해요.
ⓑ 네, 그에게 당신의 메시지를 전할게요.
ⓒ 죄송하지만 저는 할 수 없어요. ✓
ⓓ 일정이 어제 게시되었어요.

04 Suggestion Question — En

Would you like to join us for coffee?

ⓐ It's on your right.
ⓑ I joined a morning class.
ⓒ Some sugar, please.
ⓓ Not right now. ✓

join [d3ɔin] 함께 하다, 등록하다, 참여하다

저희와 커피를 함께 마시겠어요?
ⓐ 그것은 당신의 오른쪽에 있어요.
ⓑ 저는 아침 수업에 등록했어요.
ⓒ 설탕을 좀 주세요.
ⓓ 지금은 안 돼요. ✓

05 Request Question — Am

Can you tell me where the student lounge is?

ⓐ Yes, this is comfortable.
ⓑ I'll take you there. ✓
ⓒ We need more sofas.
ⓓ I'll call the event organizer.

organizer [ɔ́:rgənàizər] 기획자, 주최자

학생 라운지가 어디에 있는지 말해 주실 수 있나요?
ⓐ 네, 이것은 편안해요.
ⓑ 거기로 데려다 드릴게요. ✓
ⓒ 저희는 소파가 더 필요해요.
ⓓ 행사 기획자에게 전화할게요.

06 Suggestion Question — Nz

Why don't you ask Professor Evans for help?

ⓐ I received questions about the course.
ⓑ The science building is closed.
ⓒ Is she in her office now? ✓
ⓓ Do you want me to help you?

Evans 교수님께 도움을 요청하는 게 어때요?
ⓐ 그 과목에 대한 질문들을 받았어요.
ⓑ 과학관이 문을 닫았어요.
ⓒ 지금 그녀가 사무실에 계신가요? ✓
ⓓ 제가 도와주기를 원하시나요?

07 Offer Question — Am

Would you like a tour of our laboratory?

ⓐ Some safety goggles.
ⓑ No, I'm very curious.
ⓒ Yes, I'd love to see it. ✓
ⓓ The equipment needs updating.

laboratory [lǽbərətɔ̀:ri] 실험실

우리 실험실을 견학하시겠어요?

Ⓐ 몇몇 보안경들이요.
Ⓑ 아니요, 저는 매우 호기심이 있어요.
☑ 네, 보고 싶어요.
Ⓓ 장비가 업데이트가 필요해요.

08 Request Question En

Do you mind turning down your music?

Ⓐ I prefer classical music.
☑ Sorry, I didn't realize it was so loud.
Ⓒ He turned down the job offer.
Ⓓ I downloaded a new album.

turn down 소리를 줄이다, 거절하다

음악을 소리를 줄여 주시겠어요?
Ⓐ 저는 클래식 음악을 선호해요.
☑ 죄송해요, 그렇게 시끄러운 줄 몰랐어요.
Ⓒ 그는 일자리 제안을 거절했어요.
Ⓓ 저는 새 앨범을 다운로드했어요.

09 Request Question Am

Can you help me move my things into the dormitory?

Ⓐ The dormitory is closed for renovation.
☑ I'll be free on Saturday morning.
Ⓒ The elevator is out of service.
Ⓓ You'll need a key card to enter.

dormitory[dɔ́:rmətɔ̀:ri] 기숙사

제 물건들을 기숙사로 옮기는 것을 도와주실 수 있나요?
Ⓐ 기숙사가 보수 때문에 폐쇄되었어요.
☑ 저는 토요일 아침에 시간이 있을 거예요.
Ⓒ 엘리베이터가 고장 났어요.
Ⓓ 들어가려면 키 카드가 필요할 거예요.

10 Offer Question Nz

Would you like us to postpone the department meeting?

Ⓐ No, I'm not prepared.
☑ That seems necessary.
Ⓒ Put all the materials on the desk.
Ⓓ The department has five teams.

postpone[poustpóun] 연기하다   **necessary**[nésəsèri] 필요한

저희가 부서 회의를 연기하기를 원하시나요?
Ⓐ 아니요, 저는 준비되지 않았어요.
☑ 그것이 필요해 보여요.
Ⓒ 모든 자료를 책상에 놓으세요.
Ⓓ 부서에 다섯 개의 팀이 있어요.

11 Suggestion Question Au

Why don't we reschedule for next week?

☑ I'm free on Tuesday.
Ⓑ The schedule is on the wall.
Ⓒ Yes, I went there last week.
Ⓓ They're working late today.

reschedule[rì:skédʒu:l] 일정을 변경하다, 연기하다

다음 주로 일정을 변경하는 게 어때요?
☑ 저는 화요일에 시간이 있어요.
Ⓑ 일정이 벽에 있어요.
Ⓒ 네, 저는 지난주에 거기 갔어요.
Ⓓ 그들은 오늘 늦게까지 일해요.

12 Suggestion Question Am

How about eating at that Chinese restaurant?

Ⓐ Downtown is very crowded.
☑ I don't really like their menu.
Ⓒ Can I try on this pair?
Ⓓ Two cups of tea, please.

crowded[kráudid] 붐비는, 혼잡한

저 중국 음식점에서 먹는 게 어때요?
Ⓐ 시내가 매우 붐벼요.
☑ 저는 그들의 메뉴를 그렇게 좋아하지 않아요.
Ⓒ 이것을 신어볼 수 있나요?
Ⓓ 차 두 잔 주세요.

13 Offer Question En

Would you like some salad with your steak?

Ⓐ The chef is excellent.
☑ I'm all set with what I have.
Ⓒ Medium-rare, please.
Ⓓ The table needs cleaning.

스테이크와 함께 샐러드를 드시겠어요?
Ⓐ 요리사가 훌륭해요.
☑ 있는 것으로 충분해요.
Ⓒ 미디엄 레어로 주세요.
Ⓓ 식탁은 청소되어야 해요.

14 Request Question Am

Can you assist me with this projector?

☑ What exactly do you need help with?
Ⓑ The presentation was excellent.
Ⓒ It starts in five minutes.
Ⓓ That would be helpful.

assist[əsíst] 돕다

이 프로젝터에 있어 저를 도와주실 수 있나요?

Ⓐ 정확히 어떤 것에 도움이 필요하신가요?
Ⓑ 발표가 훌륭했어요.
Ⓒ 그것은 5분 후에 시작해요.
Ⓓ 그것이 도움이 될 거예요.

15 Request Question Au

Do you mind explaining how to use this software?
Ⓐ I prefer the previous version.
Ⓑ The software needs updating.
 The manual is available online.
Ⓓ It's quite an expensive program.

previous[príːviəs] 이전의, 앞의
available[əvéiləbl] 이용 가능한, 시간이 있는

이 소프트웨어를 어떻게 사용하는지 설명해 주시겠어요?
Ⓐ 저는 이전 버전을 선호해요.
Ⓑ 소프트웨어가 업데이트가 필요해요.
☑ 매뉴얼이 온라인에서 이용 가능해요.
Ⓓ 그것은 꽤 비싼 프로그램이에요.

16 Suggestion Question Am

Why don't you take a short break?
Ⓐ Yes, the vase is broken.
☑ I need to finish this chapter first.
Ⓒ The library is closed now.
Ⓓ My study group meets weekly.

break[breik] 휴식; 부수다

짧은 휴식을 취하는 게 어때요?
Ⓐ 네, 꽃병이 부서졌어요.
☑ 먼저 이 장을 끝내야 해요.
Ⓒ 도서관은 지금 문을 닫았어요.
Ⓓ 제 스터디 그룹이 매주 만나요.

17 Suggestion Question Au

Would you like to lead the presentation for our clients?
Ⓐ The clients arrived early.
Ⓑ The meeting room is booked.
Ⓒ New projects can be challenging.
☑ I'd be happy to handle that.

client[kláiənt] 고객
challenging[tʃælindʒiŋ] 어려운, 도전적인, 힘드는
handle[hǽndl] 담당하다, 처리하다, 다루다

고객들을 위한 발표를 진행하시겠어요?
Ⓐ 고객들이 일찍 도착했어요.
Ⓑ 회의실이 예약되어 있어요.
Ⓒ 새 프로젝트들은 어려울 수 있어요.
☑ 기꺼이 그것을 담당할게요.

18 Offer Question Am

Do you need me to explain the assignment again?
Ⓐ The professor extended the deadline.
Ⓑ No, I didn't get any information.
 Yes, I don't understand it.
Ⓓ It needs to be submitted soon.

assignment[əsáinmənt] 과제, 숙제 extend[iksténd] 연장하다

과제를 다시 설명해 드릴까요?
Ⓐ 교수님이 마감일을 연장하셨어요.
Ⓑ 아니요, 저는 어떤 정보도 받지 못했어요.
☑ 네, 이해가 안 가요.
Ⓓ 그것은 곧 제출되어야 해요.

19 Request Question En

Could you forward me that email about the lecture schedule?
Ⓐ The lecture hall is quite large.
☑ Actually, I didn't receive one.
Ⓒ You should go straight and turn right.
Ⓓ Do you have the schedule?

forward[fɔ́ːrwərd] 전달하다; 앞으로

강의 일정에 대한 그 이메일을 저에게 전달해 주실 수 있나요?
Ⓐ 강의실이 꽤 커요.
☑ 사실, 저는 그것을 받지 못했어요.
Ⓒ 직진해서 우회전하세요.
Ⓓ 시간표를 가지고 있나요?

20 Offer Question Am

Do you want me to drive you to the airport tomorrow?
 Don't you have a doctor's appointment?
Ⓑ No, he is on a business trip this week.
Ⓒ The airport has been renovated.
Ⓓ Yes, it's my driver's license.

doctor's appointment 병원 예약
renovate[rénəvèit] 개조하다, 보수하다

내일 공항까지 운전해서 데려다 드릴까요?
☑ 병원 예약이 있지 않나요?
Ⓑ 아니요, 그는 이번 주에 출장 중이에요.
Ⓒ 공항이 개조되었어요.
Ⓓ 네, 그것은 제 운전면허증이에요.

Section III. Statements

1. Informative Statements

HACKERS PRACTICE   p.73

01 Ⓐ   02 Ⓐ   03 Ⓒ   04 Ⓓ   05 Ⓒ

01 Informative Statement Am

My car broke down on the highway this morning.

Ⓐ That must have been stressful. ✓
Ⓑ I usually take the subway.
Ⓒ Yes, traffic was terrible.
Ⓓ 80 kilometers per hour.

break down 고장이 나다, 무너지다

오늘 아침 고속도로에서 제 차가 고장 났어요.
Ⓐ 그것은 스트레스였겠어요. ✓
Ⓑ 저는 보통 지하철을 타요.
Ⓒ 네, 교통체증이 끔찍했어요.
Ⓓ 시속 80킬로미터요.

02 Informative Statement En

The movie starts in twenty minutes.

Ⓐ I'll grab my coat and we can go. ✓
Ⓑ The theater is being renovated.
Ⓒ Films are expensive these days.
Ⓓ She started working there last week.

grab [græb] 챙기다, 붙잡다, 차지하다

영화가 20분 후에 시작해요.
Ⓐ 코트만 챙겨서 갈 수 있어요. ✓
Ⓑ 극장이 개조되고 있어요.
Ⓒ 요즘 영화가 비싸요.
Ⓓ 그녀가 지난주에 거기서 일을 시작했어요.

03 Informative Statement Am

I'm going to the supermarket right now.

Ⓐ In the fridge.
Ⓑ Every Sunday.
Ⓒ Can I come with you? ✓
Ⓓ The clothing store is not open.

fridge [fridʒ] 냉장고

지금 슈퍼마켓에 가려고 해요.
Ⓐ 냉장고 안에요.
Ⓑ 매주 일요일에요.
Ⓒ 함께 가도 될까요? ✓
Ⓓ 옷가게가 열려 있지 않아요.

04 Informative Statement En

This restaurant has the best seafood in town.

Ⓐ No, it's a seafood place.
Ⓑ The town hall is nearby.
Ⓒ He is out of town now.
Ⓓ I didn't really like it. ✓

이 식당은 마을에서 최고의 해산물을 가지고 있어요.
Ⓐ 아니요, 그것은 해산물 식당이에요.
Ⓑ 시청이 근처에 있어요.
Ⓒ 그는 지금 시외에 있어요.
Ⓓ 저는 그렇게 마음에 들지 않았어요. ✓

05 Informative Statement Nz

I'm not free at that time.

Ⓐ It is exactly right.
Ⓑ I already finished them.
Ⓒ What's a better time for you? ✓
Ⓓ How much is this item?

nearby [nìərbái] 근처의, 가까운

저는 그때 시간이 없어요.
Ⓐ 정확히 맞아요.
Ⓑ 저는 이미 그것들을 끝냈어요.
Ⓒ 언제가 더 좋으신가요? ✓
Ⓓ 이 물건은 얼마인가요?

HACKERS TEST   p.74

01 Ⓒ	02 Ⓐ	03 Ⓑ	04 Ⓐ	05 Ⓓ
06 Ⓑ	07 Ⓒ	08 Ⓐ	09 Ⓓ	10 Ⓒ
11 Ⓓ	12 Ⓒ	13 Ⓒ	14 Ⓓ	15 Ⓒ
16 Ⓐ	17 Ⓐ	18 Ⓒ	19 Ⓒ	20 Ⓑ

01 Informative Statement En

I forgot my student ID at home.

Ⓐ Let's try to get there early.
Ⓑ I don't feel comfortable about that.
Ⓒ Use the temporary pass system.
Ⓓ They identified the problem.

comfortable [kʌ́mfərtəbl] 편안한
temporary [témpərèri] 임시의, 일시적인
identify [aidéntəfài] 식별하다

학생증을 집에 두고 왔어요.
Ⓐ 거기에 일찍 도착하려고 노력해봅시다.
Ⓑ 그것에 대해 편안하게 느끼지 않아요.

☑ 임시 출입증 시스템을 사용하세요.
Ⓓ 그들이 문제를 식별했어요.

02 Informative Statement 🔊 Am

The campus library closes early tonight.

Ⓐ ☑ I should return my books now.
Ⓑ The librarian is very helpful.
Ⓒ The new books arrived yesterday.
Ⓓ On the other side of campus.

librarian [laibréəriən] 사서

학교 도서관이 오늘 밤에 일찍 닫아요.
☑ 지금 책들을 반납해야겠어요.
Ⓑ 사서가 매우 도움이 돼요.
Ⓒ 새 책들이 어제 도착했어요.
Ⓓ 학교 반대편에요.

03 Informative Statement 🔊 Au

Jack and Cam are on their way to the museum.

Ⓐ It closes at 5 P.M.
☑ How about joining them?
Ⓒ The exhibit starts in May.
Ⓓ Admission is ten dollars.

on one's way to ~로 가는 중인
admission [ədmíʃən] 입장료, 입학, 인정

Jack과 Cam이 박물관으로 가는 중이에요.
Ⓐ 그것은 오후 5시에 문을 닫아요.
☑ 그들과 합류하는 게 어때요?
Ⓒ 전시가 5월에 시작해요.
Ⓓ 입장료가 10달러예요.

04 Informative Statement 🔊 Am

I can't figure out how to access the campus Wi-Fi network.

☑ Ask Jonathan.
Ⓑ The map is available online.
Ⓒ Those buildings are inaccessible.
Ⓓ I usually take the bus to campus.

available [əvéiləbl] 이용 가능한, 시간이 있는
inaccessible [ìnəksésəbl] 접근할 수 없는, 도달하기 어려운

학교 와이파이 네트워크에 접속하는 방법을 모르겠어요.
☑ Jonathan에게 물어보세요.
Ⓑ 지도가 온라인에서 이용 가능해요.
Ⓒ 저 건물들은 접근할 수 없어요.
Ⓓ 저는 보통 학교에 버스를 타고 가요.

05 Informative Statement 🔊 En

Professor Jones canceled our meeting this afternoon.

Ⓐ It's getting warmer.
Ⓑ It was last week.
Ⓒ I haven't met her yet.
☑ Did she reschedule it?

reschedule [rìːskédʒuːl] 일정을 다시 세우다, 연기하다

Jones 교수님이 오늘 오후 우리 만남을 취소하셨어요.
Ⓐ 더 따뜻해지고 있어요.
Ⓑ 지난주였어요.
Ⓒ 아직 그녀를 만나지 않았어요.
☑ 그녀가 일정을 다시 세웠나요?

06 Informative Statement 🔊 Nz

Your presentation was impressive today.

Ⓐ Your present is on the table.
☑ Thanks, I worked hard on it.
Ⓒ Today is Tuesday, right?
Ⓓ I'm impressed by this sculpture.

impressive [imprésiv] 인상적인, 감명을 주는, 감동적인
sculpture [skʌ́lptʃər] 조각품

오늘 당신의 발표가 인상적이었어요.
Ⓐ 당신의 선물이 식탁 위에 있어요.
☑ 감사해요, 열심히 했어요.
Ⓒ 오늘이 화요일 맞죠?
Ⓓ 이 조각품에 감동받았어요.

07 Informative Statement 🔊 Am

The package should arrive by Friday.

Ⓐ What's your weekend schedule like?
Ⓑ The mail carrier is really friendly.
☑ That's only a few days from now.
Ⓓ I called in sick last Friday.

소포가 금요일까지 도착할 거예요.
Ⓐ 당신의 주말 일정은 어떤가요?
Ⓑ 우편 배달원이 정말로 친근해요.
☑ 지금부터 며칠 안 남았네요.
Ⓓ 지난 금요일에 병가를 냈어요.

08 Informative Statement 🔊 Fn

The rent for this apartment is quite reasonable.

☑ I think so, too.
Ⓑ Yes, it was quiet last night.
Ⓒ No, this is a dining room.
Ⓓ Let's rent this car.

rent[rent] 임대로; 빌리다　quite[kwait] 꽤, 아주
reasonable[ríːzənəbl] 합리적인, 적당한　quiet[kwáiət] 조용한

이 아파트의 임대료가 꽤 합리적이에요.
☑Ⓐ 저도 그렇게 생각해요.
Ⓑ 네, 어젯밤에 조용했어요.
Ⓒ 아니요, 여기는 식당이에요.
Ⓓ 이 차를 빌립시다.

09　Informative Statement　Am

The student cafeteria serves great vegetarian options.

Ⓐ I'm allergic to seafood.
Ⓑ It's on the second floor.
Ⓒ The server is not on the clock.
☑Ⓓ I'll have to try them sometime.

vegetarian[vèdʒətɛ́əriən] 채식의; 채식주의자
allergic[əlɚ́ːrdʒik] 알레르기가 있는

학생 식당이 훌륭한 채식주의자 메뉴를 제공해요.
Ⓐ 저는 해산물에 알레르기가 있어요.
Ⓑ 그것은 2층에 있어요.
Ⓒ 종업원이 근무 중이 아니에요.
☑Ⓓ 언젠가 그것들을 시도해봐야겠어요.

10　Informative Statement　Au

Kate told me she wants to change her major.

Ⓐ The deadline was last Friday.
Ⓑ Did you fill out the forms?
☑Ⓒ Well, I didn't know about that.
Ⓓ I'm interested in environmental science.

fill out 작성하다

Kate가 전공을 바꾸고 싶다고 저에게 말했어요.
Ⓐ 마감일이 지난 금요일이었어요.
Ⓑ 양식을 작성했나요?
☑Ⓒ 글쎄, 그것에 대해 몰랐어요.
Ⓓ 저는 환경 과학에 관심이 있어요.

11　Informative Statement　En

The campus bookstore is having a big sale.

Ⓐ The research paper is due soon.
Ⓑ Textbooks are too heavy to carry.
Ⓒ I borrowed some from the library.
☑Ⓓ Let's take advantage of it.

take advantage of (~의 이점을) 이용하다

학교 서점이 대대적인 할인을 하고 있어요.
Ⓐ 연구 논문이 곧 마감이에요.
Ⓑ 교과서들이 들고 다니기에는 너무 무거워요.
Ⓒ 도서관에서 몇 권을 빌렸어요.
☑ 그것을 이용합시다.

12　Informative Statement　Am

I've been waiting for over an hour.

Ⓐ The weight limit is 50 pounds.
☑Ⓑ I apologize for that.
Ⓒ How long will you stay?
Ⓓ Those people are waiting in line.

apologize[əpɑ́lədʒàiz] 사과하다

한 시간 이상 기다리고 있었어요.
Ⓐ 무게 제한이 50파운드예요.
☑Ⓑ 그것에 대해 사과드려요.
Ⓒ 얼마나 오래 머무를 건가요?
Ⓓ 저 사람들은 줄을 서서 기다리고 있어요.

13　Informative Statement　Nz

The client meeting has been moved to Thursday.

Ⓐ About 20 clients.
Ⓑ Don't move anything on my desk.
☑Ⓒ That works better for me.
Ⓓ This meeting room is empty.

client[kláiənt] 고객

고객 회의가 목요일로 옮겨졌어요.
Ⓐ 약 20명의 고객들이요.
Ⓑ 제 책상 위의 어떤 것도 옮기지 마세요.
☑Ⓒ 그것이 저에게 더 좋아요.
Ⓓ 이 회의실은 비어 있어요.

14　Informative Statement　Am

My flight has been delayed until tomorrow.

Ⓐ I can go and pick him up.
Ⓑ The airline serves good food.
Ⓒ When does the train arrive?
☑Ⓓ I'm sorry to hear that.

airline[ɛ́rlàin] 항공사, 정기 항공

제 항공편이 내일까지 지연되었어요.
Ⓐ 제가 가서 그를 데려올 수 있어요.
Ⓑ 그 항공사는 좋은 음식을 제공해요.
Ⓒ 기차가 언제 도착하나요?
☑Ⓓ 그것을 들으니 유감이에요.

15　Informative Statement　En

I enjoy going to the campus fitness center.

Ⓐ I lost a lot of weight.
Ⓑ Some new equipment.
☑Ⓒ I've never seen you there.

Ⓓ At the center of the campus.

저는 학교 피트니스 센터에 가는 것을 즐겨요.
Ⓐ 저는 체중을 많이 감량했어요.
Ⓑ 일부 새로운 장비요.
Ⓒ 거기서 당신을 본 적이 없는데요. ✓
Ⓓ 학교 중앙에요.

16 Informative Statement Nz

I'm not sure about the deadline for course registration.

Ⓐ It's next Friday at noon. ✓
Ⓑ There are many forms to fill out.
Ⓒ The science building is across the street.
Ⓓ I've already selected my courses.

course registration 수강 신청

수강 신청 마감일에 대해 확실하지 않아요.
Ⓐ 다음 주 금요일 정오예요. ✓
Ⓑ 작성할 양식이 많아요.
Ⓒ 과학관은 길 건너편에 있어요.
Ⓓ 저는 이미 제 과목들을 선택했어요.

17 Informative Statement En

Our quarterly reports show significant improvement.

Ⓐ That's excellent news. ✓
Ⓑ I report to the CEO directly.
Ⓒ The quarter ends next week.
Ⓓ They're improving the facilities.

significant [signífikənt] 상당한, 중요한
improvement [imprúːvmənt] 개선
directly [diréktli] 직접 facility [fəsíləti] 시설, 설비

우리의 분기 보고서들이 상당한 개선을 보였어요.
Ⓐ 훌륭한 소식이에요. ✓
Ⓑ 저는 최고경영자에게 직접 보고해요.
Ⓒ 분기가 다음 주에 끝나요.
Ⓓ 그들은 시설을 개선하고 있어요.

18 Informative Statement Au

The marketing team submitted their proposal yesterday.

Ⓐ The market conditions are challenging.
Ⓑ Let me check my calendar.
Ⓒ Let's review it this afternoon. ✓
Ⓓ Teams should work together.

submit [səbmít] 제출하다 proposal [prəpóuzəl] 제안서, 제안
challenging [tʃǽlindʒiŋ] 어려운, 도전적인, 힘드는

마케팅 팀이 어제 그들의 제안서를 제출했어요.
Ⓐ 시장 상황이 어려워요.
Ⓑ 제 달력을 확인해볼게요.
Ⓒ 오늘 오후에 그것을 검토합시다. ✓
Ⓓ 팀들은 함께 일해야 해요.

19 Informative Statement Am

My roommate is moving out at the end of the semester.

Ⓐ Did you submit your assignment?
Ⓑ Please move your car to another spot.
Ⓒ Will you look for a new one? ✓
Ⓓ I had a really busy semester.

move out 이사를 나가다 semester [siméstər] 학기
assignment [əsáinmənt] 과제, 숙제

제 룸메이트가 학기 말에 이사 나가요.
Ⓐ 당신의 과제를 제출했나요?
Ⓑ 차를 다른 곳으로 옮겨 주세요.
Ⓒ 새로운 룸메이트를 찾을 건가요? ✓
Ⓓ 정말로 바쁜 학기였어요.

20 Informative Statement En

The syllabus mentions a group project due next month.

Ⓐ November is a cold month.
Ⓑ We should start looking for partners. ✓
Ⓒ Projects are quite time-consuming.
Ⓓ Did you already finish your project?

syllabus [síləbəs] 강의 계획서

강의 계획서에 다음 달이 마감인 그룹 프로젝트가 언급되어 있어요.
Ⓐ 11월은 추운 달이에요.
Ⓑ 파트너들을 찾기 시작해야 해요. ✓
Ⓒ 프로젝트들은 시간이 꽤 많이 걸려요.
Ⓓ 이미 당신의 프로젝트를 끝냈나요?

2. Advisory Statements

HACKERS PRACTICE p.77

| 01 Ⓒ | 02 Ⓓ | 03 Ⓐ | 04 Ⓐ | 05 Ⓑ |

01 Advisory Statement Au

You should clean the lab equipment after use.

Ⓐ Equipment is expensive.
Ⓑ The lab opens at 8 A.M.
Ⓒ I'll make sure to do that. ✓
Ⓓ Using microscopes is fun.

lab [læb] 실험실, 연구실; 실습, 실험
microscope [máikrəskòup] 현미경

사용 후에 실험 장비를 청소해야 해요.
Ⓐ 장비가 비싸요.
Ⓑ 실험실이 오전 8시에 열어요.
☑ 확실히 그렇게 하겠어요.
Ⓓ 현미경을 사용하는 것이 재미있어요.

02 Advisory Statement   🔊 En

Please call me when you need me.

Ⓐ Do you need any help?
Ⓑ You have a lot of questions.
Ⓒ No, my phone is working fine.
☑ I don't have your number.

제가 필요할 때 전화해 주세요.
Ⓐ 도움이 필요한가요?
Ⓑ 질문이 많으시네요.
Ⓒ 아니요, 제 전화기는 잘 작동해요.
☑ 당신의 번호가 없어요.

03 Advisory Statement   🔊 Am

If you want to enroll, contact the admissions office directly.

☑ I'll call them this afternoon.
Ⓑ The office is on the second floor.
Ⓒ Yes, I received the confirmation email.
Ⓓ Can I call my friends over?

enroll [inróul] 등록하다   admissions office 입학처

등록하고 싶으시면, 입학처에 직접 연락하세요.
☑ 오늘 오후에 그들에게 전화할게요.
Ⓑ 사무실은 2층에 있어요.
Ⓒ 네, 확인 이메일을 받았어요.
Ⓓ 친구들을 불러도 되나요?

04 Advisory Statement   🔊 Nz

Let's have dinner at the new Italian restaurant tonight.

☑ Did you make a reservation?
Ⓑ Why not tonight instead?
Ⓒ They're on the counter.
Ⓓ Maybe it is.

reservation [rèzərvéiʃən] 예약

오늘 밤 새로운 이탈리아 음식점에서 저녁을 먹읍시다.
☑ 예약을 하셨나요?
Ⓑ 대신 오늘 밤은 어때요?
Ⓒ 그것들이 카운터 위에 있어요.
Ⓓ 아마도 그럴 거예요.

05 Advisory Statement   🔊 Am

I'd love if you could attend the holiday party next weekend.

Ⓐ The holidays are in December.
☑ I'll bring a dessert to share.
Ⓒ Your house has a nice garden.
Ⓓ They loved the gift you sent.

다음 주말 연말 파티에 참석해 주시면 좋겠어요.
Ⓐ 휴일들이 12월에 있어요.
☑ 나눠 먹을 디저트를 가져올게요.
Ⓒ 당신의 집은 좋은 정원이 있어요.
Ⓓ 그들이 당신이 보낸 선물을 좋아했어요.

HACKERS TEST   p.78

01 Ⓒ   02 Ⓑ   03 Ⓐ   04 Ⓑ   05 Ⓒ
06 Ⓑ   07 Ⓒ   08 Ⓑ   09 Ⓐ   10 Ⓐ
11 Ⓐ   12 Ⓑ   13 Ⓑ   14 Ⓑ   15 Ⓒ
16 Ⓓ   17 Ⓑ   18 Ⓐ   19 Ⓓ   20 Ⓐ

01 Advisory Statement   🔊 En

Check your email for the meeting details.

Ⓐ I'm pretty sure about it.
Ⓑ My inbox is always empty.
☑ I'll look right away.
Ⓓ Are you going to cancel it?

회의 세부 사항을 이메일로 확인하세요.
Ⓐ 그것에 대해 꽤 확신해요.
Ⓑ 제 받은 편지함은 항상 비어 있어요.
☑ 즉시 확인할게요.
Ⓓ 그것을 취소할 건가요?

02 Advisory Statement   🔊 Am

If you want to attend the seminar, register by Friday.

Ⓐ The event starts at 8 A.M.
☑ I won't be able to go there.
Ⓒ Friday works for everyone.
Ⓓ Registration desk is on the first floor.

register [rédʒistər] 등록하다; 음역

세미나에 참석하고 싶으시면, 금요일까지 등록하세요.
Ⓐ 행사는 오전 8시에 시작해요.
☑ 저는 거기에 갈 수 없을 것 같아요.
Ⓒ 금요일은 모든 사람에게 괜찮아요.
Ⓓ 등록 창구는 1층에 있어요.

03 Advisory Statement 🔊 En

Please help us organize the fundraising event.

☑ Ⓐ I can volunteer next weekend.
Ⓑ The charity raised lots of money.
Ⓒ Events are scheduled monthly.
Ⓓ Organizing requires leadership skills.

organize[ɔ́ːrgənàiz] 조직하다 fundraising event 모금 행사
volunteer[vàːləntíər] 자원봉사하다, 자원봉사자
charity[tʃǽrəti] 자선단체

모금 행사를 조직하는 것을 도와주세요.
☑ Ⓐ 다음 주말에 할 수 있어요.
Ⓑ 그 자선단체는 많은 돈을 모았어요.
Ⓒ 행사들이 매월 예정되어 있어요.
Ⓓ 조직하는 것은 리더십 기술이 필요해요.

04 Advisory Statement 🔊 Am

Let's prepare a retirement party for Mr. Clark.

Ⓐ He started working here in 2021.
☑ Ⓑ Where should we do it?
Ⓒ I like this chocolate cake better.
Ⓓ I haven't prepared the report yet.

retirement[ritáiərmənt] 은퇴

Mr. Clark을 위한 은퇴 파티를 준비합시다.
Ⓐ 그는 2021년에 여기서 일을 시작했어요.
☑ Ⓑ 어디서 해야 할까요?
Ⓒ 저는 이 초콜릿 케이크가 더 좋아요.
Ⓓ 저는 아직 보고서를 준비하지 않았어요.

05 Advisory Statement 🔊 Au

We'd love if you presented your research at the conference.

Ⓐ Research requires extensive funding.
Ⓑ The conference is in Chicago.
☑ Ⓒ I'm honored by the invitation.
Ⓓ The presentation room is booked.

extensive[iksténsiv] 광범위한, 대규모의
book[buk] 예약하다

회의에서 당신의 연구를 발표해 주시면 좋겠어요.
Ⓐ 연구는 광범위한 자금이 필요해요.
Ⓑ 회의는 시카고에서 있어요.
☑ Ⓒ 초대를 영광으로 생각해요.
Ⓓ 발표실이 예약되어 있어요.

06 Advisory Statement 🔊 En

If you need help with the online portal, contact Mr. Brown.

Ⓐ Let's meet in person.
☑ Ⓑ What is his number?
Ⓒ Do you want me to help you?
Ⓓ I already completed my courses.

in person 직접, 개인적으로

온라인 포털에 도움이 필요하시면, Mr. Brown에게 연락하세요.
Ⓐ 직접 만납시다.
☑ Ⓑ 그의 번호가 무엇인가요?
Ⓒ 제가 도와드릴까요?
Ⓓ 이미 제 과목들을 완료했어요.

07 Advisory Statement 🔊 Am

Take these documents to the third floor.

Ⓐ We don't need to document them.
Ⓑ I prefer the second floor.
☑ Ⓒ Where exactly on that floor?
Ⓓ The elevator is out of order.

document[dάkjumənt] 서류; 문서화하다, 기록하다
out of order 고장 난

이 서류들을 3층으로 가져가세요.
Ⓐ 그것들을 문서화할 필요가 없어요.
Ⓑ 저는 2층을 선호해요.
☑ Ⓒ 그 층의 정확히 어디인가요?
Ⓓ 엘리베이터가 고장 났어요.

08 Advisory Statement 🔊 Nz

I'd like you to review these articles before tomorrow.

Ⓐ How are the reviews of that diner?
Ⓑ The printer is out of paper.
Ⓒ I'm really into journalism.
☑ Ⓓ I don't have enough time today.

review[rivjúː] 검토하다; 후기

내일 전에 이 기사들을 검토해 주세요.
Ⓐ 그 식당의 후기는 어떤가요?
Ⓑ 프린터에 종이가 떨어졌어요.
Ⓒ 저는 저널리즘에 매우 관심이 있어요.
☑ Ⓓ 저는 오늘 충분한 시간이 없어요.

09 Advisory Statement 🔊 Am

Let me know when the shipment arrives.

☑ Ⓐ I'll call you immediately.
Ⓑ Shipping costs are too high.

ⓒ The package was damaged.
ⓓ We need more inventory.

shipment [ʃípmənt] 배송, 선적
immediately [imíːdiətli] 즉시, 곧
inventory [ínvəntɔ̀ːri] 재고, 재고목록

배송이 도착하면 알려주세요.
☑ 즉시 전화할게요.
ⓑ 배송비가 너무 높아요.
ⓒ 소포가 손상되었어요.
ⓓ 더 많은 재고가 필요해요.

10 Advisory Statement Au

You can use my notes if you need them.

☑ That would be really helpful.
ⓑ The professor canceled the class.
ⓒ What time is the study group meeting?
ⓓ I prefer to study in the library.

필요하시면 제 필기를 사용하실 수 있어요.
☑ 그것은 정말로 도움이 될 것 같아요.
ⓑ 교수님이 수업을 취소하셨어요.
ⓒ 스터디 그룹 모임이 몇 시인가요?
ⓓ 저는 도서관에서 공부하는 것을 선호해요.

11 Advisory Statement En

You may as well consider applying for the scholarship.

☑ When is the deadline?
ⓑ I'll take it off the calendar.
ⓒ The university has many programs.
ⓓ How much is your tuition fee?

tuition fee 등록금, 수업료

장학금 지원을 고려해 보는 게 좋겠어요.
☑ 마감일이 언제인가요?
ⓑ 달력에서 제거할게요.
ⓒ 대학교에 많은 프로그램이 있어요.
ⓓ 당신의 등록금은 얼마나 되나요?

12 Advisory Statement Am

Please explain the assignment requirements again.

ⓐ I haven't received any feedback.
☑ Which part is confusing you?
ⓒ Assignments are due next Friday.
ⓓ I finished my work early.

requirement [rikwáiərmənt] 요구사항, 필수 요건

과제 요구사항을 다시 설명해 주세요.
ⓐ 어떤 피드백도 받지 않았어요.
☑ 어떤 부분이 혼란스러우신가요?
ⓒ 과제는 다음 금요일이 마감이에요.
ⓓ 제 일을 일찍 끝냈어요.

13 Advisory Statement Nz

If you have any questions, refer to the manual first.

ⓐ Do you need more information?
☑ Where can I find the manual?
ⓒ The questions are too difficult.
ⓓ Let me answer that for you.

refer to 참조하다, 표현하다, 언급하다

질문이 있으시면, 먼저 매뉴얼을 참조하세요.
ⓐ 더 많은 정보가 필요한가요?
☑ 매뉴얼을 어디서 찾을 수 있나요?
ⓒ 질문들이 너무 어려워요.
ⓓ 당신을 위해 그것에 답해드릴게요.

14 Advisory Statement En

We should take notes during the client meeting.

ⓐ You can use my notes.
☑ That's what I'll do.
ⓒ Here is the agenda.
ⓓ Tomorrow morning.

agenda [ədʒéndə] 안건, 의제

고객 회의 동안 필기를 해야 해요.
ⓐ 제 노트를 사용할 수 있어요.
☑ 그렇게 할게요.
ⓒ 여기 안건이 있어요.
ⓓ 내일 아침이요.

15 Advisory Statement Am

I'd like to hear your thoughts on my research proposal.

ⓐ I'm revising my paper.
ⓑ The deadline is next Friday.
☑ I'll email you my feedback.
ⓓ There are five sections in total.

revise [riváiz] 수정하다   in total 총, 통틀어

제 연구 제안서에 대한 당신의 생각을 듣고 싶어요.
ⓐ 제 논문을 수정하고 있어요.
ⓑ 마감일이 다음 주 금요일이에요.
☑ 피드백을 이메일로 보내드릴게요.
ⓓ 총 다섯 개의 섹션이 있어요.

16 Advisory Statement [Nz]

We'd love if you shared your travel photos at dinner.

(A) Dinner starts at seven o'clock.
(B) The travel agency is downtown.
(C) My camera is working well.
(D) ✓ I'll bring my laptop tonight.

저녁 식사 때 여행 사진들을 공유해 주시면 좋겠어요.
(A) 저녁 식사는 7시에 시작해요.
(B) 여행사가 시내에 있어요.
(C) 제 카메라는 잘 작동해요.
(D) ✓ 오늘 밤 노트북을 가져올게요.

17 Advisory Statement [Am]

Let's schedule a virtual meeting with our clients in the morning.

(A) The schedule changed.
(B) ✓ How about in the afternoon?
(C) I think they're in the meeting room.
(D) Breakfast will be served.

schedule [skédʒuːl] 일정을 잡다; 일정   virtual [vә́ːrtʃual] 가상의

고객들과의 화상 회의 일정을 아침에 잡읍시다.
(A) 일정이 변경되었어요.
(B) ✓ 오후는 어때요?
(C) 그들이 회의실에 있는 것 같아요.
(D) 아침 식사가 제공될 거예요.

18 Advisory Statement [Nz]

Don't forget to sign the attendance sheet.

(A) ✓ Thanks for the reminder.
(B) The sheet is already full.
(C) Attendance isn't required.
(D) I prefer digital attendance systems.

reminder [rimáindәr] 알림, 상기시키는 것

출석부에 서명하는 것을 잊지 마세요.
(A) ✓ 알림에 감사해요.
(B) 용지가 이미 가득 찼어요.
(C) 출석은 필수가 아니에요.
(D) 저는 디지털 출석 시스템을 선호해요.

19 Advisory Statement [Cn]

Keep these files confidential at all times.

(A) Keeping records is difficult.
(B) The filing system is outdated.
(C) Times have changed recently.
(D) ✓ I understand the importance.

confidential [kànfәdénʃәl] 기밀의, 신임을 받는
at all times 항상, 언제나   outdated [àutdéitid] 구식인, 진부한

이 파일들을 항상 기밀로 유지하세요.
(A) 기록을 보관하는 것은 어려워요.
(B) 파일링 시스템이 구식이에요.
(C) 시대가 최근에 변했어요.
(D) ✓ 저는 그 중요성을 이해해요.

20 Advisory Statement [Am]

If you need an extension on your report, submit a request form.

(A) ✓ I already filled it out yesterday.
(B) I can give you the forms.
(C) The entry was submitted on time.
(D) Gina has an extensive collection.

extension [iksténʃәn] (기한 등의) 연장, 확장
entry [éntri] 출품작, 입장
extensive [iksténsiv] 광범위한, 대규모의
collection [kәlékʃәn] 수집품, 수거, 모금

보고서에 연장이 필요하시면, 신청서를 제출하세요.
(A) ✓ 저는 그것을 어제 이미 작성했어요.
(B) 저는 양식을 드릴 수 있어요.
(C) 출품작이 시간에 맞춰 제출되었어요.
(D) Gina는 광범위한 수집품을 갖고 있어요.

TASK 2 | Listen to a Conversation

Section I. Question Types

1. Main Topic/Purpose Questions

Example 🔊 M-Au W-Am   p.87

> M 내일 부서 회의에 대해 말씀드리고 싶어서요.
> W 네, 무슨 일인가요?
> M 핵심 팀원 3명이 내일 오후에 참석할 수 없다는 걸 방금 알았어요. 갑자기 생긴 긴급 고객 회의에 참석해야 해서요.
> W 아, 그거 좋지 않네요. 새 프로젝트 일정에 대해서는 모든 사람의 의견이 정말 필요한데요.
> M 맞아요. **일정을 변경해야 한다고 생각하고 있었어요.** 목요일 오전은 괜찮을까요? 제가 확인해봤는데 오전 10시에 회의실을 사용할 수 있어요.

key [ki:] 핵심의, 중요한   make it 참석하다
emergency [imə́ːrdʒənsi] 긴급, 비상사태
reschedule [rìːskédʒuːl] 일정을 변경하다

화자들은 주로 무엇에 대해 이야기하고 있는가?
Ⓐ 회의 효율성을 개선하는 방법들
Ⓑ 고객 피드백에 대한 우려
✓ 부서 회의 일정 변경
Ⓓ 팀원들 간의 갈등 해결

어휘 efficiency [ifíʃənsi] 효율성   concern [kənsə́ːrn] 우려, 관심
resolve [rizɔ́lv] 해결하다

HACKERS PRACTICE   p.88

01 Ⓒ   02 Ⓑ   03 Ⓐ   04 Ⓓ

01 Main Topic Question   🔊 M-Am W-En

> M **Are you going to join the gardening workshop this Saturday?**
> W Definitely! I've been wanting to learn how to grow herbs and flowers. Do you remember what time it starts?
> M 9 A.M. at the community center. They said it would include both a lecture and a hands-on session.
> W Thanks for the heads-up. I'll make sure to bring my notebook and gloves.

community center 지역 문화 센터
hands-on 실습의, 직접 해보는   make sure to 꼭 ~하다

M 이번 주 토요일 원예 워크숍에 참가하실 건가요?
W 물론이죠! 허브와 꽃을 기르는 방법을 배우고 싶었어요. 몇 시에 시작하는지 기억하세요?
M 오전 9시에 지역 문화 센터에서요. 강의와 실습 시간 둘 다 포함된다고 했어요.
W 미리 알려주셔서 감사해요. 노트와 장갑을 꼭 가져가야겠어요.

대화는 주로 무엇에 대한 것인가?
Ⓐ 중고 물품 세일
Ⓑ 꽃 축제
✓ 원예 수업
Ⓓ 농산물 직판장

어휘 yard sale 중고 물품 세일

02 Main Topic Question   🔊 M-En W-Am

> M **I've just received a message from IT about our software upgrade.**
> W They're finally updating that outdated software! It's happening on Friday, right?
> M Yes, they said it will take place after our usual work hours.
> W I see. We should back up our files before leaving the office on Friday then. Do you know what major new features will be added?
> M Well, IT mentioned we'll get a new project management feature after the upgrade.

outdated [àutdéitid] 구식의, 오래된
take place 진행하다, 일어나다
feature [fíːtʃər] 기능

M 방금 IT 부서로부터 소프트웨어 업그레이드에 대한 메시지를 받았어요.
W 드디어 그 구식 소프트웨어를 업데이트하는군요! 금요일에 하는 거죠?
M 네, 저희의 평소 근무 시간 후에 진행한다고 했어요.
W 그렇군요. 그럼 금요일에 퇴근하기 전에 파일들을 백업해야겠네요. 어떤 주요 새 기능이 추가되는지 아세요?
M 음, IT 부서에서 업그레이드 후에 새로운 프로젝트 관리 기능을 갖게 될 거라고 했어요.

화자들은 주로 무엇에 대해 이야기하고 있는가?
Ⓐ IT 부서와의 회의
✓ 직장 소프트웨어 개선
Ⓒ 업무 파일 백업 계획
Ⓓ 프로젝트 관리 전략

어휘 strategy [strǽtədʒi] 전략

03 Main Topic Question   🔊 W-Nz M-En

> W **Have you heard about the tech career fair taking place next week at the university?**

M Yes! I'm definitely planning to attend. I need to update my résumé this weekend.
W Great idea. I heard there will be more than 30 companies looking to hire interns.
M That's exciting! Why don't we meet up and go together?

career fair 진로 박람회
definitely [défənitli] 무조건, 분명히
update [ʌ̀pdéit] 갱신하다, 업데이트하다

W 다음 주에 대학교에서 열리는 기술 진로 박람회에 대해 들었어요?
M 네! 무조건 참석할 계획이에요. 이번 주말에 이력서를 갱신해야 해요.
W 좋은 생각이에요. 인턴을 채용하려는 회사가 30곳 넘게 올 거라고 들었어요.
M 흥미롭네요! 만나서 함께 가는 게 어때요?

화자들은 어떤 행사에 대해 이야기하고 있는가?
ⓐ 진로 박람회 ✓
ⓑ 이력서 워크숍
ⓒ 취업 면접
ⓓ 교류 만찬

04 Main Purpose Question   M-En W-Am

M You're taking Professor Austin's advanced statistics course, right? How are you finding it?
W Challenging but fascinating. The workload is pretty intense though.
M I'm considering signing up for the course next semester. Would you recommend it for someone who just barely passed basic statistics?
W Honestly, you might want to take the intermediate course first. Professor Austin assumes you're already comfortable with regression analysis.

advanced [ədvǽnst] 고급의, 첨단의
fascinating [fǽsənèitiŋ] 매력적인, 매혹적인
intense [inténs] 강도 높은   sign up 신청하다, 등록하다
barely [bɛ́ərli] 간신히, 거의 ~않다
intermediate [ìntərmíːdiət] 중급의, 중간의
assume [əsúːm] 상정하다, 추측하다

M Austin 교수님의 고급 통계학 수업을 듣고 계시죠? 어떠세요?
W 힘들지만 매력적이에요. 과제량이 꽤 강도 높기는 해요.
M 다음 학기에 그 수업을 신청할까 생각하고 있어요. 기초 통계학을 간신히 통과한 사람에게 추천하시겠어요?
W 솔직히, 중급 과정을 먼저 듣는 게 좋을 것 같아요. Austin 교수님은 당신이 회귀 분석에 이미 익숙하다고 상정하거든요.

남자는 왜 여자에게 이야기하고 있는가?
ⓐ 여자의 수업 노트를 빌리기 위해
ⓑ 교수님의 수업 방식에 대해 논의하기 위해
ⓒ 스터디 파트너를 찾기 위해
ⓓ 강의 선택에 대한 조언을 받기 위해 ✓

HACKERS TEST   p.90

01	ⓑ	02	ⓓ	03	ⓐ	04	ⓓ	05	ⓒ
06	ⓐ	07	ⓐ	08	ⓑ	09	ⓑ	10	ⓓ
11	ⓒ	12	ⓑ	13	ⓒ	14	ⓓ	15	ⓒ
16	ⓐ								

[01-02]   M-Am W-Au

Listen to a conversation.

M 01You are coming to the beach party this weekend, right? Everyone from our department will be there.
W I'm not sure yet. 02I have to give my younger sister a ride to the airport on Saturday morning. She's leaving to study abroad in Canada.
M Oh, really? But the party doesn't start until 3 P.M., so I think you could still make it afterward.
W Well, I'll check and get back to you tomorrow.

give someone a ride to 누군가를 ~에 태워다 주다
get back to ~에게 다시 연락하다

대화를 들으시오.

M 01이번 주말 해변 파티에 올 거죠? 저희 부서 사람들 모두 올 거에요.
W 아직 확실하지 않아요. 02토요일 아침에 여동생을 공항에 태워다 줘야 해요. 그 애가 캐나다로 유학을 떠나거든요.
M 아, 그래요? 하지만 파티는 오후 3시나 되어야 시작하니까, 그 후에는 오실 수 있을 것 같은데요.
W 글쎄요, 확인해보고 내일 다시 연락드릴게요.

01 Main Topic Question

대화는 주로 무엇에 대한 것인가?
ⓐ 가족 소풍
ⓑ 해변 파티 ✓
ⓒ 송별 만찬
ⓓ 부서 세미나

어휘   farewell [fɛ̀ərwél] 송별, 작별

02 Detail Question

여자는 토요일 아침에 무엇을 하려고 계획하는가?
ⓐ 부서 모임에 참석한다.
ⓑ 동료들과 이야기한다.
ⓒ 파티용 디저트를 만든다.
ⓓ 여동생을 공항에 데려다 준다 ✓

어휘   colleague [káliːg] 동료

[03-04]   M-Au W-Am

Listen to a conversation.

M 03How about going to the book fair together on Sunday?

W I'd love to! I heard several authors will be doing book signings.

M Yes, and there's a poetry reading at 2 P.M. that sounds interesting.

W Great! We can grab lunch before and then head to the fair.

M Sounds like a plan. Should we meet at the café across from the venue at noon?

W All right. ⁰⁴**I'm going to bring a few of my books for the signings!**

book signing 사인회
grab lunch 점심을 먹다　venue[vénju:] 행사장, 장소

대화를 들으시오.

M ⁰³일요일에 함께 도서 박람회에 가는 것은 어때요?
W 좋아요! 몇몇 작가들이 사인회를 한다고 들었어요.
M 네, 그리고 오후 2시에 흥미로울 것 같은 시 낭독회가 있어요.
W 좋네요! 먼저 점심을 먹고 박람회로 가면 되겠네요.
M 좋은 계획이에요. 정오에 행사장 맞은편 카페에서 만날까요?
W 좋아요. ⁰⁴사인회를 위해 제 책 몇 권을 가져가야겠어요!

03 Main Topic Question

화자들은 어떤 행사에 대해 이야기하고 있는가?
Ⓐ 도서 박람회 ✓
Ⓑ 시내 축제
Ⓒ 주말 시장
Ⓓ 독서 동아리 모임

04 Detail Question

여자는 행사에 무엇을 가져갈 계획인가?
Ⓐ 작가 전기
Ⓑ 도시락 통
Ⓒ 독서용 안경
Ⓓ 개인 서적 ✓

어휘　biography[baiágrəfi] 전기, 일대기
　　　container[kəntéinər] 통, 용기

[05-06]

M-Am W-En

Listen to a conversation.

M ⁰⁵**Are you going to the Summer Music Festival this weekend?**

W Yes, definitely! They've got some amazing bands playing this year. You're coming with me, right?

M I'm not sure. I've got a lot of work to finish.

W Come on, it only takes place once a year. Plus, your favorite band is headlining!

M You're right. I guess I could try to finish my work tonight and go on Saturday.

W That's the spirit! Want to meet at the entrance around noon?

M Sounds perfect. ⁰⁶**I'll buy the tickets now.**

amazing[əméiziŋ] 놀라운, 멋진
favorite[féivərit] 가장 좋아하는　entrance[éntrəns] 입구, 현관

대화를 들으시오.

M ⁰⁵이번 주말 여름 음악 축제에 가실 거예요?
W 네, 물론이죠! 올해는 몇몇 놀라운 밴드들이 공연해요. 저와 함께 가실 거죠?
M 확실하지 않아요. 끝내야 할 일이 많아서요.
W 이봐요, 일 년에 겨우 한 번만 열리는 거예요. 게다가 당신이 가장 좋아하는 밴드가 헤드라이너로 출연해요!
M 맞네요. 오늘 밤 일을 끝내고 토요일에 가도록 노력해봐야겠어요.
W 바로 그거예요! 정오쯤 입구에서 만날까요?
M 완벽해요. ⁰⁶지금 표를 사겠어요.

05 Main Topic Question

대화의 주제는 무엇인가?
Ⓐ 업무 관련 모임
Ⓑ 주말 진로 박람회
Ⓒ 여름 음악 축제 ✓
Ⓓ 유명한 밴드의 콘서트

06 Do Next Question

남자는 다음에 무엇을 할 것 같은가?
Ⓐ 축제 티켓을 구한다. ✓
Ⓑ 업무 마감일을 재조정한다.
Ⓒ 여자에게 도착 시간을 문자로 보낸다.
Ⓓ 공연하는 밴드들을 조사한다.

어휘　obtain[əbtéin] 구하다, 얻다　deadline[dédlàin] 마감일
　　　arrival time 도착 시간

[07-08]

W-En M-Au

Listen to a conversation.

W ⁰⁷**Have you reviewed the budget proposal for the new smartphone launch campaign?**

M Yes, I went through it yesterday. The digital advertising allocation seems reasonable, but I'm concerned about the TV commercial budget.

W What's your main concern? The production costs or the media buying?

M Both, actually. The production estimate is 30% higher than our last campaign, and prime time slots are getting more expensive.

W You're right. ⁰⁸**Maybe we should focus more on social media influencers** and reduce our traditional advertising spend.

budget proposal 예산 제안서　launch[lɔːntʃ] 출시, 개시
go through ~을 살펴보다, 겪다　allocation[æləkéiʃən] 배분
reasonable[ríːzənəbl] 합리적인, 합당한
estimate[éstəmèit] 추정치　prime time 황금 시간대
traditional[trədíʃənl] 전통적인

대화를 들으시오.

W ⁰⁷새로운 스마트폰 출시 캠페인을 위한 예산 제안서를 검토해보셨나요?

M 네, 어제 살펴봤어요. 디지털 광고 배분은 합리적으로 보이지만, 텔레비전 광고 예산이 걱정돼요.

W 주요 우려사항이 무엇인가요? 제작비인가요 아니면 매체 구매인가요?

M 사실 둘 다예요. 제작비 추정치가 저희 지난 캠페인보다 30% 높고, 황금 시간대는 더 비싸지고 있어요.

W 맞아요. ⁰⁸소셜 미디어 인플루언서들에게 더 집중하고 전통적 광고 지출을 줄이는 게 좋을 것 같아요.

07 Main Topic Question
화자들은 주로 무엇에 대해 이야기하고 있는가?
- Ⓐ 마케팅을 위한 예산 제안 ✓
- Ⓑ 소셜 미디어 플랫폼 선택
- Ⓒ 텔레비전 광고 제작 일정
- Ⓓ 경쟁사 분석 결과

어휘 competitor[kəmpétətər] 경쟁사, 경쟁자
       analysis[ənǽləsis] 분석   result[rizʌ́lt] 결과

08 Suggestion Question
여자는 그들이 무엇을 하라고 제안하는가?
- Ⓐ 전체 예산을 늘린다.
- Ⓑ 디지털 인플루언서에 집중한다. ✓
- Ⓒ 캠페인 시작을 연기한다.
- Ⓓ 전통적 광고에 집중한다.

어휘 overall[óuvərɔ̀:l] 전체의, 전반적인
       postpone[poustpóun] 연기하다

[09-10]   W-Am M-En
Listen to a conversation.

> W ⁰⁹Jake, I've noticed several issues with our company's updated website.
> M What kind of issues are you talking about?
> W Well, the customer login page isn't working, and some of the product images aren't loading properly.
> M That's not good. ¹⁰I'll have someone from my team look into those issues right away. We should be able to get them fixed by the end of the day.
> W Great. I hope it doesn't affect our online sales too much.

notice[nóutis] 발견하다, 알아채다
properly[prápərli] 제대로, 적절하게   affect[əfékt] 영향을 미치다

대화를 들으시오.

W ⁰⁹Jake, 저희 회사의 업데이트된 웹사이트에 몇 가지 문제를 발견했어요.

M 어떤 종류의 문제를 말씀하시는 건가요?

W 글쎄요, 고객 로그인 페이지가 작동하지 않고, 일부 제품 이미지들이 제대로 로딩되지 않아요.

M 좋지 않네요. ¹⁰제 팀의 누군가에게 그 문제들을 즉시 확인하라고 할게요. 오늘이 끝날 쯤이면 고칠 수 있을 거예요.

W 좋아요. 이게 온라인 판매에 너무 많은 영향을 미치지 않았으면 좋겠네요.

09 Main Topic Question
화자들은 주로 무엇에 대해 이야기하고 있는가?
- Ⓐ 기술 워크숍
- Ⓑ 웹사이트 문제 ✓
- Ⓒ 온라인 마케팅 전략
- Ⓓ 발표의 일부 변경사항

10 Inference Question
남자는 어느 부서에서 일하고 있을 것 같은가?
- Ⓐ 인사부
- Ⓑ 회계부
- Ⓒ 마케팅부
- Ⓓ 정보기술부 ✓

어휘 human resources 인사부   accounting[əkáuntiŋ] 회계부

[11-12]   W-En M-Nz
Listen to a conversation.

> W ¹¹I'm planning a birthday dinner for my roommate next week. Do you know any good restaurants near campus?
> M Definitely! There's Bella's Bistro on University Avenue. They have private dining rooms perfect for celebrations.
> W That sounds ideal. Do they accommodate large groups?
> M Yes, they can handle parties of up to 20 people. ¹²They also offer special birthday desserts if you mention it when booking.
> W Wonderful! I'll give them a call this afternoon to make arrangements.

private[práivət] 개별의, 사적인   ideal[aidí:əl] 이상적인
accommodate[əkɑ́:mədèit] 충분한 공간을 제공하다, 수용하다
mention[ménʃən] 말하다, 언급하다
make arrangements 일정을 잡다, 준비하다

대화를 들으시오.

W ¹¹다음 주에 제 룸메이트를 위한 생일 식사를 계획하고 있어요. 캠퍼스 근처의 좋은 식당을 아시나요?

M 그럼요! 내학로에 Bella's Bistro가 있어요. 기념 행사를 위한 완벽한 개별 식사 룸을 갖고 있어요.

W 이상적으로 들리네요. 그들은 대규모 그룹을 위한 충분한 공간을 제공하나요?

M 네, 20명까지의 일행을 받을 수 있어요. ¹²예약할 때 말씀하시면 특별한 생일 디저트도 제공해요.

W 훌륭해요! 일정을 잡기 위해 오늘 오후에 그들에게 전화할게요.

11 Main Purpose Question

여자는 왜 남자에게 이야기하고 있는가?
Ⓐ 그를 파티에 초대하기 위해
Ⓑ 캠퍼스 활동을 논의하기 위해
☑ 기념 행사 장소를 찾기 위해
Ⓓ 자신의 생일 파티를 계획하기 위해

어휘 discuss[diskʌ́s] 논의하다

12 Detail Question

남자는 식당에 대해 무엇을 언급하는가?
Ⓐ 무료 애피타이저를 제공한다.
☑ 특별한 축하 간식을 제공한다.
Ⓒ 라이브 밴드 공연이 있다.
Ⓓ 외부 장식을 허용한다.

어휘 complimentary[kɑ́mpləméntəri] 무료의
treat[tri:t] 간식, 대접 decoration[dèkəréiʃən] 장식

[13-14]

Listen to a conversation.   M-Nz W-Am

> M ¹³Have you seen the flyer for the wine tasting event this week?
> W Yes! I've been wanting to go to something like that for ages. Are you interested in going?
> M Definitely. I'm not very knowledgeable about wines, but I'd love to learn more.
> W Same here. They're also featuring food from local restaurants that pairs well with the wines.
> M What day were you thinking of going? It runs Friday through Sunday.
> W ¹⁴Saturday would work best for me. I have family commitments on Friday evening.
> M That'll probably be a popular time. We should register online soon in case it fills up.

knowledgeable[nálidʒəbl] 지식이 있는, 박식한
local[lóukəl] 지역의, 지방의 pair with ~와 어울리다
commitment[kəmítmənt] 약속, 전념

대화를 들으시오.

M ¹³이번 주 와인 시음 행사 전단지를 보셨나요?
W 네! 오랫동안 그런 곳에 가고 싶었어요. 가는 것에 관심 있으세요?
M 그럼요. 저는 와인에 대해 별로 지식은 없지만, 더 배우고 싶어요.
W 저도 마찬가지예요. 그들은 또한 와인과 잘 어울리는 지역 식당의 음식도 선보이고 있어요.
M 어느 날에 가실 생각이세요? 금요일부터 일요일까지 진행돼요.
W ¹⁴토요일이 저에게 가장 좋을 것 같아요. 금요일 저녁에 가족 약속이 있어요.
M 아마 그때는 인기 있는 시간일 거예요. 자리가 차는 경우에 대비해서 곧 온라인으로 등록해야겠어요.

13 Main Topic Question

화자들은 어떤 행사에 대해 이야기하고 있는가?
Ⓐ 음식 박람회
Ⓑ 자선 모금 행사
☑ 와인 시음 행사
Ⓓ 지역 농산물 직판장

어휘 charity fundraiser 자선 모금 행사

14 Detail Question

여자는 왜 토요일에 행사에 참석하고 싶어하는가?
Ⓐ 식당들이 주말에 특별한 음식을 제공한다.
Ⓑ 가족들이 토요일 행사에 올 것이다.
Ⓒ 금요일에 늦게까지 일해야 한다.
☑ 이미 금요일에 다른 계획이 있다.

[15-16]

Listen to a conversation.   W-Au M-En

> W ¹⁵Hey, I'm running a study group for Professor Russell's economics final. Would you like to join?
> M Thanks for the invite, but I'm not sure if group studying is my thing. I usually prefer studying alone.
> W I understand, ¹⁶but this exam covers so much material. Having different perspectives really helps clarify complex concepts.
> M That's a good point. When is the group meeting?
> W We are meeting tomorrow at the library, study room 204. The session will run from 6 to 8 P.M.
> M Alright, I'll give it a try. Maybe it'll be more effective than cramming by myself.

final[fáinəl] 기말고사; 최후의 cover[kʌ́vər] 다루다, 덮다
material[mətíəriəl] 자료, 재료
perspective[pərspéktiv] 관점 clarify[klǽrəfài] 명확히 하다
complex[kəmpléks] 복잡한, 복합의 concept[kɑ́nsept] 개념
effective[iféktiv] 효과적인 cram[kræm] 벼락치기하다

대화를 들으시오.

W ¹⁵저기, Russell 교수님의 경제학 기말고사를 위한 스터디 그룹을 운영하고 있어요. 참여하고 싶으신가요?
M 초대해주셔서 감사하지만, 그룹 스터디가 제게 맞는 것인지 확실하지 않아요. 저는 보통 혼자 공부하는 것을 선호해요.
W 이해해요. ¹⁶하지만 이 시험은 너무 많은 자료를 다뤄요. 다양한 관점을 갖는 것이 복잡한 개념들을 명확히 하는 데 정말 도움이 된답니다.
M 좋은 지적이네요. 그룹이 언제 모이나요?
W 내일 도서관의 스터디룸 204호에서 모여요. 세션은 오후 6시부터 8시까지 진행될 거예요.
M 좋아요, 해보겠어요. 혼자서 벼락치기하는 것보다 더욱 효과적일 수도 있겠네요.

15 Main Topic Question

화자들은 주로 무엇에 대해 이야기하고 있는가?
Ⓐ 교수의 교수법
Ⓑ 도서관 스터디룸
✓Ⓒ 시험을 위한 스터디 그룹
Ⓓ 경제학 강의 요구사항

어휘 course requirement 강의 요구사항

16 Inference Question

여자는 시험에 대해 무엇을 암시하는가?
✓Ⓐ 협력적인 준비가 필요하다.
Ⓑ 최근 강의에만 집중한다.
Ⓒ 이전 연도들의 것보다 쉽다.
Ⓓ 실용적 적용을 포함한다.

어휘 collaborative[kəlǽbərèitiv] 협력적인
preparation[prèpəréiʃən] 준비   recent[rí:snt] 최근의
practical[prǽktikəl] 실용적인, 실제의
application[æpləkéiʃən] 적용

2. Suggestion/Offer Questions

Example W-Am M-Au   p.95

W 다음 학기 수업 등록하셨어요?
M 아직이요. 제 일정에 대해 생각할 시간이 있는 **이번 주말에 할 계획이었어요.**
W **더 빨리 하시는 게 좋을 것 같아요.** 방금 Martinez 교수님과 얘기했는데, 환경과학 세미나가 벌써 거의 다 찼다고 하시더라고요.
M 정말요? 하지만 등록이 불과 이틀 전에 열렸잖아요!
W 학과에서 환경학 전공자들에게 조기 등록 접근 권한을 줬는데, 이제 모든 사람에게 열려 있어요. 한 시간 전에 제가 시스템을 확인했을 때 약 여덟 자리 정도만 남아 있었어요.

register[rédʒistər] 등록하다
environmental science 환경과학   spot[spɑt] 자리, 얼룩

여자는 남자에게 무엇을 하라고 제안하는가?
Ⓐ 전공을 환경학으로 바꾼다.
Ⓑ 자리 예약에 대해 교수와 이야기한다.
Ⓒ 수업 일정에 대해 신중히 생각한다.
✓Ⓓ 주말 전에 수업을 신청한다.

HACKERS PRACTICE   p.96

01 Ⓑ   02 Ⓒ   03 Ⓐ   04 Ⓓ

01 Suggestion Question M-En W-Nz

M I've been so <u>stressed with the new project</u> lately.
W You really need to take care of yourself. **How about <u>stepping away for a bit</u>?**

M I don't know... There's still so much to do, and the <u>deadline is approaching fast</u>.
W Trust me, even a short break can boost your productivity.
M You're probably right. Maybe I'll <u>take a walk in the park</u>.

take care of ~을 돌보다, 처리하다   step away 잠시 떠나다, 쉬다
approach[əpróutʃ] 다가오다, 접근하다
boost[bu:st] 증진시키다, 후원하다
productivity[prɑ̀dəktívəti] 생산성

M 최근에 새 프로젝트로 너무 스트레스를 받고 있어요.
W 정말로 자신을 돌봐야 해요. **잠시 떠나는 게 어때요?**
M 모르겠어요... 아직 해야 할 일이 너무 많고, 마감일이 빠르게 다가오고 있어요.
W 저를 믿으세요. 짧은 휴식도 당신의 생산성을 증진시킬 수 있어요.
M 당신이 맞을 거예요. 공원에서 산책이나 할까 해요.

여자는 남자에게 무엇을 하라고 제안하는가?
Ⓐ 집에서 일한다.
✓Ⓑ 휴식을 갖는다.
Ⓒ 프로젝트를 빨리 완료한다.
Ⓓ 마감일을 연장한다.

어휘 complete[kəmplí:t] 완료하다, 마치다
extend[iksténd] 연장하다

02 Offer Question W-Am M-En

W I've been trying to update the new employees' information on the company intranet, but <u>I'm having trouble with</u> the new HR system.
M I took a training session on that system last week. **Do you want me to help you upload the new hires' profiles?**
W That <u>would be a big help</u>. I've been struggling with it all morning.
M No problem. Let's set up a time this afternoon to <u>work on it together</u>.

have trouble with ~에 어려움을 겪다   training session 교육
struggle[strʌ́gl] 고생하다, 분투하다

W 회사 인트라넷에 신입 직원들의 정보를 업데이트하려고 하는데, 새 인사 시스템에 어려움을 겪고 있어요.
M 저는 지난주에 그 시스템에 대한 교육을 받았어요. **신입사원들의 프로필을 업로드하는 것을 도와드릴까요?**
W 큰 도움이 될 것 같아요. 오전 내내 고생하고 있었어요.
M 문제없어요. 오늘 오후에 함께 작업할 시간을 정해봐요.

남자는 무엇을 도와주겠다고 제안하는가?
Ⓐ 회의 일정을 세우는 것
Ⓑ 추가 교육 세션의 일정을 세우는 것
✓Ⓒ 새 시스템에 내용을 추가하는 것
Ⓓ 추가 직원을 채용하는 것

어휘 additional[ədíʃənl] 추가의   content[kántent] 내용, 함유량

recruit[rikrúːt] 채용하다, 모집하다

03 Suggestion Question W-En M-Am

W **Have you decided if you're coming to the hiking trip on Saturday?** We're going to Oakwood Trail.

M I want to, but I'm a bit worried. I've only hiked once before.

W **Why don't you give it a try?** Oakwood isn't as challenging as people say.

M I'm still a bit nervous about keeping up with everyone.

W Don't worry about that. We always stick together as a group.

give it a try 시도해보다, 한번 해보다
nervous[nə́ːrvəs] 불안한, 긴장되는 keep up with ~를 따라가다
stick together 함께 행동하다

W 토요일에 하이킹 여행에 올 건지 결정했어요? Oakwood Trail로 갈 거예요.
M 가고 싶지만, 조금 걱정돼요. 전에 한 번밖에 하이킹을 해본 적이 없어요.
W 시도해보는 게 어때요? Oakwood는 사람들이 말하는 것만큼 힘들지 않아요.
M 모든 사람들을 따라갈 수 있을지 아직 조금 불안해요.
W 그것에 대해서는 걱정하지 마세요. 우리는 항상 그룹으로 함께 행동해요.

여자는 남자에게 무엇을 하라고 권장하는가?
Ⓐ 하이킹 여행에 참여한다. ✓
Ⓑ 하이킹 장비를 산다.
Ⓒ 하이킹 전에 훈련한다.
Ⓓ 더 쉬운 길을 선택한다.

어휘 equipment[ikwípmənt] 장비

04 Suggestion Question W-Au M-En

W I've been reading this textbook for hours, but nothing seems to be sticking. I have a final exam on Monday and I'm starting to panic.

M **Don't try to memorize everything at once. Break the material into smaller sections and focus on understanding one concept before moving on to the next.**

W That makes sense. I've been trying to learn everything all at once.

M That rarely works. Remember, break it down — it's much more effective.

panic[pǽnik] 공황상태가 되다 memorize[méməraiz] 암기하다
at once 한 번에 break something into ~을 나누다
move on 넘어가다 rarely[réərli] 거의 ~않다

W 몇 시간 동안 이 교과서를 읽고 있는데, 아무것도 기억에 남지 않는 것 같아요. 월요일에 기말고사가 있는데 공황상태가 되기 시작했어요.
M 모든 것을 한 번에 암기하려고 하지 마세요. 자료를 더 작은 섹션들로 나누고 다음으로 넘어가기 전에 한 개념을 이해하는 데 집중하세요.
W 일리가 있네요. 모든 것을 한꺼번에 배우려고 했어요.
M 그건 거의 효과가 없어요. 기억하세요, 나눠서 하는 것이 훨씬 더 효과적이에요.

공부에 대한 남자의 조언은 무엇인가?
Ⓐ 여러 명의 동급생들과 공부하라.
Ⓑ 가능한 한 많이 암기하라.
Ⓒ 규칙적인 휴식이 중요하다.
Ⓓ 한꺼번이 아니라 점진적으로 학습하라. ✓

어휘 classmate[klǽsmeit] 동급생 regular[régjulər] 규칙적인
gradually[grǽdʒuəli] 점진적으로

HACKERS TEST p.98

01 Ⓑ	02 Ⓓ	03 Ⓐ	04 Ⓑ	05 Ⓒ
06 Ⓒ	07 Ⓐ	08 Ⓑ	09 Ⓐ	10 Ⓒ
11 Ⓑ	12 Ⓒ	13 Ⓑ	14 Ⓑ	15 Ⓒ
16 Ⓒ				

[01-02] W-En M-Am

Listen to a conversation.

W I've narrowed down my gym choices to either FitZone near my apartment or PowerFit by my office. Have any thoughts?

M I think PowerFit could be perfect for weekday workouts since it's closer to your workplace.

W Right. ⁰¹**It also has those new strength-training machines I want to try**, but I usually have more time for longer workouts on weekends.

M ⁰²**What about getting a trial membership at both places, and see which routine actually sticks?**

W That's brilliant! I'll sign up for trials this week and make my final decision by the end of the month.

narrow down 좁히다, 요약하다 thought[θɔːt] 의견
trial[tráiəl] 시험의, 시범적인 routine[ruːtíːn] 루틴, 일상
brilliant[bríljənt] 훌륭한, 밝은, 영리한

대화를 들으시오.

W 헬스장 선택을 제 아파트 근처의 FitZone이나 제 사무실 옆의 PowerFit 둘 중으로 좁혔어요. 의견 있으세요?
M PowerFit이 당신의 직장에 더 가깝기 때문에 평일 운동에 완벽할 것 같아요.
W 맞아요. ⁰¹그곳에는 제가 시도해보고 싶은 새로운 근력 운동기구들도 있지만, 저는 보통 주말에 더 긴 운동을 할 시간이 더 많아요.
M ⁰²두 곳 모두에서 시험 회원권을 받아서, 어떤 루틴이 실제로 계속되는지 보는 것은 어때요?
W 훌륭한 생각이네요! 이번 주에 시험 등록을 하고 이달 말까지 최종

결정을 내릴게요.

01 Detail Question
여자는 PowerFit에 대해 무엇을 말하는가?
Ⓐ 할인된 회원권을 제공한다.
☑ 최신 피트니스 장비가 있다.
Ⓒ 주말 트레이닝 세션을 제공한다.
Ⓓ 그녀가 사는 곳 가까이에 있다.

어휘 discount[dískaunt] 할인하다

02 Suggestion Question
남자는 여자에게 무엇을 하라고 권장하는가?
Ⓐ 장비 품질보다 위치를 우선시한다.
Ⓑ 오로지 근력 훈련에만 전념한다.
Ⓒ 구체적인 운동 일정을 만든다.
☑ 결정하기 전에 두 헬스장 모두 시도해본다.

어휘 prioritize[práiɔːrətàiz] 우선시하다
     location[loukéiʃən] 위치, 주소   quality[kwάləti] 품질, 특성
     exclusively[iksklúːsivli] 오로지
     specific[spisífik] 구체적인, 명확한

[03-04] 🎧 M-Am W-En

Listen to a conversation.

M You weren't at the team meeting this morning. Are you feeling okay?
W Not really. I've been having terrible migraines for over a week.
M That sounds serious. Have you seen a doctor about it?
W Not yet. But ⁰³I have an appointment scheduled for tomorrow.
M That's good. ⁰⁴Do you need me to handle your emails while you're out and forward anything urgent?
W That would be such a relief. I really appreciate your help.

terrible[térəbl] 심한, 무시무시한   migraine[máigrein] 편두통
serious[síəriəs] 심각한, 진중한
appointment[əpɔ́intmənt] 약속
handle[hǽndl] 처리하다, 다루다
urgent[ə́ːrdʒənt] 긴급한, 절박한   relief[rilíːf] 안도, 안심

대화를 들으시오.

M 당신은 오늘 아침 팀 회의에 없었죠. 괜찮으세요?
W 별로요. 일주일 넘게 심한 편두통을 앓고 있어요.
M 그것은 심각하게 들리네요. 그것에 대해 의사를 만나봤나요?
W 아직이요. 하지만 ⁰³내일로 약속을 잡아놨어요.
M 좋네요. ⁰⁴당신이 없는 동안 제가 당신의 이메일을 처리하고 긴급한 것이 있으면 전달해드릴까요?
W 그것은 정말 안도가 될 거예요. 당신의 도움에 정말 감사해요.

03 Detail Question
여자는 내일 무엇을 할 것인가?
☑ 의사를 만난다.
Ⓑ 프로젝트를 마친다.
Ⓒ 화상 회의에 참석한다.
Ⓓ 남자에게 이메일을 전달한다.

어휘 virtual meeting 화상 회의

04 Offer Question
남자는 무엇을 해주겠다고 제안하는가?
Ⓐ 의사 예약을 잡는다.
☑ 긴급한 이메일을 처리한다.
Ⓒ 혼자 회의에 참석한다.
Ⓓ 인사부에 연락한다.

어휘 contact[kάntækt] 연락하다

[05-06] 🎧 M-En W-Nz

Listen to a conversation.

M Hi, I heard the Student Volunteer Center is organizing a campus cleanup event this Saturday.
W That's right! We're meeting at 9 A.M. in front of the student union building. Are you interested in joining us?
M Definitely. ⁰⁵I need to complete some community service hours for my scholarship. How long will the event last?
W We'll work until about 2 P.M., including a lunch break. We provide gloves and equipment, but ⁰⁶you should wear comfortable clothes and bring something to drink.

organize[ɔ́ːrgənàiz] 조직하다, 준비하다
community service 지역사회 봉사
scholarship[skάːlərʃip] 장학금   last[læst] 지속되다

대화를 들으시오.

M 안녕하세요, 학생 봉사 센터에서 이번 주 토요일에 캠퍼스 청소 행사를 조직한다고 들었어요.
W 맞아요! 오전 9시에 학생회관 앞에서 만날 거예요. 저희와 함께 하시는 것에 관심이 있으세요?
M 그럼요. ⁰⁵제 장학금을 위해 지역사회 봉사 시간을 채워야 해요. 행사가 얼마나 오래 지속될까요?
W 점심 시간을 포함해서 오후 2시 정도까지 일할 거예요. 저희가 장갑과 장비를 제공하지만, ⁰⁶당신은 편한 옷을 입고 마실 것을 가져와야 해요.

05 Intention Question
남자는 왜 지역사회 봉사 시간을 언급하는가?
Ⓐ 청소 지속 기간 연장을 제안하기 위해
Ⓑ 이전 세션을 놓친 이유를 설명하기 위해
☑ 행사 참여에 대한 동기를 공유하기 위해
Ⓓ 필요한 최소 시간이 있는지 묻기 위해

어휘 **duration**[djuréiʃən] 지속 기간
motivation[mòutəvéiʃən] 동기
minimum[mínəməm] 최소의

06 Suggestion Question

여자는 남자에게 무엇을 하라고 제안하는가?
Ⓐ 새로운 청소 용품을 구매한다.
Ⓑ 다른 행사에 등록한다.
☑ 자신의 음료를 가져온다.
Ⓓ 장비 설치를 위해 일찍 도착한다.

어휘 **supply**[səplái] 용품; 공급하다　**beverage**[bévəridʒ] 음료

[07-08]　　　　　　　　　　🔊 M-Nz W-Am

Listen to a conversation.

> M I've been having trouble sleeping lately. I toss and turn for hours before finally falling asleep.
> W That's rough. Have you been using your phone or watching TV right before bed?
> M Yeah, actually I do. I usually scroll through social media or watch something to unwind.
> W ⁰⁷**That might be the problem. The blue light tricks your brain into thinking it's still daytime.**
> M Really? I had no idea that could affect my sleep so much.
> W It makes a huge difference. ⁰⁸**Try not using any screens at least an hour before bedtime.**
>
> **toss and turn** 뒤척이다　**finally**[fáinəli] 결국, 드디어
> **rough**[rʌf] 힘든　**unwind**[ənwáind] 긴장을 풀다, 느긋이 쉬다
> **trick**[trik] 속이다

대화를 들으시오.

M 최근에 잠는 데 문제가 있어요. 결국 잠들기 전에 몇 시간 동안 뒤척여요.
W 힘드시겠어요. 잠자리에 들기 직전에 휴대폰을 사용하거나 TV를 보고 계시나요?
M 네, 사실 그래요. 보통 긴장을 풀기 위해 소셜 미디어를 둘러보거나 뭔가를 봐요.
W ⁰⁷그것이 문제일 수도 있어요. 블루라이트가 당신의 뇌를 속여서 아직 낮이라고 생각하게 하는 거죠.
M 정말요? 그것이 제 잠에 그렇게 많이 영향을 줄 수 있다는 것을 전혀 몰랐어요.
W 큰 차이를 만들어요. ⁰⁸적어도 취침 시간 한 시간 전에는 화면을 사용하지 않도록 해보세요.

07 Intention Question

여자는 왜 블루 라이트를 언급하는가?
☑ 화면이 수면을 방해하는 이유를 설명하기 위해
Ⓑ 특정한 종류의 조명을 추천하기 위해
Ⓒ 블루 라이트 안경 구매를 제안하기 위해
Ⓓ 현대 기술을 비판하기 위해

어휘 **interfere with** ~을 방해하다　**criticize**[krítəsàiz] 비판하다

08 Suggestion Question

잠들기에 대한 여자의 조언은 무엇인가?
Ⓐ 매일 밤 수면제를 복용한다.
☑ 취침 전에 화면 사용을 피한다.
Ⓒ 잠들기 직전에 운동한다.
Ⓓ 저녁에 커피를 마시지 않는다.

어휘 **medication**[mèdəkéiʃən] 약물

[09-10]　　　　　　　　　　🔊 M-Am W-Nz

Listen to a conversation.

> M Have you started working on Professor Ivanov's research paper yet?
> W I've done some preliminary research, but I'm feeling a bit overwhelmed. There are just too many things to consider.
> M Same here. ⁰⁹**So, would you be interested in collaborating?** Maybe we could divide the sections.
> W That sounds like a great idea! ¹⁰**I can focus on the historical background** since I've already gathered some sources on that.
> M Perfect. I'll handle the methodology and data analysis parts then. When should we meet to coordinate our approach?
> W How about Thursday afternoon at the library?
>
> **preliminary**[prilímənèri] 예비의, 준비의
> **overwhelm**[òuvərhwélm] 압도하다
> **consider**[kənsídər] 고려하다
> **collaborate**[kəlǽbərèit] 협력하다, 협업하다
> **source**[sɔːrs] 자료, 원천
> **coordinate**[kouɔ́ːrdənèit] 조율하다, 조정하다

대화를 들으시오.

M Ivanov 교수님의 연구 논문 작업을 시작했나요?
W 예비 조사는 했지만, 조금 압도되는 느낌이에요. 고려해야 할 것들이 너무 많아요.
M 저도 마찬가지예요. ⁰⁹그럼, 협력하는 것에 관심이 있으세요? 아마 우리가 구간들을 나눌 수 있을 것 같아요.
W 정말 좋은 생각 같아요! 저는 이미 그것에 대한 몇 가지 자료를 모았기 때문에 ¹⁰역사적 배경에 집중할 수 있어요.
M 완벽해요. 그럼 제가 방법론과 데이터 분석 부분을 맡을게요. 우리의 접근법을 조율하기 위해 언제 만날까요?
W 목요일 오후에 도서관에서는 어때요?

09 Suggestion Question

남자는 여자에게 무엇을 하라고 제안하는가?
☑ 과제에서 힘을 합친다.
Ⓑ 교수님에게 기한 연장을 요청한다.
Ⓒ 데이터 분석에 더 집중한다.
Ⓓ 연구 주제를 바꾼다.

어휘 **join forces** 힘을 합치다　**extension**[iksténʃən] 기한 연장, 확장

10 Inference Question

여자는 무엇에 집중할 것 같은가?
Ⓐ 데이터 수집 방법
Ⓑ 통계 분석
☑ 과거 사건과 맥락
Ⓓ 연구 결론

어휘 method [méθəd] 방법 conclusion [kənklúːʒən] 결론

[11-12]

🔊 W-En M-Am

Listen to a conversation.

> W I've been trying to improve my cooking lately, but ¹¹everything I make turns out bland. I'm getting really frustrated.
> M Don't give up! ¹²Have you been tasting as you go? That's the key to good seasoning.
> W I never thought about tasting while cooking. I usually just follow the recipe exactly.
> M Well, recipes are just guidelines.
> W That makes sense. I guess I've been too afraid to change anything.
>
> bland [blænd] 싱거운, 온화한
> frustrated [frʌ́streitid] 좌절한, 실망한
> exactly [igzǽktli] 정확히   guideline [gáidlàin] 지침, 안내

대화를 들으시오.

W 최근에 요리 실력을 늘리려고 노력하고 있는데, ¹¹제가 만드는 모든 것이 싱겁게 나와요. 정말 좌절스러워요.
M 포기하지 마세요! ¹²요리하면서 맛을 보고 계세요? 그것이 좋은 양념의 핵심이에요.
W 요리하면서 맛을 본다는 것을 생각해본 적이 없어요. 저는 보통 요리법만 정확히 따라요.
M 글쎄요, 요리법은 그냥 지침일 뿐이에요.
W 말이 되네요. 제가 뭔가를 바꾸는 것을 너무 두려워했던 것 같아요.

11 Problem Question

여자의 문제는 무엇인가?
Ⓐ 좋은 요리 도구를 갖고 있지 않다.
☑ 음식에 맛이 부족하다.
Ⓒ 음식을 자주 태운다.
Ⓓ 요리법을 정확히 따를 수 없다.

어휘 utensil [juːténsəl] 도구   lack [læk] 부족하다
frequently [fríːkwəntli] 자주

12 Suggestion Question

남자는 여자에게 어떤 조언을 주는가?
Ⓐ 고급 요리 수업을 듣는다.
Ⓑ 요리법을 더 주의 깊게 따른다.
Ⓒ 더 좋은 주방 장비를 산다.
☑ 요리하는 동안 음식을 맛본다.

어휘 stick to ~을 따르다   carefully [kɛ́ərfəli] 주의 깊게

[13-14]

🔊 M-Am W-Au

Listen to a conversation.

> M I've been apartment hunting for months, but every place I like is way over my budget.
> W Have you considered looking in different neighborhoods?
> M Not really. ¹³I've been focusing on this one area because it's close to work.
> W ¹⁴You might want to expand your search area a bit.
> M Maybe you're right. I should also consider places near the bus station.
> W Exactly! That way you'd still have a reasonable commute, but you might find better deals.
>
> over one's budget 예산을 넘는
> neighborhood [néibərhud] 동네
> expand [ikspǽnd] 확장시키다, 팽창하다
> commute [kəmjúːt] 통근, 통학

대화를 들으시오.

M 몇 달 동안 아파트를 찾고 있는데, 제 마음에 드는 모든 곳이 제 예산을 훨씬 넘어요.
W 다른 동네들을 찾아보는 것을 고려해봤나요?
M 별로요. ¹³직장에 가깝기 때문에 이 한 지역에 집중하고 있었어요.
W ¹⁴탐색 지역을 조금 확장해보는 것이 좋을 것 같아요.
M 당신 말이 맞는 것 같아요. 정류장 근처의 장소들도 고려해봐야겠어요.
W 정확해요! 그런 식으로 하면 여전히 합리적인 통근을 하게 되지만, 더 좋은 가격들을 찾을 수도 있어요.

13 Detail Question

남자는 왜 한 지역에 집중해왔는가?
Ⓐ 안전한 동네이다.
☑ 직장과 가깝다.
Ⓒ 임대료가 가장 저렴하다.
Ⓓ 대중교통과 가깝다.

어휘 public transportation 대중교통

14 Suggestion Question

여자는 남자에게 무엇을 하라고 조언하는가?
Ⓐ 기대치를 낮춘다.
Ⓑ 임대료를 협상한다.
Ⓒ 룸메이트를 찾는다.
☑ 탐색 지역을 확장한다.

어휘 expectation [èkspektéiʃən] 기대치, 가능성
negotiate [nigóuʃièit] 협상하다

[15-16]

🎧 M-Au W-En

Listen to a conversation.

> M How are preparations coming for tomorrow's department meeting with the directors?
> W I've finished the slides, but I'm having trouble with the data charts. The formatting isn't consistent.
> M ¹⁵I can help with that, since I'm good with the presentation software. Would you like me to take a look?
> W That would be great! I should have everything ready by this afternoon. When would be a good time for you?
> M How about right after lunch? I'll have some free time around 2 P.M.
> W Perfect. ¹⁶I'll send you the file so you can review it beforehand.

director [diréktər] 관리자, 감독관
consistent [kənsístənt] 일관된　take a look 한 번 보다
right after ~ 직후

대화를 들으시오.
M 내일 있을 관리자들과의 부서 회의 준비는 어떻게 되어가고 있나요?
W 슬라이드는 완성했는데, 데이터 차트에 문제가 있어요. 서식이 일관되지 않아요.
M ¹⁵제가 프레젠테이션 소프트웨어에 능숙하기 때문에 그것을 도와드릴 수 있어요. 제가 한 번 봐드릴까요?
W 정말 좋을 것 같아요! 오늘 오후까지는 모든 것을 준비해야 해요. 언제가 당신에게 좋은 시간일까요?
M 점심 식사 직후는 어때요? 오후 2시경에 비는 시간이 있을 것 같아요.
W 완벽해요. ¹⁶당신이 미리 검토할 수 있도록 파일을 보내드릴게요.

15 Offer Question
남자는 무엇을 도와주겠다고 제안하는가?
Ⓐ 새로운 부서 로고를 디자인하는 것
Ⓑ 관리자들에게 슬라이드를 보내는 것
☑ 일관되지 않은 차트 서식을 수정하는 것
Ⓓ 회의를 위한 다과를 준비하는 것

어휘　refreshments [rifréʃmənts] 다과

16 Detail Question
여자는 그들이 만나기 전에 무엇을 할 것인가?
Ⓐ 슬라이드 복사본을 만든다.
Ⓑ 회의 일정을 잡는다.
☑ 발표 파일을 공유한다.
Ⓓ 회의실을 예약한다.

어휘　reserve [rizə́:rv] 예약하다

3. Problem Questions

Example 🎧 W-Am M-Au　　p.103

> W 내일 회의에 차를 몰고 가실 계획이신가요?
> M 그럴 계획이었는데, 오늘 아침 운전했을 때 **제 차가 이상한 소음을 내기 시작했어요**. 장거리 여행에 가져가기엔 걱정이 되네요.
> W 오, 정비공에게 전화는 하셨나요?
> M 네, 한 시간 전에 전화했어요. 내일 오후에 볼 수 있다고 하는데, 그건 너무 늦어요.
> W 원하신다면 카풀을 할 수 있어요. 저는 아침 일찍 출발하거든요.
> M 그거 좋겠네요. 제안해주셔서 정말 감사해요.

strange [streindʒ] 이상한　concerned [kənsə́:rnd] 걱정이 되는
mechanic [məkǽnik] 정비공, 수리공

남자의 문제는 무엇인가?
Ⓐ 차량에 연료가 떨어졌다.
☑ 차가 이상한 소리를 낸다.
Ⓒ 동료가 회의에 참석할 수 없다.
Ⓓ 회의 장소가 변경되었다.

HACKERS PRACTICE　　p.104

01 Ⓑ　　02 Ⓒ　　03 Ⓓ　　04 Ⓐ

01 Problem Question 🎧 M-En W-Am

> M I'm having trouble with the company email system. It keeps showing an error message when I try to attach files. Are you having the same issue?
> W Yes, it's so frustrating! We should notify the IT department about it.
> M I already called them. They said they were working on it, but they didn't give a timeline for the fix.
> W That's not good. I have important documents to send to clients before noon.

attach [ətǽtʃ] 첨부하다, 부착하다　notify [nóutəfài] 알리다
document [dákjumənt] 서류

M 회사 이메일 시스템에 문제가 있어요. 파일을 첨부하려고 할 때마다 계속 오류 메시지가 나와요. 당신도 같은 문제를 겪고 있나요?
W 네, 정말 절망적이네요! IT 부서에 알려야 해요.
M 이미 전화했어요. 그들은 작업 중이라고 했지만, 수리 일정은 알려주지 않았어요.
W 그건 좋지 않네요. 정오 전에 고객들에게 보낼 중요한 문서들이 있거든요.

화자들은 어떤 문제에 대해 이야기하고 있는가?
Ⓐ 촉박한 보고서 발송 기한
☑ 이메일 시스템 고장
Ⓒ 취소된 고객들과의 회의
Ⓓ 분실된 중요한 문서

어휘 tight [tait] 촉박한, 단단한
malfunction [mælfʌ́ŋkʃən] 고장 나다, 오작동하다

02 Problem Question 🔊 W-Nz M-En

W You look stressed today. Is everything okay?
M Not really. **I just found out I have three exams scheduled for the same day next week.**
W Wow, that's a lot of pressure. Have you talked to any of your professors about it?
M Not yet. I'm not sure if they'd be willing to adjust the schedule this late in the semester.
W Why don't you give it a try anyway? It doesn't hurt to ask.
M You're right. Thanks for the advice.

---

pressure [préʃər] 압박, 압력   adjust [ədʒʌ́st] 조정하다, 적응하다

W 오늘 스트레스를 받는 것처럼 보이네요. 모든 게 괜찮나요?
M 사실 그렇지 않아요. **다음 주 같은 날에 시험 3개가 예정되어 있다는 걸 방금 알았어요.**
W 와, 압박이 엄청나겠네요. 교수님들 중 누구와라도 얘기해보셨나요?
M 아직이요. 학기가 이렇게 늦은 시점에 일정을 조정해주실지 확신이 서지 않아요.
W 어쨌든 시도해보는 게 어때요? 물어보는 게 손해는 아니잖아요.
M 맞네요. 조언 감사해요.

남자의 문제는 무엇인가?
Ⓐ 중요한 시험에서 떨어졌다.
Ⓑ 시험에서 나쁜 점수를 받았다.
☑ 한 날에 여러 시험이 있다.
Ⓓ 이번 학기에 많은 수업을 빠졌다.

어휘 multiple [mʌ́ltipəl] 여러 개의, 복합의   skip [skip] 빠지다

03 Problem Question 🔊 W-Am M-Au

W Hey, a new fitness center just opened downtown, and I signed up.
M Really? I'm still going to the one near my apartment, but it's always so crowded after work.
W That's why I switched gyms. I could never use the equipment I wanted.
M Oh, is the new one any better?
W Much better! It's even offering a temporary discount. **The only downside is the parking situation. It's really hard to find a spot sometimes.**

---

crowded [kráudid] 붐비는, 혼잡한
switch [switʃ] 바꾸다, 교체하다
temporary [témpərèri] 일시적인   downside [dáunsàid] 단점
situation [sìtʃuéiʃən] 상황, 장소

W 이봐요, 시내에 새 헬스장이 막 오픈했는데, 저는 등록했어요.
M 정말요? 저는 여전히 아파트 근처 헬스장에 다니는데, 퇴근 후에 항상 너무 붐벼요.
W 그래서 체육관을 바꾼 거예요. 원하는 기구를 전혀 쓸 수 없었거든요.
M 아, 새로운 곳이 더 나은가요?
W 훨씬 좋아요! 일시적인 할인도 하고 있어요. **유일한 단점은 주차 상황이에요. 때때로 자리 찾기가 정말 어려워요.**

여자가 새 헬스장에서 겪고 있는 문제는 무엇인가?
Ⓐ 운동 기구가 더 적다.
Ⓑ 퇴근 후에 너무 붐빈다.
Ⓒ 높은 회원비를 요구한다.
☑ 충분한 주차 공간이 부족하다.

어휘 sufficient [səfíʃənt] 충분한, 알맞은

04 Problem Question 🔊 M-En W-Am

M I'm not sure what to do about my smartphone. **The battery drains completely in just a few hours.**
W Have you checked which apps are running in the background?
M I did, and I've closed everything unnecessary.
W Hmm... Could your phone be running low on storage?
M I don't think so. I still have more than 50GB left.
W That's strange. How old is it?
M About three years now. I'm wondering if I should just get a new one.

---

drain [drein] 소모되다   run low on ~이 부족하다
storage [stɔ́ːridʒ] 저장 공간

M 스마트폰을 어떻게 해야 할지 모르겠어요. **배터리가 단 몇 시간 만에 완전히 소모돼요.**
W 백그라운드에서 어떤 앱들이 실행되고 있는지 확인해보셨나요?
M 확인했고, 불필요한 것들은 모두 종료했어요.
W 음... 당신 폰의 저장 공간이 부족할 수도 있나요?
M 그렇지 않을 것 같아요. 아직 50GB가 넘게 남아있어요.
W 그거 이상하네요. 얼마나 오래됐나요?
M 약 3년 정도요. 그냥 새 걸 사야 하나 고민 중이에요.

남자의 스마트폰의 문제는 무엇인가?
☑ 배터리가 매우 빨리 떨어진다.
Ⓑ 저장 공간이 충분하지 않다.
Ⓒ 불필요한 앱들이 너무 많이 실행된다.
Ⓓ 여러 앱을 사용할 때 과열된다.

어휘 run out of 떨어지다   overheat [òuvərhíːt] 과열되다

HACKERS TEST p.106

01	Ⓓ	02	Ⓒ	03	Ⓑ	04	Ⓑ	05	Ⓓ
06	Ⓐ	07	Ⓑ	08	Ⓒ	09	Ⓑ	10	Ⓐ
11	Ⓓ	12	Ⓒ	13	Ⓑ	14	Ⓒ	15	Ⓑ
16	Ⓑ								

[01-02]

🎧 W-Am M-Nz

Listen to a conversation.

> W You are coming to the yoga class tonight at the community center, right?
> M Yes, ⁰¹but I just realized that I didn't bring my yoga mat today.
> W Well, do you have time to go home and get it before the class?
> M Not really.
> W ⁰²Then you can just use the shared mats they lend for free. I've been doing that since my first class.

realize [ríːəlàiz] 깨닫다   lend [lend] 빌려 주다

대화를 들으시오.
W 오늘 밤 지역 문화 센터 요가 수업에 오실 거죠?
M 네, ⁰¹하지만 오늘 제 요가 매트를 가져오지 않았다는 걸 방금 깨달았어요.
W 음, 수업 전에 집에 가서 가져올 시간이 있나요?
M 그렇지는 않아요.
W ⁰²그럼 그들이 무료로 빌려 주는 공용 매트를 사용하시면 돼요. 저는 첫 수업부터 그렇게 해왔어요.

01 Problem Question

남자의 문제는 무엇인가?
Ⓐ 요가를 연습할 시간이 충분하지 않다.
Ⓑ 지역 문화 센터가 어디에 있는지 모른다.
Ⓒ 일과 요가 수업 사이에 일정 충돌이 있다.
Ⓓ 요가 수업에 필요한 장비를 가져오지 않았다.

어휘 scheduling conflict 일정 충돌

02 Inference Question

여자에 대해 암시되는 것은?
Ⓐ 항상 요가 수업에 일찍 도착한다.
Ⓑ 커뮤니티 센터에서 요가를 가르친다.
Ⓒ 자신을 위한 요가 매트를 구입하지 않았다.
Ⓓ 남자보다 요가 경험이 더 많다.

어휘 experienced [ikspíəriənst] 경험이 많은

[03-04]

🎧 W-En M-Am

Listen to a conversation.

> W ⁰³My laptop screen suddenly went black yesterday, and I can't get it to turn back on.
> M That sounds serious. Have you tried connecting it to an external monitor?
> W Yes, and that works fine, so I think it's the display that's broken.
> M Well, the university tech center might be able to fix it.
> W Are they open on weekends? ⁰⁴I need my laptop for a presentation on Tuesday.
> M ⁰⁴They aren't, but they offer same-day repairs if you bring it in first thing in the morning.

suddenly [sʌ́dnli] 갑자기   connect [kənékt] 연결하다, 잇다
external [ekstə́ːrnəl] 외부의   same-day 당일의

대화를 들으시오.
W ⁰³제 노트북 화면이 어제 갑자기 검게 되었고, 다시 켜지게 할 수가 없어요.
M 심각하게 들리네요. 외부 모니터에 연결해보셨나요?
W 네, 그리고 그건 잘 작동해요, 그러니까 디스플레이가 고장난 것 같아요.
M 음, 대학 기술 센터에서 그것을 고칠 수 있을 것 같은데요.
W 주말에도 문을 여나요? ⁰⁴화요일에 발표 때문에 노트북이 필요해요.
M ⁰⁴안 열지만, 아침 일찍 가져가면 당일 수리를 제공해요.

03 Problem Question

여자의 노트북의 문제는 무엇인가?
Ⓐ 키보드가 고장났다.
Ⓑ 화면이 켜지지 않는다.
Ⓒ 배터리 교체가 필요하다.
Ⓓ 다른 기기에 연결되지 않는다.

어휘 replacement [ripléismənt] 교체   device [diváis] 기기

04 Intention Question

남자는 왜 당일 수리를 언급하는가?
Ⓐ 기술 센터가 비싼 이유를 설명하기 위해
Ⓑ 여자에게 이용 가능한 해결책을 알려주기 위해
Ⓒ 기술 센터의 제한된 운영 시간에 대해 불평하기 위해
Ⓓ 여자가 즉시 기술 센터를 방문하도록 격려하기 위해

어휘 explain [ikspléin] 설명하다   solution [səlúːʃən] 해결책
complain [kəmpléin] 불평하다
immediately [imíːdiətli] 즉시, 곧

[05-06]

🎧 W-Au M-En

Listen to a conversation.

> W ⁰⁵Did you book that campground for our weekend getaway?
> M I was about to, but then I just saw the weather forecast. ⁰⁵It's supposed to rain the entire weekend.
> W Oh, no. Do you think we should postpone the trip?
> M Maybe. Or we could look at indoor activities instead.
> W Good idea. I heard there's a new indoor water park that just opened near the campground.
> M Perfect! That would be fun rain or shine. ⁰⁶I'll go ahead and book the tickets.

weekend getaway 주말 나들이   weather forecast 일기 예보

be supposed to ~할 예정이다   indoor[índɔːr] 실내의
rain or shine 날씨에 상관없이

대화를 들으시오.
W ⁰⁵우리 주말 나들이를 위해 그 캠핑장을 예약하셨나요?
M 하려고 했는데, 방금 일기 예보를 봤어요. ⁰⁵주말 내내 비가 올 예정이에요.
W 오, 안 돼요. 여행을 연기해야 할까요?
M 아마도요. 아니면 대신 실내 활동을 찾아볼 수 있어요.
W 좋은 생각이에요. 캠핑장 근처에 새로 오픈한 실내 워터파크가 있다고 들었어요.
M 완벽해요! 그건 날씨에 상관없이 재미있을 거예요. ⁰⁶표를 예약하러 갈게요.

05 Problem Question
화자들은 어떤 문제에 대해 이야기하고 있는가?
Ⓐ 일부 캠핑 장비가 수리가 필요하다.
Ⓑ 주말 여행 예산이 너무 빠듯하다.
Ⓒ 캠핑장 예약 시스템이 작동하지 않는다.
✓ 주말 계획을 비 때문에 망칠 수 있다.

어휘 ruin[rúːin] 망치다

06 Do Next Question
남자는 다음에 무엇을 할 것 같은가?
✓ 표를 산다.
Ⓑ 일부 용품을 수리한다.
Ⓒ 캠핑장에 연락한다.
Ⓓ 실내 장소를 찾는다.

어휘 repair[ripɛ́ər] 수리하다

[07-08] M-Am W-Nz
Listen to a conversation.

M I can't stand it anymore. ⁰⁷I have an issue with my air conditioner, and my room feels like a sauna right now.
W Oh no! That's terrible timing with this heat wave. Is it not turning on at all?
M It turns on, but ⁰⁷cold air won't come out. Just warm air blowing around.
W You should submit a dormitory maintenance request online right away. Meanwhile, ⁰⁸do you want me to lend you a fan?
M That would save my life. I'll grab it on my way back to my room.

stand it 참다   air conditioner 에어컨   heat wave 폭염
submit[səbmít] 제출하다   maintenance request 수리 요청

대화를 들으시오.
M 더 이상 참을 수 없어요. ⁰⁷에어컨에 문제가 있어서, 제 방이 지금 사우나 같아요.
W 오 안 돼요! 이 폭염에 정말 나쁜 타이밍이네요. 아예 켜지지도 않나요?
M 켜지기는 하는데, ⁰⁷차가운 공기가 나오지 않아요. 그냥 따뜻한 공기가 돌아다녀요.
W 즉시 온라인으로 기숙사 수리 요청을 제출해야 해요. 그 동안, ⁰⁸제가 선풍기를 빌려드릴까요?
M 그게 절 살릴 거예요. 제 방으로 돌아가는 길에 가져갈게요.

07 Problem Question
남자가 에어컨으로 겪고 있는 문제는 무엇인가?
Ⓐ 시끄러운 소음을 낸다.
✓ 차가운 공기를 만들지 않는다.
Ⓒ 전기를 너무 많이 사용한다.
Ⓓ 켜지지 않는다.

어휘 produce[prədjúːs] 만들다, 생산하다
electricity[ilèktrísəti] 전기

08 Offer Question
여자는 무엇을 해주겠다고 제안하는가?
Ⓐ 건물 관리소에 연락한다.
Ⓑ 그의 에어컨을 확인한다.
✓ 냉방 기기를 빌려준다.
Ⓓ 다른 방으로 이사하는 것을 돕는다.

어휘 building maintenance 건물 관리소
cooling device 냉방 기기

[09-10] W-En M-Am
Listen to a conversation.

W I'm afraid I can't finish my part of the presentation by Friday. ⁰⁹I've been having severe headaches.
M Oh, I'm sorry to hear that. Have you seen a doctor?
W Yes, yesterday. She prescribed some medication and recommended reducing screen time.
M That makes sense. ¹⁰When do you think you'll be able to get back to work on it?
W ¹⁰Probably next Monday if the medication helps.
M All right. I'll check with the professor and see if it's possible to move the presentation to next Thursday.

severe[səvíər] 심한   prescribe[priskráib] 처방하다
possible[pásəbl] 가능한

대화를 들으시오.
W 금요일까지 제 발표 부분을 끝내지 못할 것 같아요. ⁰⁹심한 두통을 겪고 있어요.
M 오, 유감이네요. 의사를 만나보셨나요?
W 네, 어제요. 그녀는 약을 처방해주시고 화면 시청 시간을 줄이라고 추천하셨어요.
M 일리가 있네요. ¹⁰언제쯤 다시 그 작업으로 돌아갈 수 있을 것 같나요?
W 약이 도움이 된다면 ¹⁰아마 다음 주 월요일이요.
M 알겠어요. 교수님께 확인해보고 발표를 다음 주 목요일로 옮기는 것이 가능한지 알아볼게요.

09 Problem Question
여자의 문제는 무엇인가?
Ⓐ 화면 시청 시간을 줄일 수 없다.
✓ⓑ 극심한 두통을 겪고 있다.
Ⓒ 발표 날짜를 잘못 이해했다.
Ⓓ 약물 부작용으로 스트레스를 받는다.

어휘 suffer [sʌ́fər] 겪다
misunderstand [mìsʌndərstǽnd] 잘못 이해하다
side effect 부작용

10 Detail Question
여자는 언제 발표 작업을 재개할 것으로 예상하는가?
✓Ⓐ 월요일
Ⓑ 화요일
Ⓒ 목요일
Ⓓ 금요일

[11-12]
W-Am M-En

Listen to a conversation.

W Lately, ¹¹**our dorm has been way too noisy at night**. How about yours?
M The men's dorm has the same issue.
W I was thinking about bringing this up at the next dorm council meeting.
M That's a good idea, but ¹²**maybe we should gather some specific examples first**. Like what times it's the loudest and what kind of noise we hear.
W That makes sense. I'll start keeping track of it.
M Perfect. ¹²**If we have concrete details, the council will be more likely to take action rather than just dismiss it as a general complaint.**

bring something up ~을 제기하다
council meeting 의회 회의   gather [gǽðər] 모으다
example [igzǽmpl] 예시
keep track of 기록을 남기다, 추적하다
concrete [kάːnkriːt] 구체적인   detail [ditéil] 세부사항
take action 조치를 취하다   dismiss [dismís] 무시하다, 해산하다
general [dʒénərəl] 일반적인

대화를 들으시오.

W 최근에 ¹¹저희 기숙사가 밤에 너무 시끄러웠어요. 당신 쪽은 어때요?
M 남자 기숙사도 같은 문제가 있어요.
W 다음 기숙사 의회 회의에서 이것을 제기하는 것에 대해 생각하고 있었어요.
M 좋은 생각이지만, ¹²먼저 몇 가지 구체적인 예시를 모아야 할 것 같아요. 언제가 가장 시끄러운지, 어떤 종류의 소음을 듣는지 같은 것들 말이에요.
W 그게 맞는 것 같아요. 기록을 남기기 시작할게요.
M 완벽해요. ¹²구체적인 세부사항이 있다면, 의회가 그냥 일반적인 불만으로 무시하는 것보다는 조치를 취할 가능성이 더 높을 거예요.

11 Problem Question
화자들은 어떤 문제에 대해 이야기하고 있는가?
Ⓐ 기숙사 안전 문제
Ⓑ 방의 조명 부족
Ⓒ 의회 회의 시간 부족
✓Ⓓ 야간 시간대 과도한 소음

어휘 dormitory [dɔ́ːrmətɔ̀ːri] 기숙사
excessive [iksésiv] 과도한, 지나친

12 Detail Question
남자는 자신의 제안에 대해 어떤 이유를 제시하는가?
Ⓐ 회의 중 시간을 절약할 것이다.
Ⓑ 공식 보고서를 작성하는 데 도움이 될 것이다.
✓Ⓒ 불만을 더 설득력 있게 만들 것이다.
Ⓓ 구체적인 해결책을 제안할 수 있게 해줄 것이다.

어휘 formal [fɔ́ːrməl] 공식적인, 정규의
convincing [kənvínsiŋ] 설득력 있는
propose [prəpóuz] 제안하다

[13-14]
M-Nz W-Am

Listen to a conversation.

M I think there's something wrong with my bicycle. ¹³**The brakes are making a strange noise.**
W Have you tried taking it to a repair shop? There's a good one near campus.
M Not yet. I was hoping to fix it myself to save some money.
W ¹⁴**Do you want me to ask my brother?** He fixed mine last month when the chain kept falling off.
M Do you think he would be willing to take a look at mine?
W I'm sure he is. ¹⁴**I can call him and ask if he's free this weekend.**

repair shop 수리점   fall off 떨어지다
be willing to ~할 의향이 있다, 기꺼이 ~하다

대화를 들으시오.

M 제 자전거에 뭔가 문제가 있는 것 같아요. ¹³브레이크가 이상한 소음을 내요.
W 수리점에 가져가보셨나요? 캠퍼스 근처에 좋은 곳이 있어요.
M 아직이요. 돈을 절약하려고 직접 고치려고 했어요.
W ¹⁴그럼 제 오빠에게 물어보기를 원하세요? 지난달에 체인이 계속 떨어질 때 제 것을 고쳐줬어요.
M 그가 제 것도 봐주실 의향이 있을까요?
W 확실히 있을 거예요. ¹⁴전화해서 이번 주말에 시간이 있는지 물어볼게요.

13 Problem Question
남자의 자전거의 문제는 무엇인가?
Ⓐ 타이어를 교체해야 한다.
✓Ⓑ 브레이크가 소음을 낸다.

Ⓒ 체인이 계속 떨어진다.
Ⓓ 안장이 불편하다.

어휘 replace[ripléis] 교체하다, 바꾸다

14 Offer Question
여자는 무엇을 해주겠다고 제안하는가?
Ⓐ 더 저렴한 수리점을 추천한다.
Ⓑ 자전거를 수리점으로 운반하는 것을 도와준다.
✓ 도움을 위해 가족에게 연락한다.
Ⓓ 남자에게 그녀 오빠의 수리 도구를 빌려준다.

어휘 transport[trænspɔ́:rt] 운반하다, 옮기다 repair tool 수리 도구

[15-16]
W-Au M-En
Listen to a conversation.

W ¹⁵**The printer next to the meeting room is acting up again. It keeps jamming.**
M That's the third time this month. Have you tried the basic troubleshooting steps?
W Yes, I've checked the paper tray and cleared all the jams, but it's still not working properly.
M Well, then ¹⁶**we should call the maintenance company** and get them to fix it as soon as possible.
W ¹⁶**Okay, I'll do it right away.** Should I schedule a service appointment for tomorrow morning?
M Perfect. The sooner the better.

act up 말썽을 부리다, 제 기능을 못하다
troubleshooting step 문제 해결 단계
jam[dʒæm] 걸린 것; 쑤셔넣다 right away 바로

대화를 들으시오.
W ¹⁵회의실 옆 프린터가 또 말썽을 부리고 있어요. 계속 걸려요.
M 이번 달에 벌써 세 번째네요. 기본적인 문제 해결 단계들을 시도해 보셨나요?
W 네, 종이함을 확인하고 모든 걸린 것들을 치웠는데, 여전히 제대로 작동하지 않아요.
M 그럼, ¹⁶관리 회사에 전화해서 가능한 한 빨리 고치도록 해야 겠네요.
W ¹⁶알겠어요, 제가 바로 할게요. 내일 아침에 서비스 약속을 잡을까요?
M 완벽해요. 빠를수록 좋아요.

15 Problem Question
화자들이 프린터로 겪고 있는 문제는 무엇인가?
Ⓐ 페이지를 너무 천천히 인쇄한다.
✓ 지속적으로 용지가 걸린다.
Ⓒ 작동할 때 시끄러운 소음을 낸다.
Ⓓ 예기치 않게 꺼진다.

어휘 constant[kánstənt] 지속적인 operate[ápəreit] 작동하다
shut down 꺼지다, 멈추다
unexpectedly[ʌ̀nikspéktidli] 예기치 않게

16 Do Next Question
여자는 다음에 무엇을 할 것 같은가?
Ⓐ 새로운 프린터를 구입한다.
✓ 전문 수리 서비스를 주선한다.
Ⓒ 동료들에게 기본 문제 해결을 교육한다.
Ⓓ 인쇄 업무를 다른 부서로 이전한다.

어휘 professional[prəféʃənl] 전문의, 직업의
transfer[trænsfə́:r] 이전하다, 옮기다

4. Do Next Questions

Example M-En W-Am p.111

M 저기, 이웃 음식 나눔 모임에 뭘 가져갈 생각이에요?
W 완전히 잊고 있었어요! 정확히 언제죠?
M 내일 정오예요.
W 뭘 가져갈지 모르겠어요. 뭘 이바지할 예정이세요?
M 초콜릿 케이크를 가져갈 거예요. 당신은 파스타 샐러드를 만들 수도 있어요. 준비하는 데 그리 오래 걸리지 않을 거예요.
W 좋은 생각이네요. **슈퍼마켓에 가서 재료들을 살게요.**

neighborhood potluck 이웃 음식 나눔 모임
completely[kəmplí:tli] 완전히
contribute[kəntríbju:t] 이바지하다, 공헌하다
head out ~에 가다, 출발하다 ingredient[ingrí:diənt] 재료

여자는 다음에 무엇을 할 것 같은가?
✓ 슈퍼마켓에 간다.
Ⓑ 초콜릿 케이크를 만든다.
Ⓒ 다른 사람에게 도움을 요청한다.
Ⓓ 식사 준비를 시작한다.

HACKERS PRACTICE p.112

01 Ⓐ 02 Ⓓ 03 Ⓒ 04 Ⓒ

01 Do Next Question M-Am W-Au

M Have you had a chance to look at the museum exhibition schedule?
W Not really, why?
M The ancient pottery collection is being displayed until this Friday, and I really wanted to check it out.
W Oh, that's only two days away! I'm also interested in pottery, so how about going there tomorrow after lunch?
M Great! I will book our tickets on the museum website right away.

chance[tʃæns] 기회 exhibition[èksəbíʃən] 전시회
ancient[éinʃənt] 고대의, 옛날의 pottery[pátəri] 도자기
display[displéi] 전시하다

M 박물관 전시회 일정을 볼 기회가 있으셨어요?
W 아니요, 왜요?
M 고대 도자기 컬렉션이 이번 금요일까지 전시되고 있는데, 정말로 구경해보고 싶어요.
W 아, 그럼 이틀밖에 안 남았네요! 저도 도자기에 관심이 있어서, 내일 점심 후에 거기 가는 게 어떨까요?
M 좋아요! 박물관 웹사이트에서 바로 티켓을 예약할게요.

남자는 다음에 무엇을 할 것인가?
ⓐ 온라인으로 예약한다. ✓
ⓑ 오후 수업을 취소한다.
ⓒ 박물관에서 여자를 만난다.
ⓓ 친구와 점심을 먹는다.

어휘 reservation [rèzərvéiʃən] 예약

02 Do Next Question M-En W-Nz

M How's the presentation coming along for tomorrow's client meeting?
W I've got most of it done, but I'm having trouble with the projector in the conference room. It keeps shutting down randomly.
M That's frustrating. Have you tried using a different room?
W All the other rooms are booked tomorrow. I will call IT support to get this fixed.
M Good idea. They're usually pretty quick with these kinds of issues.

come along 되어 가다, 따라가다
randomly [rǽndəmli] 무작위로   pretty [príti] 꽤

M 내일 고객 회의를 위한 발표는 어떻게 되어 가고 있어요?
W 대부분 완료했는데, 회의실의 프로젝터에 문제가 있어요. 계속 무작위로 꺼져요.
M 답답하시겠네요. 다른 방을 사용해보려고 해보셨어요?
W 내일은 다른 방들이 모두 예약되어 있어요. IT 지원팀에 전화해서 이것을 고쳐달라고 할게요.
M 좋은 생각이에요. 그들은 보통 이런 종류의 문제들에 꽤 신속하죠.

여자는 다음에 무엇을 할 것 같은가?
ⓐ 발표 자료를 마무리한다.
ⓑ 다른 회의실을 찾는다.
ⓒ 고객 회의 일정을 변경한다.
ⓓ 기술 지원팀에 연락한다. ✓

어휘 finalize [fáinəlàiz] 마무리하다   technical support 기술 지원팀

03 Do Next Question W-Nz M-Am

W I missed Professor Hart's lecture yesterday because I had a doctor's appointment. Did he cover anything important?
M He went over the key concepts for next week's exam. It was pretty detailed.
W Oh no, that sounds crucial. Would you mind sharing your notes with me?
M Of course, but I can't get to them right now since class is about to start. I'll scan them and send them to you afterwards.
W No worries, thank you!

key concept 핵심 개념   detailed [díːteild] 자세한, 상세한
crucial [krúːʃəl] 중요한

W 병원 진료 예약 때문에 어제 Hart 교수님 강의를 놓쳤어요. 중요한 것을 다루셨나요?
M 다음 주 시험을 위한 핵심 개념들을 다루셨어요. 꽤 자세했어요.
W 아, 안 돼요, 그것은 중요한 것 같은데요. 당신의 필기를 저와 공유해 주실 수 있나요?
M 물론이에요, 하지만 수업이 곧 시작하기 때문에 지금은 그것들을 가져올 수 없어요. 나중에 그것들을 스캔해서 당신에게 보내드릴게요.
W 괜찮아요, 감사해요!

남자는 수업 후에 무엇을 할 것인가?
ⓐ 교수님과 만난다.
ⓑ 시험 공부를 한다.
ⓒ 여자에게 자신의 필기를 보낸다. ✓
ⓓ 여자를 병원에 데려간다.

04 Do Next Question W-Am M-En

W I just received an email about the student dormitory I applied for.
M Really? What did it say?
W I got approved! So, I need to sign the lease and pay the deposit by tomorrow.
M Congratulations! Do you have the money ready?
W Not yet. I need to transfer funds from my savings first.

apply [əplái] 신청하다, 적용되다
approve [əprúːv] 승인하다, 찬성하다   lease [liːs] 임대 계약서
deposit [dipázit] 보증금   saving [séiviŋ] 예금 계좌, 저축

W 제가 신청한 학생 기숙사에 대한 이메일을 막 받았어요.
M 정말요? 뭐라고 했나요?
W 저 승인됐어요! 그래서, 내일까지 임대 계약서에 서명하고 보증금을 지불해야 해요.
M 축하해요! 돈은 준비되어 있어요?
W 아직이요. 먼저 제 예금 계좌에서 자금을 송금해야 해요.

여자는 다음에 무엇을 할 것 같은가?
ⓐ 다른 기숙사를 찾는다.
ⓑ 남자에게 대출을 요청한다.
ⓒ 은행 계좌에 접속한다. ✓
ⓓ 기숙사 관리사무소에 전화한다.

어휘 loan [loun] 대출   bank account 은행 계좌
    administration [ədmìnistréiʃən] 관리사무소, 본부

HACKERS TEST

p.114

01 Ⓒ 02 Ⓑ 03 Ⓑ 04 Ⓓ 05 Ⓒ
06 Ⓓ 07 Ⓑ 08 Ⓐ 09 Ⓑ 10 Ⓓ
11 Ⓐ 12 Ⓒ 13 Ⓐ 14 Ⓓ 15 Ⓑ
16 Ⓑ

[01-02]

M-En W-Nz

Listen to a conversation.

M Did you hear about the new library policy?
W Not yet. Was there a big change?
M Yes, the borrowing period has been shortened to three weeks.
W Really? ⁰¹I thought it was still a month. That means my books are due tomorrow!
M They just changed the policy, so there might be some flexibility for books that were checked out before the change.
W ⁰²I'll return them right away, just to be safe. Thanks for letting me know.

policy [páləsi] 정책, 규정   period [píəriəd] 기간
shorten [ʃɔ́ːrtn] 단축하다, 줄이다
flexibility [flèksəbíləti] 융통성, 유연성
check out 대출하다, 확인하다

대화를 들으시오.

M 새로운 도서관 정책에 대해 들었어요?
W 아직이요. 큰 변화가 있었나요?
M 네, 대출 기간이 3주로 단축되었어요.
W 정말요? ⁰¹아직 한 달인 줄 알았어요. 그러면 제 책들을 내일까지 반납해야 한다는 뜻이네요!
M 그들이 막 정책을 바꿨으니까, 변경 전에 대출한 책들에 대해서는 융통성이 있을 수도 있어요.
W 안전하게 하기 위해 ⁰²바로 반납할게요. 알려주셔서 감사해요.

01 Problem Question

여자의 문제는 무엇인가?
Ⓐ 너무 많은 책을 빌렸다.
Ⓑ 도서관 웹사이트에 접속할 수 없다.
✓ⒸⒸ 자신의 책들이 반납 예정일 줄 예상하지 못했다.
Ⓓ 연체료를 내는 것을 잊었다.

어휘 overdue fine 연체료

02 Do Next Question

여자는 다음에 무엇을 할 것인가?
Ⓐ 대출 기간을 연장한다.
✓Ⓑ 자신의 책들을 즉시 반납한다.
Ⓒ 집에서 책을 찾아본다.
Ⓓ 온라인으로 새로운 정책을 확인한다.

[03-04]

W-Au M-Am

Listen to a conversation.

W I just reviewed our new company website, and I think we need to make some changes.
M What kind of changes are you thinking about?
W ⁰³The product descriptions are too technical. Our customers aren't engineers.
M I see your point. Should we simplify the language or add more explanatory graphics?
W I think both would help. ⁰⁴Could you revise the text while I work on some simple infographics?
M ⁰⁴Sure, I'll start that right away.

review [rivjúː] 검토하다   description [diskrípʃən] 설명
technical [téknikəl] 기술적인
engineer [èndʒiníər] 엔지니어, 기술자
simplify [símpəfài] 간단하게 하다, 단순화하다
explanatory [iksplǽnətɔ̀ːri] 설명의   revise [riváiz] 수정하다

대화를 들으시오.

W 제가 방금 우리의 새로운 회사 웹사이트를 검토했는데, 몇 가지를 수정해야 할 것 같아요.
M 어떤 종류의 수정사항을 생각하고 계세요?
W ⁰³제품 설명이 너무 기술적이에요. 우리 고객들은 엔지니어가 아니에요.
M 당신의 지적을 이해해요. 언어를 간단하게 하거나 더 많은 설명 도표를 추가해야 할까요?
W 둘 다 도움이 될 것 같아요. 제가 간단한 인포그래픽 작업을 하는 동안 ⁰⁴당신이 텍스트를 수정해주실 수 있나요?
M ⁰⁴물론이에요, 바로 시작할게요.

03 Intention Question

여자가 "우리 고객들은 엔지니어가 아니에요"라고 말할 때 무엇을 의도하는가?
Ⓐ 회사는 더 많은 엔지니어들을 대상으로 해야 한다.
✓Ⓑ 설명이 더 이해하기 쉬워야 한다.
Ⓒ 더 많은 기술 작가들을 고용해야 한다.
Ⓓ 그들의 제품이 너무 비싸다.

어휘 target [táːrgit] 대상으로 하다
overpriced [òuvərpráist] 비싼

04 Do Next Question

남자는 다음에 무엇을 할 것 같은가?
Ⓐ 후속 회의를 예약한다.
Ⓑ 고객 선호도를 조사한다.
Ⓒ 더 쉬운 인포그래픽을 개발한다.
✓Ⓓ 텍스트 설명을 편집한다.

어휘 follow-up 후속의   preference [préfərəns] 선호도
edit [édit] 편집하다

[05-06]

M-Am W-En

Listen to a conversation.

M Gina, are you free for lunch tomorrow? I was thinking we could try that new Japanese restaurant near campus.

W Tomorrow? ⁰⁵I have a class until 1:30. Would 2 P.M. work for you?

M That's totally fine. I heard their ramen is amazing, and they even offer student discounts.

W Great! ⁰⁶Do you know if they have vegetarian options?

M Hmm, I'm not sure. ⁰⁶Let me call and check.

amazing[əméiziŋ] 대단한, 놀라운 vegetarian option 채식 메뉴

대화를 들으시오.

M Gina, 내일 점심 시간에 시간 있어요? 캠퍼스 근처에 새로 생긴 일본 식당을 시도해볼까 생각했어요.

W 내일요? ⁰⁵1시 30분까지 수업이 있어요. 오후 2시는 괜찮으세요?

M 완전히 괜찮아요. 그들의 라멘이 대단하다고 들었고, 심지어 학생 할인도 제공한다고 해요.

W 좋아요! ⁰⁶혹시 채식 메뉴가 있는지 아세요?

M 음, 확실하지 않아요. ⁰⁶제가 전화해서 확인해볼게요.

05 Detail Question

여자는 왜 오후 2시에 만나자고 제안하는가?
Ⓐ 식당이 오후 2시까지 문을 열지 않는다.
Ⓑ 점심 전에 다른 사람을 만날 계획이다.
☑ 자신의 일정 때문에 더 일찍 만날 수 없다.
Ⓓ 식당이 오후 2시 이후에 할인을 제공한다.

06 Do Next Question

남자는 다음에 무엇을 할 것 같은가?
Ⓐ 만나는 시간을 바꾼다.
Ⓑ 두 명을 위한 테이블을 예약한다.
Ⓒ 다른 식당을 찾는다.
☑ 메뉴에 대해 문의한다.

어휘 make an inquiry 문의하다

[07-08]

M-En W-Am

Listen to a conversation.

M Excuse me, I saw your advertisement for a part-time student assistant for the campus library. Is that position still open?

W Yes, it is. We're looking for a student who can work 10 hours per week at the circulation desk.

M That sounds perfect for my schedule. ⁰⁷What kind of qualifications are you looking for?

W ⁰⁷We need someone who's organized and good with computers. Could you tell me about your availability?

M I'm available Monday through Thursday after 3 P.M.

W Great! ⁰⁸If you fill out this application form, we'll look it over and contact you soon.

M ⁰⁸I will do that, thanks!

part-time 아르바이트 assistant[əsístənt] 조교, 보조
position[pəzíʃən] 일자리, 직책 circulation desk 대출 데스크
qualification[kwὰːləfikéiʃən] 자격
availability[əvèiləbíləti] 가능한 시간, 이용할 수 있음
fill out 작성하다 application form 지원서
look something over ~을 검토하다

대화를 들으시오.

M 실례합니다, 캠퍼스 도서관 학생 조교 아르바이트에 대한 당신들의 광고를 봤어요. 그 일자리는 아직 열려 있나요?

W 네, 그래요. 우리는 대출 데스크에서 주당 10시간 일할 수 있는 학생을 찾고 있어요.

M 제 일정에 완벽할 것 같네요. ⁰⁷어떤 종류의 자격을 찾고 계세요?

W ⁰⁷우리는 체계적이고 컴퓨터에 능숙한 사람이 필요해요. 가능한 시간에 대해 말해주실 수 있나요?

M 월요일부터 목요일까지 오후 3시 이후에 가능해요.

W 좋아요! ⁰⁸이 지원서를 작성해주시면, 그것을 검토하고 곧 연락드리겠어요.

M ⁰⁸그렇게요, 감사해요!

07 Intention Question

여자는 왜 컴퓨터를 언급하는가?
Ⓐ 남자에게 컴퓨터 수업을 듣도록 조언하기 위해
☑ 일자리에 필요한 기술을 설명하기 위해
Ⓒ 온라인으로 지원서를 제출하라고 제안하기 위해
Ⓓ 도서관 시스템의 문제를 식별하기 위해

어휘 advise[ədváiz] 조언하다 necessary[nésəsèri] 필요한 identify[aidéntəfài] 식별하다

08 Do Next Question

남자는 다음에 무엇을 할 것 같은가?
☑ 양식을 작성한다.
Ⓑ 여자에게 전화한다.
Ⓒ 책들을 정리한다.
Ⓓ 자신의 일정을 바꾼다.

[09-10]

W-Am M-En

Listen to a conversation.

W ⁰⁹My computer has been freezing constantly since yesterday. I have a report due tomorrow. What am I going to do?

M Have you checked for viruses or malware?

W I ran a scan, but it didn't find anything.

M Well, I know a great repair shop downtown. They fixed my laptop when I had a bluescreen issue last month.

W That sounds promising. ¹⁰Could you send me their contact info?

M ¹⁰Sure, I'll message it to you.

W Thank you, you've saved my life!

freeze [fri:z] 멈추다, 얼다
constantly [kánstəntli] 계속, 지속적으로
promising [prámisiŋ] 유망한, 기대되는
contact info 연락처 정보

대화를 들으시오.

W ⁰⁹제 컴퓨터가 어제부터 계속 멈춰요. 내일까지 보고서를 제출해야 하는데요. 어떻게 해야 하죠?

M 바이러스나 악성 프로그램을 확인해봤어요?

W 스캔을 실행했지만, 아무것도 찾지 못했어요.

M 음, 저는 시내의 훌륭한 수리점을 알고 있어요. 지난달 제가 블루스크린 문제가 있었을 때 그들이 제 노트북을 고쳐줬어요.

W 그거 유망해 보이네요. ¹⁰그들의 연락처 정보를 보내주실 수 있나요?

M ¹⁰물론이에요, 메시지로 보내드릴게요.

W 감사해요, 절 구해주셨어요!

09 Problem Question

여자가 겪고 있는 문제는 무엇인가?
Ⓐ 보고서 마감일을 놓쳤다.
☑ 자신의 컴퓨터가 반복적으로 멈춰왔다.
Ⓒ 자신의 보고서에 너무 많은 오류가 있다.
Ⓓ 남자의 연락처 정보가 없다.

어휘 repeatedly [ripítidli] 반복적으로
      contain [kəntéin] ~가 있다, 포함하다

10 Do Next Question

남자는 다음에 무엇을 할 것인가?
Ⓐ 여자를 시내의 수리점으로 데려다 준다.
Ⓑ 컴퓨터 멈춤을 방지하는 방법을 보여준다.
Ⓒ 여자를 위해 수리점에 전화해서 예약을 잡는다.
☑ 수리점의 연락처 세부사항을 공유한다.

어휘 prevent [privént] 방지하다, 막다

[11-12] 🔊 M-En W-Am

Listen to a conversation.

M Did you choose a topic for the environmental science presentation?

W Not yet. ¹¹I've been looking at renewable energy options, but there are so many different technologies to choose from.

M I'm facing the same issue. Are you planning to go to the library for research?

W Yes, I was thinking about it. I heard the science section has some great resources.

M Perfect! Want to go together?

W That sounds great. We can help each other find relevant materials. ¹²When should we meet?

renewable energy 재생 에너지
technology [teknálədʒi] 기술   face [feis] 직면하다, 마주하다
resource [risɔ́:rs] 자료   relevant [réləvənt] 관련된, 적절한

대화를 들으시오.

M 환경과학 발표를 위한 주제를 선택했어요?

W 아직이요. ¹¹재생 에너지 옵션들을 살펴보고 있는데, 선택할 수 있는 기술이 너무 많아요.

M 저도 같은 문제에 직면하고 있어요. 조사를 위해 도서관에 갈 계획이세요?

W 네, 그렇게 생각하고 있었어요. 과학 섹션에 훌륭한 자료들이 있다고 들었어요.

M 완벽해요! 함께 가실래요?

W 그거 좋네요. 우리는 서로 관련 자료를 찾는 데 도움을 줄 수 있어요. ¹²언제 만날까요?

11 Inference Question

여자는 재생 에너지에 대해 무엇을 암시하는가?
☑ 선택하기에 많은 주제 선택지들을 제공한다.
Ⓑ 연구하기 위해 값비싼 장비가 필요하다.
Ⓒ 그들의 교과서에서 잘 다뤄지지 않는다.
Ⓓ 학생들 사이에서 더욱 인기를 얻고 있다.

12 Do Next Question

화자들은 다음에 무엇을 할 것 같은가?
Ⓐ 함께 강의에 참석한다.
Ⓑ 그들의 교수님과 상담한다.
☑ 만날 시간을 정한다.
Ⓓ 그들의 발표 주제를 바꾼다.

어휘 consult with ~와 상담하다

[13-14] 🔊 W-Am M-Au

Listen to a conversation.

W I heard there's a new express bus that goes straight to the beach. Have you tried it?

M I took it last weekend. ¹³It's much faster than the regular line since it only makes three stops.

W That sounds awesome! How much is the fare?

M It's $15 each way, but if you buy a round-trip ticket online, it's just $25.

W Sounds great! I was thinking of taking my parents to the beach. ¹⁴I should tell them right away.

express bus 급행 버스
regular [régjulər] 일반의, 보통의, 규칙적인   fare [fɛər] 요금
round-trip 왕복

대화를 들으시오.

W 해변으로 바로 가는 새로운 급행 버스가 있다고 들었어요. 타보셨나요?

M 지난 주말에 탔어요. ¹³단 3번만 정차하기 때문에 일반 노선보다 훨씬 빨라요.

W 대단해 보이네요! 요금이 얼마나 되나요?

M 편도로 15달러인데, 온라인으로 왕복 표를 사면 25달러뿐이에요.
W 좋네요! 부모님을 해변에 모시고 가려고 생각했어요. ¹⁴바로 부모님께 말씀드려야겠어요.

13 Inference Question
일반 버스 노선에 대해 암시되는 것은?
- Ⓐ 해변으로 가는 길에 최소 4번의 정차를 한다. ✓
- Ⓑ 해변으로 가는 더 경치 좋은 경로를 제공한다.
- Ⓒ 급행 버스보다 두 배 저렴하다.
- Ⓓ 사전 예약이 필요하다.

어휘 scenic[síːnik] 경치 좋은   route[ruːt] 경로
　　 in advance 사전에, 미리

14 Do Next Question
여자는 다음에 무엇을 할 것 같은가?
- Ⓐ 대안적인 교통수단 선택지들을 찾는다.
- Ⓑ 출발 시간을 위해 버스 시간표를 확인한다.
- Ⓒ 주말 해변 여행을 위한 표를 구매한다.
- Ⓓ 새로운 버스 서비스에 대해 부모님께 알린다. ✓

어휘 alternative[ɔːltə́ːrnətiv] 대안적인, 대체의
　　 departure[dipáːrtʃər] 출발   inform[infɔ́ːrm] 알리다

[15-16] 🔊 M-Au W-Am
Listen to a conversation.

M Have you confirmed the venue for next week's team workshop?
W Yes, I booked the conference room at the business center. It has all the equipment we need.
M Great. What about refreshments?
W I was thinking of ordering catering. The catering company offers various options. ¹⁵**They require a minimum order for 15 people, though.**
M That shouldn't be a problem. We have 20 people attending.
W Perfect. ¹⁶**I have a client meeting now, so I'll discuss menu options with the catering company afterwards.**
M Sounds good. Make sure to ask about dietary restrictions too.

confirm[kənfə́ːrm] 확정하다, 확인하다
refreshments[rifréʃmənts] 다과   make sure to 꼭 ~하다
dietary restriction 식단 제한

대화를 들으시오.
M 다음 주의 팀 워크숍 장소는 확정했나요?
W 네, 비즈니스 센터의 회의실을 예약했어요. 그곳은 우리가 필요한 모든 장비를 가지고 있어요.
M 좋아요. 다과는 어떻게 하죠?
W 출장연회를 주문하려고 생각했어요. 출장연회 업체가 다양한 옵션들을 제공해요. ¹⁵하지만 15명을 위한 최소 주문이 필요해요.
M 그건 문제가 되지 않을 거예요. 우리는 20명이 참석하는 걸요.
W 완벽해요. ¹⁶지금 고객 회의가 있어서, 이후에 출장연회 업체와 메뉴 옵션을 논의할게요.
M 좋네요. 식단 제한에 대해서도 꼭 물어봐 주세요.

15 Detail Question
여자는 케이터링 서비스에 대해 무엇을 말하는가?
- Ⓐ 너무 비싸다.
- Ⓑ 최소 구매를 요구한다. ✓
- Ⓒ 큰 그룹에는 이용할 수 없다.
- Ⓓ 채식주의자 옵션을 제공하지 않는다.

16 Do Next Question
여자는 회의 후에 무엇을 할 것인가?
- Ⓐ 회의 장비를 설치한다.
- Ⓑ 음식 서비스 제공업체에 연락한다. ✓
- Ⓒ 워크숍 초대장을 보낸다.
- Ⓓ 고객과 계약서에 서명한다.

어휘 send out ~을 보내다   contract[kántrækt] 계약서

5. Detail Questions

Example 🔊 W-Am M-En   p.119

W 저는 방금 새 공상과학 소설인 *Beyond the Stars*를 다 읽었어요.
M 아, 어떻게 생각하셨나요? 저는 그것을 지난달에 읽었어요.
W 대단히 흥미로웠어요! 캐릭터 개발이 정말 놀라웠어요.
M 동감해요. 저에게 가장 인상적이었던 것은 작가의 세세한 세계관 구축이었어요. **그녀가 창조한 외계 문화들은 너무나 독특하고 잘 생각해낸 것들이었어요.**
W 저는 세계관 구축에 그다지 집중하지 않았는데, 당신 말이 맞네요! 이제 반드시 그녀의 다른 책들도 읽을 거예요.
M 그러셔야 해요. 그녀의 첫 삼부작은 혁신적인 스토리텔링으로 여러 문학상을 받았어요.

---
science fiction 공상과학
fascinating[fǽsəneitiŋ] 대단히 흥미로운, 매혹적인
development[divéləpmənt] 개발
incredible[inkrédəbl] 놀라운, 굉장한
impress[imprés] 인상을 주다
unique[juːníːk] 독특한, 유일한   well-thought-out 잘 생각해낸
trilogy[tríləʒi] 삼부작   innovative[ínəvèitiv] 혁신적인

남자는 소설에 대해 무엇을 말하는가?
- Ⓐ 비평가들로부터 좋지 않은 평가를 받았다.
- Ⓑ 너무 많은 등장인물들을 포함하고 있다.
- Ⓒ 작가의 이전 작품들보다 더 좋다.
- Ⓓ 독특한 외계 문화들을 담고 있다. ✓

HACKERS PRACTICE   p.120

01 Ⓑ   02 Ⓑ   03 Ⓒ   04 Ⓓ

01 Detail Question 🎧 W-Nz M-Am

W Did you see the flyer for the campus festival? I'm interested in the outdoor movie screening and the campus e-sports tournament finals both taking place on Friday.

M Wow, they both sound fun! But I can't make it to either of them. I have dinner plans with my family.

W That's okay, I can go with Jane instead. How about the live music showcase on Saturday night? This looks pretty interesting.

M Sounds great! I'm free then.

take place 열리다, 일어나다   make it to ~에 가다
dinner plan 저녁 약속

W 캠퍼스 축제 전단지 보셨나요? 저는 금요일에 열리는 야외 영화 상영과 캠퍼스 e-스포츠 토너먼트 결승전 모두 관심이 있어요.
M 와, 둘 다 재미있을 것 같네요! 하지만 저는 둘 다 갈 수 없어요. 가족과 저녁 약속이 있거든요.
W 괜찮아요, 대신 Jane과 함께 가면 돼요. 토요일 밤 라이브 음악 쇼케이스는 어떠세요? 꽤 흥미로워 보이네요.
M 좋을 것 같네요! 그때는 시간이 돼요.

화자들은 어떤 행사에 함께 참석할 계획인가?
Ⓐ 캠퍼스 미술 쇼케이스
✓Ⓑ 라이브 음악 공연
Ⓒ 야외 영화 상영
Ⓓ 게임 토너먼트

어휘 performance [pərfɔ́:rməns] 공연

02 Detail Question 🎧 M-Am W-En

M I've been looking for a new laptop case. Do you know any good stores?

W There's a tech shop in the mall that has a great selection. It just opened last month, and they have student discounts on accessories.

M That sounds perfect! How much are the discounts?

W It's 15% off with a student ID. I bought my phone case there and saved quite a bit.

M Great! I'll check it out this weekend.

tech shop 전자제품 매장
have a great selection 다양한 상품을 갖추다

M 새 노트북 케이스를 찾고 있어요. 좋은 가게 아시나요?
W 쇼핑몰에 정말 다양한 상품을 갖춘 전자제품 매장이 있어요. 지난달에 막 열었고, 액세서리에 학생 할인을 해줘요.
M 완벽하네요! 할인은 얼마나 되나요?
W 학생증을 지니면 15% 할인이에요. 저도 거기서 휴대폰 케이스를 사서 꽤 절약했어요.
M 좋아요! 이번 주말에 가봐야겠어요.

여자는 전자제품 매장에 대해 무엇을 말하는가?
Ⓐ 작년부터 영업해왔다.
✓Ⓑ 쇼핑센터 안에 위치해 있다.
Ⓒ 디지털 기기에 학생 할인을 제공한다.
Ⓓ 학생증을 지니면 무료 액세서리를 제공한다.

어휘 be located in ~에 위치해 있다

03 Detail Question 🎧 M-En W-Am

M I'm having trouble planning my sister's surprise birthday party.

W What's the problem?

M The restaurant I reserved just canceled my booking, so now I need to find another place.

W Was there a system error at the restaurant?

M No. Apparently, they had a fire in the kitchen.

W No way, that's unfortunate. In that case, how about the café downtown that John runs? I can ask him for you.

booking [búkiŋ] 예약
apparently [əpǽrəntli] 듣자 하니, 아무래도
unfortunate [ʌnfɔ́:rtʃənət] 유감스러운, 아쉬운
run [rʌn] 운영하다, 달리다

M 제 여동생의 깜짝 생일 파티를 계획하는 데 어려움을 겪고 있어요.
W 무슨 문제인데요?
M 예약했던 식당이 막 제 예약을 취소해서, 이제 다른 장소를 찾아야 해요.
W 식당에 시스템 오류가 있었나요?
M 아니요. 듣자 하니, 주방에 화재가 있었대요.
W 말도 안 돼요, 유감스럽네요. 그렇다면 John이 운영하는 시내 카페는 어떠세요? 제가 당신을 위해 그에게 물어볼 수 있어요.

남자가 새로운 장소가 필요한 이유는 무엇인가?
Ⓐ 미리 예약을 확인하지 못했다.
Ⓑ 기존 예약이 제대로 처리되지 않았다.
✓Ⓒ 식당이 최근 화재로 손상되었다.
Ⓓ John이 남자의 카페 사용 요청을 거절했다.

어휘 original [ərídʒənl] 기존의   damage [dǽmidʒ] 손상을 입다
refuse [rifjú:z] 거절하다

04 Detail Question 🎧 W-Am M-Au

W Have you checked the company intranet? There are several sections that need updating.

M Which parts?

W The staff directory still shows employees who left months ago, and our pricing guidelines are from last year.

M I see. I'll contact our web developer today. Could you send me a detailed list of all the changes?

W Yes, I'll compile everything and email it to you by the end of the day.

staff directory 직원 명단 detailed[díːteild] 자세한, 상세한
compile[kəmpáil] 모으다, 쌓다

W 회사 인트라넷을 확인해 보셨나요? 업데이트가 필요한 섹션들이 몇 개 있어요.
M 어떤 부분들인가요?
W 직원 명단에는 몇 달 전에 퇴사한 직원들이 여전히 나와 있고, 가격 가이드라인은 작년 것이에요.
M 알겠어요. 오늘 웹 개발자에게 연락할게요. 모든 변경사항의 자세한 목록을 보내주실 수 있나요?
W 네, 모든 것을 모아서 오늘이 끝나기 전에 이메일로 보내드릴게요.

남자가 웹 개발자에게 연락할 계획인 이유는 무엇인가?
Ⓐ 제품에 대한 새로운 가격 전략을 만들기 위해
Ⓑ 웹사이트를 직접 업데이트하는 방법을 배우기 위해
Ⓒ 직원 명단을 처음부터 만드는 것에 대해 논의하기 위해
✓ 구식 정보의 업데이트를 요청하기 위해

어휘 create[kriéit] 만들다, 생산하다 from scratch 처음부터 request[rikwést] 요청하다

HACKERS TEST   p.122

01 Ⓓ   02 Ⓒ   03 Ⓑ   04 Ⓒ   05 Ⓓ
06 Ⓐ   07 Ⓒ   08 Ⓓ   09 Ⓐ   10 Ⓒ
11 Ⓓ   12 Ⓒ   13 Ⓑ   14 Ⓐ   15 Ⓓ
16 Ⓒ

[01-02]   M-En W-Am

Listen to a conversation.

> M I just received an email about our hotel reservation for the music festival. There's a problem with our booking.
> W What happened? ⁰¹We made that reservation three months ago.
> M Apparently, there was a system error, and they're overbooked. They're offering us a smaller room or a full refund.
> W ⁰²Let's just take that room. It's almost impossible to find another place this close to the festival grounds.

apparently[əpærəntli] 아무래도, 분명히
overbook[óuvərbùk] 초과 예약하다
refund[ríːfʌnd] 환불; 환불하다
impossible[impάːsəbəl] 불가능한

대화를 들으시오.
M 음악 축제를 위한 호텔 예약에 대한 이메일을 방금 받았어요. 저희 예약에 문제가 있어요.
W 무슨 일이에요? ⁰¹우리가 그 예약을 3개월 전에 했잖아요.
M 아무래도 시스템 오류가 있었나 봐요. 그래서 방이 초과 예약되었어요. 숙소에서는 우리에게 더 작은 방이나 전액 환불을 제안하고 있어요.
W ⁰²그냥 그 방을 잡죠. 축제 장소에 이렇게 가까운 다른 숙소를 찾는 것은 거의 불가능해요.

01 Detail Question

화자들은 예약에 대해 무엇을 말하는가?
Ⓐ 웹사이트를 통해 이루어졌다.
Ⓑ 이메일로 두 번 확인되었다.
Ⓒ 여자에 의해 취소되었다.
✓ 3개월 전에 이루어졌다.

02 Detail Question

여자는 왜 더 작은 방을 받아들이기로 선택하는가?
Ⓐ 더 작은 호텔 방을 선호한다.
Ⓑ 숙박비를 절약하기를 바란다.
✓ 다른 숙소를 찾는 것이 어려울 것이라고 생각한다.
Ⓓ 호텔 직원들과 상대하는 것을 피하기를 원한다.

어휘 accommodation[əkɑ̀mədéiʃən] 숙박, 숙소
deal with 상대하다, 다루다, 처리하다

[03-04]   W-Am M-En

Listen to a conversation.

> W Professor, you wanted to discuss my research assistant duties for this semester?
> M Yes. ⁰³I'd like you to focus on data collection for our climate change project rather than literature reviews.
> W I see. So my responsibilities would be working with the field sensors and organizing the incoming measurements?
> M Exactly. ⁰⁴You'll need to collect data twice a week and create summary reports.
> W I understand. When should I start with the new work?
> M Let's begin next Monday. I'll email you the detailed protocol tonight.

focus on ~에 집중하다
literature[lítərətʃər] 문헌, 논문, 문학
responsibility[rispὰnsəbíləti] 업무, 책임, 의무
summary[sʌ́məri] 요약
protocol[próutəkɔ̀ːl] 계획서, 의전, 초안

대화를 들으시오.
W 교수님, 이번 학기 제 연구 보조 업무에 대해 논의하고 싶으셨나요?
M 네. ⁰³당신이 문헌 검토보다는 저희 기후 변화 프로젝트를 위한 자료 수집에 집중했으면 좋겠어요.
W 그렇군요. 그렇다면 제 업무는 현장 센서들을 운용하고 들어오는 측정치들을 정리하는 것이 되겠네요?
M 정확해요. ⁰⁴주 2회 자료를 수집하고 요약 보고서들을 작성해야 할 거예요.
W 이해했습니다. 언제 새로운 업무를 시작해야 하나요?
M 다음 주 월요일에 시작해요. 오늘 밤에 자세한 계획서를 이메일로 보

내드릴게요.

03 Main Purpose Question
남자는 왜 여자와 이야기하고 싶어 했는가?
Ⓐ 그녀의 이전 보고서들에 대한 피드백을 제공하기 위해
✓ 그녀에게 새로운 연구 책임을 부여하기 위해
Ⓒ 회의 참석 가능 여부를 확인하기 위해
Ⓓ 그녀의 학업 성과를 논의하기 위해

어휘 provide[prəváid] 제공하다
      assign[əsáin] 부여하다, 할당하다, 내주다
      academic[ӕkədémik] 학업의, 학문적인

04 Detail Question
남자는 여자가 할 일에 대해 무엇을 말하는가?
Ⓐ 매일 실험실에서 일할 것이다.
Ⓑ 문헌 검토에 집중할 것이다.
✓ 자료를 수집하고 보고서를 작성할 것이다.
Ⓓ 발견 사항들을 회의에서 발표할 것이다.

어휘 laboratory[lӕbərətɔ̀ːri] 실험실
      finding[fáindiŋ] 발견 사항, 결과

[05-06]   M-Nz W-Am

Listen to a conversation.

> M Are you planning to attend the photography club meeting tomorrow evening?
>
> W I totally forgot about it! What time was it?
>
> M ⁰⁵**It starts at 6 P.M. in the student center.** We're going to discuss the upcoming exhibition at the auditorium and assign tasks for everyone.
>
> W Well, I can make it, but ⁰⁶**I may be a bit late since I have a study group until 5:30.** Will you be there?
>
> M Definitely! I've already volunteered to help setting up the exhibition.
>
> W Great! I'll see you there then.

totally[tóutəli] 완전히
upcoming[ʌ́pkʌ̀miŋ] 열릴 예정인, 다가오는
auditorium[ɔ̀ːditɔ́ːriəm] 강당, 대강의실
volunteer[vɑ̀ːləntíər] 자원하다; 자원봉사자

대화를 들으시오.
M 내일 저녁 사진 동아리 모임에 참석할 계획인가요?
W 완전히 잊고 있었어요! 몇 시였죠?
M ⁰⁵학생 회관에서 오후 6시에 시작해요. 강당에서 열릴 예정인 전시회와 모든 사람을 위한 업무 배정에 대해 논의할 거예요.
W 글쎄요, 참석할 수 있지만 ⁰⁶5시 30분까지 스터디 그룹이 있어서 조금 늦을지도 몰라요. 당신은 갈 건가요?
M 물론이요! 저는 이미 전시회 설치를 도와주겠다고 자원했어요.
W 좋아요! 그럼 그곳에서 봐요.

05 Detail Question
사진 동아리 모임은 어디에서 열릴 것인가?
Ⓐ 강당에서
Ⓑ 미술관에서
✓ 학생 회관에서
Ⓓ 사진 스튜디오에서

어휘 student center 학생 회관

06 Intention Question
여자는 왜 자신의 스터디 그룹을 언급하는가?
✓ 늦을 수도 있는 이유를 제시하기 위해
Ⓑ 남자를 스터디 그룹에 초대하기 위해
Ⓒ 모임 시간이 바뀔 수 있는지 묻기 위해
Ⓓ 모임에 참석할 수 없는 이유를 설명하기 위해

어휘 attend[əténd] 참석하다

[07-08]   M-Am W-Nz

Listen to a conversation.

> M I was thinking we could visit Chicago for the holiday.
>
> W Great idea! Should we drive or take the train?
>
> M The train might be more relaxing, and we won't have to worry about parking.
>
> W Good point. When should we leave? Friday evening or early Saturday?
>
> M Hmm… If we leave on Friday, we'll end up paying for one more night at the hotel. ⁰⁷**Let's leave on Saturday**, and we could return early Monday.
>
> W Perfect! ⁰⁸**I'll look up hotels in downtown Chicago.**
>
> M Great, and I'll check the train schedule and ticket prices.

relaxing[rilӕksiŋ] 편안한, 느긋한
end up ~하게 되다, 결국 ~ 되다
look up 알아보다, 찾아보다, 나아지다

대화를 들으시오.
M 저는 우리가 휴일에 시카고를 방문하면 어떨지 생각하고 있었어요.
W 좋은 생각이에요! 운전해서 갈까요, 아니면 기차를 탈까요?
M 기차가 더 편안할 것 같고, 주차 걱정을 하지 않아도 될 거예요.
W 좋은 지적이에요. 언제 떠나야 할까요? 금요일 저녁이나 토요일 이른 아침에?
M 음… 금요일에 떠나면 호텔에서 하룻밤을 더 지불하게 될 거예요. ⁰⁷토요일에 떠나서 월요일 일찍 돌아와요.
W ⁰⁸완벽해요! ⁰⁸시카고 시내의 호텔들을 알아봐야겠어요.
M 좋아요, 그리고 저는 기차 시간표와 표 가격들을 확인해볼게요.

07 Detail Question
화자들은 시카고로 언제 출발할 것 같은가?
Ⓐ 월요일
Ⓑ 금요일
✓ 토요일

Ⓓ 일요일

08 Do Next Question
여자는 다음에 무엇을 할 것 같은가?
Ⓐ 호텔 근처의 식당들을 찾는다.
Ⓑ 시카고의 일기 예보를 확인한다.
Ⓒ 기차 출발 시간과 비용을 조사한다.
☑ 시카고 시내에서 적합한 호텔을 찾는다.

어휘 look for 찾다, 구하다, 기대하다
　　suitable[súːtəbl] 적합한, 적절한

[09-10]　　　　　　　　　　W-En M-Au
Listen to a conversation.

> W　The office printer has completely stopped working. It won't even turn on now.
> M　That's frustrating. We've had it for less than a year. ⁰⁹**Is it still under warranty?**
> W　⁰⁹**Yes, it has a two-year warranty.**
> M　Great. Let's take it to the service center downtown. They should be able to repair or replace it.
> W　I can take it tomorrow morning. Do you know when they open?
> M　They open at 9 A.M., and ¹⁰**I recommend going early**. They get quite busy later in the day.
>
> frustrating[frʌ́streitiŋ] 좌절스러운, 절망적인
> warranty[wɔ́ːrənti] 보증 기간, 품질 보증서
> recommend[rèkəménd] 권하다, 추천하다
> quite[kwait] 아주, 꽤

대화를 들으시오.
W 사무실 프린터가 완전히 작동을 멈췄어요. 이제는 켜지지도 않아요.
M 좌절스럽네요. 1년도 안 가지고 있었는데요. ⁰⁹아직 보증 기간 내인가요?
W ⁰⁹네, 2년 보증이 있어요.
M 좋아요. 시내 서비스 센터에 가져갑시다. 수리하거나 교체해줄 수 있을 거예요.
W 제가 내일 아침에 가져갈 수 있어요. 가게가 몇 시에 여는지 아세요?
M 오전 9시에 열고, ¹⁰일찍 가는 것을 권해요. 거기가 오후에는 꽤 바빠지거든요.

09 Detail Question
화자들은 사무실 프린터에 대해 무엇을 말하는가?
☑ 아직 보증 기간 내에 있다.
Ⓑ 새 카트리지를 설치해야 한다.
Ⓒ 구입할 때 매우 비쌌다.
Ⓓ 2년보다 더 이전에 구매되었다.

어휘 purchase[pə́ːrtʃəs] 구입하다, 구매하다

10 Suggestion Question
남자는 여자에게 무엇을 하라고 권장하는가?
Ⓐ 교체용 프린터를 구입한다.
Ⓑ 다른 수리점들을 찾는다.
☑ 서비스 센터에 일찍 도착한다.
Ⓓ 보증이 아직 유효한지 확인한다.

어휘 valid[vǽlid] 유효한, 타당한

[11-12]　　　　　　　　　　W-Au M-Am
Listen to a conversation.

> W　¹¹**HR just announced mandatory customer service training for all sales staff next Monday.**
> M　Oh, when will the training session begin?
> W　The first group starts at 9 A.M., and ¹²**there's another session at 1 P.M.**
> M　¹²**I'll sign up for the afternoon one.** I have client calls scheduled all morning.
> W　That's smart planning. I'm actually looking forward to learning some new techniques.
> M　Same here. Some of our recent customer feedback has been challenging to address, so this should be helpful.
>
> announce[ənáuns] 발표하다, 공지하다
> mandatory[mǽndətɔ̀ːri] 의무적인　client[kláiənt] 고객
> look forward to 기대하다　technique[tekníːk] 기법, 기술
> challenging[tʃǽlindʒiŋ] 어려운, 힘든, 도전적인
> address[ǽdres] 대응하다; 주소

대화를 들으시오.
W ¹¹인사부에서 방금 다음 주 월요일에 모든 영업 직원들을 위한 의무 고객 서비스 교육을 발표했어요.
M 아, 교육 세션은 언제 시작하나요?
W 첫 번째 그룹은 오전 9시에 시작하고, ¹²오후 1시에 또 다른 세션이 있어요.
M ¹²오후 세션에 신청하겠어요. 오전 내내 고객 전화 일정이 잡혀 있거든요.
W 현명한 계획이네요. 저는 사실 새로운 기법들을 배우는 것을 기대하고 있어요.
M 저도 마찬가지예요. 최근 고객 피드백 중 일부는 대응하기 어려웠으니까, 분명 도움이 될 것 같아요.

11 Main Topic Question
화자들은 주로 무엇에 대해 이야기하고 있는가?
Ⓐ 일정 충돌
Ⓑ 최근 인사부 정책 변화
Ⓒ 부정적인 고객 피드백
☑ 의무 교육 프로그램

어휘 conflict[kánflikt] 충돌, 마찰, 갈등
　　negative[négətiv] 부정적인

12 Detail Question
남자는 언제 교육 세션에 참석할 것인가?
Ⓐ 오전 8시
Ⓑ 오전 9시
☑ 오후 1시

Ⓓ 오후 2시

[13-14]
🎧 M-Am W-Au

Listen to a conversation.

> M I'm trying to decide which laptop bag to buy. What do you think of this one?
> W It looks nice, but is it big enough for all your stuff?
> M Good question. I carry a lot of books and my charger every day.
> W How about the BookPro bag? ¹³**It has more pockets and I think it's even on sale.**
> M That sounds good. But the price tag doesn't show the exact amount.
> W ¹⁴**How about asking a store clerk over there?**
> M ¹⁴**I'll do that right away.**

exact[igzǽkt] 정확한   clerk[klə:rk] 점원, 서기

대화를 들으시오.
M 어떤 노트북 가방을 살지 결정하려고 해요. 이 제품에 대해 어떻게 생각하세요?
W 좋아 보이지만, 당신의 모든 물건들을 넣기에 충분히 큰가요?
M 좋은 질문이에요. 저는 매일 많은 책과 충전기를 가지고 다녀요.
W BookPro 가방은 어때요? ¹³더 많은 주머니가 있고 심지어 세일 중인 것 같아요.
M 좋을 것 같네요. 하지만 가격표에 정확한 금액이 나와 있지 않아요.
W ¹⁴저쪽에 있는 매장 점원에게 물어보는 것이 어때요?
M ¹⁴바로 그렇게 할게요.

13   Detail Question
여자는 BookPro 가방에 대해 무엇을 말하는가?
Ⓐ 가장 인기 있는 모델이다.
☑ 추가 수납 주머니들이 있다.
Ⓒ 남자의 예산보다 비싸다.
Ⓓ 그의 노트북 모델을 위해 설계되었다.

어휘 popular[pápjulər] 인기 있는, 대중적인   budget[bʌ́dʒit] 예산

14   Do Next Question
남자는 다음에 무엇을 할 것 같은가?
☑ 직원에게 가격에 대해 묻는다.
Ⓑ 다양한 가방 기능들을 비교한다.
Ⓒ 다른 노트북 가방을 찾는다.
Ⓓ 첫 번째 선택지를 구입한다.

어휘 compare[kəmpɛ́ər] 비교하다

[15-16]
🎧 M-En W-Nz

Listen to a conversation.

> M ¹⁵**I've been having these terrible headaches lately, especially after staring at my computer screen all day.**
> W That sounds like eye strain. How long have you been experiencing this?
> M About two weeks now. It's getting worse, and painkillers barely help.
> W ¹⁶**You should see Dr. Parker at the health center. She specializes in these issues.**
> M Do I need to make an appointment, or can I walk in?
> W Better call ahead. She has a lot of patients.

headache[hédeik] 두통   especially[ispéʃəli] 특히
painkiller[péinkilər] 진통제
specialize[spéʃəlàiz] 전공하다, 전문화하다

대화를 들으시오.
M ¹⁵최근에 끔찍한 두통이 있었는데, 특히 하루 종일 컴퓨터 화면을 쳐다본 후에요.
W 안구 피로 같네요. 언제부터 이것을 경험하고 있나요?
M 지금까지 약 2주 정도요. 점점 악화되고 있고, 진통제는 거의 도움이 안 돼요.
W ¹⁶보건 센터의 Parker 선생님을 찾아가 보세요. 그녀는 이런 문제들을 전문으로 해요.
M 예약을 해야 하나요, 아니면 그냥 가면 되나요?
W 미리 전화하는 것이 좋아요. 환자가 많거든요.

15   Problem Question
남자의 문제는 무엇인가?
Ⓐ 컴퓨터 화면이 조정이 필요하다.
Ⓑ 일부 진통제에 알레르기가 있다.
Ⓒ 업무에 집중할 수 없다.
☑ 건강상 문제를 경험하고 있다.

어휘 adjustment[ədʒʌ́stmənt] 조정
        allergic[ələ́:rdʒik] 알레르기가 있는

16   Detail Question
여자는 왜 남자에게 Parker 선생님을 찾아가라고 추천하는가?
Ⓐ 저렴한 치료 옵션들을 제공한다.
Ⓑ 유연한 예약 일정을 가지고 있다.
☑ 그의 증상 유형에 대한 전문 지식을 가지고 있다.
Ⓓ 그의 사무실 위치와 가까운 곳에서 일한다.

어휘 treatment[trí:tmənt] 치료, 처리, 대우
        flexible[fléksəbl] 유연한, 융통성 있는
        expertise[èkspərtí:z] 전문 지식

6. Intention/Attitude Questions

Example 🎧 W-Nz M-Am   p.127

> W 당신은 Kim 교수님 수업을 위한 우리 조 발표에서 당신 부분을 끝냈나요?
> M 거의요. 몇 개의 슬라이드만 더 추가하면 되는데, 마지막 부분을 위한 신뢰할 만한 자료를 찾는 데 어려움을 겪고 있어요.

W 제가 도울 수 있을 것 같아요. 지난 학기에 비슷한 연구 프로젝트를 했고 모든 참고 자료들을 저장해 뒀거든요.
M 고마워요! 그 자료들을 보내주시고 오늘 저녁에 제가 지금까지 한 것을 봐주실 수 있나요?
W 내일이 더 좋을 것 같아요. 오후 6시에 미적분 시험을 위한 스터디 그룹이 있는데, 연습 문제를 얼마나 오래 할지 모르겠어요.

reliable[riláiəbl] 신뢰할 만한, 확실한
similar[símələr] 비슷한, 유사한   semester[siméstər] 학기

여자는 왜 스터디 그룹을 언급하는가?
Ⓐ 자신의 학업적 헌신을 과시하기 위해
☑ 일정 충돌을 설명하기 위해
Ⓒ 팀워크의 중요성을 강조하기 위해
Ⓓ 남자에게 자신의 미적분 수업에 참여하라고 제안하기 위해

HACKERS PRACTICE   p.128

01 Ⓑ   02 Ⓐ   03 Ⓒ   04 Ⓓ

01 Attitude Question   M-Am W-En

M Did you book a study room in the campus library for our group project meeting tomorrow?
W I tried earlier, but all the rooms were already reserved. Is there any chance we could go to your place instead?
M Well, I don't think that's a good idea. **My house is too noisy with my little brothers always around.**
W Oh, I see. I should call the library and see if we can be put on a waiting list for any canceled rooms.

book[buk] 예약하다   noisy[nɔ́izi] 시끄러운

M 내일 우리 그룹 프로젝트 회의를 위해 캠퍼스 도서관에 스터디룸을 예약했나요?
W 전에 시도해봤는데, 모든 방이 이미 예약됐더라고요. 혹시 당신 집으로 갈 수 있을까요?
M 음, 그건 좋은 생각이 아닌 것 같아요. 제 집은 항상 어린 남동생들이 있어서 너무 시끄러워요.
W 아, 그렇군요. 도서관에 전화해서 취소된 방에 대해 대기 명단에 올려질 수 있는지 알아봐야겠어요.

자신의 집에서 공부하는 것에 대한 남자의 태도는 무엇인가?
Ⓐ 적절한 공간이 부족하다고 생각한다.
☑ 너무 산만할 것이라고 생각한다.
Ⓒ 사생활 문제에 대한 우려를 표현한다.
Ⓓ 이웃들을 방해할까봐 걱정한다.

어휘 adequate[ǽdikwət] 적절한, 충분한
distracting[distrǽktiŋ] 산만한, 산만하게 하는
disturb[distə́ːrb] 방해하다, 교란하다

02 Intention Question   W-En M-Au

W Excuse me, I'm trying to track down this sociology journal article for my research paper, but I can't seem to find it anywhere.
M Let me check for you. Hmm, it looks like that particular journal is not part of our regular subscription.
W Oh no, **my paper is due next week, and I really need that article.**
M Don't worry. We can request it through interlibrary loan.
W **But doesn't that usually take several days?**
M You're right. But for academic articles, we can get them within 24 hours. Just fill out the request form before you leave.

track down 찾다, 탐지하다   sociology[sòusiá:lədʒi] 사회학
article[á:rtikl] 기사, 논문   research paper 연구 논문
particular[pərtíkjulər] 특정한, 특별한, 까다로운
regular subscription 정기 구독

W 실례합니다만, 제 연구 논문을 위해 이 사회학 저널 기사를 찾으려고 하는데, 어디에서도 찾을 수 없네요.
M 확인해드릴게요. 흠, 그 특정 저널은 저희의 정기 구독에 포함되지 않은 것 같네요.
W 안 돼요, 제 논문이 다음 주에 마감인데, 그 기사가 정말 필요해요.
M 걱정하지 마세요. 도서관 간 대출을 통해 요청할 수 있어요.
W 하지만 그것은 보통 며칠 걸리지 않나요?
M 맞아요. 하지만 학술 기사의 경우, 24시간 내에 구할 수 있어요. 떠나시기 전에 요청서만 작성해주세요.

여자가 "하지만 그것은 보통 며칠 걸리지 않나요?"라고 말할 때 무엇을 의도하고 있는가?
☑ 기사가 마감일 전에 도착하지 않을까 봐 우려하고 있다.
Ⓑ 이전에 도서관 간 대출을 시도해본 적이 있다.
Ⓒ 남자가 서비스 속도를 과장하고 있다고 생각한다.
Ⓓ 도서관 간 대출 과정이 비효율적이라고 생각한다.

어휘 exaggerate[igzǽdʒərèit] 과장하다
inefficient[ìnifíʃənt] 비효율적인

03 Intention Question   M-Au W-Am

M Have you heard about that new Italian place that just opened downtown?
W Yeah, I actually went there yesterday. The pasta was amazing, but the staff was a bit unfriendly.
M Oh, really? **My roommate had the opposite experience. He said the food was just okay, but the staff was really attentive.**
W Well, I guess it's tough to keep everything consistent when a place just opens.

opposite[á:pəzit] 정반대의, 다른 편의
attentive[əténtiv] 친절한, 세심한

TASK 2

Hackers Updated TOEFL LISTENING

M 시내에 막 오픈한 새로운 이탈리아 식당에 대해 들어봤나요?
W 네, 사실 어제 거기 갔어요. 파스타는 훌륭했지만, 직원이 좀 불친절했어요.
M 아, 정말요? 제 룸메이트는 정반대의 경험을 했대요. 그는 음식은 그냥 그랬지만, 직원이 정말 친절했다고 했어요.
W 음, 막 오픈한 곳이면 모든 것을 일관되게 유지하기가 어려운 것 같아요.

남자는 왜 자신의 룸메이트를 언급하는가?
Ⓐ 또 다른 식당 방문을 권하기 위해
Ⓑ 새로운 식당들이 종종 실패하는 이유를 설명하기 위해
✓ⓒ 대조적인 의견을 제시하기 위해
Ⓓ 식당에서 단체 저녁 식사를 계획하기 위해

어휘 encourage[inkə́ːridʒ] 권하다, 격려하다
illustrate[íləstrèit] 설명하다, 삽화를 넣다
contrasting[kəntrǽstiŋ] 대조적인, 대비를 이루는

04 Intention Question M-En W-Nz

M What do you think of the new website design? The marketing department wants our feedback by tomorrow morning.
W I like the overall layout, but the color scheme doesn't really match our brand identity.
M You can say that again. Our company's logo is blue and silver, but they've used orange accents throughout the site.
W Exactly. Let's send in the feedback now before we forget.

scheme[skiːm] 구성, 계획   accent[ǽksent] 강조, 억양, 강세
throughout[θruːáut] 전체에, 도처에, 내내

M 새 웹사이트 디자인에 대해서 어떻게 생각하세요? 마케팅 부서에서 내일 아침까지 저희 피드백을 원해요.
W 전체적인 레이아웃은 마음에 들지만, 색상 구성이 저희 브랜드 정체성과 잘 맞지 않는 것 같아요.
M 정말 그렇네요. 저희 회사 로고는 파란색과 은색인데, 사이트 전체에 주황색 강조를 사용했어요.
W 맞아요. 잊기 전에 지금 피드백을 보내죠.

남자는 왜 회사 로고를 언급하는가?
Ⓐ 새로운 로고 제작을 추천하기 위해
Ⓑ 웹사이트에서의 로고 배치를 비판하기 위해
Ⓒ 마케팅 부서의 창의성을 칭찬하기 위해
✓Ⓓ 웹사이트 색상 변경을 제안하기 위해

어휘 praise[preiz] 칭찬하다; 칭찬   creativity[krìːeitívəti] 창의성

HACKERS TEST   p.130

01 Ⓐ   02 Ⓓ   03 Ⓑ   04 Ⓑ   05 Ⓓ
06 Ⓒ   07 Ⓓ   08 Ⓓ   09 Ⓒ   10 Ⓓ
11 Ⓑ   12 Ⓒ   13 Ⓑ   14 Ⓐ   15 Ⓑ
16 Ⓒ

[01-02] W-Am M-En

Listen to a conversation.

W Are you coming to the baseball club meeting tonight?
M I'm not sure. What time is it again?
W It starts at 7 P.M. in the main field.
M ⁰¹I have a chemistry lab that ends at 6:30. What if I'm a few minutes late?
W That would be fine. ⁰²Anyway, we're learning about how to keep baseball scorecards today.
M Sounds interesting! I'll definitely try to make it then.

chemistry[kéməstri] 화학   lab[læb] 실험, 실험실

대화를 들으시오.
W 오늘 밤 야구 동아리 모임에 오실 건가요?
M 잘 모르겠어요. 시간이 언제였죠?
W 주 경기장에서 오후 7시에 시작해요.
M ⁰¹6시 30분에 끝나는 화학 실험이 있어요. 몇 분 늦으면 어쩌죠?
W 괜찮을 거예요. ⁰²어쨌든, 오늘은 야구 기록표를 작성하는 방법을 배울 거예요.
M 흥미로운데요! 그럼 확실히 참석하려고 노력해볼게요.

01 Intention Question
남자는 왜 화학 실험을 언급하는가?
✓Ⓐ 지연 가능성에 대한 맥락을 제공하기 위해
Ⓑ 모임에 참석할 수 없는 이유를 설명하기 위해
Ⓒ 학업에 대한 자신의 헌신을 보여주기 위해
Ⓓ 자신의 시간 관리 문제들을 강조하기 위해

어휘 context[káːntekst] 맥락, 전후 사정, 문맥
demonstrate[démənstrèit] 보여주다; 설명하다
emphasize[émfəsàiz] 강조하다

02 Detail Question
여자는 오늘 밤 야구 동아리 모임에 대해 무엇을 말하는가?
Ⓐ 실내에서 열릴 예정이다.
Ⓑ 역사적인 경기의 영상을 보여줄 것이다.
Ⓒ 야구 장비를 가져와야 한다.
✓Ⓓ 경기 점수를 기록하는 것이 포함될 것이다.

어휘 historical[histɔ́ːrikəl] 역사적인, 역사의
involve[inválv] 포함하다, 수반하다, 관련시키다

[03-04]

🔊 M-En W-Nz

Listen to a conversation.

M Sarah, are you planning to attend the career development seminar tomorrow evening?
W I'm still deciding. The topic sounds useful, but ⁰³**I've heard the speaker can be quite dry and boring.**
M I thought it might be helpful for networking. A lot of industry professionals will be there.
W That's true. The networking aspect is indeed appealing.
M Plus, it's only two hours long. We could grab dinner afterward.
W All right, you've convinced me. ⁰⁴**I'll register before spots fill up.**

aspect[ǽspekt] 측면, 양상, 관점 indeed[indíːd] 정말, 참으로
appealing[əpíːliŋ] 매력적인, 마음을 끄는
convince[kənvíns] 설득시키다, 납득시키다
fill up 다 차다, 가득 차다

대화를 들으시오.

M Sarah, 내일 저녁 경력 개발 세미나에 참석할 계획이세요?
W 아직 결정 중이에요. 주제는 유용해 보이지만, ⁰³연사가 꽤 무미건조하고 지루할 수 있다고 들었어요.
M 저는 그것이 인적 네트워크 형성에 도움이 될 거라고 생각했어요. 많은 업계 전문가들이 참석할 거예요.
W 맞아요. 인적 네트워킹 형성 측면은 정말 매력적이에요.
M 게다가, 단지 2시간뿐이에요. 끝나고 저녁 식사를 할 수 있어요.
W 좋아요, 저를 설득시키셨네요. ⁰⁴자리가 다 차기 전에 등록할게요.

03 Attitude Question

세미나에 대한 여자의 태도는 무엇인가?
Ⓐ 강사가 자격이 있다고 생각한다.
☑ 발표자에 대한 우려를 가지고 있다.
Ⓒ 온라인 세미나를 선호한다.
Ⓓ 너무 늦게 시작한다고 생각한다.

어휘 qualified[kwάləfàid] 자격이 있는

04 Do Next Question

여자는 다음에 무엇을 할 것 같은가?
Ⓐ 연사의 배경을 조사한다.
☑ 세미나에 등록한다.
Ⓒ 친구들에게 의견을 물어본다.
Ⓓ 대안적인 행사들을 찾는다.

어휘 opinion[əpínjən] 의견, 견해

[05-06]

🔊 W-Au M-Am

Listen to a conversation.

W Did you know that a stress management workshop will be offered next week?
M I think I've heard of that. Are you thinking of going?
W Yes, this semester has been overwhelming, and I could use some new coping strategies.
M ⁰⁵**I agree, and the timing is perfect. Right after the midterm period when we all need it most.**
W Exactly. Plus, Dr. Lee is running it, and I heard she's excellent.
M ⁰⁶**Then what about registering right now?** I think there's limited space available.
W You're right. Let's do it.

overwhelming[òuvərwélmiŋ] 압도적인, 엄청난

대화를 들으시오.

W 스트레스 관리 워크숍이 다음 주에 제공될 거라는 걸 알고 계셨나요?
M 들어본 것 같아요. 가실 생각이세요?
W 네, 이번 학기가 압도적이었고, 제게 새로운 대처 방법들이 필요할 것 같아요.
M ⁰⁵동감하고, 시기도 완벽하네요. 우리 모두가 가장 필요로 할 때인 중간고사 기간 직후예요.
W 정확히 그래요. 게다가, Lee 박사님이 진행하는데, 그분이 훌륭하다고 들었어요.
M ⁰⁶그럼 지금 바로 등록하는 게 어떨까요? 자리가 얼마 안 남았을 것 같아요.
W 맞아요. 그렇게 해요.

05 Intention Question

남자는 왜 중간고사 기간을 언급하는가?
Ⓐ 학생들이 신체적으로 스트레스를 받는 이유를 설명하기 위해
Ⓑ 여자의 상황에 대한 이해를 보여주기 위해
Ⓒ 여자에게 다가오는 시험들을 상기시키기 위해
☑ 워크숍의 일정을 칭찬하기 위해

어휘 compliment[kάːmpləmənt] 칭찬하다; 칭찬

06 Suggestion Question

남자는 여자에게 무엇을 하라고 권장하는가?
Ⓐ 워크숍 전 모임을 조직한다.
Ⓑ 워크숍 정보를 온라인에 공유한다.
☑ 지체 없이 워크숍에 등록한다.
Ⓓ 스트레스 관리 기법들을 연구한다.

[07-08]

🔊 W-Am M-En

Listen to a conversation.

W Have you heard about the new interactive art exhibition at the National Museum?
M Yes! ⁰⁷**It opens this weekend, right?** I've been wanting to check it out.
W Actually, ⁰⁷**it opened last week**. I was thinking of going this Saturday if you'd like to join me.
M What? ⁰⁷**My mind is all over the place these days.** Anyway, that would be great! Do you know if we need to book tickets in advance?

W ⁰⁸Yes, it's recommended. The website says they're limiting visitors due to the interactive nature of the exhibits.

interactive[ìntərǽktiv] 상호작용형의, 상호적인
all over the place 산만한, 엉망인, 모든 곳에

대화를 들으시오.
W 국립 박물관의 새로운 상호작용형 미술 전시회에 대해 들어보셨나요?
M 네! ⁰⁷이번 주말에 열리죠? 살펴보고 싶었어요.
W 사실, ⁰⁷지난주에 열렸어요. 당신이 같이 가고 싶다면 이번 주 토요일에 가려고 생각 중이에요.
M 뭐라고요? ⁰⁷요즘 제 마음이 온통 산만해서요. 어쨌든, 그거 좋겠네요! 미리 티켓을 예약해야 하는지 아세요?
W ⁰⁸네, 권장사항이에요. 웹사이트에서 전시품의 상호작용적인 특성 때문에 방문객을 제한하고 있다고 해서요.

07 Intention Question

남자가 "요즘 제 마음이 온통 산만해서요"라고 말할 때 무엇을 암시하는가?
Ⓐ 박물관의 위치를 기억할 수 없었다.
Ⓑ 여러 박물관들을 방문할 계획이다.
Ⓒ 최근에 너무 많은 미술 전시회들을 봤다.
☑ 전시회의 개막일을 혼동했다.

어휘 confuse[kənfjúːz] 혼동하다, 혼란시키다

08 Inference Question

여자는 새로운 상호작용형 미술 전시회에 대해 무엇을 암시하는가?
Ⓐ 높은 수요로 인해 곧 종료될 것이다.
Ⓑ 사전 예약에 대한 할인을 제공한다.
Ⓒ 박물관에서 가장 큰 전시회이다.
☑ 사전 예약을 권장한다.

어휘 demand[dimǽnd] 수요, 요구; 요구하다
advance[ædvǽns] 사전의; 다가가다; 발전

[09-10]   W-En M-Am

Listen to a conversation.

W What do you think of this studio apartment? It's right in the heart of downtown.
M The location is fantastic, but ⁰⁹the rent is way over my budget.
W Hmm… ¹⁰But think about how much you'd save on transportation costs living here.
M That's a good point. I wouldn't need a car, and I could walk to work every day.
W Plus, look at this kitchen. It's small but has everything you need.
M You're right. Maybe I should reconsider.

studio apartment 원룸 아파트 (부엌·목욕실이 한 방에 딸린 아파트)
rent[rent] 임대료; 빌리다

대화를 들으시오.
W 이 원룸 아파트에 대해 어떻게 생각하세요? 시내 중심가 한복판에 있어요.
M 위치는 정말 좋지만, ⁰⁹임대료가 제 예산을 훨씬 초과해요.
W 음… ¹⁰하지만 여기서 사시면 교통비를 얼마나 절약하실지 생각해 보세요.
M 좋은 지적이에요. 차가 필요하지 않을 것이고, 매일 걸어서 직장에 갈 수 있어요.
W 게다가, 이 주방을 보세요. 작지만 필요한 모든 것이 있어요.
M 맞아요. 다시 고려해봐야겠네요.

09 Attitude Question

아파트에 대한 남자의 태도는 무엇인가?
Ⓐ 시끄러울 거라고 생각한다.
Ⓑ 시내 위치를 싫어한다.
☑ 그것을 감당할 수 있을지 걱정한다.
Ⓓ 더 큰 주방을 선호한다.

어휘 dislike[disláik] 싫어하다; 반감

10 Intention Question

여자는 왜 교통비를 언급하는가?
Ⓐ 임대료가 저렴한 이유를 설명하기 위해
Ⓑ 그녀 자신의 거주 상황을 설명하기 위해
Ⓒ 새 차를 사라고 제안하기 위해
☑ 더 높은 주거비를 정당화하기 위해

어휘 justify[dʒʌ́stəfài] 정당화하다

[11-12]   M-Au W-En

Listen to a conversation.

M Are you done preparing for the sales presentation?
W Yes, I just finished all the slides. How about you?
M I'm also done with the presentation part. ¹¹But could you set up the meeting room? I know I was supposed to do it, but I got an important call from my client.
W No problem. What exactly needs to be done?
M You just need to check the projector and ¹²make sure there are enough handouts for everyone.
W Got it. ¹²I'll print them out right away.

be supposed to ~할 예정이다

대화를 들으시오.
M 영업 발표를 위해 준비하는 것을 끝내셨나요?
W 네, 모든 슬라이드를 방금 끝냈어요. 당신은 어때요?
M 저도 발표 부분은 끝냈어요. ¹¹하지만 회의실을 준비해주실 수 있나요? 제가 하기로 되어 있었는데, 고객으로부터 중요한 전화가 왔거든요.
W 문제없어요. 정확히 무엇을 해야 하나요?
M 프로젝터를 점검하고 ¹²모든 사람을 위한 충분한 유인물이 있게만 해주시면 돼요.
W 알겠어요. ¹²바로 인쇄할게요.

11 Intention Question

남자는 왜 자신의 고객을 언급하는가?
Ⓐ 내일의 부서 회의를 연기하기 위해
☑ 자신의 책임을 다할 수 없는 이유를 설명하기 위해
Ⓒ 중요한 방문객에 대한 정보를 공유하기 위해
Ⓓ 발표의 중요성을 강조하기 위해

어휘 fulfill[fulfíl] 다하다, 이행하다, 성취하다
significance[signíf ikəns] 중요성, 의의

12 Do Next Question

여자는 다음에 무엇을 할 것인가?
Ⓐ 고객에게 전화한다.
Ⓑ 추가 슬라이드를 만든다.
☑ 유인물의 복사본을 만든다.
Ⓓ 고장 난 프로젝터를 수리한다.

[13-14]

🔊 M-En W-Am

Listen to a conversation.

M I see you signed up for that cooking class at the community center. Are you excited?

W ¹³**Honestly, I'm a bit nervous. I'm not very confident in the kitchen, but I really want to improve.**

M Well, everyone starts somewhere. ¹⁴**The instructor is really patient with beginners.** I took her baking class last month.

W That's reassuring. I'm hoping it will be fun and not too overwhelming.

M I'm sure you'll do great. Cooking is more about practice than natural talent.

honestly[ánistli] 솔직히, 정말로
confident[kánfədənt] 자신이 있는
improve[imprúːv] 개선하다, 발전하다
patient[péiʃənt] 인내심이 있는; 환자
reassuring[riə ʃəriŋ] 안심이 되는, 용기를 북돋는
talent[tǽlənt] 재능, 재주

대화를 들으시오.

M 지역 문화 센터에서 요리 수업을 신청하신 거 봤어요. 기대되세요?
W ¹³솔직히, 조금 긴장돼요. 저는 부엌에서 그다지 자신이 없지만, 정말 개선되고 싶어요.
M 글쎄요, 누구나 어디선가 시작하잖아요. ¹⁴강사가 초보자들에게 정말 인내심이 있어요. 지난달에 그분의 베이킹 수업을 들었거든요.
W 안심이 되네요. 즐거우면서도 너무 부담스럽지 않기를 바라요.
M 잘하실 거라고 확신해요. 요리는 타고난 재능보다는 연습이 관건이랍니다.

13 Attitude Question

여자는 요리 수업에 대해 어떻게 느끼는 것 같은가?
Ⓐ 잘할 것이라고 자신한다.
☑ 불안하지만 배우려는 동기가 있다.
Ⓒ 신청한 것을 후회한다.
Ⓓ 너무 쉬울 거라고 생각한다.

어휘 excel[iksél] 잘하다, 탁월하다
anxious[ǽŋkʃəs] 불안한, 걱정되는 regret[rigrét] 후회하다

14 Detail Question

남자는 강사에 대해 무엇을 말하는가?
☑ 새로운 요리사들과 잘 작업한다.
Ⓑ 학생들에게 매우 까다롭다.
Ⓒ 고급 기법을 전문으로 한다.
Ⓓ 베이킹 수업만 가르친다.

어휘 demanding[dimǽndiŋ] 까다로운, 벅찬

[15-16]

🔊 W-Am M-Nz

Listen to a conversation.

W Are you interested in picking up some weekend shifts at the campus cafeteria? I'm quitting next month, so they'll need someone to replace me.

M I'd like to, but I don't have a car. Is the campus shuttle bus available on weekends?

W Unfortunately, it doesn't run on weekends. ¹⁵**But several students carpool from downtown. My roommate drives here every Saturday and might be willing to give you a ride.**

M That would be fantastic. When should I submit my application?

W ¹⁶**The manager wants applications by this Friday**, so you have a few days to get everything together.

unfortunately[ʌnfɔ́ːrtʃənətli] 불행히도, 안타깝게도
application[æplǝkéiʃən] 지원서
get something together ~을 준비하다, ~을 모으다

대화를 들으시오.

W 캠퍼스 구내식당에서 주말 근무를 하는 데 관심이 있으세요? 제가 다음 달에 그만둘 예정이라 저를 대신할 사람이 필요해요.
M 하고 싶지만, 차가 없어요. 주말에 캠퍼스 셔틀버스를 이용할 수 있나요?
W 불행히도, 주말에는 운행하지 않아요. ¹⁵하지만 시내에서 몇몇 학생들이 카풀을 해요. 제 룸메이트가 매주 토요일마다 여기로 운전해오는데 당신을 태워줄 의향이 있을 거예요.
M 그거 정말 좋겠네요. 언제 지원서를 제출해야 하나요?
W ¹⁶매니저가 이번 주 금요일까지 지원서를 원해서, 모든 것을 준비할 며칠의 기간이 있어요.

15 Intention Question

여자는 왜 자신의 룸메이트를 언급하는가?
Ⓐ 자신이 일을 그만두는 이유를 설명하기 위해
☑ 대안 교통수단 선택지를 제안하기 위해
Ⓒ 그 자리에 다른 사람을 추천하기 위해
Ⓓ 일에 대한 추가 정보를 제공하기 위해

어휘 transportation[trænspərtéiʃən] 교통수단, 운송

16 Detail Question

지원 마감일은 언제인가?
Ⓐ 다음 달
Ⓑ 다음 주
✓ 이번 주 금요일
Ⓓ 이번 주 토요일

7. Inference Questions

Example W-Nz M-En   p.135

W 다음 달 업계 컨퍼런스의 준비는 어떻게 되어가고 있나요?
M 아직 기조연설자를 확정해야 해요.
W Holt 박사님이 이미 연설하기로 동의하지 않았나요? 몇 주 전에 정해진 것으로 생각했는데요.
M 그녀가 처음에는 그랬지만, 어제 그녀의 조수가 전화해서 그녀의 연구 프로젝트와 일정상 충돌이 있다고 말했어요.
W 그거 걱정되네요. 홍보 자료에 이미 그녀의 이름이 대문짝만하게 나가 있는데요.
M 그러니까요. 오늘 오후에 Chen 박사님과 만나서 그의 참석 가능 여부를 논의할 예정이에요.

industry[índəstri] 산업, 공업
keynote[kíːnout] 기조, 기본 방침, 으뜸음
settle[sétl] 정하다, 정착하다, 해결하다 initially[iníʃəli] 처음에
promotional[prəmóuʃənl] 홍보용의, 선전용의
prominently[prάmənəntli] 대문짝만하게, 눈에 잘 띄게

남자는 Holt 박사님에 대해 무엇을 암시하는가?
✓ 컨퍼런스에서 연설할 수 없다.
Ⓑ 분야에서 인정받는 전문가이다.
Ⓒ 컨퍼런스에 조수를 데려올 계획이다.
Ⓓ 발표를 위해 다른 시간대를 요청했다.

어휘 expert[ékspəːrt] 전문가; 숙련된 field[fiːld] 분야, 영역

HACKERS PRACTICE   p.136

01 Ⓓ   02 Ⓒ   03 Ⓑ   04 Ⓐ

01 Inference Question   W-Am M-Au

W I'm heading to the grocery store later. Do you need anything?
M Actually, could you pick up some vegetables for me? I'm trying to eat healthier this month.
W Sure, any specific ones you prefer? They have a great selection of organic produce.
M Maybe some spinach and bell peppers? I found some recipes online I want to try.

head to ~에 가다, ~로 향하다 grocery store 식료품점
organic[ɔːrgǽnik] 유기농의, 유기체의

W 이따 식료품점에 갈 예정이에요. 필요한 거 있나요?
M 사실, 저를 위해 채소 좀 사다 주실 수 있나요? 이번 달에는 더 건강하게 먹으려고 노력하고 있어요.
W 물론이죠, 선호하는 특정 야채들이 있나요? 그곳은 훌륭한 유기농 농산물을 구비하고 있거든요.
M 시금치와 피망은 어떨까요? 온라인에서 시도해보고 싶은 몇 가지 요리법을 찾았어요.

남자에 대해 암시되는 것은?
Ⓐ 식료품 쇼핑을 싫어한다.
Ⓑ 자신만의 채소를 기른다.
Ⓒ 특정 음식에 알레르기가 있다.
✓ 식습관을 바꿀 계획이다.

어휘 certain[sə́ːrtn] 특정한, 확신하는 eating habits 식습관

02 Inference Question   M-En W-Am

M Excuse me, I borrowed these textbooks last week. Can I renew them?
W Yes, you can extend them for another two weeks, as long as no one else has requested them. Do you want to renew all of them?
M I especially need to keep the biology reference book for my new project.
W Okay, let me check… Sorry, you can't renew that one. Three other students have already requested it.

renew[rinjúː] 연장하다, 갱신하다 as long as ~하는 한
biology[baiάlədʒi] 생물학
reference[réfərəns] 참고서, 참고, 언급

M 실례합니다, 지난주에 이 교재들을 빌렸어요. 연장할 수 있나요?
W 네, 다른 사람이 요청하지 않는 한 2주 더 연장하실 수 있어요. 모두 연장하고 싶으세요?
M 특히 제 새 프로젝트를 위해 생물학 참고서를 가지고 있어야 해요.
W 알겠어요, 확인해볼게요... 죄송해요, 그건 연장할 수 없어요. 다른 학생 세 명이 이미 요청했거든요.

여자의 직업은 무엇일 것 같은가?
Ⓐ 서점 직원
Ⓑ 생물학 교수
✓ 사서
Ⓓ 편집자

어휘 librarian[laibrɛ́əriən] 사서

03 Inference Question   M-Am W-En

M The student council said the club funding meeting is on Thursday. Are you coming too?
W Yes, I really need to get funding for the new filming equipment for my drama club.
M I heard several clubs are competing for limited funds this semester. Sounds like it won't be an easy decision.

W True. **That's why we've prepared a detailed proposal to show how that equipment would benefit multiple student productions throughout the year.**

M That sounds like a solid plan. I hope you get the funding you need.

---

student council 학생회 drama[drá:mə] 연극
compete[kəmpí:t] 경쟁하다 proposal[prəpóuzəl] 제안서, 제안
benefit[bénəfit] 도움이 되다; 혜택 solid[sálid] 탄탄한, 확실한

M 학생회에서 동아리 지원금 회의가 목요일이라고 했어요. 당신도 오나요?
W 네, 제 연극 동아리를 위한 새 촬영 장비를 위해 지원금을 정말 받아야 해요.
M 이번 학기에 여러 동아리들이 제한된 자금을 두고 경쟁한다고 들었어요. 쉬운 결정이 아닐 것 같네요.
W 맞아요. 그래서 우리는 그 장비가 일 년 내내 여러 학생 공연들에 어떻게 도움이 될지 보여주는 상세한 제안서를 준비했어요.
M 탄탄한 계획 같네요. 필요한 지원금을 받으시길 바라요.

여자는 자신의 동아리 제안서에 대해 무엇을 암시하는가?
Ⓐ 하나의 공연에만 초점을 맞춘다.
☑ 철저하게 준비되었다.
Ⓒ 예산 한도를 초과한다.
Ⓓ 늦게 제출되었다.

어휘 exceed[iksí:d] 초과하다

04 Inference Question   M-Au W-Am

M Are you planning to go to the farmers' market this weekend?

W I'm thinking about it. The produce there is so much fresher than at the supermarket.

M Definitely. **Parking is always a nightmare, though. Last time, I had to circle the lot for half an hour to get a spot.**

W That's why I usually take my bike. Bicycle parking is way easier. Plus, it forces me to be selective about what I buy, since I can only put a limited amount in my basket.

---

farmers' market 농산물 직판장 nightmare[náitmɛər] 악몽
force[fɔːrs] ~하게 하다, ~을 강요하다; 힘
selective[siléktiv] 신중하게 선택하는

M 이번 주말에 농산물 직판장에 갈 계획이에요?
W 생각해보고 있어요. 거기 농산물이 슈퍼마켓보다 훨씬 신선해요.
M 확실히요. 하지만 주차는 항상 악몽이에요. 지난번에는 자리를 잡기 위해 주차장을 30분 동안 돌아야 했어요.
W 그래서 저는 보통 자전거를 타고 가요. 자전거 주차는 훨씬 쉬워요. 게다가, 바구니에 제한된 양만 넣을 수 있어서 무엇을 살지 신중하게 선택하게 돼요.

화자들은 농산물 직판장에 대해 무엇을 암시하는가?
☑ 제한된 주차 가능성을 지닌다.
Ⓑ 슈퍼마켓보다 더 나은 가격을 제공한다.

Ⓒ 주말에만 연다.
Ⓓ 무료 주차를 제공한다.

HACKERS TEST   p.138

01 Ⓑ	02 Ⓐ	03 Ⓓ	04 Ⓑ	05 Ⓐ
06 Ⓒ	07 Ⓑ	08 Ⓒ	09 Ⓑ	10 Ⓒ
11 Ⓐ	12 Ⓑ	13 Ⓒ	14 Ⓒ	15 Ⓓ
16 Ⓐ				

[01-02]   W-En M-Au

Listen to a conversation.

W Are you interested in visiting the new exhibit at the history museum this weekend?

M I'd love to! I heard their ancient civilization display is fantastic.

W Yes, and they've added interactive elements too. Would Saturday morning work for you?

M [01]**I'm sorry, but that won't work for me. I have a family commitment.** How about Sunday afternoon?

W That works for me. Should we meet there around 2 P.M.?

M Perfect. [02]**I'll buy the tickets online to avoid the ticket office lines.**

---

civilization[sìvəlaizéiʃən] 문명
element[éləmənt] 요소, 성분, 원소 avoid[əvɔ́id] 피하다

대화를 들으시오.
W 이번 주말에 역사 박물관의 새 전시회를 관람하는 것에 관심이 있으세요?
M 그럼요! 그들의 고대 문명 전시가 훌륭하다고 들었어요.
W 맞아요, 그리고 그들은 체험형 요소들도 추가했어요. 토요일 오전 괜찮으세요?
M [01]죄송하지만, 그때는 안 될 것 같아요. 가족 약속이 있어서요. 일요일 오후는 어떠세요?
W 그때 괜찮네요. 오후 2시경에 그곳에서 만날까요?
M 완벽해요. [02]매표소 줄을 피하기 위해 온라인으로 표를 사겠어요.

01 Intention Question

남자는 왜 가족 약속을 언급하는가?
Ⓐ 박물관에 늦게 도착하는 것을 정당화하기 위해
☑ 여자에게 자신이 시간이 안 된다는 것을 알리기 위해
Ⓒ 대신 평일로 일정을 바꾸자고 제안하기 위해
Ⓓ 왜 일찍 떠나야 하는지 설명하기 위해

02 Inference Question

화자들은 역사 박물관에 대해 무엇을 암시하는가?
☑ 온라인 표 구매 옵션을 제공한다.

Ⓑ 최근에 추가 건물을 더했다.
Ⓒ 오후에 방문객 수를 제한한다.
Ⓓ 연중 현대 미술 전시회를 전시한다.

어휘 recently[ríːsntli] 최근에   year-round 연중, 일년 내내

[03-04]
🔊 M-Am W-Nz
Listen to a conversation.

M ⁰³I'm trying to decide whether to buy noise-cancelling headphones or a portable speaker.
W I think the headphones will be better since you can use them to study in the library or a café.
M Hmm… You're right. But I usually study in my dorm room. Maybe a speaker would be a better choice.
W Oh, I forgot about that. ⁰⁴Also, you often have people over to your room, so a speaker sounds like a winner.

portable[pɔ́ːrtəbl] 휴대용의, 휴대가 쉬운
have someone over ~을 초대하다

대화를 들으시오.
M ⁰³노이즈 캔슬링 헤드폰을 살지 휴대용 스피커를 살지 결정하려고 해요.
W 헤드폰이 더 나을 것 같아요. 도서관이나 카페에서 공부할 때 사용할 수 있으니까요.
M 음… 맞아요. 하지만 저는 보통 제 기숙사 방에서 공부해요. 아마 스피커가 더 나은 선택일지도 모르겠어요.
W 아, 그걸 깜빡했네요. ⁰⁴또, 당신은 자주 사람들을 방에 초대하니까, 스피커가 승자인 것 같네요.

03 Detail Question
남자는 무엇 사이에서 결정하려고 하는가?
Ⓐ 노트북과 태블릿
Ⓑ 스피커와 마이크
Ⓒ 유선과 무선 헤드폰
☑ 헤드폰과 휴대용 스피커

어휘 wired[waiərd] 유선의, 네트워크의, 긴장한
     wireless[wáiərlis] 무선의

04 Inference Question
남자에 대해 암시되는 것은?
Ⓐ 보통 방에서 음악을 듣지 않는다.
☑ 자주 친구들을 기숙사 방으로 초대한다.
Ⓒ 다른 사람들과 공부하는 것을 선호한다.
Ⓓ 이미 다른 헤드폰을 소유하고 있다.

어휘 own[oun] 소유하다; 자기 자신의

[05-06]
🔊 M-En W-Am
Listen to a conversation.

M Excuse me, ⁰⁵I saw your posting about the campus library assistant position. Is it still available?
W ⁰⁵Yes, we're still accepting applications. Do you have any prior experience?
M ⁰⁶I had a similar job in my high school. So, I'm familiar with cataloging systems.
W That's great! Our hours are weekday afternoons and some weekend shifts.
M That will work for me. What's the application process?
W Just fill out this form and submit your résumé. We'll contact you for an interview.

prior[práiər] 이전의, 앞의   experience[ikspíəriəns] 경험
résumé[rézumèi] 이력서   interview[íntərvjùː] 면접

대화를 들으시오.
M 실례합니다, ⁰⁵캠퍼스 도서관 보조 자리에 대한 당신의 게시물을 봤어요. 아직 지원 가능한가요?
W ⁰⁵네, 아직 지원서를 받고 있어요. 이전 경험이 있으세요?
M ⁰⁶고등학교 때 비슷한 일을 했어요. 그래서 목록 작성 시스템에 익숙해요.
W 훌륭해요! 저희 근무 시간은 평일 오후와 주말 교대 근무 일부예요.
M 그거면 괜찮을 것 같아요. 지원 절차는 어떻게 되나요?
W 이 양식을 작성하고 이력서를 제출하기만 하면 돼요. 면접을 위해 연락드릴게요.

05 Inference Question
여자의 직업은 무엇일 것 같은가?
☑ 도서관 직원
Ⓑ 대학교 교수
Ⓒ 서점 매니저
Ⓓ 진로 상담 센터 관리자

06 Intention Question
남자는 왜 자신의 고등학교를 언급하는가?
Ⓐ 왜 이전 직장을 그만두었는지 설명하기 위해
Ⓑ 교육 배경을 언급하기 위해
☑ 그 일에 필요한 기술을 가지고 있다는 것을 증명하기 위해
Ⓓ 고등학교와 대학교 수업을 비교하기 위해

어휘 previous[príːviəs] 이전의, 앞의
     educational[èdʒukéiʃənəl] 교육적인

[07-08]

🎧 M-Am W-Au

Listen to a conversation.

> M **⁰⁷We're still on for hiking Mount Cedar this Saturday, right?**
> W **⁰⁷Well, it doesn't look good. I just checked the weather forecast, and they're predicting heavy rain all weekend.**
> M That's disappointing. I was really looking forward to it.
> W Me too. Instead, how about trying out the indoor rock-climbing center downtown?
> M That could be fun! Have you been there before?
> W **⁰⁸No, but my roommate went last week and said it's great for beginners like us.**
>
> predict[pridíkt] 예상하다, 예측하다
> disappointing[dìsəpɔ́intiŋ] 실망스러운, 시시한

대화를 들으시오.

M ⁰⁷이번 주 토요일에 Cedar산 등반하기로 한 거 맞죠?
W ⁰⁷글쎄요, 좋지 않아 보여요. 방금 일기예보를 확인했는데, 주말 내내 폭우가 올 것으로 예상된다고 해요.
M 실망스럽네요. 정말 기대하고 있었어요.
W 저도요. 대신, 시내에 있는 실내 암벽등반 센터를 시도해보는 게 어때요?
M 재미있을 것 같아요! 거기 가본 적 있어요?
W ⁰⁸아니요, 하지만 제 룸메이트가 지난주에 갔는데 저희 같은 초보자들에게 훌륭하다고 했어요.

07 Inference Question

여자는 일기예보에 대해 무엇을 암시하는가?
Ⓐ 주말까지 바뀔 수도 있다.
☑ 그들의 야외 계획을 방해할 것이다.
Ⓒ 암벽등반 활동에 영향을 준다.
Ⓓ 보통 정확하지 않다.

어휘 inaccurate[inǽkjurət] 정확하지 않은, 틀린

08 Inference Question

화자들에 대해 암시되는 것은?
Ⓐ Cedar산 근처에 산다.
Ⓑ 전에 등반 센터를 방문한 적이 있다.
☑ 등반 경험이 많지 않다.
Ⓓ 야외 활동보다 실내 활동을 선호한다.

[09-10]

🎧 W-Nz M-En

Listen to a conversation.

> W **⁰⁹The marketing team wants the website updates completed by Friday, but I'm not sure that's realistic.**
> M What's the main challenge? Is it the product photos or the text revisions?
> W Both, actually. **¹⁰Plus, I need to coordinate with the design team for the layout changes.**
> M That does sound like a lot to juggle. How much of the content have you finished so far?
> W About 60% of the text is done, but none of the photos have been processed yet.
> M Let me talk to marketing. Maybe we can push the deadline to next week.
>
> realistic[rì:əlístik] 현실적인   challenge[tʃǽlindʒ] 문제, 도전
> revision[rivíʒən] 수정   juggle[dʒʌ́gl] 동시에 처리하다
> so far 지금까지   process[práses] 처리하다; 과정
> push something to ~을 ~로 미루다

대화를 들으시오.

W ⁰⁹마케팅팀에서 금요일까지 웹사이트 업데이트를 완료하기를 원하는데, 그게 현실적일지 확신이 안 서요.
M 주요 문제가 뭐예요? 제품 사진인가요, 아니면 텍스트 수정인가요?
W 사실, 둘 다예요. ¹⁰게다가, 레이아웃 변경을 위해 디자인팀과 조율해야 해요.
M 정말 동시에 처리해야 할 일이 많은 것 같네요. 지금까지 콘텐츠를 얼마나 완료했죠?
W 텍스트의 약 60퍼센트는 완료했는데, 사진은 아직 아무것도 처리하지 못했어요.
M 마케팅과 이야기해 볼게요. 아마 마감일을 다음 주로 미룰 수 있을 거예요.

09 Problem Question

여자의 문제는 무엇인가?
Ⓐ 필요한 기술적 능력이 부족하다.
☑ 시간 내에 완료하기에는 너무 많은 일이 있다.
Ⓒ 마케팅팀의 비전에 동의하지 않는다.
Ⓓ 디자인팀과 연락할 수 없다.

어휘 disagree[dìsəgrí:] 동의하지 않다, 일치하지 않다

10 Inference Question

여자에 대해 암시되는 것은?
Ⓐ 자주 프로젝트 마감일을 놓친다.
Ⓑ 대부분의 프로젝트에서 독립적으로 일한다.
☑ 여러 팀과 협력해야 한다.
Ⓓ 텍스트보다 사진 작업을 더 빠르게 한다.

어휘 independently[ìndipéndəntli] 독립적으로

[11-12]

🎧 M-En W-Am

Listen to a conversation.

M Did you test the microphone system for our band's performance?

W ¹¹Yes, I checked everything this morning. The sound quality is excellent, and all the cables are working properly.

M Great! ¹²What about the projector? Last semester's event had technical difficulties.

W I've already connected it to my laptop and run a full test. We should be good to go.

M Perfect. How early should we arrive to set up the stage lighting?

W I'd say around 6 P.M. That gives us an hour before the audience starts arriving, and I can double-check all the equipment.

good to go 순조로운 audience [ɔ́ːdiəns] 관객
double-check 재확인하다

대화를 들으시오.

M 우리 밴드 공연을 위한 마이크 시스템을 테스트했나요?

W ¹¹네, 오늘 아침에 모든 것을 확인했어요. 음질이 훌륭하고, 모든 케이블이 제대로 작동해요.

M 좋아요! ¹²프로젝터는 어때요? 지난 학기 행사에서는 기술적 문제가 있었거든요.

W 이미 제 노트북에 연결하고 전체 테스트를 실행했어요. 순조로운 것 같아요.

M 완벽해요. 무대 조명을 설치하기 위해 얼마나 일찍 도착해야 할까요?

W 오후 6시쯤이라고 생각해요. 그러면 관객이 도착하기 시작하는 시간 전에 한 시간이 있고, 모든 장비를 재확인할 수 있어요.

11 Inference Question

여자에 대해 결론지을 수 있는 것은?
ⓐ 기술 장비에 경험이 있다. ✓
ⓑ 오늘 밤 공연에 참석하지 않을 것이다.
ⓒ 프로젝터를 설치하는 데 도움이 필요하다.
ⓓ 행사의 성공에 대해 걱정하고 있다.

어휘 set up 설치하다, 설정하다

12 Intention Question

남자는 왜 지난 학기 행사를 언급하는가?
ⓐ 기술자 고용을 제안하기 위해
ⓑ 장비에 대한 자신의 우려를 나타내기 위해 ✓
ⓒ 여자의 준비 기술을 칭찬하기 위해
ⓓ 더 많은 관객을 끌어들이기를 추천하기 위해

어휘 attract [ətrǽkt] 끌어들이다, 유혹하다

[13-14]

🎧 W-Am M-Au

Listen to a conversation.

W Performance review season is coming up fast. ¹³I've been preparing evaluation forms and scheduling one-on-one meetings with all department heads.

M How many employees are we reviewing this quarter?

W Around 200 across all divisions. ¹⁴I also want to discuss career development opportunities with each manager during these sessions.

M That's ambitious, but it'll definitely help with employee retention. Do you need any assistance organizing the materials?

W I think I can handle it so far. Thanks!

evaluation [ivæ̀ljuéiʃən] 평가, 분석, 심사
quarter [kwɔ́ːrtər] 분기, 4분의 1
division [divíʒən] 부서, 부문, 구분
opportunity [ɑ̀pərtjúːnəti] 기회
ambitious [æmbíʃəs] 야심찬, 의욕적인
retention [riténʃən] 유지, 보유, 기억

대화를 들으시오.

W 성과 평가 기간이 빠르게 다가오고 있어요. ¹³평가 양식을 준비하고 모든 부서장들과 일대일 회의를 예약하는 중이에요.

M 이번 분기에 몇 명의 직원을 평가하나요?

W 모든 부서를 합쳐서 약 200명이에요. ¹⁴또한 이런 회의들 중에 각 관리자와 경력 개발 기회에 대해 논의하고 싶어요.

M 야심찬 계획이지만, 확실히 직원 유지에 도움이 될 거예요. 자료 정리하는 데 도움이 필요하세요?

W 지금까지는 제가 처리할 수 있을 것 같아요. 고마워요!

13 Inference Question

여자가 일하고 있는 회사의 부서는 어디인 것 같은가?
ⓐ 회계
ⓑ 광고
ⓒ 인사 ✓
ⓓ 연구개발

14 Detail Question

여자는 관리자들과 무엇에 대해 논의하고 싶어 하는가?
ⓐ 평가 절차
ⓑ 직원 일정 충돌
ⓒ 전문적인 성장 기회 ✓
ⓓ 부서 구조조정 계획

어휘 procedure [prəsíːdʒər] 절차, 진행, 경과
restructuring [riːstrʌ́kʃəriŋ] 구조조정, 개편, 재편

[15-16]

🎧 M-Nz W-Am

Listen to a conversation.

M Are you heading out somewhere?

W ¹⁵Actually, I was just about to drive to the mall. Lisa's birthday party is this weekend, and I still haven't gotten her a gift.

M Oh right, her party! What are you thinking of getting?

W I'm torn between a nice jewelry box and that art book she mentioned wanting last month.

M ¹⁶The art book sounds perfect. She's always sketching in her free time.

W You're right. Thanks for helping me decide! I should hurry before the mall closes.

be about to 막 ~ 하려던 참이다
torn between ~ 사이에서 고민하다   jewelry [dʒúːəlri] 보석

대화를 들으시오.

M 어디 나가는 길이세요?

W ¹⁵사실, 쇼핑몰로 차를 몰고 가려던 참이었어요. Lisa의 생일 파티가 이번 주말인데, 아직 선물을 사지 못했어요.

M 아, 맞다, 그녀의 파티! 뭘 사려고 생각하고 있어요?

W 예쁜 보석함과 그녀가 지난달에 갖고 싶다고 언급했던 미술 책 사이에서 고민하고 있어요.

M ¹⁶미술 책이 완벽할 것 같아요. 그녀는 항상 여가 시간에 스케치를 하잖아요.

W 맞아요. 결정하는 데 도와줘서 고마워요! 쇼핑몰이 문 닫기 전에 서둘러야겠어요.

15 Inference Question

여자는 막 하려던 것에 대해 무엇을 암시하는가?
Ⓐ Lisa의 생일 파티에 참석한다.
Ⓑ 쇼핑몰에서 친구를 만난다.
Ⓒ 미술관으로 운전해서 간다.
✓ⒹⒸ 선물을 사러 쇼핑을 간다.

16 Detail Question

남자는 왜 미술 책을 추천하는가?
✓Ⓐ Lisa의 관심사와 일치한다.
Ⓑ 무료 미술 용품과 함께 나온다.
Ⓒ 보석함보다 비용이 적게 든다.
Ⓓ 정말 좋은 후기를 받았다.

어휘 interest [íntərəst] 관심사, 흥미   cost [kɔːst] 비용이 들다; 가격

Section II. Conversation Topics

1. Daily Life

HACKERS TEST
p.148

01 Ⓒ	02 Ⓐ	03 Ⓑ	04 Ⓐ	05 Ⓒ
06 Ⓓ	07 Ⓐ	08 Ⓒ	09 Ⓐ	10 Ⓑ
11 Ⓓ	12 Ⓒ	13 Ⓑ	14 Ⓓ	15 Ⓑ
16 Ⓒ

[01-02]

🎧 W-Am M-En

Listen to a conversation.

W I've been wanting to try that new Mediterranean restaurant on Oak Street. Are you free for dinner tonight?

M ⁰¹I have a dentist appointment at 6, and my last visit took almost two hours.

W Oh, that might be too late. How about tomorrow evening instead? ⁰²I heard they have excellent seafood dishes.

M Perfect! Should we make a reservation for around 7?

W Sounds great. I'll call them right now.

Mediterranean [mèdətəréiniən] 지중해의
reservation [rèzərvéiʃən] 예약

대화를 들으시오.

W Oak가에 있는 새로운 지중해 식당을 가보고 싶었어요. 오늘 저녁 시간 괜찮으세요?

M ⁰¹6시에 치과 예약이 있는데, 지난번 방문했을 때 거의 2시간이 걸렸어요.

W 아, 그러면 너무 늦을 수도 있겠네요. 내일 저녁은 어떠세요? ⁰²훌륭한 해산물 요리가 있다고 들었어요.

M 완벽해요! 7시쯤으로 예약해야 할까요?

W 좋아요. 지금 전화해볼게요.

01 Intention Question

남자는 왜 지난번 방문을 언급하는가?
Ⓐ 다른 식당을 선호하는 이유를 설명하기 위해
Ⓑ 더 일찍 출발해야 한다고 제안하기 위해
✓Ⓒ 오늘 밤 갈 수 없는 이유를 나타내기 위해
Ⓓ 여자에게 같은 치과의사를 추천하기 위해

어휘 explain [ikspléin] 설명하다
suggest [səgdʒést] 제안하다, 암시하다
indicate [índikèit] 나타내다
recommend [rèkəménd] 추천하다

02 Detail Question

여자는 식당에 대해 무엇을 말하는가?
- ⓐ 고품질의 해산물 요리를 제공한다. ✓
- ⓑ 대부분의 사람들에게는 너무 비싸다.
- ⓒ 사전에 예약이 필요하다.
- ⓓ 그들의 지역에서 멀리 떨어져 있다.

어휘 in advance 사전에, 미리

[03-04]

🔊 M-En W-Am

Listen to a conversation.

M: ⁰³Are you planning to attend the stargazing event at the observatory this Friday night?

W: Absolutely! I've been waiting for this opportunity for months. They're allowing people to use professional telescopes.

M: That sounds amazing. What time does it start?

W: On-site registration begins at 8, but the actual observation starts around 9 when it gets darker.

M: Perfect. ⁰⁴I'm thinking of bringing my camera to capture some shots of the night sky.

---

stargazing [stάːrgèiziŋ] 별 관측, 천체 관찰
observatory [əbzə́ːrvətɔ̀ːri] 천문대, 관측소
opportunity [ὰpərtjúːnəti] 기회
professional [prəféʃənl] 전문의; 직업의
telescope [téləskòup] 망원경, 현미경
amazing [əméiziŋ] 멋진, 놀라운 on-site 현장의, 현지의
registration [rèdʒistréiʃən] 등록, 신청
capture [kǽptʃər] 찍다, (마음·관심을) 사로잡다

대화를 들으시오.

M: ⁰³이번 주 금요일 밤 천문대에서 열리는 별 관측 행사에 참석할 계획이세요?
W: 물론이에요! 몇 달 동안 이 기회를 기다렸어요. 전문 망원경을 사용할 수 있게 해준대요.
M: 정말 멋지네요. 몇 시에 시작하나요?
W: 현장 등록은 8시에 시작하지만, 실제 관측은 어두워지는 9시쯤에 시작해요.
M: 완벽하네요. ⁰⁴밤하늘 사진을 찍기 위해 카메라를 가져갈 생각이에요.

03 Main Topic Question

화자들은 어떤 행사에 대해 이야기하고 있는가?
- ⓐ 사진 워크숍
- ⓑ 별 관측 행사 ✓
- ⓒ 과학 강의
- ⓓ 캠핑 여행

어휘 lecture [léktʃər] 강의, 강연

04 Inference Question

남자는 행사에 무엇을 가져갈 것 같은가?
- ⓐ 사진 장비 ✓
- ⓑ 전문 망원경

- ⓒ 음식과 음료수
- ⓓ 휴대용 손전등

어휘 equipment [ikwípmənt] 장비 beverage [bévəridʒ] 음료(수)
portable [pɔ́ːrtəbl] 휴대용의, 휴대가 쉬운
flashlight [flǽʃlàit] 손전등

[05-06]

🔊 W-Nz M-En

Listen to a conversation.

W: ⁰⁵I have a job interview next week, and I'm torn between getting a navy blazer or a charcoal gray suit.

M: What kind of position are you interviewing for?

W: It's for a marketing coordinator role at a tech startup. The company culture seems pretty relaxed based on my research.

M: In that case, the blazer might be more appropriate. ⁰⁶You can pair it with different pairs of pants and still look professional.

W: That's a good point. I'll go with the blazer then.

---

job interview 취업 면접 torn between ~ 사이에서 고민하다
pretty [príti] 꽤 appropriate [əpróupriət] 적절한, 적당한
pair with ~와 짝을 이루다, ~와 어울리다

대화를 들으시오.

W: ⁰⁵다음 주에 취업 면접이 있는데, 네이비 블레이저를 살지 차콜 그레이 정장을 살지 고민이에요.
M: 어떤 직책으로 면접을 보시나요?
W: 기술 스타트업의 마케팅 코디네이터 역할이에요. 제가 조사한 바로는 회사 문화가 꽤 자유로운 것 같아요.
M: 그렇다면 블레이저가 더 적절할 것 같아요. ⁰⁶다른 바지와 짝을 이룰 수 있고 여전히 전문적으로 보일 수 있어요.
W: 좋은 지적이네요. 그럼 블레이저로 하겠어요.

05 Detail Question

여자는 무엇 사이에서 결정하려고 하는가?
- ⓐ 두 취업 기회
- ⓑ 두 면접 시간
- ⓒ 두 전문적인 옷차림 ✓
- ⓓ 두 다른 헤어스타일

어휘 outfit [áutfit] 옷차림

06 Detail Question

남자는 왜 블레이저를 추천하는가?
- ⓐ 정장보다 비용이 적게 든다.
- ⓑ 더 좋은 첫인상을 준다.
- ⓒ 세탁하고 관리하기가 더 쉽다.
- ⓓ 더 많은 스타일링 유연성을 제공한다. ✓

어휘 cost [kɔːst] 비용이 들다; 가격 first impression 첫인상 maintain [meintéin] 관리하다, 유지하다
flexibility [flèksəbíləti] 유연함, 융통성

[07-08]
🔊 W-En M-Au

Listen to a conversation.

> W ⁰⁷I usually take the number 42 bus to get to campus, but I heard there were some route changes.
> M I heard that too. It no longer goes directly to the campus, so you'll need to transfer to the 18 bus at Central Station.
> W How much extra time should I allow for the transfer?
> M I'd suggest adding about 15 minutes to your usual commute time.
> W Is there any other way to get there without transferring?
> M ⁰⁸You could take the express subway. It's faster but costs a bit more than the bus fare.

no longer 더 이상 ~ 않다　directly[diréktli] 직접
transfer[trænsfə́ːr] 갈아타다, 이전하다, 옮기다
commute[kəmjúːt] 통학, 통근　fare[fɛər] 요금

대화를 들으시오.

W ⁰⁷보통 캠퍼스에 가기 위해 42번 버스를 타는데, 노선 변경이 있었다고 들었어요.
M 저도 들었어요. 더 이상 캠퍼스로 직접 가지 않아서 Central역에서 18번 버스로 갈아타야 해요.
W 갈아타는 데 얼마나 더 시간을 잡아야 하나요?
M 평소 통학 시간에 15분 정도 더 잡으시는 것을 제안해요.
W 갈아타지 않고 갈 수 있는 다른 방법이 있나요?
M ⁰⁸급행 지하철을 탈 수 있어요. 더 빠르지만 버스 요금보다는 조금 더 비싸요.

07　Problem Question
여자의 문제는 무엇인가?
Ⓐ 학교 가는 정규 버스를 놓쳤다.
✓ 평소 버스 노선이 변경되었다.
Ⓒ 월정액 교통 승차권을 잃어버렸다.
Ⓓ 올바른 버스 정류장을 찾을 수 없다.

어휘　regular[régjulər] 정규의, 규칙적인
　　　usual[júːʒuəl] 평소의, 보통의　monthly[mʌ́nθli] 월간의

08　Detail Question
남자는 급행 지하철에 대해 무엇을 말하는가?
Ⓐ 사전 예약이 필요하다.
Ⓑ 버스보다 운행 빈도가 낮다.
✓ 버스를 타는 것보다 비용이 더 든다.
Ⓓ 이전보다 정거장이 적다.

어휘　require[rikwáiər] 필요로 하다, 요구하다

[09-10]
🔊 W-Am M-En

Listen to a conversation.

> W ⁰⁹I noticed water stains on the ceiling in our guest bedroom. I think there might be a leak upstairs.
> M That's concerning. Have you checked the bathroom above it yet?
> W Yes, I looked around but couldn't find anything obvious. I think we need to call a plumber.
> M You're right. It's better to address this quickly before it gets worse.
> W I'll search online for a reliable service and schedule an appointment for this week.
> M Good idea. ¹⁰Make sure to mention that it's urgent so they can prioritize our request.

stain[stein] 얼룩, 오염; 더럽히다
ceiling[síːliŋ] 천장　look around 둘러보다
obvious[ábviəs] 뚜렷한, 분명한　plumber[plʌ́mər] 배관공
address[ǽdres] 해결하다, 대응하다, 연설하다
reliable[riláiəbl] 믿을 만한, 확실한
schedule[skédʒuːl] 시간을 내주다, 예정에 넣다
make sure to 꼭 ~하다　mention[ménʃən] 언급하다
urgent[ə́ːrdʒənt] 긴급한, 절박한
prioritize[praió:rətàiz] 우선적으로 처리하다
request[rikwést] 요청; 요청하다

대화를 들으시오.

W ⁰⁹저희 손님방 천장에 물 얼룩이 보이는 걸 발견했어요. 위층에 누수가 있는 것 같아요.
M 걱정되네요. 위층 화장실은 확인해보셨나요?
W 네, 둘러봤는데 뚜렷한 것은 찾을 수 없었어요. 배관공을 불러야 할 것 같아요.
M 맞네요. 더 심해지기 전에 빨리 해결하는 게 좋겠어요.
W 온라인에서 믿을 만한 업체를 찾아서 이번 주에 예약할게요.
M 좋은 생각이에요. ¹⁰꼭 긴급하다고 언급해서 저희 요청을 우선 처리할 수 있도록 하세요.

09　Main Topic Question
화자들은 주로 무엇에 대해 이야기하고 있는가?
✓ 주택 수리 문제
Ⓑ 화장실 보수
Ⓒ 객실 장식
Ⓓ 안전점검

어휘　renovation[rènəvéiʃən] 보수, 개조, 변화
　　　decoration[dèkəréiʃən] 장식　safety inspection 안전점검

10　Suggestion Question
남자는 여자에게 무엇을 하라고 제안하는가?
Ⓐ 먼저 여러 수리 견적을 받는다.
✓ 수리가 시급하다고 나타낸다.
Ⓒ 이웃들에게 업체 추천을 요청한다.
Ⓓ 더 나은 요금을 위해 주말까지 기다린다.

어휘 **multiple**[mʌ́ltipəl] 여러, 복합의, 다수의
estimate[éstəmèit] 견적, 추정치; 추정하다
indicate[índikèit] 나타내다 **neighbor**[néibər] 이웃
recommendation[rèkəməndéiʃən] 추천
rate[reit] 요금, 비율; 평가하다

[11-12]
W-Au M-Am

Listen to a conversation.

W My younger sister's birthday is coming up next week, and I want to take my family out for dinner. ¹¹**Do you know any restaurants that would be good for a family celebration?**

M The Garden Bistro downtown would be perfect. They have excellent service there.

W That sounds promising. What time should I make the reservation for?

M I'd suggest around 7 P.M. That way you'll avoid the dinner rush, and the atmosphere is more relaxed in the evening.

W Perfect! ¹²**I'll call them today to book a table for six.**

promising[prámisiŋ] 기대되는, 유망한
atmosphere[ǽtməsfìər] 분위기, 대기 **book**[buk] 예약하다

대화를 들으시오.

W 제 여동생 생일이 다음 주에 있는데, 가족들과 함께 저녁 식사를 하러 나가고 싶어요. ¹¹가족 축하 모임에 좋은 식당을 아시나요?
M 시내에 있는 Garden Bistro가 완벽할 거예요. 거기 서비스가 훌륭해요.
W 기대되는데요. 몇 시로 예약을 해야 할까요?
M 7시쯤으로 제안할게요. 그러면 붐비는 저녁 시간을 피할 수 있고, 저녁에는 분위기가 더 편안해요.
W 완벽해요! ¹²오늘 전화해서 6명 테이블을 예약할게요.

11 Detail Question
여자는 왜 식당 추천을 요청하는가?
Ⓐ 직장용 도시락을 싸는 것을 잊었다.
Ⓑ 새로운 종류의 요리를 시도하고 싶다.
Ⓒ 친구를 위한 파티를 열고 있다.
☑ 가족 축하 모임을 계획하고 있다.

어휘 **cuisine**[kwizíːn] 요리, 요리법

12 Do Next Question
여자는 다음에 무엇을 할 것 같은가?
Ⓐ 식당 웹사이트를 방문한다.
Ⓑ 식당 가격에 대해 문의한다.
☑ 식당에 연락해서 테이블을 예약한다.
Ⓓ 다른 식당 옵션들을 찾아본다.

어휘 **look for** 찾다, 구하다, 기대하다

[13-14]
M-Am W-En

Listen to a conversation.

M ¹³**I want to start reading more books in my free time.** What genre would you recommend for someone just getting back into reading?

W Fantasy novels are really engaging. ¹⁴**They help you escape daily stress and their storylines are usually captivating.**

M That sounds interesting. Do you have any specific titles in mind?

W The *Mirror Quest* series would be perfect for you. The first book isn't too long, and it draws you in quickly.

M Great! I'll pick up a copy this weekend.

engaging[ingéidʒiŋ] 매력적인, 흥미로운
escape[iskéip] 벗어나다, 탈출하다
captivating[kǽptəvèitiŋ] 마음을 사로잡는
have something in mind ~을 염두에 두다
specific[spisífik] 특정한, 상세한 **draw in** 끌어들이다

대화를 들으시오.

M ¹³여가 시간에 독서를 더 많이 하기를 시작하고 싶어요. 독서를 막 다시 시작하는 사람에게 어떤 장르를 추천하시겠어요?
W 판타지 소설이 정말 매력적이에요. ¹⁴일상의 스트레스에서 벗어나도록 도와주고 줄거리가 보통 마음을 사로잡아요.
M 흥미롭네요. 염두에 두고 있는 특정 책 제목이 있나요?
W *Mirror Quest* 시리즈가 당신에게 완벽할 거예요. 1권은 너무 길지 않고, 당신을 빠르게 끌어들여요.
M 좋아요! 이번 주말에 한 권 사겠어요.

13 Detail Question
남자는 왜 독서를 시작하고 싶어하는가?
Ⓐ 학교 과제를 완료하기 위해
☑ 새로운 취미를 개발하기 위해
Ⓒ 독서 동아리 모임을 준비하기 위해
Ⓓ 특정 주제를 연구하기 위해

어휘 **assignment**[əsáinmənt] 과제, 숙제

14 Detail Question
여자는 판타지 소설에 대해 무엇을 말하는가?
Ⓐ 보통 매우 비싸다.
Ⓑ 다른 장르보다 짧다.
Ⓒ 복잡한 스토리라인을 가지고 있다.
☑ 일상적인 긴장을 줄이는 데 도움이 된다.

어휘 **typically**[típikəli] 보통, 대체로
complex[kəmpléks] 복잡한, 복합의
reduce[ridjúːs] 줄이다 **tension**[ténʃən] 긴장

[15-16]

Listen to a conversation. M-En W-Am

M **15Excuse me, I bought these wireless headphones here last week, but the left side isn't working properly.**

W I'm sorry to hear that. Do you have your receipt with you?

M Yes. I would like to exchange them for the same model.

W I'd be happy to help, but unfortunately we're currently out of that particular model. Our next shipment isn't expected until next Friday.

M That's not that far away. I think I can wait.

W **16In that case, I'll hold the product for you and call you when it arrives.**

wireless [wáiərlis] 무선의 properly [prápərli] 제대로, 적절하게
receipt [risí:t] 영수증, 수령 exchange [ikstʃéindʒ] 교환하다
unfortunately [ənfɔ́:rtʃənətli] 안타깝게도, 불행히도
currently [kə́:rəntli] 현재
particular [pərtíkjulər] 특정한, 특별한, 까다로운
shipment [ʃípmənt] 입고, 선적

대화를 들으시오.

M 15실례합니다만, 지난주에 여기서 이 무선 헤드폰을 샀는데, 왼쪽이 제대로 작동하지 않아요.
W 안타깝네요. 영수증을 가지고 계신가요?
M 네. 같은 모델로 교환하고 싶은데요.
W 기꺼이 도와드리고 싶지만, 안타깝게도 현재 그 특정 모델의 재고가 없어요. 다음 입고는 다음 주 금요일로 예상됩니다.
M 그렇게 멀지 않네요. 기다릴 수 있을 것 같아요.
W 16그런 경우에는, 제품을 따로 확보해두고 도착하면 전화드릴게요.

15 Problem Question

남자의 문제는 무엇인가?
Ⓐ 구매한 것에 대한 영수증을 잃어버렸다.
Ⓑ 장비의 한 부분이 작동하지 않는다. ✓
Ⓒ 원하는 헤드폰을 살 여유가 없다.
Ⓓ 매장에서 그가 선호하는 브랜드를 취급하지 않는다.

어휘 purchase [pə́:rtʃəs] 구매한 것; 구매하다
afford [əfɔ́:rd] ~을 살 여유가 있다
preferred [prifə́:rd] 선호하는

16 Offer Question

여자는 무엇을 해주겠다고 제안하는가?
Ⓐ 제조업체에 연락한다.
Ⓑ 매장 크레딧을 제공한다.
Ⓒ 상품을 따로 남겨 둔다. ✓
Ⓓ 다른 브랜드를 추천한다.

어휘 manufacturer [mæ̀njufǽktʃərər] 제조업체, 제조자
provide [prəváid] 제공하다

2. Campus Life

HACKERS TEST p.156

01 Ⓐ	02 Ⓑ	03 Ⓒ	04 Ⓐ	05 Ⓓ
06 Ⓑ	07 Ⓐ	08 Ⓑ	09 Ⓒ	10 Ⓑ
11 Ⓐ	12 Ⓓ	13 Ⓑ	14 Ⓒ	15 Ⓒ
16 Ⓓ				

[01-02]

Listen to a conversation. M-Am W-Nz

M Hi, Emma. **01I was wondering if you could share your notes from Professor Becker's marketing lecture yesterday.** I had to miss it for a doctor's appointment.

W Of course! **02But the slides he used haven't been uploaded yet.** He mentioned some technical issues with the course platform.

M That's frustrating. I really need to catch up before the midterm next week.

W Don't worry. I took detailed notes and recorded the key points. I can email them to you by tonight.

M That would be amazing. Thanks so much for helping me out!

lecture [léktʃər] 강의, 강연
doctor's appointment 병원 예약
technical [téknikəl] 기술적인
frustrating [frʌ́streitiŋ] 좌절스러운, 절망적인
catch up 따라잡다 detailed [dí:teild] 자세한, 상세한

대화를 들으시오.

M 안녕하세요, Emma. 01어제 Becker 교수님의 마케팅 강의 필기를 공유해 주실 수 있을지 궁금해요. 병원 예약 때문에 수업에 빠져야 했거든요.
W 물론이에요! 02하지만 교수님이 사용하신 슬라이드는 아직 업로드되지 않았어요. 강의 플랫폼에 기술적인 문제가 있다고 말씀하셨어요.
M 좌절스럽네요. 다음 주 중간고사 전에는 꼭 따라잡아야 하는데요.
W 걱정 마세요. 제가 자세한 필기를 했고 핵심 포인트들을 녹음했어요. 오늘 밤까지 이메일로 보내드릴게요.
M 정말 훌륭할 것 같아요. 도와주셔서 정말 감사해요!

01 Main Purpose Question

남자는 왜 여자에게 이야기하고 있는가?
Ⓐ 수업 필기를 빌리기 위해 ✓
Ⓑ 중간고사 공부 계획을 논의하기 위해
Ⓒ Becker 교수님의 상담시간에 대해 묻기 위해
Ⓓ 스터디 그룹에 초대하기 위해

02 Detail Question

여자는 슬라이드에 대해 무엇을 말하는가?
Ⓐ 오래된 것들이다.
☑ 온라인에서 접근할 수 없다.
Ⓒ 이해하기에 너무 어렵다.
Ⓓ 별도로 구매되어야 한다.

어휘 outdated [àutdéitid] 오래된, 구식의
      accessible [æksésəbl] 접근할 수 있는
      separately [sépərətli] 별도로

[03-04]   W-En M-Am

Listen to a conversation.

W Did you hear about the changes they're making to the dining hall menu for next semester?
M No, what's happening?
W They're expanding the international food options. More Asian and Mediterranean dishes, I think.
M That sounds promising. ⁰³The current selection gets pretty repetitive after a while.
W Yeah, and ⁰⁴they're also adding more plant-based alternatives. Apparently, there have been a lot of student requests for that.
M Perfect timing. I've been trying to eat less meat lately. When do these changes take effect?
W They said it'll be ready by the beginning of October.

expand [ikspǽnd] 확장시키다, 팽창하다
international [ìntərnǽʃənl] 국제적인
Mediterranean [mèdətəréiniən] 지중해의
repetitive [ripétətiv] 반복적인   plant-based 채식의, 식물성의
apparently [əpǽrəntli] 아무래도, 듣자 하니
lately [léitli] 최근에

대화를 들으시오.

W 다음 학기에 학생 식당 메뉴에 변화를 준다는 소식 들으셨나요?
M 아니요, 무슨 일이 있나요?
W 국제 음식 선택지를 확장할 거예요. 더 많은 아시아 음식과 지중해 요리인 것 같아요.
M 그거 기대되네요. ⁰³현재 선택지는 시간이 지나면 꽤 되풀이하게 되잖아요.
W 맞아요, 그리고 ⁰⁴채식 대체 음식도 더 추가할 거예요. 아무래도 그것에 대한 학생 요청이 많이 있었나 봐요.
M 완벽한 타이밍이네요. 저도 최근에 고기를 덜 먹으려고 노력하고 있거든요. 이런 변화는 언제 적용되나요?
W 10월 시작부터 준비될 것이라고 했어요.

03 Detail Question

남자는 현재 음식 선택에 대해 무엇을 말하는가?
Ⓐ 적은 양을 제공한다.
Ⓑ 학생들에게 너무 비싸다.
☑ 시간이 지나면 단조로워진다.
Ⓓ 건강한 선택지를 제공하지 않는다.

어휘 monotonous [mənátənəs] 단조로운, 지루한

04 Intention Question

여자는 왜 학생 요청을 언급하는가?
☑ 특정 변화가 이루어지는 이유를 설명하기 위해
Ⓑ 남자가 더 불평하도록 격려하기 위해
Ⓒ 학생 식당 운영진을 비판하기 위해
Ⓓ 더 많은 학생 피드백을 모으기 위해

어휘 certain [sə́ːrtn] 특정한, 확신하는
      encourage [inkə́ːridʒ] 격려하다, 권장하다
      criticize [krítəsàiz] 비판하다   gather [gǽðər] 모으다

[05-06]   M-Nz W-En

Listen to a conversation.

M I'm starting my research assistant position with Dr. Martinez next week. Since you've been working with her for two semesters now, do you have any tips?
W Well, the key is staying organized with data collection.
M What kind of tasks should I expect?
W ⁰⁵You'll mainly be recording measurements and entering data into the computer system. Just make sure to double-check everything.
M That sounds manageable. How many hours per week do you typically work?
W ⁰⁶About fifteen hours, but it can vary depending on which experiments are running.

measurement [méʒərmənt] 측정값, 양
double-check 재확인하다
manageable [mǽnidʒəbl] 감당할 수 있는
vary [vɛ́əri] 달라지다, 다양하다   depending on ~에 따라
experiment [ikspérəmənt] 실험

대화를 들으시오.

M 저는 Martinez 박사님과 함께 다음 주부터 연구 조교 일을 시작해요. 당신은 이미 두 학기 동안 그녀와 함께 일하고 계시니까, 조언이 있나요?
W 음, 핵심은 데이터 수집에서 체계적인 것을 유지하는 것이에요.
M 어떤 종류의 업무를 예상해야 하나요?
W ⁰⁵주로 측정값을 기록하고 컴퓨터 시스템에 데이터를 입력하게 될 거예요. 모든 것을 재확인하도록 하세요.
M 감당할 수 있을 것 같네요. 보통 주당 몇 시간 정도 일하세요?
W ⁰⁶약 15시간 정도인데, 어떤 실험이 진행되고 있는지에 따라 달라질 수 있어요.

05 Detail Question

남자는 주로 무엇을 담당하게 될 것인가?
Ⓐ 학부생들을 채점한다.
Ⓑ 실험실 예산을 관리한다.
Ⓒ 연구 보조금 제안서를 작성한다.
☑ 실험 데이터를 처리한다.

어휘 **grade**[greid] 채점하다; 성적, 학년
undergraduate[ʌ̀ndərgrǽʒuət] 학부
laboratory[lǽbərətɔ̀ːri] 실험실 **budget**[bʌ́dʒit] 예산
grant[grænt] 보조금; 수여하다, 승인하다
proposal[prəpóuzəl] 제안서, 제안
handle[hǽndl] 처리하다, 다루다
experimental[ikspèrəméntl] 실험의

06 Inference Question
여자는 업무량에 대해 무엇을 암시하는가?
Ⓐ 학기 내내 동일하게 유지된다.
☑ 특정 기간 동안 증가할 수 있다.
Ⓒ 주말 근무가 필요하다.
Ⓓ 정규 수업과 충돌한다.

어휘 **throughout**[θruːáut] 내내, 전체에, 도처에
semester[siméstər] 학기
require[rikwáiər] 필요로 하다, 요구하다

[07-08] W-Am M-Nz

Listen to a conversation.

> W Are you planning to attend tomorrow's chess club meeting?
> M ⁰⁷I'd love to, but I have a report due on Friday.
> W That's unfortunate. ⁰⁸**The club president mentioned they're recruiting new members this week**, and tomorrow we'll have a beginner-friendly tournament.
> M Really? That sounds like a great opportunity for newcomers. I hope we get some enthusiastic new players.
> W Me too. It would be nice to have fresh faces and different playing styles in our group.
>
> **unfortunate**[ʌnfɔ́ːrtʃənət] 아쉬운, 유감스러운
> **club president** 동아리 회장 **recruit**[rikrúːt] 모집하다, 채용하다
> **newcomer**[nuúkʌ̀mər] 신입
> **enthusiastic**[inθùːziǽstik] 열정적인

대화를 들으시오.
W 내일 체스 동아리 모임에 참석할 계획이세요?
M ⁰⁷그러고 싶지만, 금요일까지 제출해야 할 보고서가 있어요.
W 아쉽네요. ⁰⁸동아리 회장이 이번 주에 새 회원을 모집한다고 언급했고, 내일 초보자에 적합한 토너먼트가 있을 거예요.
M 정말요? 신입들에게는 훌륭한 기회인 것 같네요. 열정적인 새로운 참가자들이 생겼으면 좋겠어요.
W 저도요. 우리 그룹에 새로운 얼굴들과 색다른 경기 스타일이 있으면 좋을 것 같아요.

07 Intention Question
남자는 왜 보고서를 언급하는가?
☑ 모임에 참석할 수 없는 이유를 설명하기 위해
Ⓑ 과제에 대한 도움을 요청하기 위해
Ⓒ 토너먼트를 연기할 것을 제안하기 위해
Ⓓ 함께 공부하자고 여자를 초대하기 위해

08 Detail Question
여자는 체스 동아리에 대해 무엇을 말하는가?
Ⓐ 경험 있는 참가자만 받는다.
☑ 추가 회원을 찾고 있다.
Ⓒ 주 3회 모임을 갖는다.
Ⓓ 회비가 필요하다.

어휘 **additional**[ədíʃənl] 추가의 **membership fee** 회비

[09-10] M-En W-Am

Listen to a conversation.

> M ⁰⁹I'm trying to book the chemistry lab for next Tuesday, but the online system keeps saying it's unavailable.
> W Which time slot are you looking for? The afternoon sessions fill up really quickly, especially during midterm season.
> M I need it from 2 to 4 P.M. for my organic chemistry project. Is there any way to get on a waiting list?
> W Actually, ¹⁰you can try calling the lab coordinator directly. Sometimes there are last-minute cancellations.
> M That's a good idea.
>
> **chemistry**[kéməstri] 화학
> **unavailable**[ʌ̀nəvéiləbl] 사용할 수 없는
> **fill up** 다 차다, 가득 차다 **cancellation**[kænsəléiʃən] 취소

대화를 들으시오.
M ⁰⁹다음 주 화요일에 화학 실험실을 예약하려고 하는데, 온라인 시스템에서 계속 사용할 수 없다고 나오네요.
W 어떤 시간대를 찾고 계신가요? 오후 시간은 정말 빨리 다 차요, 특히 중간고사 기간에는요.
M 유기화학 프로젝트를 위해 오후 2시부터 4시까지 필요해요. 대기자 명단에 오를 방법이 있나요?
W 사실, ¹⁰실험실 담당자에게 직접 전화해 볼 수 있어요. 때때로 막판 취소가 있거든요.
M 좋은 생각이네요.

09 Problem Question
남자의 문제는 무엇인가?
Ⓐ 온라인 예약 시스템을 잘 사용하지 못한다.
Ⓑ 필수 안전 교육을 완료하지 않았다.
☑ 실험실 공간을 예약할 수 없다.
Ⓓ 필요한 장비를 가지고 있지 않다.

어휘 **booking**[búkiŋ] 예약 **reserve**[rizə́ːrv] 예약하다
necessary[nésəsèri] 필요한

10 Suggestion Question
여자는 남자에게 무엇을 하라고 제안하는가?
Ⓐ 다른 시간대를 시도한다.

ⓑ 실험실 담당자에게 연락한다.
ⓒ 먼저 안전 교육을 완료한다.
ⓓ 다른 건물의 다른 실험실을 사용한다.

[11-12]
W-Am M-En

Listen to a conversation.

W ¹¹I just saw a poster about a mural painting project.

M Yes! I noticed it too. ¹¹They're looking for volunteers to help create a diversity-themed mural on the main wall.

W That sounds like a really meaningful project. Do you think we need any art experience to participate?

M I'm not sure, but the poster says they welcome all skill levels. Should we look into it together?

W Definitely! I've always wanted to try something creative like this. When do you think the sessions will be?

M ¹²Let me check the details again.

mural [mjúərəl] 벽화, 벽에 붙인
volunteer [vàːləntíər] 자원봉사자; 자원봉사하다
meaningful [míːniŋfəl] 의미 있는
participate [pɑːrtísəpèit] 참가하다   creative [kriéitiv] 창의적인

대화를 들으시오.

W ¹¹벽화 그리기 프로젝트에 대한 포스터를 방금 봤어요.
M 네! 저도 봤어요. ¹¹주벽에 다양성을 주제로 한 벽화를 만드는 것을 도와줄 자원봉사자들을 찾고 있어요.
W 정말 의미 있는 프로젝트인 것 같아요. 참여하려면 미술 경험이 필요할까요?
M 확실하지 않지만, 포스터에는 모든 실력 수준을 환영한다고 해요. 함께 알아봐야 할까요?
W 물론이죠! 항상 이런 창의적인 것을 시도해보고 싶었어요. 언제 세션이 있을 것 같나요?
M ¹²세부사항을 다시 확인해볼게요.

11 Main Topic Question
화자들은 주로 무엇에 대해 이야기하고 있는가?
ⓐ 교정 봉사활동 기회
ⓑ 회화 전시회
ⓒ 주말 미술 수업
ⓓ 건물 개조

어휘 exhibition [èksəbíʃən] 전시회

12 Do Next Question
남자는 다음에 무엇을 할 것 같은가?
ⓐ 프로젝트 담당자에게 연락한다.
ⓑ 프로그램에 등록한다.
ⓒ 학생회관을 방문한다.
ⓓ 더 많은 정보를 확인한다.

[13-14]
W-Au M-Am

Listen to a conversation.

W Have you had a chance to look at the research requirements for our psychology group project?

M Yes, I have. The workload seems pretty heavy given the three-week deadline. ¹³I think we should divide the tasks more strategically.

W I agree. I was thinking I could handle the data collection and analysis since I'm comfortable with statistics.

M Perfect. I'll take care of the literature review and writing the introduction. ¹⁴Should we aim to have these tasks done by next Friday?

W ¹⁴How about Thursday? I have to start on another project on Friday.

requirement [rikwáiərmənt] 요구사항
psychology [saikáːlədʒi] 심리학
strategically [strətíːdʒikəli] 전략적으로
analysis [ənǽləsis] 분석   be comfortable with ~에 익숙하다
statistics [stətístiks] 통계
literature [lítərətʃər] 문헌, 논문, 문학
aim to ~ 하는 것을 목표로 하다

대화를 들으시오.

W 심리학 그룹 프로젝트를 위한 연구 요구사항을 살펴보셨나요?
M 네, 봤어요. 3주 마감일에 비해 업무량이 꽤 많은 것 같아요. ¹³더 전략적으로 업무를 분담해야 할 것 같아요.
W 동의해요. 제가 통계에 익숙하니까 데이터 수집과 분석을 맡을까 생각하고 있었어요.
M 완벽하네요. 저는 문헌 검토와 서론 작성을 맡을게요. ¹⁴다음 주 금요일까지 이 업무들을 완료하는 것을 목표로 해야 할까요?
W ¹⁴목요일은 어떨까요? 금요일에 다른 프로젝트를 시작해야 해서요.

13 Suggestion Question
남자는 그들이 무엇을 하라고 제안하는가?
ⓐ 마감일 연장을 요청한다.
ⓑ 작업을 더 효과적으로 분담한다.
ⓒ 추가 팀원을 찾는다.
ⓓ 연구 주제를 바꾼다.

어휘 extension [iksténʃən] 기한 연장, 확장
      effectively [iféktivli] 효과적으로

14 Detail Question
화자들은 언제 개별 업무를 완료할 것인가?
ⓐ 이달 말까지
ⓑ 3주 후에
ⓒ 다음 주 목요일에
ⓓ 다음 주 금요일에

[15-16]

🎧 W-Am M-Au

Listen to a conversation.

> W Where should we go for our nature observation trip this month?
>
> M I was considering the State Forest, but getting there requires two bus transfers. The Botanical Gardens would be easier, but it's still quite a hike from campus.
>
> W How about the Natural History Museum downtown?
>
> M I'm not really excited about that. We went there last semester, and the exhibits haven't changed much. ¹⁵**What about the Riverside Nature Center?**
>
> W ¹⁵**That's a great idea!** They have outdoor trails and an interactive learning center.
>
> M Exactly. Should we start making arrangements?
>
> W ¹⁶**I'll contact them tomorrow to check availability and group rates.**

observation[àbzərvéiʃən] 관찰 quite[kwait] 꽤, 아주
make arrangements 준비하다, 일정을 잡다

대화를 들으시오.

W 이번 달 자연 관찰 여행을 위해 어디로 가야 할까요?
M State Forest를 고려했는데, 거기에 가려면 버스를 두 번 갈아타야 해요. Botanical Gardens가 더 쉬울 텐데, 여전히 캠퍼스에서 꽤 먼 길이에요.
W 시내 Natural History Museum은 어떨까요?
M 별로 흥미롭지 않아요. 지난 학기에 거기 갔었는데, 전시물이 많이 바뀌지 않았어요. ¹⁵Riverside Nature Center는 어떨까요?
W ¹⁵좋은 생각이에요! 그곳은 야외 트레일과 상호작용 학습 센터가 있어요.
M 맞아요. 준비를 시작해야 할까요?
W ¹⁶제가 내일 연락해서 가능 여부와 단체 요금을 확인해볼게요.

15 Detail Question

견학은 어디에서 진행될 것 같은가?
Ⓐ State Forest에서
Ⓑ Natural History Museum에서
✓ Riverside Nature Center에서
Ⓓ Botanical Gardens에서

16 Offer Question

여자는 무엇을 해주겠다고 제안하는가?
Ⓐ 교통편을 준비한다.
Ⓑ 그룹 활동을 계획한다.
Ⓒ 장비를 가져온다.
✓ 센터에 연락한다.

어휘 organize[ɔ́ːrgənàiz] 준비하다, 조직하다

---

3. Work & Service

HACKERS TEST
p.164

01 Ⓐ	02 Ⓑ	03 Ⓐ	04 Ⓒ	05 Ⓑ
06 Ⓒ	07 Ⓑ	08 Ⓐ	09 Ⓒ	10 Ⓒ
11 Ⓑ	12 Ⓐ	13 Ⓑ	14 Ⓓ	15 Ⓑ
16 Ⓒ				

[01-02]

🎧 M-En W-Am

Listen to a conversation.

> M Are we all set for the client presentation on Friday morning? Everyone will be attending.
>
> W Almost. ⁰¹**I finished updating the sales figures**, but I want to double-check the proposal section one more time.
>
> M Good idea. When should we meet to go through everything together?
>
> W How about Thursday at 2? That'll give us enough time to make any final adjustments.
>
> M Actually, ⁰²**Wednesday would work better for me**. I have back-to-back meetings all day on Thursday.
>
> W Sounds good. I'll bring the printed copies and we can mark up any changes we need.

figure[fígjər] 수치, 모습 adjustment[ədʒʌ́stmənt] 조정
back-to-back 연속의, 연이은

대화를 들으시오.

M 금요일 아침 고객 발표 준비는 다 끝났나요? 모든 사람이 참석할 예정이에요.
W 거의요. ⁰¹판매 수치 업데이트는 끝냈는데, 제안서 부분을 한 번 더 재확인하고 싶어요.
M 좋은 생각이에요. 언제 만나서 모든 것을 함께 검토할까요?
W 목요일 2시는 어떠세요? 그러면 최종 조정을 할 충분한 시간이 있을 거예요.
M 사실, ⁰²수요일이 저에게는 더 나을 것 같아요. 목요일은 하루 종일 연속 회의가 있거든요.
W 좋아요. 제가 인쇄본을 가져가면 필요한 변경 사항들을 표시할 수 있을 거예요.

01 Detail Question

여자가 완료한 것은 무엇인가?
✓ 판매 데이터 업데이트
Ⓑ 발표 자료 인쇄
Ⓒ 최종 참가자 명단 확인
Ⓓ 제안서 부분 검토

어휘 update[ʌ̀pdéit] 업데이트하다, 갱신하다
     participant[pɑːrtísəpənt] 참가자 review[rivjúː] 검토하다

02 Detail Question

화자들은 언제 작업을 검토하기 위해 만날 것인가?
- Ⓐ 화요일
- ✓Ⓑ 수요일
- Ⓒ 목요일
- Ⓓ 금요일

[03-04]
M-Am W-En

Listen to a conversation.

M: ⁰³My computer has been crashing constantly since this morning. I can't get any work done.

W: That's really frustrating. Have you tried restarting it?

M: Yes, several times, but it keeps happening. ⁰³I finally called IT support about an hour ago.

W: Good thinking. While you're waiting for them, ⁰⁴why don't you use the spare laptop in the conference room?

M: That's a great idea. I completely forgot it existed.

W: That way you can at least check your urgent emails.

crash[kræʃ] 갑자기 기능을 멈추다; 충돌
constantly[kánstəntli] 계속, 지속적으로
spare[spɛər] 여분의, 남는; 할애하다
completely[kəmplí:tli] 완전히

대화를 들으시오.

M: ⁰³오늘 아침부터 제 컴퓨터가 계속 갑자기 기능을 멈추고 있어요. 일을 전혀 할 수가 없어요.
W: 정말 답답하시겠어요. 재시작해보셨나요?
M: 네, 여러 번 해봤는데 계속 그래요. ⁰³한 시간 전에 결국 IT 지원팀에 전화했어요.
W: 잘 생각하셨네요. 그들을 기다리시는 동안, ⁰⁴회의실에 있는 여분의 노트북을 사용해보시는 건 어떠세요?
M: 정말 좋은 생각이네요. 그게 있다는 걸 완전히 잊었어요.
W: 그러면 적어도 긴급한 이메일은 확인하실 수 있을 거예요.

03 Detail Question

남자는 왜 기술자에게 전화했는가?
- ✓Ⓐ 컴퓨터가 계속 제 기능을 못한다.
- Ⓑ 새로운 소프트웨어 설치가 필요하다.
- Ⓒ 인터넷 연결이 불안정하다.
- Ⓓ 업무 파일에 접근할 수 없다.

어휘 act up 제 기능을 못하다   unstable[ʌnstéibl] 불안정한

04 Suggestion Question

여자는 남자에게 무엇을 하라고 제안하는가?
- Ⓐ 수리점을 방문한다.
- Ⓑ 오늘은 집에서 일한다.
- ✓Ⓒ 대체 기기를 사용한다.
- Ⓓ IT 부서에 다시 연락한다.

어휘 alternative[ɔːltə́ːrnətiv] 대체의, 대안적인
department[dipáːrtmənt] 부서, 학부, 학과

[05-06]
W-Nz M-Am

Listen to a conversation.

W: The annual safety training compliance report shows we're falling short in some key areas. Fire safety and emergency procedures need more attention.

M: You're right. Last year's drill revealed that many employees didn't know the evacuation routes well.

W: Exactly. ⁰⁵I think we should make the training more hands-on instead of just watching videos like we did before.

M: What specific changes do you have in mind?

W: We could set up mock emergency scenarios and have employees practice the actual procedures.

M: That's a solid approach. ⁰⁶I'll contact our safety coordinator to develop realistic practice exercises for each department.

annual[ǽnjuəl] 연간의   compliance[kəmpláiəns] 준수
fall short 부족하다, 미치지 못하다   drill[dril] 훈련, 연습
reveal[riví:l] 드러내다
evacuation[ivækjuéiʃən] 피난, 비우기
hands-on 실습의, 직접 해보는   mock[mɑk] 모의의, 가짜의
solid[sɑ́lid] 확실한, 탄탄한
approach[əpróutʃ] 접근; 접근하다, 다가오다

대화를 들으시오.

W: 연간 안전 교육 준수 보고서를 보니 몇 가지 핵심 영역이 부족하네요. 화재 안전과 비상 절차에 더 많은 관심이 필요해요.
M: 맞아요. 지난해 훈련에서 많은 직원들이 피난 경로를 잘 알지 못한다는 것이 드러났잖아요.
W: 바로 그거예요. ⁰⁵전에 했던 것처럼 단지 비디오를 보는 것보다는 교육을 더 실습 위주로 만들어야 한다고 생각해요.
M: 어떤 구체적인 변화를 염두에 두고 계시나요?
W: 모의 비상 상황을 설정하면 직원들이 실제 절차를 연습하게 할 수 있을 거예요.
M: 확실한 접근법이네요. ⁰⁶각 부서를 위한 현실적인 연습을 개발하기 위해 안전 조정관에게 연락할게요.

05 Inference Question

지난해 교육에 대해 암시되는 것은?
- Ⓐ 실습 연습 시간을 포함했다.
- ✓Ⓑ 직원들이 교육 자료를 시청했다.
- Ⓒ 외부 전문가에 의해 실시되었다.
- Ⓓ 주로 피난 경로에 초점을 맞췄다.

어휘 instructional[instrʌ́kʃənl] 교육의
conduct[kəndʌ́kt] 수행하다, 처리하다
external[ekstə́ːrnəl] 외부의   expert[ékspəːrt] 전문가; 숙련된
primarily[praimérəli] 주로, 본래

06 Do Next Question

남자는 다음에 무엇을 할 것인가?
Ⓐ 안전 장비를 개선한다.
Ⓑ 준수 보고서를 검토한다.
☑ 안전 조정관에게 연락한다.
Ⓓ 비상 훈련 일정을 세운다.

[07-08]

🎧 M-En W-Au

Listen to a conversation.

> M ⁰⁷**The product launch event is scheduled for next month.** Should we invite media representatives or keep it internal?
> W I think we should include key journalists and industry bloggers. This product deserves wider attention.
> M That's a good point. If we're inviting external guests, how many people are we expecting in total?
> W ⁰⁸**Probably around 80 attendees.**
> M ⁰⁸**I'll need to look for a large conference room and upgrade our refreshments.**
> W Good thinking.
>
> representative[rèprizéntətiv] 관계자, 대표; 대표적인
> internal[íntə:rnl] 내부의, 체내의 journalist[dʒə́:rnəlist] 기자
> deserve[dizə́:rv] ~할 만하다 in total 전부, 총
> probably[prɑ́:bəbli] 아마, 십중팔구
> refreshments[rifréʃmənts] 다과

대화를 들으시오.

M ⁰⁷제품 출시 행사가 다음 달로 예정되어 있어요. 언론 관계자들을 초대해야 할까요, 아니면 내부적으로 진행해야 할까요?
W 주요 기자들과 업계 블로거들을 포함해야 한다고 생각해요. 이 제품은 더 넓은 관심을 받을 만하거든요.
M 좋은 지적이네요. 외부 손님들을 초대한다면, 전부 몇 명 정도 예상하고 있나요?
W ⁰⁸아마 80명 정도의 참석자들이요.
M ⁰⁸큰 회의실을 찾고 다과를 개선해야겠어요.
W 좋은 생각이에요.

07 Main Topic Question

화자들은 주로 무엇에 대해 이야기하고 있는가?
Ⓐ 네트워킹 세션
☑ 제품 공개 행사
Ⓒ 월간 직원 회의
Ⓓ 고객 감사 만찬

어휘 appreciation[əprì:ʃiéiʃən] 감사, 이해

08 Intention Question

남자는 왜 다과 패키지 업그레이드를 언급하는가?
☑ 더 큰 그룹 규모를 수용하기 위해
Ⓑ 잠재 고객들에게 인상을 주기 위해
Ⓒ 식단 제한을 충족하기 위해
Ⓓ 출장연회 요구사항을 만족시키기 위해

어휘 accommodate[əká:mədèit] 수용하다
impress[imprés] 인상을 주다
potential[pəténʃəl] 잠재적인; 가능성
dietary restriction 식단 제한
satisfy[sǽtisfài] 만족시키다, 충족시키다

[09-10]

🎧 W-Am M-Nz

Listen to a conversation.

> W ⁰⁹**The Internet connection in my dorm has been down since yesterday afternoon.**
> M That sounds frustrating. Is it affecting everyone in the building?
> W Yes, apparently there's an issue with the main connection. The IT department says they're working on it.
> M What about your research paper that's due tomorrow? Can you still submit it on time?
> W I'm not sure. I need to upload it to the course portal, but I can't access anything online from my room.
> M ¹⁰**Why don't you try using the library computers? They have a separate network that might still be working.**
>
> affect[əfékt] 영향을 주다 research paper 연구 논문
> on time 시간에 맞춰, 제 시간에
> separate[sépərèit] 별도의; 분리하다

대화를 들으시오.

W ⁰⁹제 기숙사의 인터넷 연결이 어제 오후부터 다운되었어요.
M 답답하시겠어요. 건물의 모든 사람에게 영향을 주고 있나요?
W 네, 메인 연결에 문제가 있는 것 같아요. IT 부서에서 작업 중이라고 해요.
M 내일이 마감인 연구 논문은 어떻게 하세요? 시간에 맞춰 제출할 수 있을까요?
W 확실하지 않아요. 강의 포털에 업로드해야 하는데, 제 방에서는 온라인으로 아무것도 접속할 수 없어요.
M ¹⁰도서관 컴퓨터를 사용해보시는 건 어떨까요? 아직 작동할 수도 있는 별도의 네트워크가 있어요.

09 Problem Question

여자의 문제는 무엇인가?
Ⓐ 연구 논문 파일을 잃어버렸다.
Ⓑ 노트북을 충전해야 한다.
☑ 인터넷에 접속할 수 없다.
Ⓓ 과제 마감일을 놓쳤다.

어휘 charge[tʃɑ:rdʒ] 충전하다, 부과하다; 요금

10 Detail Question

남자는 도서관에 대해 무엇을 말하는가?
Ⓐ 시험 주간 동안 연장 운영한다.
Ⓑ 컴퓨터 사용을 위해 사전 예약이 필요하다.

- ✓ 다른 네트워크를 사용하는 컴퓨터들이 있다.
- ⓓ 인쇄 서비스에 요금을 부과한다.

어휘 extended[iksténdid] 연장된

[11-12] 🎧 M-En W-Am
Listen to a conversation.

> M How is the website redesign coming along? I noticed the customer feedback section needs some improvement.
>
> W You're right. ¹¹**We've been getting complaints that it's too complicated to submit reviews.** The form has too many required fields.
>
> M That makes sense. ¹¹**Some of my clients have mentioned the same thing.**
>
> W Exactly! ¹²**I'd like to simplify it to just three essential fields: name, rating, and comments.** Also, we should add a thank-you message that pops up after the form is submitted.
>
> M Great idea. When can we implement these changes?
>
> W I'll have the updated version ready by Friday.
>
> ---
> improvement[imprúːvmənt] 개선하다, 발전하다
> complaint[kəmpléint] 불만
> complicated[kámpləkèitid] 복잡한, 뒤얽힌
> make sense 그럴 만하다, 의미가 통하다
> simplify[símpləfài] 간단하게 하다, 단순화하다
> pop up 뜨다, 불쑥 나타나다
> implement[ímpləmènt] 도입하다, 시행하다

대화를 들으시오.
M 웹사이트 재설계는 어떻게 진행되고 있나요? 고객 피드백 섹션에 개선이 필요하다는 것을 알았는데요.
W 맞아요. ¹¹리뷰 제출이 너무 복잡하다는 불만을 받고 있어요. 양식에 필수 입력란이 너무 많아요.
M 그럴 만하네요. ¹¹제 고객 중 몇 명도 같은 얘기를 했어요.
W 바로 그거예요! ¹²이름, 평점, 그리고 댓글의 세 개의 필수 입력란으로 간단히 하고 싶어요. 또한 양식이 제출된 후에 뜨는 감사 메시지를 추가해야 해요.
M 좋은 아이디어네요. 언제 이런 변경사항들을 도입할 수 있나요?
W 금요일까지 업데이트된 버전을 준비할게요.

11 Intention Question
남자는 왜 그의 고객을 언급하는가?
ⓐ 더 많은 고객 서비스 직원을 고용할 것을 제안하기 위해
✓ ⓑ 양식의 복잡성에 대한 증거를 제공하기 위해
ⓒ 최근 매출이 감소한 이유를 설명하기 위해
ⓓ 새로운 마케팅 전략을 제안하기 위해

어휘 hire[haiər] 고용하다 evidence[évədəns] 증거
complexity[kəmpléksəti] 복잡성
decrease[dikríːs] 감소시키다 propose[prəpóuz] 제안하다
strategy[strǽtədʒi] 전략

12 Suggestion Question
여자는 그들이 무엇을 하자고 제안하는가?
✓ ⓐ 필수 입력란의 수를 줄인다.
ⓑ 더 많은 고객 서비스 담당자를 고용한다.
ⓒ 피드백 섹션을 완전히 제거한다.
ⓓ 불필요한 팝업 메시지를 비활성화한다.

어휘 disable[diséibl] 비활성화하다
unnecessary[ʌnnésəseèri] 불필요한

[13-14] 🎧 M-Am W-En
Listen to a conversation.

> M Have you had a chance to review the candidates for the marketing position?
>
> W Yes, I've narrowed it down to five finalists. Most have strong backgrounds, ¹³**but I'm concerned about their lack of experience with digital campaigns.**
>
> M That's a valid point. However, we could provide training once they're hired. What matters more is their willingness to learn.
>
> W I suppose you're right. The recent graduate from State University seems particularly eager, though she admitted she had never managed a budget before.
>
> M Well, everyone starts somewhere. ¹⁴**Let's schedule interviews with the finalists.**
>
> ---
> candidate[kǽndidèit] 지원자, 후보자
> narrow down 좁히다, 요약하다 valid[vǽlid] 타당한, 유효한
> willingness[wílinnis] 의지
> graduate[grǽdʒuèit] 졸업생; 졸업하다
> particularly[pərtíkjulərli] 특히
> eager[íːgər] 열의가 있는, 열정적인 admit[ædmít] 인정하다

대화를 들으시오.
M 마케팅 직책 지원자들을 검토할 기회가 있으셨나요?
W 네, 5명의 최종 후보로 좁혔어요. 대부분 훌륭한 배경을 가지고 있지만, ¹³디지털 캠페인 경험 부족이 걱정돼요.
M 타당한 지적이에요. 하지만 고용된 후에 교육을 제공할 수 있어요. 더 중요한 것은 배우려는 의지예요.
W 맞는 말씀인 것 같아요. 주립 대학교 출신의 최근 졸업생은 특히 열의가 있어 보이는데, 전에 예산을 관리해본 적이 없다고 인정했어요.
M 글쎄요, 모든 사람은 어디선가 시작하잖아요. ¹⁴최종 후보자들의 면접 일정을 잡죠.

13 Attitude Question
구직 지원자들에 대한 여자의 태도는 무엇인가?
ⓐ 그들이 그 직무에 완벽하다고 생각한다.
✓ ⓑ 그들의 자격에 대해 걱정한다.
ⓒ 경험 있는 전문가를 고용하는 것을 선호한다.
ⓓ 지원자 풀에 실망했다.

어휘 consider[kənsídər] 생각하다, 고려하다
qualification[kwɑ̀ːləfikéiʃən] 자격

14 Do Next Question

화자들은 다음에 무엇을 할 것 같은가?
Ⓐ 추가 구인 공고를 게시한다.
Ⓑ 대학 취업 센터에 연락한다.
Ⓒ 회사의 교육 프로그램을 검토한다.
☑ 지원자들과의 면접 일정을 조율한다.

어휘 arrange[əréindʒ] 조율하다, 조정하다

[15-16]

🔊 W-Au M-Am

Listen to a conversation.

W The main elevator has been out of order since yesterday morning.
M I saw the maintenance notice. I'm worried it won't be fixed by tomorrow's board meeting.
W That's a problem. ¹⁵**Several executives who might have difficulty using the stairs are visiting.**
M ¹⁵**I already contacted the building manager about prioritizing this repair.** Hopefully they can get it working before the meeting starts.
W ¹⁶**Should we move the meeting to the ground floor conference room just in case?**
M That's probably our best backup plan.

out of order 고장 난 maintenance[méintənəns] 정비, 유지
executive[igzékjutiv] 임원; 집행하다
just in case 혹시 모르니, 만약을 위해 backup plan 대안

대화를 들으시오.
W 메인 엘리베이터가 어제 아침부터 고장 났어요.
M 정비 공지를 봤어요. 내일 이사회 회의까지 수리되지 않을까 봐 걱정돼요.
W 문제네요. ¹⁵계단을 이용하는 데 어려움이 있을 수 있는 임원 몇 명이 방문할 예정인데요.
M ¹⁵이미 건물 관리자에게 이 수리를 우선순위로 처리해달라고 연락했어요. 회의 시작 전에 작동시킬 수 있기를 바라요.
W ¹⁶혹시 모르니 1층 회의실로 회의를 옮겨야 할까요?
M 그게 아마 우리의 최선의 대안일 거예요.

15 Intention Question

여자는 왜 임원들을 언급하는가?
Ⓐ 회의가 중요하다는 것을 강조하기 위해
☑ 엘리베이터 수리가 긴급한 이유를 설명하기 위해
Ⓒ 회의 안건의 변경을 제안하기 위해
Ⓓ 추가 직원 고용을 권하기 위해

어휘 emphasize[émfəsàiz] 강조하다
       agenda[ədʒéndə] 안건, 의제

16 Suggestion Question

여자는 그들이 무엇을 하자고 제안하는가?
Ⓐ 이사회 회의를 완전히 취소한다.
Ⓑ 임원들의 방문을 재조율한다.
☑ 다른 회의 장소를 사용한다.
Ⓓ 엘리베이터 제조업체에 직접 연락한다.

어휘 entirely[intáiərli] 완전히

TASK 3 | Listen to an Announcement

Section I. Question Types

1. Main Topic/Purpose Questions

Example Am   p.175

> 좋은 오후입니다, 여러분. 연례 대학 취업박람회가 다음 주 목요일에 학생회관 연회장에서 열린다는 것을 알려드리는 공지입니다. 기술 대기업, 금융 기관, 그리고 의료 기관을 포함한 다양한 산업 분야의 50개 이상의 회사가 참석할 예정입니다. 이것은 인턴십과 취업 기회를 탐색할 수 있는 훌륭한 기회이므로, 이력서를 여러 부 가져오시고 전문적인 복장을 갖춰 입으시기 바랍니다.
>
> annual [ǽnjuəl] 연례의, 연간의   take place 열리다, 일어나다
> various [vɛ́əriəs] 다양한   industry [índəstri] 산업, 공업
> include [inklúːd] 포함하다   financial [fainǽnʃəl] 금융의, 재정의
> institution [ìnstitúːʃən] 기관   opportunity [ὰpərtjúːnəti] 기회
> multiple [mʌ́ltipəl] 여러   résumé [rézumèi] 이력서

공지는 주로 무엇에 대한 것인가?
Ⓐ 대학 내 채용 공고
☑ 다가오는 취업박람회
Ⓒ 이력서 작성 워크숍
Ⓓ 금융 서비스의 변화

어휘 upcoming [ʌ́pkʌ̀miŋ] 다가오는, 곧 있을

HACKERS PRACTICE   p.176

01 Ⓒ   02 Ⓑ   03 Ⓓ   04 Ⓐ

01 Main Topic Question   En

> Hello, everyone! **I'm excited to announce our annual science fair will take place this Thursday from 2 to 6 P.M. in the auditorium.** Students will showcase their research projects, and there will be interactive demonstrations throughout the afternoon. Don't miss this opportunity to see innovative work by your peers!
>
> announce [ənáuns] 발표하다
> auditorium [ɔ̀ːditɔ́ːriəm] 강당, 대강의실
> showcase [ʃóukeis] 선보이다
> interactive [ìntərǽktiv] 참여형의, 상호적인
> demonstration [dèmənstréiʃən] 시연
> throughout [θruːáut] 내내, 통하여
> innovative [ínəvèitiv] 혁신적인   peer [piər] 동료

안녕하세요, 여러분! 연례 과학 박람회가 이번 주 목요일 오후 2시부터 6시까지 강당에서 열린다는 것을 발표하게 되어 기쁩니다. 학생들이 자신들의 연구 프로젝트를 선보일 것이며, 오후 내내 참여형 시연이 있을 예정입니다. 동료들의 혁신적인 작업물을 볼 수 있는 이 기회를 놓치지 마세요!

공지는 무엇에 대한 것인가?
Ⓐ 연구 경진대회
Ⓑ 학과 회의
☑ 과학 전시회
Ⓓ 강당 보수

어휘 competition [kὰmpətíʃən] 경진대회, 경쟁
department [dipάːrtmənt] 학과, 학부, 부서
exhibition [èksəbíʃən] 전시회, 구경거리
renovation [rènəvéiʃən] 보수, 수리

02 Main Purpose Question   Am

> Quick announcement regarding tomorrow's guest lecture by Dr. Martinez. **Due to a flight delay, the talk has been moved** from 10 A.M. to 2 P.M. It will still be held in Hall C, and the topic remains "Modern Archaeological Discoveries." Please adjust your schedules accordingly, and spread the word to anyone who might have missed this update.
>
> announcement [ənáunsmənt] 공지, 발표
> regarding [rigάːrdiŋ] ~에 관한, ~에 대해
> guest lecture 초청 강연
> archaeological [ὰːrkiəládʒikəl] 고고학적인
> adjust [ədʒʌ́st] 조정하다, 적응하다
> accordingly [əkɔ́ːrdiŋli] 이에 따라, 그에 맞춰
> spread [spred] 전달하다, 펴다
> update [ʌ́pdèit] 최신 정보; 업데이트하다

Martinez 박사님의 내일 초청 강연에 관한 간단한 공지입니다. 항공편 지연으로 인해, 발표가 오전 10시에서 오후 2시로 변경되었습니다. 장소는 변함없이 C홀이며, 주제는 "현대 고고학적 발견"으로 그대로입니다. 이에 따라 여러분의 일정을 조정해 주시고 이 최신 정보를 놓쳤을 수 있는 분들께 소식을 전달하여 주시기 바랍니다.

공지의 주요 목적은 무엇인가?
Ⓐ 새로운 교수를 소개하기 위해
☑ 일정 변경을 알리기 위해
Ⓒ 고고학 수업을 홍보하기 위해
Ⓓ 강의 주제 변경을 발표하기 위해

어휘 advertise [ǽdvərtàiz] 홍보하다

03 Main Topic Question   Nz

> Attention, Environmental Club members! **We're organizing a beach cleanup this Sunday starting at 9 A.M. at Ocean Park.** We'll provide all necessary supplies, including gloves and trash bags. Please wear comfortable clothes and bring water and

sunscreen. This is a wonderful chance to help protect the marine environment while spending time outdoors.

environmental [invàiərənmént/] 환경의
organize [ɔ́ːrɡənàiz] 준비하다, 조직하다
necessary [nésəsèri] 필요한   supply [səplái] 용품, 공급; 공급하다
comfortable [kʌ́mfərtəbl] 편안한

환경 동아리 여러분 주목해 주세요! 이번 주 일요일 오전 9시부터 Ocean 공원에서 해변 청소를 준비하고 있습니다. 저희는 장갑과 쓰레기봉투를 포함한 필요한 모든 용품을 제공할 예정입니다. 편안한 옷을 입고 물과 자외선 차단제를 가져오시기 바랍니다. 이것은 야외에서 시간을 보내면서 해양 환경을 보호하는 데 도움이 되는 훌륭한 기회입니다.

공지의 주요 주제는 무엇인가?
Ⓐ 해양 생물학 현장 학습
Ⓑ 야외 수영 행사
Ⓒ 동아리 모금 활동
☑ 해변 보전 노력

어휘   marine biology 해양 생물학   field trip 현장 학습, 견학
fundraising [fʌ́ndrèisiŋ] 모금
conservation [kànsərvéiʃən] 보전, 보호

04 Main Purpose Question   🔊 Am

Attention, Drama Club members! **Auditions for our spring play** will be held this Thursday and Friday from 3 to 6 P.M. at the campus theater. We're looking for passionate actors for various roles. Please prepare a short monologue, and come ready to demonstrate your talents. This is a great opportunity to gain stage experience!

drama [drɑ́ːmə] 연극   passionate [pǽʃənət] 열정적인
monologue [mɑ́ːnəlɔːɡ] 독백   talent [tǽlənt] 재능
experience [ikspíəriəns] 경험

연극 동아리 회원들 주목해 주세요! 우리 봄 연극을 위한 오디션이 이번 주 목요일과 금요일 오후 3시부터 6시까지 캠퍼스 극장에서 열릴 예정입니다. 다양한 역할을 위한 열정적인 배우를 찾고 있습니다. 짧은 독백을 준비해 오시고 여러분의 재능을 선보일 준비를 하고 오시기 바랍니다. 이것은 무대 경험을 쌓을 수 있는 좋은 기회입니다!

행사의 목적은 무엇인가?
☑ 연극을 위한 출연자를 찾기 위해
Ⓑ 무대 뒤 스태프를 모집하기 위해
Ⓒ 제작 대본을 배포하기 위해
Ⓓ 다가오는 봄 연극을 홍보하기 위해

어휘   recruit [rikrúːt] 모집하다
distribute [distríbjuːt] 배포하다, 분배하다, 퍼뜨리다
promote [prəmóut] 홍보하다, 승진시키다

HACKERS TEST   p.178

01 Ⓐ	02 Ⓒ	03 Ⓒ	04 Ⓓ	05 Ⓑ
06 Ⓓ	07 Ⓐ	08 Ⓑ	09 Ⓑ	10 Ⓒ
11 Ⓒ	12 Ⓓ	13 Ⓒ	14 Ⓐ	15 Ⓓ
16 Ⓒ

[01-02]   🔊 En

Listen to an announcement at a university event.

Good morning, everyone! ⁰¹**I'd like to announce that our university's Health and Wellness Fair will be held this Saturday.** ⁰²**This event will take place from 10 A.M. to 3 P.M. at the Recreation Center.** We'll have free health screenings, fitness demonstrations, and wellness workshops. Don't miss this opportunity to learn more about maintaining a healthy lifestyle!

health screening 건강 검진   maintain [meintéin] 유지하다

대학교 행사에서의 공지를 들으시오.
좋은 아침입니다, 여러분! ⁰¹우리 대학교의 건강 및 웰니스 박람회가 이번 주 토요일에 열린다는 것을 안내해 드리고자 합니다. ⁰²이번 행사는 오전 10시부터 오후 3시까지 레크리에이션 회관에서 진행될 예정입니다. 무료 건강 검진, 피트니스 시연, 그리고 웰니스 워크숍이 있을 것입니다. 건강한 생활방식을 유지하는 것에 대해 더 자세히 알아볼 수 있는 이 기회를 놓치지 마세요!

01 Main Purpose Question
공지의 주요 목적은 무엇인가?
☑ 캠퍼스 건강 행사를 홍보하기 위해
Ⓑ 새로운 의료 시설에 대해 알리기 위해
Ⓒ 무료 의료 상담을 광고하기 위해
Ⓓ 캠퍼스 활동을 위한 봉사자를 모집하기 위해

어휘   publicize [pʌ́bləsàiz] 홍보하다   facility [fəsíləti] 시설, 설비
consultation [kɑ̀nsəltéiʃən] 상담
volunteer [vɑ̀ːləntíər] 봉사자; 자원봉사하다

02 Intention Question
화자는 왜 레크리에이션 회관을 언급하는가?
Ⓐ 새로운 안전 절차를 알리기 위해
Ⓑ 다른 캠퍼스 시설과 비교하기 위해
☑ 학생들을 행사 장소로 안내하기 위해
Ⓓ 시설의 최근 보수를 강조하기 위해

어휘   procedure [prəsíːdʒər] 절차, 진행   highlight [háilàit] 강조하다

[03-04]   🔊 Am

Listen to an announcement in a student lounge.

Good afternoon, everyone. ⁰³**I need to inform you that the student lounge will be closed tomorrow afternoon, from 1 to 3 P.M., due to plumbing issues.** We apologize for any inconvenience this may cause. ⁰⁴**During this time, the campus café can be your best option if you need a place to relax between classes.**

어휘 inform[infɔ́:rm] 알리다   student lounge 학생 라운지
plumbing[plʌ́miŋ] 배관   apologize[əpálədʒàiz] 사과하다
inconvenience[ìnkənvíːnjəns] 불편함

학생 라운지에서의 공지를 들으시오.
좋은 오후입니다, 여러분. ⁰³배관 문제로 인해 학생 라운지가 내일 오후 1시부터 3시까지 문을 닫는다는 것을 알려드립니다. 이로 인해 발생할 수 있는 불편함에 대해 사과드립니다. ⁰⁴이 시간 동안, 수업 사이에 휴식할 장소가 필요하시다면 캠퍼스 카페가 최선의 선택이 될 수 있습니다.

03 Main Purpose Question
공지의 주요 목적은 무엇인가?
Ⓐ 진행 중인 건설 공사에 대해 사과하기 위해
Ⓑ 학생 라운지의 새로운 시설에 대해 설명하기 위해
✓ 라운지 이용 가능 여부의 변경을 학생들에게 알리기 위해
Ⓓ 위험한 배관 상황에 대해 학생들에게 경고하기 위해

어휘 ongoing[ángòuiŋ] 진행 중인   construction[kənstrʌ́kʃən] 건설
availability[əvèiləbíləti] 이용 가능 여부

04 To Do Question
라운지 폐쇄 기간 동안 학생들은 무엇을 하라고 권고받는가?
Ⓐ 라운지 밖에서 기다린다.
Ⓑ 수리 작업에 자원한다.
Ⓒ 오후 동안 집에 머문다.
✓ 캠퍼스 카페를 대안으로 이용한다.

어휘 alternative[ɔːltə́ːrnətiv] 대안, 다른 방도

[05-06]   Au

Listen to an announcement at a university club meeting.

May I have your attention please? ⁰⁵**The University Chess Club is hosting a tournament next Wednesday evening in the Student Center.** Even if you're a beginner, don't hesitate to participate! There will be separate divisions based on experience levels. There's a small entry fee of five dollars, and ⁰⁶**the winners will receive bookstore gift cards.** Sign-up sheets are outside the club office.

student center 학생회관
hesitate[hézətèit] 주저하다, 머뭇거리다

대학교 동아리 회의에서의 공지를 들으시오.
주목해 주시겠습니까? ⁰⁵대학교 체스 동아리가 다음 주 수요일 저녁에 학생회관에서 토너먼트를 개최합니다. 여러분이 초보자이더라도 참여를 주저하지 마세요! 경험 수준에 따라 부문이 나뉘게 됩니다. 5달러의 소액 참가비가 있으며, ⁰⁶우승자들은 서점 상품권을 받을 것입니다. 신청서는 동아리 사무실 밖에 있습니다.

05 Main Topic Question
공지는 무엇에 대한 것인가?
Ⓐ 주간 체스 동아리 모임
✓ 다가오는 체스 대회
Ⓒ 체스 초보자를 위한 교육 세션
Ⓓ 체스 챔피언을 위한 시상식

어휘 weekly[wíːkli] 주간의

06 Detail Question
우승자들은 상품으로 무엇을 받을 것인가?
Ⓐ 참가비 환불
Ⓑ 트로피와 메달
Ⓒ 장학금 기회
✓ 서점 상품권

어휘 refund[ríːfʌnd] 환불; 환불하다   scholarship[skáːlərʃip] 장학금

[07-08]   En

Listen to an announcement in a classroom.

Good afternoon, everyone! ⁰⁷**I'm pleased to let you know that next week's class will feature a guest lecturer.** Professor Sarah Chandler from Glenview University will share her latest research on memory formation. As a renowned expert in behavioral psychology, she will provide valuable insights. ⁰⁸**Please prepare at least two questions for the Q&A session with her.**

latest[léitist] 최신의   renowned[rináund] 저명한, 유명한
expert[ékspəːrt] 전문가; 숙련된
behavioral psychology 행동 심리학
valuable[vǽljuəbl] 귀중한, 값비싼, 소중한   insight[ínsàit] 통찰

교실에서의 공지를 들으시오.
좋은 오후입니다, 여러분! ⁰⁷다음 주 수업에 초청 강연자가 오신다는 것을 알려드리게 되어 기쁩니다. Glenview 대학교의 Sarah Chandler 교수님이 기억 형성에 대한 그녀의 최신 연구를 공유하실 예정입니다. 행동 심리학의 저명한 전문가로서, 그녀는 귀중한 통찰을 제공하실 것입니다. ⁰⁸그녀와의 질의응답 시간을 위해 적어도 두 개의 질문을 준비해 주세요.

07 Main Topic Question
공지의 주요 주제는 무엇인가?
✓ 외부 전문가의 강연
Ⓑ 연구 프로젝트 마감일
Ⓒ 필수 읽기 과제
Ⓓ 곧 게재될 연구 논문

어휘 mandatory[mǽndətɔ̀ːri] 필수적인
assignment[əsáinmənt] 과제, 숙제
research paper 연구 논문

08 To Do Question
학생들은 무엇을 하라고 권고받는가?
Ⓐ 특별 세션에 온라인으로 등록한다.

✓ 질의응답 시간을 위한 질문을 준비한다.
ⓒ 좋은 자리를 얻기 위해 일찍 도착한다.
ⓓ Chandler 교수의 이전 연구를 살펴본다.

어휘 register[rédʒistər] 등록하다; 음역
previous[príːviəs] 앞의, 이전의

[09-10]

Am

Listen to an announcement in a classroom.

Good afternoon, everyone. Now that we've gotten through the midterms, ⁰⁹**I'd really like to hear your thoughts on how the course is going so far**. What's working for you? What could be improved? ¹⁰**I'm going to hand out surveys**, so please take five minutes to jot down your opinions. It'll help me make adjustments for the rest of the semester.

get through 마치다, 통과하다   so far 지금까지
improve[imprúːv] 개선하다   survey[sə́ːrvei] 설문조사; 살피다
jot down 적다, 메모하다   opinion[əpínjən] 의견
adjustment[ədʒʌ́stmənt] 조정   semester[siméstər] 학기

교실에서의 공지를 들으시오.
좋은 오후입니다, 여러분. 이제 중간고사를 마쳤으니, ⁰⁹지금까지 수업이 어떻게 진행되고 있는지에 대한 여러분의 생각을 듣고 싶습니다. 어떤 점이 효과적이었나요? 무엇이 개선될 수 있을까요? ¹⁰설문지를 나누어 드릴 예정이니, 5분 정도 시간을 내어 여러분의 의견을 적어주세요. 남은 학기를 조정하는 데 도움이 될 것입니다.

09 Main Purpose Question

공지의 주요 목적은 무엇인가?
ⓐ 조교의 변경을 알리기 위해
✓ 수업에 대한 학생 피드백을 요청하기 위해
ⓒ 학생들로부터 중간고사 답안지를 걷기 위해
ⓓ 학생들에게 출석 요구사항을 상기시키기 위해

어휘 teaching assistant 조교
requirement[rikwáiərmənt] 요구사항

10 Inference Question

화자는 다음에 무엇을 할 것 같은가?
ⓐ 수업을 일찍 끝낸다.
ⓑ 새로운 개념을 설명한다.
✓ 설문지를 배포한다.
ⓓ 조정된 강의 일정을 보여준다.

어휘 dismiss[dismís] 끝내다, 해산하다

[11-12]

En

Listen to an announcement in a student lounge.

Hey, everyone! ¹¹**I'd like to let you know that the vending machines in this lounge will be restocked tomorrow morning.** If you've been missing your favorite snacks, they should be available after 10 A.M. ¹²**Also, some new healthy options will be added, based on the survey many of you completed last month.**

vending machine 자판기   restock[ristɑ́k] 보충하다
available[əvéiləbl] 이용할 수 있는

학생 라운지에서의 공지를 들으시오.
안녕하세요, 여러분! ¹¹이 라운지의 자판기들이 내일 아침에 보충될 예정이라는 것을 알려드리고 싶습니다. 여러분께서 좋아하는 간식이 없어 아쉬우셨다면, 오전 10시 이후부터 이용하실 수 있을 것입니다. ¹²또한, 지난달 여러분 중 많은 분들이 작성해 주신 설문조사를 바탕으로, 몇 가지 새로운 건강한 상품들이 추가될 예정입니다.

11 Main Topic Question

공지의 주요 주제는 무엇인가?
ⓐ 새로운 구내식당 옵션
ⓑ 건강한 식생활 캠페인
✓ 간식 이용 가능 여부
ⓓ 라운지 보수 일정

어휘 refreshments[rifréʃmənts] 다과

12 Intention Question

화자는 왜 설문조사를 언급하는가?
ⓐ 추가 참여를 장려하기 위해
ⓑ 곧 있을 또 다른 설문조사를 발표하기 위해
ⓒ 시행이 지연된 것에 대해 사과하기 위해
✓ 제품 추가의 근거를 설명하기 위해

어휘 encourage[inkə́ːridʒ] 장려하다   additional[ədíʃənl] 추가적인
participation[pɑːrtìsəpéiʃən] 참여
implementation[ìmpləməntéiʃən] 시행
basis[béisis] 근거, 기초

[13-14]

Am

Listen to an announcement at a university club meeting.

Hi, Photography Club members! ¹³**I'm excited to announce that our annual Photography Exhibition will be held on October 20 at the Student Union Gallery.** Each member can submit up to three photographs on the theme of "Urban Nature." The submission deadline is October 10, and ¹⁴**prizes will be awarded to the three entries that receive the most votes from visitors**.

submit[səbmít] 제출하다   submission[səbmíʃən] 제출

대학교 동아리 회의에서의 공지를 들으시오.
안녕하세요, 사진 동아리 회원 여러분! ¹³저희의 연례 사진 전시회가 10월 20일 학생회관 갤러리에서 열린다는 것을 발표하게 되어 기쁩니다. 각 회원은 "도시 속 자연"이라는 주제로 최대 3장의 사진을 제출할 수 있습니다. 제출 마감일은 10월 10일이며, ¹⁴방문객들의 투표로 가장 많은 표를 받은 세 작품에 상이 수여될 예정입니다.

13 Main Purpose Question

공지의 주요 목적은 무엇인가?
Ⓐ 대회를 위한 사진 제출 방법을 설명하기 위해
Ⓑ 사진 동아리의 새로운 회원을 모집하기 위해
✓ 다가오는 갤러리 전시회를 홍보하기 위해
Ⓓ 사진 워크숍 참가자를 모집하기 위해

14 Detail Question

누가 수상작을 결정할 것인가?
✓ 행사 방문객들
Ⓑ 동아리 회장
Ⓒ 지도교수
Ⓓ 전문 사진작가들

어휘 attendee[əténdí:] 방문객, 참가자 club president 동아리 회장

[15-16]   Nz

Listen to an announcement on the school radio.

Hello, everyone. ¹⁵**Just a quick reminder that the university shuttle bus schedule will change starting next Monday.** Buses will run every 20 minutes instead of every 30 minutes, and ¹⁶**the last bus will depart at 11 P.M. instead of 10 P.M.** The updated schedule is available on the university website.

depart[dipá:rt] 출발하다, 떠나다

학교 라디오에서 공지를 들으시오.

안녕하세요, 여러분. ¹⁵다음 주 월요일부터 대학교 셔틀버스 시간표가 바뀔 예정이라는 것을 간단히 알려드립니다. 버스는 30분마다가 아닌 20분마다 운행될 예정이며, ¹⁶막차는 오후 10시가 아닌 오후 11시에 출발할 예정입니다. 갱신된 시간표는 대학교 웹사이트에서 확인할 수 있습니다.

15 Main Topic Question

공지는 주로 무엇에 대한 것인가?
Ⓐ 대학교 시설의 운영 시간
Ⓑ 셔틀버스의 노선 정보
Ⓒ 캠퍼스 내 새로운 교통수단 선택지
✓ 셔틀 서비스 시간표 조정

어휘 operating hours 운영 시간

16 Detail Question

새로운 스케줄에 따르면 막차는 언제 출발할 것인가?
Ⓐ 오후 10시
Ⓑ 오후 10시 30분
✓ 오후 11시
Ⓓ 오후 11시 30분

2. To Do Questions

Example En   p.183

주목해 주세요, 여러분. 아마 눈치채셨겠지만, 지난 몇 번의 발표 동안 교실 프로젝터에 몇 가지 문제가 있었습니다. 다음 주에 있을 발표에서 이러한 문제들을 피하기 위해, **발표 날에는 프로젝터를 점검하기 위해 적어도 10분 일찍 수업에 오기를 강력히 권장합니다.**

probably[prá:bəli] 아마, 십중팔구 several[sévərəl] 몇 가지의
avoid[əvɔ́id] 피하다
recommend[rèkəménd] 권장하다, 추천하다

화자는 학생들에게 무엇을 하라고 제안하는가?
Ⓐ 발표 일정을 변경한다.
Ⓑ 수업 전에 슬라이드를 제출한다.
✓ 장비를 점검하기 위해 일찍 도착한다.
Ⓓ 발표를 위해 개인 노트북을 가져온다.

어휘 reschedule[rì:skédʒu:l] 일정을 변경하다

HACKERS PRACTICE   p.184

01 Ⓐ   02 Ⓒ   03 Ⓑ   04 Ⓓ

01 To Do Question   Am

Movie lovers, get ready for our <u>outdoor movie night</u>! This Friday, <u>we're screening a classic film</u> under the stars at the main plaza starting at 7 P.M. **Bring blankets and snacks for a cozy evening.** In case of rain, we'll move to the Student Union Theater. Make sure to arrive early if you want to <u>get a good spot</u>!

cozy[kóuzi] 아늑한 in case of ~의 경우

영화 애호가 여러분, 야외 영화의 밤을 준비하세요! 이번 주 금요일, 오후 7시부터 본관 광장에서 별빛 아래 클래식 영화를 상영할 예정입니다. **아늑한 저녁을 위해 담요와 간식을 가져오세요.** 비가 올 경우, 학생회관 극장으로 이동할 예정입니다. 좋은 자리를 얻길 원하신다면 꼭 일찍 오세요!

화자는 청자들이 무엇을 하기를 바라는가?
✓ 담요와 간식을 가져온다.
Ⓑ 다른 참석자들에게 담요를 준다.
Ⓒ 영화의 밤을 널리 알린다.
Ⓓ 티켓을 구매하기 위해 일찍 도착한다.

어휘 spread the word 널리 알리다, 소문 내다
purchase[pə́:rtʃəs] 구매하다

02 To Do Question   Au

Good morning, everyone. Our campus library is implementing <u>a new reservation system</u> for the group study rooms starting next Monday. Instead of offering walk-in availability, the library will require that rooms be booked online at least two hours in advance. The maximum reservation time will be three hours per day per student. Instructions for the new system are posted near the circulation desk. **Please read them carefully to avoid any inconvenience when booking a study room.**

implement[ímpləmènt] 도입하다, 시행하다
reservation[rèzərvéiʃən] 예약
require[rikwáiər] 규정하다, 요구하다   book[buk] 예약하다
in advance ~ 전에, 미리, 앞서서
maximum[mǽksəməm] 최대의
instruction[instrʌ́kʃən] 안내, 설명서
circulation desk 대출 데스크

좋은 아침입니다, 여러분. 우리 캠퍼스 도서관은 다음 주 월요일부터 그룹 스터디룸의 새로운 예약 시스템을 도입합니다. 현장 이용 대신, 도서관은 최소 두 시간 전에 온라인으로 예약해야만 스터디룸을 사용할 수 있도록 규정할 예정입니다. 한 학생당 하루 최대 예약 시간은 3시간입니다. 새로운 시스템에 대한 안내는 대출 데스크 근처에 게시되어 있습니다. **스터디룸을 예약할 때 불편함을 피하기 위해 안내를 주의 깊게 읽어 주세요.**

학생들은 무엇을 하라고 권고받는가?
Ⓐ 대출 데스크를 방문한다.
Ⓑ 시스템에 대한 피드백을 제출한다.
✓ 게시된 안내를 읽는다.
Ⓓ 스터디룸을 사용하기 두 시간 전에 도착한다.

03 To Do Question 〔En〕

Good afternoon, everyone! Our university's debate tournament is scheduled for Thursday at 7 P.M. in Conference Room B. This year's topic is "School uniforms: Necessary or outdated?" Teams should be ready to argue for either side. **Make sure to bring your research materials** and be ready for intense discussions. Registration closes tomorrow at noon.

debate[dibéit] 토론; 토론하다
outdated[àutdéitid] 시대에 뒤떨어진
make sure to 꼭 ~하다   intense[inténs] 열띤
discussion[diskʌ́ʃən] 토론, 논의
registration[rèdʒistréiʃən] 등록, 신청

좋은 오후입니다, 여러분! 우리 캠퍼스 토론 대회가 목요일 저녁 7시에 B 회의실에서 열립니다. 올해의 주제는 "교복: 필요한가, 아니면 시대에 뒤떨어진 것인가?"입니다. 팀들은 어느 쪽 입장이든 주장할 준비를 해야 합니다. **연구 자료를 꼭 지참하시고,** 열띤 토론을 준비하세요. 등록은 내일 정오에 마감됩니다.

화자는 학생들에게 무엇을 하라고 제안하는가?
Ⓐ 교복의 역사에 대해 연구를 수행한다.
✓ 연구 자료를 가져온다.
Ⓒ 연구 자료를 미리 제출한다.
Ⓓ 구체적인 토론 주제를 요청한다.

어휘   conduct[kəndʌ́kt] 수행하다   material[mətíəriəl] 자료, 소재
request[rikwést] 요청하다; 요청   specific[spisífik] 구체적인

04 To Do Question 〔Nz〕

Attention, students. Next Wednesday, we're hosting our annual career fair in the gymnasium from 10 A.M. to 4 P.M. Over 50 companies will be present, including major tech firms and local businesses. **To make the most of this opportunity, please prepare your résumés in advance** and dress professionally. Don't miss this chance to connect with potential employers!

career fair 취업박람회   gymnasium[dʒimnéiziəm] 체육관
make the most of ~을 최대한 활용하다
potential[pəténʃəl] 잠재적인; 가능성   employer[implɔ́iər] 고용주

학생 여러분, 주목해 주세요. 다음 주 수요일에 오전 10시부터 오후 4시까지 체육관에서 연례 취업박람회를 개최합니다. 주요 기술 기업들과 지역 기업들을 포함하여 50개가 넘는 회사들이 참석할 예정입니다. **이 기회를 최대한 활용하기 위해, 미리 이력서를 준비하시고** 전문적인 복장을 갖춰 입으세요. 잠재적 고용주들과 교류할 수 있는 기회를 놓치지 마세요!

공지에 따르면 학생들은 무엇을 해야 하는가?
Ⓐ 온라인으로 등록하고 입장료를 지불한다.
Ⓑ 고용주들과의 시간대를 신청한다.
Ⓒ 미리 면접 질문을 연습한다.
✓ 이력서를 준비하고 전문적인 복장을 갖춰 입는다.

어휘   entrance fee 입장료   sign up 등록하다, 서명하다
beforehand[bifɔ́:rhænd] 미리

HACKERS TEST   p.186

01 Ⓒ	02 Ⓓ	03 Ⓓ	04 Ⓑ	05 Ⓑ
06 Ⓐ	07 Ⓐ	08 Ⓓ	09 Ⓓ	10 Ⓓ
11 Ⓒ	12 Ⓓ	13 Ⓐ	14 Ⓒ	15 Ⓑ
16 Ⓒ				

[01-02] 〔Am〕

Listen to an announcement at a university event.

Good morning, everyone! **01 I'm excited to inform you that the university's International Food Festival will be held** this Wednesday from 11 A.M. to 2 P.M. in the main hall. You'll have **02 the opportunity to taste dishes from over 20 countries prepared by our international students.** Don't miss this amazing cultural experience!

international[ìntərnǽʃənl] 국제적인
amazing[əméiziŋ] 놀라운, 멋진   cultural[kʌ́ltʃərəl] 문화의

대학교 행사에서의 공지를 들으시오.

좋은 아침입니다, 여러분! 이번 주 수요일 오전 11시부터 오후 2시까지 메인 홀에서 **01 대학 국제 음식 축제가 열린다는 것을 알려드리게 되어 기쁩니다.** 여러분은 우리 국제 학생들이 준비한 **02 20개국 이상의 요리를 맛볼 기회가 있을 것입니다.** 이 놀라운 문화 체험을 놓치지 마세요!

01 Main Topic Question

공지의 주요 주제는 무엇인가?
Ⓐ 요리 경연대회
Ⓑ 모금 활동
✓ Ⓒ 다가오는 축제
Ⓓ 식품 안전 공지

02 To Do Question

화자는 청자들이 무엇을 하기를 바라는가?
Ⓐ 요리 수업에 참여한다.
Ⓑ 행사를 위해 자원봉사한다.
Ⓒ 국제 요리를 구입한다.
✓ Ⓓ 다양한 요리를 경험한다.

어휘 cuisine[kwizíːn] 요리, 요리법

[03-04] Au

Listen to an announcement in a classroom.

> Hi everyone. Just a quick heads-up that our midterm exam has been rescheduled from next Monday to Wednesday ⁰³**due to campus-wide maintenance**. The exam will still cover the same material through Chapter 7, and will be held during our regular class time. ⁰⁴**Make sure to adjust your study plans accordingly.**

heads-up 알림   maintenance[méintənəns] 점검 작업

교실에서의 공지를 들으시오.

안녕하세요, 여러분. ⁰³캠퍼스 전체 점검 작업으로 인해 우리의 중간 고사가 다음 주 월요일에서 수요일로 일정이 변경되었다는 것을 알려 드립니다. 시험은 여전히 7장까지의 모든 동일한 내용을 다룰 것이며, 정규 수업 시간에 치러질 것입니다. ⁰⁴그에 따라 학습 계획을 조정하도록 하세요.

03 Detail Question

공지에서 설명된 변경의 이유는 무엇인가?
Ⓐ 일정 충돌
Ⓑ 교실 보수
Ⓒ 날씨 관련 응급상황
✓ Ⓓ 시설 유지보수

어휘 conflict[kánflikt] 충돌, 갈등

04 To Do Question

공지에 따라 학생들은 무엇을 하라고 권고받는가?
Ⓐ 과제를 일찍 제출한다.
✓ Ⓑ 학습 계획을 조정한다.
Ⓒ 새로운 학습 자료를 다운로드한다.
Ⓓ 추가 연습 문제를 완료한다.

어휘 modify[mádəfài] 조정하다, 변경하다   extra[ékstrə] 추가의

[05-06] Am

Listen to an announcement at a university club meeting.

> Good morning, International Students Association members. Our cultural exchange dinner in the East Hall has been rescheduled from this Friday to next Wednesday at 7 P.M. ⁰⁵**The change is due to a scheduling conflict with the university's homecoming event.** ⁰⁶**Please spread the word to anyone who might not be here today.**

homecoming[hoúmkə̀miŋ] 동창회

대학교 동아리 회의에서의 공지를 들으시오.

좋은 아침입니다, 국제 학생회 회원 여러분. 우리의 문화 교류 만찬이 동관에서 이번 금요일에서 다음 주 수요일 오후 7시로 일정이 변경되었습니다. ⁰⁵이 변경은 대학교 동창회 행사와의 일정 충돌 때문입니다. ⁰⁶오늘 여기에 오지 못한 분들에게 이 소식을 알려 주세요.

05 Intention Question

화자는 왜 대학교 동창회 행사를 언급하는가?
Ⓐ 대학교의 전통을 강조하기 위해
✓ Ⓑ 연기의 이유를 밝히기 위해
Ⓒ 문화 만찬을 완전히 취소하기 위해
Ⓓ 학생들이 두 행사 모두에 참석하도록 권장하기 위해

어휘 tradition[trədíʃən] 전통
     postponement[poustpóunmənt] 연기, 지연
     completely[kəmplíːtli] 완전히

06 To Do Question

화자는 청자들이 무엇을 하기를 바라는가?
Ⓐ 참석을 확정한다.
Ⓑ 국제 요리를 가져온다.
Ⓒ 문화 발표를 준비한다.
✓ Ⓓ 일정 변경을 전달한다.

어휘 confirm[kənfə́ːrm] 확정하다, 확인하다
     pass along 전달하다, 널리 알리다

[07-08] En

Listen to an announcement at a student meeting.

> Attention, everyone. ⁰⁷**Student council elections for next semester will take place at the end of this month.** Applications are now open for the positions of president, secretary, and treasurer. If you're interested in running, ⁰⁸**please submit your application by next Wednesday at 6 P.M.** This will be a great opportunity to develop leadership skills and have a real impact on campus.

student council 학생회   election[ilékʃən] 선거
secretary[sékrətèri] 서기, 비서   treasurer[tréʒərər] 회계 담당자
application[æ̀pləkéiʃən] 지원서

학생 회의에서의 공지를 들으시오.

여러분, 주목해 주세요. ⁰⁷다음 학기 학생회 선거가 이달 말에 치러집니다. 회장, 서기, 그리고 회계 담당자 직책의 지원서를 받고 있습니다. 출마에 관심이 있으시다면, ⁰⁸다음 주 수요일 오후 6시까지 지원서를 제출해 주세요. 이것은 리더십 역량을 개발하고 캠퍼스에 실질적인 영향을 미칠 수 있는 좋은 기회가 될 것입니다.

07 Main Topic Question
공지의 주요 주제는 무엇인가?
Ⓐ 리더십 워크숍
Ⓑ 교내 시설
Ⓒ 대학 정책
✓ 학생 선거

어휘 policy[pɑ́ləsi] 정책, 규정

08 To Do Question
공지에 따르면 관심 있는 학생들은 무엇을 해야 하는가?
Ⓐ 선거 운동을 위한 지지자들을 모집한다.
✓ 마감일 전에 입후보 신청서를 제출한다.
Ⓒ 현재 학생회 구성원들에게 의견을 제시한다.
Ⓓ 수요일 회의에서 관심을 표명한다.

어휘 turn in 제출하다 candidacy[kǽndidəsi] 입후보
declare[diklɛ́ər] 표명하다, 선언하다 interest[íntərəst] 관심

[09-10]
Listen to an announcement at a university event.

Good afternoon, students! ⁰⁹Due to the upcoming storm, tomorrow's outdoor graduation ceremony will now be held in the main gymnasium instead. The start time remains at 10 A.M. sharp. ¹⁰Please inform your family members of this venue change. Each graduate will still receive five guest tickets, which can be picked up at the Student Center today until 5 P.M.

graduation ceremony 졸업식 venue[vénju:] 장소
graduate[grǽdʒuèit] 졸업생; 졸업하다
pick up 수령하다, 포착하다

대학교 행사에서의 공지를 들으시오.
좋은 오후입니다, 학생 여러분! ⁰⁹다가올 폭풍으로 인해, 내일의 야외 졸업식은 대신에 주체육관에서 열릴 것입니다. 시간은 변동 없이 오전 10시 정각입니다. ¹⁰장소 변경을 여러분의 가족들에게 알려 주시기 바랍니다. 각 졸업생은 여전히 다섯 장의 초청권을 받게 될 것이며, 이는 오늘 오후 5시까지 학생 센터에서 수령할 수 있습니다.

09 Detail Question
공지에서 설명된 변경의 이유는 무엇인가?
Ⓐ 예산 제약
✓ 좋지 않은 날씨
Ⓒ 계획에 없던 유지보수
Ⓓ 늘어난 참석자 수

어휘 budget[bʌ́dʒit] 예산 constraint[kənstréint] 제약
unfavorable[ənféivərəbəl] 좋지 않은

10 To Do Question
화자는 청자들이 무엇을 하기를 바라는가?
Ⓐ 사용하지 않은 티켓을 반납한다.
Ⓑ 졸업식에 일찍 도착한다.
Ⓒ 실내 졸업식에 등록한다.
✓ 초청객들에게 장소 변경을 알린다.

어휘 notify[nóutəfài] 알리다

[11-12]
Listen to an announcement in a classroom.

I've finished grading your research papers, and I'm quite impressed with the overall quality. You can check your grades after class today. ¹¹**For students who received a grade below a C, I will offer an opportunity to revise.** ¹²**Please meet with me during office hours by Thursday, and submit your revision by next Monday.** I'll grade it and then average it with your original score to determine your final grade.

grade[greid] 채점하다; 등급 quite[kwait] 상당히, 꽤
overall[óuvərɔ̀ːl] 전반적인 quality[kwɑ́ləti] 수준, 특성
revise[riváiz] 수정하다 revision[rivíʒən] 수정본, 수정
average[ǽvəridʒ] 평균을 내다; 평균
determine[ditə́:rmin] 산출하다, 결정하다

교실에서의 공지를 들으시오.
저는 여러분의 연구 보고서 채점을 마쳤고 전반적인 수준은 상당히 인상 깊었습니다. 오늘 수업이 끝난 뒤에 성적을 확인하실 수 있습니다. ¹¹C 미만의 성적을 받은 학생들에게는 수정할 기회를 드리겠습니다. ¹²목요일까지 상담 시간에 저와 만나고 다음 주 월요일까지 수정본을 제출해 주세요. 그러면 제가 그것을 채점한 뒤 원래 점수와 평균을 내어 최종 성적을 산출해 드리겠습니다.

11 Main Purpose Question
공지의 주요 목적은 무엇인가?
Ⓐ 학생들에게 상담 시간의 변경을 상기시키기 위해
Ⓑ 미흡한 연구에 대해 학생들을 질책하기 위해
✓ 성적을 개선할 수 있는 기회를 제공하기 위해
Ⓓ 연구 보고서의 채점 기준을 설명하기 위해

어휘 remind[rimáind] 상기시키다 scold[skould] 질책하다, 꾸짖다
criteria[kraitíriə] 기준, 표준

12 To Do Question
C 미만의 성적을 받은 학생들은 무엇을 하도록 권고받는가?
Ⓐ 프로젝트 피드백의 요약문을 작성한다.
Ⓑ 자신들의 성적을 다른 학생들과 비교한다.
Ⓒ 초안을 제출하고 기한 연장을 요청한다.
✓ 담당 교수와 면담하고 수정본을 제출한다.

어휘 summary[sʌ́məri] 요약문 compare[kəmpɛ́ər] 비교하다
initial[iníʃəl] 처음의 extension[iksténʃən] 기한 연장, 확장

[13-14]

🎧 Am

Listen to an announcement at a university event.

Important announcement about the leadership development seminar! ¹³**Due to higher-than-expected registration, we're moving from Hamilton Hall to the larger downtown convention center.** Shuttle service will be provided at the campus main entrance. ¹⁴**Don't forget to complete your online check-in before Saturday to receive your conference materials and seat assignments.**

어휘 important[impɔ́:rtənt] 중요한

대학교 행사에서의 공지를 들으시오.

리더십 개발 세미나에 대한 중요한 공지입니다! ¹³예상보다 등록자 수가 많아 Hamilton 홀에서 더 큰 시내 컨벤션 센터로 장소를 옮깁니다. 캠퍼스 정문에서 셔틀 서비스가 제공될 예정입니다. ¹⁴컨퍼런스 자료와 좌석 배정을 받기 위해 토요일까지 온라인 체크인을 완료하는 것을 잊지 마세요.

13 Main Topic Question

공지는 무엇에 대한 것인가?
☑ Ⓐ 장소 변경
Ⓑ 행사 취소
Ⓒ 시설 업그레이드
Ⓓ 수수료 인상

어휘 cancellation[kænsəléiʃən] 취소

14 To Do Question

화자는 학생들이 무엇을 하라고 제안하는가?
Ⓐ 토요일까지 티켓을 인쇄한다.
Ⓑ 미리 질문을 준비한다.
☑ Ⓒ 온라인 체크인을 완료한다.
Ⓓ 컨벤션 센터에 일찍 도착한다.

[15-16]

🎧 Nz

Listen to an announcement at a university club meeting.

All right, everyone. I have great news! ¹⁵**Our proposal for the Campus Beautification Initiative has been accepted by the university administration.** Accordingly, we've been granted 1,800 dollars to plant eco-friendly gardens around the Science Building. The project will start on September 15. ¹⁶**If you're interested in joining the team, please sign up on the sheet I'm passing around now.**

proposal[prəpóuzəl] 제안, 논문 기획안
beautification[bjùːtəfikéiʃən] 미화
initiative[iníʃiətiv] 계획, 창시
administration[ədmìnistréiʃən] 행정처
grant[grænt] 지원하다, 수여하다   eco-friendly 친환경의
pass around 돌리다, 배포하다

대학교 동아리 회의에서의 공지를 들으시오.

자, 여러분. 좋은 소식이 있습니다! ¹⁵캠퍼스 미화 계획에 대한 우리의 제안이 대학 행정처의 승인을 받았습니다. 이에 따라, 과학관 주변에 친환경 정원을 조성하기 위해 1,800달러를 지원받았습니다. 프로젝트는 9월 15일에 시작될 것입니다. ¹⁶팀에 참여하는 데 관심이 있으시다면, 제가 지금 돌리고 있는 신청서에 이름을 적어 주세요.

15 Main Purpose Question

공지의 주요 목적은 무엇인가?
Ⓐ 과학 전시회를 광고하기 위해
☑ Ⓑ 승인된 계획에 대한 소식을 공유하기 위해
Ⓒ 캠퍼스의 식물 종을 설명하기 위해
Ⓓ 예산 배정 절차를 논의하기 위해

어휘 describe[diskráib] 설명하다, 기술하다
species[spíːʃiːz] 종, 종류   allocation[æ̀ləkéiʃən] 배정, 배분

16 To Do Question

화자는 청자들이 무엇을 하기를 바라는가?
Ⓐ 과학관을 방문한다.
Ⓑ 추가 프로젝트를 제안한다.
☑ Ⓒ 정원 프로젝트에 참가한다.
Ⓓ 식물 심기 과정을 사진으로 찍는다.

어휘 propose[prəpóuz] 제안하다   participate in ~에 참가하다

3. Detail Questions

Example 🎧 Au   p.191

좋은 아침입니다, 학생 여러분. 학기말에 제출 예정인 최종 연구 프로젝트의 참고문헌 요구사항에 대한 몇 가지 세부사항을 전달하고자 합니다. 이 과제를 위해서는 최소 5개의 학술 자료를 포함해야 하며, **그 중 최소 3개는 동료 심사를 받은 학술지 논문이어야 합니다.** 나머지 2개 자료는 도서 또는 신뢰할 만한 웹사이트가 될 수 있지만, 일반 백과사전 사이트와 비학술적 웹 자료를 주요 자료로 사용하는 것은 피하세요.

reference[réfərəns] 참고문헌   minimum[mínəməm] 최소의
academic[ækədémik] 학술의   at least 최소, 적어도
article[áːrtikl] 논문, 기사   reliable[riláiəbl] 신뢰할 만한, 확실한
encyclopedia[insàikləpíːdiə] 백과사전

화자는 프로젝트의 허용 가능한 자료에 대해 무엇을 말하는가?
Ⓐ 동료 심사를 받은 학술지 논문만 허용된다.
Ⓑ 모든 웹사이트가 주요 자료로 사용될 수 있다.
Ⓒ 모든 자료는 도서 또는 학술지 논문이어야 한다.
☑ Ⓓ 일부 자료는 동료 심사를 받은 학술지 논문이어야 한다.

HACKERS PRACTICE   p.192

01 Ⓒ   02 Ⓐ   03 Ⓑ   04 Ⓓ

01 Detail Question 〔En〕

May I have your attention? **The main computer lab will be unavailable Thursday through Sunday for software updates.** Please note that alternative computer workstations are available in the east wing of the IT Building. If you need further assistance, please contact the IT Help Center.

further[fə́ːrðər] 추가의   assistance[əsístəns] 도움, 지원

여러분, 잠시 주목해 주시기 바랍니다. **소프트웨어 업데이트로 인해 메인 컴퓨터실은 목요일부터 일요일까지 이용하실 수 없습니다.** IT 빌딩 동관에 대체 컴퓨터 워크스테이션이 마련되어 있으니 참고하시기 바랍니다. 만약 추가 도움이 필요하다면, IT 도움 센터로 연락해 주시기 바랍니다.

컴퓨터실 폐쇄의 이유는 무엇인가?
Ⓐ 건물 보수
Ⓑ 바이러스 검사
✓ 시스템 업그레이드
Ⓓ 네트워크 보안 문제

02 Detail Question 〔Am〕

Good morning, freshmen! The Student Mentoring Program is now accepting applications for next semester. **Experienced upper-year students will help you navigate academic challenges and campus life.** Mentors will meet their mentees twice a month for one-on-one sessions. A special lecture by a professional counselor will also be held for program participants. Don't miss this opportunity to adapt successfully to college life!

experienced[ikspíəriənst] 경험 있는
navigate[nǽvəgèit] 헤쳐 나가다, 적응하다
challenge[tʃǽlindʒ] 어려움, 도전   counselor[káunsələr] 상담사
adapt[ədǽpt] 적응하다

좋은 아침입니다, 1학년 여러분! 학생 멘토링 프로그램이 현재 다음 학기 신청을 받고 있습니다. **경험 있는 상급생들은 여러분이 학업상의 어려움과 대학 생활을 헤쳐 나가도록 도와줄 것입니다.** 멘토들은 한 달에 두 번 멘티들과 만나 일대일 세션을 갖게 됩니다. 프로그램 참가자들을 위한 전문 상담사의 특별 강의도 개최될 예정입니다. 대학 생활에 성공적으로 적응할 수 있는 이 기회를 놓치지 마세요!

프로그램에서 누가 멘토 역할을 할 것인가?
✓ 상급생
Ⓑ 전문 상담사
Ⓒ 선정된 교수들
Ⓓ 1학년 학생들

어휘 senior student 상급생

03 Detail Question 〔En〕

Attention, Robotics Club members. Team registration for the National Robotics Competition is due by this Wednesday. **We need to finalize our robot design and submit the technical specifications.** Practice sessions will be held daily in the engineering lab next week from 6 to 9 P.M. to prepare for the regional qualifying round.

finalize[fáinəlàiz] 완료하다, 마무리하다
specification[spèsəfikéiʃən] 사양서   lab[læb] 연구실
regional[ríːdʒənl] 지역의   qualifying round 예선

로봇 동아리 회원들, 주목해 주시기 바랍니다. 전국 로봇 대회를 위한 팀 등록이 이번 수요일까지입니다. **저희는 로봇 설계를 완료하고 기술 사양서를 제출해야 합니다.** 지역 예선을 준비하기 위해 다음 주에 오후 6시부터 9시까지 공학 연구실에서 매일 연습 세션이 열릴 예정입니다.

학생들은 팀을 등록할 때 무엇을 제출해야 하는가?
Ⓐ 동의서
✓ 기술 사양서
Ⓒ 안전 점검표
Ⓓ 연습 일정

어휘 consent[kənsént] 동의; 동의하다
technical[téknikəl] 기술적인   checklist[tʃéklìst] 점검표

04 Detail Question 〔Am〕

Photography Club members, we're hosting a landscape photography workshop this Saturday at Riverside Nature Park. Professional photographer Marian Lee will teach composition and lighting techniques. **We will depart at 8:00 A.M. from the campus's main gate on a chartered bus. Lunch and all necessary equipment for the workshop will be provided.**

landscape[lǽndskèip] 풍경
composition[kàmpəzíʃən] 구도, 구성
technique[tekníːk] 기법, 기술   chartered[tʃáːrtərd] 전세낸

사진 동아리 회원 여러분, 이번 토요일에 Riverside 자연공원에서 풍경 사진 워크숍을 개최합니다. 전문 사진작가 Marian Lee가 구도와 조명 기법을 가르쳐 주실 것입니다. **저희는 오전 8시에 캠퍼스 정문 앞에서 전세 버스로 출발할 예정입니다. 점심 식사와 워크숍에 필요한 모든 장비가 제공될 것입니다.**

다음 중 워크숍에 대해 사실인 것은 무엇인가?
Ⓐ 참가자들은 자신의 카메라를 가져와야 한다.
Ⓑ 캠퍼스 내에서 열린다.
Ⓒ 인물 사진 기법에 초점을 맞춘다.
✓ 교통편과 식사가 포함된다.

어휘 focus on ~에 초점을 맞추다, 집중하다
portrait photography 인물 사진
transportation[trænspərtéiʃən] 교통편

HACKERS TEST

p.194

01 Ⓓ	02 Ⓒ	03 Ⓒ	04 Ⓐ	05 Ⓑ
06 Ⓒ	07 Ⓐ	08 Ⓒ	09 Ⓑ	10 Ⓓ
11 Ⓓ	12 Ⓑ	13 Ⓑ	14 Ⓒ	15 Ⓒ
16 Ⓑ				

[01-02] Nz

Listen to an announcement in a student lounge.

> Attention, everyone! ⁰¹Please be advised that the student lounge will be closed this Thursday for scheduled cleaning. ⁰²For anyone looking for an alternative space to study, conference rooms in the Student Union Building will be open throughout the day. Thanks for your patience!

학생 라운지에서의 공지를 들으시오.

모두 주목해주세요! ⁰¹학생 라운지가 예정된 청소로 인해 이번 목요일에 폐쇄될 예정임을 알려드립니다. ⁰²학습을 위한 대체 공간을 찾는 분들을 위해, 학생회관의 회의실이 하루 종일 개방될 예정입니다. 양해해 주셔서 감사합니다!

01 Detail Question

학생 라운지 폐쇄의 이유는 무엇인가?
Ⓐ 리모델링 프로젝트
Ⓑ 시스템 점검
Ⓒ 카펫 설치
✓Ⓓ 청소 작업

어휘 inspection[inspékʃən] 점검 installation[ìnstəléiʃən] 설치

02 Intention Question

화자는 왜 학생회관을 언급하는가?
Ⓐ 최근 보수의 목적을 설명하기 위해
Ⓑ 진행 중인 건설에 대해 학생들에게 알리기 위해
✓Ⓒ 학생들에게 대안 공간을 추천하기 위해
Ⓓ 학생들이 다른 구역을 둘러보도록 격려하기 위해

어휘 explore[ikspló:r] 둘러보다, 탐색하다

[03-04] Am

Listen to an announcement at a university club meeting.

> I need your attention for a moment. ⁰³Our Debate Club has received an invitation to participate in the Regional University Debate Championship next month. This is a prestigious competition, with schools from five states participating. We need to select our team members by next week. If you're interested in representing our university, ⁰⁴please submit a one-page application explaining your strengths. The team list will be announced next Tuesday evening at 7 P.M. in this room.

prestigious[prestídʒəs] 권위 있는

대학교 동아리 회의에서의 공지를 들으시오.

잠깐 주목해 주세요. ⁰³저희 토론 동아리가 다음 달 지역 대학 토론 선수권 대회에 참가 초청을 받았습니다. 이것은 5개 주의 학교들이 참가하는 권위 있는 대회입니다. 저희는 다음 주까지 팀원을 선발해야 합니다. 저희 대학교를 대표하는 데 관심이 있으시다면, ⁰⁴당신의 강점을 설명하는 한 페이지 분량의 지원서를 제출해 주세요. 팀 명단은 다음 주 화요일 오후 7시에 이 교실에서 발표될 예정입니다.

03 Main Topic Question

공지의 주요 주제는 무엇인가?
Ⓐ 대학교 글쓰기 대회
Ⓑ 행사 자원봉사자 모집
✓Ⓒ 지역 토론 대회
Ⓓ 동아리 모임 장소 변경

04 Detail Question

학생들은 지원할 때 무엇을 제출해야 하는가?
✓Ⓐ 한 페이지 분량의 지원서
Ⓑ 학업 성적 증명서
Ⓒ 선호하는 주제 목록
Ⓓ 토론 전략 개요

어휘 transcript[trænskript] 성적 증명서
      preferred[prifə́:rd] 선호하는, 우선의 strategy[strǽtədʒi] 전략
      outline[áutlain] 개요

[05-06] En

Listen to an announcement at a university event.

> Attention everyone! ⁰⁵Due to the overwhelming interest in our upcoming networking event with industry professionals, the venue has been changed to the Grand Auditorium to accommodate more students. ⁰⁶Accordingly, additional registration will remain open until this Friday on the university website. This will be an excellent opportunity to connect with potential employers from over 20 companies.

overwhelming[òuvərwélmiŋ] 압도적인, 엄청난
accommodate[əkɑ́:mədèit] 수용하다

대학교 행사에서의 공지를 들으시오.

모두 주목해 주세요! ⁰⁵업계 전문가들과의 다가오는 네트워킹 행사에 대한 압도적인 관심으로 인해, 더 많은 학생을 수용할 수 있도록 행사 장소가 대강당으로 변경되었습니다. ⁰⁶이에 따라, 이번 금요일까지 대학교 웹사이트를 통해 추가 등록이 열려 있을 것입니다. 이것은 20개 이상의 기업의 잠재적 고용주들과 연결할 수 있는 훌륭한 기회가 될 것입니다.

05 Detail Question

공지에 설명된 변경의 이유는 무엇인가?
Ⓐ 예산 제약

ⓑ 행사에 대한 높은 수요
ⓒ 예치치 못한 보수 공사
ⓓ 참가 기업 수의 증가

06 Intention Question

화자는 왜 대학교 웹사이트를 언급하는가?
Ⓐ 전문적인 네트워킹 팁을 제공하기 위해
Ⓑ 장소 변경에 대한 세부 사항을 제공하기 위해
ⓒ 학생들을 등록 플랫폼으로 안내하기 위해
Ⓓ 참가하는 기업의 프로필을 게시하기 위해

어휘 direct[dirékt] 안내하다, 지도하다

[07-08]

Listen to an announcement at a university event.

Good morning, everyone! ⁰⁷**I'd like to invite you all to our International Film Festival** happening next Tuesday evening at 7 P.M. in Thompson Hall. We'll be showing award-winning short films from around the world, and free popcorn will be available for the first 30 students who arrive. ⁰⁸**Additionally, several directors of the films shown will join us online for Q&A sessions afterward.** If you have a passion for movies, don't miss this golden opportunity!

award-winning 상을 받은   afterward[ǽftərwərd] 이후
passion[pǽʃən] 열정   golden[góuldən] 절호의

대학교 행사에서의 공지를 들으시오.

좋은 아침입니다, 여러분! 다음 주 화요일 오후 7시에 Thompson홀에서 열리는 ⁰⁷**국제 영화제에 여러분 모두를 초대하고 싶습니다**. 전 세계의 상을 받은 단편 영화들을 상영할 예정이며, 먼저 도착한 30명의 학생들에게 무료 팝콘이 제공될 것입니다. ⁰⁸**또한, 상영작의 여러 감독이 이후 질의응답 시간에 온라인으로 참여할 예정입니다.** 영화에 대한 열정이 있으시다면, 이 절호의 기회를 놓치지 마세요!

07 Main Purpose Question

공지의 주요 목적은 무엇인가?
ⓐ 다가오는 영화제를 광고하기 위해
Ⓑ 학생들에게 일정이 변경된 행사를 상기시키기 위해
ⓒ 상을 받은 학생 영화 제작자들을 축하하기 위해
Ⓓ 국제 영화 대회 참여를 격려하기 위해

어휘 filmmaker[fílmeikər] 영화 제작자

08 Detail Question

감독들은 영화제에서 무엇을 할 것인가?
Ⓐ 인턴십을 위해 학생들을 모집한다.
Ⓑ 학생 영화 대회를 심사한다.
ⓒ 참석자들의 질문에 답변한다.
Ⓓ 국제 영화 트렌드에 대한 강의를 한다.

어휘 judge[dʒʌdʒ] 심사하다; 판사   lecture[léktʃər] 강의, 강연

[09-10]

Listen to an announcement in a classroom.

Attention, everyone! I'd like to inform you that ⁰⁹**Professor Alan Potter from Northwestern University will be delivering a special lecture on generative AI next Monday.** The lecture will begin at 2 P.M., and attendance, while not mandatory, is strongly encouraged due to ¹⁰**the lecture's relevance to your coursework.**

generative AI 생성형 AI   relevance[réləvəns] 관련성

교실에서의 공지를 들으시오.

모두 주목해 주시기 바랍니다! ⁰⁹Northwestern 대학교의 Alan Potter 교수님이 다음 주 월요일에 생성형 AI에 대한 특별 강의를 하실 예정임을 알려드립니다. 강의는 오후 2시에 시작되며, 출석이 의무 사항은 아니지만, ¹⁰강의의 여러분의 교과과정과의 관련성으로 인해 강력히 권장됩니다.

09 Main Topic Question

공지의 주요 주제는 무엇인가?
Ⓐ 최근 고용된 강사의 오리엔테이션
ⓑ 방문 교수의 강연
ⓒ 강의 요구사항의 변경
Ⓓ 협력 연구 프로젝트

어휘 instructor[instrʌ́ktər] 강사, 교수
      collaborative[kəlǽbərèitiv] 협력의

10 Detail Question

화자는 강의에 대해 무엇을 말하는가?
Ⓐ 2시간 동안 진행될 것이다.
Ⓑ Northwestern 대학교에서 열릴 것이다.
ⓒ 모든 학생이 참석하는 것이 필수이다.
ⓓ 교과 과정과 관련된 주제를 다룰 것이다.

어휘 last[læst] 진행되다, 계속하다   relate to 관련되다
      curriculum[kəríkjuləm] 교과과정

[11-12]

Listen to an announcement in a student lounge.

Listen up for a moment, everyone. ¹¹**The student lounge on the second floor will be closed next Monday and Tuesday so that new furniture can be installed.** I recommend using the outdoor pavilion or study rooms in Building B instead. We hope that you will find the lounge a better place to study when it reopens on Wednesday. ¹²**Please take any personal belongings from the lockers in the lounge by this Friday afternoon.**

furniture[fə́ːrnitʃər] 가구   belongings[bilɔ́ːŋiŋz] 소지품

학생 라운지에서의 공지를 들으시오.

여러분, 잠깐 들어보세요. ¹¹2층의 학생 라운지가 새 가구 설치로 인

해 다음 주 월요일과 화요일에 폐쇄될 예정입니다. 대신 야외 파빌리온이나 B관의 스터디룸을 이용하시기를 권합니다. 라운지가 수요일에 재개방하면, 여러분에게 더 좋은 학습 공간이 되길 바랍니다. ¹²이번 주 금요일 오후까지 라운지의 사물함에서 개인 소지품을 가져가 주세요.

11 Detail Question
공지에 설명된 라운지 폐쇄의 이유는 무엇인가?
Ⓐ 사물함 철거
Ⓑ 바닥 청소
Ⓒ 구조적 수리
☑ 가구 설치

어휘 removal[rimúːvəl] 철거 structural[strʌ́kʃərəl] 구조적인

12 To Do Question
화자는 청자들이 무엇을 하기를 바라는가?
Ⓐ 라운지 이용 권한을 신청한다.
☑ 개인 소지품을 가져간다.
Ⓒ 2층을 완전히 피한다.
Ⓓ 가구 선호도를 제출한다.

어휘 retrieve[ritríːv] 가져가다; 회수 preference[préfərəns] 선호도

[13-14] Au
Listen to an announcement in a classroom.

> Good morning, everyone! ¹³**I need to inform you that our class will be moved to a different room starting next week.** Since our class will focus on presentations after the midterm exams, we'll be meeting in ¹⁴**Room 619 of the Humanities Building, which includes a projector and screen for us to use during presentations.**
>
> humanities[hjuːmǽnətiz] 인문학

교실에서의 공지를 들으시오.
좋은 아침입니다, 여러분! ¹³다음 주부터 우리 수업이 다른 강의실로 이동될 것임을 알려드립니다. 중간고사 후에 저희 수업이 발표에 집중할 예정이므로, ¹⁴발표 시 사용할 프로젝터와 스크린이 갖춰진 인문관 619호에서 수업을 진행합니다.

13 Main Purpose Question
공지의 주요 목적은 무엇인가?
Ⓐ 학생들에게 일정 변경을 알리기 위해
☑ 강의실 변경을 알리기 위해
Ⓒ 학생들에게 중간고사를 상기시키기 위해
Ⓓ 발표 형식을 설명하기 위해

어휘 format[fɔ́ːrmæt] 형식

14 Detail Question
다음 중 619호에 대해 사실인 것은?
Ⓐ 중간고사 기간에만 이용이 가능하다.
Ⓑ 인문학과 학생들을 위해 최근에 보수되었다.
☑ 발표에 도움이 될 장비가 있다.
Ⓓ 현재 강의실에 비해 수용 인원이 제한적이다.

어휘 period[píəriəd] 기간 equipment[ikwípmənt] 장비
capacity[kəpǽsəti] 수용 인원, 용량

[15-16] Am
Listen to an announcement at a university event.

> Good evening, everyone. ¹⁵**I'd like to remind you that our Winter Charity Ball will be held this Friday at 8 P.M. in James Hall.** We're aiming to raise 5,000 dollars for the children's hospital this year. Entrance tickets cost five dollars, and ¹⁶**tickets are available at the Student Union Building until Thursday**. Those who purchase early-bird tickets by the end of today will receive a special commemorative badge— so don't miss this last chance.
>
> aim to ~하는 것을 목표로 하다
> commemorative[kəmémərèitiv] 기념의

대학교 행사에서의 공지를 들으시오.
좋은 저녁입니다, 여러분. ¹⁵저희의 겨울 자선 무도회가 이번 주 금요일 오후 8시에 James 홀에서 열릴 예정임을 상기시켜 드리고자 합니다. 저희는 올해 어린이병원을 위해 5,000달러를 모금하는 것이 목표입니다. 입장료는 5달러이며, ¹⁶목요일까지 학생회관에서 구입하실 수 있습니다. 오늘까지 얼리버드 티켓을 구매하시는 분들은 특별 기념 배지를 받을 수 있으니, 이 마지막 기회를 놓치지 마세요.

15 Detail Question
행사는 언제 열릴 것인가?
Ⓐ 화요일
Ⓑ 목요일
☑ 금요일
Ⓓ 일요일

16 Detail Question
청자들은 어디에서 티켓을 구매할 수 있는가?
Ⓐ James 홀
☑ 학생회관
Ⓒ 어린이병원
Ⓓ 자선 단체 본부

어휘 charity[tʃǽrəti] 자선단체 headquarters[hédkwɔ̀ːrtərz] 본부

---

4. Intention Questions

Example En
p.199

> 다음 주부터 캠퍼스 셔틀 서비스가 과학관에 새로운 정류장을 추가할 예정입니다. 노선 확장은 과학관에서 야간 실험을 하는 많은 학생들이 이전에는 어둠 속에서 기숙사까지 걸어 돌아가야 했기 때문에 시행되었습니다. 업데이트된 경로 정보는 대학 웹사이트에서 확인하실 수 있습니다.

expansion[ikspǽnʃən] 확장
dorm[dɔːrm] 기숙사(= dormitory)

화자는 왜 야간 실험을 하는 학생들을 언급하는가?
☑ⒶⒶ 새로운 정류장을 추가하는 이유를 설명하기 위해
Ⓑ 새로운 야간 수업을 알리기 위해
Ⓒ 셔틀 서비스의 추가 비용을 정당화하기 위해
Ⓓ 캠퍼스 안전 계획을 소개하기 위해

어휘 justify[dʒʌ́stəfài] 정당화하다

HACKERS PRACTICE
p.200

01 Ⓒ 02 Ⓐ 03 Ⓑ 04 Ⓓ

01 Intention Question 🔊 Am

The library's Wi-Fi system will undergo a major upgrade this weekend. The network will be unavailable from Friday evening until Monday morning. We recommend using the computer lab on the second floor if you need an Internet connection during this time. We're sorry for any inconvenience this may cause.

undergo[ʌ̀ndərgóu] 받다, 겪다 major[méidʒər] 대대적인, 큰

도서관의 Wi-Fi 시스템이 이번 주말에 대대적인 업그레이드를 받을 예정입니다. 네트워크는 금요일 저녁부터 월요일 아침까지 사용할 수 없을 것입니다. 이 시간 동안 인터넷 연결이 필요하시다면 2층의 컴퓨터실을 이용하시기를 권합니다. 이로 인해 발생할 수 있는 불편에 대해 사과드립니다.

화자는 왜 컴퓨터실을 언급하는가?
Ⓐ 새로운 소프트웨어 설치에 대해 알리기 위해
Ⓑ 건물의 최근 보수를 강조하기 위해
☑Ⓒ 인터넷에 접속할 수 있는 곳을 알리기 위해
Ⓓ 연장된 주말 운영시간을 홍보하기 위해

어휘 indicate[índikèit] 알리다, 나타내다
    extended[iksténdid] 연장된

02 Intention Question 🔊 Nz

The Regional Sculpture Exhibit opens tomorrow in our campus gallery, featuring works by emerging artists from five nearby cities. The exhibit will run for three weeks, with artist talks scheduled every Friday at noon. Visitors can purchase pieces during the exhibit, and a portion of the proceeds will go to our university's art scholarship fund.

sculpture[skʌ́lptʃər] 조각; 조각하다
feature[fíːtʃər] ~을 선보이다; 기능, 특징
emerging[imə́ːrdʒiŋ] 신진의, 떠오르는
nearby[nìərbái] 주변의 proceeds[próusiːdz] 수익금

지역 조각 전시회가 내일 저희 캠퍼스 갤러리에서 개막되며, 주변 5개 도시의 신진 작가들의 작품을 선보입니다. 전시회는 3주간 진행되며, 매주 금요일 정오에 작가 강연이 예정되어 있습니다. 방문객들은 전시회 동안 작품을 구매할 수 있으며, 수익금의 일부는 우리 대학의 미술 장학 기금에 적립될 것입니다.

화자는 왜 주변 5개 도시를 언급하는가?
☑Ⓐ 예술가들이 어디 출신인지 명시하기 위해
Ⓑ 방문객들을 위한 교통 계획을 설명하기 위해
Ⓒ 내년 확장 계획을 발표하기 위해
Ⓓ 인근 지역과의 관광 제휴를 홍보하기 위해

어휘 specify[spésəfài] 명시하다, 구체화하다 tourism[túərizm] 관광

03 Intention Question En

During finals week, the library will extend its operating hours to better serve students. We'll be open 24 hours per day on weekdays, while maintaining regular weekend hours. Additional study spaces have been set up on the third floor to accommodate increased demand. Good luck with your exams!

serve[səːrv] 지원하다, 섬기다 set up 마련하다, 설정하다
demand[dimǽnd] 수요; 요구하다

기말고사 주간 동안, 도서관은 학생들을 더 잘 지원하기 위해 운영시간을 연장합니다. 평일에는 하루 24시간 개방하며, 토요일과 일요일에는 정규 주말 시간을 유지합니다. 늘어난 수요를 수용하기 위해 3층에 추가 학습 공간이 마련되었습니다. 시험 잘 보세요!

화자는 왜 3층을 언급하는가?
Ⓐ 주말 학습 선택지를 추천하기 위해
☑Ⓑ 추가 학습 장소의 위치를 알리기 위해
Ⓒ 다과가 제공될 위치를 명시하기 위해
Ⓓ 최근 건물 보수를 강조하기 위해

04 Intention Question 🔊 Am

Important update for all chemistry students. New safety protocols will be implemented in all laboratories starting next week. Safety goggles and lab coats are now mandatory at all times during experiments. Room 201 has safety equipment available in all sizes, so please pick up your gear before Monday's session.

chemistry[kéməstri] 화학 protocol[próutəkɔ̀ːl] 규정, 계획
laboratory[lǽbərətɔ̀ːri] 실험실 experiment[ikspérəmənt] 실험
gear[giər] 장비, 톱니바퀴

모든 화학과 학생들을 위한 중요한 소식입니다. 다음 주부터 모든 실험실에서 새로운 안전 규정이 시행될 예정입니다. 실험 중에는 항상 보안경과 실험복 착용이 의무화됩니다. 201호에 모든 사이즈의 안전 장비가 준비되어 있으니, 월요일 수업 전에 장비를 가져가시기 바랍니다.

화자는 왜 201호를 언급하는가?
Ⓐ 어떤 방이 보수되었는지 보여주기 위해
Ⓑ 반납 장소를 지정하기 위해
Ⓒ 실험 보고서를 어디에 제출해야 하는지 알리기 위해

✓ 학생들을 안전 장비가 있는 곳으로 안내하기 위해

어휘 designate[dézignèit] 지정하다, 명시하다

HACKERS TEST
p.202

01 ⓒ	02 ⓑ	03 ⓒ	04 ⓐ	05 ⓓ
06 ⓐ	07 ⓑ	08 ⓑ	09 ⓒ	10 ⓑ
11 ⓐ	12 ⓐ	13 ⓒ	14 ⓒ	15 ⓓ
16 ⓒ

[01-02]
Au

Listen to an announcement in a student lounge.

Good morning, students. I need to let you know that ⁰¹the student lounge will be temporarily closed from tomorrow through to next Wednesday for some electrical work. This is necessary due to safety concerns. ⁰²Alternative spaces have been set up in the South Building. We apologize for any inconvenience this may cause.

temporarily[tèmpərérəli] 임시로, 잠시
electrical[iléktrikəl] 전기의

학생 라운지에서의 공지를 들으시오.

좋은 아침입니다, 학생 여러분. ⁰¹학생 라운지가 전기 작업으로 인해 내일부터 다음 주 수요일까지 임시 폐쇄될 예정임을 알립니다. 이는 안전상의 우려 때문에 필요한 조치입니다. ⁰²남관에 대체 공간이 마련되었습니다. 이로 인해 발생할 수 있는 불편함에 대해 사과드립니다.

01 Detail Question

공지에 설명된 라운지 폐쇄의 이유는 무엇인가?
ⓐ 예산 제약
ⓑ 계절별 보수
✓ 전기 시설 유지보수
ⓓ 정기 청소

어휘 seasonal[síːzənl] 계절의

02 Intention Question

화자는 왜 남관을 언급하는가?
ⓐ 전기 문제의 원인을 설명하기 위해
✓ 학생들에게 대체 장소를 제공하기 위해
ⓒ 정비 일정을 설명하기 위해
ⓓ 새로운 캠퍼스 시설을 강조하기 위해

[03-04]
Am

Listen to an announcement at a university event.

Good afternoon, everyone! ⁰³I'm thrilled to announce our university will be hosting the Regional A cappella Championship next weekend! Eight top college teams will compete for the title on Saturday evening in Kershaw Auditorium. ⁰⁴Given the rapid pace of ticket sales, you might want to secure your seat right now. Remember, music can bring us together!

compete[kəmpíːt] 경쟁하다   rapid[rǽpid] 빠른
pace[peis] 속도   secure[sikjúər] 확보하다; 안전한

대학교 행사에서의 공지를 들으시오.

좋은 오후입니다, 여러분! ⁰³우리 대학교가 다음 주말에 지역 아카펠라 대회를 개최한다는 소식을 알려드리게 되어 매우 기쁩니다! 8개의 최고 대학 팀들이 토요일 저녁 Kershaw 강당에서 우승을 놓고 경쟁할 것입니다. ⁰⁴빠른 티켓 판매 속도를 고려하여, 지금 바로 좌석을 확보하시는 것이 좋겠습니다. 기억하세요, 음악은 우리를 하나로 만들어 줍니다!

03 Main Topic Question

공지는 무엇에 대한 것인가?
ⓐ 악기 전시회
ⓑ 음악학과를 위한 기금 모금 행사
✓ 다가오는 아카펠라 대회
ⓓ 유명한 아카펠라 가수들과의 인터뷰

어휘 musical instrument 악기

04 Intention Question

화자는 왜 빠른 티켓 판매 속도를 언급하는가?
✓ 즉각적인 티켓 구매를 권장하기 위해
ⓑ 추가 공연 날짜를 홍보하기 위해
ⓒ 높은 티켓 가격에 대해 사과하기 위해
ⓓ 제한된 좌석 수용 능력을 설명하기 위해

어휘 immediate[imíːdiət] 즉각적인, 직접의

[05-06]
En

Listen to an announcement at a university club meeting.

Alright, let's get our University Volunteering Club meeting started. The first item on the agenda is our fundraiser next Thursday. ⁰⁵We need at least five volunteers to help organize the event and manage the booths. ⁰⁶Volunteers will be provided with a ten-dollar voucher that can be used at the campus store, so we hope you will take advantage of this opportunity to both contribute to the club and earn a nice reward.

agenda[ədʒéndə] 안건   fundraiser[fʌ́ndrèizər] 기금 모금 행사
take advantage of ~을 활용하다   contribute to ~에 기여하다
earn[əːrn] 얻다, 획득하다   reward[riwɔ́ːrd] 보상; 보상하다

대학교 동아리 회의에서의 공지를 들으시오.

좋습니다, 대학 자원봉사 동아리 회의를 시작하겠습니다. 첫 번째 안건은 다음 주 목요일에 있을 저희의 기금 모금 행사입니다. ⁰⁵행사를 조직하고 부스를 관리하는 데 도움을 줄 최소 5명의 자원봉사자가 필요합니다. ⁰⁶봉사자들은 교내 상점에서 사용할 수 있는 10달러 상품권을 제공받을 예정이므로, 여러분들이 동아리에 기여하면서 좋은 보상도 얻

는 이 기회를 활용하시기를 바랍니다.

05 To Do Question
화자는 청자들이 무엇을 하기를 바라는가?
- Ⓐ 행사 관리 전략을 논의한다.
- Ⓑ 다른 동아리에 행사를 홍보한다.
- Ⓒ 출석 기록을 위해 이름을 제공한다.
- ✓ 행사를 위한 자원봉사자로 등록한다.

어휘 management[mǽnidʒmənt] 관리, 경영

06 Intention Question
화자는 왜 10달러 상품권을 언급하는가?
- ✓ 동아리 회원들이 시간을 투자하도록 동기를 부여하기 위해
- Ⓑ 교내 상점과의 새로운 제휴를 발표하기 위해
- Ⓒ 동아리 회원들을 위한 예산 배분을 설명하기 위해
- Ⓓ 교내 상점에서 구입할 수 있는 새 상품을 소개하기 위해

어휘 motivate[móutəvèit] 동기를 부여하다
commit[kəmít] 투자하다, 자행하다

[07-08] Au
Listen to an announcement on the school radio.

> Hello, students! ⁰⁷**Starting Monday, our campus dining hall will introduce new menu options based on your survey feedback.** We've added Japanese ramen dishes and Italian risotto dishes. We'll also offer vegetarian and gluten-free versions. ⁰⁸**We hope you enjoy trying these new menu options!**
>
> dining hall 식당 vegetarian[vèdʒətɛ́əriən] 채식의; 채식주의자

학교 라디오에서의 공지를 들으시오.

안녕하세요, 학생 여러분! ⁰⁷월요일부터 우리 대학 식당에서 여러분의 설문조사의 의견을 바탕으로 새로운 메뉴 옵션을 도입할 예정입니다. 저희는 일본식 라멘 요리와 이탈리아식 리조토 요리를 추가했습니다. 저희는 채식 및 글루텐 프리 버전도 제공할 것입니다. ⁰⁸이러한 새로운 메뉴들을 즐겁게 드셔 보시길 바라겠습니다!

07 Intention Question
화자는 왜 피드백 설문조사를 언급하는가?
- Ⓐ 설문조사 마감 연장을 공지하기 위해
- ✓ 학생 의견이 결정에 어떤 영향을 미쳤는지 보여주기 위해
- Ⓒ 학생들로부터 추가 피드백을 요청하기 위해
- Ⓓ 메뉴 변경이 왜 지연되었는지 설명하기 위해

어휘 input[ínpùt] 의견; 입력하다
influence[ínfluəns] 영향을 미치다; 영향

08 To Do Question
화자는 청자들이 무엇을 하기를 바라는가?
- Ⓐ 식당을 더 자주 방문한다.
- ✓ 새로운 메뉴 옵션을 시도해본다.
- Ⓒ 변화에 대한 의견을 공유한다.
- Ⓓ 식당에서 자원봉사를 한다.

[09-10] Am
Listen to an announcement at a university event.

> Good morning, everyone! ⁰⁹**I'm pleased to announce that our technology showcase will be held next Thursday from 1 P.M. to 5 P.M. in the Innovation Center.** Students and faculty will be demonstrating their latest research projects and technological innovations. Additionally, starting at 3 P.M., ¹⁰**Dr. Robertson, a renowned expert in virtual reality, will be giving a special lecture.** Don't miss this opportunity to experience the latest advancements in technology firsthand!
>
> be pleased to ~하게 되어 기쁘다
> technological[tèknəládʒikəl] 기술적인
> innovation[ìnəvéiʃən] 혁신, 개혁 virtual reality 가상현실
> firsthand[fə́rsthǽnd] 직접

대학교 행사에서의 공지를 들으시오.

좋은 아침입니다, 여러분! ⁰⁹저희 기술 쇼케이스가 다음 주 목요일 오후 1시부터 5시까지 혁신 센터에서 열릴 예정이라는 소식을 알려드리게 되어 기쁩니다. 학생들과 교수진이 그들의 최신 연구 프로젝트와 기술 혁신을 선보일 예정입니다. 또한, 오후 3시부터 ¹⁰가상현실 분야의 저명한 전문가인 Robertson 박사님이 특별 강의를 진행할 예정입니다. 최신 기술 발전을 직접 체험할 수 있는 이 기회를 놓치지 마세요!

09 Main Topic Question
공지의 주요 주제는 무엇인가?
- Ⓐ 가상현실 강의
- Ⓑ 연구 대회
- ✓ 기술 쇼케이스
- Ⓓ 네트워킹 기회

10 Intention Question
화자는 왜 Robertson 박사님을 언급하는가?
- Ⓐ 학생 프로젝트를 평가할 사람을 명시하기 위해
- ✓ 행사의 주요 발표자가 누구인지 강조하기 위해
- Ⓒ 혁신 센터의 창립자를 축하하기 위해
- Ⓓ 행사 주최자에게 감사를 표하기 위해

어휘 evaluate[ivǽljuèit] 평가하다 founder[fáundər] 설립자

[11-12] En
Listen to an announcement at a university club meeting.

> Welcome back, Drama Club members! For our fall production, we've selected Shakespeare's *The Taming of the Shrew*. ¹¹**We will hold auditions to cast actors.** They will take place next Tuesday and Wednesday from 6 to 9 P.M. in the Black Box Theater. ¹²**No additional materials are required, as we'll provide scripts.** We look forward to your participation!
>
> look forward to 기대하다

대학교 동아리 회의에서의 공지를 들으시오.

연극 동아리 회원들, 다시 오신 것을 환영합니다! 저희 가을 공연 작품으로 셰익스피어의 The Taming of the Shrew를 선정했습니다. ¹¹배우 캐스팅을 위한 오디션을 실시할 예정입니다. 오디션은 다음 주 화요일과 수요일 오후 6시부터 9시까지 Black Box 극장에서 진행됩니다. ¹²저희가 대본을 제공할 예정이므로, 별도의 준비물은 필요하지 않습니다. 여러분의 참여를 기대합니다!

11 Main Purpose Question
공지의 주된 목적은 무엇인가?
- Ⓐ 연극 오디션 참여를 격려하기 위해 ✓
- Ⓑ 셰익스피어 연극의 줄거리를 설명하기 위해
- Ⓒ 동아리 회원들에게 특정 역할을 배정하기 위해
- Ⓓ 극장 공간의 변화를 발표하기 위해

어휘 plot [plɑt] 줄거리, 각색 assign [əsáin] 배정하다

12 Intention Question
화자는 왜 대본을 언급하는가?
- Ⓐ 준비가 왜 필요하지 않은지를 설명하기 위해 ✓
- Ⓑ 학생들에게 오디션 요구사항을 알려주기 위해
- Ⓒ 원작에서 변경된 대본을 강조하기 위해
- Ⓓ 오디션 전에 셰익스피어에 대해 공부하라고 제안하기 위해

어휘 preparation [prèpəréiʃən] 준비

[13-14]   Am

Listen to an announcement at a university club meeting.

> Good evening, Environmental Club members! I'm excited to share that we've received permission for our campus tree-planting project. ¹³**The university has allocated the area behind the Science Building for us to plant 25 trees.** We'll carry out the project this Saturday from 9 A.M. to noon. ¹⁴**Please bring gloves and sturdy shoes.** The club will provide other necessary tools and refreshments.
>
> permission [pərmíʃən] 허가   carry out 진행하다, 수행하다
> sturdy [stə́ːrdi] 튼튼한, 억센

대학교 동아리 회의에서의 공지를 들으시오.

좋은 저녁입니다, 환경 동아리 여러분! 저희 캠퍼스 나무 심기 프로젝트에 대한 허가를 받았다는 소식을 전하게 되어 기쁩니다. ¹³대학교에서 저희가 25그루의 나무를 심을 수 있도록 과학관 뒤편 지역을 배정해 주었습니다. 이번 주 토요일 오전 9시부터 정오까지 프로젝트를 진행할 예정입니다. ¹⁴장갑과 튼튼한 신발을 가져와 주세요. 동아리에서 다른 필요한 도구들과 다과를 제공할 예정입니다.

13 Intention Question
화자는 왜 과학관을 언급하는가?
- Ⓐ 건물 보수를 발표하기 위해
- Ⓑ 대안 모임 장소를 제안하기 위해
- Ⓒ 나무를 심을 장소를 확인하기 위해 ✓
- Ⓓ 장비를 보관할 장소를 알려주기 위해

어휘 identify [aidéntəfài] 확인하다

14 Detail Question
화자는 회원들에게 무엇을 가져오라고 제안하는가?
- Ⓐ 간식과 재사용 가능한 물통
- Ⓑ 땅을 파는 도구와 다과
- Ⓒ 작업용 장갑과 튼튼한 신발 ✓
- Ⓓ 학생 신분증과 서명된 허가서

어휘 reusable [riúːzəbəl] 재사용 가능한   permission form 허가서

[15-16]   Nz

Listen to an announcement at a university event.

> Hey, everyone! Just a quick reminder about our debate competition next week. ¹⁵**All team members need to submit their preferred topics by Friday at the latest.** Remember, we're focusing on environmental issues this semester. ¹⁶**Practice sessions will be held in Room 304 instead of our usual spot due to renovations.** Looking forward to seeing your brilliant ideas!
>
> usual [júːʒuəl] 평상시의   brilliant [bríljənt] 훌륭한, 밝은

대학교 행사에서의 공지를 들으시오.

안녕하세요, 여러분! 다음 주에 있을 저희 토론 대회에 대해 간단히 상기시켜 드립니다. ¹⁵모든 팀 구성원들은 늦어도 금요일까지 선호 주제를 제출해야 합니다. 이번 학기에는 환경 문제에 초점을 맞추고 있다는 점을 기억해 주세요. ¹⁶보수 작업으로 인해 연습 세션은 평상시 장소 대신 304호실에서 진행될 예정입니다. 여러분의 훌륭한 아이디어를 보기를 기대합니다!

15 To Do Question
화자는 청자들이 무엇을 하기를 바라는가?
- Ⓐ 보수 작업을 돕는다.
- Ⓑ 추가 연습 세션에 참석한다.
- Ⓒ 토론 대회를 위한 팀을 구성한다.
- Ⓓ 주제 선택을 시간 내에 제출한다. ✓

어휘 on time 시간 내에, 제시간에

16 Intention Question
화자는 왜 304호실을 언급하는가?
- Ⓐ 대회 장소를 발표하기 위해
- Ⓑ 보수가 필요한 이유를 설명하기 위해
- Ⓒ 토론 연습이 어디에서 열릴지 알려주기 위해 ✓
- Ⓓ 새로운 공간의 장점을 설명하기 위해

5. Inference Questions

Example   En   p.207

환영합니다, 여러분. 이번 주 금요일 저희 영화 동아리의 영화 감상회에 대해 간단히 알려드립니다. 작년 독립 영화제에서 여러 상을 수

상한 The Pursuit of Knowledge를 볼 예정입니다. 상영은 오후 7시에 저희 평상시 모임 장소에서 시작됩니다. **영화가 거의 3시간 30분 동안 상영되므로, 이후 평상시처럼 토론할 시간이 없을 것입니다.** 대신, 다음 주 모임에서 논의하겠습니다.

independent [ìndipéndənt] 독립적인   screening [skríːniŋ] 상영

영화 동아리의 정기 모임에 대해 암시되는 것은?
Ⓐ 매주 다른 장소에서 열린다.
☑ 일반적으로 영화 상영과 토론을 모두 포함한다.
Ⓒ 수상작 영화들만 상영한다.
Ⓓ 많은 수의 참석자들을 끌어들인다.

어휘 typically [típikəli] 일반적으로, 대체로
      attract [ətrǽkt] 끌어들이다

HACKERS PRACTICE

p.208

01 Ⓐ   02 Ⓑ   03 Ⓒ   04 Ⓓ

01 Inference Question 🎧 Am

Hello, students! We are hosting our university's first-ever gaming tournament next weekend. We've <u>partnered with several game companies</u> to offer exciting prizes, including gaming equipment and software. **Registration closes next Monday, but spots are <u>filling up so fast</u>.** This tournament is open to people of <u>all skill levels</u>, so don't hesitate to participate!

first-ever 최초의

학생 여러분, 안녕하세요! 다음 주말에 우리 대학교 최초의 게임 토너먼트를 개최합니다. 게임 장비와 소프트웨어를 포함한 흥미로운 상품을 제공하기 위해 여러 게임 회사들과 제휴를 맺었습니다. **등록은 다음 주 월요일에 마감되지만, 자리가 너무 빠르게 차고 있습니다.** 이 토너먼트는 모든 실력 수준의 사람들에게 열려 있으니, 주저하지 마시고 참여하세요!

게임 토너먼트에 대해 암시되는 것은?
☑ 상당한 학생들의 관심을 불러일으켰다.
Ⓑ 전문적인 게임 경험을 요구한다.
Ⓒ 캠퍼스를 통틀어서 여러 장소에서 열릴 것이다.
Ⓓ 참가자들이 자신의 장비를 가져와야 한다.

어휘 significant [signífikənt] 상당한, 중요한

02 Inference Question 🎧 Nz

Good afternoon, everyone! The university is <u>accepting submission for</u> this year's Student Film Festival. We welcome all kind of films <u>created by students</u>. **The creators of the winning entries will receive not only cash prizes but also the opportunity to screen <u>their works at a regional film festival</u>.** The submission deadline is March 15, and all entries must be <u>under 20 minutes in length</u>.

entry [éntri] 출품작   screen [skriːn] 상영하다

좋은 오후입니다, 여러분! 대학에서 올해의 학생 영화 축제를 위한 출품작을 접수하고 있습니다. 학생들이 제작한 모든 종류의 영화를 환영합니다. **수상작의 제작자들은 상금뿐만 아니라 지역 영화제에서의 상영 기회도 받게 될 것입니다.** 제출 마감일은 3월 15일이며, 모든 출품작은 20분 이하여야 합니다.

화자는 영화제에 대해 무엇을 암시하는가?
Ⓐ 올해 처음으로 개최된다.
☑ 캠퍼스 밖에서도 상영 기회를 제공한다.
Ⓒ 최소 20분 길이의 영화를 요구한다.
Ⓓ 개인과 팀 참가자들을 별도로 시상한다.

어휘 duration [djuréiʃən] 지속 기간
      individual [ìndəvídʒuəl] 개인의; 개인
      separately [sépərətli] 별도로

03 Inference Question 🎧 En

An important update regarding <u>your midterm examination</u>. Due to technical issues in the computer lab, you will be able to <u>use your personal computers</u> to take the test. **It will <u>still be held</u> on Tuesday at 2 P.M., but you can take it in your dorm or any location with reliable Internet access.** <u>Check your email</u> for detailed instructions.

examination [igzæmənéiʃən] 고사, 시험
detailed [díːteild] 자세한

중간고사에 관한 중요한 업데이트입니다. 컴퓨터실의 기술적 문제로 인해, 여러분은 개인 컴퓨터를 사용하여 시험을 볼 수 있게 될 것입니다. **시험은 여전히 화요일 오후 2시에 실시될 것이지만, 여러분은 기숙사나 안정적인 인터넷 접속이 가능한 장소라면 어느 곳에서든 시험을 치를 수 있습니다.** 자세한 지침은 이메일을 확인해주세요.

화자는 시험에 대해 무엇을 암시하는가?
Ⓐ 형식은 이메일을 통해 공지될 것이다.
Ⓑ 컴퓨터 실습실에서 진행될 것이다.
☑ 원래 예정된 시간에 시작될 것이다.
Ⓓ 문제들이 곧 수정될 것이다.

어휘 shortly [ʃɔ́ːrtli] 곧

04 Inference Question 🎧 Am

Good morning, students! Next weekend, the university is hosting its <u>first-ever charity marathon</u> to support local homeless shelters. The 5K run begins at 8 A.M. from the <u>campus fitness center</u>, with registration starting at 7 A.M. The entry fee is only ten dollars, and all proceeds <u>will be donated</u>. **Even if you're not running, come cheer on your fellow students and enjoy the free breakfast afterward!**

homeless [hóumlis] 노숙자   entry fee 참가비

Section I. Question Types | 5. Inference Questions **521**

TASK 3 Hackers Updated TOEFL LISTENING

좋은 아침입니다, 학생 여러분! 다음 주말에 대학교에서 지역 노숙자 쉼터를 지원하기 위한 첫 번째 자선 마라톤을 개최합니다. 5K 달리기는 오전 8시에 캠퍼스 피트니스 센터에서 시작하며, 등록은 오전 7시에 시작됩니다. 참가비는 단 10달러이고, 모든 수익금은 기부될 예정입니다. 달리기에 참여하지 않으시더라도, 동료 학생들을 응원하러 오셔서 이후 무료 조식을 즐겨주세요!

화자는 조식에 대해 무엇을 암시하는가?
Ⓐ 피트니스 센터에서 제공될 것이다.
Ⓑ 학생 자원봉사자들에 의해 만들어질 것이다.
Ⓒ 10달러에 제공될 것이다.
✓ 모든 행사 참석자들이 이용할 수 있을 것이다.

HACKERS TEST   p.210

01 Ⓒ	02 Ⓑ	03 Ⓐ	04 Ⓒ	05 Ⓓ
06 Ⓓ	07 Ⓑ	08 Ⓑ	09 Ⓐ	10 Ⓒ
11 Ⓒ	12 Ⓐ	13 Ⓑ	14 Ⓓ	15 Ⓓ
16 Ⓒ				

[01-02]   🎧 Au

Listen to an announcement in a classroom.

> Music students, ⁰¹please be informed that workers will be carrying out soundproofing work in Practice Rooms 1 through 5 next week. ⁰²Rooms 6 through 10 remain available, but we recommend reserving them in advance due to increased demand. The music department office manages the reservation schedule.

교실에서의 공지를 들으시오.
음악과 학생 여러분, ⁰¹작업자들이 다음 주에 연습실 1번부터 5번까지 방음 공사를 할 예정임을 알려드립니다. ⁰²6번부터 10번 연습실은 계속 사용 가능하지만, 수요 증가로 인해 미리 예약하실 것을 권합니다. 음악과 사무실에서 예약 일정을 관리하고 있습니다.

01 Main Topic Question
공지의 주요 주제는 무엇인가?
Ⓐ 새로운 장비 정책
Ⓑ 예약 절차의 변경
✓ 시설 개선에 대한 소식
Ⓓ 음악과의 확장

어휘 improvement[imprúːvmənt] 개선

02 Inference Question
사용 가능한 연습실에 대해 암시되는 것은?
Ⓐ 예약을 위해 요금을 필요로 한다.
✓ 평상시보다 더 붐빌 가능성이 높다.
Ⓒ 다른 건물에 위치해 있다.
Ⓓ 청소를 위해 임시로 폐쇄될 것이다.

어휘 crowded[kráudid] 붐비는, 혼잡한

[03-04]   🎧 Am

Listen to an announcement in a classroom.

> Attention students. ⁰³Due to an unexpected shortage of proctors, tomorrow's scheduled exam has been postponed until next Tuesday at the same time. ⁰⁴I hope you will use this extra time to review the material thoroughly.
>
> unexpected[ʌnikspéktid] 예상치 못한
> shortage[ʃɔ́ːrtidʒ] 부족, 결핍   proctor[práktər] 시험 감독관
> postpone[poustpóun] 연기하다   review[rivjúː] 검토하다
> thoroughly[θə́ːrouli] 철저히, 완전히

교실에서의 공지를 들으시오.
학생 여러분 주목해 주세요. ⁰³예상치 못한 시험 감독관 부족으로 인해, 내일 예정된 시험이 다음 주 화요일의 같은 시간으로 연기되었습니다. ⁰⁴이 추가 시간을 활용해서 교재를 철저히 검토하길 바랍니다.

03 Detail Question
공지에서 설명된 변경 사유는 무엇인가?
✓ 시험 감독관 부족
Ⓑ 교육과정 요구사항의 변경
Ⓒ 시험 시설의 유지보수 문제
Ⓓ 부족한 학생들의 준비 시간

어휘 supervisor[súːpərvàizər] 감독관
     insufficient[ìnsəfíʃənt] 부족한

04 Inference Question
화자는 연기에 대해 무엇을 암시하는가?
Ⓐ 대학교의 비상 프로토콜을 따른다.
Ⓑ 시험 문제의 난이도에 영향을 줄 수 있다.
✓ 학생들에게 학업적 이점을 제공한다.
Ⓓ 추가적인 일정 문제를 야기할 수 있다.

어휘 complication[kàmpləkéiʃən] 문제

[05-06]   🎧 Nz

Listen to an announcement at a university event.

> Good morning, everyone! ⁰⁵Just a quick reminder that the Research Symposium registration deadline is this Friday at 5 P.M. ⁰⁵/⁰⁶This is your chance to showcase your academic work to faculty and potential employers. Don't miss this opportunity to build your professional network and strengthen your résumé!
>
> faculty[fǽkəlti] 교수진, 교직원   strengthen[stréŋkθən] 강화하다

대학교 행사에서의 공지를 들으시오.
좋은 아침입니다, 여러분! ⁰⁵연구 심포지엄 등록 마감이 이번 주 금요일 오후 5시라는 것을 간단히 상기시켜드립니다. ⁰⁵/⁰⁶이것은 여러분의 학업 성과를 교수진과 잠재적 고용주들에게 선보일 기회입니다. 여러분의 전문적 네트워크를 구축하고 이력서를 강화할 이 기회를 놓치지 마세요!

05 Main Purpose Question

공지의 주요 목적은 무엇인가?
Ⓐ 캠퍼스 취업박람회를 홍보하기 위해
Ⓑ 새로운 연구 지침을 설명하기 위해
Ⓒ 연구 시설의 개방을 발표하기 위해
☑ 학술 쇼케이스를 홍보하기 위해

06 Inference Question

행사에 대해 암시되는 것은?
Ⓐ 외국의 초청 연사들이 참여한다.
Ⓑ 졸업을 위해 의무적으로 참석해야 한다.
Ⓒ 등록을 위해 지도 교수의 허가가 필요하다.
☑ 대학교 외부의 사람들이 참석할 것이다.

어휘 foreign[fɔ́:rən] 외국의 approval[əprú:vəl] 허가, 승인

[07-08]

Listen to an announcement in a student lounge.

Students, please note that the student lounge will be inaccessible this Thursday because the windows are being replaced. ⁰⁷The construction crew will install energy-efficient windows as part of our university's sustainability initiative. The lounge will be completely closed while the work is in progress, so ⁰⁸please be sure to take all important belongings from the lounge lockers in advance.

inaccessible[inæksésəbl] 접근할 수 없는
sustainability[səstèinəbíləti] 지속가능성

학생 라운지에서의 공지를 들으시오.

학생 여러분, 창문 교체로 인해 이번 주 목요일에 학생 라운지에 접근할 수 없음을 알려드립니다. ⁰⁷건설팀은 우리 대학교의 지속가능성 계획의 일환으로 에너지 효율적인 창문을 설치할 예정입니다. 라운지는 공사 기간 동안 완전히 폐쇄될 예정이므로, ⁰⁸미리 라운지 사물함에서 모든 중요한 소지품을 가져가시기 바랍니다.

07 Inference Question

화자는 작업에 대해 무엇을 암시하는가?
Ⓐ 건물의 외관을 개선할 것이다.
☑ 환경적 목표를 지원한다.
Ⓒ 예산 증액이 필요할 것이다.
Ⓓ 자연 채광을 향상시킬 것이다.

어휘 appearance[əpíərəns] 외관, 외형
     enhance[inhǽns] 향상시키다

08 To Do Question

라운지 폐쇄 기간 동안 학생들은 무엇을 하라고 권고받는가?
Ⓐ 라운지에 대한 개선사항을 제안한다.
Ⓑ 시설에 대한 임시 접근을 요청한다.
☑ 소지품을 미리 챙긴다.
Ⓓ 교내에서 대안 학습 공간을 찾는다.

어휘 temporary[témpərèri] 임시의

[09-10]

Listen to an announcement at a university club meeting.

Community Service Club members, this Saturday ⁰⁹we're volunteering at the downtown food bank from 10 A.M. to 2 P.M. Tasks include sorting donations, packing food boxes, and assisting with distribution. ⁰⁹Our bus will leave from the main gate 30 minutes before our work starts. ¹⁰This is a great opportunity to have a meaningful impact in our local community while earning service hours.

sort[sɔ:rt] 분류하다; 종류 distribution[dìstrəbjú:ʃən] 배급
meaningful[mí:niŋfəl] 의미 있는 local community 지역 사회
service hours 봉사 시간

대학교 동아리 회의에서의 공지를 들으시오.

봉사 동아리 회원 여러분, 이번 주 토요일에 ⁰⁹오전 10시부터 오후 2시까지 시내 푸드 뱅크에서 자원봉사를 할 예정입니다. 업무에는 기부품 분류하기, 음식 상자 포장하기, 그리고 배급 돕기가 포함됩니다. ⁰⁹우리의 버스는 저희 일이 시작하기 30분 전에 정문에서 출발할 예정입니다. ¹⁰이것은 봉사 시간을 얻으면서 우리 지역 사회에 의미 있는 영향을 미칠 수 있는 좋은 기회입니다.

09 Detail Question

동아리원들은 출발을 위해 몇 시에 준비되어 있어야 하는가?
☑ 오전 9시 30분
Ⓑ 오전 10시
Ⓒ 오후 1시 30분
Ⓓ 오후 2시

10 Inference Question

자원봉사 기회에 대해 암시되는 것은?
Ⓐ 개별 가정에 음식을 배달하는 것을 포함한다.
Ⓑ 학생들이 참여하기 전에 특별한 훈련이 필요하다.
☑ 지역 사회와 학생들 모두에게 도움이 된다.
Ⓓ 매주 참여 의무가 있는 프로그램으로 운영된다.

어휘 involve[inválv] 포함하다
     commitment[kəmítmənt] 의무, 약속

[11-12]

Listen to an announcement in a classroom.

Good morning, everyone. Starting today, meeting with professors during office hours will be available by appointment only using our new online booking system. In other words, walk-in visits will no longer be accepted. ¹¹Please visit your department's website to schedule your meetings. ¹²This change will help ensure professors can dedicate adequate time to each student.

appointment[əpɔ́intmənt] 예약, 약속 no longer 더 이상 ~않다

ensure [inʃúər] 보장하다   dedicate [dédikèit] 할애하다
adequate [ǽdikwət] 충분한

교실에서의 공지를 들으시오.

좋은 아침입니다, 여러분. 오늘부터 교수님들과의 면담은 새로운 온라인 예약 시스템을 통해 사전 예약제로만 가능합니다. 즉, 예고 없는 방문은 더 이상 받지 않을 것입니다. ¹¹미팅을 예약하기 위해 여러분의 학과 웹사이트를 방문해 주세요. ¹²이 변화는 교수님들이 각 학생에게 충분한 시간을 할애할 수 있도록 보장하는 데 도움이 될 것입니다.

11   Intention Question
화자는 왜 학과 웹사이트를 언급하는가?
Ⓐ 잦은 방문을 권장하기 위해
Ⓑ 새로운 강의 일정을 공유하기 위해
✓ 학생들에게 예약할 페이지를 안내하기 위해
Ⓓ 연장된 상담 시간을 알리기 위해

어휘   frequent [frí:kwənt] 잦은

12   Inference Question
화자는 새로운 시스템에 대해 무엇을 암시하는가?
✓ 교수님들이 학생들에게 더 나은 서비스를 제공할 수 있게 할 것이다.
Ⓑ 기존의 이메일 소통을 완전히 대체할 것이다.
Ⓒ 더 긴 예약 대기 시간을 만들 것이다.
Ⓓ 이용 가능한 상담 시간을 줄일 것이다.

어휘   existing [igzístiŋ] 기존의   entirely [intáiərli] 완전히

[13-14]   🔊 En
Listen to an announcement in a classroom.

Good afternoon, students! I'm pleased to announce that ¹³**Professor Jimmy Jones will lead a special seminar on cognitive behavioral therapy.** This will be held on this Thursday at 2 P.M. in Hall B. This is an excellent opportunity to learn from one of the leading experts in the field. ¹⁴**The seminar will include a question-and-answer session.**

cognitive [kágnətiv] 인지적인   behavioral [bihéivjərəl] 행동의
therapy [θérəpi] 치료, 치료법   leading [lí:diŋ] 주요의, 선도적인

교실에서의 공지를 들으시오.

좋은 오후입니다, 학생 여러분! ¹³Jimmy Jones 교수님이 인지 행동 치료에 관한 특별 세미나를 진행하실 것이라는 점을 알려드리게 되어 기쁩니다. 이는 이번 주 목요일 오후 2시에 B홀에서 열릴 예정입니다. 이것은 그 분야의 주요 전문가 중 한 분으로부터 배울 수 있는 훌륭한 기회입니다. ¹⁴세미나는 질의응답 시간을 포함할 예정입니다.

13   Main Purpose Question
공지의 주요 목적은 무엇인가?
Ⓐ 목요일 강의의 장소를 변경하기 위해
Ⓑ 특별 심리학 프로그램을 홍보하기 위해
✓ 전문가의 학술 세미나를 알리기 위해
Ⓓ 인지 행동 치료 기법을 설명하기 위해

어휘   psychology [saikáːlədʒi] 심리학

14   Inference Question
행사에 대해 암시되는 것은?
Ⓐ 심리학 전공자들에게 필수일 것이다.
Ⓑ 여러 초청 연사들을 포함할 것이다.
Ⓒ 향후 참고를 위해 녹화될 것이다.
✓ 연사와의 상호작용이 포함될 것이다.

어휘   interaction [ìntərǽkʃən] 상호작용

[15-16]   🔊 Am
Listen to an announcement at a university club meeting.

Attention, astronomy lovers! ¹⁵**The Stargazing Club will invite Dr. Rachel Marie, a planetary scientist, to the university observatory next Tuesday at 7 P.M. She'll discuss recent efforts to explore Mars** and share insights about future space missions. We'll also conduct telescope observations of Jupiter after her presentation. ¹⁶**If the weather conditions are unfavorable, we will show a documentary on astronomy instead.**

observatory [əbzáːrvətɔ̀:ri] 천문대
telescope [téləskòup] 망원경, 현미경

대학교 동아리 회의에서의 공지를 들으시오.

천문학 애호가 여러분, 주목해 주세요! ¹⁵천문학 동아리에서 행성 과학자인 Rachel Marie 박사님을 다음 주 화요일 오후 7시에 대학교 천문대로 모실 예정입니다. 그녀는 최근 화성 탐사를 위한 노력에 대해 논의하고 미래 우주 임무에 대한 통찰을 공유할 예정입니다. 또한 그녀의 발표 후에 목성의 망원경 관측을 실시할 예정입니다. ¹⁶만약 날씨 상황이 좋지 않다면, 대신 천문학 다큐멘터리를 상영할 것입니다.

15   Main Topic Question
공지의 주요 주제는 무엇인가?
Ⓐ 망원경 유지보수 워크숍
Ⓑ 신규 회원을 위한 오리엔테이션
Ⓒ 우주 임무 기념식
✓ 화성 탐사에 관한 전문가의 강연

어휘   exploration [èksplərèiʃən] 탐사, 조사

16   Inference Question
화자는 망원경 관측에 대해 무엇을 암시하는가?
Ⓐ 사전 등록이 필요하다.
Ⓑ 참가자들에게 선택사항이 될 것이다.
✓ 날씨 상황에 달려 있다.
Ⓓ 대학원생들이 관리할 것이다.

어휘   optional [ápʃənl] 선택적인   depend on ~에 달려 있다
graduate student 대학원생

Section II. Announcement Topics

1. Campus Events

HACKERS TEST   p.220

01	ⓑ	02	ⓐ	03	ⓓ	04	ⓐ	05	ⓒ
06	ⓐ	07	ⓑ	08	ⓐ	09	ⓒ	10	ⓒ
11	ⓑ	12	ⓑ	13	ⓒ	14	ⓐ	15	ⓓ
16	ⓒ								

[01-02]   Au

Listen to an announcement on the school radio.

Everyone, your attention please. ⁰¹**The Campus Wellness Center is offering free flu vaccinations tomorrow from 9 A.M. to 3 P.M. in the east wing lobby.** No appointment necessary, just bring your student ID card. The process only takes about five minutes, so ⁰²**please come by and take advantage of this healthy opportunity.**

vaccination[væksənéiʃən] 예방접종
appointment[əpɔ́intmənt] 예약, 약속
necessary[nésəsèri] 필요한   take advantage of ~을 활용하다

학교 라디오에서의 공지를 들으시오.

모두 주목해 주세요. ⁰¹캠퍼스 건강 센터가 내일 오전 9시부터 오후 3시까지 동관 로비에서 무료 독감 예방접종을 제공합니다. 예약은 필요 없고, 학생증만 가져오시면 됩니다. 과정은 약 5분 정도만 걸리니, ⁰²들러서 이 건강한 기회를 활용해 주세요.

01   Main Topic Question
공지의 주요 주제는 무엇인가?
ⓐ 임시 시설 폐쇄
✓ⓑ 무료 예방접종 프로그램
ⓒ 건강 센터 이전
ⓓ 의무 건강 검진

어휘   temporary[témpərèri] 일시적인   facility[fəsíləti] 시설
closure[klóuʒər] 폐쇄   relocation[rì:loukéiʃən] 이전
mandatory[mǽndətɔ̀:ri] 의무적인
health screening 건강 검진

02   To Do Question
화자는 청자들이 무엇을 하기를 바라는가?
✓ⓐ 예방접종을 받으러 온다.
ⓑ 건강 센터에 연락한다.
ⓒ 동관 로비에서 자원봉사한다.
ⓓ 미리 예약을 한다.

어휘   volunteer[vὰ:ləntíər] 자원봉사하다; 자원봉사자
beforehand[bifɔ́:rhænd] 미리

[03-04]   Nz

Listen to an announcement at a university event.

Good morning, everyone! I'm excited to announce that our university's first vocal competition will be held this Friday at 5 P.M. in the main auditorium. ⁰³**The winner will receive a cash prize along with a golden microphone trophy!** Students from all departments are welcome to participate and showcase their vocal talents, and both solo and team entries are allowed. ⁰⁴**If you're interested, please submit your application forms through the university's mobile app before tomorrow's deadline.**

announce[ənáuns] 알리다, 공지하다
competition[kὰmpətíʃən] 경연대회
auditorium[ɔ̀:ditɔ́:riəm] 강당, 대강의실
department[dipά:rtmənt] 학과, 학부, 부서
participate[pɑ:rtísəpèit] 참여하다
showcase[ʃóukèis] 선보이다   talent[tǽlənt] 재능
entry[éntri] 참가   submit[səbmít] 제출하다
application form 지원서

대학교 행사에서의 공지를 들으시오.

좋은 아침입니다, 여러분! 우리 대학교의 첫 번째 노래 경연대회가 이번 주 금요일 오후 5시에 메인 강당에서 열릴 것을 알려드리게 되어 기쁩니다. ⁰³우승자는 황금 마이크 트로피와 함께 상금을 받게 될 것입니다! 모든 학과의 학생들이 참여하여 노래 재능을 선보이는 것을 환영하며, 솔로와 팀 참가 모두 허용됩니다. ⁰⁴관심이 있으시다면, 내일 마감일 전에 대학교 모바일 앱을 통해 지원서를 제출해 주세요.

03   Detail Question
경연대회 우승자들은 무엇을 받을 수 있는가?
ⓐ 헤드폰과 마이크
ⓑ 전문가들과 녹음할 기회
ⓒ 금메달과 리본
✓ⓓ 상금과 트로피

어휘   opportunity[ὰpərtjú:nəti] 기회

04   Intention Question
화자는 왜 대학교 모바일 앱을 언급하는가?
✓ⓐ 지원서 제출 방법을 안내하기 위해
ⓑ 행사 알림 시스템을 홍보하기 위해
ⓒ 새로운 디지털 플랫폼 기능을 광고하기 위해
ⓓ 기한 변경을 알리기 위해

어휘   indicate[índikèit] 안내하다, 나타내다
submission[səbmíʃən] 제출   method[méθəd] 방법
promote[prəmóut] 홍보하다   notification[nòutəfikéiʃən] 알림
advertise[ǽdvərtàiz] 광고하다   feature[fí:tʃər] 기능

[05-06]   Am

Listen to an announcement on the school radio.

Excuse me, everyone. ⁰⁵**I need to inform you that the Student Support Center is offering free group tutoring services for all first-year courses**

starting this week. Sessions are available Monday through Thursday from 3 to 6 P.M. We are confident that this will be a great help in adjusting to your college life, ⁰⁶**so don't miss this opportunity!**

어휘 inform[infɔ́:rm] 알리다 available[əvéiləbl] 이용 가능한
confident[kάnfədənt] 확신하는

학교 라디오에서의 공지를 들으시오.
실례합니다, 여러분. ⁰⁵학생 지원 센터에서 이번 주부터 모든 1학년 과정에 대해 무료 그룹 튜터링 서비스를 제공한다는 것을 알려드립니다. 세션은 월요일부터 목요일까지 오후 3시부터 6시까지 이용 가능합니다. 저희는 이것이 여러분의 대학 생활에 적응하는 데 큰 도움이 될 것이라고 확신합니다. ⁰⁶그러니 이 기회를 놓치지 마세요!

05 Main Topic Question
공지의 주요 주제는 무엇인가?
Ⓐ 지도 교수 미팅
Ⓑ 1학년 학생 요구사항
✓ 이용 가능한 튜터링 세션
Ⓓ 수강 신청 정보

어휘 academic advisor 지도 교수
requirement[rikwáiərmənt] 요구사항
course registration 수강 신청

06 To Do Question
학생들은 무엇을 하라고 권고받는가?
✓ 프로그램에 참여한다.
Ⓑ 수강 일정을 제출한다.
Ⓒ 개별 미팅을 예약한다.
Ⓓ 지도 교수들을 만난다.

어휘 participate in ~에 참가하다
schedule[skédʒu:l] 예약하다, 일정을 잡다
individual[ìndəvídʒuəl] 개별의

[07-08] 🔊 En
Listen to an announcement at a university event.

Ladies and gentlemen, ⁰⁷**we're thrilled to announce a last-minute addition to our university literature festival.** Award-winning poet Maya Richardson will be giving her poetry reading tomorrow at 3 P.M. in the Humanities Auditorium. She'll also have a book signing afterward. ⁰⁸**Given her rapidly growing fame since receiving an award last year, we recommend arriving early to secure a spot.**

literature[lítərətʃər] 문학, 논문 award-winning 상을 받은
poet[póuit] 시인 poetry[póuitri] 시, 운문
humanities[hju:mǽnətiz] 인문학
afterward[ǽftərwərd] 그 후에
given[gívən] ~을 고려하여, ~을 감안하면
rapidly[rǽpidli] 빠르게 fame[feim] 명성
recommend[rèkəménd] 권하다
secure[sikjúər] 확보하다; 안전한

대학교 행사에서의 공지를 들으시오.
신사 숙녀 여러분, ⁰⁷우리 대학교 문학 축제에 막판 추가된 내용을 알려드리게 되어 기쁩니다. 상을 받은 시인 Maya Richardson이 내일 오후 3시에 인문학 강당에서 시 낭독을 해줄 예정입니다. 그녀는 또한 그 후에 사인회도 가질 예정입니다. ⁰⁸지난해 상을 받은 이후에 그녀의 빠르게 증가하는 명성을 고려하여, 자리를 확보하기 위해 일찍 도착하시기를 권합니다.

07 Main Purpose Question
공지의 주요 목적은 무엇인가?
Ⓐ 대학교 미술 전시회를 광고하기 위해
✓ 다가오는 문학 행사를 홍보하기 위해
Ⓒ 문학 콘테스트의 수상자들을 발표하기 위해
Ⓓ 학생들이 그들의 시를 제출하도록 격려하기 위해

어휘 exhibition[èksəbíʃən] 전시회 publicize[pʌ́bləsàiz] 홍보하다
upcoming[ʌ́pkʌ̀miŋ] 다가오는 literary[lítərèri] 문학의
encourage[inkə́:ridʒ] 격려하다

08 Intention Question
화자는 왜 Maya Richardson의 명성을 언급하는가?
✓ 좌석을 일찍 확보하라고 권하기 위해
Ⓑ 티켓이 왜 비싼지 설명하기 위해
Ⓒ 학생들이 문학을 공부하도록 설득하기 위해
Ⓓ 참석자들이 그녀의 책을 구매하도록 설득하기 위해

어휘 convince[kənvíns] 설득하다 persuade[pərswéid] 설득하다
attendee[ətèndí:] 참석자, 방문객 purchase[pə́:rtʃəs] 구매하다

[09-10] 🔊 Au
Listen to an announcement at a university event.

Good afternoon, everyone. For tomorrow's career fair, we've arranged the employers by industry in different sections of the hall. ⁰⁹**Tech companies are in the north section, healthcare in the east, finance in the west, and education in the south.** ¹⁰**Please make sure you have your résumés ready and professional attire on before approaching the booths.**

career fair 취업박람회 arrange[əréindʒ] 배치하다
industry[índəstri] 산업, 공업 résumé[rézumèi] 이력서
attire[ətáiər] 복장

대학교 행사에서의 공지를 들으시오.
좋은 오후입니다, 여러분. 내일의 취업박람회를 위해, 우리는 홀의 각기 다른 구역에 업계별로 고용주들을 배치했습니다. ⁰⁹기술 회사들은 북쪽 구역에, 의료는 동쪽에, 금융은 서쪽에, 교육은 남쪽에 있습니다. ¹⁰부스에 접근하기 전에 반드시 이력서를 준비하고 전문적인 복장을 갖추시길 바랍니다.

09 Detail Question
금융 회사들은 어디에 위치해 있는가?
Ⓐ 북쪽 구역
Ⓑ 동쪽 구역

☑ 서쪽 구역
Ⓓ 남쪽 구역

10 Detail Question
화자는 청자들에게 무엇을 가져오라고 제안하는가?
Ⓐ 학생증
Ⓑ 추천서
☑ 이력서
Ⓓ 학업 성적 증명서

어휘 recommendation[rèkəmendéiʃən] 추천
transcript[trǽnskript] 성적 증명서

[11-12]
Listen to an announcement at a university event.

> Good afternoon, everyone! I'm excited to share that ¹¹**our annual football game will take place next Saturday at 2 P.M. at Memorial Stadium.** We're facing our longtime rival, and ¹¹**we need your energy to cheer our team to victory.** ¹²**The first 200 students will receive free T-shirts featuring our university's mascot, so hurry up if you want to get this special item!**

annual[ǽnjuəl] 연례의, 연간의 take place 열리다, 일어나다

대학교 행사에서의 공지를 들으시오.
좋은 오후입니다, 여러분! ¹¹우리의 연례 미식축구 경기가 다음 주 토요일 오후 2시에 Memorial 경기장에서 열릴 것을 알려드리게 되어 기쁩니다. 우리는 오랜 라이벌과 경기를 하며, ¹¹우리 팀이 승리할 수 있도록 응원하기 위해 여러분들의 에너지가 필요합니다. ¹²첫 200명의 학생들은 우리 대학교 마스코트가 들어간 무료 티셔츠를 받을 것이므로, 이 특별한 아이템을 원한다면 서둘러 주세요!

11 Main Purpose Question
공지의 주요 목적은 무엇인가?
Ⓐ 미식축구팀의 새로운 선수들을 모집하기 위해
☑ 캠퍼스 행사 참석을 장려하기 위해
Ⓒ 다가오는 경기를 위한 자원봉사자들을 요청하기 위해
Ⓓ 다른 학교와의 새로운 라이벌 관계를 발표하기 위해

어휘 recruit[rikrúːt] 모집하다 request[rikwést] 요청하다

12 Intention Question
화자는 왜 무료 티셔츠를 언급하는가?
Ⓐ 새로운 학교 마스코트를 소개하기 위해
☑ 학생들이 일찍 나타나도록 설득하기 위해
Ⓒ 선수들의 성과에 대해 보상하기 위해
Ⓓ 참석자들을 위한 통일된 모습을 만들기 위해

어휘 unified[júːnifàid] 통일된

[13-14]
Listen to an announcement at a university event.

> Hello students! ¹³**I'm excited to announce our Sustainability Week starting Monday.** We'll have daily workshops in the auditorium from 10 A.M. to 2 P.M., covering topics like recycling, energy saving, and sustainable eating. If you attend three or more workshops, you'll receive a free reusable water bottle. Sign-up sheets are available in the lobby on the first floor of the Engineering Building. ¹⁴**Please join us for this meaningful time!**

sustainability[səstèinəbíləti] 지속가능성
reusable[riúːzəbəl] 재사용의, 재사용 가능한
engineering[èndʒəníəriŋ] 공학
meaningful[míːniŋfəl] 의미 있는

대학교 행사에서의 공지를 들으시오.
학생 여러분 안녕하세요! ¹³월요일부터 시작하는 우리의 지속가능성 주간을 발표하게 되어 기쁩니다. 우리는 오전 10시부터 오후 2시까지 강당에서 재활용, 에너지 절약, 그리고 지속가능한 식습관과 같은 주제들을 다루는 워크숍을 매일 가질 것입니다. 세 개 이상의 워크숍에 참석하시면, 무료 재사용 물병을 받으실 것입니다. 신청서는 공학관 1층 로비에 있습니다. ¹⁴이 의미 있는 시간에 우리와 함께 해주세요!

13 Main Purpose Question
공지의 주요 목적은 무엇인가?
Ⓐ 캠퍼스 행사를 위한 자원봉사자들을 요청하기 위해
Ⓑ 학생들에게 무료 물병을 배포하기 위해
☑ 환경 인식 활동들에 대해 알리기 위해
Ⓓ 행사의 장소 변경을 발표하기 위해

어휘 distribute[distríbjuːt] 배포하다

14 To Do Question
화자는 청자들이 무엇을 하기를 바라는가?
☑ 예정된 워크숍에 등록한다.
Ⓑ 다른 학생들에게 행사를 홍보한다.
Ⓒ 지속가능한 식습관을 실천한다.
Ⓓ 워크숍을 위해 자원봉사한다.

어휘 practice[prǽktis] 실천하다, 연습하다 eating habits 식습관

[15-16]
Listen to an announcement at a university event.

> Good evening, everyone! ¹⁵**We're pleased to announce that this year's spring music festival will take place next Friday at 7 P.M. in the main auditorium.** Several student bands and our university orchestra will be performing a wide range of music from classical to contemporary. ¹⁶**Admission fee is five dollars, but it's free for students who bring their student ID card.** We hope to see you there for a night of incredible music!

several [sévərəl] 여러 a wide range of 다양한 범위의
admission fee 입장료 incredible [inkrédəbl] 놀라운, 굉장한

material [mətíəriəl] 자료, 소재 sign up 신청하다, 등록하다
Student Affairs 학생처

대학교 행사에서의 공지를 들으시오.

좋은 저녁입니다, 여러분! ¹⁵올해의 봄 음악 축제가 다음 주 금요일 오후 7시에 메인 강당에서 열릴 것을 발표하게 되어 기쁩니다. 여러 학생 밴드들과 우리 대학교 오케스트라가 클래식부터 현대음악까지 다양한 범위의 음악을 연주할 예정입니다. ¹⁶입장료는 5달러이지만, 학생증을 가져오는 학생들에게는 무료입니다. 놀라운 음악의 밤에 그곳에서 여러분들을 만나기를 바랍니다!

학생 회의에서의 공지를 들으시오.

안녕하세요 여러분, 오늘 와주셔서 감사합니다. ⁰¹우리는 10월 12일에서 14일까지 Wildwood 캠프에서 예정된 가을 리더십 수련회의 계획을 마무리하고 있습니다. 올해의 주제는 "내일의 리더 만들기"입니다. 등록 비용은 45달러이며 식사, 숙박, 그리고 자료들이 포함됩니다. 마감일은 10월 5일이고, 우리의 학생 포털이나 학생처 사무실에서 신청할 수 있습니다.

15 Main Topic Question

공지의 주요 주제는 무엇인가?
Ⓐ 콘서트 일정의 변경
Ⓑ 학술 회의
Ⓒ 학생 밴드 오디션
☑ 다가오는 음악 행사

01 Main Topic Question

공지의 주요 주제는 무엇인가?
Ⓐ 학생 포털 업데이트
Ⓑ 사무실 건물 보수
☑ 리더십 훈련 행사
Ⓓ Wildwood 캠프 시설들

어휘 renovation [rènəvéiʃən] 보수

16 Intention Question

화자는 왜 신분증을 언급하는가?
Ⓐ 학점 인정을 위한 참여 여부를 기록하기 위해
Ⓑ 대학교의 신분증 시스템을 홍보하기 위해
☑ 학생들의 무료 입장을 가능하게 하기 위해
Ⓓ 행사에서 보안을 보장하기 위해

어휘 track [træk] 기록하다, 추적하다
      participation [pɑ:rtìsəpéiʃən] 참여 ensure [inʃúər] 보장하다

02 Intention Question

화자는 왜 학생처 사무실을 언급하는가?
☑ 등록 장소를 언급하기 위해
Ⓑ 수련회가 어디에서 열릴지 보여주기 위해
Ⓒ 학생들에게 어디에서 결제할지 말해주기 위해
Ⓓ 등록 문제를 어디에 신고할지 설명하기 위해

어휘 mention [ménʃən] 언급하다
      report [ripɔ́:rt] 신고하다, 보고하다; 보고서

[03-04] En

Listen to an announcement at a university event.

Hi everyone! Just a quick reminder about our short-story competition. ⁰³Remember, your stories should cover the "friendship" theme in some way, and the deadline is the end of November. The submission portal is now open on our website, so ⁰⁴you can upload your work whenever it's ready. Don't leave it until the last minute!

theme [θi:m] 주제

2. Student Activities

HACKERS TEST   p.228

01 Ⓒ	02 Ⓐ	03 Ⓓ	04 Ⓐ	05 Ⓑ
06 Ⓐ	07 Ⓓ	08 Ⓑ	09 Ⓓ	10 Ⓓ
11 Ⓓ	12 Ⓒ	13 Ⓓ	14 Ⓒ	15 Ⓒ
16 Ⓑ				

[01-02] Am

Listen to an announcement at a student meeting.

Hey everyone, thanks for coming today. ⁰¹We're finalizing plans for the Fall Leadership Retreat scheduled from October 12 to 14 at Camp Wildwood. This year's theme is "Building Tomorrow's Leaders." Registration costs 45 dollars and includes meals, lodging, and materials. ⁰²The deadline is October 5th, and you can sign up through our student portal or at the Student Affairs office.

finalize [fáinəlàiz] 결말을 짓다, 최종적으로 승인하다
retreat [ritrí:t] 수련회 include [inklú:d] 포함하다

대학교 행사에서의 공지를 들으시오.

안녕하세요 여러분! 우리 단편소설 경연대회에 대해 간단히 상기시켜 드립니다. ⁰³기억하세요, 여러분들의 이야기는 어떤 식으로든 "우정" 주제를 다루어야 하고, 마감일은 11월 말입니다. 제출 포털이 현재 우리 웹사이트에서 열려 있으니, ⁰⁴작품이 준비되는 대로 언제든지 업로드할 수 있습니다. 마지막 순간까지 미루지 마세요!

03 Main Purpose Question

공지의 주요 목적은 무엇인가?
Ⓐ 글쓰기 대회의 우승자들을 축하하기 위해
Ⓑ 제출 마감일의 연기를 발표하기 위해
Ⓒ 월간 모임의 새로운 주제를 제안하기 위해
☑ 경연대회의 제출 지침을 설명하기 위해

어휘 suggest[səgdʒést] 제안하다

04 To Do Question
학생들은 무엇을 하라고 권고받는가?
Ⓐ 인쇄된 사본을 가져온다.
Ⓑ 여러 이야기를 제출한다.
✓ⓒ 출품을 완료한다.
Ⓓ 워크숍에 참석한다.

어휘 multiple[mʌ́ltipəl] 여러 entry[éntri] 출품, 출품작

[05-06] Am
Listen to an announcement at a university club meeting.

> Now, let's begin our weekly Tennis Club meeting. ⁰⁵**I'm pleased to announce that our application to host the Inter-University Tennis Tournament has been approved.** The tournament will be held on October 15th and 16th here at our campus tennis court. ⁰⁶**The winner will receive a custom tennis racket engraved with their name.** If you're confident in your skills, go ahead and take on the challenge!
>
> approve[əprúːv] 승인하다 custom[kʌ́stəm] 맞춤형의
> engrave[ingréiv] 새기다 confident[kánfədənt] 자신 있는

대학교 동아리 회의에서의 공지를 들으시오.
자, 이제 우리의 주간 테니스 동아리 모임을 시작하겠습니다. ⁰⁵대학 간 테니스 경기를 개최하겠다는 우리의 신청이 승인되었다고 발표하게 되어 기쁩니다. 경기는 10월 15일과 16일에 우리 교내 테니스 코트에서 열릴 예정입니다. ⁰⁶우승자는 그들의 이름이 새겨진 맞춤형 테니스 라켓을 받을 것입니다. 여러분의 실력에 자신이 있다면, 도전해보세요!

05 Main Topic Question
공지의 주요 주제는 무엇인가?
Ⓐ 테니스 장비 판매
✓Ⓑ 대학교 스포츠 행사
ⓒ 테니스 수업 일정
Ⓓ 코트 유지보수 공지

어휘 equipment[ikwípmənt] 장비
     maintenance[méintənəns] 유지보수

06 Detail Question
우승자들은 상으로 무엇을 받을 수 있는가?
✓Ⓐ 특별한 테니스 라켓
Ⓑ 테니스 모자
ⓒ 현금 상금
Ⓓ 트로피와 메달

[07-08] Nz
Listen to an announcement in a classroom.

> ⁰⁷**I'd like to let everyone know that the deadline for applying to the university's study abroad program for next semester is October 1st.** ⁰⁸**Information sessions will be held this Wednesday and Thursday at noon in Room 302.** These programs fill up quickly, so don't hesitate if you're interested.
>
> study abroad program 해외 연수 프로그램
> semester[siméstər] 학기 noon[nuːn] 정오
> hesitate[hézəteit] 망설이다

교실에서의 공지를 들으시오.
⁰⁷다음 학기 대학교의 해외 연수 프로그램에 지원하는 마감일이 10월 1일이라는 것을 모든 분들께 알려드리고자 합니다. ⁰⁸정보 설명회가 이번 수요일과 목요일 정오에 302호실에서 열릴 예정입니다. 이러한 프로그램들은 자리가 빨리 차므로, 관심이 있으시다면 망설이지 마세요.

07 Main Topic Question
공지의 주요 주제는 무엇인가?
Ⓐ 언어 숙달 시험 등록
Ⓑ 국제학생 오리엔테이션
ⓒ 졸업 요건 업데이트
✓Ⓓ 해외 연수 지원 마감일

어휘 proficiency[prəfíʃənsi] 숙달, 능숙
     international[intərnǽʃənl] 국제적인
     graduation requirement 졸업 요건
     application[æpləkéiʃən] 지원 due date 마감일

08 Intention Question
화자는 왜 302호실을 언급하는가?
Ⓐ 학생들에게 장소 변경을 알리기 위해
✓Ⓑ 행사가 열릴 장소를 명시하기 위해
ⓒ 지원서를 제출할 곳을 보여 주기 위해
Ⓓ 스터디 그룹이 이용 가능한 공간을 보여주기 위해

어휘 specify[spésəfài] 명시하다, 구체화하다

[09-10] Am
Listen to an announcement at a university club meeting.

> Attention Chess Club members! ⁰⁹**I'm pleased to inform you that we've finally received funding for new chess equipment.** So, we'll be purchasing ten tournament-quality chess sets and five digital chess clocks. ¹⁰**If anyone has suggestions for specific brands or models, please email me by this Sunday so I can place the order next week.**
>
> finally[fáinəli] 드디어, 마침내 funding[fʌ́ndiŋ] 자금, 지원

대학교 동아리 회의에서의 공지를 들으시오.
체스 동아리 회원들 주목하세요! ⁰⁹우리가 드디어 새로운 체스 장비를 위한 자금을 받았다고 알려드리게 되어 기쁩니다. 그래서, 우리는 토너먼트급 체스 세트 10개와 디지털 체스 시계 5개를 구매할 예정입니다. ¹⁰특정 브랜드나 모델에 대한 제안이 있으시다면, 다음 주에 주문을 할 수 있도록 이번 일요일까지 저에게 이메일을 보내주세요.

09 Main Purpose Question

공지의 주요 목적은 무엇인가?
Ⓐ 체스 대회를 조직하기 위해
Ⓑ 토너먼트 날짜를 변경하기 위해
Ⓒ 체스 경기 기술을 시연하기 위해
☑ 새로운 장비를 살 계획을 발표하기 위해

어휘 demonstrate [démənstrèit] 시연하다, 보여주다
technique [tekní:k] 기술, 기법

10 To Do Question

화자는 청자들이 무엇을 하기를 바라는가?
Ⓐ 배송비를 나누어 낸다.
Ⓑ 다음 토너먼트에 참석한다.
Ⓒ 장비 공급업체에 연락한다.
☑ 장비 브랜드를 추천한다.

어휘 supplier [səpláiər] 공급업체, 공급자

[11-12]　　　　　　　　　　　　　Au

Listen to an announcement at a university club meeting.

> Welcome to the Robotics Club's weekly meeting! I need to share some important details about the regional robotics competition at the end of the month. ¹¹**All teams who want to participate should submit complete blueprints**, and the deadline is August 5th. ¹²**The winning team will receive funding for next semester's projects.** Let's aim for the winner to be from our club!
>
> blueprint [blú:prìnt] 설계도

대학교 동아리 회의에서의 공지를 들으시오.

로봇공학 동아리의 주간 모임에 오신 것을 환영합니다! 이달 말 지역 로봇공학 경연대회에 대한 몇 가지 중요한 세부사항을 공유해야 합니다. ¹¹참여하고 싶은 모든 팀들은 완전한 설계도를 제출해야 하고, 마감일은 8월 5일입니다. ¹²우승팀은 다음 학기 프로젝트들을 위한 자금을 받을 것입니다. 우승자가 우리 동아리에서 나오도록 목표해봅시다!

11 Detail Question

화자는 완전한 설계도에 대해 어떤 점을 언급하는가?
Ⓐ 업계 전문가들에 의해 검토될 것이다.
Ⓑ 다음 모임에서 자세히 논의될 것이다.
Ⓒ 성공적인 이전 프로젝트들의 예시를 보여준다.
☑ 대회를 위한 필수 제출물이다.

어휘 in detail 자세히　previous [prí:viəs] 이전의

12 Detail Question

우승팀은 상으로 무엇을 받을 수 있는가?
Ⓐ 다음 학기 등록금 면제
Ⓑ 전국 대회 자동 진출권
☑ 미래 프로젝트들을 위한 재정적 지원
Ⓓ 전문적인 멘토십 기회

어휘 exemption [igzémpʃən] 면제　tuition fee 등록금, 수업료

automatic [ɔ̀:təmǽtik] 자동의　financial [fainǽnʃəl] 재정적인

[13-14]　　　　　　　　　　　　　Am

Listen to an announcement at a university club meeting.

> I'm excited to share some great news with you. ¹³**Our Environmental Club's proposal for a campus-wide recycling initiative has been officially approved by the administration!** Starting next month, new recycling stations will be installed in every building. ¹⁴**We're now looking for volunteers to assist with the installation and to help create promotional flyers.** If you're interested, please email me by this Friday.
>
> environmental [invàiərənméntl] 환경의
> proposal [prəpóuzəl] 제안　initiative [iníʃiətiv] 계획
> administration [ədminəstréiʃən] 행정부
> promotional flyer 홍보 전단지

대학교 동아리 회의에서의 공지를 들으시오.

여러분께 좋은 소식을 공유하게 되어 기쁩니다. ¹³우리 환경 동아리의 캠퍼스 전체 재활용 계획에 대한 제안이 행정부에 의해 공식적으로 승인되었습니다! 다음 달부터 새로운 재활용 시설들이 모든 건물에 설치될 것입니다. ¹⁴우리는 지금 설치를 도와줄 자원봉사자들과 홍보 전단지 제작을 도와줄 자원봉사자들을 찾고 있습니다. 관심이 있으시다면, 이번 주 금요일까지 저에게 이메일을 보내주세요.

13 Main Purpose Question

공지의 주요 목적은 무엇인가?
Ⓐ 동아리의 새로운 회원들을 모집하기 위해
Ⓑ 환경 인식 개선 캠페인을 시작하기 위해
Ⓒ 캠퍼스에서 재활용의 이점을 설명하기 위해
☑ 동아리 제안의 승인을 알리기 위해

어휘 launch [lɔ:ntʃ] 시작하다, 개시하다　awareness [əwɛ́ərnis] 인식
benefit [bénəfit] 이점, 이익

14 To Do Question

화자는 청자들이 무엇을 하기를 바라는가?
Ⓐ 소셜 미디어에서 계획을 홍보한다.
Ⓑ 새로운 환경 제안서들을 개발한다.
☑ 캠퍼스 재활용 노력에 참여한다.
Ⓓ 새로운 재활용 장소의 사용을 감독한다.

어휘 monitor [mánətər] 감독하다

[15-16]　　　　　　　　　　　　　Nz

Listen to an announcement at a university club meeting.

> Hi everyone. ¹⁵**I'm pleased to let you know that our Photography Club has secured permission to hold our annual exhibition in the main university gallery this year!** ¹⁶**This is a significant upgrade from our usual space in the Student Center.** The exhibition will run from October 15th to October 30th. If

you want to submit photos, the deadline is October 1st. Each member can submit up to three photographs. Let's make this our best exhibition yet!

permission[pərmíʃən] 허가 significant[signífikənt] 상당한
student center 학생회관

대학교 동아리 회의에서의 공지를 들으시오.

안녕하세요 여러분. ¹⁵우리 사진 동아리가 올해 대학교의 메인 갤러리에서 연례 전시회를 개최할 수 있는 허가를 받았다는 것을 알려드리게 되어 기쁩니다! ¹⁶이것은 우리의 평소 공간인 학생회관에 비해 상당한 업그레이드입니다. 전시회는 10월 15일부터 10월 30일까지 진행될 예정입니다. 사진을 제출하고 싶으시다면, 마감일은 10월 1일입니다. 각 회원은 최대 세 장의 사진을 제출할 수 있습니다. 이번 전시회를 우리의 최고의 전시회로 만들어봅시다!

15 Main Topic Question
공지의 주요 주제는 무엇인가?
Ⓐ 새로운 사진 대회
Ⓑ 사진 장비의 구매
☑ 연례 사진 전시회
Ⓓ 갱신된 회원 요건

어휘 updated[ʌ̀pdéitid] 갱신된

16 Intention Question
화자는 왜 학생회관을 언급하는가?
Ⓐ 전시회가 열리는 장소를 보여 주기 위해
☑ 동아리가 이룬 발전을 보여주기 위해
Ⓒ 등록이 이루어질 장소를 설명하기 위해
Ⓓ 추가 정보를 찾을 수 있는 곳을 알리기 위해

어휘 illustrate[íləstrèit] 보여주다, 설명하다
progress[prágres] 발전, 진전
describe[diskráib] 설명하다, 기술하다 advise[ədváiz] 알리다
additional[ədíʃənl] 추가의

3. Lectures & Facilities

HACKERS TEST   p.236

01 Ⓑ	02 Ⓒ	03 Ⓓ	04 Ⓑ	05 Ⓓ
06 Ⓓ	07 Ⓒ	08 Ⓑ	09 Ⓓ	10 Ⓒ
11 Ⓒ	12 Ⓑ	13 Ⓓ	14 Ⓑ	15 Ⓓ
16 Ⓐ

[01-02]   Am

Listen to an announcement in a student lounge.

Attention everyone! ⁰¹**The student lounge will be closed this weekend for an electrical inspection.** ⁰²**You can use the west wing study area or the library's third floor as alternatives during this time.** Thank you for your understanding.

student lounge 학생 라운지 electrical[ilέktrikəl] 전기의
inspection[inspέkʃən] 점검
alternative[ɔːltə́ːrnətiv] 대안, 다른 방도

학생 라운지에서의 공지를 들으시오.

여러분 주목하세요! ⁰¹학생 라운지가 전기 점검으로 인해 이번 주말에 문을 닫을 것입니다. ⁰²이 시간 동안 서관 학습 공간이나 도서관 3층을 대안으로 이용하실 수 있습니다. 양해해 주셔서 감사합니다.

01 Detail Question
공지에서 설명된 라운지 폐쇄의 이유는 무엇인가?
Ⓐ 긴급 안전 수리
☑ 전기 점검
Ⓒ 와이파이 시스템 유지보수
Ⓓ 정기 주말 유지보수

어휘 emergency[imə́ːrdʒənsi] 긴급의

02 To Do Question
공지에 따라 학생들은 무엇을 하라고 권고받는가?
Ⓐ 대신 야외에서 공부한다.
Ⓑ 유지보수 작업에 자원한다.
☑ 대안적인 학습 공간들을 이용한다.
Ⓓ 주말 계획을 재조정한다.

어휘 reschedule[rìːskédʒuːl] 재조정하다, 일정을 변경하다

[03-04]   Au

Listen to an announcement in a classroom.

Attention, students! ⁰³**We have a special guest lecture by Dr. Victor Davidson**, the environmental policy expert, this Friday at 2 P.M. right here in this classroom. He will be discussing climate legislation for about an hour. ⁰⁴**There will be a Q&A session afterward, so prepare your questions in advance.** Attendance will be counted toward your participation grade.

guest lecture 초청 강연 policy[páləsi] 정책, 규정
legislation[lèdʒisléiʃən] 법률, 법령 in advance 미리, 앞서서

교실에서의 공지를 들으시오.

학생 여러분 주목하세요! 환경 정책 전문가인 ⁰³Victor Davidson 박사님의 특별 초청 강연이 이번 금요일 오후 2시에 바로 이 교실에서 있습니다. 그는 약 한 시간 동안 기후 관련 법률에 대해 논의할 것입니다. ⁰⁴이후에 질의응답 시간이 있을 예정이니, 미리 질문을 준비해 두세요. 출석은 여러분의 참여 점수에 포함될 것입니다.

03 Main Purpose Question
공지의 주요 목적은 무엇인가?
Ⓐ 새로운 지도교수를 소개하기 위해
Ⓑ 학생들에게 출석 요건을 알리기 위해
Ⓒ 캠퍼스 환경 계획을 홍보하기 위해

✓ 다가오는 학술 행사를 알리기 위해

어휘 notify[nóutəfài] 알리다   attendance[əténdəns] 출석
      publicize[pʌ́bləsàiz] 홍보하다

04 Intention Question

화자는 왜 질의응답 시간을 언급하는가?
Ⓐ 강연이 평소보다 길어질 이유를 설명하기 위해
✓ 학생들에게 미리 질문을 만들어 두라고 조언하기 위해
Ⓒ 참여 점수가 어떻게 계산될지 보여주기 위해
Ⓓ 학생들의 행사 참여를 독려하기 위해

어휘 formulate[fɔ́ːrmjulèit] 만들다, 공식화하다
      inquiry[ínkwəri] 질문, 문의
      calculate[kǽlkjulèit] 계산하다, 평가하다

[05-06]   🔊 Am

Listen to an announcement in a classroom.

I'm pleased to inform you that next week's class will be held in the university's new Digital Media Lab instead of our regular classroom. ⁰⁵This will give you hands-on experience with the equipment we've been discussing. Please arrive on time as we'll need the entire period for our activities. ⁰⁶Don't forget to bring your student ID to access the building!

instead of ~ 대신에   hands-on 실습의, 직접 해보는
entire[intáiər] 전체의

교실에서의 공지를 들으시오.
다음 주 수업이 우리의 정규 교실 대신 대학교의 새로운 디지털 미디어 연구실에서 열릴 것이라는 것을 알려드리게 되어 기쁩니다. ⁰⁵이것은 우리가 논의해왔던 장비들에 대한 실습 경험을 제공할 것입니다. 우리의 활동을 위해 전체 시간이 온전히 필요하므로 시간에 맞춰 도착해 주세요. ⁰⁶건물에 출입하기 위해 학생증을 가져오는 것을 잊지 마세요!

05 Detail Question

공지에서 설명된 변경의 이유는 무엇인가?
Ⓐ 날씨 관련 우려
Ⓑ 캠퍼스 건설 작업
Ⓒ 장비 유지보수 문제
✓ 체험 학습 기회

어휘 construction[kənstrʌ́kʃən] 건설
      experiential[ikspìəriénʃəl] 체험의, 실험의

06 Suggestion Question

화자는 구성원들에게 무엇을 가져오라고 제안하는가?
Ⓐ USB 저장 드라이브
Ⓑ 디지털 미디어 프로젝트
Ⓒ 완성된 과제
✓ 개인 신분증

어휘 assignment[əsáinmənt] 과제, 숙제
      identification card 신분증

[07-08]   🔊 Nz

Listen to an announcement in a student lounge.

Attention, everyone using the student lounge. ⁰⁷Starting next week, we'll be extending our hours until midnight from Sunday through Thursday to provide longer study hours during midterm season. The coffee shop inside the lounge will also remain open until 11 P.M. on these nights. ⁰⁸Please remember to clean up after yourselves so we can keep the space tidy for everyone.

extend[iksténd] 연장하다   midnight[mídnàit] 자정, 한밤중
tidy[táidi] 깔끔한

학생 라운지에서의 공지를 들으시오.
학생 라운지를 사용하는 모든 분들 주목하세요. ⁰⁷다음 주부터, 중간고사 기간동안 더 긴 학습 시간을 제공하기 위해 일요일부터 목요일까지 자정까지 운영시간을 연장합니다. 라운지 내부의 커피숍도 이 기간에는 오후 11시까지 열려 있을 것입니다. ⁰⁸모든 사람을 위해 공간을 깔끔하게 유지할 수 있도록 사용하신 뒤에는 정리하는 것을 기억해 주시기 바랍니다.

07 Main Topic Question

공지의 주요 주제는 무엇인가?
Ⓐ 라운지 폐쇄
Ⓑ 청소 일정
✓ 라운지 운영시간의 변경
Ⓓ 커피숍 메뉴 변경

08 To Do Question

학생들은 무엇을 하라고 권고받는가?
Ⓐ 소음 수준을 낮게 유지한다.
✓ 쓰레기를 제대로 처리한다.
Ⓒ 직원에게 어떤 문제든 신고한다.
Ⓓ 떠날 때 불을 끈다.

어휘 dispose of ~을 처리하다   properly[prápərli] 제대로, 적절하게

[09-10]   🔊 Am

Listen to an announcement in a classroom.

Before we end today's class, ⁰⁹I want to remind everyone that your midterm papers are due next Monday by midnight through the online submission system. ¹⁰Make sure you follow the formatting guidelines in the syllabus: twelve-point font, double-spaced, with proper citations. I won't accept late submissions except for documented emergencies, so please plan accordingly. My office hours this week are extended until 5 P.M. if anyone needs help.

syllabus[síləbəs] 강의계획서   proper[prápər] 적절한
citation[saitéiʃən] 인용   except for ~을 제외하고
accordingly[əkɔ́ːrdiŋli] 그에 따라

교실에서의 공지를 들으시오.

오늘 수업을 마치기 전에, ⁰⁹여러분의 중간 보고서가 다음 주 월요일 자정까지 온라인 제출 시스템을 통해 제출되어야 한다는 것을 모든 분들께 상기시키고 싶습니다. ¹⁰강의계획서에 있는 형식 지침인 12포인트 글꼴, 더블 스페이스, 적절한 인용을 따르도록 하세요. 증빙 서류가 있는 응급상황을 제외하고는 늦은 제출을 받지 않을 것이므로, 그에 따라 계획해 주세요. 도움이 필요하다면 이번 주 제 상담시간은 오후 5시까지 연장되어 있습니다.

09 Main Purpose Question

공지의 주요 목적은 무엇인가?
Ⓐ 수업을 위한 새로운 과제를 소개하기 위해
Ⓑ 학생들에게 연장된 상담시간을 알리기 위해
Ⓒ 제출 형식의 변경을 발표하기 위해
☑ 학생들에게 중간 보고서 마감일을 상기시키기 위해

10 Intention Question

화자는 왜 강의계획서를 언급하는가?
Ⓐ 학생들에게 출석 정책을 검토하라고 제안하기 위해
Ⓑ 온라인에서 강의 자료에 접근하는 방법을 설명하기 위해
☑ 학생들에게 보고서 형식 기준을 안내하기 위해
Ⓓ 강의에 최근 이루어진 변경사항들을 강조하기 위해

어휘 course material 강의 자료 standard[stǽndərd] 기준
highlight[háilàit] 강조하다

[11-12]

Listen to an announcement in a student lounge.

Attention, everyone! ¹¹**The student lounge will be temporarily closed due to construction work.** ¹²**They're adding a coffee shop, and the administration is asking for your feedback on potential menus.** You just need to visit the school website to vote. The three most voted options will be included when the coffee shop opens! Please take a moment to share your preferences.

potential[pəténʃəl] 후보의, 잠재적인
preference[préfərəns] 선호, 선호도

학생 라운지에서의 공지를 들으시오.

여러분 주목하세요! ¹¹학생 라운지는 공사 작업으로 인해 임시적으로 문을 닫을 것입니다. ¹²커피숍을 추가하고 있으며, 행정부는 후보 메뉴에 대한 여러분들의 피드백을 요청합니다. 여러분은 투표하기 위해 학교 웹사이트를 방문하기만 하면 됩니다. 가장 많은 표를 받은 세 가지 옵션이 커피숍이 개장할 때 포함될 것입니다! 여러분들의 선호를 공유하기 위해 잠시 시간을 내어 주세요.

11 Main Topic Question

공지는 무엇에 관한 것인가?
Ⓐ 구내식당의 보수 지연
Ⓑ 학생 만족도에 대한 설문조사
☑ 학생 시설의 공사
Ⓓ 시내에서의 새로운 커피숍 개장

어휘 satisfaction[sæ̀tisfǽkʃən] 만족도

12 To Do Question

라운지 폐쇄 기간 동안 학생들은 무엇을 하라고 권고받는가?
Ⓐ 새로운 커피숍의 일자리에 지원한다.
☑ 온라인 투표 시스템에 참여한다.
Ⓒ 라운지 재설계를 위한 의견을 제공한다.
Ⓓ 임시적으로 대안 캠퍼스 시설들을 이용한다.

어휘 apply for ~에 지원하다 contribute[kəntríbju:t] 제공하다
re-design[rì:dizáin] 재설계

[13-14]

Listen to an announcement in a classroom.

¹³**I'd like to inform everyone that we've secured Dr. Thompson as our keynote speaker for next month's leadership conference.** He's a renowned expert in organizational psychology and will speak about effective team management. ¹⁴**Registration opens next Monday on our website**, and the first 50 students to register will receive a free copy of Dr. Thompson's latest book.

keynote speaker 기조연설자
renowned[rináund] 저명한, 유명한
expert[ékspə:rt] 전문가; 숙련된
organizational psychology 조직 심리학
effective[iféktiv] 효과적인 latest[léitist] 최신의

교실에서의 공지를 들으시오.

¹³다음 달 리더십 회의 기조연설자로 Thompson 박사님을 확보했다는 것을 모든 분들께 알려드리고 싶습니다. 그는 조직 심리학의 저명한 전문가이며 효과적인 팀 관리에 대해 연설할 것입니다. ¹⁴등록은 다음 주 월요일에 우리 웹사이트에서 시작되며, 등록하는 첫 50명의 학생들은 Thompson 박사님의 최신 저서 한 권을 무료로 받을 것입니다.

13 Main Topic Question

공지의 주요 주제는 무엇인가?
Ⓐ 책 사인회 행사
Ⓑ 등록 마감일
☑ 리더십 회의
Ⓓ 심리학 강의 수강 신청

어휘 enrollment[inróulmənt] 등록

14 Intention Question

화자는 왜 웹사이트를 언급하는가?
Ⓐ 연설자 자격을 설명하기 위해
☑ 등록 정보를 제공하기 위해
Ⓒ 컨퍼런스 장소에 대한 세부사항을 공유하기 위해
Ⓓ 디지털 컨퍼런스 자료를 배포하기 위해

어휘 qualification[kwὰ:ləfikéiʃən] 자격

[15-16]

🔊 Au

Listen to an announcement in a classroom.

Attention, students. There has been a change to next week's class location. Instead of our regular classroom, we'll be meeting in the computer lab in Room 302. **¹⁵Since you'll be working on the data analysis portion of your research projects, I've made sure you all have access to the statistical software.** **¹⁶Please bring your data sets and research questions with you.** Don't forget, it's room 302 next Wednesday.

analysis[ənǽləsis] 분석   statistical[stətístikəl] 통계의

교실에서의 공지를 들으시오.

주목해주세요, 학생 여러분. 다음 주 수업 장소에 변경이 있습니다. 기존 강의실 대신, 302호 컴퓨터 실습실에서 만날 것입니다. ¹⁵여러분이 연구 프로젝트의 데이터 분석 부분을 진행할 예정이므로, 모두가 통계 소프트웨어를 사용할 수 있도록 했습니다. ¹⁶여러분의 데이터 세트와 연구 질문들을 가져와 주세요. 잊지 마세요, 다음 수요일은 302호입니다.

15   Detail Question

공지에서 설명된 변경의 이유는 무엇인가?
Ⓐ 초청 강연
Ⓑ 일정 충돌
Ⓒ 시설 유지보수
☑ 소프트웨어 접근 필요

어휘   conflict[kɑ́nflikt] 충돌, 갈등

16   Detail Question

화자는 학생들이 무엇을 가져와야 한다고 강조하는가?
☑ 프로젝트 데이터
Ⓑ 강의계획서
Ⓒ 참고 도서
Ⓓ 학생증

어휘   reference[réfərəns] 참고

TASK 4 | Listen to an Academic Talk

Section I. Question Types

1. Main Topic/Purpose Questions

Example 🎧 Nz   p.247

> 오늘 우리는 부화 후 새의 발달에 대해 논의하려고 합니다. 구체적으로, 우리는 부화한 새의 두 범주인 조숙성과 만숙성 새끼에 대해 이야기할 것입니다. 이미 논의했듯이, 대부분의 새들은 알에서 생명을 시작하고 부화라고 불리는 과정을 통해 세상에 나옵니다. 음, 그것은 알을 먹는 우리 누구에게나 충분히 명백해 보이지만, 새끼들이 부화한 후에는 무엇이 일어날까요? 그것은 그들이 어떤 종류의 새인지에 달려 있습니다.
>
> development[divéləpmənt] 발달, 개발 hatch[hætʃ] 부화하다

강의는 주로 무엇에 대한 것인가?
ⓐ 부화 전 새 배아의 형성
ⓑ 알을 낳는 동물의 진화
✓ⓒ 두 가지 유형의 새끼 발달
ⓓ 각 부화 전략의 생존 우위

어휘 embryo[émbriòu] 배아 evolution[èvəlúːʃən] 진화

HACKERS PRACTICE   p.248

01 Ⓐ   02 Ⓒ   03 Ⓓ   04 Ⓑ

01 Main Topic Question 🎧 En

> **Let's explore more about enzymes**. Enzymes are proteins that act as biological catalysts. In other words, they help complex reactions occur within all living organisms. **Essentially, what they do is they increase the speed of a chemical reaction.** Now, to help you understand what an enzyme does, I'd like to look a little more closely into the actual process of how an enzyme works.
>
> enzyme[énzaim] 효소   biological[bàiəládʒikəl] 생물학적인
> catalyst[kǽtəlist] 촉매   occur[əkə́ːr] 일어나다
> chemical[kémikəl] 화학의

효소에 대해 더 살펴보겠습니다. 효소는 생물학적 촉매 역할을 하는 단백질입니다. 다시 말해, 효소는 모든 생명체 내에서 복잡한 반응이 일어나도록 도와줍니다. 본질적으로, 효소가 하는 일은 화학 반응의 속도를 높이는 것입니다. 이제 효소가 실제로 무엇을 하는지 여러분이 이해할 수 있도록, 효소가 작용하는 실제 과정을 좀 더 자세히 살펴보고자 합니다.

강의는 주로 무엇에 대한 것인가?
✓ⓐ 효소 작용의 메커니즘
ⓑ 효소 기능의 발견
ⓒ 산업에서의 효소 응용
ⓓ 다양한 종류의 생물학적 물질

어휘 discovery[diskʌ́vəri] 발견 function[fʌ́ŋkʃən] 기능; 기능하다
application[æ̀pləkéiʃən] 응용, 적용
substance[sʌ́bstəns] 물질, 재질, 재료

02 Main Topic Question 🎧 Am

> A lot of the traditional arts by Native North Americans <u>have been collected and traded</u> over the centuries by European travelers. **These artworks were also <u>refashioned to suit</u> the public's taste in art.** Originally, they were produced in a completely different cultural context. In some cases, native people gave a blanket or piece of pottery qualities that weren't related to <u>its primary function</u>. And some groups produced items that revealed <u>the status of their owners</u>.
>
> traditional[trədíʃənəl] 전통의   refashion[riːfǽʃən] 개조하다
> quality[kwɑ́ləti] 특성, 질   relate to ~와 관련이 있는
> primary[práiməri] 주된, 주요한   reveal[rivíːl] 드러내다
> status[stéitəs] 지위, 상태

많은 북미 원주민의 전통 예술품들이 수 세기에 걸쳐 유럽 여행자들에 의해 수집되고 거래되어 왔습니다. 이러한 예술 작품들은 또한 대중의 예술 취향에 맞게 개조되기도 했습니다. 원래 이것들은 완전히 다른 문화적 맥락에서 제작되었습니다. 어떤 경우에는, 원주민들이 담요나 도자기에 그것의 주된 기능과 관련이 없는 특성을 부여했습니다. 그리고 어떤 집단들은 소유자의 지위를 드러내는 물품들을 제작했습니다.

강의의 주제는 무엇인가?
ⓐ 원주민 공동체의 문화적 변화
ⓑ 아메리카 원주민의 제작 기법
✓ⓒ 토착 예술의 재맥락화
ⓓ 원주민 수공예품의 기능적 가치

어휘 indigenous[indídʒənəs] 토착의 functional[fʌ́ŋkʃənəl] 기능적인

03 Main Topic Question 🎧 Nz

> **I'm going to focus on <u>how the Moon was formed</u>. Actually, there are <u>several theories</u> about it.** Some people argue that the Moon <u>split off from</u> Earth, while others believe it formed elsewhere and was later captured by Earth's gravity. In recent decades, the theory that the Moon formed from debris produced <u>by a giant impact</u> between Earth and another body has gained wide acceptance.
>
> theory[θíːəri] 이론   argue[áːrgjuː] 주장하다, 논하다

split off 분리되다, 떨어지다　capture[kǽptʃər] 포획하다, 사로잡다
gravity[grǽvəti] 중력　decade[dékeid] 10년
debris[dəbríː] 잔해

달이 어떻게 형성되었는지에 집중해보겠습니다. 사실, 이에 대한 여러 이론이 있습니다. 어떤 이들은 달이 지구에서 분리되었다고 주장하는 반면, 다른 이들은 달이 다른 곳에서 형성되었다가 나중에 지구의 중력에 의해 포획되었다고 생각합니다. 최근 수십 년 동안에는 지구와 다른 천체의 거대한 충돌로 생성된 잔해로부터 달이 형성되었다는 이론이 널리 받아들여지고 있습니다.

강의의 주요 주제는 무엇인가?
Ⓐ 달의 물리적 특성
Ⓑ 달 연구가 행성 과학에 미치는 영향
Ⓒ 최근 달 탐사 임무들의 결과
Ⓓ 달의 형성에 대한 다양한 이론

어휘　property[prápərti] 특성　planetary[plǽnətèri] 행성의

04 Main Topic Question

Today, we're discussing diamond formation and volcanic transport. You might wonder, if ancient volcanoes brought diamonds to the surface, why can't modern eruptions do the same?
Diamonds form 150 kilometers below Earth's surface under extreme conditions. Ancient volcanic eruptions originated from these depths, but modern eruptions originate from shallow magma chambers within the crust, at depths less than 30 kilometers. This explains why diamond mining focuses on ancient formations rather than current volcanic activity.

volcanic[valkǽnik] 화산의　transport[trænspɔ́ːrt] 운반하다
ancient[éinʃənt] 고대의　surface[sɔ́ːrfis] 지표면
eruption[irʌ́pʃən] 분화, 분출　extreme[ikstríːm] 극한의
shallow[ʃǽlou] 얕은　chamber[tʃéimbər] 저장소
crust[krʌst] 지각

오늘은 다이아몬드 형성과 화산 운반에 대해 논의하겠습니다. 고대 화산이 다이아몬드를 지표면으로 운반했다면, 현대의 분화가 같은 일을 할 수 없는 이유가 무엇인지 궁금할 것입니다.
다이아몬드는 극한 조건 하에서 지구 표면 아래 150킬로미터에서 형성됩니다. 고대 화산 분화는 이러한 깊이에서 시작되었지만, 현대 분화는 지구 지각의 30킬로미터보다 얕은 깊이의 마그마 저장소에서 발생합니다. 이것이 다이아몬드 채굴이 현재의 화산 활동보다는 고대 형성물에 집중하는 이유를 설명합니다.

강의의 주제는 무엇인가?
Ⓐ 지각층 간의 깊이 차이
Ⓑ 화산 작용과 다이아몬드 형성
Ⓒ 현대 다이아몬드 채굴 기법
Ⓓ 지구 화산 진화의 연대표

어휘　crustal[krʌ́stl] 지각의

HACKERS TEST　p.250

01 Ⓒ	02 Ⓐ	03 Ⓒ	04 Ⓓ	05 Ⓓ
06 Ⓑ	07 Ⓒ	08 Ⓐ	09 Ⓓ	10 Ⓐ
11 Ⓑ	12 Ⓒ	13 Ⓓ	14 Ⓑ	15 Ⓒ
16 Ⓐ				

[01-04]　Au

Listen to a talk in a psychology class.

[01]Today, let's talk about the specific ways that psychologists get their information. Well, the best place to begin is with observation. There are two kinds of observation: natural and controlled. [02]Naturalistic observation is done by all of us. If you watch birds flying in a V-pattern, you get the point. Naturalistic observation was likely the first kind of scientific research. Controlled observation, in contrast, means observing subjects in a laboratory or other controlled setting.
Both methods have pros and cons. For instance, naturalistic observation allows you to watch something in its natural environment. If you're studying churchgoers, what better way than observing at church! However, this isn't easy, as people move around or your view may get blocked. That's why controlled observation is preferable when precise, timely results are needed.
Beyond observation methods, psychologists also employ case studies as another research approach. In this method, a researcher examines a unique case, group, person, or situation. These are common when studying rare diseases or exceptional abilities, like a two-year-old who can read. [03]The major drawback is that case studies usually only look at exceptions, making it difficult to apply results broadly. So, [04]now that we have briefly learned about the three research methods, let's look at successful cases for each of them.

observation[ὰbzərvéiʃən] 관찰　controlled[kəntróuld] 통제된
pros and cons 장단점　employ[implɔ́i] 사용하다, 고용하다
examine[igzǽmin] 조사하다
exceptional[iksépʃənl] 예외적인, 특별한
drawback[drɔ́ːbæk] 단점, 결점　exception[iksépʃən] 예외

심리학 강의를 들으시오.

[01]오늘은 심리학자들이 정보를 얻는 구체적인 방법들에 대해 이야기해 보겠습니다. 음, 시작하기 가장 좋은 곳은 관찰입니다. 관찰에는 두 종류가 있는데, 자연 관찰과 통제 관찰입니다. [02]자연 관찰은 우리 모두가 하는 것입니다. 여러분이 새들이 V자 패턴으로 날아가는 것을 본다면, 요점을 아시겠죠. 자연 관찰은 아마도 최초의 과학적 연구 종류였을 것입니다. 반면, 통제 관찰은 실험실이나 기타 통제된 환경에서 피험자들을 관찰하는 것을 의미합니다.

두 방법 모두 장단점이 있습니다. 예를 들어, 자연 관찰은 여러분이 자연 환경에서 무언가를 관찰할 수 있게 해줍니다. 만약 여러분이 교회에 다니는 사람들을 연구한다면, 교회에서 관찰하는 것보다 더 좋은 방법이 있을까요! 하지만 사람들이 돌아다니거나 여러분의 시야가 가려질 수 있기 때문에 이것은 쉽지 않습니다. 그래서 정확하고 시기적절한 결과가 필요할 때는 통제 관찰이 더 바람직합니다.

관찰 방법들 외에도, 심리학자들은 또 다른 연구 접근법으로 사례 연구도 사용합니다. 이 방법에서는 연구자가 독특한 사례, 집단, 사람, 또는 상황을 조사합니다. 이들은 희귀 질병이나 두 살에 글을 읽는 아이와 같은 예외적 능력을 연구할 때 흔히 사용됩니다. 03주요 단점은 사례 연구가 보통 예외적인 것들만 살펴보기 때문에 결과를 널리 적용하기 어렵다는 것입니다. 그래서, 04이제 세 가지 연구 방법에 대해 간단히 배웠으니, 각각에 대한 성공적인 사례들을 살펴보겠습니다.

01 Main Topic Question

강의의 주요 주제는 무엇인가?
Ⓐ 과학적 연구의 한계
Ⓑ 어린 아이들의 이례적인 능력
☑ 심리학자들이 정보를 수집하는 방법
Ⓓ 심리학적 관찰의 역사

어휘 gather[gǽðər] 수집하다, 이해하다
     psychological[sàikəládʒikəl] 심리적인

02 Intention Question

화자는 왜 V자 패턴을 언급하는가?
☑ 자연 관찰의 예시를 보여주기 위해
Ⓑ 왜 새들이 이상적인 연구 대상인지 설명하기 위해
Ⓒ 새의 행동을 인간의 행동과 비교하기 위해
Ⓓ 자연에서 관찰하는 것의 한계를 소개하기 위해

어휘 subject[sʌ́bdʒikt] (실험) 대상

03 Detail Question

화자에 따르면, 사례 연구를 사용하는 것의 문제는 무엇인가?
Ⓐ 다른 연구 방법들보다 더 비용이 많이 든다.
Ⓑ 연구자들이 피험자들을 명확히 보는 데 어려움을 겪을 수 있다.
☑ 결과를 일반 인구에 적용하기 어렵다.
Ⓓ 실험실 환경에서만 실시될 수 있다.

어휘 method[méθəd] 방법

04 Discuss Next Question

화자는 다음에 무엇을 논의할 것 같은가?
Ⓐ 예외적인 능력을 가진 개인들의 사례 연구
Ⓑ 아직 언급되지 않은 대안적 연구 접근법들
Ⓒ 관찰 연구에 사용되는 현대 기술
☑ 각 연구 방법론의 주목할 만한 결과들

어휘 observational[àbzərvéiʃənl] 관찰의
     notable[nóutəbl] 주목할 만한
     methodology[mèθədálədʒi] 방법론

[05-08]

Listen to a talk in an environmental science class.

05**Today, we're going to discuss the past and present uses of charcoal. The production of charcoal is one of the oldest chemical processes known to humankind, having been used for thousands of years to refine metals.** Charcoal played a central role in the Bronze and Iron Ages.

While it had already been used industrially, archaeological evidence suggests that charcoal began to be used more broadly as a domestic fuel around 5,500 BC. 06**Well, today, its primary use remains as fuel, as it yields more heat relative to its weight than wood.** Its porous structure also makes it highly effective in filtration, ideal for applications such as sugar refining, water purification, factory air filtration, and gas masks.

Now, let me talk about a special type of charcoal known as activated charcoal. Activated charcoal is treated with oxygen through heating or chemical processes. This creates millions of tiny pores between carbon atoms, significantly increasing its surface area and adsorptive capacity. When a material is adsorbed, it binds to the surface of the activated charcoal through chemical attraction. Activated charcoal's vast surface area provides numerous bonding sites, and 07**it is excellent for protecting against poisonous gases in battlefield conditions.** So, 08**is charcoal a "dream resource" without any disadvantages?** Well, let's find out together from the next slide.

charcoal[tʃɑ́:rkòul] 목탄, 숯   refine[rifáin] 정제하다, 제련하다
Bronze Age 청동기 시대   Iron Age 철기 시대
archaeological[ὰ:rkiəládʒikəl] 고고학적인
evidence[évədəns] 증거   yield[ji:ld] 발생시키다, 산출하다
porous[pɔ́:rəs] 다공성의, 스며드는
purification[pjùərəfikéiʃən] 정화
adsorptive[ædsɔ́:rptiv] 흡착의   adsorb[ædsɔ́:rb] 흡착하다
bind[baind] 결합하다   poisonous[pɔ́izənəs] 독성의

환경과학 강의를 들으시오.

05오늘은 목탄의 과거와 현재 용도에 대해 논의하겠습니다. 목탄의 생산은 인류에게 알려진 가장 오래된 화학적 과정 중 하나로, 수천 년 동안 금속을 정제하는 데 사용되어 왔습니다. 목탄은 청동기 시대와 철기 시대에 중심적인 역할을 했습니다.

이미 산업적으로 사용되고 있었지만, 고고학적 증거는 목탄이 기원전 5,500년경부터 가정용 연료로 더 널리 사용되기 시작했다는 것을 시사합니다. 06음, 오늘날 그것의 주요 용도는 여전히 연료로, 나무보다 무게 대비 더 많은 열을 발생시킵니다. 그것의 다공성 구조는 또한 여과에도 매우 효과적이어서, 설탕 정제, 물 정화, 공장 공기 여과, 그리고 방독면과 같은 용도에 이상적입니다.

자, 활성탄으로 알려진 특별한 종류의 목탄에 대해 얘기해 봅시다. 활성탄은 가열이나 화학적 과정을 통해 산소로 처리됩니다. 이것은 탄소 원자 사이에 수백만 개의 작은 구멍들을 만들어, 그것의 표면적과 흡착 능력을 상당히 증가시킵니다. 물질이 흡착될 때, 그것은 화학적 인력을

통해 활성탄의 표면에 결합됩니다. 활성탄의 광대한 표면적은 수많은 결합 부위들을 제공하며, [07]전장 상황에서 독성 가스로부터 보호하는 데 탁월합니다. 그럼, [08]목탄은 어떤 단점도 없는 "꿈의 자원"일까요? 음, 다음 슬라이드에서 함께 알아보겠습니다.

05 Main Topic Question
강의는 주로 무엇에 대한 것인가?
Ⓐ 활성탄의 다양한 산업적 사용
Ⓑ 연료원과 관련된 고고학적 발견
Ⓒ 목탄 활성화에 관여하는 화학 반응
✓ 인류 역사 전반에 걸친 목탄의 이용

어휘 **industrial**[indʌ́striəl] 산업적인 **activation**[æktəvéiʃən] 활성화

06 Intention Question
화자는 왜 나무를 언급하는가?
Ⓐ 나무를 목탄으로 변환하는 과정을 설명하기 위해
✓ 목탄의 무게 대 열 비율 장점에 주목하기 위해
Ⓒ 전통적인 연료원의 지속가능성 문제를 논의하기 위해
Ⓓ 한 연료원에서 다른 연료원으로의 역사적 변화를 살펴보기 위해

어휘 **convert**[kənvə́ːrt] 변환하다 **ratio**[réiʃou] 비율
historical[histɔ́ːrikəl] 역사적인

07 Detail Question
화자는 활성탄이 전장 상황에서 어떻게 도움이 된다고 언급하는가?
Ⓐ 의사소통을 위한 연기 신호를 만듦으로써
Ⓑ 가벼운 연료 운반을 가능하게 함으로써
✓ 독성 가스로부터 보호를 제공함으로써
Ⓓ 어두운 색을 통해 위장을 제공함으로써

어휘 **lightweight**[láitweit] 가벼운 **camouflage**[kǽməflàːʒ] 위장

08 Discuss Next Question
화자는 다음에 무엇을 논의할 것인가?
✓ 목탄 사용의 잠재적 부정적 영향
Ⓑ 활성탄의 환경적 이점
Ⓒ 가장 효율적인 목탄 활성화 방법
Ⓓ 선사시대 목탄 사용에 대한 고고학적 증거

어휘 **prehistoric**[prìːhistɔ́ːrik] 선사시대의

[09-12]

Listen to a talk in an art class.

[09]Among the art movements included in postmodern art, earth art and site-specific art share two common characteristics. First, anyone can be an artist because it's the individual that interprets his or her environment. And second, since the 1970s, both earth art and site-specific art have become common forms of production. Then, what are the differences between these two art forms? Well, [10]earth art is large-scale and is set in nature like the desert or forest, and it's usually located in some remote place. The focus of earth art is to make a design out of the land itself, not to use the land as an environment for the artwork. That is, earth artists work with natural materials like water, snow, grass, leaves, rock, and even wind.
On the other hand, site-specific art is designed for a specific location, and the artist attempts to integrate the artwork with its surroundings. So, [11]**the surroundings function as a kind of backdrop for the actual work of art. It's like an exploration of the relationship of the artwork to the features of its locale, whether that locale is urban or rural, indoors or outdoors.**
Representative artists of these techniques include Robert Smithson and [12]Lawrence Weiner. Today, let's learn more about the latter.

movement[múːvmənt] 사조, 운동
postmodern[pòustmádərn] 포스트모더니즘의
interpret[intə́ːrprit] 해석하다, 통역하다
remote[rimóut] 외딴, 먼 **attempt**[ətémpt] 시도하다
integrate[íntəgrèit] 통합시키다, 통합하다
surrounding[səráundiŋ] 주변 환경
backdrop[bǽkdràp] 배경
exploration[èkspləréiʃən] 탐구, 조사 **locale**[loukǽl] 장소

미술 강의를 들으시오.
[09]포스트모던 미술에 포함되는 미술 사조 중 대지 미술과 장소 특정적 미술은 두 가지 공통된 특성을 공유합니다. 첫째, 누구나 예술가가 될 수 있는데 왜냐하면 자신의 환경을 해석하는 것은 개인이기 때문입니다. 그리고 둘째, 1970년대 이후로 대지 미술과 장소 특정적 미술 모두 일반적인 창작 형태가 되었습니다. 그렇다면, 이 두 예술 형태의 차이점은 무엇일까요?
음, [10]대지 미술은 대규모이고 사막이나 숲과 같은 자연에 설치되며, 보통 어떤 외딴 곳에 위치합니다. 대지 미술의 초점은 토지 자체로부터 디자인을 만드는 것이지, 토지를 예술작품의 환경으로 사용하는 것이 아닙니다. 즉, 대지 예술가들은 물, 눈, 풀, 나뭇잎, 바위, 그리고 심지어 바람과 같은 자연 재료들로 작업합니다.
반면에, 장소 특정적 미술은 특정 장소를 위해 설계되며, 예술가는 예술작품을 그 주변 환경과 통합시키려고 시도합니다. 그래서 [11]**주변 환경은 실제 예술작품을 위한 일종의 배경 역할을 합니다. 그것은 그 장소가 도시든 시골이든, 실내든 야외든, 그 장소의 특징과 예술작품의 관계를 탐구하는 것과 같습니다.**
이런 기법들의 대표적인 예술가들로는 로버트 스미스슨과 [12]로렌스 와이너가 있습니다. 오늘은 후자에 대해 더 알아보겠습니다.

09 Main Topic Question
강의의 주제는 무엇인가?
Ⓐ 풍경 기반 미술에서 자연 재료의 역할
Ⓑ 뉴욕 미술에서 포스트모더니즘의 역사
Ⓒ 포스트모던 예술가들이 사용한 유명한 기법들
✓ 포스트모던 예술적 실천의 두 가지 독특한 형태

어휘 **distinct**[distíŋkt] 독특한

10 Intention Question
화자는 왜 사막이나 숲을 언급하는가?
- ☑ⒶⒶ 대지 미술의 전형적인 배경을 보여주기 위해
- Ⓑ 도시와 자연의 예술적 배경을 비교하기 위해
- Ⓒ 미술 재료가 어디로부터 조달되는지 설명하기 위해
- Ⓓ 왜 일부 미술이 대중에게 접근하기 어려운지 설명하기 위해

어휘 typical[típikəl] 전형적인

11 Intention Question
화자는 왜 배경을 언급하는가?
- Ⓐ 미술에서 조명의 중요성을 보여주기 위해
- ☑Ⓑ 장소 특정적 예술이 장소 맥락을 어떻게 고려하는지 보여주기 위해
- Ⓒ 포스트모던 미술의 회화 기법을 설명하기 위해
- Ⓓ 조각의 배경 요소들과 대조하기 위해

어휘 lighting[láitiŋ] 조명   sculpture[skʌ́lptʃər] 조각

12 Discuss Next Question
화자는 다음에 무엇을 논의할 것 같은가?
- Ⓐ 로버트 스미슨의 예술적 기법들
- Ⓑ 세계 각지의 유명한 대지 미술 설치물들
- ☑Ⓒ 로렌스 와이너의 예술적 기법들과 작품들
- Ⓓ 스미슨과 다른 대지 예술가들의 비교

어휘 comparison[kəmpǽrəsn] 비교

[13-16]
🔊 Am

Listen to a talk in a literature class.

[13]**Romantic poetry of the late 18th and early 19th centuries marked a significant shift in literary expression, particularly in how poets approached the natural world.** Romantic poets like William Wordsworth viewed nature not merely as a backdrop for human activity, but as a source of inspiration and truth. [14]**Unlike the preceding Neoclassical movement, Romantic poets emphasized spontaneous emotion and personal experience.** Wordsworth, for example, described poetry as "the spontaneous overflow of powerful feelings." This approach led to more personal, emotional verse that celebrated the beauty and mystery of the natural world.
[15]**Romantic poets often used nature imagery to explore psychological states and philosophical ideas. For instance, Samuel Taylor Coleridge's poem *The Rime of the Ancient Mariner* uses a sea voyage to examine themes of guilt, redemption, and humanity's relationship with the natural world.** Finally, [16]**Romantic poets also emphasized the importance of imagination over reason, believing that intuitive understanding could reveal deeper truths than rational analysis.** This shift toward emotion and imagination influenced not only literature but also art, music, and philosophy throughout the 19th century.

Romantic[roumǽntik] 낭만주의의   poetry[póuitri] 시
particularly[pərtíkjulərli] 특히   poet[póuit] 시인
inspiration[ìnspəréiʃən] 영감
preceding[prisí:diŋ] 이전의, 앞서는
Neoclassical[nì:ouklǽsikəl] 신고전주의의
spontaneous[spɑntéiniəs] 자발적인
philosophical[fìləsɑ́:fikəl] 철학적인   guilt[gilt] 죄책감
redemption[ridémpʃən] 구원   intuitive[intjú:ətiv] 직관적인

문학 강의를 들으시오.
[13]18세기 말과 19세기 초의 낭만주의 시는 문학적 표현에서 상당한 변화를 보여주었는데, 특히 시인들이 자연 세계에 접근하는 방식에서 그랬습니다. 윌리엄 워즈워스와 같은 낭만주의 시인들은 자연을 단순히 인간 활동의 배경으로 보지 않고, 영감과 진실의 원천으로 보았습니다. [14]이전 사조인 신고전주의와는 달리, 낭만주의 시인들은 자발적인 감정과 개인적 경험을 강조했습니다. 예를 들어, 워즈워스는 시를 "강력한 감정들의 자발적 넘침"이라고 묘사했습니다. 이런 접근법은 자연 세계의 아름다움과 신비를 찬양하는 더 개인적이고 감정적인 시로 이어졌습니다.
[15]낭만주의 시인들은 종종 자연 이미지를 사용해 심리적 상태와 철학적 사상을 탐구했습니다. 예를 들어, 사무엘 테일러 콜리지의 시 *The Rime of the Ancient Mariner*는 바다 항해를 사용하여 죄책감, 구원, 그리고 자연 세계와 인류의 관계라는 주제들을 탐구합니다.
마지막으로, [16]낭만주의 시인들은 또한 이성보다 상상력의 중요성을 강조했는데, 직관적 이해가 이성적 분석보다 더 깊은 진실을 드러낼 수 있다고 믿었습니다. 감정과 상상력 쪽으로의 이런 변화는 19세기 전반에 걸쳐 문학뿐만 아니라 미술, 음악, 그리고 철학에도 영향을 미쳤습니다.

13 Main Topic Question
강의는 주로 낭만주의 시의 어떤 측면에 대한 것인가?
- Ⓐ 주요 낭만주의 시인들의 전기적 세부사항
- Ⓑ 낭만주의 시대의 역사적 맥락
- Ⓒ 다른 예술 형태들에 대한 낭만주의 시의 영향
- ☑Ⓓ 낭만주의 시인들이 자연을 바라본 방식

어휘 biographical[baiəgrǽfikəl] 전기적인
   period[píəriəd] 시대, 기간

14 Organization Question
화자는 낭만주의 시인들의 특성을 어떻게 설명하는가?
- Ⓐ 시간순으로 시를 분석함으로써
- ☑Ⓑ 낭만주의 시를 이전 전통과 비교함으로써
- Ⓒ 개별 시인들의 생활 경험에 초점을 맞춤으로써
- Ⓓ 낭만주의 시에 대한 정치적 영향들을 살펴봄으로써

어휘 chronological[krɑ̀nəlɑ́dʒikəl] 시간순의, 연대기의
   political[pəlítikəl] 정치적인

15 Intention Question
화자는 왜 *The Rime of the Ancient Mariner*를 언급하는가?
- Ⓐ 낭만주의 시인들이 종교적 주제들을 어떻게 사용했는지 보여주기 위해
- Ⓑ 콜리지의 서사시 숙련을 강조하기 위해
- ☑Ⓒ 자연 이미지가 더 깊은 주제들을 어떻게 탐구했는지 보여주기 위해
- Ⓓ 바다 이미지가 낭만주의 문학에서 얼마나 인기가 있었는지 보여주

기 위해

어휘 religious[rilídʒəs] 종교의, 독실한
narrative[nǽrətiv] 서사적인; 묘사 theme[θi:m] 주제

16 Detail Question

화자에 따르면, 낭만주의 시인들은 왜 이성보다 상상력을 우선시했는가?
ⓐ 직관적 통찰이 깊은 진실을 드러낼 수 있다고 느꼈다.
Ⓑ 이성적 접근법이 인간의 감정을 무시한다고 믿었다.
Ⓒ 논리적 분석이 시적 영감을 제한한다고 생각했다.
Ⓓ 학문보다 개인적 경험을 강조하기를 원했다.

어휘 profound[prəfáund] 깊은 restrict[ristríkt] 제한하다

2. Discuss Next Questions

Example Nz   p.255

미국 노동운동은 고용주와 피고용인 간의 불평등 때문에 발생했습니다. 근로자들은 자신들의 근무시간과 보상에 대해 더 많은 통제권을 원했습니다. 파업을 처음 시작한 사람들은 인쇄업자들이었고, 이어서 가구 제작자와 목수들이 따랐으며, 이는 다양한 노동조합으로 이어졌습니다. 정부가 임금을 규제하는 서유럽 국가들과 달리, 미국 노동조합들은 근로자와 고용주가 직접 협상해야 한다고 생각했습니다. 이러한 차이점은 미국 근로자들이 8시간 근무제와 최저임금과 같은 기본권을 얻기 위해 종종 투쟁해야 했으며, 때로는 목숨을 걸어야 했다는 것을 의미했습니다. 이제 이러한 근로자들의 투쟁이 실제로 무엇을 포함했는지 살펴보겠습니다.

labor[léibər] 노동 arise[əráiz] 발생하다
inequality[ìnikwáləti] 불평등
compensation[kàmpənséiʃən] 보상 labor union 노동조합
regulate[régjuleit] 규제하다, 통제하다
wage[weidʒ] 임금; (전쟁을) 일으키다
negotiate[nigóuʃièit] 협상하다 struggle[strʌ́gl] 투쟁하다

화자는 다음에 무엇을 논의할 것 같은가?
ⓐ 노동 분쟁 중 갈등의 구체적 사례들
Ⓑ 유럽 노동운동이 미국 노동조합에 미친 영향
Ⓒ 현대 노동협상에서 정부의 역할
Ⓓ 저명한 노동 지도자들의 전기적 기록

어휘 dispute[dispjú:t] 분쟁, 다툼 prominent[prámənənt] 저명한

HACKERS PRACTICE   p.256

01 Ⓑ   02 Ⓓ   03 Ⓒ   04 ⓐ

01 Discuss Next Question Am

While quilting originated in Egypt and Mongolia, European colonists brought quilting traditions to America in the 1600s. The real transformation occurred in the 1800s when American textile mills began producing diverse, high-quality fabrics. Revolutionary printing methods and synthetic dyes created unprecedented color palettes, inspiring quilters to develop uniquely American patterns. This combination of industrial innovation and domestic creativity established quilting as a truly American art form. Next, we will explore how quilting techniques spread westward with American pioneers and evolved into distinct regional styles.

originate in ~에서 시작되다 colonist[kάlənist] 식민지 개척자
textile[tékstail] 직물의 mill[mil] 공장
synthetic[sinθétik] 합성의
unprecedented[ʌ̀nprésədèntid] 전례가 없는
establish[istǽbliʃ] 확립하다 pioneer[pàiəníər] 개척자; 개척하다

퀼팅은 이집트와 몽골에서 시작되었지만, 유럽 식민지 개척자들이 1600년대에 퀼팅 전통을 미국으로 가져왔습니다. 진정한 변화는 1800년대에 미국 섬유 공장들이 다양하고 고품질의 직물을 생산하기 시작하면서 일어났습니다. 혁신적인 인쇄 방법과 합성 염료가 전례 없는 색상 팔레트를 만들어내며, 퀼트를 만드는 사람들이 독특한 미국 패턴을 개발하도록 영감을 주었습니다. 이러한 산업 혁신과 가정 내 창의성의 결합이 퀼팅을 진정한 미국 예술 형태로 확립했습니다. 다음으로, 우리는 퀼팅 기법이 미국 개척자들과 함께 서쪽으로 어떻게 퍼져나갔으며 독특한 지역 스타일로 어떻게 발전했는지 탐구할 것입니다.

화자는 다음에 미국 퀼팅의 어떤 측면에 대해 논의할 것인가?
ⓐ 섬유 제조 과정에 어떻게 영향을 미쳤는지
ⓑ 어떻게 다른 지역적 특성을 발전시켰는지
Ⓒ 유럽 퀼팅 전통과 어떻게 경쟁했는지
Ⓓ 산업 혁명 이후 어떻게 쇠퇴했는지

어휘 manufacturing[mæ̀njufǽktʃəriŋ] 제조의

02 Discuss Next Question Au

Today, we're examining food chains and their vulnerability. Charles Elton introduced this concept in 1927, describing energy flow from plants to herbivores to carnivores. Remove one link, and entire system collapses. Consider sea turtles: these coastal animals lay eggs containing fluids that nourish dune vegetation, preventing erosion. When conservationists relocated eggs for safety, vegetation died, coastlines eroded, and marine animals disappeared. This demonstrates a concept called ecological interconnectedness. Let's take a closer look at the cases of this interesting concept.

vulnerability [vʌ̀lnərəbíləti] 취약성 나약함
herbivore[hə́:rbəvɔ̀:r] 초식동물 carnivore[ká:rnəvɔ̀:r] 육식동물
collapse[kəlǽps] 무너지다, 붕괴하다 fluid[flú:id] 액체
nourish[nə́:riʃ] 영양을 공급하다 dune[dju:n] 모래언덕
vegetation[vèdʒitéiʃən] 식생, 식물 erosion[iróuʒən] 침식
ecological[ìkəlάdʒikəl] 생태학적인

오늘 우리는 먹이사슬과 그 취약성을 살펴보겠습니다. Charles Elton은 1927년에 이 개념을 도입하여 식물에서 초식동물, 그리고 육식동물

로의 에너지 흐름을 설명했습니다. 한 고리를 제거하면 전체 시스템이 무너집니다. 바다거북을 생각해보세요. 이 연안 동물들은 모래언덕 식생에 영향을 공급하는 액체가 들어있는 알을 낳아 침식을 방지합니다. 보존론자들이 안전을 위해 알을 옮겼을 때, 식생이 죽고 해안선이 침식되었으며 해양 동물들이 사라졌습니다. 이것은 생태학적 상호연결성이라는 개념을 보여줍니다. 이 흥미로운 개념의 사례들을 자세히 살펴보겠습니다.

화자는 다음에 무엇을 논의할 것 같은가?
Ⓐ 전지구적 먹이사슬에 대한 기후변화의 영향
Ⓑ 생태학에 대한 Charles Elton의 다른 기여
Ⓒ 포식자-피식자 관계의 상세한 분석
☑ 생태학적 상호연결성의 구체적인 예시들

어휘 ecology[ikάlədʒi] 생태학 predator[prédətər] 포식자
prey[prei] 피식자, 먹이

03 Discuss Next Question

Alright, I want to challenge a common misconception about the Great Depression. Most think it was simply free market's failure, but the government actually played a crucial role. US authorities lowered interest rates and increased money supply in the 1920s, creating artificial expansion. This easy money led to poor investment decisions and unstable businesses that inevitably collapsed, triggering widespread unemployment and economic hardship. **Then, why did the government make such mistakes back then? Let's explore the reasons behind it.**

Great Depression 대공황 authority[əθɔ́:rəti] 당국, 권한
interest rate 금리 artificial[ὰːrtəfíʃəl] 인위적인
investment[invéstmənt] 투자 inevitably[inévətəbli] 필연적으로
unemployment[ə̀nimplɔ́imənt] 실업(률), 실직

좋습니다, 저는 대공황에 대한 일반적인 오해에 도전하고 싶습니다. 대부분은 그것이 단순히 자유시장의 실패였다고 생각하지만, 정부가 실제로 중요한 역할을 했습니다. 미국 당국은 1920년대에 금리를 낮추고 통화 공급량을 늘려 인위적인 성장을 조성했습니다. 이러한 느슨한 통화 정책은 부실한 투자 결정과 불안정한 사업체들로 이어졌고, 이것들이 필연적으로 무너지면서 광범위한 실업과 경제적 어려움을 촉발했습니다. 그렇다면, 정부는 왜 그 당시 그런 실수를 했을까요? 그 이유를 탐구해보겠습니다.

화자는 다음에 무엇을 논의할 것인가?
Ⓐ 경제적 어려움에 대한 노동조합의 반응
Ⓑ 회복 일정과 복구 노력
☑ 당국의 정책 결정 뒤의 근거
Ⓓ 그 시기 동안의 국제 무역 영향

어휘 restoration[rèstəréiʃən] 복구, 회복
rationale[ræ̀ʃənǽl] 근거, 근본적 이유

04 Discuss Next Question

Today, we'll explore one of humanity's oldest meteorological tools, which is the weathervane. Archaeological evidence shows they existed before the first century BC, with the famous Tower of Winds in Athens featuring a spectacular bronze Triton statue holding a directional wand. This was an elaborate representation demonstrating the importance of wind direction in ancient societies. Before modern forecasting existed, people worldwide relied on these devices to predict weather patterns. **These were crucial for agricultural success. Now, let's take a look at how they specifically predicted the weather using a weathervane.**

humanity[hju:mǽnəti] 인류
meteorological[mì:tiərəládʒikəl] 기상학의
weathervane[wéðərvèin] 풍향계
spectacular[spektǽkjulər] 장엄한, 호화스러운
statue[stǽtʃu:] (조각)상 elaborate[ilǽbərət] 정교한
predict[pridíkt] 예측하다 agricultural[ǽgrəkʌ́ltʃərəl] 농업의

오늘 우리는 인류의 가장 오래된 기상학 도구 중 하나인 풍향계를 탐구해보겠습니다. 고고학적 증거에 따르면 그것들은 기원전 1세기 이전에 존재했으며, 아테네의 유명한 바람의 탑에는 방향을 가리키는 지팡이를 들고 있는 장엄한 청동 트리톤상이 있었습니다. 이것은 고대 사회에서 풍향의 중요성을 보여주는 정교한 표현이었습니다. 현대적인 예보가 존재하기 전에, 전 세계 사람들은 날씨 패턴을 예측하기 위해 이러한 장치들에 의존했습니다. 이는 농업의 성공에 필수적이었습니다. 이제, 그들이 구체적으로 어떻게 풍향계를 이용해 날씨를 예측했는지 살펴보겠습니다.

화자는 다음에 무엇을 논의할 것 같은가?
☑ 풍향계를 사용한 날씨 예측 방법
Ⓑ 기상학의 역사적 발전
Ⓒ 초기 기상학 장비에 사용된 재료
Ⓓ 날씨 예측 도구의 사회적 영향

HACKERS TEST

01 Ⓑ	02 Ⓒ	03 Ⓐ	04 Ⓒ	05 Ⓐ
06 Ⓓ	07 Ⓐ	08 Ⓑ	09 Ⓑ	10 Ⓒ
11 Ⓐ	12 Ⓑ	13 Ⓒ	14 Ⓓ	15 Ⓐ
16 Ⓑ				

[01-04]

Listen to a talk in a biology class.

⁰¹I'd like to draw your attention to marsupials, which are commonly thought of as pouched animals, and do not have long gestation periods like placental mammals. A representative marsupial is, yes, the kangaroo. Anyway, ⁰²marsupials

give birth soon after conception, that is, after the baby marsupials have spent about four to five weeks in the uterus. And the young animal, which is actually still in an embryonic stage, climbs from the birth canal onto its mother's nipples. So it's nourished in this manner for weeks or months until it fully develops. When it reaches a certain stage, though, it'll sometimes venture outside of the pouch, but eventually it will return to get food and warmth. ⁰¹Placental mammals, however, are nourished by the mother's blood through an embryonic organ known as the placenta, which allows for a longer gestation period and a live birth. ⁰³It is misleading to use the descriptive term "placental" to categorize these animals because marsupials also have placentas. It is just that the placentas of marsupials are short-lived and cannot nourish the young as well as those of placental animals. ⁰⁴So, why do you think these differences exist? Let's find out together.

marsupial[mɑːrsúːpiəl] 유대류 gestation[dʒestéiʃən] 잉태
placental[pləséntəl] 태반의, 태반이 있는
mammal[mǽməl] 포유류 conception[kənsépʃən] 임신
uterus[júːtərəs] 자궁 embryonic[èmbriɑ́nik] 태아의, 배의
birth canal 산도 descriptive[diskríptiv] 서술적인, 설명적인
categorize[kǽtəgəràiz] 분류하다

생물학 강의를 들으시오.

⁰¹저는 주머니 동물로 보통 여겨지고, 태반 포유동물처럼 긴 잉태 기간을 갖지 않는 유대류에 대해 여러분의 주의를 끌고자 합니다. 대표적인 유대류는, 네, 바로 캥거루입니다. 어쨌든, ⁰²유대류는 수정 직후에, 즉 새끼 유대류가 자궁에서 약 4~5주를 보낸 후 출산합니다. 그리고 실제로 여전히 배아 단계인 새끼 동물은 산도에서 어미의 젖꼭지로 기어 올라갑니다. 그래서 완전히 발달할 때까지 이런 방식으로 몇 주에서 몇 달 동안 영양을 공급받습니다. 특정 단계에 도달하면, 가끔 주머니 밖으로 모험을 떠나지만, 결국 음식과 따뜻함을 얻기 위해 돌아옵니다. ⁰¹하지만 태반 포유동물은 태반이라고 알려진 배아 기관을 통해 어미의 혈액으로부터 영양을 공급받으며, 이는 더 긴 임신 기간과 완전히 발달한 새끼의 출산을 가능하게 합니다. ⁰³이러한 동물들을 분류하기 위해 "태반이 있는"이라는 서술적 용어를 사용하는 것은 오해를 불러일으키는데, 유대류도 태반을 가지고 있기 때문입니다. 단지 유대류의 태반은 수명이 짧고 태반 동물의 태반만큼 새끼에게 영양을 잘 공급할 수 없을 뿐입니다. ⁰⁴그렇다면, 왜 이런 차이가 존재한다고 생각하십니까? 함께 알아봅시다.

01 Main Topic Question
강의는 주로 무엇에 대한 것인가?
Ⓐ 주머니의 진화적 이점
Ⓑ 포유동물의 서로 다른 번식 전략 ✓
Ⓒ 암컷 유대류의 양육 행동
Ⓓ 동물 번식에서 태반의 중요성

어휘 evolutionary[èvəlúːʃənèri] 진화적인
reproductive[rìːprədʌ́ktiv] 번식의, 생식의

02 Inference Question
화자는 새끼 유대류에 대해 무엇을 암시하는가?
Ⓐ 태반 포유동물보다 더 빨리 발달한다.
Ⓑ 주머니를 떠난 후 돌아오지 않는다.
Ⓒ 매우 덜 발달된 상태로 태어난다. ✓
Ⓓ 생존하기 위해 어미의 젖이 필요하지 않다.

어휘 underdeveloped[ʌ̀ndərdivéləpt] 덜 발달된, 저개발의

03 Detail Question
화자에 따르면, "태반 포유동물"이라는 용어를 사용하는 것이 왜 오해를 불러일으킬 수 있는가?
Ⓐ 태반은 유대류가 아닌 포유동물에게만 고유한 것이 아니다. ✓
Ⓑ 태반 동물들도 유대류처럼 주머니를 가질 수 있다.
Ⓒ 이 용어는 번식의 한 측면에만 너무 집중한다.
Ⓓ 두 동물군 모두 발달을 위해 태반에 동등하게 의존한다.

어휘 equally[íːkwəli] 동등하게

04 Discuss Next Question
화자는 다음에 무엇을 논의할 것 같은가?
Ⓐ 태반 포유동물의 구체적인 예시들
Ⓑ 기후 변화가 포유동물에게 미치는 영향
Ⓒ 번식 방법의 분화를 설명하는 요인들 ✓
Ⓓ 유대류 번식에 대한 일반적인 오해들

어휘 divergence[divə́ːrdʒəns] 분화, 분기
misconception[mìskənsépʃən] 오해

[05-08]　　　　　　　　　　Am
Listen to a talk in a music class.

⁰⁵Today, we're going to explore Impressionism in music, a movement that emerged in France during the late 19th century. I guess you've heard of Impressionist painting, and you may think of artists like Monet or Renoir, right? Today's subject, musical Impressionism, shares some similar characteristics. The leading figure was Claude Debussy. Unlike the dramatic, structured compositions of the Romantic period, Debussy created music that was more suggestive than explicit. ⁰⁶He used unconventional scales, particularly the whole-tone scale that creates a floating, dreamlike quality you hear in pieces like *Clair de Lune*.
What made Impressionist music revolutionary was its approach to harmony and timbre. Traditional music moved from tension to resolution, but Impressionists were more interested in atmosphere and mood. ⁰⁷They used parallel chords, often shifting entire chord progressions up or down. Well, this was considered quite radical at the time.
This movement influenced countless 20th-century composers and helped bridge the gap between Romantic and modern music. ⁰⁸Next, we will

discuss Neoclassicism, a musical movement that emerged as a reaction against Impressionism, and examine its key characteristics.

Impressionism[impréʃənìzm] 인상주의
figure[fígjər] 인물, 모습   composition[kàmpəzíʃən] 작곡, 구성
suggestive[səgdʒéstiv] 암시적인   explicit[iksplísit] 명시적인
unconventional[ʌ̀nkənvénʃənəl] 독특한, 비전통적인
scale[skeil] 음계   timbre[támbər] 음색
resolution[rèzəlúːʃən] 해소   chord[kɔːrd] 화음
radical[rǽdikəl] 급진적인

어휘 evolve from ~에서 진화하다

08 Discuss Next Question

화자는 다음에 무엇을 논의할 것 같은가?
Ⓐ 현대 음악에서 인상주의의 유산
☑ 신고전주의의 핵심 특징과 역사적 맥락
Ⓒ 신고전주의 작곡가들의 전기적 세부사항
Ⓓ 인상주의 운동의 급속한 쇠퇴

어휘 contemporary[kəntémpərèri] 현대의, 현대적인
rapid[rǽpid] 급속한, 빠른

음악 강의를 들으시오.

⁰⁵오늘, 우리는 19세기 후반 프랑스에서 등장한 운동인 음악에서의 인상주의를 탐구할 것입니다. 인상주의 회화에 대해 들어보셨을 것이고, 모네나 르누아르 같은 예술가들을 생각하실 수 있을 것입니다, 그렇죠? 오늘의 주제인 음악적 인상주의는 몇 가지 유사한 특징을 공유합니다. 주도적인 인물은 클로드 드뷔시였습니다. 낭만주의 시대의 극적이고 구조화된 작곡과 달리, 드뷔시는 명시적이기보다는 더 암시적인 음악을 창조했습니다. ⁰⁶그는 독특한 음계, 특히 *Clair de Lune* 같은 작품에서 듣는 떠다니는 듯하고 꿈같은 느낌을 만드는 온음계를 사용했습니다. 인상주의 음악을 혁신적으로 만든 것은 화성과 음색에 대한 접근법이었습니다. 전통 음악은 긴장에서 해소로 전개되었지만, 인상주의자들은 분위기와 정서에 더 관심이 있었습니다. ⁰⁷그들은 평행 화음을 사용했으며, 종종 전체 화음 진행을 위아래로 이동시켰습니다. 음, 이것은 당시에 꽤 급진적으로 여겨졌습니다.

이 운동은 수많은 20세기 작곡가들에게 영향을 미쳤고 낭만주의와 현대 음악 사이의 간극을 메우는 데 도움을 주었습니다. ⁰⁸다음으로, 우리는 인상주의에 대한 반작용으로 등장한 음악 운동인 신고전주의를 논의하고, 그 핵심 특징들을 살펴볼 것입니다.

05 Main Topic Question

강의의 주요 주제는 무엇인가?
☑ 음악적 인상주의의 독특한 요소들
Ⓑ 시각 예술과 음악 예술 형태 간의 관계
Ⓒ 고전 음악에서 화음 진행의 진화
Ⓓ 음악사에서 혁신적인 작곡 기법들

어휘 distinctive[distíŋktiv] 독특한, 특별한

06 Inference Question

화자는 드뷔시에 대해 무엇을 암시하는가?
Ⓐ 의도적으로 모든 전통적인 음악 원칙을 거부했다.
Ⓑ 주로 낭만주의 작곡가들의 영향을 받았다.
Ⓒ 자신의 독특한 기법으로 비판을 받았다.
☑ 온음계를 사용해 떠다니는 듯한 감각을 만들어냈다.

어휘 deliberately[dilíbərətli] 의도적으로
composer[kəmpóuzər] 작곡가

07 Intention Question

화자는 왜 평행 화음을 언급하는가?
☑ 독특한 인상주의적 접근법을 강조하기 위해
Ⓑ 후대 작곡가들이 왜 이런 기법들을 포기했는지 설명하기 위해
Ⓒ 인상주의 음악이 연주하기 어려웠던 이유를 강조하기 위해
Ⓓ 현대 음악이 인상주의에서 어떻게 진화했는지 보여주기 위해

[09-12]

Listen to a talk in a business management class.

⁰⁹**The service recovery paradox occurs when a company responds so effectively to a customer's problem that the customer ends up more satisfied than if no problem had occurred.** Strange, right? But studies confirm that customer loyalty can actually increase with positive recovery experiences.

¹⁰**Let me illustrate with a real example. My daughter purchased a laptop right before her first semester at university started, but it turned out to be defective.** This, of course, caused a major inconvenience. However, when she contacted the manufacturer, their response was impressive. They arranged free return shipping, expedited a replacement via courier, and offered a complimentary software upgrade to compensate for the delay. ¹⁰**As a result, her confidence in the manufacturer grew stronger than before.**

¹¹**So, why does this work? Research shows customers appreciate when businesses demonstrate genuine concern for their specific needs. When companies go beyond expectations to resolve issues, customers feel especially valued and believe the company will continue prioritizing their satisfaction.** However, this paradox doesn't apply universally. While customers typically appreciate one-time problem resolution, recurring product failures don't build loyalty. ¹²**Well, next, let's take a look at some research findings that address these limitations.**

paradox[pǽrədàks] 역설   loyalty[lɔ́iəlti] 충성도
defective[diféktiv] 결함이 있는
expedite[ékspədàit] 신속히 처리하다   courier[kúriər] 택배
complimentary[kàmpləméntəri] 무료의
genuine[dʒénjuin] 진정한   resolve[rizɑ́lv] 해결하다
universally[jùːnəvə́ːrsəli] 보편적으로
recurring[rikə́ːriŋ] 반복되는

경영학 강의를 들으시오.

⁰⁹서비스 회복 역설은 회사가 고객의 문제에 매우 효과적으로 대응하여 고객이 아무런 문제도 발생하지 않았을 때보다 더 만족하게 되는 현상

입니다. 이상하죠? 하지만 연구들은 고객 충성도가 실제로 긍정적인 회복 경험으로 증가할 수 있다는 것이 사실임을 보여주었습니다.

[10]실제 예시로 설명해드리겠습니다. 제 딸이 첫 대학 학기가 시작되기 직전에 노트북을 구매했는데, 결함이 있었습니다. 이것은 물론 큰 불편을 초래했죠. 그런데 그녀가 제조사에 연락했을 때, 그들의 대응은 인상적이었습니다. 그들은 무료 반품 배송을 준비하고, 택배를 통해 교체품을 신속히 처리했으며, 지연에 대한 보상으로 무료 소프트웨어 업그레이드를 제공했습니다. [10]결과적으로, 그 제조사에 대한 그녀의 신뢰는 이전보다 더 강해졌습니다.

[11]그렇다면, 왜 이것이 효과가 있을까요? 연구는 고객들이 기업이 그들의 특정한 필요에 대해 진정한 관심을 보일 때 감사하게 여긴다는 것을 보여줍니다. 회사들이 문제를 해결하기 위해 기대를 넘어설 때, 고객들은 특별히 존중받고 있다고 느끼고 회사가 계속해서 그들의 만족을 우선시할 것이라고 믿습니다. 하지만, 이 역설은 보편적으로 적용되지는 않습니다. 고객들은 일반적으로 일회성 문제 해결에 대해서는 감사하게 여기지만, 반복되는 제품 고장은 충성도를 구축하지 못하죠. [12]음, 다음으로, 이런 한계들을 다루는 몇 가지 연구 결과들을 살펴보겠습니다.

09 Main Topic Question
강의는 주로 무엇에 대한 것인가?
Ⓐ 고객 실망 뒤의 심리학
☑ⓑ 고객 만족에서 직관에 반하는 개념
Ⓒ 광고가 고객 경험에 미치는 영향
Ⓓ 서비스 실패와 그것이 기업 평판에 미치는 영향

어휘 counterintuitive[kàuntərintjúːitiv] 반하는, 반대되는

10 Intention Question
화자는 왜 자신의 딸을 언급하는가?
Ⓐ 서비스 회복 역설의 한계를 보여주기 위해
Ⓑ 기술 고장으로 인한 스트레스를 강조하기 위해
☑ⓒ 효과적인 문제 해결의 사례를 제시하기 위해
Ⓓ 회사의 초기 제품 품질을 비판하기 위해

11 Detail Question
화자에 따르면, 서비스 회복 역설이 왜 효과가 있는가?
☑ⓐ 기업들이 문제를 해결하는 과정에서 고객의 기대를 뛰어넘는다.
Ⓑ 제조업체들이 고객의 관심을 본래 문제에서 다른 곳으로 돌린다.
Ⓒ 결함 있는 제품이 더 나은 품질의 대체품으로 교환된다.
Ⓓ 기업들이 그 문제가 일회성 사건이었다고 고객을 설득한다.

어휘 exceed[iksíːd] 뛰어넘다   isolated[áisəlèitid] 일회성의, 단발의

12 Discuss Next Question
화자는 다음에 무엇을 논의할 것 같은가?
Ⓐ 서비스 실패의 장기적 결과들
☑ⓑ 서비스 회복의 제약에 대한 과학적 연구들
Ⓒ 손상된 기업 평판을 재구축하기 위한 전략들
Ⓓ 성공적인 위기 관리 접근법을 가진 회사들

어휘 consequence[kánsəkwèns] 결과
constraint[kənstréint] 제약   reputation[rèpjutéiʃən] 평판
crisis management 위기 관리

[13-16]
Listen to a talk in a physics class.

> [13]**Noise is generally considered a disagreeable and bothersome auditory experience.** Imagine your neighbor mowing the lawn or the sound of construction around your house. Noise becomes harmful when it exceeds 85 decibels, which is about the level of an alarm or busy street noise. Prolonged exposure to such noise can damage hearing and cause stress. It can even lead to heart disease.
>
> [13]**So, is noise always such a bad thing? Actually, it's not, at least in physics. In physics, noise refers to an acoustic or electronic signal containing a random mixture of frequencies, and it comes in various forms.** [14]**One example is white noise, which contains all audible frequencies simultaneously.** This sounds like a humming or static and can be soothing. I'm sure you've heard this at least once in your life. You know, the sound of falling rain or the crackling of a bonfire.
>
> [15]**The concept of white noise is similar to white light, which contains all visible wavelengths.** Other types of noise include pink noise, which is stronger in lower frequencies and sounds lower pitched. And there is blue noise, which has higher frequencies and a higher pitch. [16]**Next, we will listen to each of them and discuss the differences.**

---

disagreeable[dìsəgríːəbl] 불쾌한
bothersome[báðərsəm] 성가신   auditory[ɔ́ːditɔ̀ːri] 청각의; 청각
mow[móu] (풀을) 깎다, 베다   prolonged[prəlɔ́ːŋd] 장시간의
acoustic[əkúːstik] 음향적인   frequency[fríːkwənsi] 주파수
audible[ɔ́ːdəbl] 가청의, 들리는
simultaneously[sàiməltéiniəsli] 동시에
static[stǽtik] (수신기의) 잡음   soothing[súːðiŋ] 진정시키는
wavelength[wéivlèŋkθ] 파장

물리학 강의를 들으시오.

[13]소음은 일반적으로 불쾌하고 성가신 청각적 경험으로 여겨집니다. 여러분의 이웃이 잔디를 깎는 것이나 여러분의 집 주변의 건설 소음을 상상해보세요. 소음은 85데시벨을 초과할 때 해로워지는데, 이는 대략 알람이나 바쁜 거리 소음의 수준입니다. 그런 소음에 장시간 노출되면 청력을 손상시키고 스트레스를 유발할 수 있습니다. 심지어 심장병으로 이어질 수도 있어요.

[13]그렇다면, 소음이 항상 그렇게 나쁜 것일까요? 꼭 그렇지 않습니다, 적어도 물리학에서는 말입니다. 물리학에서 소음은 주파수의 무작위 혼합을 포함하는 음향적 또는 전자적 신호를 의미하며, 다양한 종류가 있습니다. [14]한 예시는 모든 가청 주파수를 동시에 포함하는 화이트 노이즈입니다. 이것은 윙윙거리거나 잡음처럼 들리며 진정시킬 수 있습니다. 저는 여러분이 인생에서 적어도 한 번은 이것을 들어 보았을 거라고 확신합니다. 그러니까, 떨어지는 빗소리나 모닥불의 탁탁거리는 소리 말입니다.

[15]화이트 노이즈의 개념은 모든 가시 파장을 포함하는 백색광과 유사합니다. 다른 종류의 소음에는 낮은 주파수에서 더 강하고 더 낮은 음조로 들리는 핑크 노이즈가 있습니다. 그리고 더 높은 주파수와 더 높은 음

조를 가진 블루 노이즈가 있습니다. ¹⁶다음으로, 우리는 각각을 듣고 차이점들을 논의할 것입니다.

13 Main Topic Question
강의는 주로 무엇에 대한 것인가?
Ⓐ 소음이 인간의 지각에 어떻게 영향을 미치는가
Ⓑ 환경 소음의 해로운 영향들
☑ 소음의 다양한 유형과 인식들
Ⓓ 소음의 물리적 분류 기준

어휘 perception[pərsépʃən] 지각, 인식
classification[klæ̀səfikéiʃən] 분류
criteria[kraitíriə] 기준, 표준

14 Detail Question
화자는 화이트 노이즈에 대해 무엇을 말하는가?
Ⓐ 수면 시간 동안 피해야 한다.
Ⓑ 혼잡한 거리 교통의 소리와 유사하다.
Ⓒ 대부분의 사람들이 인식하기에는 너무 복잡하다.
☑ 모든 가청 주파수를 동시에 포함한다.

15 Intention Question
화자는 왜 백색광을 언급하는가?
☑ 결합된 주파수의 개념을 시각화하기 위해
Ⓑ 감각 지각에 대한 유사한 연구를 소개하기 위해
Ⓒ 자연광과 인공광의 원천을 구별하기 위해
Ⓓ 화이트 노이즈가 스펙트럼 디스플레이에서 왜 하얗게 나타나는지 설명하기 위해

어휘 visualize[víʒuəlaiz] 시각화하다 sensory[sénsəri] 감각의
distinguish[distíŋgwiʃ] 구별하다

16 Discuss Next Question
화자는 다음에 무엇을 논의할 것 같은가?
Ⓐ 다양한 소음 유형들의 건강에 대한 영향
☑ 블루와 핑크 노이즈의 오디오 시연
Ⓒ 인간의 소음 민감도 변화에 대한 연구
Ⓓ 즐겁고 불쾌한 소리에 대한 문화적 인식

어휘 demonstration[dèmənstréiʃən] 시연
sensitivity[sènsətívəti] 민감도

3. Detail Questions

Example 🔊 En p.263

털부처꽃, 학명으로는 *Lythrum salicaria*에 대해 이야기해보겠습니다. 이 침입성 식물은 토착 식생을 밀어내고 습지 생태계를 교란시켜 미국에서 생태학적 우려 사항이 되었습니다. 그렇다면 이 식물은 어떻게 그곳에 도달했을까요? 아마도 1800년대 초에 털부처꽃이 유럽에서 미국으로 들어온 것으로 보입니다. 몇몇 연구자들이 1830년대에 이를 "토착" 식물로 분류했지만, 지금은 그것이 사실이 아니라는 것을 알고 있습니다. 어쨌든, 이 식물은 배를 안정화시키기 위해 사용된 배의 하부에 있던 바위나 물과 함께 도착한 것으로 알려져 있습니다. 그 배들은 미국과의 무역을 위한 주요 수출 중심지였던 북유럽에서 항해해 왔습니다.

invasive[invéisiv] 침입성의
outcompete[àutkəmpí:t] 밀어내다, 경쟁에서 이기다
disrupt[disrʌ́pt] 교란시키다, 파괴하다 wetland[wétlænd] 습지
ecosystem[í:kousìstəm] 생태계 identify[aidéntəfài] 식별하다
stabilize[stéibəlàiz] 안정화시키다

강의에 따르면, 털부처꽃은 어떻게 미국에 도달했는가?
Ⓐ 관상용 식물로 수입되어서
Ⓑ 대서양을 가로질러 자연적으로 이주해서
Ⓒ 미국 식물학자들에 의해 들여와져서
☑ 배의 하부에 있는 물에 실려 들어와서

어휘 ornamental[ɔ̀:rnəméntl] 장식적인 migrate[máigreit] 이주하다
Atlantic[ætlǽntik] 대서양 botanist[bátənist] 식물학자

HACKERS PRACTICE p.264

01 Ⓐ   02 Ⓒ   03 Ⓓ   04 Ⓑ

01 Detail Question 🔊 Am

Today, we'll discuss insomnia, <u>a difficulty falling asleep</u> or staying asleep. There are two types: acute and chronic.

Acute insomnia, which is caused by <u>temporary factors</u>, lasts only a few days and typically resolves on its own. On the other hand, chronic insomnia occurs at least three nights a week for over three months. Various physical and psychological factors <u>can cause this condition</u>.

Now, **treatment for insomnia focuses on sleep hygiene.** This includes consistent bedtimes, <u>avoiding daytime naps</u>, limiting caffeine, and maintaining cool, dark sleeping environments without distractions.

insomnia[insá:mniə] 불면증 fall asleep 잠에 들다
acute[əkjú:t] 급성의 chronic[kránik] 만성의
treatment[trí:tmənt] 치료, 처리, 대우 sleep hygiene 수면 습관
consistent[kənsístənt] 일정한
distraction[distrǽkʃən] 주의를 산만하게 하는 것

오늘 우리는 잠드는 것이나 잠을 유지하는 데 어려움을 겪는 불면증에 대해 논의하겠습니다. 두 가지 유형이 있는데, 바로 급성과 만성입니다. 급성 불면증은 일시적 요인에 의해 발생하는데, 며칠만 지속되며 보통 스스로 해결됩니다. 반면, 만성 불면증은 3개월 이상 최소 주 3회 발생합니다. 다양한 신체적 및 심리적 요인이 이 질환을 유발할 수 있습니다. 이제, **불면증 치료는 수면 습관에 초점을 맞춥니다.** 여기에는 일정한 취침 시간, 낮잠 피하기, 카페인 제한, 그리고 주의를 산만하게 하는 것 없이 시원하고 어두운 수면 환경을 유지하는 것이 포함됩니다.

불면증 치료로 언급되지 않은 것은 무엇인가?
☑ 격렬한 운동
Ⓑ 카페인 제한

ⓒ 일정한 취침 시간
ⓓ 온도 조절

어휘 strenuous [strénjuəs] 격렬한   restriction [ristríkʃən] 제한, 한정

02 Detail Question   Nz

The history of solar activity is of great interest to scientists. **Out of the past 1,150 years, the Sun has been extremely active during the last sixty.** With the increase in sunspots, the Earth has been getting warmer. This information suggests that changes in solar activity may influence global climate. In fact, historical data and climate records support the idea that variations in solar activity have played a role in long-term climate changes.

solar [sóulər] 태양의   sunspot [sʌ́nspɑ̀t] 흑점
influence [ínfluəns] 영향을 미치다; 영향
variation [vɛ̀əriéiʃən] 변화   long-term 장기적인

태양 활동의 역사는 과학자들에게 큰 관심사입니다. **지난 1,150년 중, 태양은 지난 60년 동안 극도로 활발했습니다.** 흑점의 증가와 함께, 지구는 점점 더워지고 있습니다. 이 정보는 태양 활동의 변화가 지구 기후에 영향을 미칠 수 있음을 시사합니다. 실제로, 역사적 데이터와 기후 기록은 태양 활동의 변화가 장기적인 기후 변화에 역할을 했다는 의견을 뒷받침합니다.

화자는 태양 활동에 대해 무엇을 말하는가?
ⓐ 약 1,150년 전에 정점에 달했다.
ⓑ 60년마다 예측 가능한 주기를 따른다.
✓ⓒ 최근 수십 년간 특히 강했다.
ⓓ 지구 날씨 패턴에 최소한의 영향을 미친다.

어휘 peak [pi:k] 정점에 달하다; 정점
approximately [əpráksəmətli] 약, 대략
predictable [pridíktəbl] 예측 가능한   intense [inténs] 강한
minimal [mínəməl] 최소한의

03 Detail Question   En

Bubonic plague is a long-standing disease. During the reign of the Roman Emperor Justinian, about 50% of the Mediterranean population died from the plague. This clearly shows that the plague was a fast-spreading and highly deadly disease.
Improved hygiene and quarantine measures have helped control it, but **it remains prevalent in parts of Asia, such as India, where around 5,000 cases were reported in 1994.**

bubonic plague 흑사병   long-standing 오랜
reign [rein] 통치 기간   Mediterranean [mèdətəréiniən] 지중해의
population [pɑ̀:pjuléiʃən] 인구   plague [pleig] 질병
hygiene [háidʒi:n] 위생   quarantine [kwɔ́:rənti:n] 격리
prevalent [prévələnt] 만연한, 흔한

흑사병은 오랜 역사를 지닌 질병입니다. 로마 황제 유스티니아누스의 통치 기간 동안, 지중해 인구의 약 50퍼센트가 흑사병으로 사망했습니다. 이는 흑사병이 전염 속도가 매우 빠르고 치명성이 높은 질병이었음을 잘 보여줍니다.
개선된 위생과 격리 조치가 이를 통제하는 데 도움을 주었지만, 1994년에 약 5,000건의 사례가 보고된 인도와 같은 아시아 일부 지역에서는 여전히 만연해 있습니다.

화자에 따르면, 흑사병의 핵심 특징은 무엇인가?
ⓐ 수년에 걸친 느린 진행
ⓑ 현대적 격리 조치에 대한 저항
ⓒ 어린이에게만 영향을 미치는 치명적 감염
✓ⓓ 특정 지역에서의 지속적인 존재

어휘 infection [infékʃən] 감염

04 Detail Question   Am

Absolute dating is a method that establishes the age of an object or event in terms of calendar years. **It often relies on the decay of radioactive isotopes, such as carbon-14 and uranium-238, to calculate the age.** For example, geologists may find three layers of different types of rock. Determining the relative age of these layers is straightforward: the deepest layer is the oldest, the middle layer is younger, and the uppermost layer is the youngest. However, if a piece of pottery is found in the middle layer and the geologists want to know exactly which period it belongs to, absolute dating can be used to determine its precise age.

in terms of ~으로, ~에 있어서
calendar year 역년 (달력 기준 1년)
decay [dikéi] (방사성 물질의) 붕괴
radioactive [rèidiouǽktiv] 방사성의   isotope [áisətòup] 동위원소
calculate [kǽlkjulèit] 계산하다, 평가하다
geologist [dʒiɑ́lədʒist] 지질학자
determine [ditə́:rmin] 측정하다, 결정하다
relative [rélətiv] 상대적인
uppermost [ʌ́pərmòust] 최상의, 가장 높은
precise [prisáis] 정확한

절대 연대 측정은 역년으로 물체나 사건의 연령을 확정하는 방법입니다. **이는 종종 탄소-14와 우라늄-238과 같은 방사성 동위원소의 붕괴에 의존하여 연령을 계산합니다.** 예를 들어, 지질학자들은 서로 다른 종류의 암석으로 이루어진 세 개의 층을 발견할 수 있습니다. 이러한 층들의 상대적 연령을 측정하는 것은 간단한데, 가장 깊은 층이 가장 오래된 것이고, 중간 층이 더 젊으며, 최상층이 가장 젊습니다. 하지만, 만약 중간 층에서 도자기 조각이 발견되고 지질학자들이 그것이 정확히 어느 시대에 속하는지 알고 싶다면, 그것의 정확한 연령을 측정하기 위해 절대 연대 측정이 사용될 수 있습니다.

강의에 따르면, 과학자들은 물체의 정확한 연령을 어떻게 측정하는가?
ⓐ 주변 암석층과 비교하여
✓ⓑ 방사성 동위원소의 붕괴를 분석하여
ⓒ 물리적 외관을 조사하여
ⓓ 광물 성분을 규명하여

어휘 analyze [ǽnəlàiz] 분석하다
characterize [kǽrəktəràiz] 규명하다, 특징을 나타내다
mineral [mínərəl] 광물, 무기물

HACKERS TEST   p.266

01 ⓒ	02 Ⓐ	03 Ⓑ	04 Ⓓ	05 Ⓐ
06 ⓒ	07 Ⓓ	08 Ⓑ	09 Ⓑ	10 Ⓓ
11 ⓒ	12 Ⓓ	13 Ⓑ	14 ⓒ	15 Ⓐ
16 Ⓓ				

[01-04]

Listen to a talk on a podcast about sociology.

⁰¹**Social mobility refers to the ability of individuals or groups to move between different socioeconomic positions within society. Education has traditionally been viewed as the great equalizer, providing opportunities for people from lower-income families to improve their circumstances.** However, ⁰²**recent research reveals that the relationship between education and social mobility is more complex than previously thought.** While higher education generally increases earning potential, the cost of college has risen dramatically, creating barriers for low-income students. Even when financial aid is available, hidden costs like textbooks, transportation, and housing can prevent completion. Additionally, the quality of elementary and secondary education varies significantly based on neighborhood wealth, creating unequal starting points. For instance, ⁰³**students from affluent families benefit from resources like tutoring, test preparation, and extracurricular activities that enhance college applications.** They also have access to social networks that provide information about opportunities and career advancement. These advantages are often inaccessible to students from lower-income families. Despite these challenges, education remains one of the most reliable paths to upward mobility. To support this, there are programs that provide comprehensive assistance, including mentoring, financial aid, and academic preparation. ⁰⁴**Next, we'll examine specific programs that have successfully increased college graduation rates among low-income students.**

social mobility 사회적 이동성
equalizer[í:kwəlàizər] 평등화 도구, 평등하게 하는 것
circumstance[sə́:rkəmstæns] 형편, 상황
complex[kəmpléks] 복잡한, 복합의
dramatically[drəmǽtikəli] 극적으로   financial aid 재정 지원
completion[kəmplí:ʃən] 졸업, 수료, 완성
elementary[èləméntəri] 초등의, 기본의
secondary[sékəndèri] 중등의, 부차적인
affluent[ǽfluənt] 부유한
extracurricular[èkstrəkəríkjələr] 과외의
enhance[inhǽns] 강화하다, 높이다

inaccessible[ìnəksésəbl] 접근할 수 없는, 도달하기 어려운
upward[ʌ́pwərd] 상향의
comprehensive[kɔ̀mprihénsiv] 포괄적인

사회학에 관한 팟캐스트에서의 강의를 들으시오.

⁰¹사회적 이동성은 개인이나 집단이 사회 내에서 서로 다른 사회경제적 위치 사이를 이동할 수 있는 능력을 의미합니다. 교육은 전통적으로 위대한 평등화 도구로 여겨져 왔으며, 저소득 가정 출신의 사람들이 그들의 형편을 개선할 기회를 제공해 왔습니다. 하지만 ⁰²최근 연구는 교육과 사회적 이동성 사이의 관계가 이전에 생각했던 것보다 더 복잡하다는 것을 보여줍니다. 고등교육이 일반적으로 소득 잠재력을 증가시키는 반면, 대학 비용은 극적으로 상승했고, 저소득 학생들에게 장벽을 만들었습니다. 재정 지원이 가능할 때조차도, 교과서, 교통비, 주거비와 같은 숨겨진 비용들이 졸업을 방해할 수 있습니다.
게다가, 초등 및 중등교육의 질은 지역의 경제적 수준에 따라 상당히 다르며, 불평등한 출발점을 만들어냅니다. 예를 들어, ⁰³부유한 가정 출신의 학생들은 대학 입학원서를 강화하는 과외, 시험 준비, 그리고 비교과 활동과 같은 자원으로부터 혜택을 받습니다. 그들은 또한 기회와 경력 발전에 대한 정보를 제공하는 사회적 네트워크에도 접근할 수 있습니다. 이러한 장점들은 보통 저소득 가정 출신의 학생들은 접근할 수 없습니다.
이러한 도전에도 불구하고, 교육은 상향 이동성을 위한 가장 신뢰할 만한 경로 중 하나로 남아 있습니다. 이를 지원하기 위해, 멘토링, 재정 지원, 그리고 학업 준비를 포함한 포괄적인 지원을 제공하는 프로그램들이 있습니다. ⁰⁴다음으로, 우리는 저소득 학생들 사이에서 대학 졸업률을 성공적으로 증가시킨 구체적인 프로그램들을 살펴보겠습니다.

01 Main Topic Question

강의의 주요 주제는 무엇인가?
Ⓐ 치솟고 있는 대학 교육 비용
Ⓑ 저소득 학생들을 위한 재정 지원 프로그램
🗹 교육과 사회 이동성의 관계
Ⓓ 고등교육기관의 숨겨진 비용

어휘 institution[ìnstətjú:ʃən] 기관, 제도

02 Detail Question

화자는 교육에 대한 최근 연구에 대해 무엇이라고 주장하는가?
🗹 교육과 사회적 이동성 간의 관계가 복잡하다고 제안한다.
Ⓑ 재정적 장벽이 완전히 제거되었다는 것을 보여준다.
ⓒ 부유한 가정들이 교육적 장점을 갖지 않는다는 것을 보여준다.
Ⓓ 교육이 더 이상 사회적 이동성 기회를 제공하지 않는다는 것을 증명한다.

어휘 complicated[kʌ́mpləkèitid] 복잡한, 뒤얽힌
       eliminate[ilímənèit] 제거하다, 삭제하다

03 Detail Question

화자는 부유한 가정 출신의 학생들에 대해 무엇을 말하는가?
Ⓐ 학업 성공을 위해 멘토링 프로그램에 의존한다.
🗹 대학 지원서를 강화하는 요소들을 가지고 있다.
ⓒ 학문적 준비보다 직업 훈련에 더 중점을 둔다.
Ⓓ 교육이 사회적 이동에 미치는 역할을 과소평가하는 경향이 있다.

어휘 tend to ~하는 경향이 있다
       underestimate[ʌ̀ndəréstəmeit] 과소평가하다

04 Discuss Next Question

화자는 다음에 무엇을 논의할 것인가?
Ⓐ 교육 불평등에 대한 연구 결과
Ⓑ 불우한 학생들을 위한 진로 상담 전략
Ⓒ 교육 시스템의 국제적 비교
✓ 효과적인 교육 지원 프로그램의 예시

어휘 counseling [káunsəliŋ] 상담
   disadvantaged [dìsədvǽntidʒd] 불우한, 가난한

[05-08]　　　　　　　　　　🎧 Am

Listen to a talk in an anthropology class.

> ⁰⁵Homo Ludens, meaning "Playing Man," examines the importance of play in human culture. Unlike traditional views that humans are primarily rational beings, the Homo Ludens theory suggests play is a fundamental cultural activity that predates civilization itself. That is, play isn't just recreational. Rather, it serves crucial social functions.
> ⁰⁶Consider how children's games like hide-and-seek establish important social skills. Through these seemingly simple activities, children learn rule-following, cooperation, and conflict resolution. In many cultures, ritualized games teach social classes and expected behaviors. You see, even in adult contexts, games and play-like activities reinforce cultural values. Just think of how formal debates follow game-like structures with specific rules that participants should respect.
> ⁰⁷The significance of play extends beyond obvious entertainment. It shapes our social structures, legal systems, and even warfare. Well, for instance, many ancient societies had ritualized forms of conflict resolution that resembled games with specific rules. This demonstrates how elements for play are embedded in serious cultural institutions.
> ⁰⁸What's particularly interesting is how play transcends necessity. Unlike basic survival behaviors, play is voluntary and exists outside ordinary life while still following strict rules. This paradox, serious activities with non-serious purposes, reveals something fundamental about human nature.

rational [rǽʃənl] 이성적인　fundamental [fʌ̀ndəméntl] 근본적인
predate [prideít] 앞서다　civilization [sìvəlaizéiʃən] 문명
recreational [rèkriéiʃənəl] 오락적인
crucial [krúːʃəl] 중요한, 결정적인
seemingly [síːmiŋli] 겉보기에, ~듯한
cooperation [kouɑ́pəréiʃən] 협력
ritualize [rítʃuəlàiz] 의식화하다
reinforce [rìːinfɔ́ːrs] 강화하다, 보강하다　warfare [wɔ́ːrfɛr] 전쟁
resemble [rizémbəl] 유사하다, 닮다
embed [imbéd] 내재되다; 내장
transcend [trænsénd] 초월하다　necessity [nəsésəti] 필요성

인류학 강의를 들으시오.

⁰⁵호모 루덴스는 "놀이하는 인간"을 의미하며, 인간 문화에서 놀이의 중요성을 탐구합니다. 인간이 주로 이성적 존재라는 전통적 견해와 달리, 호모 루덴스 이론은 놀이가 문명 자체보다 앞서는 근본적인 문화 활동이라고 제안합니다. 즉, 놀이는 단순히 오락적이지 않습니다. 오히려, 그것은 중요한 사회적 기능을 수행합니다.
⁰⁶숨바꼭질과 같은 아이들의 게임이 어떻게 중요한 사회적 기술을 확립하는지 생각해보세요. 이러한 겉보기에 단순한 활동들을 통해, 아이들은 규칙 준수, 협력, 그리고 갈등 해결을 배웁니다. 많은 문화에서, 의식화된 게임들은 사회적 계층과 기대되는 행동들을 가르칩니다. 성인의 맥락에서도 게임과 놀이 같은 활동들이 문화적 가치를 강화한다는 것을 알 수 있죠. 공식적인 토론이 참가자들이 존중해야 하는 특정한 규칙을 가진 게임 같은 구조를 따르는 방식을 생각해보세요.
⁰⁷놀이의 중요성은 명백한 오락을 넘어 확장됩니다. 그것은 우리의 사회 구조, 법적 시스템, 그리고 심지어 전쟁까지도 형성합니다. 예를 들어, 많은 고대 사회들은 특정한 규칙이 있는 게임과 유사한 의례화된 갈등 해결 형태를 가지고 있었습니다. 이것은 놀이 요소들이 어떻게 진지한 문화적 제도들에 내재되어 있는지를 보여줍니다.
⁰⁸특히 흥미로운 것은 놀이가 어떻게 필요성을 초월하는가입니다. 기본적인 생존 행동과 달리, 놀이는 자발적이며 엄격한 규칙을 따르면서도 일상적인 삶 밖에 존재합니다. 진지하지 않은 목적을 가진 진지한 활동이라는 역설은 인간 본성에 대한 근본적인 무언가를 보여줍니다.

05 Main Topic Question

강의의 주요 주제는 무엇인가?
✓ 인간의 문화와 문명에서 놀이의 역할
Ⓑ 업무와 여가 활동의 구별
Ⓒ 사회적 맥락에서 규칙 준수의 중요성
Ⓓ 게임과 법적 시스템 사이의 관계

어휘 distinction [distíŋkʃən] 구별, 특별함　leisure [líːʒər] 여가

06 Intention Question

화자는 왜 숨바꼭질을 언급하는가?
Ⓐ 문화가 게임 선택에 어떻게 영향을 미치는지 제안하기 위해
Ⓑ 아이들의 놀이의 보편적 성격을 보여주기 위해
✓ 게임이 중요한 사회적 행동을 가르친다는 것을 보여주기 위해
Ⓓ 아동기 발달에서 규칙은 불필요하다고 주장하기 위해

어휘 universal [jùːnəvə́ːrsəl] 보편적인
   unnecessary [ʌnnésəsèri] 불필요한

07 Detail Question

놀이가 형성할 수 있는 요소로 언급되지 않은 것은 무엇인가?
Ⓐ 군사적 갈등
Ⓑ 법적 제도
Ⓒ 사회 조직
✓ 필수적인 생존 기술

어휘 organization [ɔ̀ːrgənizéiʃən] 조직

08 Intention Question

화자는 왜 일상적인 삶을 언급하는가?
Ⓐ 성인과 아이들의 게임을 대조하기 위해
✓ 놀이가 필요성을 초월한다는 것을 보여주기 위해
Ⓒ 문화적 제도의 진지함을 강조하기 위해

Ⓓ 게임이 구조화된 규칙을 요구하는 이유를 설명하기 위해

어휘 contrast[káːntræst] 대조

[09-12]

🎧 Au

Listen to a talk in an astronomy class.

> [09]Gamma rays are the highest-energy photons in the electromagnetic spectrum, with the shortest wavelengths and the highest energy levels known. [10]So, where do these waves come from? Gamma rays originate from the hottest, most extreme regions of the universe. They're produced when radioactive atoms decay, and we believe that many come from distant galaxies where superheated matter spirals into massive black holes.
>
> Here's the thing, though: when gamma rays reach Earth, our atmosphere acts like a natural shield, absorbing most of them at different altitudes. This actually makes studying them quite challenging. [11]How do we observe something that's blocked by our own atmosphere? That's where technology comes to the rescue. Scientists use specialized instruments mounted on high-altitude balloons and satellites, such as the Compton Gamma Ray Observatory, to detect these rays from space.
>
> So, why should we care about gamma rays? Well, if we could see the universe through gamma vision, everything would look completely different. The moon would appear brighter than the sun, and we could peer into the regions around black holes and witness the most violent cosmic events. [12]Understanding gamma radiation will help us unlock secrets about the universe's origin and expansion.

gamma ray 감마선 photon[fóutɑn] 광자
electromagnetic[ilèktroʊmæɡnétik] 전자기의
atom[ǽtəm] 원자 atmosphere[ǽtməsfìər] 대기
absorb[æbsɔ́ːrb] 흡수하다 altitude[ǽltətjùːd] 고도, 높이
mount[maunt] 장착하다, 탑재하다 peer into ~을 들여다 보다
witness[wítnis] 목격하다; 증언
violent[váiələnt] 격렬한, 폭력적인

천문학 강의를 들으시오.

[09]감마선은 전자기 스펙트럼에서 가장 높은 에너지를 가진 광자들로서, 알려진 것 중 가장 짧은 파장과 가장 강한 에너지 수준을 가지고 있습니다. [10]그렇다면, 이러한 파동들은 어디서 오는 것일까요? 감마선은 우주에서 가장 뜨거운 극한의 지역에서 기원합니다. 그것들은 방사능 원자가 붕괴할 때 생성되며, 우리는 많은 것들이 과열된 물질이 거대한 블랙홀로 나선형으로 빨려 들어가는 먼 은하들로부터 온다고 여깁니다. 하지만 여기서 중요한 것은 감마선이 지구에 도달할 때, 우리의 대기가 자연 방패처럼 작용하여, 대부분을 서로 다른 고도에서 흡수한다는 것입니다. 이것은 실제로 감마선을 연구하는 것을 상당히 어렵게 만듭니다. [11]우리 대기에 의해 차단된 대상을 어떻게 관찰할까요? 그 지점에서 기술이 문제 해결에 도움을 줍니다. 과학자들은 콤프턴 감마선 관측선과 같이 고고도 풍선과 위성에 장착된 특수 장비를 사용하여 우주에서 이러한 감마선을 탐지합니다.

그렇다면, 왜 우리가 감마선에 대해 신경 써야 할까요? 만약 우리가 감마선 시야로 우주를 볼 수 있다면, 모든 것이 완전히 다르게 보일 것입니다. 달이 태양보다 더 밝게 나타날 것이고, 우리는 블랙홀 주변을 들여다 보고 가장 격렬한 우주적 사건들을 목격할 수 있을 것입니다. [12]감마선을 이해하는 것은 우주의 기원과 팽창에 대한 비밀을 푸는 데 도움을 줄 것입니다.

09 Main Topic Question

강의는 주로 무엇에 대한 것인가?
Ⓐ 보이지 않는 방사선을 위한 관측 기법
✓ 고에너지 광자의 특성과 중요성
Ⓒ 천문학적 관측을 수행하는 것의 어려움
Ⓓ 서로 다른 전자파들 간의 비교

어휘 observational[ɑ̀bzərvéiʃənl] 관측의
    invisible[invízəbl] 보이지 않는
    astronomical[æ̀strənɑ́mikəl] 천문학적인

10 Inference Question

화자는 감마선에 대해 무엇을 암시하는가?
Ⓐ 자연적이라기보다는 주로 인공적이다.
Ⓑ 지상 기반 장비로 쉽게 탐지된다.
Ⓒ X선과 비교했을 때 보통의 에너지 수준을 가진다.
✓ 극한 조건의 지역에서 발생한다.

어휘 moderate[mɑ́dərèit] 보통의, 적당한
    emerge from ~에서 발생하다

11 Intention Question

화자는 왜 콤프턴 감마선 관측선을 언급하는가?
Ⓐ 위성의 궤도 특성을 묘사하기 위해
Ⓑ 현재 장비들의 한계를 논의하기 위해
✓ 대기 간섭에 대한 해결책을 설명하기 위해
Ⓓ 전자기 탐지의 원리를 설명하기 위해

어휘 satellite[sǽtəlàit] 위성 atmospheric[æ̀tməsférik] 대기의

12 Detail Question

화자에 따르면, 왜 감마선이 연구되어야 하는가?
Ⓐ 행성 대기에 대한 정보를 제공한다.
Ⓑ 지구의 지질학적 과정에 대한 통찰을 제공한다.
Ⓒ 진보된 의료 영상 기법을 개발하는 데 도움을 준다.
✓ 우주 팽창 과정에 대한 정보를 보여준다.

[13-16]

🎧 Am

Listen to a talk in a biology class.

> [13]Identical twins originate from one ovum, which means that they come from a single fertilized egg. They divide into two zygotes sometime during the first thirteen days. You might think that identical twins are truly identical in every way because they share the same DNA, [14]but the only similarity they actually share is their sex. Their personalities will likely be different, and if they're exposed to divergent

environments, their appearances may even be somewhat dissimilar.

¹³Fraternal twins, on the other hand, ¹⁵form from two separate eggs and two different sperm cells. They develop side by side in the womb and may actually be as similar or as dissimilar as siblings are. For same-sex twins, it's harder to determine whether they're identical or fraternal. In some cases, whether twins are identical or fraternal cannot even be determined during pregnancy. Why is this so? Well, identical twins form in a single sac and they typically share a single placenta. But the number of placentas isn't always a clear indicator because the separate placentas of fraternal twins can actually fuse together and appear to be one. And at times, identical twins develop with completely separate placentas. In such cases, ¹⁶how can we tell whether twins are identical or fraternal? Let's find out.

identical [aidéntikəl] 일란성의, 똑같은   ovum [óuvəm] 난자
fertilized egg 수정란   zygote [záigout] 접합자
similarity [sìməlǽrəti] 유사점   divergent [daivə́ːrdʒənt] 서로 다른
somewhat [sʌ́mwɑt] 다소   fraternal [frətə́ːrnl] 이란성의, 형제의
sperm [spəːrm] 정자   side by side 나란히   womb [wuːm] 자궁
sibling [síbliŋ] 형제자매   pregnancy [prégnənsi] 임신 (기간)
sac [sæk] 주머니, 낭   indicator [índikèitər] 지표, 지시

생물학 강의를 들으시오.

¹³일란성 쌍둥이는 하나의 난자에서 기원하는데, 이는 그들이 단일한 수정란에서 나온다는 것을 의미합니다. 그들은 처음 13일 동안의 어느 시점에서 두 개의 접합자로 분할됩니다. 여러분은 일란성 쌍둥이가 같은 DNA를 공유하기 때문에 모든 면에서 진정으로 동일하다고 생각할지도 모르지만, ¹⁴그들이 실제로 공유하는 유일한 유사점은 그들의 성별입니다. 그들의 성격은 아마도 다를 것이고, 만약 그들이 서로 다른 환경에 노출된다면, 그들의 외형조차도 다소 다를 수 있습니다.

¹³반면에, 이란성 쌍둥이는 ¹⁵두 개의 분리된 난자와 두 개의 다른 정자로부터 형성됩니다. 그들은 자궁에서 나란히 발달하며 실제로 형제자매만큼 유사하거나 다를 수 있습니다.

같은 성별의 쌍둥이의 경우, 그들이 일란성인지 이란성인지 판단하기가 더 어렵습니다. 어떤 경우에는 쌍둥이가 일란성인지 이란성인지를 임신 중에도 판단할 수 없습니다. 왜 그럴까요? 음, 일란성 쌍둥이는 하나의 주머니에서 형성되고 그들은 보통 단일한 태반을 공유합니다. 하지만 태반의 수가 항상 명확한 지표는 아닌데, 왜냐하면 이란성 쌍둥이의 분리된 태반들이 실제로 함께 융합되어 하나로 보일 수 있기 때문입니다. 그리고 때때로, 일란성 쌍둥이가 각각 완전히 분리된 태반을 가진 채로 발달하기도 합니다. 그러한 경우에, ¹⁶우리는 쌍둥이가 일란성인지 이란성인지를 어떻게 구별할 수 있을까요? 알아봅시다.

13 Main Topic Question

강의의 주요 주제는 무엇인가?
Ⓐ 임신 중 쌍둥이 유형을 판단하는 방법
✓ 서로 다른 쌍둥이 유형의 형성과 특성
Ⓒ 쌍둥이 발달에 대한 부모의 유전적 기여
Ⓓ 쌍둥이 성격 형성에 대한 환경적 영향

어휘 parental [pəréntl] 부모의   genetic [dʒənétik] 유전적인, 유전자의
contribution [kɑ̀ntrəbjúːʃən] 기여

14 Detail Question

화자에 따르면, 일란성 쌍둥이가 실제로 공유하는 것은 무엇인가?
Ⓐ 성격 발달
Ⓑ 신체적 외형
✓ 성별 특성
Ⓓ 환경적 적응

어휘 gender [dʒéndər] 성별
characteristic [kæ̀riktərístik] 특성; 특징적인
adaptation [æ̀dəptéiʃən] 적응

15 Detail Question

화자는 이란성 쌍둥이에 대해 무엇이라고 주장하는가?
✓ 분리된 난자와 분리된 정자로부터 발달한다.
Ⓑ 발달 중에 단일한 태반을 공유한다.
Ⓒ 같은 성격 특성을 보여준다.
Ⓓ 일반적으로 일란성 쌍둥이보다 더 많은 유사점을 공유한다.

어휘 trait [treit] 특성, 특징

16 Discuss Next Question

화자는 다음에 무엇을 논의할 것인가?
Ⓐ 쌍둥이 특이적 질환에 대한 치료 선택지
Ⓑ 쌍둥이 임신에 영향을 미치는 부모의 유전적 요인
Ⓒ 서로 다른 쌍둥이 유형에 대한 장기적 건강 결과
✓ 쌍둥이 유형을 판단하기 위한 진단적 접근법

어휘 diagnostic [dàiəgnɑ́stik] 진단적인

4. Intention Questions

Example

저는 다차원 공간을 제시한 첫 번째 이론인 Kaluza-Klein 이론에 대해 이야기하고자 합니다. 이 이론은 중력과 전자기력을 통일하려고 했지만, 이론이 성립하려면 네 번째 공간 차원의 존재를 가정해야 했습니다. Theodor Kaluza는 차원이 작고 보이지 않을 수 있다는 발상을 내놓았습니다. 정원 호스를 생각해보세요. **멀리서 보면 호스는 1차원으로 보이지만, 가까이 다가가면 원형의 추가 차원이 있음을 알 수 있습니다.** Kaluza-Klein 이론은 우주에 정원 호스의 원형 차원처럼 감겨 있는 다른 차원들이 매우 작은 규모로 존재할 수 있다고 말합니다.

spatial [spéiʃəl] 공간의   dimension [diménʃən] 차원
unify [júːnəfai] 통일하다   assume [əsúːm] 가정하다
existence [igzástəns] 존재   one-dimensional 1차원의

교수는 왜 정원 호스를 언급하는가?
Ⓐ 알려진 우주의 차원들을 설명하기 위해
✓ 보이지 않는 추가 차원의 예시를 제공하기 위해
Ⓒ 물체가 어떻게 네 개의 차원을 가질 수 있는지 명확히 하기 위해
Ⓓ 공간 차원과 시간 차원을 비교하기 위해

어휘 clarify[klǽrəfài] 명확히 하다 temporal[témpərəl] 시간의

HACKERS **PRACTICE**   p.272

01 ⓒ   02 ⓓ   03 ⓑ   04 ⓐ

01 Intention Question   Am

Originally, coyotes were wild animals with minimal human contact. However, as suburban development expanded, some coyote populations began inhabiting urban fringes and residential areas.
What's interesting is their behavioral shift. These urban coyotes have learned that humans pose little threat, and this has led to increasingly bold behavior. They've started hunting during daylight hours and venturing into residential yards. **Some even approach children directly, which represents** a significant departure from their traditionally cautious nature.

suburban[səbə́:rbən] 교외의 fringe[frindʒ] 변두리
residential area 주거 지역 behavioral[bihéivjərəl] 행동의
shift[ʃift] 변화; 바꾸다 pose a threat 위협을 가하다
bold[bould] 대담한 venture into ~을 감행하다
nature[néitʃər] 본성, 습성, 자연

원래 코요테는 인간과의 접촉이 최소한인 야생 동물이었습니다. 하지만 교외 개발이 확장되면서, 일부 코요테 집단은 도시 변두리와 주거 지역에 서식하기 시작했습니다.
흥미로운 점은 그들의 행동 변화입니다. 이러한 도시 코요테들은 인간이 거의 위협을 가하지 않는다는 것을 학습했고, 이는 점점 더 대담한 행동을 하도록 이끌었습니다. 그들은 낮 시간대에 사냥하기 시작했고 주택가의 마당으로 들어가는 것을 감행하기 시작했습니다. **일부는 심지어 아이들에게 직접 접근하기도 하는데, 이는 전통적으로 조심스러운 그들의 본성에서의 상당한 이탈을 나타냅니다.**

화자는 왜 아이들을 언급하는가?
Ⓐ 도시 코요테의 자연적인 먹이 선호도를 설명하기 위해
Ⓑ 부모들이 아이들을 제대로 감독하지 않는다고 비판하기 위해
✓ 도시 코요테의 전례 없는 대담함을 강조하기 위해
Ⓓ 야생동물 조우에 대한 교육 프로그램을 제안하기 위해

어휘 criticize[krítəsàiz] 비판하다 supervise[sú:pərvàiz] 감독하다
properly[prápərli] 제대로, 적절하게

02 Intention Question   Nz

Today, let's examine the fundamental assumptions underlying the Big Bang theory. Many people believe the Big Bang occurred at a single point in space. But scientists actually assume the universe is infinite and has no boundaries or edges. This means the Big Bang occurred throughout all space simultaneously. That is, what's expanding isn't the universe itself, but the space-time continuum within it. Additionally, **the Big Bang theory relies on Einstein's theory of relativity, which describes** space and time as relative **rather than absolute. This not only explains gravitational interactions between all matter in our universe but also serves as** a fundamental basis for the Big Bang theory itself.

assumption[əsʌ́mpʃən] 가설, 추측 infinite[ínfənət] 무한한
boundary[báundəri] 경계 edge[edʒ] 가장자리, 끝
space-time continuum 시공간 연속체, 4차원
gravitational[grӕvətéiʃənl] 중력의 matter[mǽtər] 물질
basis[béisis] 토대, 근거

오늘은 빅뱅 이론의 근본 가정을 살펴보겠습니다. 많은 사람들은 빅뱅이 우주의 한 지점에서 발생했다고 믿습니다. 하지만 과학자들은 실제로 우주가 무한하며 경계나 가장자리가 없다고 가정합니다. 이는 빅뱅이 우주 전역에서 동시에 발생했다는 것을 의미합니다. 즉, 팽창하는 것은 우주 자체가 아니라 그 안의 시공간 연속체입니다. 또한 **빅뱅 이론은 공간과 시간을 절대적이 아닌 상대적으로 기술하는 아인슈타인의 상대성 이론에 기반합니다. 이는 우주의 모든 물질 간 중력 상호작용을 설명할 뿐만 아니라 빅뱅 이론 자체의 근본적인 토대 역할도 합니다.**

교수는 왜 아인슈타인의 상대성 이론을 언급하는가?
Ⓐ 중력이 우주 팽창에 어떻게 영향을 미치는지 설명하기 위해
Ⓑ 시간이 서로 다른 속도로 흐른다는 것을 증명하기 위해
Ⓒ 우주가 하나의 지점에서 시작되었다는 것을 증명하기 위해
✓ 빅뱅 이론에 과학적 근거를 제공하기 위해

어휘 cosmic[kázmik] 우주의

03 Intention Question   Am

Scientists create climate models using historical data and computer simulations to forecast future climate patterns. **A fascinating case involves research on** ice cores. Climate scientist Lonnie Thompson analyzed thousands of samples worldwide and discovered evidence of a massive climate shift approximately 5,200 years ago. **Remarkably, he claims that current climate patterns** mirror those ancient conditions, **suggesting we're approaching a similar dramatic change.**

forecast[fɔ́:rkæst] 예측하다
fascinating[fǽsənèitiŋ] 흥미로운, 멋진 ice core 빙핵
massive[mǽsiv] 대규모의, 거대한
remarkably[rimá:rkəbli] 놀랍게도
mirror[mírər] 반영하다, 비추다; 거울
dramatic[drəmǽtik] 극적인

과학자들은 역사적 데이터와 컴퓨터 시뮬레이션을 사용하여 미래의 기후 패턴을 예측하는 기후 모델을 만듭니다. **흥미로운 사례는 빙핵 연구와 관련이 있습니다.** 기후 과학자 Lonnie Thompson은 전 세계 수천 개의 샘플을 분석하여 약 5,200년 전 대규모 기후 변화의 증거를 발견했습니다. 놀랍게도, 그는 현재의 기후 패턴이 그 고대 조건들을 반영한다고 주장하며, 우리가 유사한 극적인 변화에 다가가고 있음을 시사합니다.

교수는 왜 빙핵을 언급하는가?
Ⓐ 대안적인 연구 방법론을 제안하기 위해

Ⓐ 기후 패턴의 순환적 특성을 보여주기 위해
Ⓒ 기존의 기후 변화 이론들에 도전하기 위해
Ⓓ 기후 모델이 신뢰할 수 없다는 것을 증명하기 위해

어휘 cyclical[sáiklikəl] 순환적인
unreliable[ʌ̀nrilɑiə́bəl] 신뢰할 수 없는

04 Intention Question 🔊 En

When psychologists first began mapping the brain's emotional circuits, they discovered fascinating connections between our neural pathways and fear responses. They found that some people show heightened activity in the amygdala, the brain's alarm center, making them more susceptible to anxiety. Are these differences genetic or learned? Current research suggests that both factors play a role. People with overactivated fear circuits often have family histories of anxiety, which indicates possible inherited traits. However, environmental experiences also shape these neural networks.

circuit[sə́:rkit] 회로   neural[njúərəl] 신경의
pathway[pǽθwei] 경로   heighten[haitn] 높이다, 강화하다
susceptible[səséptəbl] 취약한, 민감한   anxiety[æŋzáiəti] 불안
inherited[inhéritid] 유전적인
environmental[invàiərənméntl] 환경적인

심리학자들이 처음 뇌의 감정 회로를 매핑하기 시작했을 때, 그들은 우리의 신경 경로와 공포 반응 사이의 흥미로운 연결을 발견했습니다. 그들은 일부 사람들이 뇌의 경보 센터인 편도체에서 높아진 활동을 보여 불안에 더 취약하게 만든다는 것을 발견했습니다. 이러한 차이점이 유전적인 것일까요, 아니면 학습된 것일까요? 현재의 연구는 두 요인 모두가 역할을 한다고 시사합니다. 과도하게 활성화된 공포 회로를 가진 사람들은 종종 불안의 가족력을 가지고 있으며, 이는 유전적 특성을 시사합니다. 하지만 환경적 경험들도 이러한 신경망을 형성합니다.

화자는 왜 환경적 경험을 언급하는가?
Ⓐ 공포 반응을 형성하는 요인을 설명하기 위해
Ⓑ 환경적 요인이 유전적 요인보다 우세함을 증명하기 위해
Ⓒ 심리학 연구의 새로운 방향을 제안하기 위해
Ⓓ 불안 장애에 대한 전통적인 견해에 도전하기 위해

어휘 outweigh[àutwéi] 우세하다, 중대하다
disorder[disɔ́:rdər] 장애

HACKERS TEST   p.274

01 Ⓒ	02 Ⓓ	03 Ⓑ	04 Ⓐ	05 Ⓓ
06 Ⓒ	07 Ⓑ	08 Ⓒ	09 Ⓐ	10 Ⓒ
11 Ⓓ	12 Ⓑ	13 Ⓓ	14 Ⓑ	15 Ⓒ
16 Ⓒ				

[01-04] 🔊 Au

Listen to a talk in a biology class.

⁰¹So it was really a big surprise to scientists in 1977 that animals could live at the bottom of the ocean. And we aren't talking about just a few animals. More than three hundred species of animals have been discovered living at deep-sea hydrothermal vents. Now, scientists continue to discover more, ⁰¹but for today, let's focus on tubeworm, the most abundant of the vent animals. ⁰²The really interesting thing about tubeworms is that while the baby worms or larvae are able to move around, adult worms stay in one place. In fact, scientists have observed that they are attached to the seafloor beneath them. It's quite a strange adaptation, isn't it?

⁰³Anyhow, adult tubeworms have no mouth or anus, or intestines. ⁰¹/⁰³This means that they don't eat and they don't remove waste as other animals do. Yet, they survive. How is this possible? You're probably thinking there's some symbiosis involved. ⁰⁴And you're absolutely right, there are special bacteria. But how do they get inside the worm if there's no mouth and no anus? Let's find out that now.

hydrothermal[hàidrəθə́:rməl] 열수의   vent[vent] 분출구
tubeworm[tjú:bwə̀:rm] 관벌레
abundant[əbʌ́ndənt] 흔한, 풍부한   larva[lɑ́:rvə] 유충, 애벌레
seafloor[sí:flɔ̀:r] 해저 바닥   anus[éinəs] 항문
intestine[intéstin] 장, 창자   symbiosis[sìmbaióusis] 공생 관계

생물학 강의를 들으시오.

⁰¹1977년에 과학자들에게 동물들이 바다 밑바닥에서 살 수 있다는 것이 정말 큰 놀라움이었습니다. 그리고 우리는 단지 몇 마리의 동물들에 대해 이야기하는 것이 아닙니다. 실제로 심해 열수 분출구에서 살고 있는 동물 종이 300종 이상 발견되었습니다. 현재, 과학자들은 계속해서 더 많은 것을 발견하고 있지만, ⁰¹오늘은 가장 흔한 분출구 동물인 관벌레에 집중해봅시다. ⁰²관벌레에 대해 정말 흥미로운 것은 새끼 벌레나 유충들은 돌아다닐 수 있는 반면, 성체 벌레들은 한 곳에 머물러 있다는 것입니다. 실제로, 과학자들은 그것들이 해저 바닥에 붙어 있는 것을 관찰했습니다. 꽤 이상한 적응이지 않나요?
⁰³어쨌든, 성체 관벌레들은 입, 항문, 장이 없습니다. ⁰¹/⁰³이는 그것들이 먹지도 않고 다른 동물들이 하는 것처럼 노폐물을 제거하지도 않는다는 것을 의미합니다. 그러나, 그것들은 살아남습니다. 어떻게 이것이 가능할까요? 여러분들은 아마도 어떤 공생 관계가 관련되어 있다고 생각하고 있을 것입니다. ⁰⁴그리고 여러분들이 절대적으로 옳아요, 특별한 박테리아가 있습니다. 하지만 입도 항문도 없다면 그것들이 어떻게 긴 벌레의 내부로 들어갈까요? 이제 그것에 대해 알아봅시다.

01 Main Topic Question

강의는 주로 무엇에 대한 것인가?
Ⓐ 해양 생물학의 과학적 연구 방법
Ⓑ 1977년 과학자들이 한 발견의 중요성
Ⓒ 놀라운 생존 적응을 지닌 독특한 종

Ⓓ 박테리아와 해양 동물 간의 관계

어휘 marine biology 해양 생물학

02 Intention Question
화자는 왜 새끼 벌레들을 언급하는가?
Ⓐ 관벌레들이 혹독한 환경에서 어떻게 번식하는지 설명하기 위해
Ⓑ 해양 생물의 변태 개념을 소개하기 위해
Ⓒ 어린 관벌레들의 섭식 습관을 보여주기 위해
✓ 생애 단계별 이동성을 대조하기 위해

어휘 reproduce[rì:prədjú:s] 번식하다 harsh[hɑ:rʃ] 혹독한, 가혹한
metamorphosis[mètəmɔ́:rfəsis] 변태

03 Inference Question
화자는 관벌레에 대해 무엇을 암시하는가?
Ⓐ 근처의 다른 관벌레들과 소통할 수 있다.
✓ 기본적인 해부학적 특징들이 부족함에도 불구하고 생존했다.
Ⓒ 다른 심해 생물들과 다르게 진화했다.
Ⓓ 열수 분출구에서 가장 최근에 발견된 종이다.

어휘 vicinity[visínəti] 근처 anatomical[ænətámikəl] 해부학적인

04 Discuss Next Question
화자는 다음에 무엇을 논의할 것 같은가?
✓ 박테리아가 관벌레로 들어가는 메커니즘
Ⓑ 심해 생물을 연구하기 위한 과학적 연구 기법
Ⓒ 관벌레에서 발견되는 박테리아 종의 분류
Ⓓ 관벌레가 입과 소화 기관이 없는 이유

어휘 digestive[didʒéstiv] 소화의

[05-08]   Am

Listen to a talk in a sociology class.

⁰⁵A cohort is a group of people who share a significant life experience during the same time period, typically being born in the same year or a span of years.
Well, cohorts are important in sociological research ⁰⁶because people from the same cohort often share similar experiences, values, and perspectives. For instance, the Baby Boomer cohort, those born between 1946 and 1964, experienced post-war economic growth, the Civil Rights Movement, and significant technological advances during their formative years.
When sociologists study cohorts, they're examining how historical events and social changes affect different generations. ⁰⁷This is what we call cohort analysis. It helps us understand why certain attitudes or behaviors might be more prevalent among specific age groups.
⁰⁸An interesting aspect of cohort studies is that they allow us to distinguish between age effects and cohort effects. Are certain behaviors simply the result of being a certain age? Or are they unique to a particular generation's experiences? For example, is digital technology use among young people an age effect that will change as they grow older, or a cohort effect that will persist throughout their lives? Well, ⁰⁸let's take a look at what sociological experts have to say about this.

span[spæn] 범위, 기간 sociological[sòusiəládʒikəl] 사회학적인
perspective[pərspéktiv] 관점 post-war 전후의, 전쟁 뒤의
formative[fɔ́:rmətiv] 성장의, 형성의
sociologist[sòusiáládʒist] 사회학자
generation[dʒènəréiʃən] 세대 analysis[ənǽləsis] 분석
attitude[ǽtitjù:d] 태도 persist[pərsíst] 지속하다

사회학 강의를 들으시오.
⁰⁵코호트는 같은 시기에 중요한 삶의 경험을 함께 겪은 사람들의 집단으로, 보통은 같은 해 또는 몇 년의 범위에 태어난 사람들을 가리킵니다.
음, 코호트들은 사회학적 연구에서 중요한데 ⁰⁶같은 코호트 출신의 사람들이 종종 비슷한 경험, 가치, 그리고 관점을 공유하기 때문입니다. 예를 들어, 1946년과 1964년 사이에 태어난 베이비붐 코호트는 그들의 성장기 동안 전후 경제 성장, 시민권 운동, 그리고 상당한 기술적 진보를 경험했습니다.
사회학자들이 코호트를 연구할 때, 그들은 역사적 사건들과 사회적 변화들이 각기 다른 세대들에게 어떻게 영향을 미치는지를 살펴봅니다. ⁰⁷이것이 우리가 코호트 분석이라고 부르는 것입니다. 그것은 왜 특정한 태도나 행동들이 특정 연령 집단들 사이에서 더 널리 퍼져 있을 수 있는지를 이해하는 데 도움을 줍니다.
⁰⁸코호트 연구의 흥미로운 측면은 우리가 연령 효과와 코호트 효과를 구별할 수 있도록 해줍니다. 특정한 행동들이 단순히 특정 연령이 되는 결과일까요? 아니면 그것들이 특정 세대의 경험들에 독특한 것일까요? 예를 들어, 젊은 사람들 사이의 디지털 기술 사용은 그들이 나이가 들면서 변화할 연령 효과일까요, 아니면 그들의 삶 전체에 걸쳐 지속될 코호트 효과일까요? 음, ⁰⁸이것에 대해 사회학 전문가들이 무엇이라고 말하는지 살펴봅시다.

05 Main Topic Question
강의의 주요 주제는 무엇인가?
Ⓐ 사회학에서 연구 방법의 진화
Ⓑ 전후 세대의 형성적 경험
Ⓒ 연령 관련 행동을 구별하는 것의 어려움
✓ 연령 집단 내의 공유된 경험의 중요성

06 Intention Question
화자는 왜 베이비붐 코호트에 대해 논의하는가?
Ⓐ 기술적 진보에 대한 그들의 반응을 비판하기 위해
Ⓑ 코호트 분석의 발전 과정에 대한 연대표를 제시하기 위해
✓ 코호트 집단의 구체적인 예시를 제시하기 위해
Ⓓ 베이비붐 코호트를 다른 집단과 비교하기 위해

어휘 advancement[ædvǽnsmənt] 발전
concrete[kɑ́:nkri:t] 구체적인

07 Detail Question

코호트 분석은 사회학에 무엇을 기여할 수 있는가?
Ⓐ 사회들 간의 문화적 차이의 분류
✓Ⓑ 세대들 간의 행동 차이의 설명
Ⓒ 사회에서 미래 기술 채택 동향의 예측
Ⓓ 모든 연령 집단에 걸친 보편적 행동 패턴의 인식

어휘 categorization [kæ̀təgərizéiʃən] 분류
explanation [èksplənéiʃən] 설명 prediction [pridʌ́kʃən] 예측
recognition [rèkəgníʃən] 인식

08 Discuss Next Question

화자는 다음에 무엇을 논의할 것인가?
Ⓐ 전통적인 코호트 분석의 한계
Ⓑ 세대에 걸친 디지털 기술 사용의 예시
✓Ⓒ 세대적 행동 패턴에 대한 전문가적 관점
Ⓓ 다른 효과들을 구별하는 방법론

어휘 viewpoint [vjúːpɔint] 관점
generational [dʒènəréiʃənl] 세대적인

[09-12] 🎧 En

Listen to a talk in a psychology class.

> ⁰⁹**The Barnum effect refers to the phenomenon where individuals believe that personality descriptions apply specifically to them.** This is true even when those descriptions are actually vague and general enough to apply to almost anyone.
> ¹⁰**This effect is named after P.T. Barnum, a 19th-century showman renowned for his skill in appealing to the general public.** When people read generic personality statements like "You have a tendency to be critical of yourself" or "You have a great need for other people to like and admire you," they often rate these statements as highly accurate descriptions of themselves. I bet some of you were thinking, 'That sounds like me.'
> ⁰⁹**Anyhow, the Barnum effect explains why many people find horoscopes, fortune cookies, and certain personality tests convincing.** These typically consist of statements broad enough to fit most people, yet readers perceive them as uniquely insightful. ¹¹**Psychologists have found that statements are particularly effective when they're mostly positive, with just enough negative traits to seem balanced and honest.** So, understanding this cognitive bias is important because it helps us recognize when we might be falling for general information presented as personalized insight. ¹²**Of course, there are also some drawbacks of this effect. Let's briefly take a look at what they are.**

phenomenon [finάmənὰn] 현상

description [diskrípʃən] 묘사, 설명 vague [veig] 모호한, 막연한
renowned for ~로 유명한 have a tendency to ~의 경향이 있다
admire [ædmáiər] 감탄하다 statement [stéitmənt] 진술
accurate [ǽkjurət] 정확한 horoscope [hɔ́ːrəskὰup] 별자리 운세
consist of ~로 구성되다 insightful [ínsàitfəl] 통찰력 있는
cognitive bias 인지 편향

심리학 강의를 들으시오.

⁰⁹바넘 효과는 개인이 성격 묘사가 구체적으로 자신들에게 적용된다고 믿는 현상을 가리킵니다. 그 묘사들이 실제로는 거의 누구에게나 적용될 만큼 모호하고 일반적일 때조차 이는 유효합니다.
¹⁰이 효과는 일반 대중에게 어필하는 기술로 유명한 19세기 흥행업자 P.T. Barnum의 이름을 따서 명명되었습니다. 사람들이 "당신은 자신을 비판하는 경향이 있다"나 "당신은 다른 사람들이 당신을 좋아하며 감탄하기를 매우 필요로 한다"와 같은 일반적인 성격 진술들을 읽을 때, 그들은 종종 이런 진술들을 자신에 대한 매우 정확한 묘사로 평가합니다. 여러분들 중 일부는 '그거 나 같은데.'라고 생각하셨을 것이라 장담합니다.
⁰⁹어쨌든, 바넘 효과는 왜 많은 사람들이 별자리 운세, 포춘 쿠키, 그리고 특정 성격 테스트들을 설득력 있다고 여기는지를 설명합니다. 이것들은 전형적으로 대부분의 사람들에게 맞을 만큼 충분히 광범위한 진술들로 이루어져 있지만, 읽는 사람들은 그것들을 고유한 통찰력이 있는 것으로 인식합니다. ¹¹심리학자들은 진술들이 대부분 긍정적이면서, 균형 잡히고 정직해 보이기 충분할 정도의 부정적 특성들과 함께할 때 특히 효과적이라는 것을 발견했습니다.
그래서, 이 인지적 편향을 이해하는 것은 중요한데 그것이 우리가 개인화된 통찰로 제시된 일반적인 정보에 속을 수 있는 때를 인식하는 데 도움을 주기 때문입니다. ¹²물론, 이 효과 역시 일부 단점들이 있습니다. 그것들이 무엇인지 간단히 살펴봅시다.

09 Main Topic Question

강의는 주로 무엇에 대한 것인가?
✓Ⓐ 바넘 효과의 심리적 메커니즘
Ⓑ 긍정적이고 부정적인 피드백의 심리적 효과
Ⓒ 별자리 운세와 자아 정체성 간의 연결
Ⓓ 점술에서 사용되는 조작 기법

어휘 manipulation [mənìpjuléiʃən] 조작

10 Detail Question

화자는 P.T. Barnum에 대해 무엇을 말하는가?
Ⓐ 현대 심리학에서 사용되는 성격 테스트의 창조자였다.
Ⓑ 자기확증 편향의 심리학적 원리를 확립했다.
✓Ⓒ 대중에게 어필하는 능력으로 유명했다.
Ⓓ 성격 연구에 관해 초기 심리학자들과 협력했다.

어휘 collaborate with ~와 협력하다

11 Intention Question

화자는 왜 심리학자들을 언급하는가?
Ⓐ 성격 심리학에서의 논란이 된 견해들을 소개하기 위해
Ⓑ 성격을 이해하는 더 나은 접근법을 제안하기 위해
Ⓒ 성격 테스트가 비판에도 불구하고 왜 인기를 유지하는지 설명하기 위해
✓Ⓓ 바넘 효과의 효과성에 대한 근거를 제공하기 위해

어휘 controversial [kὰntrəvə́ːrʃəl] 논란이 되는

despite[dispáit] ~에도 불구하고

12 Discuss Next Question
화자는 다음에 무엇을 논의할 것 같은가?
Ⓐ 성격 특성에 대한 고급 심리학적 연구
☑ 바넘 효과의 잠재적 해로운 영향
Ⓒ 심리학적 테스트 방법의 진화
Ⓓ 유명한 성격 심리학자들의 사례

[13-16] 🎧 Am
Listen to a talk in a geology class.

---

¹³Soil formation begins with parent material—inorganic matter that forms most of the soil. This material results from weathering, where rocks break down into smaller particles due to external forces.

¹⁴There are two main types of weathering. First, physical weathering breaks down rocks through wind, rain, and temperature changes. Heating causes expansion, cooling leads to contraction, forming cracks. Next, chemical weathering occurs when slightly acidic rainwater dissolves certain rocks, especially limestone and chalk.

Well, ¹⁵environmental changes can also significantly influence soil formation over long periods. For example, in the Makgadikgadi Pans of the Kalahari Desert, a shift in an ancient river's course caused millennia of salinity buildup, leading to the formation of calcretes and silcretes—hard layers within the soil.

Anyhow, these processes produce rock particles that become the soil's parent material. Its composition affects soil properties—particles with water-soluble ions like calcium and magnesium often yield more fertile soil.

Despite making up less than 6% of soil, organic matter has the greatest impact on fertility. It forms during decomposition, when microorganisms break down plant and animal remains. Well, ¹⁶organic matter is categorized as active, slow, or passive, each contributing differently to soil's ability to support plant growth over time.

---

parent material 모재 inorganic[ìnɔːrgǽnik] 무기체의
weathering[wéðəriŋ] 풍화(작용)
particle[páːrtikəl] 입자, 작은 조각 external[ekstə́ːrnəl] 외부의
force[fɔːrs] 힘 break down 부수다
contraction[kəntrǽkʃən] 수축 crack[kræk] 균열; 갈라지다
acidic[əsádik] 산성의 dissolve[dizáːlv] 용해시키다, 녹이다
limestone[láimstòun] 석회암 chalk[tʃɔːk] 백악
salinity[səlǽnəti] 염분 water-soluble 수용성의
fertile[fə́ːrtl] 비옥한 organic[ɔːrgǽnik] 유기체의
decomposition[dìːkɑ̀mpəzíʃən] 분해, 부패
microorganism[màikrouɔ́ːrgənìzm] 미생물

지질학 강의를 들으시오.
¹³토양 형성은 토양의 대부분을 이루는 무기물질인 모재로 시작됩니다. 이 물질은 암석이 외부의 힘에 의해 더 작은 입자들로 분해되는 풍화에 의해 생성됩니다.
¹⁴풍화에는 두 가지 주요 유형이 있습니다. 첫째, 물리적 풍화는 바람, 비, 그리고 온도 변화를 통해 암석을 부숩니다. 가열은 팽창을 초래하고, 냉각은 수축을 이끌며, 균열을 형성합니다. 다음으로, 화학적 풍화는 약간 산성인 빗물이 특정 암석들, 특히 석회암과 백악을 용해시킬 때 발생합니다.
음, ¹⁵환경적 변화들도 긴 기간에 걸쳐 토양 형성에 상당히 영향을 미칠 수 있습니다. 예를 들어, 칼라하리 사막의 막가디가디 판에서는, 고대 강의 경로 변화가 수천 년간의 염분 축적을 야기하여, 토양 내의 단단한 층인 칼크리트와 실크리트의 형성으로 이어졌습니다.
어쨌든, 이런 과정들은 토양의 모재가 되는 암석 입자들을 형성합니다. 그것의 구성은 토양 특성에 영향을 미치는데, 칼슘과 마그네슘 같은 수용성 이온들을 가진 입자들은 종종 더 비옥한 토양을 만들어냅니다.
토양의 6% 미만을 구성함에도 불구하고, 유기물은 비옥도에 가장 큰 영향을 미칩니다. 유기물은 미생물들이 식물과 동물의 잔해를 분해하는 과정에서 형성됩니다. 음, ¹⁶유기물은 활성, 완만, 또는 불활성으로 분류되며, 각각은 시간이 지남에 따라 식물 성장을 뒷받침하는 토양의 능력에 다르게 기여합니다.

13 Main Topic Question
강의의 주요 주제는 무엇인가?
Ⓐ 토양 형성에서 미생물의 역할
Ⓑ 토양 형성에서 모재의 중요성
Ⓒ 물과 토양 형성 간의 관계
☑ 토양 발달 과정과 그 구성 요소

어휘 component[kəmpóunənt] 구성 요소, 성분

14 Detail Question
화자는 두 가지 주요 풍화 유형에 대해 무엇을 말하는가?
Ⓐ 대부분의 환경에서 동시에 발생한다.
☑ 별개의 분해 과정을 통해 토양을 형성한다.
Ⓒ 물리적 풍화는 주로 석회암과 백악에 영향을 미친다.
Ⓓ 화학적 풍화는 사막 환경에서 더 흔하다.

어휘 affect[əfékt] 영향을 미치다

15 Intention Question
화자는 왜 막가디가디 판을 언급하는가?
Ⓐ 물리적 풍화와 화학적 풍화 과정을 대조하기 위해
Ⓑ 칼슘과 마그네슘이 토양 비옥도를 개선하는 이유를 설명하기 위해
☑ 토양에 대한 장기적인 환경 효과의 증거를 제공하기 위해
Ⓓ 극한 조건에서 유기물이 어떻게 형성되는지 보여주기 위해

16 Detail Question
유기물의 범주로 언급되지 않은 것은 무엇인가?
Ⓐ 완만
Ⓑ 활성
☑ 용해성
Ⓓ 불활성

5. Organization Questions

Example 🎧 Au p.281

20세기 초, 사진은 픽토리얼리즘과 같은 운동을 통해 정당한 순수 예술 형식으로 등장했습니다. 픽토리얼리스트들은 1902년 Alfred Stieglitz에 의해 설립된 Photo-Secession이라고 알려진 그룹을 형성했습니다. 또한 구성원이었던 Clarence White는 Stieglitz가 픽토리얼리즘을 거부한 후 사조의 리더가 되었습니다. Stieglitz는 마음을 바꾸고 픽토리얼리즘과 정반대인 스트레이트 사진을 선호하게 되었습니다. 스트레이트 사진은 효과를 위해 사용되는 방법이나 장비보다는 피사체에 중점을 둡니다. 반면에, 픽토리얼리즘은 Clarence White가 강력히 지지한 순수한 사진적 또는 회화적 특성을 강조합니다. 픽토리얼리즘에서는 피사체가 아니라 사진가가 피사체를 어떻게 제시하고 다루는지에 중점을 두었습니다.

emerge [imə́ːrdʒ] 등장하다, 생기다
legitimate [lidʒítəmət] 정당한, 합법적인   fine art 순수예술
found [faund] 설립하다   reject [ridʒékt] 거부하다, 탈락시키다
opposite [ɑ́ːpəzit] 정반대의, 다른 편의   scenic [síːnik] 회화적인
manipulate [mənípjuleit] 다루다, 조정하다

화자는 사진 촬영에 대한 Clarence White의 생각을 어떻게 소개하는가?
Ⓐ ✓ 그것들을 Stieglitz의 것들과 대조함으로써
Ⓑ White가 촬영한 사진들의 예시를 제공함으로써
Ⓒ 사진가이자 예술가로서 White의 삶의 세부사항을 제공함으로써
Ⓓ Photo-Secession이 어떻게 그리고 왜 설립되었는지 설명함으로써

HACKERS PRACTICE p.282

01 Ⓒ   02 Ⓐ

03

	Red muscle	White muscle
Does not tire easily	✓	
Relies on glycolytic enzymes		✓
Releases energy quickly		✓
Contracts slowly	✓	

04

	Mother	Father	Neighbors/Visitors
Bigger words		✓	
Special language	✓		
Higher-pitched speech			✓

01 Organization Question 🎧 Am

We are considering two types of celestial bodies, comets and asteroids, which can be hard to distinguish with the naked eye. To tell them apart, we look at their size, composition, and orbits. Comets are usually a few kilometers to tens of kilometers across and may show a bright head and a long tail when near Earth. Asteroids range from pebble-sized to about one thousand kilometers in diameter. Asteroids are rocky and metallic, while comets are mostly ice, dust, carbon dioxide, and methane. Comets follow highly elliptical orbits, moving in and out of the solar system. Most asteroids remain within the solar system, primarily in the asteroid belt between Jupiter and Mars.

celestial body 천체   comet [kɑ́ːmit] 혜성
asteroid [ǽstərɔid] 소행성   naked eye 육안
orbit [ɔ́ːrbit] 궤도; 궤도를 그리며 돌다
diameter [daiǽmətər] 지름, 직경
elliptical [ilíptikəl] 타원형의, 타원의   solar system 태양계

우리는 육안으로 구별하기 어려울 수 있는 두 종류의 천체인 혜성과 소행성을 살펴보고 있습니다. 이들을 구별하기 위해, 우리는 그들의 크기, 구성, 그리고 궤도를 살펴봅니다. 혜성은 보통 지름이 몇 킬로미터에서 수십 킬로미터에 이르고, 지구 근처에 있을 때 밝은 머리와 긴 꼬리를 보일 수 있습니다. 소행성은 지름이 자갈 크기에서 약 천 킬로미터까지 다양합니다. 소행성은 암석과 금속으로 이루어져 있는 반면, 혜성은 대부분 얼음, 먼지, 이산화탄소, 그리고 메탄으로 이루어져 있습니다. 혜성은 매우 타원형인 궤도를 따라 태양계 안팎으로 이동합니다. 대부분의 소행성은 태양계 내에, 주로 목성과 화성 사이의 소행성대에 존재합니다.

화자는 두 종류의 천체를 어떻게 설명하는가?
Ⓐ 다른 천체들과 대조함으로써
Ⓑ 어떻게 발견되었는지 설명함으로써
Ⓒ ✓ 일련의 기준에 따라 그것들을 비교함으로써
Ⓓ 형성에 대한 이론들을 제시함으로써

02 Organization Question 🎧 En

Amartya Sen has been a strong critic of free markets because of their role in man-made famines. His work showed empirically that famines are due to the maldistribution of food—for example, when traders hoard food for speculation and profit—rather than to inadequate supplies. As a result, Amartya Sen emphasized entitlement—that is, access to the means to acquire food—over food availability alone, as a strategy to address poverty and famine.

man-made 인위적인   famine [fǽmin] 기근
empirically [impǽrikəli] 경험적으로
maldistribution [mæ̀ldistrəbjúːʃən] 분배   hoard [hɔːrd] 비축하다
speculation [spèkjuléiʃən] 투기
inadequate [inǽdikwət] 부적절한
entitlement [intáitlmənt] 권리   means [miːnz] 수단
address [ǽdres] 해결하다   poverty [pɑ́ːvərti] 빈곤

아마르티아 센은 인위적인 기근에서의 자유 시장의 역할 때문에 자유 시장의 강력한 비판자입니다. 그의 연구는 기근이 부적절한 공급보다는 식량의 잘못된 분배 때문이라는 것을 경험적으로 보여주었는데, 예컨대 상인들이 투기와 이익을 위해 식량을 비축하는 경우를 들 수 있습

니다. 결과적으로, 아마르티아 센은 빈곤과 기근을 해결하기 위한 방식으로 식량 가용성만이 아니라 권리, 즉 식량을 획득할 수단에 대한 접근성의 역할을 강조했습니다.

화자는 식량의 잘못된 분배를 어떻게 명확히 하는가?
- ✓ 잘못된 분배의 사례를 제시함으로써
- ⓑ 전 세계 식량 생산에 대한 통계 데이터를 분석함으로써
- ⓒ 도시와 농촌의 식량 접근 패턴을 비교함으로써
- ⓓ 식량 공급에 영향을 미치는 환경적 요인들을 논의함으로써

어휘 statistical[stətǽstikəl] 통계의 rural[rúərəl] 시골의 factor[fǽktər] 요인

03 Organization Question 🎧 Au

There are two types of muscle tissue: red muscle and white muscle. Red muscle fibers get their red color from myoglobin, which stores and delivers oxygen within muscle tissue. ^Red^These muscles contract slowly and use oxygen to release energy. ^Red^Red muscle fibers are resistant to fatigue. ^White^White muscle fibers, on the other hand, contract rapidly but tire quickly. ^White^White muscle fibers rely on anaerobic pathways and glycolytic enzymes to release energy without oxygen, causing their energy reserves to deplete more quickly.

muscle fiber 근섬유 contract[kəntrǽkt] 수축하다; 계약
release[rilíːs] 방출하다; 발매 resistant to ~에 강한, ~에 저항하는
fatigue[fətíːg] 피로 rapidly[rǽpidli] 빠르게
anaerobic[ænɛəróubik] 무산소의
glycolytic[glàikəlátik] 당분해의
deplete[diplíːt] 고갈시키다, 다 써버리다

적근과 백근, 두 종류의 근섬유가 있습니다. 적근 섬유는 근육 조직 내에서 산소를 저장하고 전달하는 미오글로빈으로 인해 붉은색을 띕니다. ^Red^이러한 근육은 천천히 수축하며, 저장된 에너지를 방출하는 데 산소를 사용합니다. ^Red^적근 섬유는 피로에 강합니다. ^White^반면에 백근 섬유는 빠르게 수축하지만 빨리 피로해집니다. ^White^백근 섬유는 무산소 대사 경로와 당분해 효소를 사용하여 에너지를 빠르게 방출하므로, 에너지 비축량이 더 빨리 고갈됩니다.

다음 문구들이 설명하는 근육의 유형이 무엇인지 각 예시에 대해 표시하십시오.

올바른 칸에 클릭하십시오.

	적근	백근
쉽게 피로하지 않는다.	✓	
당분해 효소에 의존한다.		✓
에너지를 빠르게 방출한다.		✓
천천히 수축한다.	✓	

04 Organization Question 🎧 En

Today we'll examine how different people communicate with infants. Research reveals that "baby talk" follows distinct patterns based on the speaker's relationship to the child. ^Mo^Mothers use well-structured, short sentences, speaking slowly with special vocabulary for body parts and bodily functions, such as "poo." ^Fa^Fathers employ more direct communication with a broader vocabulary than mothers do. ^Neigh/Vis^Non-family members, such as neighbors and visitors, use simplified, higher-pitched speech. These variations serve important functions in early language development.

infant[ínfənt] 유아, 유아의 based on ~에 기반하여
simplified[símpləfàid] 단순화된

오늘 우리는 각기 다른 사람들이 유아와 어떻게 소통하는지를 살펴보겠습니다. 연구에 따르면 "아기 말"은 화자와 아이의 관계에 기반한 뚜렷한 패턴을 따릅니다. ^Mo^어머니들은 잘 구조화된 짧은 문장으로 천천히 말하며, 신체 부위나 생리 현상에 관한 특별한 어휘인 "응가"와 같은 말을 사용합니다. ^Fa^아버지들은 어머니들보다 더 직접적으로 말하며 더 폭넓은 어휘를 사용합니다. ^Neigh/Vis^이웃이나 방문객 같은 가족 외 사람들은 단순화된, 더 높은 음조로 말합니다. 이러한 차이들은 초기 언어 발달에서 중요한 기능을 합니다.

각 개인이 아기와 대화하는 특징적인 방식을 표시하십시오.

올바른 칸에 클릭하십시오.

	어머니	아버지	이웃/방문객
더 폭넓은 어휘		✓	
특별한 어휘	✓		
더 높은 음조			✓

HACKERS TEST p.284

01 Ⓐ 02 Ⓑ 03 Ⓒ 04 Ⓑ 05 Ⓑ
06 Ⓒ 07 Ⓐ 08 Ⓓ 09 Ⓑ 10 Ⓒ
11 Ⓐ 12 Ⓓ 13 Ⓑ 14 Ⓐ 15 Ⓓ
16

Step 1	The Old Babylonian Empire fell to invaders.
Step 2	A revolt established Babylonia's independence from Assyrian rule.
Step 3	The Hanging Gardens and the Ishtar Gate were built.
Step 4	Neo-Babylonia faced instability and weak rulers.

[01-04] 🎧 Am

Listen to a talk in a linguistics class.

^01^The Critical Period Hypothesis is one of the most debated theories in linguistics, proposing that there is a specific time window during which humans can acquire language most effectively. It suggests that language acquisition becomes significantly more difficult after puberty due to

neurological changes in the brain.
⁰²**The theory is based on observations of brain plasticity, which refers to the brain's ability to reorganize and form new neural connections.** During childhood, the brain exhibits high plasticity, making it easier for children to learn multiple languages simultaneously without formal instruction. But as individuals mature, this plasticity decreases, potentially making second language acquisition more challenging.
Evidence supporting the critical period comes from studies of feral children and individuals who experienced delayed language exposure due to extreme social isolation. ⁰³**These cases often show significant difficulties in achieving native-like proficiency when language learning begins after the proposed critical period.**
⁰¹/⁰⁴**However, critics of the hypothesis argue that adult language learners can still achieve high levels of proficiency** ⁰⁴**with adequate motivation and appropriate learning environments.** They question whether the observed difficulties are truly due to biological constraints or to other factors such as reduced learning opportunities or different learning strategies.

linguistics [liŋgwástiks] 언어학   acquire [əkwáiər] 습득하다
puberty [pjú:bərti] 사춘기   neurological [njùərəládʒikəl] 신경의
plasticity [plæstísəti] 가소성
reorganize [ri:ɔ́:rgənaiz] 재조직하다   mature [mətjúər] 성숙하다
feral [fǽərəl] 야생의   exposure [ikspóuʒər] 노출
isolation [àisəléiʃən] 고립   proficiency [prəfíʃənsi] 유창함
adequate [ǽdikwət] 적절한, 충분한
motivation [mòutəvéiʃən] 동기   appropriate [əpróupriət] 적합한

언어학 강의를 들으시오.

⁰¹임계기 가설은 언어학에서 가장 논쟁이 많은 이론 중 하나로, 인간이 언어를 가장 효과적으로 습득할 수 있는 특정한 시간 창이 있다고 제안합니다. 이 가설은 뇌의 신경학적 변화로 인해 사춘기 이후에는 언어 습득이 현저히 더 어려워진다고 시사합니다.

⁰²이 이론은 뇌가 재조직되고 새로운 신경 연결을 형성하는 능력을 가리키는 뇌 가소성에 대한 관찰에 기반합니다. 아동기 동안 뇌는 높은 가소성을 보이며, 이는 아이들이 공식적인 교육 없이도 여러 언어를 동시에 더 쉽게 학습할 수 있게 합니다. 하지만 개인이 성숙해지면서 이러한 가소성은 감소하여 잠재적으로 제2언어 습득을 더 어렵게 만듭니다. 임계기 가설을 지지하는 증거는 극도의 사회적 고립으로 인해 언어 노출이 지연된 야생 아동들과 개인들에 대한 연구에서 나옵니다. ⁰³이러한 사례들은 제안된 임계기 이후에 언어 학습이 시작될 때 원어민 수준의 유창함을 달성하는 데 상당한 어려움을 겪는 것을 종종 보여줍니다.

⁰¹/⁰⁴하지만 가설의 비판자들은 성인 언어 학습자들도 적절한 동기와 적합한 학습 환경이 있으면 여전히 높은 수준의 유창함을 달성할 수 있다고 주장합니다. 그들은 관찰된 어려움들이 진정으로 생물학적 제약 때문인지 아니면 감소된 학습 기회와 다른 학습 전략 등 다른 요인들 때문인지 의문을 제기합니다.

01 Organization Question
강의는 주로 어떻게 구성되는가?
☑ 이론에 대해 지지하는 의견과 반대되는 의견을 모두 제시한다.
Ⓑ 어린 시절부터 성인기까지의 정보를 시간순으로 설명한다.
Ⓒ 가설이 만들어진 이후의 발전을 추적한다.
Ⓓ 제1언어와 제2언어 습득 과정을 대조한다.

어휘 chronologically [krάnəládʒikəli] 시간순으로
trace [treis] 추적하다, 거슬러 올라가다

02 Detail Question
화자는 뇌 가소성에 대해 무엇을 말하는가?
Ⓐ 청소년기 동안 현저히 증가한다.
☑ 뇌가 신경 경로를 재조직화할 수 있게 한다.
Ⓒ 언어 습득에서 공식적인 교육이 필수적인 이유를 보여준다.
Ⓓ 말하기 능력보다 읽기 기술에 더 영향을 미친다.

어휘 adolescence [ædəlésns] 청소년기

03 Intention Question
화자는 왜 야생 아동들을 언급하는가?
Ⓐ 동물과 인간의 언어 습득을 비교하기 위해
Ⓑ 언어 발달에 대한 전통적인 견해에 도전하기 위해
☑ 지연된 언어 노출의 어려움을 보여주기 위해
Ⓓ 성공적인 늦은 언어 습득의 예시를 제안하기 위해

04 Detail Question
가설의 비판자들은 무엇을 강조하는가?
Ⓐ 성숙 중에 일어나는 신경학적 변화
☑ 언어 습득을 위한 적절한 학습 환경
Ⓒ 성인에서 감소된 신경 연결 형성
Ⓓ 성인 언어 학습의 생물학적 제약

어휘 maturation [mætʃuréiʃən] 성숙

[05-08]

Listen to a talk in an environmental science class.

Ecosystem services are the benefits that humans receive from the natural ecosystems. ⁰⁵**These services can be categorized into four main types: provisioning, regulating, cultural, and supporting services.** Each of them is essential for human well-being and economic prosperity.
Provisioning services include the tangible products we obtain from ecosystems, such as food, fresh water, timber, and medicine. ⁰⁶**Regulating services involve the control of environmental conditions, including climate regulation, water purification, and disease control.** Cultural services encompass the non-material benefits people gain from ecosystems, such as recreational opportunities, spiritual value, and aesthetic enjoyment. Finally, supporting services are the fundamental processes that maintain ecosystem functioning, including nutrient cycling and soil formation.

However, ⁰⁷**human activities are threatening these valuable services through habitat destruction, pollution, and climate change. In particular, the loss of biodiversity directly impacts the ability of ecosystems to provide these essential services.** When species disappear, ecosystem stability decreases, making the remaining services less reliable and less effective. ⁰⁸**Now, we'll discuss specific strategies that communities and governments are implementing to protect and restore ecosystem services.**

prosperity [prɑspérəti] 번영, 번창   tangible [tǽndʒəbl] 유형의
obtain [əbtéin] 얻다   timber [tímbər] 목재
encompass [inkʌ́mpəs] 포괄하다, ~을 둘러싸다
spiritual [spíritʃuəl] 정신적인   aesthetic [esθétik] 미적인
nutrient [njúːtriənt] 영양소   threaten [θrétn] 위협하다
valuable [vǽljuəbl] 귀중한   habitat [hǽbitæt] 서식지
pollution [pəlúːʃən] 오염   in particular 특히
biodiversity [bàioudivə́ːrsəti] 생물 다양성
stability [stəbíləti] 안정성

환경과학 강의를 들으시오.

생태계 서비스는 인간이 자연 생태계에서 얻는 혜택입니다. ⁰⁵이러한 서비스들은 네 가지 주요 유형으로 분류될 수 있는데, 공급, 조절, 문화, 그리고 지지 서비스입니다. 이들 각각은 인간의 복지와 경제적 번영에 필수적입니다.

공급 서비스는 우리가 생태계에서 얻는 유형의 산물들을 포함하며, 식량, 담수, 목재, 그리고 의약품 등이 있습니다. ⁰⁶조절 서비스는 환경 조건을 통제하는 기능으로, 기후 조절, 수질 정화, 질병 통제가 있습니다. 문화 서비스는 사람들이 생태계에서 얻는 비물질적 혜택들을 포괄하며, 휴양 기회, 정신적 가치, 그리고 미적 즐거움 등이 있습니다. 마지막으로, 지지 서비스는 영양소 순환과 토양 형성을 포함하는 생태계 기능을 유지하는 기본적인 과정입니다.

하지만 ⁰⁷인간 활동들이 서식지 파괴, 오염, 그리고 기후 변화를 통해 이러한 귀중한 서비스들을 위협하고 있습니다. 특히, 생물 다양성의 손실은 생태계가 이러한 필수적인 서비스들을 제공하는 능력에 직접적으로 영향을 미칩니다. 종들이 사라지면 생태계 안정성이 감소하여 남은 서비스들을 덜 안정적이고 덜 효과적으로 만듭니다. ⁰⁸이제 우리는 지역 사회와 정부들이 생태계 서비스를 보호하고 복원하기 위해 실시하고 있는 구체적인 전략들에 대해 논의하겠습니다.

05 Organization Question
화자는 생태계 서비스를 어떻게 설명하는가?
Ⓐ 특정 생태계의 예시들을 제공함으로써
☑ 명확한 범주들로 구성함으로써
Ⓒ 인공적인 서비스들과 대조함으로써
Ⓓ 과학적 메커니즘을 조사함으로써

06 Detail Question
조절 서비스의 요소로 언급되지 않은 것은 무엇인가?
Ⓐ 수질 정화
Ⓑ 기후 조절
☑ 영양소 순환
Ⓓ 질병 통제

어휘   regulation [règjuléiʃən] 통제

07 Detail Question
화자에 따르면, 인간 활동은 어떻게 생태계 서비스를 위협하는가?
☑ 종 다양성을 감소시킴으로써
Ⓑ 정부 자금을 줄임으로써
Ⓒ 인공적인 대안들을 개발함으로써
Ⓓ 불충분한 야생동물 통로를 만듦으로써

어휘   corridor [kɔ́ːridər] 통로, 회랑

08 Discuss Next Question
화자는 다음에 무엇을 논의할 것인가?
Ⓐ 생태계 유형의 상세한 분류
Ⓑ 생물 다양성을 측정하는 과학적 방법들
Ⓒ 자연 경관의 문화적 중요성
☑ 구체적인 보존 및 복원 접근법들

어휘   landscape [lǽndskèip] 경관
         conservation [kɑ̀nsərvéiʃən] 보존

[09-12]
Listen to a talk in a chemistry class.

Catalysis is a fundamental process in chemistry where a substance called a catalyst increases the rate of a chemical reaction without being consumed in the process. ⁰⁹**Catalysts work by providing an alternative pathway for the reaction that requires less energy to proceed. This concept is essential for understanding many chemical processes in both nature and industry.**

There are two main types of catalysts: homogeneous and heterogeneous. Homogeneous catalysts exist in the same phase as the reactants, typically in solution, ¹⁰**while heterogeneous catalysts exist in a different phase, usually as solids in contact with liquid or gas reactants.** Each type has distinct advantages and applications.

Catalysis in industry is particularly important. ¹¹**It is estimated that about 90% of all industrial chemicals produced worldwide use catalysts in the manufacturing process.** For example, the production of ammonia for fertilizers uses the Haber-Bosch process, which employs iron catalysts to combine nitrogen and hydrogen. Without this catalytic process, it would be impossible to produce fertilizers at the scale needed to feed the world's population.

Finally, catalysts also play a crucial role in environmental protection. For instance, ¹²**catalytic converters in automobiles use platinum and other metals to convert harmful exhaust gases into less toxic substances.** This technology has significantly reduced air pollution in urban areas since its widespread adoption.

catalysis [kətǽlisis] 촉매작용   chemistry [kéməstri] 화학

catalyst[kǽtəlist] 촉매　consume[kənsúːm] 소비하다
homogeneous[hòumədʒíːniəs] 균질의, 동종의
heterogeneous[hètərədʒíːniəs] 불균질의, 이종의
reactant[riǽktənt] 반응물　solution[səlúːʃən] 용액, 해액책
solid[sálid] 고체; 고체의　liquid[líkwid] 액체; 액체의
gas[gæs] 기체, 가스　estimate[éstəmèit] 추정하다, 추산하다
combine[kəmbáin] 결합하다, 모으다　harmful[háːrmfəl] 해로운
exhaust gas 배기가스　toxic[táksik] 독성의
widespread[wáidsprèd] 광범위한　adoption[ədápʃən] 채택

화학 강의를 들으시오.
촉매작용은 촉매라고 불리는 물질이 과정에서 소비되지 않으면서 화학 반응의 속도를 증가시키는 화학의 기본적인 과정입니다. [09]촉매들은 반응이 진행되는 데 더 적은 에너지를 필요로 하는 반응의 대안적 경로를 제공함으로써 작동합니다. 이 개념은 자연과 산업 모두에서 많은 화학 과정들을 이해하는 데 필수적입니다.
촉매에는 균질과 불균질 촉매의 두 가지 주요 유형이 있습니다. 균질 촉매는 반응물과 같은 상태로 존재하며, 일반적으로 용액 상태이고, [10]불균질 촉매는 다른 상태로 존재하며, 보통 액체나 기체 반응물과 접촉하는 고체입니다. 각 유형은 고유한 장점과 적용 분야를 가지고 있습니다.
산업에서 촉매작용은 특히나 중요합니다. 전 세계적으로 생산되는 [11]모든 산업 화학물질의 약 90퍼센트가 제조 과정에서 촉매를 사용하는 것으로 추정됩니다. 예를 들어, 비료를 위한 암모니아 생산은 질소와 수소를 결합하기 위해 철 촉매를 사용하는 하버-보슈법을 사용합니다. 이 촉매 과정 없이는 세계 인구를 먹여 살리는 데 필요한 규모로 비료를 생산할 수 없을 것입니다.
마지막으로, 촉매들은 환경 보호에서도 중요한 역할을 합니다. 예를 들어, [12]자동차의 촉매 변환기는 백금과 다른 금속들을 사용하여 해로운 배기가스를 독성이 적은 물질로 변환합니다. 이 기술은 광범위한 채택 이후 도시 지역의 대기 오염을 현저히 줄였습니다.

09　Main Topic Question
강의의 주요 주제는 무엇인가?
Ⓐ 도시 대기의 화학적 구성
✓ 화학 촉매의 종류와 역할
Ⓒ 실험실 환경에서의 화학 반응 메커니즘
Ⓓ 철 기반 촉매 시스템의 산업적 적용

10　Detail Question
화자는 불균질 촉매에 대해 무엇을 말하는가?
Ⓐ 일반적으로 액체 반응 혼합물에 녹아있는 상태로 발견된다.
Ⓑ 균질 시스템과 같은 에너지 수준을 필요로 한다.
✓ 반응하는 물질들과 다른 상태로 존재한다.
Ⓓ 질소와 수소 결합에서만 독점적으로 작용한다.

어휘　mixture[míkstʃər] 혼합물　exclusively[iksklúːsivli] 독점적으로

11　Organization Question
화자는 촉매작용의 산업적 중요성을 어떻게 소개하는가?
✓ 보급률에 대한 통계적 수치를 제공함으로써
Ⓑ 암모니아 생산을 위한 하버-보슈법을 시연함으로써
Ⓒ 촉매 시스템에서의 상태 차이를 논의함으로써
Ⓓ 균질과 불균질 촉매의 효과를 비교함으로써

어휘　prevalence[prévələns] 보급률

12　Detail Question
강의에 따르면, 촉매 변환기는 어떻게 환경 보호에 기여하는가?
Ⓐ 화학 반응의 에너지 요구사항을 줄임으로써
Ⓑ 배출 통제를 위한 균질 촉매 시스템을 제공함으로써
Ⓒ 비료 생산 과정의 효율성을 증가시킴으로써
✓ 독성 배기 배출물을 더 안전한 화합물로 변환함으로써

어휘　emission[imíʃən] 배출　efficiency[ifíʃənsi] 효율성
　　　compound[kəmpáund] 화합물

[13-16]

Listen to a talk in a history class.

[13]The Neo-Babylonian Empire was one of the most significant civilizations of the ancient world. To understand this empire, [16-Step1]we first need to look at its predecessor, the Old Babylonian Empire. It flourished around 1800 BC but eventually fell to various invaders. The Neo-Babylonian Empire emerged much later, around 626 BC, when [16-Step2]Nabopolassar successfully revolted against the Assyrian Empire and established Babylon as an independent kingdom once again. Under his rule, Babylon began to regain its former glory.
[13]The empire reached its peak during the reign of Nebuchadnezzar II, who ruled from 605 to 562 BC. He transformed Babylon into the most magnificent city of the ancient world. [16-Step3]He even constructed the famous Hanging Gardens, one of the Seven Wonders of the Ancient World. These terraced gardens, filled with exotic plants and sophisticated irrigation systems, demonstrated the empire's engineering prowess and wealth. [16-Step3]Nebuchadnezzar II also built the impressive Ishtar Gate and expanded the city's defensive walls. [13/16-Step4]However, the empire's decline began after Nebuchadnezzar II's death, leading to political instability and weak rulers. [14]This culminated in the reign of Nabonidus, who alienated the powerful priesthood by favoring the moon god Sin over Marduk, Babylon's guardian deity. This religious turmoil weakened the empire from within.
In 539 BC, Cyrus the Great of Persia conquered Babylon with relatively little resistance. [13]This eventually marked the end of the Neo-Babylonian Empire. Okay, [15]next, we will examine how Persian rule affected Mesopotamian culture and administration.

predecessor[prédəsesər] 전신, 조상　flourish[fləːriʃ] 번영하다
invader[invéidər] 침입자　revolt[rivóult] 반란을 일으키다
rule[ruːl] 통치하다; 통치　magnificent[mægnífəsnt] 웅장한
terraced[térəst] 계단식의　exotic[igzátik] 이국적인
sophisticated[səfístəkèitid] 정교한　irrigation[irəgéiʃən] 관개
prowess[práuis] 기량, 역량　instability[ìnstəbíləti] 불안정

culminate[kʌ́lmənèit] 절정에 달하다
alienate[éiljənèit] 소외시키다, 멀리하다
priesthood[prí:sthud] 사제층   guardian deity 수호신
turmoil[tə́:rmɔil] 혼란   conquer[káŋkər] 정복하다
relatively[rélətivli] 상대적으로, 비교적으로
resistance[rizístəns] 저항, 방해   mark[mɑ:rk] 알리다, 나타내다

역사 강의를 들으시오.

¹³신바빌로니아 제국은 고대 세계의 가장 중요한 문명 중 하나였습니다. 이 제국을 이해하기 위해서는 ¹⁶⁻ˢᵗᵉᵖ¹먼저 그 전신인 고바빌로니아 제국을 살펴볼 필요가 있습니다. 그것은 기원전 1800년경에 번영했지만 결국 다양한 침입자들에게 멸망했습니다. 신바빌로니아 제국은 기원전 626년경 훨씬 후에 등장했는데, ¹⁶⁻ˢᵗᵉᵖ²나보폴라사르가 아시리아 제국에 대해 성공적으로 반란을 일으키고 바빌론을 다시 한 번 독립 왕국으로 세웠을 때였습니다. 그의 통치 하에서 바빌론은 이전의 영광을 되찾기 시작했습니다.

¹³제국은 기원전 605년부터 562년까지 통치한 네부카드네자르 2세의 통치 기간 동안 절정에 달했습니다. 그는 바빌론을 고대 세계의 가장 웅장한 도시로 변모시켰습니다. ¹⁶⁻ˢᵗᵉᵖ³그는 심지어 고대 세계 7대 불가사의 중 하나인 유명한 공중정원을 건설했습니다. 이색적인 식물들과 정교한 관개 시설로 가득 찬 이 계단식 정원은 제국의 공학적 기량과 부를 보여주었습니다. ¹⁶⁻ˢᵗᵉᵖ³네부카드네자르 2세는 또한 인상적인 이슈타르 문을 건설했고 도시의 방어벽을 확장했습니다.

¹³/¹⁶⁻ˢᵗᵉᵖ⁴하지만 제국의 쇠퇴는 네부카드네자르 2세의 죽음 이후에 시작되어 정치적 불안정과 약한 통치자들로 이어졌습니다. ¹⁴이것은 바빌론의 수호신인 마르두크보다 달의 신 신을 선호함으로써 강력한 사제층을 소외시킨 나보니두스의 통치에서 절정에 달했습니다. 이 종교적 혼란은 제국을 내부에서 약화시켰습니다.

기원전 539년에 페르시아의 키루스 대왕이 상대적으로 적은 저항으로 바빌론을 정복했습니다. ¹³이것은 결국 신바빌로니아 제국의 종말을 알렸습니다. 좋아요, ¹⁵다음으로 우리는 페르시아의 통치가 메소포타미아의 문화와 행정에 어떤 영향을 미쳤는지 살펴보겠습니다.

13 Main Topic Question

강의의 주요 주제는 무엇인가?
Ⓐ 고대 바빌론의 건축적 경이로움
✓ 신바빌로니아 제국의 흥망성쇠
Ⓒ 메소포타미아 제국들의 역사적 중요성
Ⓓ 아시리아와 바빌로니아 사이의 종교적 갈등

어휘 architectural[ɑ̀:rkətéktʃərəl] 건축적인

14 Intention Question

화자는 왜 나보니두스를 언급하는가?
✓ 그의 정책이 바빌로니아를 내부적으로 어떻게 약화시켰는지를 보여주기 위해
Ⓑ 바빌로니아의 독립에서 그의 역할을 설명하기 위해
Ⓒ 페르시아에 대한 그의 승리를 보여주기 위해
Ⓓ 그가 바빌로니아의 방어 시설을 강화한 것을 묘사하기 위해

어휘 strengthen[stréŋkθən] 강화하다

15 Discuss Next Question

화자는 다음에 무엇을 논의할 것인가?
Ⓐ 메소포타미아에서 페르시아 영향력의 쇠퇴
Ⓑ 새로운 지도자 아래서의 바빌론 재건
Ⓒ 바빌론의 유명한 기념물들의 파괴
✓ 메소포타미아 사회에 대한 페르시아 통치의 영향

어휘 destruction[distrʌ́kʃən] 파괴
monument[má:njumənt] 기념물

16 Organization Question

화자는 신바빌로니아 제국의 발전 단계를 설명한다. 이 단계들을 순서대로 배치하시오.

각 문장을 알맞은 빈칸에 끌어오시오.

1단계	고바빌로니아 제국이 침입자들에게 멸망했다.
2단계	반란으로 바빌로니아가 아시리아의 지배에서 독립을 이루었다.
3단계	공중 정원과 이슈타르 문이 건설되었다.
4단계	신바빌로니아는 불안정과 약한 통치자들에 직면했다.

6. Inference Questions

Example   Am   p.289

오늘 우리는 디플레이션에 대해 논의하겠습니다. 인플레이션이 일반적인 물가 상승을 의미하는 반면, **디플레이션은 소비자 물가 수준의 지속적인 하락입니다**. 물가가 하락하는 것이 소비자들에게는 좋을 것이라고 생각할 수도 있지만, 디플레이션은 많은 사람들이 깨닫는 것보다 훨씬 복잡하고 잠재적으로 위험합니다. 물가가 내려가면, 생산자들은 같은 수익을 내기 위해 더 많이 생산할 수밖에 없습니다. 그래서 시장이 범람하고, 가격은 더욱 하락하며, 생산자는 더욱 적은 수익을 올리게 됩니다.

persistent[pərsístənt] 지속적인   in order to ~하기 위해
profit[práfit] 수익, 이익   flood[flʌd] 범람하다, 넘쳐나다

화자는 디플레이션에 대해 무엇을 암시하는가?
Ⓐ 인플레이션보다 통제하기 쉽다.
Ⓑ 주로 국제 무역 관계에 영향을 받는다.
✓ 상품 가치의 하락을 초래한다.
Ⓓ 생산자들에게 해를 끼치는 것보다 소비자들에게 더 많은 이익을 준다.

어휘 international[ìntərnǽʃənl] 국제적인
benefit[bénəfit] 이익을 주다; 이익

HACKERS PRACTICE   p.290

01 Ⓓ   02 Ⓑ   03 Ⓒ   04 Ⓐ

01 Inference Question   Au

Let's talk about one of nature's most underrated creatures, the earthworm. They are, in fact, like ecosystem engineers. When they tunnel through compacted soil, they're essentially plowing it. **This creates pathways for air and water circulation, which is crucial for plant root penetration and**

soil health.
Here's a fascinating statistic. Researchers found that on just one acre of cultivated land, earthworms deposit about 16,000 pounds of nutrient-rich castings annually, sometimes up to 30,000 pounds! These castings contain essential nutrients like nitrogen, calcium, and phosphorus.

어휘 underrated[ʌndərréitid] 과소평가된   creature[krí:tʃər] 생물
earthworm[ə́:rθwə:rm] 지렁이   tunnel[tʌ́nl] 굴을 파다
compacted[kəmpǽktid] 다져진   plow[plau] 갈다, 경작하다
circulation[sə̀:rkjuléiʃən] 순환   penetration[pènətréiʃən] 관통
casting[kǽstiŋ] 배설물, 주조

자연에서 가장 과소평가된 생물 중 하나인 지렁이에 대해 이야기해봅시다. 지렁이들은 사실 생태계 엔지니어와 같습니다. 지렁이들이 다져진 흙을 뚫고 굴을 팔 때, 본질적으로는 땅을 갈고 있는 것입니다. 이것은 공기와 물의 순환을 위한 통로를 만들어내며, 이는 식물 뿌리의 관통과 토양 건강에 중요합니다.
여기 흥미로운 통계가 있습니다. 연구자들은 단 1에이커의 경작지에서 지렁이들이 연간 약 16,000파운드의 영양이 풍부한 배설물을 남기며, 때로는 30,000파운드까지 남긴다는 것을 발견했습니다! 이 배설물들은 질소, 칼슘, 인과 같은 필수 영양소를 포함하고 있습니다.

농업에서 지렁이에 대해 암시되는 것은?
Ⓐ 농업 전문가들의 신중한 관찰이 필요하다.
Ⓑ 토양에서 너무 많은 유기물을 소비한다.
Ⓒ 농업 시스템에서 물의 필요성을 줄인다.
☑ 식물 성장을 위한 토양 조건을 자연스럽게 개선한다.

어휘 expert[ékspə:rt] 전문가; 숙련된

02 Inference Question 🎧 Am

Sunspots are relatively cool, darkish spots that appear in groups on the Sun's surface. Between 1645 and 1715, astronomers of the time reported very little, or even zero, sunspot activity. Sunspots seemed to have disappeared during those years. In relation to this, the English astronomer Edward Walter Maunder observed that temperatures fell so drastically in that period that the world, particularly Europe, appeared to have undergone a Little Ice Age. Consequently, scientists speculated that **there might be an association between the Earth's climate and the lack of sunspots on the Sun's surface**.

astronomer[əstrá:nəmər] 천문학자   of the time 당시의
in relation to ~와 관련하여   drastically[drǽstikəli] 급격하게
undergo[ʌ̀ndərgóu] 겪다, 경험하다
consequently[kánsəkwèntli] 따라서
speculate[spékjulèit] 추정하다
association[əsòusiéiʃən] 연관성

흑점은 태양 표면에 무리를 이루어 나타나는, 주변보다 상대적으로 온도가 낮고 어둡게 보이는 영역입니다. 1645년부터 1715년 사이에는 당시의 천문학자들이 흑점 활동이 매우 적거나 아예 없었다고 보고했습니다. 그 시기에는 흑점이 사라진 것처럼 보였습니다. 이와 관련하여, 영국의 천문학자 Edward Walter Maunder는 그 기간 동안 기온이 매우 급격하게 하락하여 전 세계, 특히 유럽이 소빙하기를 겪은 듯했다고 관찰했습니다. 따라서 과학자들은 지구의 기후와 태양 표면의 흑점 부족 사이에 연관성이 있을 수 있다고 추정했습니다.

흑점에 대해 결론지을 수 있는 것은?
Ⓐ 겨울철에만 나타나는 것으로 보인다.
☑ 전 세계의 기온 하락과 연관이 있을 수 있다.
Ⓒ 추운 시기에는 크기가 커진다.
Ⓓ 일정한 기간이 지나면 영구적으로 사라질 수도 있다.

어휘 permanently[pə́:rmənəntli] 영구적으로

03 Inference Question 🎧 En

The ancient Egyptians used geometry for land measurement, especially when the Nile floods destroyed boundaries. They applied these techniques to mapmaking. Meanwhile, the Greeks advanced further. Greek mapmakers began creating more systematic and scientific maps based on the concept of a spherical Earth.
By the seventeenth century, mapmakers sought greater accuracy. While calculating latitude became easier with the sextant, determining longitude remained problematic. It was not until the 1884 Washington conference that the Greenwich Meridian was established as zero longitude, creating our global reference system.

geometry[dʒiá:mətri] 기하학
measurement[méʒərmənt] 측정   destroy[distrɔ́i] 파괴하다
systematic[sìstəmǽtik] 체계적인   accuracy[ǽkjurəsi] 정확성
latitude[lǽtətjù:d] 위도   sextant[sékstənt] 육분의
longitude[lá:ndʒətjù:d] 경도
problematic[prɑ̀bləmǽtik] 문제인, 문제가 되는

고대 이집트인들은 특히 나일강 홍수가 경계를 파괴했을 때 토지 측정을 위해 기하학을 사용했습니다. 그들은 이런 기법들을 지도 제작에 적용했습니다. 한편, 그리스인들은 더 발전했습니다. 그리스 지도 제작자들은 구형 지구의 개념에 기반한 더 체계적이고 과학적인 지도를 만들기 시작했습니다.
17세기에 이르러, 지도 제작자들은 더 높은 정확성을 추구했습니다. 육분의로 위도 계산이 더 쉬워진 반면, 경도 측정은 여전히 문제였습니다. 1884년 워싱턴 회의에서야 비로소 그리니치 자오선이 경도 0도로 확정되어, 오늘날의 전 세계 기준 체계가 마련되었습니다.

화자는 1884년 워싱턴 회의에 대해 무엇을 암시하는가?
Ⓐ 그리니치 천문대의 천문학자들에 의해 조직되었다.
Ⓑ 위도 측정을 위한 새로운 기법들을 확립했다.
☑ 지도 제작에서 오랫동안 지속된 문제를 다루었다.
Ⓓ 구형 지구에 기반한 지도 제작의 개념을 도입했다.

어휘 spherical[sférikl] 구형의, 원 모양의

04 Inference Question 🎧 Am

Today we'll examine dowsing rods, an interesting folk practice that generates considerable debate in scientific circles. These Y-shaped tools, made of wood or metal, are claimed to detect underground water, minerals, or even missing persons. Dowsers hold the rods close to their bodies and believe they move in response to subtle energies. **Despite some reported successes, scientific testing has generally yielded negative results.** For instance, in one experiment, a dowser completely failed to identify which beaker contained water across multiple trials. Nevertheless, the practice remains a popular cultural tradition.

folk[fouk] 민속의 considerable[kənsídərəbl] 상당한
debate[dibéit] 논쟁, 토론; 논쟁하다
circle[sə́ːrkl] ~계 (특정 분야 사람들의 집단)
detect[ditékt] 탐지하다 in response to ~에 반응하여
subtle[sʌ́tl] 미묘한 experiment[ikspérəmənt] 실험

오늘 우리는 과학계에서 상당한 논쟁을 불러일으키는 흥미로운 민속 관습인 다우징 막대를 살펴보겠습니다. 나무나 금속으로 만들어진 이 Y자 모양의 도구들은 지하수, 광물, 심지어 실종자까지 탐지한다고 주장됩니다. 다우징 탐사자들은 막대를 몸에 가깝게 잡고 그것이 미묘한 에너지에 반응하여 움직인다고 믿습니다. 일부 보고된 성공에도 불구하고, 과학적 실험은 일반적으로 부정적인 결과를 낳았습니다. 예를 들어, 한 실험에서 다우징 탐사자는 여러 번의 시행에 걸쳐 어떤 비커에 물이 들어있는지 식별하는 데 완전히 실패했습니다. 그럼에도 불구하고, 이 관습은 인기 있는 문화적 전통으로 남아있습니다.

다우징의 보고된 성공 사례에 대해 암시되는 것은?
ⓐ 체계적인 실험적 증거와 모순되는 것으로 보인다. ✓
Ⓑ 문화 보존의 중요성을 보여준다.
Ⓒ 다우징을 정당한 과학적 실천으로 확립한다.
Ⓓ 다우징이 예상보다 더 신뢰할 만하다는 것을 시사한다.

어휘 contradict[kɑ̀ntrədíkt] 모순되다
experimental[ikspèrəméntl] 실험적인
preservation[prèzərvéiʃən] 보존

HACKERS **TEST**
p.292

01 Ⓑ	02 Ⓓ	03 Ⓒ	04 Ⓑ	05 Ⓒ
06 Ⓑ	07 Ⓒ	08 Ⓑ	09 Ⓑ	10 Ⓓ
11 Ⓒ	12 Ⓐ	13 Ⓑ	14 Ⓓ	15 Ⓒ
16 Ⓑ				

[01-04]   En

Listen to a talk in an archaeology class.

⁰¹Palynology is the study of pollen and other microscopic organic particles. These microscopic particles are incredibly valuable for understanding our past.
Unlike most organic materials that decompose quickly, ⁰²pollen has a remarkable ability to survive for thousands, even millions of years. This durability makes it perfect for archaeological research. When archaeologists excavate sites, they often find pollen grains embedded in soil around ancient artifacts. By identifying these pollen types, researchers can actually date objects and reconstruct past environments.
Well, a few years ago in the Caucasus Mountains of Russia, archaeologists discovered an ancient bone spear tip in a cave. By analyzing the artifact and surrounding sediments, they determined that it dated to around 70,000 to 80,000 years ago. It was created by Neanderthals who carefully crafted it from bison bone and attached it to a wooden shaft using tar.
Palynology goes beyond just dating artifacts. It reveals how human societies interacted with their environment. ⁰³**For example, soil samples from Belize show dramatic vegetation changes around 2500 BC—less tree pollen, more grass and weed pollen, with cultivated plants like maize appearing. This clearly indicates when humans first settled and began farming in the region.** ⁰⁴Now, let's look at some important considerations when collecting and analyzing pollen samples.

palynology[pælənálədʒi] 화분학 pollen[pɑ́ːlən] 꽃가루
microscopic[mài krəskɑ́pik] 미세한
incredibly[inkrédəbli] 믿을 수 없을 만큼
durability[djùərəbǽləti] 내구성
archaeologist[ɑ̀ːrkiɑ́lədʒist] 고고학자
excavate[ékskəvèit] 발굴하다 site[sait] 유적지
grain[grein] 입자 artifact[ɑ́ːrtəfækt] 유물
sediment[sédəmənt] 토양 bison[bɑ́isn] 들소
shaft[ʃæft] 자루, 축 maize[meiz] 옥수수
consideration[kənsìdəréiʃən] 고려 사항

고고학 강의를 들으시오.
⁰¹화분학은 꽃가루와 다른 미세한 유기 입자들을 연구하는 학문입니다. 이러한 미세한 입자들은 우리의 과거를 이해하는 데 있어 믿을 수 없을 만큼 가치가 있어요.
빠르게 분해되는 대부분의 유기 물질과는 달리, ⁰²꽃가루는 수천 년, 심지어 수백만 년 동안 보존될 수 있는 놀라운 능력을 가지고 있습니다. 이러한 내구성이 고고학 연구에 완벽하게 적합하죠. 고고학자들이 유적지를 발굴할 때, 그들은 종종 고대 유물 주변의 토양에 박혀 있는 꽃가루 입자들을 발견합니다. 이러한 꽃가루의 유형들을 식별함으로써, 연구자들은 실제로 유물의 연대를 측정하고 과거 환경을 재구성할 수 있습니다.
음, 몇 년 전 러시아의 캅카스 산맥에서, 고고학자들은 동굴에서 고대 뼈로 만든 창촉을 발견했습니다. 유물과 주변 퇴적물을 분석해서, 그들은 그것이 약 7만-8만 년 전의 것임을 알아냈습니다. 이것은 네안데르탈인들이 들소 뼈로 세심하게 만들고 타르를 사용해 나무 자루에 붙인 것이었습니다.
화분학은 단순히 유물의 연대 측정을 넘어섭니다. 그것은 인간 사회가 어떻게 그들의 환경과 상호작용했는지를 보여줍니다. ⁰³예를 들어, 벨리즈에서 나온 토양 샘플들은 기원전 2500년경 극적인 식생 변화를 보여주는데, 나무 꽃가루는 적어지고, 풀과 잡초 꽃가루는 많아지며, 더불어 옥수수 같은 재배 식물들이 나타나는 것입니다. 이것은 인간들이

언제 처음 정착하고 그 지역에서 농업을 시작했는지를 명확히 나타냅니다. ⁰⁴이제, 꽃가루 시료를 수집하고 분석할 때의 몇 가지 중요한 고려 사항을 살펴봅시다.

01 Main Topic Question
강의는 주로 무엇에 대한 것인가?
Ⓐ 네안데르탈인들의 도구 제작 기법
☑ 꽃가루와 기타 미세 입자들에 관한 연구
Ⓒ 선사 고고학의 연구 방법들
Ⓓ 서로 다른 연대 측정 방법들 간의 비교

02 Inference Question
화자는 꽃가루에 대해 무엇을 암시하는가?
Ⓐ 다른 방법들보다 더 정확한 연대 측정을 제공한다.
Ⓑ 특정한 지리적 지역에서만 발견될 수 있다.
Ⓒ 고대 인간 활동에 대한 제한적인 통찰을 제공한다.
☑ 극도로 긴 기간 동안 그대로 남아있다.

어휘 geographical[dʒì:əgrǽfikəl] 지리적인 intact[intǽkt] 그대로
extraordinarily[ikstrɔ̀:rdənérəli] 극도로

03 Intention Question
화자는 왜 벨리즈를 언급하는가?
Ⓐ 서로 다른 고고학적 발굴 방법들을 비교하기 위해
Ⓑ 중앙아메리카에서 사용되는 연대 측정 기법들을 설명하기 위해
☑ 화분학이 어떻게 인간 정착 패턴을 보여주는지 예를 들기 위해
Ⓓ 열대 고고학 유적지에서 작업의 어려움을 묘사하기 위해

어휘 excavation[èkskəvéiʃən] 발굴
exemplify[igzémpləfài] 예를 들다 tropical[trɑ́:pikəl] 열대의

04 Discuss Next Question
화자는 다음에 무엇을 논의할 것인가?
Ⓐ 고고학 유물들을 위한 고급 연대 측정 기법들
☑ 꽃가루 시료들을 수집하고 연구하는 절차들
Ⓒ 추가적인 고고학적 발굴들로부터의 사례 연구들
Ⓓ 다른 고대 문명들의 환경 재구성

어휘 specimen[spésəmən] 시료, 표본

[05-08]
Listen to a talk in an economics class.

⁰⁵**The Lipstick Effect refers to the tendency of consumers to purchase small, affordable luxuries during economic downturns, even while cutting back on major expenses.** This concept was first popularized in the early 2000s when Leonard Lauder, the chairman of Estée Lauder, noticed that lipstick sales actually increased during economic recessions. Why would this happen? Well, when consumers face financial constraints, they still desire some form of self-reward or emotional boost. Rather than buying expensive items like designer clothing or taking vacations, they opt for smaller luxury items that provide a psychological lift without significantly impacting their budget. And yes, lipstick is a perfect product to meet this demand.

So, ⁰⁶**the Lipstick Effect has been observed across various economic downturns. During the 2008 financial crisis, for example, lipstick sales remained strong while sales of other cosmetics declined.** Of course, this phenomenon isn't limited to cosmetics. We can see similar patterns with chocolate, affordable accessories, and streaming service subscriptions during recessions. ⁰⁷**These small pleasures help consumers maintain a sense of normalcy and well-being during challenging economic times.**

Then what makes this concept particularly valuable to businesses? Understanding this consumer behavior allows companies to adjust their product offerings and marketing strategies during economic downturns. ⁰⁸**Now, let's examine some specific case studies that illustrate this phenomenon in different markets.**

tendency[téndənsi] 경향
affordable[əfɔ́:rdəbl] 저렴한, 감당할 수 있는
luxury[lʌ́kʃəri] 사치품; 호화로운
downturn[dáuntərn] 침체, 하락 cut back 줄이다, 삭감하다
expense[ikspéns] 지출, 비용
popularize[pɑ́:pjuləràiz] 대중화하다
recession[riséʃən] 침체, 불경기 desire[dizáiər] 원하다, 바라다
opt for ~을 선택하다 cosmetic[kɑːzmétik] 화장품
subscription[səbskrípʃən] 구독 normalcy[nɔ́:rməlsi] 일상감
well-being 안녕, 행복 challenging[tʃǽlindʒiŋ] 어려운, 도전적인

경제학 강의를 들으시오.

⁰⁵립스틱 효과는 주요 지출을 줄이면서도 경제 침체기 동안 소비자들이 작고 저렴한 사치품을 구매하는 경향을 가리킵니다. 이 개념은 2000년대 초반에 에스티 로더의 회장인 레너드 로더가 경기 침체 동안 립스틱 판매가 실제로 증가하는 것을 알아차리면서 처음 대중화되었습니다. 왜 이런 일이 일어날까요? 음, 재정적 제약에 직면할 때, 소비자들은 여전히 어떤 형태의 자기 보상이나 정서적 위안을 원합니다. 디자이너 옷 같은 비싼 물건을 사거나 휴가를 떠나는 대신, 그들은 예산에 크게 영향을 주지 않으면서 심리적 만족을 제공하는 더 작은 사치품들을 선택합니다. 그리고 맞아요, 립스틱은 이러한 수요에 완벽한 제품이죠.

그래서, ⁰⁶립스틱 효과는 여러 차례의 경제 침체기 동안 관찰되어 왔습니다. 예를 들어, 2008년 금융 위기 동안, 다른 화장품 판매가 감소하는 동안 립스틱 판매만은 강세를 유지했죠. 물론, 이 현상은 화장품에만 국한되지 않습니다. 우리는 침체기 동안 초콜릿, 저렴한 액세서리들, 그리고 스트리밍 서비스 구독에서 비슷한 패턴을 볼 수 있습니다. ⁰⁷이러한 작은 즐거움들은 소비자들이 어려운 경제 시기 동안 일상감과 정서적 안녕을 유지하는 데 도움을 줍니다.

그렇다면 무엇이 이 개념을 기업들에게 특히 가치 있게 만들까요? 이러한 소비자 행동을 이해하면 기업은 경제 침체기에 제품 구성과 마케팅 전략을 조정할 수 있습니다. ⁰⁸이제, 다른 시장에서 이 현상을 설명하는 몇 가지 구체적인 사례 연구를 살펴보겠습니다.

05 Main Topic Question
강의의 주요 주제는 무엇인가?
Ⓐ 사치품 마케팅 전략의 진화
Ⓑ 침체기에 기업들이 비용을 줄이는 일반적인 방법
✓Ⓒ 불황기에 관찰되는 경제 현상
Ⓓ 재정적 제약이 소비자 감정에 미치는 심리적 영향

06 Inference Question
화자는 립스틱 효과에 대해 무엇을 암시하는가?
Ⓐ 침체기 동안 소비자들의 좋지 않은 재정 관리를 반영한다.
✓Ⓑ 경제 침체기 동안 비즈니스 전략에 대한 통찰을 제공한다.
Ⓒ 주로 젊은 소비자 인구 집단에서 관찰되었다.
Ⓓ 특정한 수십 년 동안 화장품 산업에만 적용된다.

어휘 reflect[riflékt] 반영하다, 나타내다
poor[puər] 좋지 않은, 부족한, 가난한

07 Detail Question
강의에 따르면, 립스틱 효과는 경제 침체기 동안 어떻게 사람들에게 도움이 될 수 있는가?
Ⓐ 침체에도 불구하고 소비자 트렌드에 참여함으로써
Ⓑ 더 비싼 물건들의 충동 구매를 줄임으로써
✓Ⓒ 안정감과 정서적 안녕감을 보존함으로써
Ⓓ 특정 회사들에 대한 더 강한 브랜드 충성도를 개발함으로써

어휘 participate in ~에 참여하다 impulse[ímpʌls] 충동

08 Discuss Next Question
화자는 다음에 무엇을 논의할 것 같은가?
✓Ⓐ 다양한 산업에서의 립스틱 효과의 예시들
Ⓑ 소비자 지출 습관에 대한 대안적 이론들
Ⓒ 립스틱 효과를 측정하기 위한 시장 조사 방법들
Ⓓ 경제 침체기 동안 광고 전략의 변화들

[09-12]
Listen to a talk on a podcast about music.

You know, I was cleaning out my garage last weekend and found my old saxophone case. I haven't touched that thing in years! But seeing it got me thinking about this common misconception I hear all the time. ⁰⁹So here's the thing—most people assume that because saxophones are made of shiny brass, they belong to the brass family. But the saxophone is actually a woodwind instrument.
The saxophone was invented in 1846 by a Belgian named Adolphe Sax. ¹⁰Sax basically created a hybrid instrument. He took a clarinet mouthpiece and attached it to a conical brass body. This unique combination gives the saxophone its distinctive sound. ¹¹The clarinet mouthpiece uses a single reed that vibrates—that's classic woodwind mechanics. But here's where it gets interesting: ¹²even though it has a clarinet mouthpiece, the saxophone's conical body actually makes it sound more like an oboe than a clarinet.
Think about it—a clarinet has this smooth, fluid tone, while an oboe sounds reedier and more piercing. The saxophone falls somewhere in between, which is why it's so versatile. So, next time someone tells you the sax is a brass instrument, you can set them straight. It's all about that reed!

garage[gərá:dʒ] 차고, 수리공장 brass[bræs] 황동
woodwind instrument 목관 악기 conical[kánikəl] 원뿔의
vibrate[váibreit] 진동하다 smooth[smu:ð] 매끈한
versatile[vɔ́:rsətl] 다재다능한 brass instrument 금관 악기

음악에 관한 팟캐스트에서의 강의를 들으시오.

있잖아요, 저는 지난 주말에 차고를 정리하다가 제 오래된 색소폰 케이스를 발견했어요. 몇 년 동안 그것에 손도 대지 않았죠! 하지만 그걸 보고 제가 늘 듣던 흔한 오해가 떠올랐어요. ⁰⁹자, 대부분의 사람들은 색소폰이 반짝이는 황동으로 만들어졌기 때문에 금관악기로 분류된다고 생각해요. 하지만 색소폰은 실제로는 목관악기랍니다.
색소폰은 1846년에 Adolphe Sax라는 벨기에 사람에 의해 발명되었어요. ¹⁰Sax는 사실상 하이브리드 악기를 만든 셈이죠. 그는 클라리넷 마우스피스를 가져와서 원뿔형의 황동 몸체에 붙였어요. 이 독특한 조합이 색소폰 특유의 소리를 만들어 줍니다. ¹¹클라리넷 마우스피스는 진동하는 단일 리드를 사용하는데, 이는 전형적인 목관악기의 특성이죠. 하지만 여기서부터 흥미로워지는데요, ¹²클라리넷의 마우스피스를 쓰지만, 색소폰의 원뿔형 몸체는 실제로 클라리넷보다는 오보에에 더 가까운 소리가 나게 만들어요.
생각해보세요, 클라리넷은 부드럽고 흐르는 듯한 음색을 내는 반면, 오보에는 좀 더 거칠고 날카로운 소리가 나죠. 색소폰은 그 중간 어딘가에 위치하는데, 그래서 그렇게 다재다능한 거예요. 그래서, 다음번에 누군가가 여러분에게 색소폰이 금관악기라고 말하면, 여러분은 그들을 바로잡아 줄 수 있어요. 관건은 바로 리드랍니다!

09 Main Topic Question
강의의 주요 주제는 무엇인가?
Ⓐ 클라리넷과 오보에의 음색 차이
✓Ⓑ 색소폰 분류에 대한 흔한 오해
Ⓒ 리드 악기들의 발명 과정
Ⓓ 색소폰 구성 요소들의 제조 과정

10 Inference Question
화자는 Adolphe Sax에 대해 무엇을 암시하는가?
Ⓐ 주로 클라리넷 연주로 알려져 있었다.
Ⓑ 오직 벨기에 악기 제조업체들과만 작업했다.
Ⓒ 악기들의 내구성을 개선하는 데 집중했다.
✓Ⓓ 악기 제작에 혁신적인 접근법을 개발했다.

어휘 primarily[praimérəli] 본래 innovative[ínəvèitiv] 혁신적인

11 Intention Question
화자는 왜 클라리넷 마우스피스를 언급하는가?
Ⓐ 색소폰 구성 요소들의 시각적 외관을 묘사하기 위해
Ⓑ 색소폰이 클라리넷보다 연주하기 쉬운 이유를 설명하기 위해
✓Ⓒ 색소폰이 왜 목관악기로 분류되는지 명확히 하기 위해
Ⓓ 서로 다른 악기 부품들의 비용을 비교하기 위해

어휘 classify[klǽsəfài] 분류하다

12 Intention Question

화자는 왜 오보에를 언급하는가?
- ⓐ 색소폰의 소리가 무엇과 닮았는지 묘사하기 위해 ✓
- ⓑ 오보에의 연주 기법을 색소폰의 것과 대조하기 위해
- ⓒ 오보에가 클래식 오케스트라에서 선호되는 이유를 설명하기 위해
- ⓓ 서로 다른 관악기들의 음역 제한을 논의하기 위해

어휘 range [réindʒ] 음역, 범위

[13-16]

Listen to a talk in a literature class.

¹³**Gothic literature emerged in the late 18th century as a reaction against the rationalism of the Enlightenment period.** This genre introduced elements of mystery, supernatural events, and psychological terror into fiction. ¹⁴**Gothic novels typically feature dark, atmospheric settings such as crumbling castles, ancient monasteries, or isolated mansions that create a sense of foreboding and unease.** They often explore themes of decay, death, and the struggle between good and evil.

One of the most enduring examples is Mary Shelley's *Frankenstein*. This classic novel combines scientific inquiry with Gothic horror to examine questions about creation, responsibility, and what it means to be human. Its monster represents both scientific achievement and moral failure, embodying the Gothic fascination with the boundaries between life and death.

¹⁵**Gothic literature also frequently employs unreliable narrators** and complex plot structures that keep readers uncertain about reality versus imagination. This psychological ambiguity has become one of the genre's most influential contributions to literature. Elements of Gothic fiction can be found in many modern horror stories, psychological thrillers, and even contemporary literary fiction. ¹⁶**The genre's emphasis on atmosphere, psychological complexity, and moral ambiguity continues to captivate writers and readers alike. This demonstrates its lasting relevance in exploring human fears and desires.**

Enlightenment [inláitnmənt] 계몽주의
monastery [mánəstèri] 수도원   enduring [indjúəriŋ] 불후의
inquiry [ínkwəri] 탐구, 문의   embody [imbádi] 구현하나
unreliable narrator 신뢰할 수 없는 화자
uncertain [ʌnsə́ːrtn] 불확실한   imagination [imædʒənéiʃən] 상상
ambiguity [æmbigjúːəti] 모호함
influential [influénʃəl] 영향력 있는   emphasis [émfəsis] 강조
moral [mɔ́ːrəl] 도덕적인   captivate [kǽptəvèit] ~을 매혹하다
relevance [réləvəns] 관련성

문학 강의를 들으시오.

¹³고딕 문학은 계몽주의 시대의 합리주의에 대한 반작용으로 18세기 후반에 등장했습니다. 이 장르는 소설에 신비, 초자연적 사건들, 그리고 심리적 공포의 요소를 도입했습니다. ¹⁴고딕 소설들은 일반적으로 무너져가는 성들, 고대 수도원들, 또는 불길한 예감과 불안감을 조성하는 고립된 저택들과 같은 어둡고 분위기 있는 배경들을 특징으로 합니다. 이 장르는 종종 부패, 죽음, 그리고 선과 악 간의 투쟁의 주제들을 탐구합니다.

가장 불후의 작품 중 하나는 메리 셸리의 '프랑켄슈타인'입니다. 이 고전 소설은 창조, 책임, 그리고 인간이란 무엇인가라는 물음을 탐구하기 위해 과학적 탐구와 고딕 호러를 결합했습니다. 작품 속 괴물은 과학적 성취와 도덕적 실패를 동시에 나타내며, 삶과 죽음 사이의 경계에 대한 고딕 장르의 매혹을 구현합니다.

¹⁵고딕 문학은 또한 자주 신뢰할 수 없는 화자를 제시하고, 독자들을 현실과 상상에 대해 불확실하도록 만드는 복잡한 플롯 구조를 사용합니다. 이러한 심리적 모호함은 이 장르가 문학에 끼친 가장 영향력 있는 기여 중 하나가 되었습니다. 고딕 픽션의 요소들은 많은 현대 공포 소설, 심리 스릴러, 그리고 심지어 현대 문학 작품에서도 발견될 수 있습니다. ¹⁶분위기, 심리적 복잡성, 그리고 도덕적 모호함에 대한 이 장르의 강조는 작가들과 독자들을 계속해서 매혹시킵니다. 이는 인간의 두려움과 욕망을 탐구하는 데 있어 그 지속적인 관련성을 보여주죠.

13 Main Purpose Question

강의의 주요 목적은 무엇인가?
- ⓐ 메리 셸리의 서술 기법을 분석하기 위해
- ⓑ 고전 문학의 특정 장르를 탐구하기 위해 ✓
- ⓒ 고딕 건축에서 사용되는 상징주의를 논의하기 위해
- ⓓ 공포 소설의 진화를 설명하기 위해

14 Detail Question

화자에 따르면, 고딕 문학은 어떻게 불길한 예감을 조성하는가?
- ⓐ 직접적이고 명시적인 설명을 사용함으로써
- ⓑ 과학적 설명을 포함함으로써
- ⓒ 빛과 그림자 이미지를 대조함으로써
- ⓓ 모호하고 불안감을 주는 이미지를 사용함으로써 ✓

어휘 ambiguous [æmbígjuəs] 모호한

15 Detail Question

화자는 고딕 소설들의 서술 기법에 대해 무엇이라고 주장하는가?
- ⓐ 현실적인 묘사에 크게 의존한다.
- ⓑ 직접적인 연대순 구조를 사용한다.
- ⓒ 종종 신뢰할 수 없는 화자를 특징으로 한다. ✓
- ⓓ 주로 등장인물들 간의 대화에 집중한다.

어휘 dialogue [dáiəlɔ̀ːg] 대화, 대사

16 Inference Question

고딕 문학의 영향에 대해 결론지을 수 있는 것은?
- ⓐ 현대 문학 스타일에 의해 빠르게 대체되었다.
- ⓑ 지속적인 인간의 두려움과 욕망을 반영한다. ✓
- ⓒ 감정적 깊이의 탐구를 방해한다.
- ⓓ 작품 속에 합리주의적 가치관을 포함했다.

어휘 discourage [diskə́ːridʒ] 방해하다, 실망시키다
incorporate [inkɔ́ːrpərèit] 포함하다, 결합하다

Section II. Academic Topics

1. Humanities

HACKERS TEST

p.302

01 Ⓓ	02 Ⓑ	03 Ⓐ	04 Ⓒ	05 Ⓑ
06 Ⓓ	07 Ⓒ	08 Ⓐ	09 Ⓓ	10 Ⓐ
11 Ⓑ	12 Ⓒ	13 Ⓒ	14 Ⓒ	15 Ⓐ
16 Ⓓ	17 Ⓒ	18 Ⓒ	19 Ⓓ	20 Ⓐ
21 Ⓓ	22 Ⓑ	23 Ⓐ	24 Ⓒ	

[01-04]

Listen to a talk in a philosophy class.

Today, we'll examine Utilitarianism, a moral philosophy that judges actions based on their consequences. **01Utilitarianism holds that the best action is the one that produces the greatest happiness for the greatest number of people. Two key figures shaped this philosophy: Jeremy Bentham and John Stuart Mill.**

Bentham, who established the foundational principles in the late 18th century, proposed a simple formula called the "greatest happiness principle." **02He believed that all pleasures and pains could be measured and compared using what he called the "hedonic calculus."** According to Bentham, a child's simple joy from playing was essentially equal to an adult's satisfaction from reading poetry, as long as the intensity and duration were the same.

Mill, writing in the 19th century, refined Bentham's ideas by introducing qualitative differences between pleasures. **03He argued that "it is better to be a human being dissatisfied than a pig satisfied." Mill distinguished between higher pleasures, like intellectual and moral satisfactions, and lower pleasures, such as physical enjoyments.**

So, while both philosophers agreed on maximizing overall happiness, their approaches to measuring and ranking different types of pleasure differed significantly. **04Next, we'll explore how these different interpretations of utilitarianism influence modern ethical debates.**

어휘 Utilitarianism[juːtìlətéəriənìzm] 공리주의 moral[mɔ́ːrəl] 도덕의
philosophy[filάːsəfi] 철학 judge[dʒʌdʒ] 판단하다; 심판
consequence[kάnsəkwèns] 결과 figure[fígjər] 인물, 수치
establish[istǽbliʃ] 정립하다
foundational[faundéiʃənl] 기초적인, 기본의

principle[prínsəpl] 원칙 formula[fɔ́ːrmjulə] 공식
intensity[inténsəti] 강도 duration[djuréiʃən] 지속 시간
refine[riːfáin] 다듬다, 정련하다 qualitative[kwάlitèitiv] 질적인
distinguish[distíŋgwiʃ] 구분하다
intellectual[ìntəléktʃuəl] 지적인
interpretation[intə̀ːrprətéiʃən] 해석 ethical[éθikəl] 윤리적인

철학 강의를 들으시오.

오늘 우리는 결과에 따라 행동을 판단하는 도덕철학인 공리주의를 살펴볼 것입니다. **01공리주의는 가장 많은 사람들에게 가장 큰 행복을 가져다주는 행동이 최선의 행동이라고 주장합니다. 두 명의 주요 인물들이 이 철학을 형성했는데, 제러미 벤담과 존 스튜어트 밀입니다.**

18세기 말에 기초 원칙을 정립한 벤담은 "최대 행복 원칙"이라고 불리는 간단한 공식을 제안했습니다. **02그는 "쾌락 계산법"이라고 부르는 방법으로 모든 즐거움과 고통을 측정하고 비교할 수 있다고 믿었죠.** 벤담에 따르면, 아이가 놀이에서 얻는 단순한 기쁨은 강도와 지속 시간이 같다면 어른이 시를 읽는 것에서 얻는 만족과 본질적으로 동일했습니다.

19세기에 활동한 밀은 즐거움 사이의 질적 차이를 도입함으로써 벤담의 사상을 다듬었습니다. **03그는 "만족한 돼지보다는 불만족한 인간이 되는 것이 낫다"라고 주장했습니다. 밀은 지적이고 도덕적인 만족과 같은 고차원적 즐거움과 육체적 즐거움과 같은 저차원적 즐거움을 구분했죠.**

따라서, 두 철학자 모두 전체적인 행복을 최대화하는 것에 동의했지만, 다양한 유형의 즐거움을 측정하고 순위를 매기는 그들의 접근법은 상당히 달랐습니다. **04다음으로, 우리는 공리주의의 이러한 다른 해석들이 현대 윤리적 논쟁에 어떻게 영향을 미치는지 살펴볼 것입니다.**

01 Main Topic Question

강의의 주요 주제는 무엇인가?
Ⓐ 도덕 철학의 역사적 발전
Ⓑ 행복과 도덕성 사이의 관계
Ⓒ 공리주의의 실용적 적용
Ⓓ 두 공리주의 철학자 간의 비교

어휘 historical[histɔ́ːrikəl] 역사의, 역사적인
morality[mərǽləti] 도덕성 practical[prǽktikəl] 실용적인
comparison[kəmpǽrəsn] 비교

02 Detail Question

화자는 쾌락 계산법에 대해 무엇을 말하는가?
Ⓐ 벤담 시대의 대부분 철학자들에 의해 거부되었다.
Ⓑ 즐거움을 평가하는 체계적인 방법을 제공했다.
Ⓒ 질적 차이의 인정에서 혁명적이었다.
Ⓓ 실제 상황에서 실행하기 위해 광범위한 훈련이 필요했다.

어휘 reject[ridʒékt] 거부하다 systematic[sìstəmǽtik] 체계적인
revolutionary[rèvəlúːʃənèri] 혁명적인
recognition[rèkəgníʃən] 인정, 인지
extensive[iksténsiv] 광범위한
implement[ímpləmənt] 실행하다, 도입하다

03 Intention Question

화자는 왜 돼지를 언급하는가?
Ⓐ 만족과 성취의 다른 수준들을 대조하기 위해
Ⓑ 동물들이 진정한 행복을 경험할 수 있다는 것을 보여주기 위해
Ⓒ 단순한 즐거움이 종종 더 확실하다는 것을 제안하기 위해
Ⓓ 육체적 즐거움을 완전히 피해야 하는 이유를 설명하기 위해

어휘 fulfillment [fulfílmənt] 만족 genuine [dʒénjuin] 진정한
authentic [ɔːθéntik] 확실한

04 Discuss Next Question
화자는 다음에 무엇을 논의할 것인가?
Ⓐ 벤담과 밀에 대한 전기적 세부사항
Ⓑ 쾌락 계산법 방법의 자세한 설명
✓ 공리주의 원칙의 현대적 적용
Ⓓ 밀 이후 공리주의 사상의 진화

어휘 contemporary [kəntémpərèri] 현대적인
evolution [èvəlúːʃən] 진화, 진화론

[05-08]
Listen to a talk in a literature class.

⁰⁵**Stream of consciousness is a narrative technique that depicts the continuous flow of thoughts and feelings in a character's mind.** This method revolutionized modern fiction by breaking away from traditional linear storytelling.
The technique seeks to capture the random, associative nature of thought processes as they occur in real time, without the logical organization typically found in conventional narrative structures. ⁰⁵**One of the most famous examples of stream-of-consciousness technique is found in James Joyce's *Ulysses*, particularly in the final section known as Molly Bloom's soliloquy.** This passage presents an uninterrupted flow of thoughts as the character lies in bed, moving seamlessly between memories, observations, and reflections without traditional punctuation or paragraph breaks. ⁰⁶Joyce's technique demonstrates how human thought rarely follows strictly logical sequences but instead shifts between topics via personal associations and emotional triggers.
Meanwhile, Virginia Woolf employed stream-of-consciousness differently, using it to explore the subjective experiences of her characters and the fluid nature of time and memory. ⁰⁵**In her novel *Mrs. Dalloway*,** Woolf moves fluidly between different characters' perspectives. ⁰⁷This shows how external events trigger internal reflections and how past and present intermingle in consciousness. This approach allows readers to experience the psychological depth and complexity of characters in ways that traditional third-person narration cannot achieve. ⁰⁸Next, we will examine the influence of the stream-of-consciousness technique on contemporary literature.

stream of consciousness 의식의 흐름
narrative [nǽrətiv] 서술의; 이야기 depict [dipíkt] 묘사하다
break away from ~로부터 벗어나다

linear [líniər] 선형적인, 일직선의 nature [néitʃər] 특성
organization [ɔ̀ːrɡənizéiʃən] 조직
conventional [kənvénʃənl] 전통적인
uninterrupted [ʌ̀nintərʌ́ptid] 중단되지 않는
seamlessly [síːmlisli] 매끄럽게 paragraph [pǽrəɡræf] 단락, 절
rarely [réərli] 거의 ~않다 via [víːə] ~을 통해, ~으로
association [əsòusiéiʃən] 연상 trigger [tríɡər] 촉발하다
employ [implɔ́i] 활용하다 subjective [səbdʒéktiv] 주관적인
perspective [pərspéktiv] 관점 external [ekstə́ːrnəl] 외부의
internal [intə́ːrnl] 내적, 내부의 intermingle [ìntərmíŋɡl] 섞이다

문학 강의를 들으시오.

⁰⁵의식의 흐름은 등장인물의 마음에서 생각과 감정의 연속적인 흐름을 묘사하는 서술 기법입니다. 이 방법은 전통적인 선형적 스토리텔링에서 벗어나 현대 소설을 혁신했습니다.
이 기법은 일반적으로 전통적인 이야기 구조에서 흔히 볼 수 있는 논리적 조직 없이, 실시간으로 발생하는 사고 과정의 무작위적이고 연상적인 특성을 포착하려고 합니다. ⁰⁵의식의 흐름 기법의 가장 유명한 예시 중 하나는 제임스 조이스의 '율리시스', 특히 Molly Bloom의 독백이라고 알려진 마지막 부분에서 발견됩니다. 이 구절은 등장인물이 침대에 누워 있을 때의 중단되지 않는 사고의 흐름을 보여주며, 전통적인 문장부호나 단락 구분 없이 기억, 관찰, 성찰 사이를 매끄럽게 이동합니다. ⁰⁶조이스의 기법은 인간의 사고가 논리적 순서를 거의 따르지 않고 대신 개인적 연상과 감정적 자극을 통해 주제들 사이를 옮겨 간다는 것을 보여줍니다.
한편, 버지니아 울프는 의식의 흐름 기법을 다르게 활용하여 그녀의 등장인물들의 주관적 경험과 시간과 기억의 유동적 특성을 탐구했습니다. ⁰⁵그녀의 소설 '댈러웨이 부인'에서, 울프는 다른 등장인물들의 관점 사이를 유동적으로 이동합니다. ⁰⁷이것은 어떻게 외부 사건들이 내적 성찰을 촉발하고 과거와 현재가 의식에서 섞이는지를 보여줍니다. 이 접근법은 독자들이 전통적인 3인칭 서술이 달성할 수 없는 방식으로 등장인물들의 심리적 깊이와 복잡성을 경험할 수 있게 합니다. ⁰⁸다음으로, 우리는 의식의 흐름 기법이 현대 문학에 미치는 영향을 살펴볼 것입니다.

05 Organization Question
화자는 의식의 흐름 기법을 어떻게 소개하는가?
Ⓐ 비교 문학 분석을 수행함으로써
✓ 기법을 설명하기 위해 예시를 제시함으로써
Ⓒ 역사적인 발전을 설명함으로써
Ⓓ 등장인물 개발에 어떻게 영향을 미치는지 보여줌으로써

어휘 conduct [kəndʌ́kt] 수행하다, 처리하다
comparative [kəmpǽrətiv] 비교의
literature [lítərətʃər] 문학, 논문 analysis [ənǽləsis] 분석

06 Detail Question
화자에 따르면, Molly Bloom의 독백은 의식의 흐름 기법을 어떻게 보여주는가?
Ⓐ 포괄적인 등장인물 배경을 제공함으로써
Ⓑ 논리적 사고 순서를 주의 깊게 따름으로써
Ⓒ 기억을 연대기적 순서로 정리함으로써
✓ 사고의 무작위적이고 연상적인 특성을 보여줌으로써

어휘 comprehensive [kɔ̀mprihénsiv] 포괄적인
chronological [krɑ̀nəlɑ́dʒikəl] 연대기적인, 시간 순의

07 Intention Question

화자는 왜 3인칭 서술을 언급하는가?
Ⓐ 두 방법을 결합한 혼합 접근법을 제안하기 위해
Ⓑ 인물 형상화에서의 효과성을 보여주기 위해
☑ 심리적 복잡성을 포착하지 못함을 보여주기 위해
Ⓓ 현대 기법들과의 호환성을 보여주기 위해

어휘 effectiveness[iféktivnis] 효과성
inability[ìnəbíləti] 못함, 무능

08 Discuss Next Question

화자는 다음에 무엇을 논의할 것 같은가?
☑ 이 기법을 활용한 현대 소설
Ⓑ 현대 문학에 대한 조이스의 영향
Ⓒ 문학 기법에 대한 학술적 논쟁
Ⓓ 인간 의식에 관한 심리적 이론

어휘 debate[dibéit] 논쟁, 토론; 논쟁하다

[09-12]

Listen to a talk in a history class.

Alright, we'll examine coffeehouses as unexpected catalysts during the 17th and 18th century Enlightenment. [09]**These establishments, particularly near universities, created unique intellectual spaces where scholars engaged in rational discourse outside formal academic settings.**
[10]**Unlike taverns where alcohol impaired judgment, coffeehouses promoted clear thinking through the consumption of coffee while fostering focused conversations.** Influential philosophers like Jean-Jacques Rousseau used these venues to discuss revolutionary concepts such as the general will, which emphasized the collective pursuit of common interests to achieve equality. These ideas spread rapidly among patrons and later influenced French Revolutionary leaders.
Each coffeehouse developed distinct characteristics, attracting specialized communities of scientists, writers, musicians, or merchants. [11]**This specialization earned some venues the nickname "penny universities," as anyone who could afford the penny admission fee gained access to scholarly discussions with prominent intellectuals.**
[12]**The proliferation of uncensored newspapers, particularly after England granted press freedom in the late 17th century, further amplified coffeehouses' impact.** Owners encouraged journalists to distribute publications, so that coffeehouses could provide diverse reading materials that fostered critical thinking about traditional authorities.

examine[igzǽmin] 검토하다, 조사하다, 살펴보다

catalyst[kǽtəlist] 촉매제   scholar[skɑ́:lər] 학자
engage in 참여하다   discourse[dískɔ:rs] 담론, 강의
impair[impέər] 손상시키다   promote[prəmóut] 촉진하다, 홍보하다
consumption[kənsʌ́mpʃən] 섭취   foster[fɔ́:stər] 조성하다
venue[vénju:] 장소   collective[kəléktiv] 집단적인
pursuit[pərsú:t] 추구   rapidly[rǽpidli] 빠르게
patron[péitrən] 고객   distinct[distíŋkt] 고유한
prominent[prɑ́mənənt] 저명한   proliferation[prəlìfəréiʃən] 확산
grant[grǽnt] 인정하다, 보장하다   amplify[ǽmpləfài] 증폭하다
distribute[distríbju:t] 배포하다, 분배하다
diverse[dáivə:rs] 다양한   authority[əθɔ́:rəti] 권위, 권한

역사 강의를 들으시오.

좋습니다, 우리는 17세기와 18세기 계몽주의의 예상치 못한 촉매제로서의 커피하우스를 살펴볼 것입니다. [09]이러한 시설, 특히 대학 근처에 있는 곳들은, 학자들이 공식적인 학문적 환경 밖에서 이성적 담론에 참여하는 독특한 지적 공간을 만들었습니다.
[10]알코올이 판단력을 손상시키는 술집과 달리, 커피하우스는 커피 섭취를 통해 명료한 사고를 촉진하면서 집중된 대화를 조성했습니다. 장자크 루소와 같은 영향력 있는 철학자들은 이러한 장소들을 이용하여 평등을 달성하기 위한 공동 이익의 집단적 추구를 강조한 일반 의지와 같은 혁명적 개념들을 논의했습니다. 이러한 아이디어들은 고객들 사이에서 빠르게 퍼졌고 나중에 프랑스 혁명 지도자들에게 영향을 미쳤습니다. 각 커피하우스는 고유한 특징을 갖추어, 과학자, 작가, 음악가, 또는 상인들로 이루어진 전문화된 공동체를 끌어들였습니다. [11]이 전문화는 일부 장소들에게 "페니 대학교"라는 별명을 얻게 했는데, 1페니의 입장료를 지불할 수 있는 사람이면 누구나 저명한 지식인들과의 학술적 토론을 접할 수 있었기 때문입니다.
[12]검열되지 않은 신문의 확산, 특히 영국이 17세기 말에 언론의 자유를 인정한 이후, 커피하우스의 영향을 더욱 증폭시켰습니다. 소유자들은 언론인들이 출판물을 배포하도록 격려했고, 이에 따라 커피하우스는 전통적인 권위에 대한 비판적 사고를 조성하는 다양한 읽을거리를 제공할 수 있었습니다.

09 Main Topic Question

강의는 주로 커피하우스의 어떤 측면에 대한 것인가?
Ⓐ 공공 모임 공간의 건축적 진화
Ⓑ 커피 섭취 습관의 발전
Ⓒ 커피 로스팅과 양조의 기술적 혁신
☑ 이성적 담론과 학습의 중심지로서의 역할

어휘 innovation[ìnəvéiʃən] 혁신

10 Intention Question

화자는 왜 술집을 언급하는가?
☑ 커피하우스의 비교우위를 나타내기 위해
Ⓑ 두 시설의 고객층을 비교하기 위해
Ⓒ 커피하우스의 주요 경쟁자들을 식별하기 위해
Ⓓ 공공 모임 장소의 역사적 기원을 묘사하기 위해

어휘 advantage[ædvǽntidʒ] 우위, 이점

11 Detail Question

커피하우스는 어떻게 "페니 대학교"로 알려지게 되었는가?
Ⓐ 근처 대학들과 파트너십을 설립함으로써
☑ 학술적 대화에 대한 저렴한 접근을 제공함으로써
Ⓒ 경쟁하는 학자들 사이의 공식적인 토론을 조직함으로써

Ⓓ 교육 장학금을 지원하기 위해 수수료를 징수함으로써

12 Detail Question

17세기 말에 커피하우스의 영향을 증폭시킨 것은 무엇인가?
Ⓐ 수입된 읽을거리의 이용 가능성 증가
Ⓑ 유럽 전역의 커피하우스 확산
✓ 다양하고 검열되지 않은 읽을거리의 유통
Ⓓ 교육 계획에 대한 정부 지원

어휘 **circulation**[sə̀ːrkjuléiʃən] 유통 **initiative**[iníʃiətiv] 계획

[13-16]

Listen to a talk in a literature class.

> In literature, Classicism refers to the tradition that emerged from ancient Greece and Rome, establishing principles that have influenced Western literature for centuries. ¹³**The classical period produced works that emphasized universal themes, moral instruction, and artistic excellence**. Greek writers like Homer created epic poems such as the Iliad and the Odyssey, which explored heroism, fate, and human nature. These works established narrative structures and character archetypes that continue to appear in modern storytelling.
> ¹⁴**Classicism was characterized by its adherence to specific forms and conventions, such as the unity of time, place, and action in drama.** The works often featured noble characters facing moral dilemmas and emphasized the importance of virtue, honor, and civic duty. ¹⁵**During the Renaissance, scholars rediscovered many classical texts, and this led to renewed interest in these ancient literary principles.** This vitality of Classicism was revived once again in the neoclassical movement of the 17th and 18th centuries. This movement explicitly revived classical ideals, with writers like John Dryden and Alexander Pope emphasizing reason, order, and dignity in their works. Classical literature's emphasis on enduring human experiences and moral lessons has ensured its continued relevance and inclusion in educational curricula worldwide. ¹⁶**In contemporary literature, such themes are often reinterpreted and transformed. Let's look at some examples.**
>
> **Classicism**[klǽsəsìzm] 고전주의 **emerge from** ~에서 나타나다
> **emphasize**[émfəsàiz] 강조하다
> **universal**[jùːnəvə́ːrsəl] 보편적인 **epic poem** 서사시
> **archetype**[ɑ́ːrkitàip] 원형 **convention**[kənvénʃən] 관습
> **unity**[júːnəti] 통일성 **noble**[nóubəl] 고귀한; 귀족
> **virtue**[və́ːrtʃuː] 덕 **civic duty** 시민적 의무 **lead to** ~로 이어지다
> **vitality**[vaitǽləti] 생명력 **revive**[riváiv] 되살아나다
> **dignity**[dígnəti] 위엄

문학 강의를 들으시오.

문학에서 고전주의는 고대 그리스와 로마에서 나타난 전통을 가리키며, 이 전통은 수세기 동안 서구 문학에 영향을 미친 원칙들을 확립했습니다. ¹³고전 시대는 보편적 주제, 도덕적 교훈, 그리고 예술적 우수성을 강조한 작품들을 만들어냈습니다. 호메로스와 같은 그리스 작가들은 영웅주의, 운명, 그리고 인간 본성을 탐구한 일리아드와 오디세이아와 같은 서사시를 창작했습니다. 이러한 작품들은 현대 스토리텔링에서 계속 나타나는 서술 구조와 등장인물 원형들을 확립했습니다. ¹⁴고전주의는 드라마에서 시간, 장소, 그리고 행동의 통일성과 같은 특정한 형식과 관습에 대한 준수로 특징지어졌습니다. 작품들은 종종 도덕적 딜레마에 직면한 고귀한 등장인물들을 내세웠고 덕, 명예, 그리고 시민적 의무의 중요성을 강조했습니다. ¹⁵르네상스 동안, 학자들은 많은 고전 텍스트들을 재발견했고, 이는 이러한 고대 문학 원칙들에 대한 새로운 관심으로 이어졌습니다. 고전주의의 이와 같은 생명력은 17세기와 18세기의 신고전주의 운동에서 되살아났습니다. 이 운동은 고전적 이상들을 명시적으로 부활시켰고, 존 드라이든과 알렉산더 포프와 같은 작가들은 그들의 작품에서 이성, 질서, 그리고 위엄을 강조했습니다. 보편적 인간 경험과 도덕적 교훈에 대한 고전 문학의 강조는 고전 문학의 지속적인 관련성과 전 세계 교육과정에서의 편성을 보장해왔습니다. ¹⁶현대 문학에서는 그러한 주제들이 종종 재해석되고 변환되곤 합니다. 예시들을 살펴봅시다.

13 Detail Question

화자에 따르면, 고전주의 시대의 작품들은 다음 중 어느 것을 제외한 모든 것을 강조하였는가?
Ⓐ 도덕적 교훈
Ⓑ 예술적 우수성
✓ 낭만적 관계
Ⓓ 지속적인 주제들

어휘 **aesthetic**[esθétik] 예술적인 **brilliance**[bríljəns] 우수성, 우수함
romantic[roumǽntik] 낭만적인 **enduring**[indjúəriŋ] 지속적인

14 Detail Question

화자에 따르면, 고전주의 문학을 특징짓는 것은 무엇인가?
Ⓐ 개인적 심리적 경험에 대한 강조
✓ 특정한 구조와 규칙의 준수
Ⓒ 전통적인 서술 구조의 거부
Ⓓ 지역적 방언과 관습에 대한 집착

어휘 **dialect**[dáiəlèkt] 방언 **custom**[kʌ́stəm] 관습

15 Intention Question

화자는 왜 르네상스를 언급하는가?
✓ 고전주의 원리의 부활을 설명하기 위해
Ⓑ 고전적 글쓰기의 정점으로 지목하기 위해
Ⓒ 중세와 고전 문학을 대조하기 위해
Ⓓ 고전 문학적 영향의 쇠퇴를 묘사하기 위해

어휘 **pinnacle**[pínəkl] 정점 **medieval**[miːdíːvəl] 중세(풍)의

16 Discuss Next Question

화자는 다음에 무엇을 논의할 것인가?
Ⓐ 신고전주의 운동의 쇠퇴
Ⓑ 고전 작품들의 교육적 사용 예시
Ⓒ 후대 작가들에 대한 호메로스의 영향
✓ 고전주의 영향의 현대적 사례

어휘 **instance**[ínstəns] 사례, 예시

[17-20]

Listen to a talk in a history class.

> [17]During the Industrial Revolution in the early 19th century, England experienced rapid technological advancement and mechanization. However, this progress came with significant social consequences, particularly for skilled workers.
> The Luddite movement emerged between 1811 and 1816 as a response to these changes. Named after a possibly fictional figure called Ned Ludd, the Luddites were groups of textile workers who destroyed machinery they believed threatened their livelihoods. These workers, primarily weavers and knitters, had spent years developing their craft skills. [18]When new machines like power looms and spinning frames were introduced, factory owners could hire unskilled workers at much lower wages. To resist this, the Luddites organized secret raids, breaking into factories at night to smash the machines. [19]They weren't anti-technology in general, but rather opposed to technology that displaced skilled labor without providing alternative employment. The government responded harshly, deploying troops to industrial areas to suppress the movement. Many Luddites were arrested, executed, or transported to Australia.
> Though the movement was eventually suppressed, it highlighted the human cost of rapid industrialization and raised important questions about technological progress and worker protection. [20]Next, we'll examine how similar concerns about automation continue to influence labor movements today.

Industrial Revolution 산업혁명　significant [signífikənt] 중대한
response to ~에 대응하여　threaten [θrétn] 위협하다
introduce [intrədjúːs] 도입하다, 소개하다
wage [weidʒ] 임금; (전쟁을) 일으키다　resist [rizíst] 저항하다
in general 전반적으로　displace [displéis] 대체하다
alternative [ɔːltə́ːrnətiv] 대체의; 대안　harshly [hɑ́ːrʃli] 강경하게
troop [truːp] 군대　suppress [səprés] 진압하다
highlight [háilàit] 부각시키다
industrialization [indʌ̀striəlizéiʃən] 산업화
automation [ɔ̀ːtəméiʃən] 자동화　labor movement 노동 운동

역사 강의를 들으시오.

[17]19세기 초 산업혁명 동안, 영국은 급속한 기술 발전과 기계화를 경험했습니다. 그러나 이 발전은 특히 숙련 노동자들에게 중대한 사회적 파장을 가져왔습니다.
러다이트 운동은 1811년과 1816년 사이에 이러한 변화에 대응하여 나타났습니다. 아마도 허구의 인물인 Ned Ludd의 이름을 따서 명명된 러다이트들은 그들의 생계를 위협한다고 믿었던 기계를 파괴한 직물 노동자들의 집단이었습니다. 주로 직조공과 편직공이었던 이 노동자들은 그들의 기술을 익히는 데 수년을 들였습니다. [18]동력 직조기와 방적기와 같은 새로운 기계들이 도입되었을 때, 공장 소유주들은 훨씬 낮은 임금으로 비숙련 노동자들을 고용할 수 있었습니다. 이에 저항하기 위해, 러다이트들은 비밀 습격을 조직하여 밤에 공장에 침입해 기계들을 부쉈습니다. [19]그들은 전반적으로 기술에 반대한 것이 아니라, 대체 일자리를 제공하지 않고 숙련 노동을 대체하는 기술에 반대했습니다. 정부는 강경하게 대응하여 운동을 진압하기 위해 산업 지역에 군대를 배치했습니다. 많은 러다이트들이 체포되거나, 처형되거나, 형벌로 호주로 이송되었습니다.
운동은 결국 진압되었지만, 그것은 급속한 산업화의 인간적 대가를 부각시켰고 기술 발전과 노동자 보호에 대한 중요한 질문들을 제기했습니다. [20]다음으로, 우리는 자동화에 대한 유사한 우려들이 오늘날의 노동 운동에 어떻게 계속 영향을 미치는지 살펴볼 것입니다.

17　Main Topic Question

강의의 주요 주제는 무엇인가?
Ⓐ 현대 노동조합 운동의 기원
☑ 숙련된 기술자들과 새로운 기술 사이의 갈등
Ⓒ 산업혁명 동안의 사회 개혁
Ⓓ 영국의 노동 운동에 대한 정부 정책

어휘　labor union 노동조합　reform [rifɔ́ːrm] 개혁; 개혁하다

18　Intention Question

화자는 왜 동력 직조기를 언급하는가?
Ⓐ 그 시대의 가장 발전된 기술을 묘사하기 위해
Ⓑ 초기 공장의 근로 조건을 설명하기 위해
☑ 무엇이 노동자들에게 파괴적 행동의 동기를 부여했는지 설명하기 위해
Ⓓ 기계로 만든 제품의 우수한 품질을 강조하기 위해

어휘　motivate [móutəvèit] 동기를 부여하다
　　　destructive [distrʌ́ktiv] 파괴적인, 해를 끼치는
　　　superior [supíəriər] 우수한, 뛰어난

19　Detail Question

화자는 러다이트들에 대해 무엇을 말하는가?
Ⓐ 성공적으로 공장 기계화를 막았다.
Ⓑ 근무 조건 개선에 집중했다.
Ⓒ 점진적인 기술 변화를 옹호했다.
☑ 주로 일자리를 잃는 것에 대해 걱정했다.

어휘　advocate [ǽdvəkət] 옹호하다, 지지하다
　　　gradual [grǽdʒuəl] 점진적인

20　Discuss Next Question

화자는 다음에 무엇을 논의할 것 같은가?
☑ 오늘날의 노동 운동에서 영향을 미치는 자동화 우려
Ⓑ 유죄 판결을 받은 러다이트들의 호주 이송
Ⓒ 대체된 노동자들을 위한 대안적 고용 기회
Ⓓ 다른 나라들로의 유사한 운동의 확산

어휘　convicted [kənvíktid] 유죄 판결을 받은

[21-24]

Listen to a talk in a linguistics class.

> [21]The Sapir-Whorf hypothesis suggests that the language we speak influences how we think

about and perceive the world. There are two versions of this theory: a strong version and a weak version. The former claims that language determines thought, while the latter suggests that language simply influences thought patterns.

Research has provided mixed evidence for this hypothesis. Some studies show that speakers of different languages categorize colors, spatial relationships, and time concepts differently. For example, Russian speakers, who have distinct words for light blue and dark blue, can distinguish between these shades faster than English speakers. [22]Similarly, some Aboriginal Australian languages use absolute directions like north and south instead of relative terms like left and right, and speakers of these languages exhibit exceptional spatial awareness.

[23]However, critics argue that cognitive differences might reflect cultural practices rather than linguistic structures alone. Building on this, modern research suggests that while language doesn't completely determine thought, it can influence attention and memory in subtle ways. This ongoing debate has significant implications for education, translation, and cross-cultural communication. [24]Next, we'll look at how bilingualism affects cognitive processes and thinking patterns.

---

hypothesis [haipɑ́:θəsis] 가설, 가정
influence [ínfluəns] 영향을 미치다; 영향
perceive [pərsíːv] 인식하다   claim [kleim] 주장하다
spatial [spéiʃəl] 공간적인
Aboriginal [æbərídʒənəl] 오스트레일리아 원주민의
absolute [ǽbsəlùːt] 절대적인   relative [rélətiv] 상대적인
exhibit [igzíbit] 보이다, 나타나다
exceptional [iksépʃənl] 뛰어난, 예외적인
awareness [əwέərnis] 인식   critic [krítik] 비판자, 비평가
argue [ɑ́ːrgjuː] 주장하다   cognitive [kɑ́gnətiv] 인지적인
linguistic [liŋgwístik] 언어적인   subtle [sʌ́tl] 미묘한
ongoing [ɑ́ngòuiŋ] 진행 중인
bilingualism [bailíŋgwəlìzm] 이중언어 사용

언어학 강의를 들으시오.

[21]사피어-워프 가설은 우리가 말하는 언어가 우리가 세상에 대해 생각하고 인식하는 방식에 영향을 미친다고 주장합니다. 이 이론에는 두 가지 버전이 있는데, 강한 버전과 약한 버전입니다. 전자는 언어가 사고를 결정한다고 주장하는 반면, 후자는 언어가 단순히 사고 패턴에 영향을 미친다고 제안합니다.

연구는 이 가설에 대해 엇갈린 증거를 제공했습니다. 일부 연구들은 다른 언어의 화자들이 색깔, 공간적 관계, 그리고 시간 개념을 다르게 분류한다는 것을 보여줍니다. 예를 들어, 밝은 파랑과 어두운 파랑을 가리키는 서로 다른 단어를 가진 러시아어 화자들은 영어 화자들보다 이러한 색조들을 더 빠르게 구별할 수 있습니다. [22]마찬가지로, 일부 호주 원주민 언어들은 좌우와 같은 상대적 용어 대신 북쪽과 남쪽과 같은 절대적 방향을 사용하며, 이러한 언어의 화자들은 뛰어난 공간 인식을 보입니다.

[23]하지만, 비판자들은 인지적 차이가 언어적 구조만이 아니라 문화적 관습을 반영할 수도 있다고 주장합니다. 이에 기반하여, 현대 연구는 언어가 사고를 완전히 결정하지는 않지만, 주의와 기억에 미묘한 방식으로 영향을 미칠 수 있다고 제안합니다. 이 진행 중인 논쟁은 교육, 번역, 그리고 문화 간 소통에 중요한 시사점을 가집니다. [24]다음으로, 우리는 이중언어 사용이 인지 과정과 사고 패턴에 어떻게 영향을 미치는지 살펴볼 것입니다.

21 Main Topic Question

강의는 주로 무엇에 대한 것인가?
Ⓐ 여러 언어를 말하는 것의 인지적 장점
Ⓑ 사피어-워프 가설의 역사적 기원
Ⓒ 언어학 연구의 실용적 적용
☑ 언어적 구조가 인간 사고에 끼치는 영향

어휘 application [ӕpləkéiʃən] 적용

22 Detail Question

화자는 호주 원주민 화자들에 대해 무엇을 말하는가?
Ⓐ 독특한 색깔 지각 능력을 가지고 있다.
☑ 뛰어난 공간 지각 능력을 보인다.
Ⓒ 고대 언어 전통을 더 효과적으로 보존한다.
Ⓓ 문화적 고립을 통해 그들의 언어를 발전시켰다.

어휘 possess [pəzés] 가지다   remarkable [rimɑ́ːrkəbl] 뛰어난

23 Inference Question

사피어-워프 가설에 대해 암시되는 것은?
☑ 연구자들 사이에서 계속 논쟁을 발생시킨다.
Ⓑ 원래 교육적 적용을 위해 의도되었다.
Ⓒ 보편 문법의 전통적 견해에 도전한다.
Ⓓ 현대 언어학에 제한된 관련성을 가진다.

어휘 generate [dʒénərèit] 발생시키다, 생기게 하다
intend [inténd] 의도하다   challenge [tʃǽlindʒ] 도전하다; 도전

24 Discuss Next Question

화자는 다음에 무엇을 논의할 것인가?
Ⓐ 언어적 구조를 형성하는 데 있어서 문화의 역할
Ⓑ 언어와 사고 간의 관계
☑ 여러 언어를 말하는 것의 인지적 영향
Ⓓ 기억과 언어적 다양성 사이의 연결

어휘 diversity [daivə́ːrsəti] 다양성, 변화

2. Arts

HACKERS TEST
p.314

01 ⓒ	02 ⓑ	03 ⓓ	04 ⓐ	05 ⓐ
06 ⓒ	07 ⓐ	08 ⓓ	09 ⓐ	10 ⓐ
11 ⓑ	12 ⓒ	13 ⓓ	14 ⓐ	15 ⓒ
16 ⓑ	17 ⓓ	18 ⓐ	19 ⓓ	20 ⓑ
21 ⓑ	22 ⓑ	23 ⓐ	24 ⓒ	

[01-04]
Au

Listen to a talk in a film class.

⁰¹Today, I'd like to discuss the sound recording process in films. ⁰²The complete movie soundtrack consists of three key elements: dialogue, sound effects, and music. ⁰¹Let's focus specifically on dialogue recording today.

Dialogue is typically recorded during the production phase, when the main filming occurs. Getting clean, clear dialogue without background noise presents significant challenges. A boom operator usually positions a microphone on a boom pole as close as possible to the actors without creating visible shadows in the frame. ⁰³Sometimes, microphones are hidden on actors' clothing, but this method often produces lower-quality sound and picks up unwanted noises like passing vehicles. So, to create authentic sound, the recordist must capture what we call room tone, the ambient sound of a location when nobody is speaking. This room tone gets added to dialogue in post-production to match the filmed environment.

After filming is complete, sound editors thoroughly review every second of footage. They note sounds that need to be removed, replaced, or modified. After that, they eliminate distractions like camera squeaks. This process is precise because sounds are strategically manipulated to create emotional impact on the audience. It is so meticulous that viewers rarely notice that they're being influenced by these skillfully crafted sounds! ⁰⁴Now, since you'll need to take a practical exam, let's look at what software is mainly used in this process.

consist of ~로 구성되다 dialogue[dáiəlɔ̀ːg] 대화, 대사
specifically[spisífikəli] 특히 production[prədʌ́kʃən] 제작
visible[vízəbl] 보이는 authentic[ɔːθéntik] 자연스러운
ambient[ǽmbiənt] 주변의 thoroughly[θə́ːrouli] 철저히
review[rivjúː] 검토하다 footage[fútidʒ] 장면
modify[mɑ́dəfài] 수정하다
eliminate[ilímənèit] 제거하다, 삭제하다

distraction[distrǽkʃən] 방해 요소
strategically[strətǽdʒikəli] 전략적으로
manipulate[mənípjulèit] 조작하다
meticulous[mətíkjuləs] 세심한 practical[prǽktikəl] 실습의

영화 강의를 들으시오.

⁰¹오늘은 영화의 음향 녹음 과정에 대해 논의하고자 합니다. ⁰²완전한 영화 사운드트랙은 대화, 음향 효과, 음악의 세 가지 핵심 요소로 구성되는데요. ⁰¹오늘은 특히 대화 녹음에 중점을 두겠습니다.

대화는 일반적으로 주요 촬영이 이루어지는 제작 단계에서 녹음됩니다. 배경 소음 없이 깨끗하고 명확한 대화를 얻는 것은 상당히 어렵습니다. 붐 오퍼레이터는 보통 프레임에 보이는 그림자를 만들지 않으면서 배우들에게 가능한 한 가까이 붐 폴에 마이크를 위치시킵니다. ⁰³때때로 마이크를 배우들의 옷에 숨기기도 하지만, 이 방법은 보통 품질이 더 낮은 음향을 만들어내고 지나가는 차량과 같은 원치 않는 소음까지 잡아내죠. 그래서 자연스러운 소리를 만들기 위해, 녹음 기사는 우리가 룸 톤이라고 부르는 것, 즉 아무도 말하지 않을 때 장소의 주변 소리를 잡아내야 합니다. 이 룸 톤은 촬영된 환경과 맞추기 위해 후반 작업에서 대화에 추가됩니다.

촬영이 완료된 후, 음향 편집자들은 모든 장면을 초 단위로 철저히 검토합니다. 그들은 제거, 교체, 또는 수정이 필요한 소리들을 기록합니다. 그 다음에, 그들은 카메라 삐걱거림과 같은 방해 요소들을 제거합니다. 이 과정은 정밀하게 이루어지는데, 왜냐하면 음향은 관객에게 감정적 영향을 주기 위해 전략적으로 조작되기 때문입니다. 이것은 너무나도 세심해서 시청자들은 자신들이 이렇게 정교하게 설계된 음향에 의해 영향을 받고 있다는 것을 거의 눈치채지 못할 정도랍니다! ⁰⁴이제, 여러분이 실습 시험을 치를 예정이므로, 이 과정에서 주로 사용되는 소프트웨어가 무엇인지 살펴보겠습니다.

01 Main Topic Question
강의의 주요 주제는 무엇인가?
ⓐ 붐 오퍼레이터가 사용하는 기술 장비
ⓑ 영화 음향 녹음 방법의 발전
✓ⓒ 영화 대화를 포착하고 처리하는 방법
ⓓ 전문 영화 제작에서의 다양한 마이크 유형

어휘 equipment[ikwípmənt] 장비

02 Detail Question
완전한 영화 사운드트랙의 핵심 요소로 언급되지 않은 것은 무엇인가?
ⓐ 음향 효과
✓ⓑ 음향 균형
ⓒ 음악
ⓓ 대사

어휘 line[lain] 대사, 선

03 Detail Question
화자에 따르면, 배우들의 옷에 마이크를 숨기는 것의 문제는 무엇인가?
ⓐ 촬영 중에 배우들을 불편하게 만든다.
ⓑ 배우들이 특정 유형의 옷을 입어야 한다.
ⓒ 카메라 프레임에 보이는 그림자를 만든다.
✓ⓓ 대화의 명확성을 방해하는 원치 않는 소음을 잡아낸다.

어휘 disrupt[disrʌ́pt] 방해하다

04 Discuss Next Question
화자는 다음에 무엇을 논의할 것 같은가?
- ☑ⓐ 오디오 후반 작업을 위한 디지털 도구
- ⓑ 소프트웨어 기반 볼륨 정규화
- ⓒ 실습 시험의 평가 기준
- ⓓ 고급 음향 믹싱 기술

[05-08] 🔊 Am
Listen to a talk in an architecture class.

⁰⁵Today, we'll explore ancient Greek theater architecture. ⁰⁶Theatrical performances were central to Greek culture. This was so important that every Greek town had its own theater by the Hellenistic period. So, what made these theaters remarkable? Greek architects developed a three-part design accommodating thousands of spectators while ensuring perfect visibility and acoustics.
⁰⁷⁻ᴮFirst, the orchestra—this circular center area was where plays were actually performed, not just music, as in modern theaters. Actors and the chorus shared this space, with the chorus providing background information and commentary.
⁰⁷⁻ᴰBehind the orchestra stood the skene—a rectangular building serving as both backdrop and storage for props and costumes. Decorated like a palace, it had a flat roof where actors portraying gods would appear to help human characters below.
⁰⁷⁻ᶜFinally, the theatron, which refers to all the seating, was built into hillsides in semi-circular arrangements. This created amazing acoustics. Even back-row spectators could hear everything! Recent research suggests that limestone seats acted as acoustic filters, emphasizing actors' voices while blocking background noise. You see, this wasn't just architecture—it was sophisticated acoustic engineering. ⁰⁸Now, let's take a look at how these theaters differ from today's theaters.

architecture[ɑ́ːrkitèktʃər] 건축
Hellenistic period 헬레니즘 시대
accommodate[əkɑ́məadèit] 수용하다
spectator[spékteitər] 관중, 구경꾼
ensure[inʃúər] 보장하다, ~을 책임지다
acoustics[əkúːstiks] 음향 commentary[kɑ́məntèri] 해설
rectangular[rektǽŋgjulər] 직사각형 palace[pǽlis] 궁전
portray[pɔːrtréi] 묘사하다, 그리다 semi-circular 반원형의
arrangement[əréindʒmənt] 배치
sophisticated[səfístəkèitid] 정교한, 세련된
engineering[èndʒəníəriŋ] 공학

건축학 강의를 들으시오.

⁰⁵오늘 우리는 고대 그리스 극장 건축을 탐구해보겠습니다. ⁰⁶극장 공연은 그리스 문화의 중심이었습니다. 극장 공연은 너무 중요해서 헬레니즘 시대에는 모든 그리스 도시에 자신들만의 극장이 있었을 정도입니다. 그렇다면, 이 극장들을 놀랍게 만든 것은 무엇이었을까요? 그리스 건축가들은 완벽한 시야와 음향을 보장하면서 수천 명의 관중을 수용하는 세 부분으로 이루어진 설계를 개발했습니다.
⁰⁷⁻ᴮ첫째는 오케스트라로, 이 원형 중앙 구역은 현대 극장의 오케스트라처럼 음악만을 위한 공간이 아니라 실제로 연극이 공연되는 곳이었습니다. 배우들과 코러스가 이 공간을 공유했으며, 코러스는 배경 정보와 해설을 제공했습니다.
⁰⁷⁻ᴰ오케스트라 뒤에는 스케네가 서 있었는데, 그것은 소품과 의상을 위한 저장소이자 배경 역할을 하는 직사각형 건물이었습니다. 궁전처럼 장식된 스케네는 신들을 묘사하는 배우들이 아래의 인간 등장인물들을 돕기 위해 나타나는 평평한 지붕을 가지고 있었습니다.
⁰⁷⁻ᶜ마지막으로, 모든 좌석을 의미하는 테아트론은 반원형 배치로 언덕 비탈에 건설되었습니다. 이것은 놀라운 음향을 만들어냈습니다. 심지어 뒷줄 관중들도 모든 것을 들을 수 있었습니다! 최근 연구는 석회암 좌석이 음향 필터 역할을 하여 배경 소음을 차단하면서 배우들의 목소리를 강조했다고 제안합니다. 보시다시피, 이것은 단순한 건축이 아닌 정교한 음향 공학이었습니다. ⁰⁸이제, 이 극장들이 오늘날의 극장과 어떻게 다른지 살펴보겠습니다.

05 Main Topic Question
강의는 주로 무엇에 대한 것인가?
- ☑ⓐ 그리스 극장의 건축적 요소
- ⓑ 고대 그리스에서 사용된 건축 재료
- ⓒ 그리스 공연에서의 신들과 신화
- ⓓ 고대 그리스에서 극장의 문화적 중요성

어휘 element[éləmənt] 요소, 원소 material[mətíəriəl] 재료, 소재
mythology[miθɑ́lədʒi] 신화

06 Intention Question
화자는 왜 헬레니즘 시대를 언급하는가?
- ⓐ 다른 건축 시대들을 비교하기 위해
- ⓑ 그리스 사회의 문화적 변화를 강조하기 위해
- ☑ⓒ 극장이 얼마나 일반적이 되었는지 보여주기 위해
- ⓓ 극장 건축이 언제 표준화되었는지 설명하기 위해

어휘 standardize[stǽndərdàiz] 표준화하다

07 Detail Question
고대 그리스 극장의 세 가지 주요 부분 중 하나로 언급되지 않은 것은 무엇인가?
- ☑ⓐ 합창
- ⓑ 오케스트라
- ⓒ 관람석
- ⓓ 배경 건물

08 Discuss Next Question
화자는 다음에 무엇을 논의할 것 같은가?
- ⓐ 과학자들이 사용한 음향 연구 방법
- ⓑ 시간이 지남에 따른 연극 공연의 발전
- ⓒ 로마 건축에 대한 그리스 극장의 영향
- ☑ⓓ 고대와 현대 극장의 비교

어휘 acoustic[əkúːstik] 음향의

[09-12]
Listen to a talk in an art class.

Paleolithic cave painters used natural pigments like red ochre and charcoal. [09]**But notably, no blue appears in prehistoric art.** This absence tells us something important—blue was simply too difficult to produce from readily available natural sources. [09/10]**The first major breakthrough came with lapis lazuli, a semi-precious stone primarily mined in Afghanistan since the Neolithic period.** This deep blue gemstone became highly prized by ancient artists. You can see its striking effect in Tutankhamun's funerary mask, where lapis lazuli creates bold blue accents against the gold background. However, there was a significant problem. [11]**Importing this material from Afghanistan was extremely costly and risky.** This challenge spurred Egyptian artists to innovate. [12]**Around 2500 BCE, they developed the world's first synthetic blue pigment by mixing copper, sand, and other substances. This Egyptian blue was used for centuries by Egyptian, Greek, and Roman civilizations.** Interestingly, when the Roman Empire collapsed, much knowledge was lost, including the formula for Egyptian blue. [09]**Medieval European artists then relied on plant-based alternatives like woad**, which produced only a grayish-blue color. The real turning point came during the Scientific Revolution when, in 1709, a German chemist accidentally discovered Prussian blue while experimenting with iron compounds. This marked the beginning of affordable, mass-produced blue paint that remains widely used today.

Paleolithic[pèiliəlíθik] 구석기 시대의 pigment[pígmənt] 안료
prehistoric[prì:histɔ́:rik] 선사 시대의 readily[rédəli] 쉽게
breakthrough[bréikθrù:] 돌파구
Neolithic[nì:əlíθik] 신석기 시대의 gemstone[dʒémstòun] 보석
ancient[éinʃənt] 고대의 striking[stráikiŋ] 놀라운
bold[bould] 선명한, 대담한 spur[spəːr] 촉발하다
synthetic[sinθétik] 합성의, 인공의
substance[sʌ́bstəns] 재료, 소재
collapse[kəlǽps] 무너지다, 멸망하다 rely on ~에 의존하다
plant-based 식물성의 Scientific Revolution 과학 혁명
accidentally[æ̀ksidéntəli] 우연히
compound[kámpaund] 화합물 affordable[əfɔ́:rdəbl] 저렴한
mass-produced 대량 생산된

미술 강의를 들으시오.

구석기 시대 동굴 화가들은 적철석과 목탄과 같은 천연 안료를 사용했습니다. [09]하지만 주목할 점은, 선사 시대 예술에는 파란색이 나타나지 않습니다. 이 부재는 우리에게 중요한 것을 말해주는데, 바로 파란색은 쉽게 구할 수 있는 천연 자원으로부터 생산하기에는 너무 어려웠다는 점이죠. [09/10]첫 번째 주요 돌파구는 신석기 시대부터 주로 아프가니스탄에서 채굴된 준보석인 라피스 라줄리에서 비롯되었습니다. 이 진한 파란색 보석은 고대 예술가들에 의해 매우 귀중하게 여겨졌습니다. 투탕카멘의 장례용 가면에서 그 놀라운 효과를 볼 수 있는데, 라피스 라줄리가 금 배경 위에서 대담한 파란색 장식을 만들어냅니다. 하지만 중대한 문제가 있었습니다. [11]아프가니스탄에서 이 재료를 수입하는 것은 극도로 비싸고 위험했다는 것이죠.

이런 어려움은 이집트 예술가들의 혁신을 촉발했습니다. [12]기원전 2500년경, 그들은 구리, 모래, 그리고 다른 물질들을 혼합하여 세계 최초의 합성 파란색 안료를 개발했습니다. 이 이집트 청색은 이집트, 그리스, 로마 문명에 의해 수세기 동안 사용되었습니다. 흥미롭게도, 로마 제국이 무너졌을 때 이집트 청색의 제조법을 포함한 많은 지식이 손실되었습니다. [09]중세 유럽 예술가들은 그 후 대청 같은 식물성 대안에 의존했는데, 이는 회색빛 파란색만을 만들어낼 뿐이었습니다. 진정한 전환점은 과학 혁명 시기인 1709년에, 독일 화학자가 철 화합물로 실험하던 중 우연히 프러시안 블루를 발견했을 때 일어났습니다. 이것은 오늘날까지 널리 사용되고 있는 저렴하고 대량 생산된 파란색 페인트의 시작을 의미했습니다.

---

09 Main Topic Question
강의의 주요 주제는 무엇인가?
Ⓐ 파란색 안료 생산의 기술적 어려움
Ⓑ 고대 안료의 화학적 구성
☑ 파란색 안료의 시대순 발전
Ⓓ 천연색과 합성색의 비교

어휘 chemical[kémikəl] 화학적인 composition[kàmpəzíʃən] 구성

10 Intention Question
화자는 왜 아프가니스탄을 언급하는가?
☑ 라피스 라줄리의 지리적 원산지를 보여주기 위해
Ⓑ 그 시대의 운송 방법을 묘사하기 위해
Ⓒ 고대 채굴 작업의 위험을 보여주기 위해
Ⓓ 문화 간의 다른 채굴 기법을 비교하기 위해

어휘 geographic[dʒì:əgrǽfik] 지리적인

11 Detail Question
화자에 따르면, 라피스 라줄리의 문제는 무엇이었는가?
Ⓐ 왕실 예술품에만 사용되었다.
☑ 수입하기에 비싸고 위험했다.
Ⓒ 바위에서 추출하기 어려웠다.
Ⓓ 햇빛에 노출되면 빨리 바랬다.

어휘 fade[feid] (빛깔이) 바래다

12 Detail Question
화자는 이집트 청색에 대해 무엇을 말하는가?
Ⓐ 현대 파란색 페인트보다 더 내구성이 있었다.
Ⓑ 오로지 종교적 목적으로만 사용되었다.
☑ 인공적으로 생산된 최초의 파란색 안료였다.
Ⓓ 그 생산 방법이 현대에 재발견되었다.

어휘 durable[djúərəbl] 내구성이 있는, 튼튼한
exclusively[iksklú:sivli] 오로지
religious[rilídʒəs] 신앙심이 깊은

[13-16]

Listen to a talk in an architecture class.

> ¹³**Today we will examine American Gothic architecture and contrast it with authentic European Gothic architecture, which flourished between the 12th and 15th centuries.** Let's start with European Gothic architecture. This style began at the abbey church of Saint-Denis near Paris, designed by Abbot Suger to represent the Heavenly Jerusalem. ¹⁴**These massive structures served a specific purpose: to remind people of God's greatness and human insignificance.**
>
> Around the late 18th century, a movement known as the Gothic Revival began in England. It later spread to America, but it wasn't a faithful reproduction of medieval churches and castles. This difference becomes clear when we compare two examples. ¹⁵**Notre Dame Cathedral in Paris, a prime example of Gothic architecture, features a grid-like facade pattern, soaring verticality, flying buttresses, enlarged windows, and elaborate ornamentation.** Now compare this to Lyndhurst Mansion, a representative example of American Gothic, which partially incorporates Gothic elements from European architecture. The mansion applied Gothic elements primarily for decorative purposes. For example, the pointed arches, which in traditional Gothic architecture serve to distribute structural loads, are used here only to decorate windows and doorways. Other Gothic features, such as steeply pitched roofs and decorative finials, are treated in the same way.
>
> Such structures satisfied the public's desire for ornate Gothic decoration rather than embodying genuine Gothic principles. This trend illustrates how architectural styles can lose their original functional and symbolic meaning when adapted across cultures. ¹⁶**Next, let's look at another architectural style that reflects this same tendency.**

contrast [kɑ́ntræst] 대비하다, 대조하다   flourish [flə́ːriʃ] 번영하다
abbey [ǽbi] 수도원   massive [mǽsiv] 거대한
insignificance [ìnsignífikəns] 미미함   faithful [féiθfəl] 충실히
reproduction [rìːprədʌ́kʃən] 재현   prime [praim] 대표적인
enlarged [inláːrdʒd] 커진, 확장된   elaborate [ilǽbərət] 정교한
representative [rèprizéntətiv] 대표적인
decorative [dékərətiv] 장식적인, 외사인
steeply [stíːpli] 뾰족하게, 가파르게   ornate [ɔːrnéit] 화려한
functional [fʌ́ŋkʃənl] 기능적인
symbolic [simbɑ́lik] 상징적인, 표상하는
tendency [téndənsi] 경향

건축학 강의를 들으시오.

¹³오늘 우리는 미국 고딕 건축을 살펴보고 12세기와 15세기 사이에 번영했던 정통 유럽 고딕 건축과 대비해보겠습니다. 유럽 고딕 건축부터 시작해봅시다. 이 양식은 천상의 예루살렘을 표현하기 위해 Abbot Suger에 의해 설계된 파리 근처의 생드니 수도원 교회에서 시작되었습니다. ¹⁴이 거대한 구조물들은 특정한 목적을 수행했는데, 사람들에게 신의 위대함과 인간의 미미함을 상기시키는 것이었습니다.

18세기 후반경, 고딕 부흥이라고 알려진 운동이 영국에서 시작되었습니다. 이 운동은 나중에 미국으로 퍼졌지만, 이것은 중세 교회와 성을 충실히 재현한 것이 아니었습니다. 이 차이는 두 가지 예를 비교할 때 명확해집니다. ¹⁵고딕 건축의 대표적 예시인 파리의 노트르담 대성당은 격자 형태의 파사드 패턴, 치솟는 수직성, 공중부벽, 커진 창문, 그리고 정교한 장식을 보여줍니다. 이제 유럽 건축에서 고딕 요소를 부분적으로 차용한 미국 고딕의 대표적 사례인 Lyndhurst 저택과 비교해보죠. 이 저택은 주로 장식 목적으로 고딕 요소들을 적용했습니다. 예를 들어, 전통적인 고딕 건축에서 구조적 하중을 분산시키는 역할을 하는 뾰족한 아치들이 여기서는 창문과 출입구를 장식하는 데에만 사용됩니다. 가파르게 경사진 지붕과 끝장식과 같은 다른 고딕 특징들도 같은 방식으로 다뤄집니다.

그런 구조물들은 진정한 고딕 원칙을 구현하기보다는 화려한 고딕 장식에 대한 대중의 욕구를 만족시켰습니다. 이 경향은 건축 양식이 문화 간에 적용될 때 원래의 기능적, 상징적 의미를 어떻게 잃을 수 있는지를 보여줍니다. ¹⁶다음으로, 이와 같은 경향을 반영하는 또 다른 건축 양식을 살펴봅시다.

13 Main Purpose Question

강의의 목적은 무엇인가?
Ⓐ 관광을 위한 고딕 부흥 건물을 홍보하기 위해
Ⓑ 중세 설계의 현대적 해석을 비판하기 위해
Ⓒ 진정한 고딕 건물의 보존을 장려하기 위해
☑ 건축적 적용에서의 문화적 차이를 보여주기 위해

어휘 encourage [inkə́ːridʒ] 권장하다, 격려하다

14 Inference Question

유럽 고딕 건축에 대해 암시되는 것은?
☑ 건축적 형태를 종교적 목적과 통합했다.
Ⓑ 귀족들을 위한 편안한 생활공간 창조에 중점을 두었다.
Ⓒ 주로 기술적 건설 기술을 과시하기 위해 건설되었다.
Ⓓ 구조적 무결성보다 장식적 특징을 우선시했다.

어휘 integrate [íntəgrèit] 통합시키다, 통합하다
prioritize [praiɔ́ːrətàiz] 우선순위를 매기다
integrity [intégrəti] 무결성

15 Detail Question

노트르담 대성당의 고딕 양식의 특징으로 언급되지 않은 것은 무엇인가?
Ⓐ 정교한 장식
Ⓑ 격자 모양의 파사드 패턴
☑ 좁은 창문
Ⓓ 공중부벽

16 Discuss Next Question

화자는 다음에 무엇을 논의할 것 같은가?
Ⓐ 고딕 부흥 건축가들의 전기 정보
☑ 문화적으로 변형된 건축 양식의 추가 사례
Ⓒ 고딕 구조 요소의 기술적 세부사항
Ⓓ 유럽 고딕 대성당의 복원 프로젝트

어휘 biographical[baiágrəfikəl] 전기적인
specification[spèsəfikéiʃən] 세부사항
cathedral[kəθí:drəl] 대성당

[17-20]

Listen to a talk in a music class.

---

[17]**Baroque music emerged in Europe around 1600 and flourished until approximately 1750, representing a dramatic shift from the Renaissance musical style.** This period is characterized by ornate musical decoration, complex counterpoint, and emotional intensity. Baroque composers like Johann Sebastian Bach and Antonio Vivaldi developed sophisticated techniques that emphasized contrast and drama in their compositions. [18]**The primary venues for Baroque performances were churches and royal courts, and this influenced the grandiose and ceremonial character of much of Baroque music.**

[19]**One defining feature of Baroque music is the use of basso continuo, a continuous bass line that provides a harmonic foundation throughout a piece.** This period saw the development of major-minor tonality, which replaced the older modal systems and created clearer harmonic progressions. Baroque music often featured elaborate ornamentation, with performers expected to add decorative flourishes to the written melodies.

Additionally, the era witnessed the rise of instrumental music to equal importance with vocal music, with the establishment of the violin family and improvements to keyboard instruments. Concertos became a popular form during this time, featuring solo instruments accompanied by orchestras. [20]**The Baroque period also established many musical forms that remain important today, including fugue, suite, and sonata.** These forms laid the groundwork for the symphony, which would become a major form in the Classical period.

---

approximately[əpráksəmətli] 약, 대략
dramatic[drəmǽtik] 극적인
characterize[kǽrəktəraiz] 특징짓다
counterpoint[káuntərpɔ̀int] 대위법
ceremonial[sèrəmóuniəl] 의례적인
continuous[kəntínjuəs] 지속적인 tonality[tounǽləti] 조성
modal[móudl] 선법 be accompanied by ~을 동반하다
groundwork[gráundwə̀:rk] 토대, 기초

음악 강의를 들으시오.

[17]바로크 음악은 1600년경 유럽에서 등장하여 약 1750년까지 번영했으며, 르네상스 음악 양식으로부터의 극적인 변화를 나타냈습니다. 이 시대는 화려한 음악적 장식, 복잡한 대위법, 그리고 감정적 강렬함으로 특징지어집니다. 요한 제바스티안 바흐와 안토니오 비발디 같은 바로크 작곡가들은 자신들의 작품에서 대조와 드라마를 강조하는 정교한 기법들을 개발했습니다. [18]바로크 공연의 주요 장소는 교회와 왕실 궁정이었으며, 이는 많은 바로크 음악의 웅장하고 의례적인 성격에 영향을 미쳤습니다.

[19]바로크 음악의 한 가지 결정적 특징은 basso continuo의 사용인데, 이는 곡 전반에 걸쳐 화성적 기초를 제공하는 지속적인 저음성부입니다. 이 시대에는 장조-단조 조성이 정립되었고, 이는 오래된 선법 체계를 대체하고 더 명확한 화성 진행을 만들어냈습니다. 바로크 음악은 종종 정교한 꾸밈을 특징으로 했으며, 연주자들은 쓰여진 선율에 장식적 기교를 추가할 것을 요구받았습니다.

또한, 이 시대는 기악음악이 성악음악과 동등한 중요성을 갖게 되었으며, 바이올린족의 확립과 건반악기의 개선이 이루어졌습니다. 협주곡은 이 시기에 인기 있는 형식이 되었으며, 오케스트라를 동반하는 독주 악기를 특징으로 했습니다. [20]바로크 시대는 또한 푸가, 모음곡, 그리고 소나타를 포함하여 오늘날까지 중요한 많은 음악 형식들을 확립했습니다. 이 형식들은 고전 시대에 주요 형식이 될 교향곡의 토대를 마련했습니다.

17 Main Topic Question

강의의 주요 주제는 무엇인가?
Ⓐ 유럽에서 기악음악의 발전
Ⓑ 현대 음악에 대한 요한 제바스티안 바흐의 영향
Ⓒ 르네상스와 고전 시대의 비교
☑ 유럽의 극적인 음악적 변혁의 시대

어휘 development[divéləpmənt] 발전

18 Intention Question

화자는 왜 교회와 왕실 궁정을 언급하는가?
☑ 공연 장소가 음악적 양식에 어떻게 영향을 미쳤는지 보여주기 위해
Ⓑ 바로크 작품에서 종교적 주제를 강조하기 위해
Ⓒ 공연을 위한 다른 음향 환경을 비교하기 위해
Ⓓ 바로크 작곡가들의 후원 제도를 설명하기 위해

어휘 patronage[péitrənidʒ] 후원

19 Detail Question

화자에 따르면, basso continuo는 무엇인가?
Ⓐ 극적인 음악적 대조를 강조하는 연주 양식
Ⓑ 장조와 단조 사이를 전환하는 방법
☑ 화성적 지원을 제공하는 지속적인 저음부
Ⓓ 바이올린족 악기를 특징으로 하는 기악 앙상블

어휘 transition[trænzíʃən] 전환

20 Detail Question

바로크 시대에 확립된 음악 형식으로 언급되지 않은 것은 무엇인가?
Ⓐ 푸가
☑ 교향곡
Ⓒ 소나타
Ⓓ 모음곡

[21-24]

Listen to a talk in a photography class.

²¹Before we had sophisticated cameras with multiple lenses, there was something much simpler yet equally remarkable—the camera obscura. This literally means "dark room" in Latin, and it operates on a principle that dates back thousands of years. ²¹When light passes through a tiny opening into a darkened space, an inverted image of the outside world is projected onto the opposite wall. This isn't magic—it's physics. Light travels in straight lines, so when rays from different parts of an object pass through that small hole, they cross over and create a flipped image. ²²What's truly amazing is how this simple concept revolutionized our understanding of optics and vision. Medieval scholars like Ibn al-Haytham used this principle to study how our eyes work. ²³Think about it: the human eye is essentially a biological camera obscura, with the pupil acting as that tiny opening. ²²This ancient discovery eventually led to portable camera obscuras, which artists used for centuries to trace accurate drawings. ²⁴So, when and how did it become possible to actually take photographs? Let's find out about that.

equally [í:kwəli] 똑같이 operate [ápərèit] 작동하다
date back 거슬러 올라가다 darken [dá:rkən] 어둡게 하다
inverted [invə́:rtid] 거꾸로 된 opposite [á:pəzit] 반대편의
physics [fíziks] 물리학 ray [rei] 광선 cross over 교차하다
optics [ápiks] 광학 biological [bàiəládʒikəl] 생물학적인
pupil [pjú:pl] 동공 portable [pɔ́:rtəbl] 휴대용의
find out 알아보다

사진학 강의를 들으시오.

²¹우리가 여러 렌즈를 가진 정교한 카메라를 갖기 전에, 훨씬 더 단순하지만 똑같이 놀라운 것이 있었는데, 카메라 옵스큐라입니다. 이것은 라틴어로 문자 그대로 "어두운 방"을 의미하며, 수천 년 전으로 거슬러 올라가는 원리로 작동합니다. ²¹빛이 작은 구멍을 통해 어두운 공간으로 들어갈 때, 바깥 세계의 거꾸로 된 이미지가 반대편 벽에 투영됩니다. 이것은 마법이 아닌 물리학입니다. 빛은 직선으로 이동하므로, 물체의 다른 부분들로부터 온 광선들이 그 작은 구멍을 통과할 때, 그들은 서로 교차하여 뒤집힌 이미지를 만들어냅니다. ²²정말 놀라운 것은 이 단순한 개념이 광학과 시각에 대한 우리의 이해를 어떻게 혁신했는지입니다. Ibn al-Haytham과 같은 중세 학자들은 이 원리를 사용하여 우리의 눈이 어떻게 작동하는지 연구했습니다. ²³생각해 보세요, 인간의 눈은 본질적으로 생물학적 카메라 옵스큐라이며, 동공이 그 작은 구멍 역할을 합니다. ²²이 고대의 발견은 결국 휴대용 카메라 옵스큐라로 이어졌고, 예술가들은 수세기 동안 정확한 그림을 따라 그리기 위해 이것을 사용했습니다. ²⁴그렇다면, 언제 그리고 어떻게 실제로 사진을 찍을 수 있게 되었을까요? 그것에 대해 알아봅시다.

21 Detail Question

화자는 카메라 옵스큐라에 대해 무엇이라고 주장하는가?
Ⓐ 라틴어로 문자 그대로 "밝은 방"으로 번역된다.
☑ 반대편 벽에 뒤집힌 이미지를 투영한다.
Ⓒ 기능하려면 정교한 기술이 필요하다.
Ⓓ 중세 학자들이 과학적 연구를 위해 발명했다.

어휘 translate [trænsléit] 번역하다

22 Inference Question

카메라 옵스큐라의 역사적 중요성에 대해 암시되는 것은?
Ⓐ 과학보다는 마법의 한 형태로 여겨졌다.
☑ 예술과 과학의 발전에 기여했다.
Ⓒ 고대 기술적 성취의 정점을 나타냈다.
Ⓓ 인체에 대한 중세 학자들의 이해를 향상시켰다.

어휘 contribute [kəntríbju:t] 기여하다

23 Intention Question

화자는 왜 인간의 눈을 언급하는가?
☑ 영상 형성의 생물학적 기초를 묘사하기 위해
Ⓑ 현대 이전에 카메라가 불필요했던 이유를 설명하기 위해
Ⓒ Ibn al-Haytham이 광학 연구에 집중한 이유를 강조하기 위해
Ⓓ 고대와 현대의 광학 이해를 비교하기 위해

어휘 basis [béisis] 기초 unnecessary [ʌnnésəsèri] 불필요한

24 Discuss Next Question

화자는 다음에 무엇을 논의할 것 같은가?
Ⓐ 현대 예술에서의 카메라 옵스큐라 응용
Ⓑ 현대에 카메라 옵스큐라 사용의 쇠퇴
☑ 관찰에서 이미지 포착으로의 역사적 발전
Ⓓ 광학 시스템에서 광선의 거동에 대한 상세한 분석

어휘 detailed [dí:teild] 상세한

3. Social Science

HACKERS TEST p.326

01	Ⓓ	02	Ⓐ	03	Ⓒ	04	Ⓑ	05	Ⓐ
06	Ⓒ	07	Ⓑ	08	Ⓒ	09	Ⓒ	10	Ⓓ
11	Ⓐ	12	Ⓑ	13	Ⓒ	14	Ⓓ	15	Ⓐ
16	Ⓐ	17	Ⓑ	18	Ⓒ	19	Ⓒ	20	Ⓓ
21	Ⓐ	22	Ⓑ	23	Ⓓ	24	Ⓐ		

[01-04]

Listen to a talk in an anthropology class.

⁰¹**Today I want to focus on one of history's greatest mysteries—the sudden collapse of the Maya civilization. Around AD 900, a thriving society of 15 million people suddenly vanished.** Cities were abandoned, pyramids left to decay. What could cause such a dramatic downfall?

For years, archaeologists debated various theories, such as overpopulation, warfare, and economic collapse. ⁰²**But recently, compelling evidence has emerged in support of the drought theory. Scientists analyzed ocean sediment layers near the Maya region.** These sediments contain levels of titanium that indicate annual rainfall, much like tree rings, except that they form underwater.

⁰³**The data reveals three severe droughts lasting about a decade each, around AD 810, AD 860, and AD 910.** These dates precisely match the periods when many southern Maya cities were abandoned. Drought triggered a devastating chain reaction. Crop failures led to famine, which sparked warfare between city-states. Meanwhile, people cleared more forests for farming, using slash-and-burn methods that destroyed topsoil.

This deforestation worsened the drought by raising regional temperatures up to six degrees Celsius. It was a vicious cycle that leaders failed to address, instead focusing on building monuments. The result? In some regions, the population may have declined by 70–90% over the course of two centuries. ⁰⁴**The rapid collapse of the Maya civilization serves as a powerful lesson to modern nations of the importance of responsible resource management.** Next, we'll discuss this a bit further.

---

collapse[kəlǽps] 붕괴   abandon[əbǽndən] 버리다
downfall[dáunfɔːl] 몰락   archaeologist[ɑ̀ːrkiəládʒist] 고고학자
warfare[wɔ́ːrfɛr] 전쟁   compelling[kəmpéliŋ] 설득력 있는
in support of ~을 뒷받침하는   drought[draut] 가뭄
reveal[rivíːl] 보여주다, 드러내다
devastating[dévəstèitiŋ] 파괴적인   famine[fǽmin] 기근
spark[spɑːrk] 일으키다; 불꽃   topsoil[tɑpsɔ̀il] 표토
deforestation[diːfɔ̀ːristéiʃən] 삼림 벌채
worsen[wɔ́ːrsn] 악화시키다   vicious cycle 악순환
address[ǽdres] 해결하다; 주소
monument[mɑ́ːnjumənt] 기념물
lesson[lésn] 교훈, 수업; 가르치다

인류학 강의를 들으시오.

⁰¹오늘 저는 역사상 가장 큰 수수께끼 중 하나인 마야 문명의 갑작스러운 붕괴에 집중하고자 합니다. 서기 900년경, 1천 5백만 명 규모의 번영하던 사회가 갑자기 사라졌습니다. 도시들은 버려졌고, 피라미드들은 퇴락하도록 방치되었습니다. 무엇이 그런 극적인 몰락을 일으킬 수 있었을까요?

수년간, 고고학자들은 인구 과잉, 전쟁, 경제 붕괴와 같은 다양한 이론을 논의했습니다. ⁰²하지만 최근에, 가뭄 이론을 뒷받침하는 설득력 있는 증거가 나타났습니다. 과학자들은 마야 지역 인근의 해양 퇴적층을 분석했습니다. 이러한 퇴적물들은 연간 강우량을 나타내는 티타늄 수치를 포함하고 있는데, 수중에서 형성된다는 점만 제외하면 나무의 나이테와 비슷합니다.

⁰³데이터는 810년, 860년, 그리고 910년경에 각각 약 십 년간 지속된 세 번의 심각한 가뭄을 보여주는데요. 이 날짜들은 많은 남부 마야 도시들이 버려진 시기와 정확히 일치합니다. 가뭄은 파괴적인 연쇄 반응을 유발했습니다. 흉작은 기근으로 이어졌고, 이는 도시국가들 간의 전쟁을 일으켰습니다. 한편, 사람들은 농업을 위해 더 많은 숲을 개간했고, 표토를 파괴하는 화전 방식을 사용했습니다.

이러한 삼림 벌채는 지역 기온을 최대 섭씨 6도까지 올려 가뭄을 악화시켰습니다. 그것은 지도자들이 해결하지 못한 악순환이었고, 대신 그들은 기념물 건설에 집중했습니다. 그 결과는? 어떤 지역에서는, 인구가 2세기에 걸쳐 70-90퍼센트까지 감소했을지도 모릅니다. ⁰⁴마야 문명의 급속한 붕괴는 현대 국가들에게 책임감 있는 자원 관리의 중요성에 대한 강력한 교훈이 됩니다. 다음으로, 우리는 이에 대해 좀 더 논의할 것입니다.

01 Main Topic Question

강의의 주요 주제는 무엇인가?
Ⓐ 고대 마야 도시들의 인구 증가
Ⓑ 유적지 연구를 위한 고고학적 방법들
Ⓒ 마야 기념물들의 건설 기법들
Ⓓ 마야 도시 중심지들의 갑작스러운 방치

어휘   archaeological[ɑ̀ːrkiəládʒikəl] 고고학적인
   ruin[rúːin] 유적지, 폐허

02 Detail Question

강의에 따르면, 과학자들은 고대 기후 패턴을 어떻게 발견했는가?
Ⓐ 수중 퇴적물 표본을 조사함으로써
Ⓑ 다른 고고학적 이론과 비교함으로써
Ⓒ 수세기에 걸친 인구 변화를 계산함으로써
Ⓓ 고대 나무들의 성장 패턴을 조사함으로써

어휘   calculate[kǽlkjulèit] 계산하다

03 Detail Question

마야 문명의 가뭄 시기로 언급되지 않은 것은 무엇인가?
Ⓐ 810년
Ⓑ 860년
Ⓒ 900년
Ⓓ 910년

04 Discuss Next Question

화자는 다음에 무엇을 논의할 것 같은가?
Ⓐ 마야 유적지에서 사용된 고고학적 발굴 기법들
Ⓑ 현대 자원 보존에 대한 시사점
Ⓒ 현대 멕시코에 대한 마야 문화의 영향
Ⓓ 다른 붕괴된 문명들의 사례

어휘   excavation[èkskəvéiʃən] 발굴   site[sait] 유적지
   implication[ìmplikéiʃən] 시사점, 함축

[05-08]

Listen to a talk in a psychology class.

⁰⁵**Today we'll examine the famous Marshmallow experiment, a landmark study in self-control and delayed gratification.** This experiment, conducted at Stanford University, gave young children a simple choice—eat one marshmallow immediately or wait 15 minutes to receive two marshmallows.

The researchers observed how children coped with temptation. Some ate the marshmallow immediately, while others used various strategies to resist. They covered their eyes, turned away, or distracted themselves by singing or talking.

What made this study remarkable was its follow-up findings. Several years later, children who delayed gratification showed better outcomes, such as higher SAT scores, better academic performance, and healthier body mass indices. ⁰⁶**This demonstrated a strong correlation between early self-control and future success.**

⁰⁷**This research connects to behavioral economics concepts like temporal discounting.** It describes our tendency to value immediate rewards over larger future benefits. Unlike traditional economic theory, which assumes rational decision-making, the Marshmallow experiment showed how emotional and cognitive factors influence decision-making, particularly regarding immediate versus delayed rewards.

However, whether this ability can be developed solely through training or strategy instruction remains a topic of debate. ⁰⁸**Follow-up studies, including one conducted in 2018, have offered various critical perspectives. Let's take a look at some of them.**

---

landmark [lǽndmɑːrk] 획기적인
gratification [græ̀təfikéiʃən] 만족 immediately [imíːdiətli] 즉시
cope with ~에 대처하다 temptation [temptéiʃən] 유혹
strategy [strǽtədʒi] 전략 turn away 돌아서다
follow-up 후속의 finding [fáindiŋ] 연구 결과
outcome [áutkʌ̀m] 결과 correlation [kɔ̀ːrəléiʃən] 상관관계
behavioral economics 행동경제학
temporal discounting 시간 할인 rational [rǽʃənl] 합리적인
decision-making 의사결정 regarding [rigɑ́ːrdiŋ] ~에 관한
solely [sóulli] 오직 critical [krítikəl] 비판적인, 중요한

심리학 강의를 들으시오.

⁰⁵오늘 우리는 자제력과 지연된 만족에 관한 획기적인 연구인 유명한 마시멜로 실험을 살펴보겠습니다. 스탠포드 대학교에서 실시된 이 실험은 어린아이들에게 마시멜로 하나를 즉시 먹거나 15분을 기다려 두 개를 받는 간단한 선택지를 제시했습니다.

연구자들은 아이들이 유혹에 어떻게 대처하는지 관찰했습니다. 일부는 마시멜로를 즉시 먹었고, 다른 아이들은 저항하기 위해 다양한 전략을 사용했습니다. 그들은 눈을 가리거나, 돌아서거나, 노래하거나 말하며 스스로를 산만하게 했습니다.

이 연구를 주목할 만하게 만든 것은 후속 연구 결과였습니다. 몇 년 후, 만족을 지연시킨 아이들은 더 높은 SAT 점수, 더 나은 학업 성과, 그리고 더 건강한 체질량 지수와 같은 더 나은 결과를 보였습니다. ⁰⁶이것은 초기 자제력과 미래 성공 사이의 강한 상관관계를 보여주었습니다.

⁰⁷이 연구는 시간 할인과 같은 행동경제학 개념과 연결되는데요. 그것은 더 큰 미래 이익보다 즉각적인 보상을 가치 있게 여기는 우리의 경향을 설명하죠. 합리적 의사결정을 상정하는 전통적인 경제 이론과 달리, 마시멜로 실험은 감정적이고 인지적인 요인들이 특히 즉각적 보상과 지연된 보상에 관한 의사결정에 어떻게 영향을 미치는지 보여주었습니다.

하지만 이러한 능력이 오직 훈련이나 전략 지도를 통해서만 개발될 수 있는지는 논의의 주제로 남아있습니다. ⁰⁸2018년에 실시된 연구를 포함한 후속 연구들은 다양한 비판적 관점을 제시했습니다. 그중 일부를 살펴보겠습니다.

05 Main Topic Question

강의는 주로 무엇에 대한 것인가?
Ⓐ ✓ 지연된 만족과 그 결과에 대한 연구
Ⓑ 성공과 식이 습관 사이의 상관관계
Ⓒ 다양한 양육 방식과 결과의 비교
Ⓓ 현대 연구에서 전통적인 심리학 이론에 대한 비판

어휘 dietary [dáiətèri] 식이의

06 Detail Question

화자는 마시멜로 실험에 대해 무엇을 말하는가?
Ⓐ 결과는 다양한 연령대에 걸쳐 비교되었다.
Ⓑ 연구자들은 아이들이 유혹에 저항하도록 돕기 위해 장난감을 제공했다.
✓ 초기 자제력을 이후의 삶의 성공과 연결했다.
Ⓓ 방법론이 너무 복잡하다고 비판받았다.

어휘 methodology [mèθədάlədʒi] 방법론
complex [kəmpléks] 복잡한, 복합의

07 Intention Question

화자는 왜 행동경제학을 언급하는가?
Ⓐ 마시멜로 실험의 모순을 강조하기 위해
✓ 감정적 요인들이 의사결정에 어떻게 영향을 미치는지 보여주기 위해
Ⓒ 다른 분야들이 연구를 어떻게 잘못 해석하는지 보여주기 위해
Ⓓ 아이들이 성인들보다 더 나은 경제적 결정을 한다고 주장하기 위해

어휘 contradiction [kɑ̀ntrədíkʃən] 모순, 상충
factor [fǽktər] 요인, 요소 field [fiːld] 분야, 영역
misinterpret [mìsintə́rprət] 잘못 해석하다, 오해하다

08 Discuss Next Question

화자는 다음에 무엇을 논의할 것 같은가?
Ⓐ 지연된 만족의 신경학적 기초
Ⓑ 유사한 실험에서 사용된 대체 보상
✓ 마시멜로 실험에 대한 비판적 관점
Ⓓ 성인 참가자를 대상으로 한 실험 확장

어휘 neurological [njùərəlɑ́dʒikəl] 신경학적인

[09-12]

Listen to a talk in an economics class.

⁰⁹**Today, we're going to discuss an important marketing strategy known as art-based marketing, also called cultural branding.** This approach uses artistic elements and cultural associations to create powerful brand identities in the marketplace.

Art-based marketing differs from conventional marketing in a fundamental way. While traditional marketing focuses primarily on product features or immediate sales goals, ¹⁰**cultural branding builds deeper connections by tapping into artistic and cultural meanings that resonate with consumers.** ¹²⁻ᴬ**For example, a company might collaborate with local artists to design limited-edition packaging that reflects regional cultural values.**

What makes this approach particularly effective is how it creates emotional engagement. When brands associate themselves with artistic expressions, they don't just sell products—they sell experiences and identities. ¹¹**Consider how luxury fashion houses often sponsor art exhibitions or** ¹¹/¹²⁻ᴮ**collaborate with renowned artists.** These partnerships aren't random. ¹²⁻ᶜ**They're strategic efforts to position these brands within cultural conversations.**

Research shows that art-based marketing can significantly enhance brand equity and customer loyalty. A recent experiment demonstrated that consumers exposed to products with artistic elements were willing to pay 15% more than those who were shown standard commercial designs. This illustrates how cultural branding can transform ordinary products into meaningful items that can command premium prices in the marketplace.

---

association [əsòusiéiʃən] 연상 differ from ~와 다르다
tap into ~을 활용하다 resonate with ~와 공명하다
limited-edition 한정판의; 한정판
engagement [ingéidʒmənt] 몰입 sponsor [spánsər] 후원하다
renowned [rináund] 유명한, 저명한
strategic [strətí:dʒik] 전략적인 equity [ékwəti] 자산, 공평
willing to ~할 의향이 있다 commercial [kəmə́:rʃəl] 상업적인
ordinary [ɔ́:rdənèri] 표준의, 보통의
meaningful [mí:niŋfəl] 의미 있
command [kəmǽnd] (가격 등을) 받다, 명령하다; 명령

경제학 강의를 들으시오.

⁰⁹오늘 우리는 예술 기반 마케팅, 혹은 문화적 브랜딩이라고도 불리는 중요한 마케팅 전략에 대해 논의할 것입니다. 이 접근법은 시장에서 강력한 브랜드 정체성을 만들기 위해 예술적 요소와 문화적 연상을 사용합니다.

예술 기반 마케팅은 본질적으로 기존 마케팅과 다릅니다. 전통적인 마케팅이 주로 제품의 특징이나 즉각적인 판매 목표에 집중하는 반면, ¹⁰문화적 브랜딩은 소비자와 공명하는 예술적, 문화적 의미를 활용해 더 깊은 유대를 구축합니다. ¹²⁻ᴬ예를 들어, 회사는 지역의 문화적 가치를 반영하는 한정판 패키지를 디자인하기 위해 지역 예술가와 협력할 수도 있습니다.

이 접근법이 특히 효과적인 이유는 정서적 몰입을 이끌어내는 방식에 있습니다. 브랜드가 자신을 예술적 표현과 연관시킬 때, 단지 제품을 파는 것이 아니라 경험과 정체성을 판매하는 것입니다. ¹¹럭셔리 패션 하우스들이 종종 미술 전시회를 후원하거나 ¹¹/¹²⁻ᴮ유명한 예술가들과 협력하는 방식을 생각해보세요. 이러한 파트너십들은 임의적인 것이 아닙니다. ¹²⁻ᶜ이는 브랜드를 문화적 담론 속에 위치시키려는 전략적 노력입니다.

연구는 예술 기반 마케팅이 브랜드 자산과 고객 충성도를 상당히 향상시킬 수 있음을 보여줍니다. 최근 실험에서는 예술적 요소가 있는 제품에 노출된 소비자들이 표준 상업적 디자인을 본 소비자보다 15퍼센트 더 지불할 의향이 있는 것으로 나타났습니다. 이는 문화적 브랜딩이 평범한 제품을 시장에서 프리미엄 가격을 받을 수 있는 의미 있는 물품으로 변화시킬 수 있다는 것을 보여줍니다.

09 Main Topic Question

강의의 주요 주제는 무엇인가?
Ⓐ 비즈니스에서의 문화적 상징주의
Ⓑ 전통적인 마케팅의 한계
✓ 예술적 요소를 통한 마케팅
Ⓓ 예술 후원의 경제적 영향

어휘 symbolism [símbəlìzm] 상징주의

10 Detail Question

회사는 예술 기반 마케팅으로부터 무엇을 얻을 수 있는가?
Ⓐ 시장 점유율의 즉각적인 증가
Ⓑ 단순화된 제품 디자인 요구 사항
Ⓒ 시장에서 경쟁의 제거
✓ 소비자와의 더 깊은 정서적 연결

어휘 simplified [símpləfàid] 단순화된
　　　elimination [ilìmənéiʃən] 제거

11 Intention Question

화자는 왜 럭셔리 패션 하우스들을 언급하는가?
✓ 전략적인 예술적 파트너십을 보여주기 위해
Ⓑ 그들의 제조 기법을 설명하기 위해
Ⓒ 그들의 영향력 쇠퇴를 강조하기 위해
Ⓓ 그들의 과도한 지출을 비판하기 위해

어휘 excessive [iksésiv] 과도한

12 Detail Question

예술 기반 마케팅을 위한 회사의 노력으로 언급되지 않은 것은 무엇인가?
Ⓐ 한정판 예술적 디자인
Ⓑ 예술가와의 협력
Ⓒ 문화적 담론에서의 전략적 포지셔닝
✓ 디지털 마케팅 캠페인에 대한 투자

어휘 investment [invéstmənt] 투자

[13-16]

Listen to a talk in a business management class. 🎧 Au

Today we're discussing the Ringelmann effect, an important concept in productivity economics. ¹³**The Ringelmann effect describes how individual productivity tends to decrease as group size increases.** ¹⁴**This was first observed in the early 1900s when French engineer Maximilien Ringelmann studied a rope-pulling task.**

¹⁴**What Ringelmann found was interesting: as more people joined the rope-pulling task, each person's effort actually declined.** For example, when eight people pulled together, they didn't produce eight times the force of one person working alone. This reduction in individual effort in group settings happens for two main reasons: coordination losses and motivation losses.

¹⁵**Coordination losses occur because it becomes harder to synchronize efforts as groups grow larger.** And motivation losses happen when individuals feel less responsible for the outcome, which we call social loafing. This explains why adding more workers to a project doesn't always increase productivity proportionally.

This concept has significant implications for workplace management and team organization. Understanding the Ringelmann effect helps businesses determine optimal team sizes and create better accountability structures to maintain productivity levels in group settings. Accordingly, ¹⁶**some companies have introduced the concept of the "Directly Responsible Individual," called DRI. Now, let's explore what that is.**

productivity economics 생산성 경제학
tend to ~하는 경향이 있다   decline[dikláin] 감소하다, 쇠퇴하다
reduction[ridʌ́kʃən] 감소, 하락
coordination[kouɔ̀ːrdənéiʃən] 조정
motivation[mòutəvéiʃən] 동기
synchronize[síŋkrənaiz] 조율하다   social loafing 사회적 태만
proportionally[prəpɔ́ːrʃənli] 비례적으로
optimal[áptəməl] 최적의, 최상의
accountability[əkàuntəbíləti] 책임

경영학 강의를 들으시오.

오늘 우리는 생산성 경제학의 중요한 개념인 링겔만 효과에 대해 논의하고 있습니다. ¹³링겔만 효과는 집단 크기가 증가함에 따라 개인 생산성이 감소하는 경향이 있음을 설명합니다. ¹⁴이것은 1900년대 초에 프랑스 엔지니어 막시밀리앙 링겔만이 밧줄 당기기 과제를 연구하며 처음 관찰되었습니다.

¹⁴링겔만이 발견한 것은 흥미로웠는데, 더 많은 사람들이 밧줄 당기기 작업에 참여함에 따라, 각 사람의 노력은 실제로 감소했습니다. 예를 들어, 여덟 명이 함께 당길 때, 그들은 혼자 일하는 한 사람의 힘의 여덟 배를 만들어내지 못했습니다. 집단 환경에서 개별 노력의 이러한 감소는 조정 손실과 동기 손실이라는 두 가지 주요 이유로 발생합니다.

¹⁵조정 손실은 집단이 더 커짐에 따라 노력을 조율하는 것이 더 어려워지기 때문에 발생합니다. 그리고 동기 손실은 개인들이 결과에 대해 덜 책임감을 느낄 때 발생하는데, 우리는 이를 사회적 태만이라고 부릅니다. 이것은 프로젝트에 더 많은 근로자를 추가하는 것이 항상 비례적으로 생산성을 증가시키지 않는 이유를 설명합니다.

이 개념은 직장 관리와 팀 조직에 중요한 시사점을 갖습니다. 링겔만 효과를 이해하는 것은 기업들이 최적의 팀 크기를 결정하고 집단 환경에서 생산성 수준을 유지하기 위한 더 나은 책임 구조를 만드는 데 도움이 됩니다. 따라서 ¹⁶일부 회사들은 DRI라고 불리는 "직접적인 책임을 지는 개인"의 개념을 도입했습니다. 이제 그것이 무엇인지 살펴보겠습니다.

13 Main Topic Question

강의는 주로 무엇에 대한 것인가?
Ⓐ 현대 직장에서의 동기 부여 문제
Ⓑ 팀 조정 전략의 발전
☑ 팀 크기와 생산성 사이의 관계
Ⓓ 현대 관리 기법의 개발

어휘 motivational[mòutəvéiʃənl] 동기의

14 Intention Question

화자는 왜 밧줄 당기기 작업을 언급하는가?
Ⓐ 초기 과학적 연구의 한계를 보여주기 위해
Ⓑ 산업 심리학의 역사적 맥락을 소개하기 위해
Ⓒ 팀의 힘을 측정하는 다양한 방법을 비교하기 위해
☑ 집단 환경에서 개별 노력이 어떻게 감소하는지 예를 들기 위해

어휘 exemplify[igzémpləfài] 예를 들다

15 Detail Question

화자에 따르면, 조정 손실은 왜 발생하는가?
Ⓐ 팀 구성원들이 같은 작업에 대해 경쟁적인 접근법을 개발한다.
☑ 팀 크기가 증가함에 따라 동기화가 더 어려워진다.
Ⓒ 리더들이 여러 사람이 함께하는 작업에서 명확한 방향을 제공하지 못한다.
Ⓓ 집단은 가장 빠른 구성원의 속도로 일하는 경향이 있다.

어휘 synchronization[síŋkrənizéiʃən] 동기화
pace[peis] 속도; 보조를 맞추다

16 Discuss Next Question

화자는 다음에 무엇을 논의할 것 같은가?
☑ 명확한 책임을 부여하는 관리 접근법
Ⓑ 집단 환경에서 개별 생산성을 측정하는 방법
Ⓒ 링겔만의 원래 발견을 확장하는 추가 연구
Ⓓ 대규모 팀에서의 조정 손실 사례

어휘 assign[əsáin] 부여하다   extend[iksténd] 확장하다

[17-20]

Listen to a talk in an archaeology class. 🎧 Am

¹⁷**Today we'll be exploring the record-keeping systems used by the ancient Assyrians.** The Assyrians developed one of the most sophisticated record-keeping methods in the ancient world,

primarily using clay tablets inscribed with cuneiform script. This writing system consisted of wedge-shaped marks pressed into soft clay using a reed stylus.

Well, what made Assyrian record-keeping particularly notable was its comprehensive nature. Royal archives contained detailed administrative records, diplomatic correspondence, and religious texts. [18]**The most famous collection comes from King Ashurbanipal's library at Nineveh, dating to the 7th century BC. This library housed thousands of tablets covering subjects from astronomy to medicine.**

So, [19]**Assyrian scribes were highly trained professionals who typically worked in dedicated rooms within palaces or temples.** They used a standardized format for their records that typically included date formulae, the names of witnesses, and official seals to verify authenticity.

Interestingly, these clay tablets have proven remarkably durable. Unlike papyrus or parchment used by other civilizations, fired clay tablets could survive fires and floods, which is why we have such extensive records from Assyrian civilization today. These tablets provide us with an unparalleled window into ancient Mesopotamian society and governance. [20]**Now, we'll examine how these record-keeping systems influenced later civilizations.**

sophisticated [səfístəkèitid] 정교한, 세련된　clay tablet 점토판
inscribed with ~로 새겨진　reed [ri:d] 갈대
stylus [stáiləs] 첨필　notable [nóutəbl] 주목할 만한
administrative [ədmínistrèitiv] 행정의
diplomatic [dìpləmǽtik] 외교의
correspondence [kɔ̀:rispándəns] 서신
come from ~에서 나오다　house [haus] 보관하다; 집
astronomy [əstrá:nəmi] 천문학　scribe [skráib] 서기관
dedicated [dédikèitid] 전용의　witness [wítnis] 증인; 목격하다
seal [si:l] 인장　verify [vérəfài] 확인하다
authenticity [ɔ̀:θentísəti] 진위　parchment [pá:rtʃmənt] 양피지
unparalleled [ənpǽrəlèld] 더할 나위 없는

고고학 강의를 들으시오.

[17]오늘 우리는 고대 아시리아인들이 사용한 기록 보관 시스템을 탐구할 것입니다. 아시리아인들은 주로 쐐기 문자로 새겨진 점토판을 사용하여 고대 세계에서 가장 정교한 기록 보관 방법들 중 하나를 개발했습니다. 이 문자 시스템은 갈대 첨필을 사용하여 부드러운 점토에 눌러진 쐐기 모양의 기호들로 구성되었습니다.

음, 아시리아의 기록 보관을 특히 주목할 만하게 만든 것은 그 포괄적인 성격이었습니다. 왕실 기록 보관소들은 상세한 행정 기록들, 외교 서신들, 그리고 종교 텍스트들을 포함했습니다. [18]가장 유명한 컬렉션은 기원전 7세기로 거슬러 올라가는 니네베에 있는 아슈르바니팔 왕의 도서관에서 나온 것입니다. 이 도서관은 천문학에서 의학까지의 주제들을 다루는 수천 개의 점토판들을 보관했습니다.

그래서, [19]아시리아의 서기관들은 일반적으로 궁전이나 신전 내의 전용 방에서 일한 고도로 훈련된 전문가들이었습니다. 그들은 기록들을 위한 표준화된 형식을 사용했는데, 형식에는 일반적으로 연대 공식, 증인들의 이름, 그리고 진위를 확인하기 위한 공식 인장이 포함되었습니다. 흥미롭게도, 이러한 점토판들은 놀랍도록 내구성이 있다는 것이 증명되었습니다. 다른 문명들이 사용한 파피루스나 양피지와 달리, 구워진 점토판들은 화재와 홍수를 견딜 수 있었는데, 이것이 우리가 오늘날 아시리아 문명으로부터 온 방대한 기록을 가지고 있는 이유입니다. 이러한 점토판들은 우리에게 고대 메소포타미아 사회와 통치에 대한 더할 나위 없는 통찰을 제공합니다. [20]이제, 우리는 이러한 기록 보관 시스템들이 어떻게 후대 문명들에 영향을 미쳤는지 살펴볼 것입니다.

17　Main Topic Question

강의의 주요 주제는 무엇인가?
Ⓐ 니네베에서의 고고학적 발견들
☑ 아시리아의 기록 관리와 기록 보관 시스템
Ⓒ 고대 문명에서 기록의 발전
Ⓓ 니네베 왕실 기록 보관소의 역사적 중요성

어휘　archival [á:rkáivəl] 기록의

18　Intention Question

화자는 왜 아슈르바니팔 왕을 언급하는가?
Ⓐ 아시리아와 바빌로니아의 기록 보관의 차이점을 구별하기 위해
Ⓑ 서기관 직업의 중요성에 대한 증거를 제시하기 위해
☑ 그의 도서관에서 다루어진 다양한 주제를 강조하기 위해
Ⓓ 아시리아 통치자의 정치적 권력을 보여주기 위해

어휘　diverse [dáivə:rs] 다양한

19　Detail Question

화자는 아시리아 서기관들에 대해 무엇을 말하는가?
Ⓐ 주로 귀족 가문에서 모집되었다.
Ⓑ 외국어 번역을 책임졌다.
☑ 중요한 건물들 내의 전용 공간에서 일했다.
Ⓓ 다양한 목적을 위해 다양한 문자 시스템을 사용했다.

어휘　recruit [rikrú:t] 모집하다, 채용하다

20　Discuss Next Question

화자는 다음에 무엇을 논의할 것 같은가?
Ⓐ 주요 아시리아 문학 작품의 구체적인 내용
Ⓑ 점토판 생산의 기술적 발전
Ⓒ 인근 문명들의 비슷한 문자 시스템
☑ 후대 사회들에 대한 아시리아 기록 시스템의 영향

어휘　technological [tèknəládʒikəl] 기술적인
　　　 neighboring [néibəriŋ] 인근의

[21-24]

Listen to a talk on a podcast about economics.

Hey everyone! So last weekend, my friend invited me to this amazing concert by my favorite band. [22]**But I had an important project due Monday morning that I'd been putting off. Well, I chose the concert,** and let me tell you, it was incredible! But in the end, I turned in the project past the deadline, which slightly lowered my grade in that class. [21]**My story**

perfectly illustrates today's topic: opportunity cost. Opportunity cost is an economic concept that's actually pretty simple once you get it. [23]**It's basically the value of the best alternative you give up when you make a decision.** When I chose that concert over working on my project, the opportunity cost was the better grade I might've gotten if I'd spent those hours working on my project instead.

Now, this isn't just about personal choices. Countries face opportunity costs too. [24]**Let's say a country can produce either cars or computers with its resources. If it decides to make cars, the opportunity cost is the computers it can't produce.** It's like you can't be in two places at once, right?

The cool thing is, understanding opportunity cost helps us make smarter decisions. Next time you're choosing between something really fun and that workout you've been avoiding, just ask yourself, 'What am I really giving up here?' Sometimes the answer might surprise you and help you make a better choice!

incredible [inkrédəbl] 놀라운, 굉장한　turn in 제출하다
slightly [sláitli] 살짝　illustrate [íləstrèit] 설명하다, 삽화를 넣다
opportunity cost 기회비용　face [feis] 직면하다
workout [wɔ́ːrkàut] 운동, 연습

경제학에 관한 팟캐스트에서의 강의를 들으시오.

안녕하세요 여러분! 지난 주말에, 제 친구가 제가 가장 좋아하는 밴드의 멋진 콘서트에 저를 초대했어요. [22]하지만 저는 월요일 아침 마감인 중요한 프로젝트가 있었는데 미루고 있었어요. 음, 저는 콘서트를 선택했고, 말씀드리자면, 정말 놀라웠어요! 하지만 결국 프로젝트를 기한이 지난 뒤에 제출했고, 그 과목의 점수가 살짝 깎이고 말았죠. [21]저의 이야기는 오늘의 주제인 기회비용을 완벽하게 설명합니다.

기회비용은 일단 이해하면 실제로 꽤 간단한 경제 개념입니다. [23]그것은 기본적으로 여러분이 결정을 내릴 때 포기하는 최선의 대안의 가치입니다. 그래서 제가 프로젝트를 하는 것보다 그 콘서트를 선택했을 때, 기회비용은 그 시간을 프로젝트에 썼다면 받았을 수도 있는 더 나은 성적이었던 셈이죠.

자, 이것은 단지 개인적인 선택에 관한 것이 아닙니다. 국가들도 기회비용에 직면합니다. [24]어떤 국가가 자국의 자원으로 자동차나 컴퓨터 중 하나를 생산할 수 있다고 해봅시다. 만약 그 나라가 자동차를 만들기로 결정한다면, 기회비용은 생산하지 못하는 컴퓨터입니다. 여러분이 동시에 두 곳에 있을 수 없는 것과 같죠, 그렇지 않나요?

좋은 점은 기회비용을 이해하는 것이 우리가 더 현명한 결정을 내리는 데 도움이 된다는 것입니다. 여러분도 다음에 정말 재미있는 것과 미뤄왔던 운동 사이에서 선택할 때, 그냥 스스로에게 '내가 여기서 정말로 포기하는 것은 무엇일까?'라고 물어보세요. 때때로 답은 여러분을 놀라게 할 수도 있고 더 나은 선택을 하는 데 도움이 될 수도 있답니다!

21　Main Topic Question

강의의 주요 주제는 무엇인가?
- ☑ 선택에 수반되는 교환
- Ⓑ 잘못된 의사결정의 결과
- Ⓒ 학생들을 위한 시간 관리의 중요성
- Ⓓ 더 현명한 결정을 내리는 것의 이점

어휘　trade-off 교환, 거래

22　Detail Question

화자는 지난 주말 자신의 경험에 대해 무엇을 말하는가?
- Ⓐ 콘서트 때문에 프로젝트를 제출하지 못했다.
- ☑ 학업보다 자신이 가장 좋아하는 밴드를 보는 것을 우선시했다.
- Ⓒ 자신이 가장 좋아하는 밴드의 공연에 실망했다.
- Ⓓ 콘서트 휴식 시간 동안 프로젝트 작업을 했다.

어휘　disappoint [dìsəpɔ́int] 실망시키다
　　　intermission [ìntərmíʃən] 휴식 시간

23　Detail Question

화자는 기회비용에 대해 무엇이라고 주장하는가?
- Ⓐ 경제 공식을 사용하여 정확히 계산될 수 있다.
- Ⓑ 사람들이 어려운 결정을 내리는 것을 피하도록 도와준다.
- Ⓒ 신중한 시간 관리를 통해 제거될 수 있다.
- ☑ 지나간 대안의 가치를 반영한다.

어휘　precisely [prisáisli] 정확히　foregone [fɔːrgɔ́ːn] 지나간, 앞선

24　Intention Question

화자는 왜 컴퓨터를 언급하는가?
- Ⓐ 자동차가 컴퓨터보다 더 비싸다는 것을 설명하기 위해
- Ⓑ 산업 간의 기회비용을 비교하기 위해
- Ⓒ 국가들이 기술에 집중해야 한다고 주장하기 위해
- ☑ 자원 배분에서의 기회비용을 보여주기 위해

어휘　allocation [æ̀ləkéiʃən] 배분

4. Physical Science

HACKERS TEST　p.338

01 Ⓒ	02 Ⓓ	03 Ⓑ	04 Ⓒ	05 Ⓑ
06 Ⓓ	07 Ⓐ	08 Ⓑ	09 Ⓓ	10 Ⓒ
11 Ⓑ	12 Ⓐ	13 Ⓑ	14 Ⓒ	15 Ⓑ
16 Ⓓ	17 Ⓑ	18 Ⓒ	19 Ⓒ	20 Ⓑ
21 Ⓑ	22 Ⓒ	23 Ⓓ	24 Ⓐ	

[01-04]　Am

Listen to a talk in an engineering class.

[01]**Today we're exploring how the bicycle evolved to become more efficient over time.** As we know, efficiency means getting maximum output with minimum energy input. [02]**Let's start with the earliest version—the "running machine" from 1818. This German invention had two wheels and a wooden frame, but no pedals! Riders literally pushed off the ground with their feet.** While faster than

walking, it was heavy and impractical.
The next development was the "velocipede" in the 1860s. This added pedals to the front wheel, but here's the problem—one pedal rotation only moved you five or six feet. Plus, these iron machines weighed up to 100 pounds!

[03]Then came the "penny-farthing" around 1870. Its distinctive feature was the huge front wheel. The larger the wheel, the further you'd travel per pedal rotation. So, this was much more efficient! However, it had a serious drawback. Riders had to sit at a dangerous height and often fell forward. Finally, the modern "safety bicycle" emerged in the late 1800s with equal-sized wheels and, most importantly, [04]a chain drive system. This innovation made bicycles incredibly efficient, transferring 98% of pedaling energy directly to motion. Next, let's take a closer look at exactly how it works.

evolve[iválv] 발전하다, 진화하다
efficient[ifíʃənt] 효율적인, 능률적인   efficiency[ifíʃənsi] 효율성
maximum[mǽksəməm] 최대한의; 최대
minimum[mínəməm] 최소한의; 최소
literally[lítərəli] 말 그대로, 정확히
impractical[imprǽktikəl] 비실용적인
weigh[wei] 무게가 나가다, 작용하다
distinctive[distíŋktiv] 독특한, 특별한
drawback[drɔ́ːbæ̀k] 단점, 결점

공학 강의를 들으시오.

[01]오늘 우리는 자전거가 시간이 지남에 따라 어떻게 더 효율적으로 발전했는지 탐구할 겁니다. 아시다시피, 효율성이란 최소한의 에너지 투입으로 최대한의 산출을 얻는다는 의미죠. [02]가장 초기 버전인 1818년의 "running machine"부터 시작해봅시다. 이 독일 발명품은 두 개의 바퀴와 나무 프레임을 가지고 있었지만, 페달이 없었습니다! 탑승자들은 말 그대로 발로 땅을 밀어냈어요. 걷는 것보다는 빨랐지만, 무겁고 비실용적이었습니다.

다음 발전은 1860년대의 "velocipede"였습니다. 이것은 앞바퀴에 페달을 추가했지만, 여기에 문제가 있었어요. 페달을 한 번 돌리면 5~6피트밖에 이동하지 못했던 거죠. 게다가, 이런 철제 기계들은 100파운드까지 무게가 나갔습니다!

[03]그러고 나서 1870년경 "penny-farthing"이 등장했습니다. 그것의 독특한 특징은 거대한 앞바퀴였습니다. 바퀴가 클수록, 페달을 한 번 돌릴 때마다 더 멀리 이동할 수 있었습니다. 그래서, 이것은 훨씬 더 효율적이었습니다! 하지만, 심각한 단점이 있었습니다. 탑승자들이 위험한 높이에 앉아야 했고 종종 앞으로 넘어졌던 것입니다.

마침내, 1800년대 후반에 같은 크기의 바퀴와, 가장 중요하게는, [04]체인 구동 시스템을 갖춘 현대적인 "safety bicycle"이 등장했습니다. 이 혁신은 자전거를 믿을 수 없을 정도로 효율적으로 만들어, 페달링 에너지의 98퍼센트를 바로 운동으로 전달했습니다. 다음으로, 그것이 정확히 어떻게 작동하는지 자세히 살펴봅시다.

01 Main Topic Question
강의는 주로 무엇에 대한 것인가?
Ⓐ 1800년대 자전거의 인기
Ⓑ 19세기 운송수단의 안전 우려
✓ 자전거 기술의 점진적 개선
Ⓓ 독일에서의 현대 자전거 발명

어휘 improvement[imprúːvmənt] 개선

02 Detail Question
화자는 1818년의 "running machine"에 대해 무엇을 말하는가?
Ⓐ 전부 철로 만들어졌다.
Ⓑ 대략 100파운드의 무게가 나갔다.
Ⓒ 1800년대 초 프랑스에서 발명되었다.
✓ 탑승자들이 발을 사용해 스스로를 추진해야 했다.

어휘 entirely[intáiərli] 전부, 완전히
propel[prəpél] 추진하다, 몰고 가다

03 Detail Question
화자에 따르면, "penny-farthing"의 문제는 무엇이었는가?
Ⓐ 페달이 조작하기에 너무 어려웠다.
✓ 탑승자들이 위험한 높이에 앉아야 했다.
Ⓒ 대부분의 탑승자들이 다루기에 너무 무거웠다.
Ⓓ 페달을 한 번 돌리면 5피트 미만으로 이동했다.

04 Discuss Next Question
화자는 다음에 무엇을 논의할 것 같은가?
Ⓐ 1800년대 자전거의 비용
Ⓑ 엔진이 달린 운송수단과의 비교
✓ 체인 구동 시스템의 작동 원리
Ⓓ 현대 자전거 제조업

어휘 motorized[móutəràizd] 엔진이 달린
mechanics[məkǽniks] 작동 원리, 구조

[05-08]
Listen to a talk in an astronomy class.

[05]Today we're going to explore one of the most spectacular features in our solar system—planetary rings. Now, when I mention planetary rings, what's the first planet that comes to mind? That's right, Saturn. But here's something interesting. [06]Saturn isn't the only planet with rings. Jupiter, Neptune, and Uranus all have ring systems too. [05]However, Saturn's rings are truly exceptional. They're massive, highly visible, and have fascinated astronomers for centuries. When Galileo Galilei first observed Saturn in 1610, he actually thought he was seeing three separate objects! It wasn't until 1659 that astronomers realized these were rings encircling the planet.

For a long time, people believed Saturn's rings were solid bands of material. But in the 19th century, astronomers made a crucial discovery. Specifically, the rings were somewhat transparent. You could actually see Saturn's surface through them! [07]This observation led to James Clerk Maxwell's groundbreaking calculations in 1859, proving that solid rings would have been torn apart by Saturn's gravity long ago. So what are the rings made of? **They're actually composed of countless individual particles,** mostly ice and rock, orbiting the planet like tiny moons. [08]**Now, let's take a closer look at the composition of these rings.**

spectacular[spektǽkjulər] 장관을 이루는
planetary ring 행성 고리 come to mind 떠오르다
fascinate[fǽsəneit] 매혹시키다 encircle[insə́ːrkl] 둘러싸다
solid[sάlid] 고체의; 고체 somewhat[sʌ́mwʌ̀t] 다소
transparent[trænspέərənt] 투명한, 명쾌한
groundbreaking[gráundbrèikiŋ] 획기적인
tear apart 산산조각내다, 찢어놓다 made of ~로 만든
compose[kəmpóuz] 구성하다, 작곡하다
countless[káuntlis] 수많은, 셀 수 없는
orbit[ɔ́ːrbit] ~의 궤도를 돌다; 궤도

천문학 강의를 들으시오.
[05]오늘 우리는 태양계에서 가장 장관을 이루는 특징 중 하나인 행성 고리를 탐구할 것입니다. 이제, 제가 행성 고리를 언급할 때, 가장 먼저 떠오르는 행성은 무엇인가요? 맞습니다, 토성입니다. 하지만 흥미로운 점이 있습니다. [06]토성이 고리를 가진 유일한 행성이 아니라는 것입니다. 목성, 해왕성, 그리고 천왕성 모두 고리 시스템을 가지고 있습니다.
[05]하지만, 토성의 고리는 정말 예외적입니다. 그것들은 거대하고, 매우 눈에 잘 띄며, 수세기 동안 천문학자들을 매혹시켜 왔습니다. 갈릴레오 갈릴레이가 1610년에 토성을 처음 관찰했을 때, 그는 실제로 세 개의 별개의 물체를 보고 있다고 생각했습니다! 1659년에 이르러서야 천문학자들이 이것이 행성을 둘러싸고 있는 고리라는 사실을 깨달았습니다. 오랫동안, 사람들은 토성의 고리가 고체로 된 띠라고 믿었습니다. 하지만 19세기에, 천문학자들은 중요한 발견을 했습니다. 구체적으로 말하면, 고리는 다소 투명했습니다. 실제로 그 고리를 통해 토성의 표면을 볼 수 있었습니다! [07]이 관찰은 1859년 제임스 맥스웰의 획기적인 계산으로 이어졌고, 고체 고리들은 오래전에 토성의 중력에 의해 산산조각났을 것이라는 사실을 증명했습니다. 그렇다면 고리들은 무엇으로 만들어져 있을까요? 그것들은 실제로 수많은 개별 입자들로 구성되어 있으며, 대부분 얼음과 암석으로 이루어져 있고, 작은 달처럼 행성의 궤도를 돕니다. [08]이제, 이 고리들의 구성을 자세히 살펴봅시다.

05 Main Topic Question
강의의 주요 주제는 무엇인가?
Ⓐ 토성 주위 작은 달들의 궤도
✓Ⓑ 토성 고리 시스템의 독특한 특징
Ⓒ 암석 고리와 얼음 고리 사이의 차이점
Ⓓ 여러 행성의 고리 시스템 비교

06 Detail Question
화자는 행성 고리에 대해 무엇을 말하는가?
Ⓐ 온전히 고체 물질로 구성되어 있다.
Ⓑ 강력한 망원경을 통해서만 볼 수 있다.
Ⓒ 1610년에 동시에 발견되었다.
✓Ⓓ 여러 행성 주변에서 발견될 수 있다.

어휘 telescope[téləskòup] 망원경
      simultaneously[sàiməltéiniəsli] 동시에

07 Intention Question
화자는 왜 맥스웰을 언급하는가?
✓Ⓐ 고리의 입자 구성 이론을 뒷받침하기 위해
Ⓑ 궤도 역학의 개념을 소개하기 위해
Ⓒ 토성의 고리를 처음 발견한 사람이 누구인지 설명하기 위해
Ⓓ 서로 다른 천문학 이론들을 비교하기 위해

어휘 orbital[ɔ́ːrbitl] 궤도의 astronomical[æstrənάmikəl] 천문학의

08 Discuss Next Question
화자는 다음에 무엇을 논의할 것 같은가?
Ⓐ 목성과 해왕성의 고리들
Ⓑ 행성 고리의 형성 과정
Ⓒ 토성 근처의 대기 조건
✓Ⓓ 고리들의 원소와 화합물

어휘 atmospheric[ætməsférik] 대기의

[09-12]   Am
Listen to a talk in a geology class.

[09]**Today we're going to examine how Earth's materials can be classified based on their origins— specifically, the distinction between inorganic minerals and organically derived materials.** This classification system is fundamental to understanding our planet's composition and geological history.
[10]**First, inorganic minerals form the majority of Earth's crust through geological processes without biological involvement.** These include quartz, feldspar, and metal ores, which typically form through crystallization from molten rock or precipitation from solutions under intense heat and pressure.
Organically derived materials contain carbon compounds from once-living organisms. Here, coal serves as a good example, forming when plant material undergoes pressure and heat over millions of years without fully decomposing. [11]**Amber is another fascinating example. Though not a mineral in the strict sense**, it's a fossilized tree resin that sometimes preserves ancient insects and plant fragments. This gives us glimpses into prehistoric ecosystems.
Well, this classification is crucial for interpreting Earth's history. [12]**Inorganic minerals tell us about purely geological processes like volcanic activity and tectonic movements**, while organically influenced materials reveal interactions between biological and geological forces. The distinction helps us trace the evolution of Earth's composition and provides insights into ancient environments.

classify[klǽsəfài] 분류하다 inorganic[ìnɔːrgǽnik] 무기물의
mineral[mínərəl] 광물
fundamental[fʌ̀ndəméntl] 핵심적인, 기본적인

geological [dʒìəládʒikəl] 지질학적인
majority [mədʒɔ́ːrəti] 대부분   crust [krʌst] 지각
involvement [invɑ́ːlvmənt] 개입
crystallization [krìstəlizéiʃən] 결정화
molten [móultən] 용융된, 녹은
precipitation [prisìpətéiʃən] 침전, 강우량
solution [səlúːʃən] 용액, 해결책   pressure [préʃər] 압력
organism [ɔ́ːrgənìzm] 유기체, 생물
undergo [ʌ̀ndərgóu] 받다, 겪다
decompose [dìːkəmpóuz] 분해하다
in the strict sense 엄격한 의미에서
fossilize [fɑ́səlàiz] 화석화하다
fragment [frǽgmənt] 조각; 부서지다
interpret [intə́ːrprit] 해석하다, 통역하다
volcanic [valkǽnik] 화산의   tectonic [tektɑ́nik] 지반의

지질학 강의를 들으시오.

⁰⁹오늘 우리는 지구의 물질이 기원에 따라 어떻게 분류되는지, 구체적으로 무기 광물과 유기 기원 물질 간의 구별을 살펴볼 것입니다. 이 분류 시스템은 우리 행성의 구성과 지질학적 역사를 이해하는 데 핵심적입니다.

¹⁰먼저, 무기 광물들은 생물학적 개입 없이 지질학적 과정을 통해 지구 지각의 대부분을 형성합니다. 이것들은 일반적으로 용융된 암석으로부터의 결정화나 고온과 고압 하에서 용액으로부터의 침전을 통해 형성되는 석영, 장석, 그리고 금속 광석을 포함합니다.

유기 기원 물질은 한때 살아있던 유기체에서 유래한 탄소 화합물을 포함합니다. 여기서 석탄은 좋은 예로, 석탄은 식물 물질이 완전히 분해되지 않은 채 수백만 년 동안 압력과 열을 받으며 형성됩니다. ¹¹호박은 또 다른 매혹적인 예입니다. 엄격한 의미에서 광물은 아니지만, 때때로 고대 곤충과 식물 조각을 보존하는 화석화된 나무 수지입니다. 이것은 우리에게 선사시대 생태계에 대한 통찰을 제공합니다.

음, 이 분류는 지구의 역사를 해석하는 데 중요합니다. ¹²무기 광물들은 화산 활동과 지반 운동과 같은 순수하게 지질학적인 과정에 대해 알려주는 반면, 유기 기원 물질은 생물학적 힘과 지질학적 힘 사이의 상호작용을 드러냅니다. 이 구별은 우리가 지구 구성의 진화를 추적하는 것에 도움이 되고 고대 환경에 대한 통찰을 제공합니다.

09 Main Topic Question

강의는 주로 무엇에 대한 것인가?
Ⓐ 지구 지각 형성에서 결정화의 역할
Ⓑ 광물 형성에 영향을 미치는 환경 요인들
Ⓒ 선사시대 생명을 이해하는 데 있어서 화석의 중요성
☑ 지구 물질들의 기원에 따른 분류

어휘 fossil [fɑ́səl] 화석   classification [klæ̀səfikéiʃən] 분류

10 Detail Question

화자에 따르면, 무기 광물에 대해 사실인 것은?
Ⓐ 시간이 지남에 따라 형성되기 위해 생물학적 과정이 필요하다.
Ⓑ 고대 유기체의 화석화된 잔해를 포함한다.
☑ 용융된 암석으로부터의 결정화를 통해 형성된다.
Ⓓ 일반적인 광물 연구에서 흔히 간과된다.

어휘 overlook [òuvərlúk] 간과하다

11 Detail Question

화자는 호박에 대해 무엇을 말하는가?
Ⓐ 주로 압력 하에서 석탄으로부터 형성된다.
☑ 엄격한 의미에서 광물로 간주되지 않는다.
Ⓒ 식물 물질이 완전히 분해될 때 형성된다.
Ⓓ 주로 무기 화합물로 구성되어 있다.

어휘 primarily [praimérəli] 주로, 본래

12 Intention Question

화자는 왜 지각 운동을 언급하는가?
☑ 무기 광물들이 드러내는 지질학적 과정을 설명하기 위해
Ⓑ 식물 물질의 분해 과정을 보여주기 위해
Ⓒ 고대 환경이 시간이 지남에 따라 어떻게 변했는지 설명하기 위해
Ⓓ 생물학적 물질이 어떻게 화석화되는지 보여주기 위해

어휘 matter [mǽtər] 물질

[13-16]

Listen to a talk in an earth science class.

¹³Today we're going to discuss fjords, which are one of Earth's most dramatic geological formations. Fjords are long, narrow, deep inlets of the sea between high cliffs, typically formed by glacial erosion. They're particularly common in Norway, but are also found in places like New Zealand, Chile, and Alaska.

¹³Well, fjord formation is quite fascinating. During ice ages, massive glaciers slowly carved out U-shaped valleys. These glaciers, sometimes over a mile thick, had tremendous erosive power. ¹⁴As they moved, they ground away at the underlying rock, deepening and widening pre-existing river valleys. When the glaciers eventually retreated during warming periods, seawater flooded these carved valleys. This created the fjords we see today.

So, fjords have some distinctive characteristics that set them apart from other coastal features. In particular, they typically have steep walls that extend far below the water's surface. Some fjords have depths exceeding 4,000 feet! ¹⁵The water in fjords often exhibits interesting layering, with freshwater from rivers floating on top of the denser seawater. This creates unique ecosystems where various marine species thrive. ¹⁶Now, any questions before we examine famous fjords around the world?

narrow [nǽrou] 좁은   inlet [ínlet] 입구   cliff [klif] 절벽
glacial [gléiʃəl] 빙하의   erosion [iróuʒən] 침식, 침식작용
quite [kwait] 상당히, 꽤   Ice Age 빙하기
glacier [gléiʃər] 빙하   carve out 조각하다, 새기다
valley [vǽli] 계곡, 골짜기   tremendous [triméndəs] 엄청난
erosive [iróusiv] 침식의
underlying [ʌ̀ndərlàiiŋ] 밑바닥의, 기저의   retreat [ritríːt] 후퇴
flood [flʌd] 침수하다, 범람하다   set apart from ~와 구별하다
feature [fíːtʃər] 특성   in particular 특히
steep [stiːp] 가파른; 경사   dense [dens] 밀도가 높은
thrive [θraiv] 번성하다

지구과학 강의를 들으시오.

¹³오늘 우리는 지구의 가장 극적인 지질학적 형성물 중 하나인 피오르드에 대해 논의할 것입니다. 피오르드는 높은 절벽 사이의 길고, 좁고, 깊은 바다 입구로, 일반적으로 빙하 침식에 의해 형성됩니다. 피오르드는 특히 노르웨이에서 자주 발견되지만, 뉴질랜드, 칠레, 알래스카와 같은 곳에서도 발견됩니다.

¹³음, 피오르드의 형성 과정은 상당히 매혹적입니다. 빙하기 동안, 거대한 빙하들이 천천히 U자 모양의 계곡들을 조각해냈습니다. 때때로 1마일 이상 두꺼운 이 빙하들은 엄청난 침식력을 가지고 있었습니다. ¹⁴그 빙하들이 움직이면서 밑바닥 암석을 갈아내 기존 강 계곡을 더 깊고 넓게 만들었습니다. 빙하들이 결국 온난화 기간 동안 후퇴했을 때, 바닷물이 이 조각된 계곡들을 침수시켰습니다. 이렇게 해서 오늘날의 피오르드가 형성된 것이죠.

그래서, 피오르드는 다른 해안 지형과 구별되는 독특한 특성들을 가지고 있습니다. 특히, 피오르드에는 일반적으로 수면 아래 깊숙이 이어지는 가파른 절벽이 있죠. 일부 피오르드들은 4,000피트를 초과하는 깊이를 보입니다! ¹⁵피오르드의 물은 종종 흥미로운 층상 구조를 특징으로 하는데, 강에서 온 민물이 더 밀도가 높은 바닷물 위에 떠 있습니다. 이것은 다양한 해양 종들이 번성하는 독특한 생태계를 만듭니다. ¹⁶이제, 전 세계의 유명한 피오르드들을 살펴보기 전에 질문이 있나요?

13 Main Topic Question

강의의 주제는 무엇인가?
ⓐ 다양한 풍경에 대한 빙하기의 영향
☑ 극적인 바다 입구의 기원과 주목할 만한 측면
ⓒ 피오르드 보존이 직면한 환경적 도전
ⓓ 피오르드와 다른 계곡들 사이의 지질학적 차이점

어휘 landscape[lǽndskèip] 풍경

14 Detail Question

화자는 빙하에 대해 무엇을 말하는가?
ⓐ 노르웨이의 특정 기후 조건에서만 형성되었다.
ⓑ 현대에 해수면 상승에 기여했다.
☑ 움직이면서 계곡들을 넓히고 깊게 만들었다.
ⓓ 중요한 침식을 일으키기에는 너무 천천히 움직였다.

어휘 specific[spisífik] 특정한, 구체적인　contribute to ~에 기여하다

15 Detail Question

화자가 말하는 피오르드의 어떤 특징이 독특한 생태계에 기여하는가?
ⓐ 암석의 지질학적 구성
☑ 강물이 바닷물 위에 층을 이루는 효과
ⓒ 빙하 퇴적물로부터의 영양분이 풍부한 침전물
ⓓ 해수와 담수 해류의 공존

어휘 deposit[dipázit] 퇴적물; 쌓다
coexistence[kòuigzístəns] 공존
current[kə́:rənt] 해류; 현재의

16 Discuss Next Question

화자는 다음에 무엇을 논의할 것 같은가?
ⓐ 피오르드 생태계에 대한 환경적 위협
ⓑ 피오르드 지역에서 인기 있는 레크리에이션 활동
ⓒ 피오르드 깊이를 측정하는 과학적 방법
☑ 전 세계의 유명한 피오르드들

어휘 threat[θret] 위협, 협박　prominent[prámənənt] 유명한, 현저한

[17-20]

Listen to a talk on a podcast about physics.

Have you ever stared up at the night sky and wondered how the universe actually works? I was doing exactly that last weekend while camping, and the countless stars were so… breathtakingly beautiful. Plus, out of nowhere, it got me thinking about Einstein's Theory of Relativity that I learned about back in high school. ¹⁷You know, it completely revolutionized our understanding of physics in the early 1900s! So what's the big deal? Well, Einstein basically showed us that space and time aren't separate things: they're actually connected as "spacetime." ¹⁸Imagine placing a bowling ball on a trampoline— see how it creates a curve? That's similar to how massive objects like our sun curve the fabric of spacetime, creating what we call gravity. What's more surprising is that time isn't constant either! ¹⁹Time actually passes more slowly for objects moving at high speeds or in strong gravitational fields. This means if you traveled near the speed of light, you'd age more slowly than people on Earth! ²⁰This concept helped scientists understand everything from GPS satellites to black holes.
²⁰So, next time you check your smartphone's navigation, remember that without Einstein's relativistic corrections, your directions would be completely off! Isn't it amazing how abstract theories end up affecting our everyday lives?

out of nowhere 갑자기　revolutionize 변혁시키다
big deal 대단한 것, 큰일　separate[sépərèit] 분리하다
space-time 시공　fabric[fǽbrik] 구조, 직물
constant[kánstənt] 일정한　gravitational[grævətéiʃənl] 중력의
speed of light 빛의 속도　satellite[sǽtəlàit] 위성
relativistic[rèlətivístik] 상대론적인　correction[kərékʃən] 보정
abstract[ǽbstrækt] 추상적인　end up ~하게 되다, 결국 ~ 되다

물리학에 관한 팟캐스트에서의 강의를 들으시오.

당신은 밤하늘을 올려다보며 우주가 실제로 어떻게 작동하는지 궁금했던 적이 있나요? 저는 지난 주말 캠핑을 하면서 정확히 그런 생각을 하고 있었는데, 수많은 별들이 너무나… 숨막히게 아름다웠습니다. 게다가, 갑자기 고등학교 때 배운 아인슈타인의 상대성 이론에 대해 생각하게 되었습니다. ¹⁷아시다시피, 그것은 1900년대 초에 물리학에 대한 우리의 이해를 완전히 변혁시켰습니다.

그렇다면 뭐가 그렇게 대단한 것일까요? 글쎄요, 아인슈타인은 기본적으로 공간과 시간이 분리된 것들이 아니라 실제로 "시공"으로 연결되어 있다는 것을 우리에게 보여주었습니다. ¹⁸트램펄린에 볼링공을 올려놓는 것을 상상해보세요, 어떻게 휘어지는지 보이시나요? 그것은 우리 태양과 같은 거대한 물체들이 시공의 구조를 굽혀서, 우리가 중력이라고 부르는 것을 만드는 방식과 비슷합니다. 더 놀라운 것은 시간도 일정하지 않다는 것입니다! ¹⁹시간은 실제로 고속으로 움직이거나 강한 중력장에 있는 물체들에게는 더 천천히 흘러갑니다. 이것은 당신이 빛의

속도 근처로 여행한다면, 지구에 있는 사람들보다 더 천천히 늙을 것이라는 의미이죠! [20]이 개념은 과학자들이 GPS 위성부터 블랙홀까지의 모든 것을 이해하는 데 도움이 되었습니다. [20]그러니, 다음번에 당신의 스마트폰 내비게이션을 확인할 때, 아인슈타인의 상대론적 보정 없이는 당신의 길 안내가 완전히 틀렸을 것이라는 것을 기억하세요! 추상적인 이론들이 우리의 일상생활에 영향을 미치게 된다는 사실이 놀랍지 않나요?

17 Main Topic Question
강의는 주로 무엇에 대한 것인가?
Ⓐ GPS 기술의 실용적 응용
☑ 물리학에서 시공의 혁명적 개념
Ⓒ 밤하늘의 별들의 시각적 아름다움
Ⓓ 천문학과 일상생활 사이의 관계

18 Intention Question
화자는 왜 볼링공을 언급하는가?
Ⓐ 우주의 구식 모델들을 비판하기 위해
Ⓑ 아인슈타인의 계산의 복잡성을 강조하기 위해
☑ 태양이 시공간에 미치는 영향을 트램펄린과 비교하기 위해
Ⓓ 상대성 이론의 수학적 원리들을 강조하기 위해

어휘 outdated [àutdéitid] 구식인, 진부한
mathematical [mæ̀θəmǽtikəl] 수학적인

19 Detail Question
화자는 시간에 대해 무엇을 말하는가?
Ⓐ 물체의 속도와 관계없이 일정하게 유지된다.
Ⓑ 과학자들이 지도에서 정확한 위치를 계산하는 데 도움이 된다.
☑ 운동과 중력에 따라 다른 속도로 흐른다.
Ⓓ 별들이 우주에서 관측할 때 왜 다르게 보이는지 설명한다.

어휘 regardless of ~와 관계없이

20 Intention Question
화자는 왜 GPS 위성을 언급하는가?
Ⓐ 현재 내비게이션 기술의 한계를 비판하기 위해
☑ 상대성 이론이 일상생활에 어떻게 적용되는지 보여주기 위해
Ⓒ 거대한 물체들이 시공에 어떻게 영향을 미치는지 설명하기 위해
Ⓓ 아인슈타인의 예측을 현대 발견들과 비교하기 위해

어휘 criticize [krítəsàiz] 비판하다

[21-24]
Listen to a talk in a chemistry class. 🔊 Am

[21]**Carbon rarely exists in its pure atomic form. Instead, it bonds with other carbon atoms to create what we call allotropes, which are different structural forms of the same element.** I'll give you two examples.
First, there's graphite—the material in your pencil lead. Then we have diamonds, which are known as the hardest natural substance on Earth. The difference between them lies entirely in their atomic structure. ↻

In graphite, each carbon atom bonds with three neighbors. They form flat, hexagonal sheets that can slide past each other—hence the softness. [22]**This structure also leaves extra electrons, making graphite an excellent electrical conductor.** Diamonds, however, have each carbon atom bonded to four others in a three-dimensional lattice. No extra electrons means no electrical conductivity, making diamonds perfect insulators. They are made of the same atoms but have completely different properties based purely on arrangement. That's why it is also possible to convert an allotrope like graphite into diamond. [23/24]**One method is called high pressure high temperature, or HPHT, which subjects graphite to hundreds of thousands of atmospheres of pressure and temperatures above 1,500°C.** [24]**There's another method, called chemical vapor deposition, or CVD**. Instead of starting with graphite, it uses carbon-containing gases such as methane to grow synthetic diamonds. [24]**Let's take a closer look at these two fascinating techniques.**

bond with ~와 결합하다 allotrope [ǽlətròup] 동소체
neighbor [néibər] 이웃한; 이웃 hexagonal [heksǽgənl] 육각형의
hence [hens] 그렇기 때문에, 따라서 electron [iléktran] 전자
conductor [kəndʌ́ktər] 전도체 three-dimensional 3차원의
lattice [lǽtis] 격자 insulator [ínsəlèitər] 절연체
property [prápərti] 성질, 특징 convert [kənvə́ːrt] 변환하다

화학 강의를 들으시오.

[21]탄소는 순수한 원자 형태로 거의 존재하지 않습니다. 대신, 다른 탄소 원자들과 결합해 우리가 동소체라고 부르는 것, 즉 같은 원소의 서로 다른 구조적 형태들을 이룹니다. 제가 두 가지 예를 들어드리겠습니다. 첫째, 연필심의 재료인 흑연이 있습니다. 그 다음에는 지구상에서 가장 단단한 천연 물질로 알려진 다이아몬드가 있습니다. 그들 사이의 차이는 전적으로 그들의 원자 구조에 있습니다. 흑연에서, 각 탄소 원자는 세 개의 이웃한 원자와 결합합니다. 그들은 서로 미끄러질 수 있는 평평하고 육각형의 시트들을 형성하며, 그렇기 때문에 부드럽습니다. [22]이 구조는 또한 여분의 전자들을 남겨두어, 흑연을 우수한 전기 전도체로 만듭니다. 하지만 다이아몬드에서는 각 탄소 원자가 3차원 격자에서 네 개의 다른 탄소 원자와 결합합니다. 여분의 전자가 없다는 것은 전기 전도성이 없다는 의미로, 다이아몬드를 완벽한 절연체로 만듭니다. 그들은 같은 원자들로 이루어져 있지만 순전히 배열에 따라 성질이 완전히 달라지는 거죠. 그래서 흑연과 같은 동소체를 다이아몬드로 변환하는 것도 가능합니다. [23/24]한 가지 방법은 고압 고온, 즉 HPHT라고 불리는데, 이것은 흑연을 수십만 기압의 압력과 1,500°C 이상의 온도에 노출시킵니다. [24] 화학 증착법, 즉 CVD라고 불리는 또 다른 방법도 있습니다. 흑연으로 시작하는 대신, 메탄과 같은 탄소 함유 기체를 사용해 합성 다이아몬드를 성장시킵니다. [24]이 두 가지 매혹적인 기술을 자세히 살펴봅시다.

21 Main Topic Question
강의는 주로 무엇에 대한 것인가?
Ⓐ 흑연과 다이아몬드의 산업적 응용
☑ 탄소 동소체와 그들의 독특한 특성

ⓒ 서로 다른 탄소 기반 물질들을 식별하는 방법
ⓓ 흑연을 다이아몬드 형태로 변환하는 과정

22 Detail Question
화자는 흑연에 대해 무엇을 말하는가?
ⓐ 대부분의 응용에서 전기 절연체 역할을 한다.
ⓑ 탄소 원자들의 3차원 격자 배열을 형성한다.
☑ 여분의 전자들로 인해 전기를 전도한다.
ⓓ 자연 형성 과정을 위해 극한의 온도가 필요하다.

어휘 serve as ~의 역할을 하다

23 Detail Question
HPHT 기법의 특성으로 언급되지 않은 것은 무엇인가?
ⓐ 흑연을 시작 재료로 사용한다.
ⓑ 극도로 높은 압력 조건을 활용한다.
ⓒ 1000°C를 초과하는 온도에서 작동한다.
☑ CVD법보다 다이아몬드를 더 빠르게 생산한다.

어휘 utilize[júːtəlàiz] 사용하다

24 Discuss Next Question
화자는 다음에 무엇을 논의할 것 같은가?
☑ 두 다이아몬드 생성 방법의 추가 탐구
ⓑ 인공 다이아몬드 생산의 경제적 이점
ⓒ 흑연과 다이아몬드를 넘어선 다른 탄소 동소체
ⓓ 합성 다이아몬드 제조의 환경적 영향

어휘 artificial[àːrtəfíʃəl] 인공의

5. Life Science

HACKERS TEST   p.348

01 ⓑ	02 ⓒ	03 ⓒ	04 ⓑ	05 ⓒ
06 ⓓ	07 ⓑ	08 ⓓ	09 ⓓ	10 ⓐ
11 ⓓ	12 ⓒ	13 ⓒ	14 ⓑ	15 ⓒ
16 ⓐ	17 ⓓ	18 ⓐ	19 ⓓ	20 ⓑ
21 ⓒ	22 ⓑ	23 ⓓ	24 ⓒ	

[01-04]

Listen to a talk in a biology class.

⁰¹**Today, I'm going to talk about the butterfly life cycle. This process is divided into four distinct stages.**

The first stage is the egg stage, where female butterflies attach eggs to plant leaves using a special adhesive substance. ⁰²**Interestingly, the number of eggs varies greatly depending on environmental factors. Butterflies in colder climates tend to lay fewer, larger eggs that are more resistant to frost. Butterflies in warmer regions lay numerous smaller eggs more frequently.**

After several weeks, the process reaches the larval stage, when larvae emerge by breaking through the egg's outer shell—the chorion. ⁰³**These larvae feed constantly on leaves, which explains why female butterflies must select appropriate plants, as incorrect choices could be fatal.** Larvae undergo multiple growth periods called instars, shedding their cuticle after each one. ⁰⁴**Following the final instar, larvae enter the pupal stage, ceasing to feed and attaching themselves to the undersides of leaves with silk threads.** They form a protective chrysalis where transformation occurs over approximately two weeks. During this immobile state, they're highly vulnerable, so chrysalises are typically camouflaged in colors such as green, brown, or gray. Finally, at the adult stage, the butterfly emerges at full size. Its wings need about an hour to expand, dry, and harden before flight is possible.

divide into ~로 나뉘다 adhesive[ædhíːsiv] 접착 물질
vary[vέəri] 달라지다 lay[lei] (알을) 낳다, 놓다 frost[frɔːst] 서리
numerous[njúːmərəs] 다수의 frequently[fríːkwəntli] 자주
larva[láːrvə] 유충, 애벌레 chorion[kɔːriàn] 난각
constantly[kánstəntli] 끊임없이
appropriate[əpróupriət] 적절한 incorrect[ìnkərékt] 잘못된
fatal[féitl] 치명적인 shed[ʃed] (표피를) 벗다
cuticle[kjúːtikl] 표피
instar[ínstɑːr] 령(곤충의 탈피와 탈피 사이의 기간)
pupal[pjúːpəl] 번데기의 cease[siːs] 멈추다 thread[θred] 실
chrysalis[krísəlis] 번데기 immobile[imóubəl] 움직이지 않는
vulnerable[válnərəbl] 취약한

생물학 강의를 들으시오.

⁰¹오늘 저는 나비의 생활사에 대해 이야기해보겠습니다. 이 과정은 네 개의 뚜렷한 단계로 나뉩니다.

첫 번째는 알 단계인데, 암컷 나비들이 특별한 접착 물질을 사용하여 식물 잎에 알을 붙입니다. ⁰²흥미롭게도, 알의 개수는 환경적 요인에 따라 크게 달라집니다. 추운 기후의 나비들은 더 적고, 서리에 더 저항성이 강한 더 큰 알을 낳는 경향이 있습니다. 더 따뜻한 지역의 나비들은 다수의 더 작은 알을 더 자주 산란합니다.

몇 주 후, 이 과정은 애벌레들이 알의 외피인 난각을 뚫고 나오는 유충 단계에 도달합니다. ⁰³이 애벌레들은 잎을 끊임없이 먹는데, 이는 암컷 나비가 적절한 식물을 선택해야 하는 이유를 설명해 주는데, 잘못된 선택은 치명적일 수 있기 때문입니다. 애벌레들은 령이라고 불리는 여러 성장 기간을 거치며 각 령이 끝날 때마다 큐티클을 벗습니다. ⁰⁴마지막 령 이후, 애벌레들은 번데기 단계에 들어가서, 먹는 것을 멈추고 실로 잎의 뒷면에 자신을 붙입니다. 그들은 약 2주에 걸쳐 변태가 일어나는 보호용 번데기를 형성합니다. 이 움직이지 않는 상태 동안 매우 취약하기 때문에, 번데기는 주로 녹색, 갈색, 또는 회색과 같은 위장색을 띱니다. 마지막으로, 성체 단계에서, 나비는 완전한 크기로 나옵니다. 성체의 날개는 비행이 가능하기 전에 펼쳐지고, 말리고, 굳어지는데 약 1시간이 소요됩니다.

01 Main Topic Question

강의는 주로 무엇에 대한 것인가?
Ⓐ 나비 번데기의 보호 메커니즘
Ⓑ 나비의 완전한 발달 과정 ✓
Ⓒ 다양한 생활 단계 동안 나비의 취약성
Ⓓ 다양한 환경에서 나비의 적응 전략

어휘 vulnerability[vÀlnərəbíləti] 취약성

02 Intention Question

화자는 왜 알의 개수를 언급하는가?
Ⓐ 나비 개체군의 생존율을 계산하기 위해
Ⓑ 어떤 나비 종이 가장 많은 알을 낳는지 파악하기 위해
Ⓒ 기후가 번식 적응에 어떻게 영향을 미치는지 보여주기 위해 ✓
Ⓓ 왜 알을 세는 것이 연구자들에게 중요한지 설명하기 위해

어휘 reproductive[rì:prədÁktiv] 번식의

03 Detail Question

화자에 따르면, 암컷 나비가 올바른 식물을 선택하는 것이 왜 중요한가?
Ⓐ 식물들이 각 발달 단계의 지속 기간을 결정한다.
Ⓑ 향기가 나는 식물들이 미래 교미를 위해 더 많은 수컷 나비들을 끌어들인다.
Ⓒ 부적절한 식물 선택이 애벌레의 사망을 초래할 수 있다. ✓
Ⓓ 식물의 화학적 구성이 나비의 최종 색깔에 영향을 미친다.

어휘 mating[méitiŋ] 교미, 짝짓기

04 Detail Question

화자는 애벌레에 대해 무엇을 말하는가?
Ⓐ 에너지를 보존하기 위해 추운 날씨에 동면한다.
Ⓑ 번데기 단계에 들어가기 전에 먹는 것을 멈춘다. ✓
Ⓒ 매일 밤 보호용 실크 덮개를 낸다.
Ⓓ 다양한 온도 조건에서 생존할 수 있다.

어휘 hibernate[háibərnèit] 동면하다, 겨울잠을 자다
spin[spin] (실을) 내다, 돌다; 회전

[05-08]

Listen to a talk in an environmental science class.

> **05Today we'll discuss the causes of global warming.** Many associate it with general pollution, but it's specifically caused by excess carbon dioxide and other greenhouse gases emitted by everyday activities, particularly from burning fossil fuels.
> Deforestation is another significant contributor. Rainforests provide over 20% of the world's oxygen, and trees naturally absorb CO2. **06Alarmingly, about 50% of the world's rainforests have been destroyed in just forty years**, dramatically reducing this natural carbon sink.
> **07Global warming isn't solely human-caused, though. Earth has a long history of warming and cooling trends—consider how the Ice Age ended.** Some scientists point out that the oceans are heating much faster than the atmosphere, suggesting that the heat originates from Earth's interior rather than from atmospheric changes.
> Since warm oceans release CO2 while cool oceans absorb it, this dynamic creates a significant feedback loop. Water has a much higher heat capacity than air. That is, water can heat air, but air can't effectively heat water.
> **08Well, the scientific community remains divided. Some researchers attribute warming oceans to atmospheric pollution from human activities. But others insist that only processes within Earth's core could heat the oceans to this degree.** Most likely, our current global warming results from both human intervention and natural phenomena acting in combination.

emit[imít] 내뿜다, 방출하다   contributor[kəntríbjutər] 원인
rainforest[réinfɔ̀:rist] 열대우림   absorb[æbsɔ́:rb] 흡수하다
carbon sink 탄소 흡수원(대기 중 이산화탄소를 흡수하는 저장소)
point out 지적하다   originate from ~에서 나오다
interior[intíəriər] 내부   attribute[ətríbju:t] ~의 탓이라고 생각하다
insist[insíst] 주장하다   intervention[ìntərvénʃən] 개입, 간섭

환경과학 강의를 들으시오.

05오늘 우리는 지구온난화의 원인들에 대해 논의하겠습니다. 많은 사람들이 지구 온난화를 일반적인 오염과 연관시키지만, 구체적으로는 일상 활동, 특히 화석 연료를 태우는 과정에서 배출되는 과도한 이산화탄소와 기타 온실가스가 원인이 됩니다.
삼림 벌채는 또 다른 중요한 요인입니다. 열대우림은 세계 산소의 20% 이상을 공급하고, 나무들은 자연적으로 이산화탄소를 흡수합니다. 06놀랍게도, 전 세계 열대우림의 약 50%가 불과 40년 만에 파괴되면서, 이 자연적인 탄소 흡수원이 크게 줄었습니다.
07하지만 지구온난화가 전적으로 인간이 야기한 것은 아닙니다. 지구는 온난화와 냉각 경향이 반복되어 온 오랜 역사를 가지고 있는데, 빙하기가 어떻게 끝났는지 생각해보세요. 일부 과학자들은 바다가 대기보다 훨씬 더 빠르게 가열되고 있다는 점을 지적하는데, 이는 대기 변화보다는 지구 내부에서 나오는 열을 시사합니다.
따뜻한 바다는 이산화탄소를 방출하고 차가운 바다는 그것을 흡수하므로, 이 역학은 중요한 피드백 루프를 형성합니다. 물은 공기보다 훨씬 더 높은 열용량을 가집니다. 다시 말해, 물은 공기를 가열할 수 있지만, 공기는 물을 효과적으로 가열할 수 없습니다.
08음, 과학계는 여전히 의견이 갈려 있습니다. 일부 연구자들은 바다의 온난화를 인간 활동으로 인한 대기 오염 탓이라고 생각합니다. 하지만 다른 이들은 오직 지구 핵 내부의 과정만이 바다를 이 정도까지 가열할 수 있다고 주장합니다. 가장 가능성이 높은 설명은, 현재의 지구온난화가 인간의 개입과 자연 현상이 결합하여 작용한 결과라는 것입니다.

05 Main Topic Question

강의의 주요 주제는 무엇인가?
Ⓐ 환경 문제에 대한 해결책
Ⓑ 환경에 대한 인간의 영향
Ⓒ 기후 변화에 기여하는 요인들 ✓
Ⓓ 오염에 대한 과학적 논쟁

어휘 disagreement[dìsəgríːmənt] 논쟁

06 Detail Question
화자는 삼림 벌채에 대해 무엇을 말하는가?
Ⓐ 화석 연료를 태우는 것보다 덜 해롭다.
Ⓑ 자연적인 온난화와 냉각 주기에 기여한다.
Ⓒ 주로 이산화탄소 흡수보다는 산소 생산에 영향을 미친다.
☑ 40년 만에 전 세계 열대우림의 약 절반을 파괴했다.

07 Intention Question
화자는 왜 빙하기를 언급하는가?
Ⓐ 자연적 영향과 인간의 영향 사이의 차이점을 강조하기 위해
☑ 지구가 자연적인 기후 변이를 경험한다는 것을 보여주기 위해
Ⓒ 삼림 벌채가 선사시대에는 요인이 아니었다는 것을 증명하기 위해
Ⓓ 기후에 대한 인간 활동의 영향을 강조하기 위해

어휘 variation[vɛ̀əriéiʃən] 변이, 변화

08 Intention Question
화자는 왜 과학계를 언급하는가?
Ⓐ 특정 연구 방향을 추천하기 위해
Ⓑ 주류 기후 변화 이론에 도전하기 위해
Ⓒ 연구 그룹들 간의 협력을 촉진하기 위해
☑ 기후 변화 원인에 대한 여러 관점이 존재한다는 것을 나타내기 위해

어휘 mainstream[méinstrìːm] 주류의; 주류
causation[kɔːzéiʃən] 원인

[09-12]
Listen to a talk in a biology class.

[09]Many of you have probably seen fish jump. Both freshwater and saltwater fish exhibit this behavior, so let's explore the reasons by examining different species.
First, predator-prey interactions are a major factor. When fish leap out of the water, predators are often nearby. [11-A]Jumping helps fish escape quickly and unpredictably, since they face less resistance in the air than in the water.
Jumping can also benefit some hunters. Certain fish leap to catch organisms above the surface. [10]The silver arowana from South American rivers contorts its body into an S-shape before straightening rapidly, generating thrust to snatch prey with its sharp teeth. These fish can leap almost 2 meters!
For migrating fish, especially anadromous species, [11-B]jumping helps them overcome obstacles. When encountering rapids, jumping can be more efficient than swimming through strong currents. Salmon, for instance, can jump up to 3.7 meters at Scotland's Orrin Falls. Deep pools at waterfall bases allow them to gather speed, and upward currents assist them like hydraulic lifts.
Finally, [11-C]jumping may serve as a form of communication. Large fish like sturgeon produce loud splashes when they hit the water, which may signal feeding areas or attract others during mating. Now, we've seen the reasons behind fish jumping. [12]Next, we'll take a look at the mechanics that make such leaps possible.

freshwater[fréʃwɔːtər] 민물의 saltwater[sɔ́ːltwɔːtər] 바닷물의
predator[prédətər] 포식자, 육식동물 prey[prei] 먹이
leap out of ~에서 튀어오르다 contort[kəntɔ́ːrt] 비틀다
straighten[stréitn] 곧게 펴다 thrust[θrʌst] 추진력
snatch[snætʃ] 빼앗아 달아나다, 강탈하다
migrating[máigreitiŋ] 이동하는, 이주하는
anadromous species 소하성 종
overcome[òuvərkʌ́m] 극복하다 obstacle[ábstəkl] 장애물
rapids[rǽpidz] 급류 waterfall[wɔ́ːtərfɔːl] 폭포
hydraulic lift 수압 상승기

생물학 강의를 들으시오.
[09]여러분들 중 많은 분들이 아마 물고기가 튀어오르는 것을 본 적이 있을 겁니다. 민물고기와 바닷물고기 모두 이런 행동을 보이므로, 다양한 종들을 살펴봄으로써 그 이유들을 탐구해봅시다.
첫째로, 포식자-피식자 상호작용이 주요 요인입니다. 물고기가 물에서 튀어오를 때, 포식자들이 종종 근처에 있습니다. [11-A]튀어오르는 것은 물고기가 빠르고 예측하기 어렵게 탈출하는 데 도움이 되는데, 그들이 물에서보다 공기에서 저항을 덜 받기 때문입니다.
튀어오르는 것은 또한 일부 사냥꾼들에게도 도움이 될 수 있습니다. 특정 물고기들은 수면 위의 생물체를 잡기 위해 뜁니다. [10]남미의 강에 사는 은빛 아로와나는 몸을 S자 모양으로 비틀었다가 빠르게 곧게 펴서 추진력을 만들어 날카로운 이빨로 먹이를 낚아챕니다. 이 물고기들은 거의 2미터까지 튀어오를 수 있죠!
이동하는 물고기들, 특히 소하성 종에게는 [11-B]튀어오르는 것이 장애물을 극복하는 데 도움이 됩니다. 급류를 마주했을 때, 튀어오르는 것이 강한 조류를 통과해 헤엄치는 것보다 더 효율적일 수 있죠. 예를 들어, 연어는 스코틀랜드의 Orrin 폭포에서 최대 3.7미터까지 튀어오를 수 있습니다. 폭포 바닥의 깊은 웅덩이들이 그들이 속도를 모으도록 해주고, 상승 조류가 수압 상승기처럼 도움을 주죠.
마지막으로, [11-C]튀어오르는 것은 의사소통의 한 형태로 작용할 수 있습니다. 철갑상어와 같은 큰 물고기들은 물에 부딪힐 때 큰 물튀김 소리를 내는데, 이는 먹이터를 신호하거나 짝짓기 동안 다른 개체들을 끌어들일 수 있습니다. 자, 우리는 물고기의 튀어오름 뒤에 숨겨진 이유들을 살펴보았습니다. [12]다음으로, 그런 도약을 가능하게 하는 역학을 살펴보겠습니다.

09 Main Topic Question
강의는 주로 무엇에 대한 것인가?
Ⓐ 다양한 물고기 종과 그들의 독특한 특성
☑ 민물고기와 바닷물고기의 생존 전략
Ⓒ 다양한 물고기 종의 신체적 능력
☑ 물고기가 물 밖으로 튀어오르는 이유에 대한 설명

어휘 capability[kèipəbíləti] 능력

10 Detail Question

화자는 은빛 아로와나에 대해 무엇을 말하는가?
- Ⓐ 추진력을 만들기 위해 몸을 빠르게 곧게 편다. ✓
- Ⓑ 산란 이동 중 장애물을 극복하기 위해 튀어오른다.
- Ⓒ 튀어오름을 짝짓기 의사소통의 한 형태로 사용한다.
- Ⓓ 수중 포식자들로부터 탈출하기 위해 몸을 비튼다.

어휘 courtship[kɔ́ːrtʃip] 짝짓기

11 Detail Question

물고기 튀어오름의 효과로 언급되지 않은 것은 무엇인가?
- Ⓐ 포식자로부터 탈출하기
- Ⓑ 물리적 장벽 극복하기
- Ⓒ 다른 물고기와 의사소통하기
- Ⓓ 체온 조절하기 ✓

어휘 regulate[régjulèit] 조절하다

12 Discuss Next Question

화자는 다음에 무엇을 논의할 것 같은가?
- Ⓐ 튀어오르는 물고기 종의 추가 예시
- Ⓑ 이동 물고기의 번식 전략
- Ⓒ 물고기 튀어오름을 가능하게 하는 물리적 과정 ✓
- Ⓓ 물고기 튀어오름 행동의 생태학적 중요성

어휘 ecological[ìkəlɑ́ːdʒikəl] 생태학적인, 생태의

[13-16] Am

Listen to a talk in a physiology class.

[13]**You might think your brain just shuts down when you sleep, but that's not true at all.** We can actually measure brain activity using an instrument called an EEG—an electroencephalogram—which records electrical activity.

When you're awake, your brain produces beta waves—these are irregular because your mental activity is constantly changing. As you relax, these shift to slower alpha waves, like when you're meditating.

[13]**So, sleep occurs in distinct stages.** [14]**Stage one is light sleep with theta waves.** They are slower than alpha waves but larger in amplitude. You drift in and out easily and might have fragmented dream images. [15]**Have you ever felt those sudden muscle jerks that wake you up? That's a typical property of this stage.** [14]**Stage two still features theta waves.** But now we see sleep spindles, rapid bursts of brain activity, and K-complexes, which are sudden increases in wave amplitude.

Now, stages three and four feature delta waves—the slowest, largest brain waves. This is deep sleep where sleepwalking occurs. Finally, there's REM sleep when vivid dreaming happens. Your eyes dart around, but your muscles become paralyzed. If awakened during REM, you'll likely remember your dreams clearly. [16]**So, there's a common belief that if you dream, it means you didn't sleep well. But is that really true? Let's find out together.**

shut down 꺼지다, 멈추다   at all 전혀
irregular[irégjulər] 불규칙한   meditate[médəteit] 명상하다
amplitude[ǽmplətjùːd] 진폭   jerk[dʒəːrk] 경련
spindle[spíndl] 방추파   burst[bəːrst] 폭발
sleepwalking[slíːpwɔːkiŋ] 몽유병   vivid[vívid] 생생한
paralyzed[pǽrəlàizd] 마비된

생리학 강의를 들으시오.

[13]여러분은 잠잘 때 뇌가 그냥 꺼진다고 생각할 수도 있지만, 그건 전혀 사실이 아닙니다. 우리는 실제로 EEG 또는 뇌전도라고 불리는 장치를 사용하여 뇌 활동을 측정할 수 있는데, 이것은 전기적 활동을 기록합니다.

여러분이 깨어 있을 때, 여러분의 뇌는 베타파를 생성하는데, 이는 여러분의 정신적 활동이 끊임없이 변하기 때문에 불규칙하죠. 여러분이 휴식을 취하면서, 이것들은 여러분이 명상할 때처럼 더 느린 알파파로 바뀝니다.

[13]자, 수면은 뚜렷한 단계로 진행됩니다. [14]1단계는 세타파가 나타나는 얕은 잠입니다. 세타파는 알파파보다 더 느리지만 진폭은 더 큽니다. 여러분은 잠에서 쉽게 깨어났다가 다시 잠들곤 하며, 단편적인 꿈의 이미지를 볼 수 있습니다. [15]갑자기 근육이 경련하면서 잠에서 깬 경험이 있나요? 그것은 이 단계의 전형적인 특징입니다. [14]2단계는 여전히 세타파를 가집니다. 하지만 이제 우리는 뇌 활동의 빠른 폭발인 수면 방추파와 파형 진폭의 갑작스러운 증가인 K-복합파를 관찰합니다.

이제, 3단계와 4단계는 가장 느리고 가장 큰 뇌파인 델타파를 특징으로 합니다. 이것은 몽유병이 일어나는 깊은 잠입니다. 마지막으로, 생생한 꿈이 일어나는 REM 수면이 있습니다. 여러분의 눈은 이리저리 빠르게 움직이지만, 여러분의 근육은 마비됩니다. REM 수면 중에 깨어나면, 여러분은 아마 여러분의 꿈을 명확히 기억할 것입니다. [16]자, 꿈을 꾸면 숙면을 취하지 못했다는 일반적인 믿음이 있죠. 하지만 그게 정말 사실일까요? 함께 알아봅시다.

13 Main Topic Question

강의의 주요 주제는 무엇인가?
- Ⓐ 뇌파 패턴의 발견
- Ⓑ EEG 기술의 의학적 응용
- Ⓒ 수면 단계의 진행 과정 ✓
- Ⓓ 명상과 수면 사이의 관계

어휘 meditation[mèditéiʃən] 명상

14 Detail Question

화자는 세타파에 대해 무엇을 말하는가?
- Ⓐ 오직 REM 수면 동안에만 나타난다.
- Ⓑ 수면의 첫 두 단계를 특징짓는다. ✓
- Ⓒ 뇌가 생성하는 가장 큰 뇌파이다.
- Ⓓ 사람들이 완전히 깨어있고 주의 깊을 때 나타난다.

어휘 alert[əláːrt] 주의 깊은

15 Intention Question

화자는 왜 근육 경련을 언급하는가?
- Ⓐ 방해받는 수면의 위험성에 대해 경고하기 위해

Ⓑ 깊은 잠에서 근육이 어떻게 이완되는지 보여주기 위해
✓ 1단계 수면의 쉽게 알아볼 수 있는 예시를 제공하기 위해
Ⓓ 왜 일부 사람들이 잠들기 어려워하는지 설명하기 위해

어휘 **interrupted**[ìntərʌ́ptid] 방해받는
recognizable[rékəgnàizəbl] 쉽게 알아볼 수 있는

16 Discuss Next Question
화자는 다음에 무엇을 논의할 것 같은가?
✓ 꿈과 편안한 수면에 대한 진실
Ⓑ 꿈 분석의 치료적 활용
Ⓒ 나쁜 수면의 건강상 결과
Ⓓ 수면의 질을 개선하는 기법

어휘 **restful**[réstfəl] 편안한 **therapeutic**[θèrəpjúːtik] 치료적인

[17-20] 🎧 Au
Listen to a talk in an environmental science class.

[17]Today, we're going to compare fossil fuels and biofuels by examining their environmental impacts and future roles in our energy landscape.
Fossil fuels, such as coal, oil, and natural gas, have powered industrial development for centuries. These energy sources were formed over millions of years from decomposed plant and animal remains. While they've been reliable energy providers, their combustion releases significant amounts of carbon dioxide. This contributes to climate change. Additionally, fossil fuel reserves are finite, raising concerns about long-term availability.
[18]In contrast, biofuels are derived from recently living organisms or their metabolic byproducts. Common examples include ethanol from corn or sugarcane, and biodiesel from vegetable oils. What makes biofuels appealing? Well, they're renewable since we can grow more feedstock crops each year. They also typically produce fewer greenhouse gas emissions when burned than fossil fuels do.
However, biofuels aren't without challenges. Production often requires significant agricultural land, potentially competing with food crops. [19]There are also concerns about water use and the large amount of energy required in the production process. So, [20]are biofuels truly the sustainable alternative we're looking for? That's what we'll explore next as we analyze their complete environmental footprint.

biofuel[báioufjùːəl] 바이오 연료
environmental[invàiərənméntl] 환경의
power[páuər] ~에 동력을 공급하다; 힘 **remains**[riméinz] 잔해
combustion[kəmbʌ́stʃən] 연소 **finite**[fáinait] 유한한
metabolic[mètəbálik] 대사의 **byproduct**[báiprɑ̀dəkt] 부산물
appealing[əpíːliŋ] 매력적인 **renewable**[rinúːəbl] 재생 가능한
feedstock[fíːdstɑ̀k] 공급 원료 **crop**[krɑːp] 작물

agricultural[ægrikʌ́ltʃərəl] 농업의 **compete with** ~와 경쟁하다
large amount of 대량의 **sustainable**[səstéinəbl] 지속 가능한
analyze[ǽnəlàiz] 분석하다 **footprint**[fútprìnt] 발자국

환경과학 강의를 들으시오.
[17]오늘, 우리는 환경 영향과 우리 에너지 분야에서의 미래 역할을 살펴봄으로써 화석 연료와 바이오 연료를 비교해보겠습니다.
석탄, 석유, 천연가스와 같은 화석 연료는 수 세기 동안 산업 발전에 동력을 공급해왔습니다. 이 에너지원들은 분해된 동식물 잔해로부터 수백만 년에 걸쳐 형성되었습니다. 화석 연료는 신뢰할 만한 에너지 공급원이지만, 이들의 연소는 상당한 양의 이산화탄소를 배출합니다. 이것은 기후 변화에 기여합니다. 게다가, 화석 연료 매장량은 유한하여, 장기적 공급 가능성에 대한 우려를 불러일으킵니다.
[18]대조적으로, 바이오 연료는 최근에 살았던 유기체나 대사 부산물로부터 유래됩니다. 일반적인 예로 옥수수나 사탕수수에서 얻는 에탄올과 식물성 기름에서 얻는 바이오디젤이 포함됩니다. 바이오 연료가 매력적인 이유는 무엇일까요? 음, 우리가 매년 더 많은 공급 원료 작물을 재배할 수 있기 때문에 바이오 연료는 재생 가능합니다. 또한 일반적으로 이들은 연소될 때 화석 연료보다 더 적은 온실가스를 배출합니다.
하지만, 바이오 연료도 문제가 전혀 없는 것은 아닙니다. 생산에는 보통 상당한 농지가 필요하므로, 잠재적으로 식량 작물과 경쟁하게 됩니다. [19]물 사용과 생산 과정에서 필요한 대량의 에너지에 대한 우려도 있습니다. 그렇다면 [20]바이오 연료가 정말로 우리가 찾고 있는 지속 가능한 대안일까요? 이는 다음으로 우리가 바이오 연료의 전체 환경 발자국을 분석하면서 탐구할 내용입니다.

17 Main Topic Question
강의는 주로 무엇에 대한 것인가?
Ⓐ 전통적인 에너지원의 가용성 감소
Ⓑ 에너지 소비로 인한 환경 문제
Ⓒ 재생 불가능한 에너지원의 미래 고갈
✓ 다양한 연료 유형의 장점과 단점

어휘 **depletion**[diplíːʃən] 감소

18 Intention Question
화자는 왜 에탄올을 언급하는가?
✓ 최근에 살았던 유기체로 만든 연료를 소개하기 위해
Ⓑ 연료 유형 간의 비용 차이를 강조하기 위해
Ⓒ 재생 에너지에 대한 가정에 반박하기 위해
Ⓓ 비효율적인 에너지 대안을 비판하기 위해

어휘 **inefficient**[ìnifíʃənt] 비효율적인

19 Detail Question
화자에 따르면, 바이오 연료의 문제는 무엇인가?
Ⓐ 기존 차량 엔진에 사용될 수 없다.
Ⓑ 화석 연료보다 더 많은 이산화탄소를 방출한다.
✓ 제조 과정에서 상당한 에너지를 소비한다.
Ⓓ 전 세계 수요를 충족할 정도의 충분한 양으로 생산될 수 없다.

어휘 **quantity**[kwɑ́ntəti] 양

20 Discuss Next Question
화자는 다음에 무엇을 논의할 것 같은가?
Ⓐ 다양한 국가들의 에너지 정책 비교

- 바이오 연료 대안의 종합적인 생태학적 평가
- ⓒ 에너지 소비에 대한 미래 예측
- ⓓ 연료 효율성의 기술적 혁신

어휘 assessment[əsésmənt] 평가
      projection[prədʒékʃən] 예측, 투영

[21-24]
Listen to a talk in a biology class.

> Coral polyps are tiny marine animals that secrete limestone to form the hard structures we call coral reefs. [21]**But what makes them fascinating is their dependence on microscopic algae called zooxanthellae.** [22]**These algae actually live inside the coral tissues**. In fact, up to 30% of a polyp's body mass consists of these tiny plants.
>
> [21]**Here's how this partnership works**: The zooxanthellae use photosynthesis to convert sunlight into sugar, just like other plants. The coral then consumes this sugar, which provides an incredible 90% of its nutritional needs. In exchange, the coral provides the algae with a protected environment and essential nutrients.
>
> However, this efficient system has a critical weakness. When ocean temperatures rise beyond the coral's tolerance range, the zooxanthellae stop producing food and are expelled from the coral tissues. [23]**This process is called coral bleaching because the reef loses its vibrant colors and turns white. Without their algal partners, coral colonies become nutritionally stressed, weakened, and much more susceptible to disease.** [24]**If bleaching persists, entire coral colonies can die, which is why global warming poses a severe threat to these ecosystems. Next, let's explore the efforts that marine biologists are making to prevent such disasters.**
>
> marine[mərí:n] 해양의 secrete[sikrí:t] 분비하다
> dependence[diǽndəns] 의존성
> microscopic[màikrəskápik] 미세한 tissue[tíʃuː] 조직
> consume[kənsú:m] 소비하다 nutritional[njuːtríʃənl] 영양의
> in exchange 그 대가로 essential[isénʃəl] 필수의, 중요한
> tolerance[tὰlərəns] 내성 be expelled from ~에서 방출되다
> bleaching[blí:tʃiŋ] 탈색 vibrant[váibrənt] 생생한
> susceptible[səséptəbl] 약한, 민감한 persist[pərsíst] 지속되다
> severe[səvíər] 심각한 disaster[dizǽstər] 재앙

생물학 강의를 들으시오.

산호 폴립은 우리가 산호초라고 부르는 단단한 구조를 형성하기 위해 석회석을 분비하는 작은 해양 동물입니다. [21]하지만 그들을 매혹적으로 만드는 것은 황록공생조류라고 불리는 미세한 조류에 대한 그들의 의존성입니다. [22]이 조류들은 실제로 산호 조직 안에 살고 있습니다. 사실, 폴립 체질량의 최대 30퍼센트가 이 작은 식물들로 구성되죠.

[21]이 파트너십이 작동하는 방식은 다음과 같은데요, 황록공생조류는 다른 식물들처럼 광합성을 사용하여 햇빛을 당으로 변환합니다. 그러면 산호가 이 당을 소비하는데, 이것이 산호의 영양 요구량 중 무려 90퍼센트를 충족시킵니다. 그 대가로, 산호는 조류에게 보호된 환경과 필수 영양소를 제공합니다.

하지만, 이 효율적인 시스템은 중요한 약점을 가지고 있습니다. 바다 온도가 산호의 내성 범위를 넘어 올라가면, 황록공생조류는 먹이 생산을 멈추고 산호 조직에서 방출됩니다. [23]이 과정을 산호 탈색이라고 부르는데, 산호초가 생생한 색깔을 잃고 하얗게 변하기 때문입니다. 조류 파트너가 없이는, 산호는 영양 결핍 상태에 빠지고, 약해지며 질병에 훨씬 더 취약해집니다. [24]탈색이 지속되면, 전체 산호 군체가 죽을 수 있는데, 이것이 지구 온난화가 이러한 생태계에 심각한 위협을 가하는 이유입니다. 다음으로, 해양 생물학자들이 그런 재앙을 막기 위해 하고 있는 노력을 탐구해봅시다.

21 Main Topic Question
강의의 주요 주제는 무엇인가?
- ⓐ 해양 동물의 온도 내성
- ⓑ 해양 조류를 위한 보호 환경
- ✓ 산호 생태계에서의 상리공생 관계
- ⓓ 해양 동물이 형성한 석회석 구조

어휘 protective[prətéktiv] 보호의
      mutualistic[mjúːtʃuəlistik] 상리공생의

22 Detail Question
화자는 황록공생조류에 대해 무엇을 말하는가?
- ⓐ 산호 조직 외부에 군체를 형성한다.
- ✓ 산호의 조직 안에서 서식한다.
- ⓒ 정상적인 조건에서 산호를 약화시킨다.
- ⓓ 물로부터 필수 영양소를 흡수한다.

어휘 reside[rizáid] 서식하다, 거주하다 weaken[wíːkən] 약화시키다

23 Detail Question
화자에 따르면, 산호 탈색이 문제인 이유는 무엇인가?
- ⓐ 조류가 산호 내부에서 너무 빠르게 번식한다.
- ⓑ 산호 조직이 해로운 물질을 생산한다.
- ⓒ 바다 온도가 내성 수준 아래로 떨어진다.
- ✓ 산호가 먹이 부족과 약화로 고통을 받는다.

어휘 multiply[mʌ́ltiplai] 번식하다, 증가시키다
      suffer from ~으로 고통 받다 deprivation[dèprivéiʃən] 부족

24 Discuss Next Question
화자는 다음에 무엇을 논의할 것 같은가?
- ⓐ 해양 식물에서의 당 생산
- ⓑ 바다 온도의 측정
- ✓ 산호 생태계를 위한 보존 노력
- ⓓ 해양 연구자들이 사용하는 다이빙 기법

어휘 measurement[méʒərmənt] 측정, 양, 치수

ACTUAL TEST 1

p.356

Module 1

01 Ⓐ	02 Ⓓ	03 Ⓑ	04 Ⓓ	05 Ⓒ
06 Ⓐ	07 Ⓐ	08 Ⓓ	09 Ⓐ	10 Ⓑ
11 Ⓑ	12 Ⓓ	13 Ⓐ	14 Ⓑ	15 Ⓓ
16 Ⓒ	17 Ⓑ	18 Ⓓ	19 Ⓐ	20 Ⓒ

Module 2

01 Ⓑ	02 Ⓐ	03 Ⓓ	04 Ⓑ	05 Ⓓ
06 Ⓑ	07 Ⓐ	08 Ⓑ	09 Ⓑ	10 Ⓒ
11 Ⓒ	12 Ⓐ	13 Ⓒ	14 Ⓓ	15 Ⓑ

Module 1

01 Request Question En

Would you mind helping me set up the projector?

☑ Ⓐ Let me wrap up this email first.
Ⓑ Yes, the project was a success.
Ⓒ I really like the setup in here.
Ⓓ No, further from the screen.

wrap up 마무리하다   success[səksés] 성공

제가 프로젝터를 설치하는 것을 도와주시겠어요?
☑ 먼저 이 이메일부터 마무리할게요.
Ⓑ 네, 그 프로젝트는 성공이었어요.
Ⓒ 여기 구조가 정말 마음에 들어요.
Ⓓ 아니요, 스크린에서 더 멀리요.

02 Auxiliary Verb Question Am

Did you reserve the seminar room?

Ⓐ Who can reserve it?
Ⓑ Either room is available.
Ⓒ Yes, I should.
☑ Ⓓ It's already booked by someone else.

reserve[rizə́ːrv] 예약하다

세미나실을 예약했나요?
Ⓐ 누가 그것을 예약할 수 있나요?
Ⓑ 둘 중 어느 방도 이용 가능해요.
Ⓒ 네, 저는 그래야 해요.
☑ 그것은 이미 다른 사람이 예약했어요.

03 Where Question Am

Where is the desk to register for membership?

Ⓐ It opens at 9 A.M.

☑ Ⓑ I believe it's in the main lobby.
Ⓒ You should bring your ID to register.
Ⓓ I'm thinking about joining next month.

register[rédʒistər] 등록하다

회원권을 등록하는 데스크는 어디에 있나요?
Ⓐ 그곳은 오전 9시에 문을 열어요.
☑ 메인 로비에 있는 것 같아요.
Ⓒ 등록하려면 당신의 신분증을 가져와야 해요.
Ⓓ 다음 달에 가입하려고 생각 중이에요.

04 Informative Statement En

I'm not satisfied with this blender.

Ⓐ So am I.
Ⓑ I recommend a microwave.
Ⓒ It blends in well.
☑ Ⓓ Oh, I didn't expect that.

satisfied[sǽtisfàid] 만족하는
recommend[rèkəménd] 추천하다   blend in 어울리다

저는 이 믹서기에 만족하지 않아요.
Ⓐ 저도 그래요.
Ⓑ 저는 전자레인지를 추천해요.
Ⓒ 그것은 잘 어울려요.
☑ 아, 그러실 줄 몰랐어요.

05 Who Question Nz

Who is attending the board meeting tomorrow?

Ⓐ They provided a broad agenda.
Ⓑ It's at 10 o'clock.
☑ Ⓒ The executives will be there.
Ⓓ Keep me posted.

broad[brɔːd] 광범위한, 넓은   agenda[ədʒéndə] 안건
executive[igzékjutiv] 임원

내일 이사회 회의에 누가 참석하나요?
Ⓐ 그들이 광범위한 안건을 제공했어요.
Ⓑ 10시 정각이에요.
☑ 임원들이 참석할 거예요.
Ⓓ 계속 알려줘요.

06 Be Verb Question En

Are you all ready for the company's product rollout tomorrow?

☑ Ⓐ We're all set to go.
Ⓑ No need to try explaining that.

ⓒ I've actually already tried it out.
ⓓ Take a look at the sales projections.

product rollout 제품 공개　all set 모든 준비가 된
projection[prədʒékʃən] 예상치, 추정

내일 회사의 제품 공개에 모두 준비되셨나요?
ⓐ 모든 준비가 되었어요.
ⓑ 그걸 설명하려고 하실 필요는 없어요.
ⓒ 사실 이미 시도해봤어요.
ⓓ 판매 예상치를 보세요.

07　How Question　　　　　　　　　Au

How many sessions are going to be offered this semester in total?

ⓐ It depends mainly on the professor's teaching schedule.
ⓑ Twelve classrooms on each floor of the building.
ⓒ Beginning right at the end of August this year.
ⓓ Covering various topics divided into four modules.

in total 총　cover[kʌ́vər] 다루다　divided into ~으로 나누어진

이번 학기에 총 몇 개의 수업이 제공될 예정인가요?
ⓐ 그것은 주로 교수님의 수업 일정에 달려 있어요.
ⓑ 건물 각 층마다 12개의 교실이요.
ⓒ 올해 8월 말에 바로 시작해요.
ⓓ 4개의 모듈로 나누어진 다양한 주제들을 다뤄요.

08　Advisory Statement　　　　　　En

Please bring copies of the revised handbook to this afternoon's training session.

ⓐ Several errors in the old employee manual, actually.
ⓑ The training room was used earlier this morning.
ⓒ In the storage facility until they can be recycled.
ⓓ George is collecting them from the print shop tomorrow.

revise[riváiz] 수정하다　storage facility 보관 시설
print shop 인쇄소

오늘 오후 교육 세션에 수정된 핸드북 사본들을 가져와 주세요.
ⓐ 사실, 옛 직원 매뉴얼에서의 몇 개의 오류요.
ⓑ 교육실은 오늘 오전 일찍 사용되었어요.
ⓒ 재활용될 수 있을 때까지 보관 시설에서요.
ⓓ George가 내일 인쇄소에서 그것들을 가져올 거예요.

[09-10]　　　　　　　　　　W-Am M-En

Listen to a conversation.

W　Did you hear the announcement this morning?
M　Yes, I just got the email from HR. ⁰⁹**So we're officially combining with TechSolutions next month?**

W　That's right. The CEO mentioned there might be some restructuring in the marketing and IT departments.
M　I'm a bit concerned about job security. Do you know if the company is planning any layoffs?
W　According to the announcement, ¹⁰**they're focusing on getting rid of jobs that are very similar to each other. I believe they'll try to relocate employees to other departments when possible.**

announcement[ənáunsmənt] 공지, 발표
officially[əfíʃəli] 공식적으로
combine[kəmbáin] 합병하다, 모이다　job security 고용 안정성
focus on ~에 집중하다　get rid of ~을 없애다
similar[símələr] 유사한　relocate[rìloukéit] 재배치하다

대화를 들으시오.
W　오늘 아침 공지 들으셨나요?
M　네, 방금 인사부로부터 이메일을 받았어요. ⁰⁹그래서 우리가 다음 달에 TechSolutions와 공식적으로 합병한다는 거죠?
W　맞아요. CEO가 마케팅과 IT 부서에서 약간의 구조조정이 있을 수 있다고 언급했어요.
M　고용 안정성에 대해 좀 걱정이 되네요. 회사가 해고를 계획하고 있는지 아시나요?
W　공지에 따르면, ¹⁰그들은 서로 매우 유사한 직무를 없애는 데 집중하고 있어요. 가능하면 직원들을 다른 부서로 재배치하려고 노력할 거라고 생각해요.

09　Main Topic Question

화자들은 어떤 사건에 대해 이야기하고 있는가?
ⓐ 회사 합병
ⓑ 제품 출시
ⓒ 직원 승진
ⓓ 부서 회의

어휘　merger[mə́:rdʒər] 합병

10　Attitude Question

여자는 해고에 대해 어떻게 생각하는가?
ⓐ 유감이지만 불가피하다.
ⓑ 시행되지 않을 것이다.
ⓒ 직원 재배치와 동시에 발생할 것이다.
ⓓ 특정 부서에만 계획되어 있다.

어휘　unfortunate[ʌnfɔ́:rtʃənət] 유감인, 불행한
inevitable[inévətəbl] 불가피한
implement[ímpləmənt] 시행하다

[11-12]　　　　　　　　　　W-Nz M-Am

Listen to a conversation.

W　Did you make the reservation for dinner with the clients next week?
M　I did, ¹¹**but the restaurant just called to say they have to cancel it due to a kitchen emergency.** They say they'll be closed for two weeks

because of a plumbing problem.

W That's terrible timing. We need somewhere nice to take them.

M Actually, I've already found a few options downtown that can accommodate us. ¹²**Why don't you check them out in advance? I'll send you the names and menu highlights.**

reservation[rèzərvéiʃən] 예약
emergency[imə́:rdʒənsi] 응급상황
accommodate[əkámədèit] 수용하다, 부응하다
in advance 미리, 사전에

대화를 들으시오.
W 다음 주에 고객들과 함께 할 저녁 식사를 위해 예약하셨나요?
M 했지만, ¹¹레스토랑에서 방금 주방 응급상황 때문에 취소해야 한다고 전화했어요. 배관 문제 때문에 2주 동안 문을 닫을 거라고 해요.
W 최악의 타이밍이네요. 그들을 데려갈 좋은 곳이 필요해요.
M 사실, 우리를 수용할 수 있는 시내의 몇 가지 선택지들을 이미 찾았어요. ¹²미리 확인해보는 게 어때요? 이름들과 메뉴에서 가장 좋은 것을 보내드릴게요.

11 Detail Question
남자는 왜 저녁 식사 예약을 지킬 수 없는가?
Ⓐ 예약을 확인하는 것을 잊었다.
☑ 긴급 휴업 통보를 받았다.
Ⓒ 고객들의 일정 변경을 알게 되었다.
Ⓓ 집에 배관 문제가 있다.

어휘 confirm[kənfə́:rm] 확인하다 be informed of ~을 알게 되다

12 Suggestion Question
남자는 여자가 무엇을 하라고 제안하는가?
Ⓐ 다른 레스토랑들을 찾는다.
Ⓑ 그와 함께 저녁을 먹는다.
Ⓒ 고객 미팅을 취소한다.
☑ 대안이 되는 장소들을 미리 방문한다.

어휘 alternative[ɔ:ltə́:rnətiv] 대안이 되는
venue[vénju:] 장소 ahead of time 미리

[13-14]
Listen to an announcement at a university event.

Good afternoon, everyone. ¹³**I'd like to remind you that the campus talent show registration closes this Friday at 5 P.M. in the Student Center.** ¹⁴**Please remember to bring your student ID when you sign up.** We look forward to seeing your performances and supporting our talented students!

remind[rimáind] 알리다, 상기시키다 sign up 등록하다
look forward to ~하기를 기대하다

대학교 행사에서의 공지를 들으시오.
좋은 오후입니다, 여러분. ¹³캠퍼스 장기자랑 등록이 이번 주 금요일 오후 5시에 학생회관에서 마감됨을 알려드립니다. ¹⁴등록하실 때 학생증을 지참해 주시기 바랍니다. 여러분의 공연을 보고 재능 있는 학생들을 응원하기를 기대합니다!

13 Main Topic Question
공지의 주요 주제는 무엇인가?
☑ 다가오는 마감일
Ⓑ 새로운 공연 장소
Ⓒ 수강 등록 절차
Ⓓ 학생증 정책 변경

어휘 deadline[dédlàin] 마감일 enrollment[inróulmənt] 등록
process[práses] 절차 policy[páləsi] 정책, 규정

14 Detail Question
학생들은 무엇을 가져오라고 권고받는가?
Ⓐ 등록비
☑ 신분증
Ⓒ 공연 영상
Ⓓ 추천서

[15-16]
Listen to an announcement on the school radio.

Attention, students. This is your student council president with an important announcement. ¹⁵**The school library will be hosting a free Study Skills Workshop this Friday from 2 to 4 P.M. in the main conference room.** Professional learning coaches will share effective study techniques and time management strategies. All students are welcome to attend, and ¹⁶**you can get even more out of it by preparing a study plan in advance and discussing it with the coaches.** Don't miss this valuable opportunity!

host[houst] 개최하다 professional[prəféʃənl] 전문적인, 직업의
effective[iféktiv] 효과적인 in advance 미리, 사전에

학교 라디오에서의 공지를 들으시오.
주목해주세요, 학생 여러분. 학생회장으로서 중요한 공지를 드립니다. ¹⁵학교 도서관은 이번 주 금요일 오후 2시부터 4시까지 메인 회의실에서 무료 학습법 워크숍을 개최합니다. 전문 학습 코치들이 효과적인 공부 기법과 시간 관리 전략을 공유할 것입니다. 모든 학생들의 참여를 환영하며, ¹⁶미리 학습 계획을 준비하여 코치들과 논의하면 더욱 많은 것을 얻을 수 있습니다. 이 소중한 기회를 놓치지 마세요!

15 Main Purpose Question
공지의 주요 목적은 무엇인가?
Ⓐ 학교 도서관의 새로운 자료를 설명하기 위해
Ⓑ 효과적인 시간 관리 전략을 홍보하기 위해
Ⓒ 회의실 예약 절차를 설명하기 위해
☑ 다가오는 행사에 대한 정보를 제공하기 위해

어휘 describe[diskráib] 설명하다, 기술하다
resource[risɔ́:rs] 자료 procedure[prəsí:dʒər] 절차, 방법

16 To Do Question

공지에 따르면 학생들은 무엇을 하라고 권고받는가?
Ⓐ 다른 사람들과 행사에 대해 논의한다.
Ⓑ 자리를 확보하기 위해 일찍 도착한다.
☑ 계획을 준비해서 온다.
Ⓓ 질문 목록을 작성한다.

어휘 secure a seat 자리를 확보하다

[17-20]

Listen to a talk in an archaeology class.

> [17]**Experimental archaeology is a research method where archaeologists recreate ancient technologies and processes to better understand how people lived in the past.** Instead of just studying artifacts in museums, researchers actually make and use replicas of ancient tools, build structures using historical techniques, and practice traditional crafts. [17]**One attractive aspect of this hands-on approach is that it allows us to very specifically gauge our ancestors' capabilities in particular fields.** For example, researchers have recreated Stone Age flint-knapping techniques to understand how prehistoric peoples made cutting tools. They've also built replica Viking ships to test their seaworthiness and navigation methods. [18]**Another project involved constructing Iron Age houses using only materials and techniques available to ancient builders, which taught us about their insulation properties.** [17]**The method does have limitations, though.** While modern researchers have contemporary knowledge and physical conditioning that ancient people might not have had, [19]**it's nearly impossible to fully replicate the cultural context of a past era and the accumulated generational knowledge that guided past societies.** Despite these constraints, experimental archaeology is expanding into new areas, including digital simulations and biochemical analyses of ancient processes. [20]**Let's now explore the ways researchers are using modern technology to enhance these traditional experimental approaches.**

artifact [á:rtəfækt] 유물   aspect [ǽspekt] 측면, 양상
hands-on 체험적인   particular [pərtíkjulər] 특정의
flint-knapping 부싯돌 가공   navigation method 항해법
property [prápərti] 특성
limitation [lìmətéiʃən] 한계, 제한
replicate [réplikèit] 재현하다, 복제하다
constraint [kənstréint] 제약
accumulate [əkjú:mjulèit] 축적하다

고고학 강의를 들으시오.

[17]실험 고고학은 고고학자들이 과거 사람들이 어떻게 살았는지 더 잘 이해하기 위해 고대 기술과 과정을 재현하는 연구 방법입니다. 박물관에서 유물을 연구하는 것에 그치지 않고, 연구자들은 실제로 고대 도구의 복제품을 만들고 사용하며, 역사적 기법을 사용하여 구조물을 건설하고, 전통 공예를 실습합니다. [17]이러한 체험적 접근법의 매력적인 측면 중 하나는 특정 분야에서 우리 조상들의 능력을 매우 구체적으로 측정할 수 있다는 것입니다. 예를 들어, 연구자들은 선사 시대 사람들이 어떻게 절삭 도구를 만들었는지 이해하기 위해 석기 시대의 부싯돌 가공 기법을 재현했습니다. 그들은 또한 바이킹 선박의 복제품을 건조하여 항해 적합성과 항해법을 테스트했습니다. [18]또 다른 프로젝트는 고대 건축업자들이 사용할 수 있었던 재료와 기법만을 사용하여 철기 시대 주택을 건설하는 것이었는데, 이는 우리에게 그들의 단열 특성에 대해 가르쳐 주었습니다. [17]하지만 이 방법에는 한계가 있습니다. 현대 연구자들이 고대 사람들이 갖지 못했을 수도 있는 현대적 지식과 신체적 컨디션을 가지고 있는 반면, [19]과거 시대의 문화적 맥락과 과거 사회를 이끌었던 축적된 세대별 지식을 완전히 재현하는 것은 거의 불가능합니다. 이러한 제약에도 불구하고, 실험 고고학은 디지털 시뮬레이션과 고대 과정의 생화학적 분석을 포함한 새로운 영역으로 확장되고 있습니다. [20]이제 연구자들이 이러한 전통적인 실험 접근법을 향상시키기 위해 현대 기술을 사용하는 방법들을 탐구해봅시다.

17 Main Topic Question

강의의 주요 주제는 무엇인가?
Ⓐ 역사를 연구하는 데 사용되는 전통적 방법들의 부적절성
☑ 실험 고고학의 장점과 단점
Ⓒ 철기 시대 건물 재건과 관련된 어려움들
Ⓓ 실험 고고학과 전통 고고학 간의 차이점들

18 Detail Question

연구자들은 철기 시대 주택을 건설함으로써 무엇에 대해 배울 수 있는가?
Ⓐ 절삭 도구
Ⓑ 항해법
Ⓒ 부싯돌 가공 기법
☑ 단열 특성

19 Intention Question

화자는 왜 과거 시대의 문화적 맥락을 언급하는가?
☑ 실험 고고학의 단점을 강조하기 위해
Ⓑ 과거 사회를 이끄는 데 있어서 문화의 중요성을 설명하기 위해
Ⓒ 지식이 세대를 거쳐 어떻게 전달되었는지 설명하기 위해
Ⓓ 현대적 지식이 과거를 이해하는 것을 촉진한다고 제안하기 위해

어휘 shortcoming [ʃɔ́:rtkʌ̀miŋ] 단점
  transmit [trænsmít] 전달하다, 전송하다
  facilitate [fəsílətèit] 촉진하다

20 Discuss Next Question

화자는 다음에 실험 고고학의 어떤 측면에 대해 논의할 것인가?
Ⓐ 그것의 발전 역사
Ⓑ 실험 프로젝트에서 예상되는 어려움들
☑ 현대 기술이 전통적 방법들과 어떻게 통합되는지
Ⓓ 실험 고고학자들을 훈련시키는 방법들

어휘 integrate [íntəgrèit] 통합시키다

Module 2

01 Informative Statement En

Alex and Maria are talking over our travel budget.

Ⓐ Have you seen the report?
Ⓑ Should we join the discussion? ✓
Ⓒ Tomorrow morning.
Ⓓ The best financial plan.

talk over ~에 대해 의논하다 discussion[diskʌ́ʃən] 논의

Alex와 Maria가 우리의 여행 예산에 대해 의논하고 있어요.
Ⓐ 보고서 보셨나요?
Ⓑ 우리도 논의에 참여해야 할까요? ✓
Ⓒ 내일 오전이에요.
Ⓓ 최고의 재정 계획이요.

02 Be Verb Question Am

Hold on, isn't the bill due next Friday?

Ⓐ No, it's this Friday. ✓
Ⓑ No, I don't have time.
Ⓒ Yes, I could.
Ⓓ Yes, that's reasonable.

reasonable[ríːzənəbl] 합리적인, 합당한

잠깐만요, 고지서 만기일이 다음 주 금요일 아닌가요?
Ⓐ 아니요, 이번 주 금요일이에요. ✓
Ⓑ 아니요, 저는 시간이 없어요.
Ⓒ 네, 할 수 있어요.
Ⓓ 네, 그게 합리적이네요.

03 Why Question Nz

Why did the alumni gathering get postponed?

Ⓐ Last Friday.
Ⓑ The auditorium on campus.
Ⓒ Can you join next time?
Ⓓ As a matter of fact, it was canceled. ✓

alumni gathering 동문회 postpone[poustpóun] 연기하다
as a matter of fact 사실

동문회가 왜 연기되었나요?
Ⓐ 지난 주 금요일이요.
Ⓑ 캠퍼스의 강당이요.
Ⓒ 다음에 참여할 수 있나요?
Ⓓ 사실, 취소되었어요. ✓

[04-05] W-Au M-Am

Listen to a conversation.

W I hope you've been enjoying your stay with us, sir. Is the room to your liking?
M The room is just fine, but I'm afraid I nearly lost it this morning. ⁰⁴**I didn't receive the wake-up call I requested.**
W Oh, I am so sorry. One of our new staff members is still learning the system. ⁰⁵**Would you like me to set up a wake-up call for tomorrow?**
M Yes, for 7:30 A.M. I really can't afford to oversleep. I have an important event to attend.
W Absolutely. I'm entering your request into the system as we speak.

to one's liking 만족스러운, 좋아하는
lose it 참지 못하다, 화가 나다 afford[əfɔ́ːrd] 감당하다

대화를 들으시오.
W 저희와 함께 머물러 주셔서 즐거우시기를 바라요. 객실은 만족스러우신가요?
M 객실은 괜찮은데, 오늘 아침에 거의 참지 못할 뻔했어요. ⁰⁴제가 요청했던 모닝콜을 받지 못했거든요.
W 아, 정말 죄송합니다. 저희 신입 직원 중 한 명이 아직 시스템을 배우고 있어요. ⁰⁵내일 모닝콜을 설정해 드릴까요?
M 네, 오전 7시 30분으로요. 저는 정말 늦잠을 감당할 수가 없어요. 참석해야 할 중요한 행사가 있거든요.
W 물론이죠. 지금 당신의 요청을 시스템에 입력하고 있어요.

04 Main Topic Question

화자들은 주로 무엇에 대해 이야기하고 있는가?
Ⓐ 호텔 객실의 상태
Ⓑ 이행되지 않은 고객 요청 ✓
Ⓒ 고장 난 전화 시스템
Ⓓ 놓친 환영 행사

어휘 malfunction[mælfʌ́ŋkʃən] 고장 나다

05 Offer Question

여자는 무엇을 해주겠다고 제안하는가?
Ⓐ 행사 일정을 변경해달라고 요청한다.
Ⓑ 신입 직원을 훈련시킨다.
Ⓒ 남자에게 식사를 제공한다.
Ⓓ 남자를 위해 서비스를 준비한다. ✓

[06-07] W-En M-Am

Listen to a conversation.

W Hey, do you have Miranda's phone number? I have to contact her for a meeting tomorrow.
M ⁰⁶**Oh, right! We have a meeting tomorrow. My mind's all over the place. I've been juggling three different projects lately.**
W No problem. So, do you have her number?
M Sure, let me grab my phone from my bag. It's around here somewhere.
W Never mind. I'll just email her. Don't stress yourself out any more than you need to. ⁰⁷**Actually, I think you should step away for a bit to clear your**

head.

M Maybe you're right. If I took a short walk or got some coffee, I might be able to focus better.

step away 쉬다, 물러나다

대화를 들으시오.
W 저기, Miranda 전화번호 갖고 있어요? 내일 회의 때문에 그녀에게 연락해야 해요.
M ⁰⁶아, 맞다! 우리 내일 회의가 있군요. 제 마음이 온통 이곳저곳에 가 있어요. 요즘 세 가지 다른 프로젝트를 동시에 처리하고 있거든요.
W 괜찮아요. 그래서, 그녀의 번호를 갖고 있나요?
M 물론이죠, 가방에서 제 전화기를 꺼낼게요. 여기 어딘가에 있을 거예요.
W 신경 쓰지 마세요. 그냥 그녀에게 이메일을 보낼게요. 필요 이상으로 스트레스받지 마세요. ⁰⁷사실, 당신은 머리를 맑게 하기 위해 잠시 쉬어야 할 것 같아요.
M 아마 당신 말이 맞을 거예요. 짧게 산책을 하거나 커피를 마시면, 더 잘 집중할 수 있을지도 모르겠어요.

06 Intention Question
남자는 왜 "제 마음이 온통 이곳저곳에 가 있어요"라고 말하는가?
Ⓐ Miranda에게 어떻게 연락할지 확신하지 못한다.
☑ 한번에 너무 많은 것들을 처리하고 있다.
Ⓒ 자신의 가방이 어디 있는지 알지 못한다.
Ⓓ Miranda가 어디에 있을 수 있는지 생각하고 있다.

어휘 handle[hǽndl] 처리하다

07 Suggestion Question
여자는 남자가 무엇을 하라고 권장하는가?
☑ 긴장을 풀기 위해 휴식을 취한다.
Ⓑ 그의 가방이 책상에 있는지 확인한다.
Ⓒ Miranda에게 이메일을 보낸다.
Ⓓ 그녀와 함께 커피를 마신다.

[08-11]

Listen to a talk in a psychology class.

⁰⁸**Stereotype threat is a psychological phenomenon where individuals fear confirming negative stereotypes about the group they identify with, resulting in an adverse effect on performance.** The concept was introduced in the 1990s through a study showing that the academic performance of Black students diminished—but only when they were specifically told a test measured intellectual ability. This occurred because of the stereotype in Western society that Black students are less intellectually capable than other students. ⁰⁹**Stereotype threat is not limited to race, however. A 2021 study found that students from lower socioeconomic backgrounds also scored worse on tests described as measuring intellectual ability but did as well as their wealthier peers when no specific testing purpose was given.** The study supports the idea that stereotype threat creates anxiety, which can ¹⁰⁻ᴬ**reduce academic focus** because of the high cognitive load associated with it and ¹⁰⁻ᴮ**produce self-doubt**. This can cause people to disengage from interests or alter career paths, essentially ¹⁰⁻ᴰ**creating a self-fulfilling prophecy in which they appear to confirm the stereotypes they fear**. One explanation for stereotype threat is an idea called ¹¹**"belonging uncertainty." Because individuals want to feel socially accepted, they may do everything they can to fit in and avoid embarrassing themselves by confirming stereotypes about their identity, such as those about intellectual ability.** When people experience this, they drain mental resources, which affects their performance.

stereotype[stériətaip] 고정관념
phenomenon[finámənàn] 현상
performance[pərfɔ́:rməns] 성과
intellectual ability 지적 능력   race[reis] 인종
anxiety[æŋzáiəti] 불안   self-doubt 자기 의심
prophecy[práfəsi] 예언   uncertainty[ʌnsə́:rtnti] 불확실성
drain[drein] 소모하다

심리학 강의를 들으시오.
⁰⁸고정관념 위협은 개인들이 자신들이 동일시하는 집단에 대한 부정적인 고정관념을 확인하게 될까 봐 두려워하여 성과에 악영향을 미치는 심리적 현상입니다. 이 개념은 1990년대에 한 연구를 통해 소개되었는데, 그 연구는 흑인 학생들의 학업 성과가 시험이 지적 능력을 측정한다고 구체적으로 들었을 때만 저하되었음을 보여줬습니다. 이것은 서구 사회에서 흑인 학생들이 다른 학생들보다 지적으로 덜 유능하다는 고정관념 때문에 발생했습니다. ⁰⁹하지만 고정관념 위협은 인종에 국한되지 않습니다. 2021년 연구에서는 낮은 사회경제적 배경의 학생들 또한 지적 능력을 측정한다고 설명된 시험에서 더 낮은 점수를 받았지만, 구체적인 시험 목적이 주어지지 않았을 때는 더 부유한 또래들과 마찬가지로 잘 수행했다는 것을 발견했습니다. 이 연구는 고정관념 위협이 불안을 조성하고, 이와 관련된 높은 인지 부하 때문에 ¹⁰⁻ᴬ학업 집중력을 감소시키고 ¹⁰⁻ᴮ자기 의심을 생산할 수 있다는 생각을 뒷받칩니다. 이것은 사람들이 관심사에서 이탈하거나 진로를 바꾸게 할 수 있으며, 본질적으로 ¹⁰⁻ᶜ그들이 두려워하는 고정관념을 확인하는 것처럼 보이는 자기 실현적 예언을 만들어냅니다. 고정관념 위협에 대한 한 가지 설명은 ¹¹"소속감 불확실성"이라고 불리는 개념입니다. ¹¹개인들은 사회적으로 받아들여지기를 원하기 때문에, 그들은 어울리고 지적 능력에 대한 것과 같은 자신들의 정체성에 대한 고정관념을 확인함으로써 자신들을 창피하게 만드는 것을 피하기 위해 모든 것을 할 수 있습니다. 사람들이 이것을 경험할 때, 그들은 정신적 자원을 소모하게 되고, 이것이 그들의 성과에 영향을 미칩니다.

08 Main Topic Question
강의의 주요 주제는 무엇인가?
Ⓐ 학업 성취도 저하의 이유들
☑ 고정관념 위협의 원인과 효과
Ⓒ 학생 학습에 대한 시험의 영향들
Ⓓ 학업 환경에 만연한 고정관념들

어휘 prevalent[prévələnt] 만연한, 유행하는

09 Intention Question

화자는 왜 2021년의 연구에 대해 논의하는가?
Ⓐ 고정관념 위협이 사회에 미치는 광범위한 결과들을 보여주기 위해
✓ 고정관념 위협이 정체성의 어떤 측면에 대한 인식으로부터도 야기될 수 있다고 제안하기 위해
Ⓒ 1990년대 이후 연구 방법론이 어떻게 변화했는지 보여주기 위해
Ⓓ 인종과 사회경제적 배경 사이에 상관관계가 있다고 주장하기 위해

어휘 far-reaching 광범위한 consequence[kάnsəkwèns] 결과
perception[pərsépʃən] 인식, 지각
correlation[kɔ̀:rəléiʃən] 상관관계

10 Detail Question

화자에 따르면, 고정관념 위협은 다음 중 어느 것을 제외한 모든 것을 야기할 수 있는가?
Ⓐ 학업 집중력 감소
Ⓑ 개인적 능력에 대한 의심
✓ 인지 발달 손상
Ⓓ 두려워하는 고정관념의 실현

11 Inference Question

개인들에 대한 "소속감 불확실성"의 영향에 대해 결론지을 수 있는 것은?
Ⓐ 스트레스를 다루는 그들의 능력을 향상시킨다.
Ⓑ 그들을 어울려야 한다는 압박에서 해방시켜준다.
✓ 그들의 정신적 에너지를 다른 곳으로 돌린다.
Ⓓ 그들의 정체성 의식을 강화한다.

어휘 reinforce[rì:infɔ́:rs] 강화하다

[12-15] 🔊 Am

Listen to a talk in a meteorology class.

> ¹²The urban heat island effect is a phenomenon where cities experience significantly warmer temperatures than their surrounding rural areas. This happens because urban materials like concrete, asphalt, and steel absorb and retain solar radiation much more effectively than natural surfaces like grass, trees, and soil. ¹³How do we measure this urban heat island effect? Well, scientists use networks of weather stations placed throughout metropolitan areas and compare readings between downtown locations and nearby countryside. The data consistently shows that the center of cities tends to be the warmest, with temperatures gradually decreasing toward suburban and rural boundaries. ¹⁴The urban heat island effect has serious implications for both energy consumption and public health. Cities require significantly more air conditioning during the summer months, leading to increased electricity demand and higher greenhouse gas emissions. Additionally, extreme heat events become more dangerous in urban areas, particularly affecting vulnerable populations like the elderly and those without access to cooling systems. ¹⁵But what factors determine how intense an urban heat island becomes? Well, there are several key variables, so let's take a look at some of them.

surrounding[səráundiŋ] 주변의
rural[rú:ərəl] 농촌의, 시골의   absorb[əbsɔ́:rb] 흡수하다
retain[ritéin] 보유하다, 유지하다   solar radiation 태양 복사열
gradually[grǽdʒuəli] 점차, 점진적으로
implication[ìmplikéiʃən] 영향, 암시, 함축
energy consumption 에너지 소비   greenhouse gas 온실가스
vulnerable[vʌ́lnərəbl] 취약한   variable[vέəriəbl] 변수

기상학 강의를 들으시오.

¹²도시 열섬 효과는 도시들이 주변 농촌 지역보다 현저히 더 따뜻한 기온을 경험하는 현상입니다. 이것은 콘크리트, 아스팔트, 강철과 같은 도시 재료들이 풀, 나무, 토양과 같은 자연 표면보다 태양 복사열을 훨씬 더 효과적으로 흡수하고 보유하기 때문에 발생합니다. 우리는 ¹³이 도시 열섬 효과를 어떻게 측정할까요? 음, 과학자들은 대도시 전역에 배치된 기상 관측소 네트워크를 사용하고 시내 중심가 위치와 인근 시골 지역 간의 측정치를 비교합니다. 데이터는 일관되게 도시의 중심부가 가장 따뜻한 경향이 있으며, 교외와 농촌 경계 쪽으로 갈수록 기온이 점차 감소한다는 것을 보여줍니다. ¹⁴도시 열섬 효과는 에너지 소비와 공중 보건 모두에 심각한 영향을 미칩니다. 도시들은 여름철에 상당히 더 많은 에어컨을 필요로 하며, 이는 전력 수요 증가와 더 높은 온실가스 배출로 이어집니다. 게다가, 극한 폭염 사건들은 도시 지역에서 더 위험해지며, 특히 노인들과 냉방 시스템에 접근할 수 없는 사람들과 같은 취약한 인구에게 영향을 미칩니다. ¹⁵하지만 도시 열섬이 얼마나 강렬해지는지를 결정하는 요인들은 무엇일까요? 음, 몇 가지 핵심 변수들이 있으므로, 그 중 일부를 살펴보겠습니다.

12 Main Topic Question

강의의 주로 무엇에 대한 것인가?
Ⓐ 온도 차이가 어떻게 측정되는지
✓ 농촌 지역과 비교한 도시의 더 높은 기온
Ⓒ 태양 복사열과 도시 재료들 간의 관계
Ⓓ 도시에서 기후 변화의 원인

13 Detail Question

화자에 따르면, 과학자들은 도시 온도 차이를 어떻게 연구하는가?
Ⓐ 도시 지역의 온실가스 배출을 분석함으로써
Ⓑ 다른 재료들에서 태양 복사열 흡수를 측정함으로써
✓ 다른 장소들에서 수집된 기상 데이터를 비교함으로써
Ⓓ 냉방 시스템의 사용 패턴을 추적함으로써

어휘 track[træk] 추적하다

14 Intention Question

화자는 왜 에어컨을 언급하는가?
Ⓐ 도시들이 어떻게 그들의 에너지 소비를 측정하는지 설명하기 위해
Ⓑ 도시와 농촌 지역 간의 에너지 사용을 비교하기 위해
Ⓒ 도시에서 공중 보건의 취약성을 강조하기 위해
✓ 도시 열섬 효과가 어떻게 에너지 소비에 영향을 미치는지 설명하기 위해

15 Discuss Next Question

화자는 다음에 무엇을 논의할 것 같은가?
Ⓐ 도시에서 열섬의 일반적인 패턴들
Ⓑ 열섬 강도에 영향을 미치는 주요 요소들
Ⓒ 도시 지역의 극한 폭염 사건 사례들
Ⓓ 다양한 기후대에서 열섬들 간의 차이점들

어휘 **element**[éləmənt] 요소 **intensity**[inténsəti] 강도
climate zone 기후대

ACTUAL TEST 2

p.368

Module 1				
01 ⓒ	02 ⓑ	03 ⓒ	04 ⓐ	05 ⓓ
06 ⓑ	07 ⓐ	08 ⓓ	09 ⓓ	10 ⓒ
11 ⓐ	12 ⓓ	13 ⓓ	14 ⓓ	15 ⓑ
16 ⓑ	17 ⓑ	18 ⓒ	19 ⓓ	20 ⓑ
21 ⓑ	22 ⓒ	23 ⓑ	24 ⓓ	25 ⓐ
26 ⓒ	27 ⓓ	28 ⓑ		

Module 2				
01 ⓐ	02 ⓓ	03 ⓑ	04 ⓑ	05 ⓒ
06 ⓒ	07 ⓐ	08 ⓒ	09 ⓓ	10 ⓒ
11 ⓐ	12 ⓑ	13 ⓑ	14 ⓐ	15 ⓓ

Module 1

01 Advisory Statement　　En

Let's arrange transportation for the field visit next week.

Ⓐ They can use the visitor parking lot.
Ⓑ We'll discuss the goals of the visit.
☑ How many people are supposed to come?
Ⓓ From our most recently opened branch.

transportation [trænspərtéiʃən] 교통편
be supposed to ~할 예정이다

다음 주 현장 방문을 위한 교통편을 준비합시다.
Ⓐ 그들은 방문객 주차장을 사용할 수 있어요.
Ⓑ 방문 목표에 대해 논의할게요.
☑ 얼마나 많은 사람들이 올 예정인가요?
Ⓓ 가장 최근에 문을 연 우리 지점에서요.

02 Auxiliary Verb Question　　Am

Does the company offer health insurance benefits?

Ⓐ The HR department is in charge of hiring.
☑ Only for full-time staff.
Ⓒ Claims must be filed promptly.
Ⓓ Yes, it provides paid time off.

health insurance 건강보험　in charge of ~을 담당하는
full-time staff 정규직

회사에서 건강보험 혜택을 제공하나요?
Ⓐ HR 부서가 채용을 담당해요.
☑ 정규직만요.
Ⓒ 청구는 즉시 제출되어야 해요.
Ⓓ 네, 유급휴가를 제공해요.

03 What Question　　Nz

What time do the fireworks begin?

Ⓐ In front of City Hall.
Ⓑ They're really colorful.
☑ At 9 P.M.
Ⓓ To celebrate the holiday.

celebrate [séləbrèit] 축하하다, 기념하다

불꽃놀이는 몇 시에 시작하나요?
Ⓐ 시청 앞에서요.
Ⓑ 정말 화려해요.
☑ 오후 9시에요.
Ⓓ 공휴일을 축하하기 위해서요.

04 Request Question　　Au

Can you explain the new software features?

☑ Which part is hard for you to understand?
Ⓑ You're quite skilled.
Ⓒ The software needs an update.
Ⓓ That works fine for me.

feature [fíːtʃər] 기능

새로운 소프트웨어 기능들을 설명해 주실 수 있나요?
☑ 어떤 부분이 이해하기 어려운가요?
Ⓑ 당신은 꽤 숙련되어 있어요.
Ⓒ 그 소프트웨어는 업데이트가 필요해요.
Ⓓ 그건 저에게는 괜찮아요.

05 How Question　　En

How do I access the online training materials?

Ⓐ It was developed online last year.
Ⓑ Yes, training is mandatory for all staff.
Ⓒ No, the materials aren't very informative.
☑ Log in with your employee ID and the password we emailed you.

material [mətíəriəl] 자료　mandatory [mǽndətɔ̀ːri] 의무인

온라인 교육 자료에 어떻게 접근하나요?
Ⓐ 작년에 온라인으로 개발되었어요.
Ⓑ 네, 모든 직원에게 교육은 의무예요.
Ⓒ 아니요, 자료들은 그리 유익하지 않아요.
☑ 당신의 직원 ID와 우리가 이메일로 보낸 비밀번호로 로그인하세요.

06 Tag Question   En

You finally got the job promotion you wanted, didn't you?

Ⓐ Employees are evaluated once a year.
☑ It was a long time coming.
Ⓒ The promotion helped boost sales.
Ⓓ I do not like my current schedule.

evaluate [ivǽljuèit] 평가하다   boost [buːst] 증대하다

당신이 원했던 승진을 마침내 받았죠, 그렇지 않나요?
Ⓐ 직원들은 1년에 한 번 평가를 받아요.
☑ 오랜 시간이 걸렸어요.
Ⓒ 홍보가 매출 증대에 도움이 되었어요.
Ⓓ 저는 현재 일정이 마음에 들지 않아요.

07 When Question   Au

When will the swimming pool be up and running again?

☑ This Saturday.
Ⓑ Are you up for some running?
Ⓒ Next to the golf course.
Ⓓ Keep the door open.

be up and running 운영하다   be up for ~할 의향이 있다

수영장이 언제 다시 운영되나요?
☑ 이번 주 토요일에요.
Ⓑ 달리기를 할 의향이 있나요?
Ⓒ 골프장 옆에요.
Ⓓ 문을 열어 두세요.

08 Who Question   Am

Who's covering the morning shift tomorrow?

Ⓐ It starts at 8 in the morning.
☑ The schedule should say.
Ⓒ We need to shift our focus.
Ⓓ Terry called in sick today.

shift [ʃift] 근무, 근무 조; 바꾸다

내일 오전 근무는 누가 담당하나요?
Ⓐ 아침 8시에 시작해요.
☑ 일정표에 나와 있을 거예요.
Ⓒ 우리는 초점을 바꿔야 해요.
Ⓓ Terry는 오늘 아파서 못 왔어요.

09 Informative Statement   Am

I'm afraid I won't be able to take a day off on Friday.

Ⓐ Yes, that's why I hate downtown.
Ⓑ I'll be on vacation next month.
Ⓒ I usually take off around 6 on Fridays.
☑ Then, how about Saturday instead?

take a day off 하루 쉬다   take off 퇴근하다, 이륙하다

유감스럽게도 금요일에 하루 쉴 수 없을 것 같아요.
Ⓐ 네, 그래서 제가 시내를 싫어해요.
Ⓑ 저는 다음 달에 휴가를 갈 예정이에요.
Ⓒ 보통 금요일에는 6시쯤 퇴근해요.
☑ 그러면, 토요일은 어떨까요?

10 Request Question   Nz

Would you mind closing the window?

Ⓐ We're getting close.
Ⓑ The one next to you.
☑ Of course not.
Ⓓ That's not mine.

창문 좀 닫아주시겠어요?
Ⓐ 저희는 거의 다 왔어요.
Ⓑ 당신 옆에 있는 것요.
☑ 물론이죠.
Ⓓ 그건 제 것이 아니에요.

[11-12]   W-En M-Am

Listen to a conversation.

W ¹¹Have you booked the conference room for this afternoon yet?
M ¹¹I tried to earlier, but it's being used until 3 P.M. Should we push back our presentation?
W That would really mess up our schedule. What about using the smaller room on the second floor instead?
M Good thinking! I'll check it out and let you know after this meeting.
W Perfect. ¹²I'll wrap up the slides in the meantime.

push back 미루다   mess up ~을 엉망으로 만들다
wrap up ~을 마무리하다

대화를 들으시오.
W ¹¹오늘 오후를 위해 회의실을 예약하셨나요?
M ¹¹일찍 시도했는데, 오후 3시까지 사용 중이에요. 우리 발표를 미뤄야 할까요?
W 그럼 우리 일정이 정말 엉망이 될 것 같아요. 대신 2층에 있는 더 작은 방을 사용하는 건 어떨까요?
M 좋은 생각이에요! 확인해보고 이 회의 후에 알려드릴게요.
W 완벽해요. ¹²그동안 제가 슬라이드를 마무리할게요.

11 Detail Question

남자는 왜 발표를 미루자고 제안하는가?
☑ 회의실이 나중까지 사용할 수 없다.
Ⓑ 그가 발표를 너무 일찍 예약했다.

Ⓒ 그가 2층의 작은 방을 선호한다.
Ⓓ 발표 슬라이드가 준비되지 않았다.

12 Do Next Question
여자는 다음에 무엇을 할 것인가?
Ⓐ 다른 방을 예약한다.
Ⓑ 다른 사람들에게 새로운 장소에 대해 알린다.
Ⓒ 회의 시간을 연기한다.
✓Ⓓ 발표 자료를 완성한다.

어휘 **postpone** [poustpóun] 연기하다

[13-14]
🔊 M-Am W-En
Listen to a conversation.

> M Did you sort out the marketing campaign's budget issue?
> W Not yet. I'm still crunching the numbers, but ¹³we're definitely over budget.
> M ¹³I'd like to help. Mind if I share an idea?
> W Not at all! I'd love to hear your thoughts. Honestly, any input would be really helpful. I'm kind of stuck right now.
> M ¹⁴Then, how about cutting back on the print ads? We may be used to them, but digital ads are way more cost-effective.

sort out 해결하다   **crunch the numbers** 수치를 계산하다
input [ínput] 의견; 입력하다   **cut back on** ~을 줄이다

대화를 들으시오.
M 마케팅 캠페인의 예산 문제를 해결하셨나요?
W 아직이에요. 여전히 수치를 계산하고 있는데, ¹³확실히 예산을 초과했어요.
M ¹³도와드리고 싶어요. 제가 아이디어를 공유해도 될까요?
W 물론이에요! 당신의 생각을 듣고 싶어요. 솔직히, 어떤 의견이든 정말 도움이 될 것 같아요. 지금 좀 막혀 있거든요.
M ¹⁴그러면, 인쇄 광고를 줄이는 건 어떨까요? 우리가 그것에 익숙할 수는 있지만, 디지털 광고가 훨씬 더 비용 효율적이에요.

13 Offer Question
남자는 무엇을 해주겠다고 제안하는가?
Ⓐ 디지털 광고를 제작한다.
Ⓑ 제품 출시 행사를 계획한다.
Ⓒ 인쇄 자료를 디자인한다.
✓Ⓓ 비용을 낮추는 방법을 공유한다.

어휘 **expense** [ikspéns] 비용, 경비

14 Intention Question
남자는 왜 디지털 광고를 언급하는가?
Ⓐ 전체 마케팅 예산을 증가시킬 것을 제안하기 위해
Ⓑ 인쇄 광고가 왜 선호되는지 설명하기 위해
Ⓒ 마케팅 분야에서 자신의 전문성을 강조하기 위해
✓Ⓓ 더 저렴한 대안을 제안하기 위해

어휘 **overall** [òuvərɔ́:l] 전체의, 전반적인
affordable [əfɔ́:rdəbl] 저렴한, 감당할 수 있는

[15-16]
🔊 W-Nz M-En
Listen to a conversation.

> W Did you see the flyer about the farmers' market this Saturday? It runs from 8 A.M. to 3 P.M.
> M Yes! I've wanted to check it out for a while. There's going to be organic produce, as well as fresh flowers and homemade bread.
> W That sounds amazing! ¹⁵What if it rains, though? The weather hasn't been great.
> M ¹⁵Don't worry about that. The market is at the plaza, under a big canopy, so we'll stay dry.
> W OK, then. ¹⁶I'll meet you in front of the library next to the plaza at 9 o'clock. It should be easier to find each other there.

farmers' market 농산물 직거래 장터   **produce** [prədjú:s] 농산물

대화를 들으시오.
W 이번 토요일 농산물 직거래 장터에 대한 전단지를 보셨나요? 오전 8시부터 오후 3시까지 열려요.
M 네! 한동안 확인해보고 싶었어요. 유기농 농산물뿐만 아니라 신선한 꽃과 수제 빵도 있을 거예요.
W 정말 멋져요! ¹⁵그런데 비가 오면 어떨까요? 날씨가 좋지 않았거든요.
M ¹⁵그건 걱정하지 마세요. 장터는 광장에 있고, 큰 천막 아래에 있어서 우리는 비에 젖지 않을 거예요.
W 그럼 좋네요. ¹⁶9시에 광장 옆 도서관 앞에서 만나요. 거기서 서로를 찾기가 더 쉬울 것 같아요.

15 Detail Question
남자는 여자에게 무엇에 대해 확신을 주는가?
Ⓐ 농산물이 유기농일 것이라는 것
✓Ⓑ 비가 와도 쇼핑하는 데 문제가 없을 것이라는 것
Ⓒ 오전 9시가 가기 좋은 시간이라는 것
Ⓓ 위치를 찾기 쉬울 것이라는 것

16 Detail Question
화자들은 어디에서 만날 것인가?
Ⓐ 광장에서
✓Ⓑ 도서관에서
Ⓒ 빵집에서
Ⓓ 꽃집에서

[17-18]
🔊 Am
Listen to an announcement in a classroom.

> I'd like to get your attention for a moment. Several additional guest speakers have confirmed their participation in our upcoming class discussions this semester. ¹⁷Therefore, we need to adjust our

syllabus accordingly. [18]The updated syllabus has been posted on the course website under the announcements section. Please review the changes and prepare questions for our distinguished visitors.

---

guest speaker 초청 연사
confirm[kənfə́ːrm] 확정하다, 확인하다
adjust[ədʒʌ́st] 조정하다, 적응하다
syllabus[síləbəs] 강의 계획서

교실에서의 공지를 들으시오.

잠시 주목해 주세요. 몇 명의 추가 초청 연사들이 이번 학기 우리의 다가오는 수업 토론에 참여를 확정했습니다. [17]**따라서, 우리는 그에 따라 강의 계획서를 조정해야 합니다.** [18]**업데이트된 강의 계획서는 공지사항 섹션 아래 강의 웹사이트에 게시되었습니다.** 변경사항들을 검토하고 우리의 저명한 방문객들을 위한 질문들을 준비해주세요.

17 Main Topic Question
공지의 주요 주제는 무엇인가?
Ⓐ 추가 초청 연사 모집
☑ 과목 일정에 이루어진 변경사항들
Ⓒ 강의계획서에 대한 검토 절차들
Ⓓ 수업 토론을 준비하는 방법

18 Intention Question
화자는 왜 공지사항 섹션을 언급하는가?
Ⓐ 학생들이 다른 과목을 수강하도록 격려하기 위해
Ⓑ 학생들에게 온라인 자료에 대해 알리기 위해
☑ 학생들이 업데이트된 정보를 찾도록 돕기 위해
Ⓓ 학생들에게 새로운 과제를 주기 위해

어휘 assignment[əséinmənt] 과제

[19-20]

Listen to an announcement at a student meeting.

I'm excited to announce our new peer tutoring program launching next month. [19]**Unlike previous years, it will offer both in-person and online tutoring sessions to accommodate different schedules.** Students can receive help in math, science, English, and foreign languages from certified student tutors who have maintained a 3.5 GPA or higher. Each tutoring session lasts one hour and is completely free for all enrolled students. We also provide study materials and practice tests. [20]**Don't miss out! Simply visit our website to book your first session.**

---

peer[piər] 또래, 동료   launch[lɔːntʃ] 시작하다, 개시하다
accommodate[əkámədèit] 수용하다, 부응하다
miss out 놓치다

학생 회의에서의 공지를 들으시오.

다음 달에 시작되는 우리의 새로운 또래 튜터링 프로그램을 발표하게 되어 기쁩니다. [19]이전 연도들과 다르게, 그것은 다른 일정들을 수용하기 위해 대면과 온라인 튜터링 세션 모두를 제공할 것입니다. 학생들은 3.5 평점 이상을 유지한 공인된 학생 튜터들로부터 수학, 과학, 영어, 그리고 외국어에서 도움을 받을 수 있습니다. 각 튜터링 세션은 한 시간 지속되며 모든 등록된 학생들에게 완전히 무료입니다. 저희는 학습 자료와 모의고사 또한 제공합니다. [20]놓치지 마세요! 당신의 첫 번째 세션을 예약하려면 저희 웹사이트를 방문하세요.

19 Detail Question
다음 중 또래 튜터링 프로그램에 대해 사실인 것은?
Ⓐ 각 튜터링 세션 시간은 과목에 따라 다르다.
Ⓑ 3.5 미만의 평점을 가진 학생들만 튜터링 도움을 요청할 수 있다.
Ⓒ 참여하는 학생들은 등록비를 지불한다.
☑ 이 프로그램은 작년에 단 한 가지 유형의 형식으로만 제공되었다.

어휘 vary[vέːəri] 다르다, 차이가 있다   depending on ~에 따라
enrollment fee 등록비

20 To Do Question
화자는 청자들이 무엇을 하기를 바라는가?
Ⓐ 모의고사를 본다.
Ⓑ 학습 자료를 구매한다.
☑ 튜터링 세션을 예약한다.
Ⓓ 공인된 튜터를 선택한다.

[21-24]

Listen to a talk on a podcast about psychology.

Have you ever tried to memorize your friend's phone number while someone was talking to you? I bet you found it nearly impossible. [21]**That's because of what psychologists call Cognitive Load Theory.** This theory explains how our brain processes and stores information and why we sometimes feel mentally overwhelmed. Our working memory—think of it as your brain's temporary workspace—can only handle a limited amount of information at once... Usually, around seven pieces of information, give or take two. When we exceed this capacity, we experience cognitive overload. It's like trying to juggle too many balls at once. Eventually, you'll drop them all. Now, there are three types of cognitive load. [22]**First is intrinsic load—this is the mental effort required by the task itself. Learning to drive a car, for instance, has high intrinsic load because it involves multiple complex skills.** [23]**Second is extraneous load, which comes from outside factors, such as poor instructional design or distractions. Imagine trying to study in a place where loud music is playing—it would be really hard to concentrate.** [24]**Finally, there's germane load—this is the productive mental effort that helps you build understanding and create lasting memories.** The key is managing these loads effectively. When intrinsic and extraneous loads are too high, there's no room left for germane load, and real learning can't happen.

memorize [méməraiz] 외우다, 암기하다
psychologist [saikálədʒist] 심리학자
overwhelm [òuvərhwélm] 압도하다
temporary [témpərèri] 임시의   capacity [kəpǽsəti] 용량, 능력

심리학에 관한 팟캐스트에서의 강의를 들으시오.

누군가가 당신에게 말을 거는 동안 친구의 전화번호를 외우려고 노력한 적이 있나요? 거의 불가능하다는 것을 알았을 것입니다. ²¹그것은 심리학자들이 인지 부하 이론이라고 부르는 것 때문입니다. 이 이론은 우리의 뇌가 어떻게 정보를 처리하고 저장하는지, 그리고 왜 때때로 정신적으로 압도당한다고 느끼는지를 설명합니다. 우리의 작업 기억은, 뇌의 임시 작업 공간이라고 생각하면 되는데, 한 번에 제한된 양의 정보만 처리할 수 있습니다... 일반적으로, 대략 7개의 정보 조각이고, 2개 정도 차이가 날 수 있습니다. 이 용량을 초과하면, 우리는 인지 과부하를 경험합니다. 그것은 한 번에 너무 많은 공을 저글링하려고 하는 것과 같습니다. 결국, 당신은 모든 공을 떨어뜨리겠죠. 이제, 인지 부하에는 세 가지 유형이 있습니다. ²²첫 번째는 내재적 부하인데, 이것은 과제 자체에 의해 요구되는 정신적 노력입니다. 예를 들어, 자동차 운전을 배우는 것은 여러 복잡한 기술들을 포함하기 때문에 높은 내재적 부하를 갖습니다. ²³두 번째는 외재적 부하인데, 이것은 부실한 교육 설계나 방해 요소 같은 외부 요인들에서 나옵니다. 큰 음악이 연주되는 곳에서 공부하려고 한다고 상상해본다면, 집중하기가 정말 어려울 것입니다. ²⁴마지막으로, 관련 부하가 있는데, 이것은 이해를 구축하고 지속적인 기억을 만드는 데 도움이 되는 생산적인 정신적 노력입니다. 핵심은 이러한 부하들을 효과적으로 관리하는 것입니다. 내재적 부하와 외재적 부하가 너무 높으면, 관련 부하를 위한 여지가 남지 않고, 진정한 학습은 일어날 수 없습니다.

21 Main Topic Question
강의의 주제는 무엇인가?
Ⓐ 기억이 우리의 일상 활동에 영향을 미치는 법
☑ 세 가지 유형의 인지 부하
Ⓒ 작업 기억 용량의 중요성
Ⓓ 집중력 기술을 향상시키는 방법

22 Detail Question
화자에 따르면, 내재적 부하란 무엇인가?
Ⓐ 처리될 수 있는 것을 초과하는 정보
Ⓑ 집중하기 어렵게 만드는 관련 없는 세부 사항들
☑ 과제를 완료하는 데 필요한 인지적 힘
Ⓓ 새로운 정보를 처리하는 데 전념하는 에너지

어휘   irrelevant [iréləvənt] 관련 없는
dedicated to ~하는 데 전념하는

23 Intention Question
화자는 왜 주위에서 큰 음악이 연주되는 상황에서 공부하는 것을 언급하는가?
Ⓐ 방해받으면서 공부하는 것이 흔하다고 제안하기 위해
☑ 외부 영향에 의해 야기되는 인지 부하의 예를 제공하기 위해
Ⓒ 나쁜 학습 습관이 어떻게 발달하는지 설명하기 위해
Ⓓ 현명한 교육 설계의 중요성을 강조하기 위해

어휘   external [ikstə́ːrnl] 외부의

24 Detail Queston
화자는 관련 부하에 대해 무엇을 말하는가?
Ⓐ 내재적 부하와 외재적 부하가 높을 때 발생한다.
Ⓑ 더 나은 학습을 위해 최소화되어야 한다.
Ⓒ 정신적 피로와 스트레스를 만든다.
☑ 이해와 기억을 만드는 데 도움이 된다.

어휘   minimize [mínəmàiz] 최소화하다   fatigue [fətíːg] 피로

[25-28]
Listen to a talk in an art class.

Our focus today is Dadaism. Dadaism began in 1916 in Zurich, Switzerland, at the Cabaret Voltaire. ²⁵The name "Dada" itself was deliberately meaningless. Some say it came from a child's word for a hobbyhorse, while others claim it was chosen from a dictionary at random. This randomness perfectly embodied the movement's rejection of logic and reason. This revolutionary art movement emerged during World War I as a radical response to the senselessness of global conflict and the devastation it caused. Considering traditional art had failed to prevent or address the horrors of war, ²⁶Dada artists employed startling and often unorthodox techniques to provoke a reaction from audiences. ²⁷Let's take a look at Marcel Duchamp's "Fountain." In 1917, he turned an ordinary porcelain urinal upside down, signed it with the pseudonym "R. Mutt," and submitted it to an art exhibition. By presenting everyday objects as art, Duchamp challenged society's fundamental assumptions about what constitutes artistic creation and value. The movement's anti-rational philosophy extended beyond the visual arts into poetry, performance, and theater. Artists like Kurt Schwitters created collages from discarded materials, while Tristan Tzara developed poems by randomly cutting up newspaper articles and rearranging the words. ²⁸Dadaism's significance lies not in creating beautiful objects but in entirely undermining how we think about art, meaning, and society. The movement's emphasis on chance, absurdity, and rebellion against authority laid crucial groundwork for later avant-garde movements, particularly Surrealism, and continues to influence contemporary conceptual art today. Next, we'll examine how Surrealism evolved from Dadaist principles to explore the unconscious mind and dream imagery in artistic expression.

deliberately [dilíbərətli] 의도적으로, 신중히
embody [imbádi] 구현하다
revolutionary [rèvəlúːʃənèri] 혁신적인
radical [rǽdikəl] 급진적인

devastation [dèvəstéiʃən] 파괴, 대참사
provoke [prəvóuk] 불러일으키다
pseudonym [súːdənim] 가명, 필명
fundamental [fʌ̀ndəméntl] 근본적인
assumption [əsʌ́mpʃən] 가정, 가설
discard [diskɑ́ːrd] 버리다, 폐기하다
undermine [ʌ̀ndərmáin] 뒤흔들다, 약화시키다
rebellion [ribéljən] 반항 **unconscious** [ʌ̀nkɑ́nʃəs] 무의식의

미술 강의를 들으시오.

오늘 우리가 집중할 내용은 다다이즘입니다. 다다이즘은 1916년 스위스 취리히의 카바레 볼테르에서 시작되었습니다. ²⁵"Dada"라는 이름 자체는 의도적으로 무의미했습니다. 어떤 이들은 그것이 목마를 가리키는 아이의 말에서 나왔다고 하고, 다른 이들은 사전에서 무작위로 선택되었다고 주장합니다. 이 무작위성은 논리와 이성의 거부라는 운동의 정신을 완벽하게 구현했습니다. 이 혁신적인 예술 운동은 제1차 세계 대전 중에 전세계적 갈등의 무의미함과 그것이 야기한 파괴에 대한 급진적 반응으로 등장했습니다. 전통 예술이 전쟁의 공포를 예방하거나 다루는 데 실패한 점을 고려했을 때, ²⁶다다 예술가들은 관객으로부터 반응을 불러일으키기 위해 충격적이고 종종 비정통적인 기법들을 사용했습니다. ²⁷마르셀 뒤샹의 "샘"을 살펴봅시다. 1917년에, 그는 평범한 도자기 소변기를 뒤집어 놓고, "R. Mutt"라는 가명으로 서명한 후, 미술 전시회에 출품했습니다. 일상적인 물건들을 예술로 제시함으로써, 뒤샹은 예술적 창조와 가치를 구성하는 것이 무엇인지에 대한 사회의 근본적인 가정들에 도전했습니다. 이 운동의 반이성적 철학은 시각 예술을 넘어 시, 공연, 연극으로 확장되었습니다. 쿠르트 슈비터스같은 예술가들은 버려진 재료들로 콜라주를 만들었고, 트리스탕 차라는 신문 기사들을 무작위로 잘라내고 단어들을 재배열하여 시를 개발했습니다. ²⁸다다이즘의 중요성은 아름다운 객체들을 창조하는 데 있는 것이 아니라 예술, 의미, 그리고 사회에 대해 우리가 생각하는 방식을 완전히 뒤흔드는 데 있습니다. 우연, 부조리, 그리고 권위에 대한 반항을 강조하는 이 운동은 후기 전위 운동들, 특히 초현실주의를 위한 중요한 토대를 마련했으며, 오늘날 현대 개념 예술에 계속해서 영향을 미치고 있습니다. 다음으로, 우리는 초현실주의가 어떻게 다다이스트 원칙들로부터 발전하여 예술적 표현에서 무의식과 꿈의 이미지를 탐구하게 되었는지 살펴보겠습니다.

25 Intention Question

교수는 강의 시작 부분에서 왜 목마를 언급하는가?
☑ 한 이름의 가능한 기원을 설명하기 위해
Ⓑ 예술에서 자주 사용되는 상징을 묘사하기 위해
Ⓒ 전통이 시대에 뒤떨어진 가치를 나타낸다고 제안하기 위해
Ⓓ 예술가들이 어떻게 유치함과 무작위성을 받아들였는지 보여주기 위해

어휘 **embrace** [imbréis] 받아들이다

26 Detail Question

화자에 따르면, 다다이즘의 핵심 특징은 무엇인가?
Ⓐ 미적으로 아름다운 구성의 창조
Ⓑ 확립된 예술적 관례의 준수
☑ 충격적이고 비전통적인 방법들의 사용
Ⓓ 전세계적 전쟁과 갈등의 묘사에 대한 집중

어휘 **depict** [dipíkt] 묘사하다

27 Inference Question

화자는 뒤샹의 "샘"을 예술작품으로 출품한 것이 무엇의 예라고 암시하는가?
Ⓐ 전통적인 조각 기법
Ⓑ 3차원 작품에서의 기술적 숙달
Ⓒ 현대 예술에서의 종교적 상징주의
☑ 예술에 대한 기본적 믿음의 전복

28 Inference Question

후기 전위 운동들에 대해 암시되는 것은?
Ⓐ 아름다운 객체들을 창조하는 것으로 돌아갔다.
☑ 다다이즘에 의해 도입된 개념들을 기반으로 했다.
Ⓒ 다다이스트들이 예술의 의미를 탐구하도록 영향을 미쳤다.
Ⓓ 다다이즘만큼 관련성이 없었다.

Module 2

01 Advisory Statement   🔊 En

If you need access to the system, submit the authorization form.

☑ Where exactly can I get it from?
Ⓑ I'll take part in the authorization process.
Ⓒ You need to complete some paperwork.
Ⓓ And what form should I submit?

submit [səbmít] 제출하다   **authorization form** 승인 양식

시스템에 접근이 필요하시면, 승인 양식을 제출하세요.
☑ 정확히 어디서 구할 수 있나요?
Ⓑ 승인 과정에 참여할게요.
Ⓒ 몇 가지 서류 작업을 완료해야 해요.
Ⓓ 근데 어떤 양식을 제출해야 하나요?

02 Auxiliary Verb Question   🔊 Am

Have you checked the weather for tomorrow?

Ⓐ I doubt whether it will work.
Ⓑ Yes, I remembered my umbrella.
Ⓒ The local news.
☑ I'll do that now.

doubt [daut] 의심하다   **local** [lóukəl] 지역의

내일 날씨를 확인해보셨나요?
Ⓐ 그것이 효과가 있을지 의심스러워요.
Ⓑ 네, 우산을 챙겼어요.
Ⓒ 지역 뉴스요.
☑ 지금 할게요.

03 How Question   🔊 En

How long before we hear back from the prospective buyers?

Ⓐ We're asking for a good price.   ○

Ⓑ They've got lots of other options to see.
Ⓒ That puts the matter into perspective.
Ⓓ More people are coming to take a look.

hear back 답변을 듣다
prospective[prəspéktiv] 잠재적인, 미래의

잠재적 구매자들로부터 답변을 듣기까지 얼마나 걸릴까요?
Ⓐ 저희는 좋은 가격을 요구하고 있어요.
Ⓑ 그들은 볼 다른 선택지들이 많아요.
Ⓒ 그것으로 상황이 명확해지네요.
Ⓓ 더 많은 사람들이 보러 오고 있어요.

[04-05]　　　🎧 M-Am W-Au

Listen to a conversation.

M Have you submitted your student visa application?
W Not yet. ⁰⁴**They want so many supporting documents.**
M I hear you. The visa application process can be a real pain, not to mention quite expensive. When I applied last year, it took me over three weeks to collect everything because the instructions were so confusing.
W ⁰⁵**Maybe I should make an appointment with the International Student Office to see if they can help me.**
M ⁰⁵**Yeah. That's what I ended up doing.** They probably saved my application from getting rejected.

not to mention ~을 말할 것도 없다
instructions[instrʌ́kʃəns] 지침
make an appointment 예약을 잡다
reject[ridʒékt] 거절하다, 탈락시키다

대화를 들으시오.
M 학생 비자 신청서를 제출하셨나요?
W 아직이에요. ⁰⁴지원 서류가 너무 많이 필요해요.
M 공감해요. 비자 신청 과정은 정말 고통스러울 수 있는데, 비싼 것은 말할 것도 없고요. 작년에 제가 신청할 때는 지침이 너무 혼란스러워서 모든 것을 수집하는 데 3주가 넘게 걸렸어요.
W ⁰⁵국제학생처에 예약을 잡고 도움을 받을 수 있는지 알아봐야겠어요.
M ⁰⁵네. 저도 결국 그렇게 했어요. 그들이 아마 제 신청서가 거절되는 것을 막아주었을 거예요.

04　Detail Question

여자는 비자 신청의 어떤 측면에 대해 이야기하는가?
Ⓐ 불분명한 지침
Ⓑ 첨부 서류
Ⓒ 높은 처리 비용
Ⓓ 승인 대기 기간

05　Detail Question

남자는 국제학생처에 대해 무엇을 말하는가?
Ⓐ 그의 신청서를 거절했다.
Ⓑ 그에게 예약을 잡을 것을 요구했다.
Ⓒ 그가 신청서 도움을 위해 찾아갔다.
Ⓓ 도움을 받기가 어려웠다.

어휘 assistance[əsístəns] 도움　obtain[əbtéin] 받다, 얻다

[06-07]　　　🎧 W-Am M-Nz

Listen to a conversation.

W I finally signed up for that new fitness center downtown, but I'm already having second thoughts about it.
M Really? What's wrong with it? I heard it's great.
W It is. I especially like that there are plenty of different classes. ⁰⁶**But whenever I drive there, the lot is always packed.**
M That sounds really inconvenient. Have you talked to the management about it?
W Yes, they said they're looking into partnering with nearby businesses for additional parking, but there's no timeline yet.
M Maybe you could try going at different times when it's less crowded? ⁰⁷**It's hard to find a gym with equipment of that quality in the whole city, so I wouldn't switch gyms.**

sign up for ~에 등록하다　have second thoughts 후회하다
plenty of 많은　inconvenient[ìnkənvíːnjənt] 불편한
switch[switʃ] 바꾸다, 교체하다

대화를 들으시오.
W 드디어 시내 새 피트니스 센터에 등록했는데, 벌써 후회가 되고 있어요.
M 정말요? 뭐가 문제인가요? 정말 좋다고 들었는데요.
W 맞아요. 특히 다양한 수업들이 많이 있다는 점이 마음에 들어요. ⁰⁶하지만 그곳에 차를 몰고 갈 때마다 주차장이 항상 꽉 차 있어요.
M 정말 불편할 것 같네요. 관리사무소에 그것에 대해 이야기해보셨나요?
W 네, 그들은 추가 주차를 위해 인근 업체들과 제휴하는 것을 검토하고 있다고 했지만, 아직 일정은 없어요.
M 덜 붐비는 다른 시간에 가보시는 건 어떨까요? ⁰⁷시내 전체에서 그런 품질의 장비를 갖춘 헬스장을 찾기는 어려우니까, 저라면 헬스장을 바꾸지는 않을 것 같아요.

06　Problem Question

피트니스 센터에 대한 여자의 문제는 무엇인가?
Ⓐ 집에서 너무 멀리 위치해 있다.
Ⓑ 다양한 수업을 제공하지 않는다.
Ⓒ 충분한 주차 공간이 부족하다.
Ⓓ 회원비를 너무 많이 청구한다.

어휘 lack[læk] 부족하다　sufficient[səfíʃənt] 충분한, 알맞은

해커스인강 **HackersIngang.com**
본 교재 인강 · 교재 MP3 · 단어암기 MP3 · iBT 리스닝 실전모의고사 · 쉐도잉 프로그램

고우해커스 **goHackers.com**
토플 보카 외우기 · 토플 스피킹/라이팅 첨삭 게시판 · 토플 공부전략 강의 · 토플 자료 및 유학 정보

type of result. Trickle-down economics is based on the theory that cutting taxes for corporations and wealthy individuals will eventually benefit everyone. The idea is that when the wealthy have more money, they will invest it in ways that create more jobs and economic opportunities for lower-income groups, which then leads to more consumer spending. [13]While this theory sounds logical, it can widen the gap between the wealthy and everyone else. Research shows that high-income individuals tend to save additional money or use it to build their personal wealth through investments. [14]Corporations, likewise, often do not use tax breaks to benefit the average worker. For instance, many use extra funds for stock buybacks, which raise share prices and reward existing investors. Understanding these potential outcomes has become particularly important as policymakers seek strategies that can promote both economic growth and equitable wealth distribution. [15]Next, we will discuss how different policy perspectives have shaped debates about taxation in the United States.

stimulate [stímjuleit] 촉진하다　expansion [ikspǽnʃən] 확장
prosperity [prɑspérəti] 번영　consistent [kənsístənt] 일관된
eventually [ivéntʃuəli] 결국, 결과적으로
consumer spending 소비자 지출　stock buyback 자사주 매입
potential [pəténʃəl] 잠재적인

13 Detail Question

화자에 따르면, 기업과 부유층에 대한 세금 감면의 문제는 무엇인가?
Ⓐ 개인들이 저축하는 것보다 더 많이 지출하도록 격려한다.
✓ 사회의 부의 격차를 증가시킬 수 있다.
Ⓒ 경제가 감당할 수 있는 것보다 더 많은 일자리 창출로 이어진다.
Ⓓ 항상 일반 대중에게 보고되지는 않는다.

어휘　wealth disparity 부의 격차　general public 일반 대중

14 Intention Question

화자는 왜 자사주 매입을 언급하는가?
✓ 기업 세금 감면이 근로자들에게 도움이 되지 않을 수 있다는 것을 보여주기 위해
Ⓑ 기업들이 수익을 증대시키는 효율적인 방법을 강조하기 위해
Ⓒ 기업들이 어떻게 일자리를 창출할 수 있지만 하지 않는지 보여주기 위해
Ⓓ 기업들이 어떻게 소비자 지출을 격려하는지 보여주기 위해

15 Discuss Next Question

화자는 다음에 무엇을 논의할 것 같은가?
Ⓐ 부의 분배가 성장에 미치는 긍정적 효과
Ⓑ 낙수 경제학에 의해 촉발된 논쟁들
Ⓒ 서로 다른 세금 구조의 잠재적 결과들
✓ 세금 정책 담론을 형성해온 관점들

어휘　discourse [dískɔːrs] 담론

경제학 강의를 들으시오.

성장 촉진 전략들은 경제 확장을 촉진하고 전반적인 번영을 증가시키기 위해 고안된 정부 행동들입니다. 인프라 구축과 교육 자금 지원 같은 일부 접근법들은 일관된 성공을 보여주었습니다. [12]낙수 경제학은 한때 성장 촉진 정책으로 널리 홍보되었지만, 같은 유형의 결과를 만들어내지는 못했습니다. 낙수 경제학은 기업과 부유한 개인들에 대한 세금을 줄이는 것이 결국 모든 사람에게 이익이 될 것이라는 이론에 기반합니다. 이 아이디어는 부유한 사람들이 더 많은 돈을 가지게 되면, 그들이 저소득층을 위한 더 많은 일자리와 경제적 기회를 창출하는 방식으로 투자할 것이고, 이것이 더 많은 소비자 지출로 이어진다는 것입니다. [13]이 이론이 논리적으로 들리지만, 부유한 사람들과 다른 모든 사람들 사이의 격차를 넓힐 수 있습니다. 연구는 고소득자들은 추가적인 돈을 저축하거나 투자를 통해 개인 재산을 구축하는 데 사용하는 경향이 있다는 것을 보여줍니다. [14]기업들도 마찬가지로 종종 세금 감면을 평균적인 근로자에게 도움이 되도록 사용하지 않습니다. 예를 들어, 많은 기업들이 주가를 올리고 기존 투자자들에게 보상하는 자사주 매입에 추가 자금을 사용합니다. 이러한 잠재적 결과들을 이해하는 것은 정책 입안자들이 경제 성장과 공평한 부의 분배를 모두 촉진할 수 있는 전략들을 추구하면서 특히 중요해졌습니다. [15]다음으로, 우리는 서로 다른 정책 관점들이 미국의 세금에 대한 논쟁들을 어떻게 형성해왔는지 논의할 것입니다.

12 Main Topic Question

강의의 주요 주제는 무엇인가?
Ⓐ 기업 세율 인하의 이익
✓ 낙수 경제학이 실패하는 이유
Ⓒ 성공적인 성장 촉진 전략들
Ⓓ 경제 성장에 영향을 미치는 요인들

07 Detail Question

피트니스 센터의 어떤 점이 남자에게 인상을 주는가?
Ⓐ 운영 시간이 편리하다.
Ⓑ 장비가 훌륭하다. ✓
Ⓒ 개인 트레이너를 이용할 수 있다.
Ⓓ 다른 업체들과 협력한다.

어휘 impress[imprés] 인상을 주다, 감동을 주다
       collaborate[kəlǽbərèit] 협력하다

[08-11]

Listen to a talk in a biology class.

⁰⁸Convergent evolution refers to the process where unrelated species independently develop similar characteristics in response to comparable environmental pressures. This means that organisms with different evolutionary backgrounds can end up looking or functioning remarkably alike, even though they didn't get these traits from a common ancestor. ⁰⁹A striking example is echolocation, which evolved separately in both dolphins and bats. Both species use sound waves to navigate and hunt in environments where vision is limited, yet their echolocation systems operate through completely different biological mechanisms. Another case is flight development in different animal groups. Birds and insects evolved wings independently to navigate through air, but their wing structures are fundamentally different. ¹⁰Bird wings came about through modifications to arm bones over time, while insect wings are thought to have developed from gill plates. The phenomenon also occurs in plants facing similar survival challenges. For instance, desert plants like cacti in the Americas and euphorbias in Africa both developed thick, waxy stems and reduced leaves to conserve water, despite being only distantly related. ¹¹This demonstrates how environmental pressures can shape evolution in predictable ways, leading to "evolutionary solutions" to common problems.

similar[símələr] 유사한
characteristic[kæ̀riktərístik] 특성, 특징
in response to ~에 대한 반응으로
organism[ɔ́ːrgənìzm] 유기체   ancestor[ǽnsestər] 조상
sound wave 음파   conserve[kənsə́ːrv] 보존하다

생물학 강의를 들으시오.

⁰⁸수렴 진화는 관련이 없는 종들이 비교 가능한 환경적 압력에 대한 반응으로 독립적으로 유사한 특성을 발달시키는 과정을 말합니다. 이것은 서로 다른 진화적 배경을 가진 유기체들이 공통 조상으로부터 이러한 특성들을 얻지 않았음에도 불구하고 놀랍도록 비슷하게 보이거나 기능할 수 있다는 것을 의미합니다. ⁰⁹인상적인 예는 반향정위인데, 이것은 돌고래와 박쥐 모두에서 별도로 진화했습니다. 두 종 모두 시각이 제한된 환경에서 탐색하고 사냥하기 위해 음파를 사용하지만, 그들의 반향정위 시스템은 완전히 다른 생물학적 메커니즘을 통해 작동합니다. 또 다른 사례는 서로 다른 동물 집단에서의 비행 발달입니다. 새와 곤충은 공기를 통해 나아가기 위해 날개를 독립적으로 진화시켰지만, 그들의 날개 구조는 근본적으로 다릅니다. ¹⁰새의 날개는 시간이 지남에 따라 팔뼈의 변형을 통해 생겨났고, 곤충의 날개는 아가미 판에서 발달한 것으로 여겨집니다. 이 현상은 또한 유사한 생존 도전에 직면하는 식물에서도 발생합니다. 예를 들어, 아메리카의 선인장과 아프리카의 유포르비아 같은 사막 식물들은 멀리 관련되어 있음에도 불구하고 물을 보존하기 위해 두꺼운 왁스질 줄기와 축소된 잎을 모두 발달시켰습니다. ¹¹이것은 환경적 압력이 예측 가능한 방식으로 진화를 형성할 수 있어서, 공통 문제들에 대한 "진화적 해결책들"을 이끈다는 것을 보여줍니다.

08 Main Topic Question

강의는 주로 무엇에 대한 것인가?
Ⓐ 서로 다른 종들이 어떻게 공통 조상을 공유하는지
Ⓑ 동물 행동에서 환경적 요인의 역할
Ⓒ 관련 없는 종들에서 독립적으로 발달하는 유사한 특성들의 예 ✓
Ⓓ 종들이 환경적 압력에서 생존하는 방법들

어휘 trait[treit] 특성   method[méθəd] 방법

09 Detail Question

화자에 따르면, 돌고래와 박쥐가 탐색과 사냥을 위해 음파를 사용하도록 야기하는 것은 무엇인가?
Ⓐ 공유된 진화적 조상
Ⓑ 제한된 환경적 가시성 ✓
Ⓒ 유사한 뇌 구조
Ⓓ 비교 가능한 사회적 구조

10 Detail Question

화자는 새의 날개에 대해 무엇이라고 주장하는가?
Ⓐ 곤충의 날개보다 더 효율적이다.
Ⓑ 곤충의 것과 같은 구조를 가지고 있다.
Ⓒ 팔뼈의 변화로부터 진화했다. ✓
Ⓓ 비행 시 서로 독립적으로 움직인다.

11 Inference Question

화자는 환경적 압력에 대해 무엇을 암시하는가?
Ⓐ 서로 다른 종들에서 유사한 진화적 결과를 만들어낼 수 있다. ✓
Ⓑ 동물보다 식물에 더 중요하게 영향을 미친다.
Ⓒ 종 진화의 주요 원인이다.
Ⓓ 예측 가능한 해결책들로 줄어들 수 있다.

어휘 primary[práiməri] 주요한

[12-15]

Listen to a talk in an economics class.

Pro-growth strategies are government actions designed to stimulate economic expansion and increase overall prosperity. Some approaches, like building infrastructure and funding education, have demonstrated consistent success. ¹²Trickle-down economics was once widely promoted as a pro-growth policy, but it has not produced the same

고우해커스

토플 시험부터
학부·석박사, 교환학생,
중·고등 유학정보까지

고우해커스에 다 있다!

유학전문포털 235만개 정보 보유
고우해커스 내 유학 관련 컨텐츠 누적게시물 수 기준 (~2022.04.06.)

200여 개의 유학시험/생활 정보 게시판

17,200여 건의 해외 대학 합격 스펙 게시글
고우해커스 사이트 어드미션포스팅 게시판 게시글 수 기준 (~2022.10.14.)

goHackers.com

1위 해커스어학원
260만이 선택한 해커스 토플

단기간 고득점 잡는 해커스만의 체계화된 관리 시스템

01 토플 무료 배치고사
현재 실력과 목표 점수에 딱 맞는 학습을 위한 무료 반배치고사 진행!

02 토플 Trial Test
월 2회 실전처럼 모의테스트 가능한 TRIAL test 응시기회 제공!

03 1:1 개별 첨삭시스템
채점표를 기반으로 약점파악 및 피드백, 1:1 개인별 맞춤 첨삭 진행!

[260만] 해커스어학원 누적 수강생 수, 해커스인강 토플 강의 누적 수강신청건수 합산 기준 (2003.01~2018.09.05. 환불자/중복신청 포함)
[1위] 한경비즈니스 2024 한국브랜드만족지수 교육(온·오프라인 어학원) 1위

해커스어학원 단기 졸업 시스템으로
빠르게 토플 졸업 go ▶